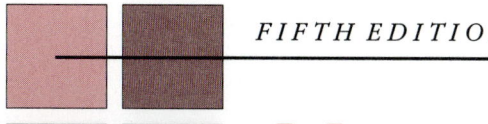

FIFTH EDITION

Mental Retardation

FIFTH EDITION

Mental Retardation

Mary Beirne-Smith
University of Alabama

Richard F. Ittenbach
University of Mississippi

James R. Patton
Pro-Ed, Austin, Texas

Merrill,
an imprint of Prentice Hall

Upper Saddle River, New Jersey   Columbus, Ohio

Cover art: Amanda Vernon, West Central School, Columbus, Ohio. Franklin County Board of Mental Retardation and Developmental Disabilities
Editor: Ann Castel Davis
Production Editor: Mary M. Irvin
Photo Coordinator: Nancy Harre Ritz
Design Coordinator: Karrie M. Converse
Text Designer: John Edeen
Cover Designer: Ceri Fitzgerald
Production Manager: Deidra M. Schwartz
Director of Marketing: Kevin Flanagan
Advertising/Marketing Coordinator: Julie Shough
Marketing Manager: Suzanne Stanton

This book was set in Garamond by Carlisle Communications, Inc., and was printed and bound by R. R. Donnelley & Sons Company. The cover was printed by Phoenix Color Corp.

 © 1998 by Prentice-Hall, Inc.
Simon & Schuster/A Viacom Company
Upper Saddle River, New Jersey 07458

Photo credits: Barbara Schwartz/Merrill, pp. 1, 123, 197, 202, 245, 274; Anne Vega/Merrill, pp. 189, 191, 202, 237, 254, 263, 280, 356, 362, 366, 392, 402, 415, 424, 432, 445, 448; Tom Watson/Merrill, pp. 52, 346; Todd Yarrington/Merrill, pp. 61, 101, 220, 271, 323, 462, 482, 489, 513, 551; Scott Cunningham/Merrill, pp. 92, 121, 137, 313, 389, 490, 520; Eugene E. Doll, p. 127; Dr. Kenneth Salyer, Dallas, TX, p. 223; Lloyd Lemmerman/Merrill, p. 437; The Ohio Historical Society, p. 495; Human Policy Press, p. 506; v/DIA Editorial Photo Archives, p. 532.

Printed in the United States of America

10 9 8 7 6 5 4 3 2

ISBN: 0-13-894908-5

Library of Congress Cataloging-in-Publication Data

Mental retardation / [edited by] Mary Beirne-Smith, Richard F. Ittenbach, James R. Patton. — 5th ed.
   p.   cm.
   Includes bibliographical references and index.
   ISBN 0-13-894908-5
   1. Mental retardation.   I. Beirne-Smith, Mary.
II. Ittenbach, Richard F.   III. Patton, James R.
   RC570.M386   1998
   362.3—dc21   97-30617
                                     CIP

Prentice-Hall International (UK) Limited, *London*
Prentice-Hall of Australia Pty. Limited, *Sydney*
Prentice-Hall of Canada, Inc., *Toronto*
Prentice-Hall Hispanoamericana, S. A., *Mexico*
Prentice-Hall of India Private Limited, *New Delhi*
Prentice-Hall of Japan, Inc., *Tokyo*
Simon & Schuster Asia Pte. Ltd., *Singapore*
Editora Prentice-Hall do Brasil, Ltda., *Rio de Janeiro*

To our parents,
Dorothy and John Patton;
Mary and John Ittenbach;
in memory of Harold and Mary Beirne;

and in loving memory of Smitty, Catie, and Billy

Preface

For the past 200 years, a considerable body of knowledge has been compiled about individuals who are mentally retarded: how they learn, how and what to teach them, and how society treats people who are retarded. The recent move toward inclusion of individuals who are disabled in general education settings is changing the face of education as we know it. Consequently, we are changing the ways in which we serve students who are mentally retarded and the ways in which we train prospective teachers of these students. In addition, such recent developments in the field of special education and in the area of mental retardation as community-based instruction, transitional planning, and supported employment have made critical the need for informed, educated professionals in this area.

Our purpose in writing the fifth edition of this text is to provide educators and other service providers with timely information about the many facets of mental retardation from a life cycle perspective. We have tried to digest the literature and add what we have learned from our own experiences. We believe that it is exciting to be involved in the area of mental retardation, and we hope that our interest and enthusiasm about individuals who are retarded, their families, their friends, others with whom they come in contact, and the society in which they live come through in this book.

Our challenge as we worked on the fifth edition of this text was to retain what was valuable from previous editions, add what is current in this edition, and integrate it all into a meaningful whole. Throughout the revision process, we have been mindful of our goal of producing a text that is useful for all professionals who work with individuals who are mentally retarded. As is true in previous editions of this text, we attempt to show relationships between theory and practice; we decode the terminology used in the literature on mental retardation, particularly that associated with causes of retardation; and we relate these terms to the reality of the classroom, the work world, and the community. In addition, we point out many valuable resources in the field of special education and the area of mental retardation.

We have retained the features in previous editions for which we received positive feedback from reviewers and users. We begin each chapter with a list of key words and learning objectives. Each key word is defined in the chapter and included in the glossary for easy reference. Each chapter has been substantially revised, and, where appropriate, we have increased the focus on developmental disabilities, multiculturalism, and technology. Each chapter ends with bulleted summary statements. Finally, we have continued to use short features in each chapter to broaden the coverage of topics.

We have organized the text in four parts. In Part 1, we concentrate on basic concepts about mental retardation. In this section, we have chapters on perspectives on mental retardation history, definition, assessment, and causes and prevention. In Part 2, we focus on the characteristics of individuals who have different levels of retardation. Here, we have chapters about individuals who are mildly retarded and individuals who are severely or profoundly retarded. In Part 3, we look at programming and issues across the lifespan of individuals who are retarded. In this section, we have chapters about infancy and early childhood, the school years, transition from school to life after school, and adulthood. Finally, in Part 4, we address ongoing concerns with chapters about family concerns, individual rights and legal issues, institutional and community living, and current and emerging issues.

ACKNOWLEDGMENTS

In revising this text, we were inspired by many individuals. Jim Payne's mentorship and vision for this text motivated us. Our family and friends offered unconditional love and the support we needed to complete the task.

We are indebted to those who contributed their time, energies, and expertise to previous editions: Diane M. Browder, Frances E. Butera, Lawrence J. Coleman, Jill C. Dardig, Robert M. Davis, Keith Hume, Eric D. Jones, Allen K. Miller, John A. Nietupski, Ruth Ann Payne, Greg A. Robinson, Tommy Russell, Janis Spiers, Carol Thomas, Thomas J. Zirpoli, and Vicki Knight.

We are grateful to our colleagues who contributed to this edition of the text: Mitylene B. Arnold, Gary Clark, Dan Ezell, Shannon H. Kim, Cynthia Jackson, Fay and David Jackson, Veda Jairrels, Jerry Saiz Nunnally, Edward Polloway, J. David Smith, and H. Monroe Snider. Their willingness to participate, their expertise, and their excellent work are appreciated.

We are especially grateful to the people who contributed to the research and development of this edition. We could not have completed the revision without the assistance of Dean Creel, Mary Ann Crumly, Cynthia Jackson, and Michelle Moses. We also wish to express our appreciation to Charlotte A. Sonnier, who spent many hours completely revising the Instructor's Manual.

We also want to thank the reviewers for their guidance and constructive criticism: Charlotte Erickson, University of Wisconsin at LaCrosse; Pam Gent, Clarion University; and Sr. Gabrielle Kowalski, Cardinal Stritch College.

Finally, we wish to express our sincere appreciation to the individuals at Merrill/Prentice Hall who encouraged and supported our efforts. Their patience, understanding, and professionalism are unequaled. We thank Ann Castel Davis, Pat Grogg, Mary Irvin, Deidra Schwartz, and Karrie Converse.

MBS, RFI, JRP

Contents

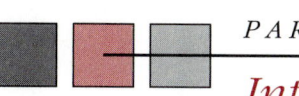

PART **2**

Introduction to the Different Levels of Mental Retardation   *197*

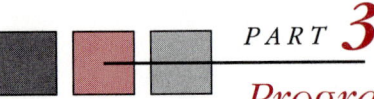

PART *3*

Programming and Issues
across the Lifespan   263

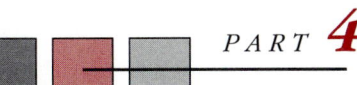

PART **4**

Continuing Concerns 415

PART **1**

Basic Concepts

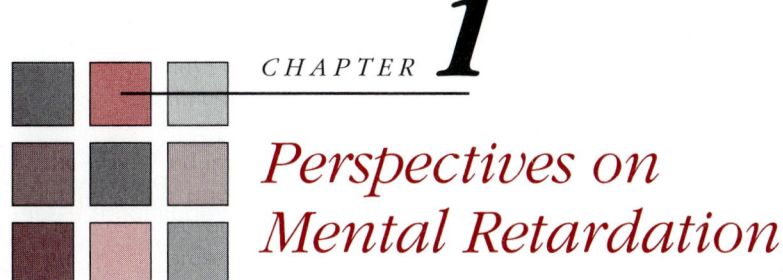

CHAPTER **1**

Perspectives on Mental Retardation

Mental retardation means different things to different people. The purpose of this book is to describe the many facets of mental retardation by providing factual information on an extensive range of topics. This information is essential to individuals who will be working with persons who are mentally retarded.

Having a basic level of factual understanding of mental retardation, however, is not sufficient. Anyone studying the topic of mental retardation needs to be aware of personal dimensions related to this disability; facts alone do not provide a complete picture of what mental retardation is about.

This chapter is devoted to a series of personal reflections that address many issues and topics relating to mental retardation: what to teach, where and how to teach, what role the family plays, and what we can and should expect from community service providers. All of the perspectives offer glimpses of important facets related to mental retardation.

The following perspectives were contributed by persons who have dedicated a significant part of their lives and careers to acting as educators and advocates for individuals who are retarded. Individuals who contributed their thoughts are Dr. Gary Clark, University of Kansas, Lawrence, KS; Mr. H. Monroe Snider, North Mississippi Regional Center, Oxford, MS; Mr. and Mrs. David Jackson, Tuscaloosa, AL; Dr. Dan Ezell, The University of Alabama, Tuscaloosa, AL; and Ms. Jerry Nunnally, Tuscaloosa City Schools, Tuscaloosa, AL. We are grateful to these individuals for sharing their thoughts and insights. We believe that their stories provide an engaging way of introducing the topic of mental retardation.

DR. GARY CLARK: A HISTORICAL PERSPECTIVE

The reader is referred to Chapter 10 for a discussion of career education programs.

Dr. Gary Clark is one of the foremost leaders in the field of special education. He is second to none in terms of contributions in the area of career development and transition. His scholarly activities include the authorship of many books, chapters, and articles. He has been a consultant to numerous schools and agencies throughout the country. His influence on the field is dramatically evidenced by the number of people he has trained who are now in leadership positions.

As teachers are key players in the lives of individuals who are mentally retarded, Dr. Clark's comments are noteworthy, since they focus on important elements of training. He identifies a number of important trends that have dominated the field at various times. He also notes that many issues in this area tend to reappear and points out that the context for addressing these issues also changes substantially over time.

In the personal perspective that follows, Dr. Clark describes important trends that he has observed in his work in preparing professionals over the past thirty years.

"What should I be teaching my students?" That simple, yet profound question in 1962 from a high school teacher of students then classified as "educable mentally retarded" gave my professional career a direction that it had never had before. I was at that time a vocational rehabilitation counselor for the Texas Education Agency, assigned to work with all students referred for rehabilitation services under the Texas Cooperative Work Study Program. I had been a secondary English teacher and a guidance counselor before taking on what was for me a new professional role. I had one general survey course on exceptional children in my bachelor-level teacher-education program and one introductory course on mental retardation during the first few months of my new job. I give this as background to put into perspective the special education teacher's question.

Who was I, an outsider with only minimal experience or training in the fields of special education or exceptionality, to be asked such a question? It was appalling to me at the time, but it set in motion my thinking and my ultimate decision to go back to graduate school in special education to become a secondary special education teacher educator, focusing on high school programming. I was convinced that the need for emphasis on special education teacher training for secondary teachers was so desperate that perhaps even I could make a contribution.

Since my introduction to the field of special education about thirty-five years ago, some major teacher education thrusts are identifiable. Each of the ones I recall most vividly deserves at least brief mention.

The 1950s and the early 1960s were years of identification of children and youths who needed special intervention and the establishment of classes and programs for them. The knowledge base for the field at that time was, for the most part, causes and characteristics of mental retardation. Teachers and school psychologists had to be trained to participate in the identification process, so courses were offered in characteristics and testing. Most of the conceptual base for these courses was from abnormal psychology, intelligence testing, and research on the causes of mental retardation and resulting characteristics of those causes. There were invariably references to early efforts to educate children and youths with mental retardation (Itard, Seguin, Montessori, Descoeudres, Ingram, and others) and to the attempt to bridge the gap between theoretical approaches, past and present, and appropriate instruction. Given the state of the field, this resulted in a variety of approaches being presented in teacher education and, subsequently, a variety of approaches used in the field.

The term "six-hour retarded child" refers to a student whose retardation is evident only in school-related areas.

Teacher education during the mid-1960s was in a transition period when I began my doctoral study. The field of mental retardation was experiencing extraordinarily rapid growth due to the impact of President John F. Kennedy and his family through the Joseph P. Kennedy Foundation and the initiatives of the federal government. Public schools were adding classes rapidly to meet the needs of the thousands of children and youths who were being identified as "mentally deficient," "mentally retarded," "slow learners," and many later referred to as "the six-hour retarded child."

Instructional programs were gearing up to meet the wave of new optimism as well as responding to the new close scrutiny of their treatments and general care. In this national milieu, teacher educators were trying to prepare teachers in numbers sufficient to meet the demand in public schools and institutions, but because the field of special education lacked a sound knowledge base in curriculum and instruction, questions from teachers in training frequently focused on who "belonged" in special classes and how they could be administratively organized.

The logical shift away from a focus on identification and organization of segregated special class environments in the 1960s was to emphasize curriculum. Debates within the field on what was special about special education grew out of the hodgepodge of instructional practices that had evolved. There were the "happiness" class curricula (characterized by recreational therapy activities and arts and crafts), "watered-down academics" curricula, functional academics curricula, and specialized curricula for individuals believed to have Strauss syndrome, exogenous mental retardation, perceptual-motor disorders, or brain injury, or who were institutionalized. Teacher education courses dealing with methods and materials for teaching changed with this shift, moving from *whom* to teach to *what* to teach. Curriculum models such as the Illinois Curriculum Guide and the Iowa Curriculum for Persisting Life Needs were frequently studied in methods and materials classes.

During the last half of the 1960s and into the early 1970s, teacher educators felt the influence of the efficacy studies (segregated special class vs. regular class) and the Civil Rights movement. Teacher educators, some of whom were engaged in efficacy study research, began to doubt the wisdom of some of the previously advocated theoretical models and the segregated special class delivery system based on a specialized curriculum. New ideas such as criterion-referenced assessment, behavior modification, competency-based education, behavioral objectives, culture-fair testing, and mainstreaming permeated teacher education, and the pendulum began to swing away from curriculum (*what* to teach) back to better identification and placement practices, better instructional interventions, and different instructional delivery environments (*how* to teach and, to some extent, *where*).

In the early 1970s, a change in the definitional interpretation of mental retardation (from 1 standard deviation below the mean to 2), as well as the rapid emergence of the new areas of learning disabilities and emotional disturbance/behavior disorders, added to the movement away from special curricula for special needs to specialized instructional environments and special interventions. This period is the one I recall as the "hardening of the categories" period, with teacher educators committing themselves to one categorical camp or the other and one instructional intervention or the other, and the beginnings of the differentiation between elementary and secondary special education. It was also the period when teacher education was being directed primarily at undergraduates and graduates in preservice programs rather than summer "re-tread" workshops and programs for those already in the field. These students were asking over and again, "What do you do with a student who can't _____?" "Where do you place a student who has an IQ of _____ and can't read?"

Teacher education from 1975 to 1980 was largely a continuation of the earlier period (*how* to teach) but with a much stronger emphasis on *where* to teach it. Most teacher education programming during this time was done within the massive effort to communicate the mandate of PL 94-142 to a current generation of special and general education teachers who had to learn new skills and new values, and a future generation of special and general education teachers who had entered their respective fields without any hint of the new roles and responsibilities that would be theirs. Many teacher education programs in mental retardation during this period were discontinued and merged into noncategorical or cross-categorical teacher education programs. The programs that managed to survive, because of state certification policies, typically showed dramatic losses in enrollment.

The new language of PL 94-142 (nondiscriminatory testing, individualized, appropriate education, zero reject, individualized educational program, least restrictive environment, and due process) dominated teacher education courses. The themes of compliance monitoring and avoidance of due process hearings added another layer of stress for students preparing to be special education teachers

Discussions of PL 94-142 can be found in Chapters 8 and 9.

in their learning of how to teach and where to teach it—that is, *how to comply with and document* the instructional planning process. Teachers in in-service and preservice teacher education programs were asking questions on how to complete Individualized Education Programs (IEPs), how to individualize for students when they were moving into and out of the self-contained or resource classrooms, and how to find regular education teachers who would take students previously considered too mentally retarded to be taught outside a self-contained classroom or, in some cases, outside an institution.

It took about six or seven years for teacher training to move out of the "how to comply" and "how to individualize instruction" phase. By the mid-1980s, two things had happened to prompt some teacher education programs to diverge in their philosophies and personnel preparation approaches. First, many of the children who had gone through elementary special education programs were having difficulty in high school programs, finding the delivery system and personal attention quite different from what they had experienced in elementary school. Many dropped out, and some had to go back to more self-contained programming. Second, follow-up studies of those who had spent six to seven years in secondary special education programs found that they were too frequently unemployed or under-employed, still living at home, and not making satisfactory personal and interpersonal social adjustments to the community.

The reaction to these events and the conclusions drawn as to the best teacher education response prompted the formation of advocacy camps along two basic lines. One group of teacher educators is advocating full inclusion and a restructuring of general education to accommodate full-inclusion practices. Teacher educators in such programs are shifting away from an individualized approach under a full-continuum-of-services model to an advocacy model calling for an end to present systems of assessment and classification and any segregated, self-contained instruction. These teacher educators use methods courses to present full-inclusion policies and procedures, with special emphasis on accommodation and support for individual students to reach their current individualized goals and objectives. Students in full-inclusion teacher training programs are asking, "How do I teach _____ within the context of someone else's ninth-grade general math class?" and "How can I collaborate with Ms. _____ to make this instructional program work?"

The other primary response group within teacher education questions both the capability and the will of general educators to restructure current instructional practices to meet the individual needs of students with disabilities in general ed-ucation settings. The basic concern of this group is the question of the extent to which schools can or will accommodate every student while still achieving the critical outcomes required for adult adjustment. Members of this group advocate a return to an emphasis on curriculum and direct instruction for those students, particularly during the secondary school years, who need relevant, reinforcing schooling that works on life skills for survival now and in the future. Methods classes for this group focus on comprehensive curriculum development, functional curriculum, community-based instruction, vocational training, and training in transition from school to adult life. Students in these programs are asking again, "What is a functional curriculum, and how can we develop one?"

If it appears that professional preparation in the field of mental retardation has come full circle, I would have to agree somewhat: We are back to asking some of the same questions that faced us years ago. However, the difference lies in the message of the following old story: A long-tenured professor was asked, "How is it you can continue to use the same exam questions year in and year out?" His answer was simple: "The answers change each year." When the field comes back around to some of the same questions of earlier times, it is not the same field as it was before.

The field of mental retardation has changed and will continue to change as we learn more and are able to move to different levels of response to some of the old, familiar questions. It is frightening to some that we do not know enough to have all the answers by now. It is disconcerting to young people to be told that they are going to be pioneering in this field, when they come in expecting that the answers to all challenges are available. Under these conditions, professional preparation must seem amorphous and inadequate to students entering the field. It *is* amorphous and inadequate, and it always will be. Still, we have come a long way from the days when we accepted institutional warehousing, assumed children and youths with mental retardation could learn only the simplest of tasks, believed we knew all the causes and characteristics of mental retardation, and thought we had most of the answers to education and treatment. If I did not believe that, I would have real difficulty trying to respond to a question a student asked again just last week in class: "What should I be teaching?"

H. MONROE SNIDER:
A COMMUNITY PERSPECTIVE

H. Monroe Snider is currently employed in the Community Services Department of one of Mississippi's five residential facilities for persons with developmental disabilities. He has worked as a state employee in the mental health field for the past twenty years, beginning as a teacher's aide, then as a special educator, then as a program director, and currently as a community services administrator.

Mr. Snider received a B.S. in anthropology from The University of Southern Mississippi, and an M.Ed. in special education from The University of Mississippi. He is currently pursuing a Ph.D. in educational leadership at The University of Mississippi.

In his perspective, Mr. Snider recounts changes in the field that resulted from the movement away from institutionalization and toward the provision of community-based services for individuals who are retarded.

A discussion of deinstitutionalization can be found in Chapter 14.

As the movement toward deinstitutionalization has grown, I have seen the Community Services Department in which I work grow from one of the smallest at my facility, with only a handful of staff and clients, to one that now serves more community-based clients than does the larger facility. Now the largest department of the facility, we are proof that the emphasis on more community-based services continues to grow.

The Community Services Department offers assistance in a number of areas. These include case management, alternative living arrangements, work activity, and supported employment.

The case management program is a service acquisition system for individuals with developmental disabilities. Needs are identified through an evaluation process, and clients are then referred to an available program in their own community for services.

The alternative living arrangements program includes group homes and supervised apartments as residential alternatives to institutionalization for individuals with developmental disabilities. House Managers provide training that focuses on self-help, socialization, and communication skills, and accessing community resources and services.

The work activity centers program is designed to provide sheltered employment, and prevocational and vocational training to individuals with developmental disabilities who demonstrate outstanding needs in areas such as appropriate work behavior, dress, and actual performance of jobs for which the clients receive compensation.

The supported employment program is designed to function as an extension of work activity. In this program, clients ready to make the transition to employment in the community are identified and provided necessary support, including on-the-job training, transportation, counseling, and intervention services necessary to ensure successful community employment.

As one of two primary administrators within my department who work directly under the Department Director, I coordinate the work activity and supported employment service areas. My counterpart (the Case Management Coordinator) and I serve as liaisons between the seventeen programs we administer and my supervisor, the Department Director. Basically, my work consists of several functions, which include quality assurance, technical assistance, program enhancement, cyclical projects, and special projects.

I will make some brief observations on how things have changed over the years in the special education profession.

Service has become more client-centered. Gone are the days of large, isolated institutions. You no longer see large, imposing, and impersonal dormitories divided into wards where row upon row of iron beds stood without provisions for privacy or human dignity. You no longer see a large, tile-floored room, stripped of furnishings and known as the "playhall" into which persons were herded and confined, to pass their days and years with only custodial care. Now, you rarely see food for clients delivered to dormitories in large vats while significantly better food is offered to staff in the institution cafeteria. In the past, students had little or no say about how they were housed, cared for, fed, or educated. When I entered the field twenty years ago, I did see these practices, but over the years I have seen them change for the better. Students and their families have gradually come to be viewed as consumers of service, which they certainly are. The students' ideas, input, desires, thoughts, goals, and dreams have gradually come to take on an increasingly important role in the education of students with special needs.

Special education has also become significantly more functional. When I began, little thought was given to why a skill was being taught. Developmental sequences were of primary concern, and relatively little attention was given to the question of whether clients would ever need the skill or would benefit from their knowledge of it. We took a "train and hope" approach; we taught first and thought later. Today, in contrast, much instruction is functional in nature. We are less concerned with teaching the student to count mixed change aloud; instead, we emphasize such skills as teaching the student to pick out sufficient money for a vending machine, a pay phone, or a washing machine. We now look toward tomorrow much earlier in our students' lives and are more concerned with how their education will prepare them for their private lives and work lives in the future.

Finally, we have come to share the responsibility for educating individuals with developmental disabilities. Once purely training or instructionally oriented, we in special education no longer take a he-gets-it-or-he-doesn't attitude, placing responsibility for learning on the student alone. It is up to us to determine what supports would allow our students to succeed and then to provide those supports.

More services, more client-centered services, more boundary-spanning services, and more innovative training services are available to adults with developmental disabilities now than at any other time in history. Yet, there remain individuals who are not yet served, and whose needs remain unmet. The field needs more genuinely caring people to take on the challenge of educating these individuals and making a real difference in the quality of their lives.

FAY AND DAVID JACKSON: A FAMILY PERSPECTIVE

Fay and David Jackson are the legal guardians of David's brother Charles, an adult who is moderately retarded. David earned a B.S. in chemistry from Gardner Webb College, Boiling Springs, NC, and recently retired from Michelin North America. Fay received a B.A. in speech pathology and an M.Ed. and a Ph.D. in special education, mental retardation from the University of Alabama, Tuscaloosa. She is currently employed at Wayne State College in Wayne, Nebraska.

Mr. and Mrs. Jackson describe the joys and frustrations of acting as guardian and advocate for an adult who is retarded.

Family concerns are discussed in Chapter 12; legal concerns are discussed in Chapter 13.

In 1987, on Christmas Day, Lena Jackson died. She left a house, some land, and a forty-year-old son with mental retardation, our brother Charles. After the hurt and shock passed, my husband and I began to get down to the duties of guardianship.

The first things that had to be faced were the legal aspects. We lived in Alabama. Charles was a resident of South Carolina. There was no reciprocity between those states, so everything that had been handled in South Carolina had to be handled again, and differently, in Alabama. In South Carolina, for instance, we were called "conservators." That caused a lot of problems in Alabama when we were setting up accounts. We had to explain each and every time that conservator and guardian were virtually the same thing.

Another consideration was health insurance. Charles had Medicare, but that was very limited. We would have to legally adopt him before he could be claimed on my husband's group insurance. We discovered that it could be done, but it would be a very lengthy process. It also meant that he would lose the Social Security benefits he was receiving. After a long and hard decision-making time, we decided that it would be better not to initiate adoption procedures.

In order for Charles to receive his Social Security payments, new accounts had to be arranged. The bureaucracy within the Social Security system was incredible. The people were helpful, but it became our opinion that the national debt could be lowered if there were less paperwork. It did take patience. We had to answer questions and fill in blanks until we both saw them in our sleep. However, Charles's checks did come on time. We still have to fill out a yearly report for him, but after the first year or so, we got pretty good at filling out those forms.

We also wanted to consider a will for Charles. A state can rip any resources away, even a small amount, if a person is ever in the care of a state-supported facility. However, a will can deter that process. We both wished we had known many years ago what we know now about estate planning. It sounds harsh, but in the case of small estates, it is so much better if parents do not leave anything to children who are mentally retarded. They can put a statement of obligation within their own wills requesting that other children accept the responsibility of their brother or sister who is disabled. If Charles's mother had known about the possible danger to Charles's resources, we feel sure that she would have done just that; however, there was no one to tell her.

We used our family lawyer to draw up the document. Charles made his mark on it. We felt better. We knew that it could be challenged, but the cost of such a challenge would be a deterrent to anyone who might consider it.

After the legal, insurance, and financial problems were dealt with, there came a much larger concern, one we call just plain Monday-through-Sunday living.

Our daughter had moved to an apartment only a few months before Charles came to live with us. It was strange having someone in the house so soon when we had looked forward to being on our own again. I will not say it was all bad, but it was not all good either. We had some wonderful times, and we had some difficult times.

Charles had never had any education at all. There had been nothing in that little South Carolina town for him. By the time PL 94-142 was passed, Charles was close to thirty years old. Charles's mother had done the best she could for him. She taught him to be honest, to try hard, and to be polite. Those are lessons that some very intelligent people never grasp. However, he did not know how to associate with his peers. He did not know how to make up a bed efficiently, shave himself, wash his hair, or hang up his clothes. He also did not know how to bowl, how to play basketball, or baseball, or how to start a conversation with a stranger.

We decided that he needed to have some kind of life to help him gain some of these skills. In our town, Tuscaloosa, Alabama, we are quite fortunate to have a Parks and Recreation Authority (PARA) that provides some activities for adults with mental retardation.

The first thing we did was to enroll Charles in the PARA basketball program. David was working in the afternoons, so I took Charles. I will never forget the first time we went. He was wearing his new basketball shoes. I had been talking about going since I had come home that day. He had seemed to be really excited about it, but when it came time to go, he was frightened. All he could say was, "You're not going to leave me, are you?" I assured him I would not. For the next five weeks, we both learned how to play basketball. Then one night, he came over to me, smiling, and told me I could come back and pick him up later. One hurdle had been crossed.

Our next endeavor was to enroll Charles in some kind of training program. For this task, David and I had one advantage. I had taught in special education for a number of years and had a Master's degree in mental retardation. I also had made a few contacts at the local mental health service.

Initially, we thought Charles would be placed in a program that taught only basic living skills; however, after testing and informal evaluation, the director of the mental retardation services decided that he would be better in a more advanced program. She was right!

After transportation problems were worked out, Charles began "going to school." The first day brought the same fear that the basketball outing had, but not quite as much. He was beginning to gain some confidence.

Charles became involved in a sheltered workshop that also provided some other training. He learned to cross streets, to recognize denominations of money, and not to hug strangers. After a while, he began to make friends, his own friends. That was when we began to consider other living arrangements for him.

For twenty months Charles lived in our home. As time passed, it became clear that it was not a good situation for us or for him. We would never tell anyone else what they should do, but for us, a group home placement seemed to be the answer.

We began by letting Charles visit the home. He would go and have supper with them. We had to pay for his meals, and it took some talking to persuade the mental health personnel to let us do things this way, but they gave in. We are really glad they did.

At first Charles did not like it much, but by the third or fourth visit, we would find him talking to people when we came to pick him up. After that, he began to spend some weekends at the home. We arranged this through the respite care program that was offered through the mental health services. For about three or four months, Charles spent every other weekend at the group home. When they had an opening for him to move in, he was delighted. We visited him often, but he never made any effort to come with us when we left. We were both glad that he was happy and a little hurt that he did not want to come back.

In October, Charles was supposed to move to a new group home. The house had been purchased and the arrangements had been made for five men to live in the new house. The night before moving day, the house burned. Arson was suspected. Charles had been staying in a semi-independent apartment while his belongings were being moved to the new house. The representatives from mental health services suggested that Charles become a permanent resident at that facility. We were terribly troubled. We did not think that he was ready for that environment. We were afraid that he would not have the supervision or care that he needed. However, it was either that, or have Charles come back to live with us. Charles did come back for about two weeks. He was miserable. All he wanted to do was to go back with his friends. When we let him go, we discovered another aspect of guardianship: advocacy.

I supposed that the personnel who supervised the apartments had never dealt with anyone who even knew what Section 504 of the Rehabilitation Act was, much less knew how to get it to work for them. They were horrified at first. They did not know what to do when David and I both asked about Individual Prescriptive Plan (IPP) meetings. They were surprised when we asked to have copies sent within thirty days for our approval. They got upset when we reminded them that anything in the IPP is binding, such as transportation to special events.

When we saw that we might have some trouble, we selected our local advocacy group. This is a state-supported service that offers legal counseling at no charge. Our local agency is very powerful. We never actually had to use the service, but we did use their advice. We made agendas for meetings. We documented problems and sent copies of the documentation to the mental health representatives. Without the mention of the advocacy group behind us, we doubt that problems would have been solved so quickly. It is not that the personnel did not care, it was just that they did only what they had to do and no more. Since then, the situation has changed for the better.

Now, Charles is living alone, in his own apartment. David and I visit him often, but he does not want to come home with us. He has his own home, his own friends, and his own life.

It is amazing when I think about the person who came to live with us those years ago. That person was frightened. He had no self-confidence, no friends, nothing. Now Charles goes to Hardees with his group of buddies for supper on Fridays. He goes bowling and was even a runner-up in bowling at the State Special Olympics last year. He knows how to count money and cook some meals. Actually, he's become quite a neat person to know.

It has been three years since we wrote our perspective on life with Charles, and we can honestly still say that we are happy that he has come into our lives. It would not, however, be fair to indicate that everything is all good. There are two problems facing us: money and mobility.

When Charles came to live with us, his mother had left her estate to both of her children equally. We wish that there had been someone to tell her that leaving any amount of money to Charles would end up hurting him. For instance, Charles is not eligible for the amount of housing assistance other adults who are retarded have because of this money. It certainly is not much, and if Charles had to face a medical crisis, the money in the account would not last long. We know that it sounds cruel to disinherit a child with a disability, but having part of an estate can actually hurt the child's future.

The second problem, mobility, is one we did not consider until recently. We have been planning to move west for several years. We dreamed that one day I would finish my doctorate and David would retire. Then, we would pick a place and send out resumes. I have earned my doctorate, David has retired, and the dream is almost a reality. Now we must think not only of our futures but of the facilities and services available for Charles. It is important that we find a place where he will be happy and continue to make progress.

We have been doing some scouting over the past few years, and we have made some rather startling discoveries. In one area, for instance, the waiting period for getting services for Charles is two days, in another, it is two years.

A further concern is the quality of assistance available. In some states, the state-supported services are minimal, but the private services are excellent. Of course, the private facilities are usually very expensive. In other areas, state and private group homes and workshops are equal, and usually very good. There are many problems facing families that include individuals who are disabled, but most of them can be surmounted by planning, information, and consideration.

DR. DAN EZELL: AN EDUCATIONAL PERSPECTIVE

Dr. Dan Ezell is a newcomer to higher education. He is a newly appointed Assistant Professor at The University of Alabama in Programs in Mental Retardation and Developmental Disabilities. Dr. Ezell has classroom experience working with students who are mentally retarded or who have other disabilities in the public school system in Louisiana. He also has had personal experience with a nephew who was diagnosed as severely mentally retarded and physically disabled. His professional interests include alternative forms of assessment, appropriate transitional services, availability of recreational and leisure activities, and vocational training for individuals who are disabled.

Following are Dr. Ezell's reflections on his personal experiences with family members as well as his professional experiences in the public school classroom and at the University level. He shares his beliefs and convictions concerning working with individuals who are retarded.

So often I am asked the question "Why are you in special education?" I cannot help but smile with confidence because I have no doubts as to why I chose this career: Shondell Shay Powell was born to my sister, Sherlyn Ezell-Powell on August 30, 1979. His many physical and health complications forced my sister to decide whether to institutionalize Shondell or provide round-the-clock monitoring for him herself. She chose the latter. I lived with my sister and her family during my high school years. I know how it feels to get the stares in department stores, the looks of pity, and the "What's wrong with him?" look. I learned much from Shondell, and I view the world differently because of him. Although he passed away when he was six years old, he still has a tremendous influence on my life. The way I care about the field of special education is the way Shondell would have cared if he were still here. Since Shondell's death, philosophies of educating individuals who are retarded have changed significantly. The American Association on Mental Retardation (AAMR) has adopted a new definition of mental retardation that places emphasis on the level of support needed for individuals to function in their environment. Community living, transitional services, and inclusive settings have also emerged as important issues in the field of mental retardation. Transitional services are at the forefront of interest due to the mandated requirements of the Individuals with Disabilities Education Act (IDEA) for students aged sixteen and over. Treatments in the field of mental retardation have evolved from such practices as inappropriate institutionalization, involuntary sterilization, and euthanasia to more positive and humane accommodations.

See the discussion of Carrie Buck in Chapter 5.

We need to understand, however, that not all change is good, nor is all new necessarily better. Newcomers to the field often cling to their own view of how things are done, believing that today's practices are superior. We must, however, consider our beliefs in their historical context. Take, for instance, involuntary sterilization. Our view of the Carrie Buck story is skewed because we now know "the rest of the story." Our place in history determines, to a great extent, our perspective. We may be making philosophical and trendy mistakes now that we will not know about until many years down the road.

We need to continue to evaluate our current perspective and philosophy, taking into account the current needs of individuals who are retarded and the situational and environmental demands involved in working with these individuals. I try to impress on my college students that we are all products of our experiences, and our philosophies and perspectives today may not be what our philosophies and perspectives will be five years from today. I relate that my own perspective and philosophy of special education is to some degree based on my classroom experiences but largely based on my experiences with Shondell.

I also have had many valuable experiences during my appointment at The University of Alabama—not only through my teaching and research but also in my supervision of practicum students and teacher interns. These experiences have reinforced my commitment to make a positive contribution to the field of mental retardation. As I view what is going on currently in the classroom settings, the effective as well as the not-so-effective practices, I take the opportunity to address what I perceive to be the components necessary for effectively teaching individuals who are mentally retarded.

I relay to students preparing a career of working with individuals who are retarded the following tenants, which I call "Teacher Do's." These suggestions are culminations of my personal and professional experience and reflections.

- *Focus on the abilities of your students, not their disabilities.* Even though my nephew was severely disabled, he could smile and blink. Focus on the positives. Adhere to the philosophy that every child can learn. My sister, who is now a successful teacher of students who are mentally retarded, expounds on this idea by saying, "If they walk in my door, that is an ability that I treasure, since I had a child of my own who could not walk." It is through the students' strengths that we can help them overcome their weaknesses.

- *Keep the lines of communication open to everyone involved.* When writing Individualized Education Programs (IEPs), it is necessary to communicate with the parent, previous teachers, and the student to determine the specific capabilities and interests that may go unnoticed unless identified by someone who knows the student personally. This can save a teacher from writing an inappropriate goal. A parent of a child who was retarded once explained to the child's teacher that the objective "the student will recognize the numbers 1–10" was not appropriate, because her child could already recognize those numbers. When the teacher asked the parent, "How do you know that he can recognize those numbers?" (since apparently the teacher had tried previously), the parent reported that her child could tell you any basketball or football player's jersey number and point to it and tell you the player's name. Because the mother related recognizing numbers in the context of what her son enjoyed—watching sports—she was able to share this with his teacher. Everyone can benefit by keeping the lines of communication open.

- *Do not jump to conclusions.* What you see may not be what you think. We tend to assume to know the reasons for other people's actions, when in reality we do not know all of the factors or the context. I witnessed a special education teacher's lesson on rain and precipitation in which she spent half of the thirty-minute lesson listening to a student share his experience about being caught in a rainstorm. At the time, I thought that this was a bit extreme. Afterward, however, I learned that this one student had been reluctant to talk or share with his classmates or teacher. He seldom spoke in class and less often carried on a conversation. Another example of hasty judgment comes from a practicum student who complained of preschool children who played all the time in the class in which she was observing. She assumed that no formal instruction was taking place. I explained to her that young children learn through the avenue of play and that, through play, these students were learning to communicate, share, count, recognize shapes, and letters, and so on. As a teacher of students who are mentally retarded, one needs to step back and get all of the facts to avoid jumping to the wrong conclusion.

- *Educate the public in order to dispel the myths concerning individuals who are retarded.* Some myths are prevalent among persons who have not had a family member who is retarded or who have not had personal involvement with an individual who is retarded. A person who has not had a personal experience with someone who is retarded is more likely to believe the myths associated with mental retardation. An isolated event with one individual who is retarded may become generalized to all individuals who are retarded. The consequences of such myths as "most people who are retarded are sexually maladjusted," "mental illness and mental retardation are synonymous terms," or "an individual is diagnosed as mentally retarded based on the results of an IQ test" can be detrimental. In such instances as a criminal trial in which an individual who is retarded is the accused, fairness can be difficult if the jury believes some of the prevalent myths. It is our obligation as professionals in the field to educate society in order to prevent the unjust and prevalent myths associated with individuals who are retarded.

- *Put more emphasis on what you as a teacher can do than on what the child who is retarded can not do.* Blaming the cognitive limits of students who are retarded or blaming the parents benefits no one. The goal of the teachers should be to improve their own teaching skills that can have an impact on enhancing the potential of each child. It is the responsibility of teachers to be aware of and use the most effective teaching methods available. Like all individuals, students who are retarded have various learning styles and individual needs. Teachers need to be able to efficiently and effectively teach each student. When faced with a student who is failing academically, responsible teachers focus on how to improve the learning environment in the classroom instead of on factors over which they have no control.

■ *Find students' comfort zones and make learning fun.* For students to be successful, teachers must present learning as an enjoyable experience. For learning to be enjoyable, I believe that the teacher must find the students' comfort zone. It is when the student is most comfortable that true learning occurs. Every child should have the opportunity to grow intellectually, physically, vocationally, and emotionally. It is the responsibility of teachers to create the type of environment that induces a pleasant climate for learning. Making learning fun encourages students to learn and to enjoy the learning experience.

■ *Classroom management is essential for learning.* In the field of mental retardation, it does not matter at what cognitive levels students function if the teacher cannot manage the students' behavior and create an environment conducive to learning. The teacher has to have the knowledge and ability to maintain classroom behavior in order to teach each student to his or her fullest potential. I recall teaching an overage student to read by implementing a strong behavior modification program combined with effective teaching strategies. I believe that this student could have learned to read years before, but he was unsuccessful because of his severe behavior problems. The missing element for this student, I believe, was the necessary classroom management at the onset of his education.

■ *Teach tasks and skills in an authentic context.* Students who are mentally retarded experience difficulty when generalizing concepts from one situation to another. It is important to teach skills in a context in which little generalization is needed. When appropriate, orchestrate the learning environment to resemble real-life experiences that the student will encounter later. Instead of having students complete a worksheet with clock faces, use real clocks to help the students understand the concept of time. Teaching students to tell time with real clocks eliminates the need for students to generalize the skill from worksheets to clocks. Teaching tasks in authentic contexts is sensible not only because it uses true-to-life situations but also is less time-consuming because the student does not have to be taught to generalize the skill.

■ *Ownership is an important concept, especially for students who are mentally retarded.* Some may believe that the concept of ownership is difficult to evoke in students who are retarded. Even so, students who are retarded should be given the opportunity to choose and decide on certain activities, tasks, and/or goals. The teacher should have an overall strategic plan to guide and prompt the student in selecting appropriate goals and activities to induce ownership. The more severely retarded the student, the more guidance and prompting the teacher will need to provide. Using portfolio assessment is one way in which ownership can be enhanced in students who are mentally retarded. Students who are retarded should be taught that their interests and concerns are worthwhile and should be communicated to others. Portfolio assessment is a good investment and is not in opposition to direct teaching or task analysis but could enhance such proven methods of teaching students who are retarded. It is possible to teach ownership to students who are retarded, and it is a good way to enhance self-esteem in these students.

■ *Be open to changing your opinion.* It is important to have a viewpoint or opinion because no one should float like a feather in the wind. Stand firm in your convictions, and share them with others. Expressing your viewpoints allows others to reflect and share their thoughts. Together, we can broaden our way of thinking. It is important to place oneself in a particular situation before passing judgment. Because we cannot experience everything, we can listen to others' stories of mistakes and successes and broaden our own life experiences. Keep in mind that we need the viewpoint of extremists; that is how we are provoked into reexamining our own philosophy and making adjustments as needed. I think that everyone should have a soapbox on which to stand, but I also think that we should be wise enough to step down when shown a better way.

■ *Understand that you cannot change the whole world by yourself.* This, however, does not mean that you should not try to make a difference. Even if you touch just one life, it is worth the effort. I am reminded of the story of the young man who was caught throwing starfish that had washed up on the shore back into the ocean. When asked why he was making such an effort when there was no way he could make a difference, he replied as he threw a starfish back in to the safety of the water, "For that one, I made all the difference in the world." We can only do what we can do, and we need the collaborative efforts of all to help make the necessary changes for the world. In preparing future teachers, I hope always to be sensitive to this issue concerning change and strive to improve what I can change after constructively evaluating whether it should be changed. Although as a newcomer, I am inclined to cling to my viewpoints, I do practice what I teach in that I keep an open mind and appreciate the accomplishments of those who came before us in the field of mental retardation so that I can better adjust my way of doing things.

As a newcomer to higher education, I am filled with great expectations and aspirations that I, as a professional, can provide effective teacher training programs. I believe that we should place the emphasis in such programs on maintaining quality services for individuals who are disabled, assisting these individuals in gaining more independence, and increasing community awareness, support, and involvement for individuals who are retarded. I believe that our ultimate goal should be to improve the quality of life for individuals who are retarded.

JERRY NUNNALLY: A CLASSROOM PERSPECTIVE

Ms. Jerry Nunnally earned a B.S. in psychology and an M.S. in special education, mental retardation from The University of Alabama, Tuscaloosa. She recently completed her eighth year as a teacher of students categorized as educable mentally retarded by the Alabama State Department of Education.

Descriptions of school-based programs are located in Chapter 9.

Ms. Nunnally relates her beliefs about teaching students who are retarded and describes how she adapts instruction and materials to meet the individual needs of students in her classroom.

Teachers of children who are retarded must be not only educators but also advocates. I have found that general education teachers, students, and administrators, as well as the general public, sometimes have negative preconceived ideas about these special children. The primary difference between general education children and "my kids" is the time and effort needed to learn. It is important to convey the message to others that children who are retarded are in more ways than not "just regular kids."

I have found that the best way to be an advocate is to assimilate into everything I do—from academics to self-help and social skills— the basic idea that children who are retarded are first and foremost children. This does not mean that the special needs of these children should be overlooked, but it does mean that the teacher must insist on and expect mastery of reading, writing, math, and all subject areas, depending on the potential of each child. One child, for example, may not be able to write her name, and for that child, mastery in handwriting may come to mean being able to accomplish this most basic task.

The teacher must never accept another teacher's or other professional's assessment that a particular child will not learn to accomplish a particular skill. I have been told that I should not waste my time trying with some children, but I have never accepted this. I have found that if you believe that each student is capable of learning, use the student's desire to learn, employ effective teaching techniques, provide sufficient instruction and practice, and reinforce success, then you can teach all students to achieve at their highest level of potential.

"If at first you don't succeed, try, try again" may sound like a cliché to us, but to my students it is a motto to live by. I start off every year by reading *The Little Engine that Could* (Piper, 1930/1976). I stress the importance of trying your hardest and the fact that mastery comes only with practice and only after many mistakes. The teacher must always praise effort but should never accept anything less than the child's personal best. If this is done correctly, then the child will learn that the teacher appreciates effort as well as success. Verbal praise, sharing achievements with others, and occasional tangible rewards such as stickers or popcorn parties also are powerful reinforcers. Such rewards work to reinforce academic concepts as well as good behavior. Mastery requires continual reinforcement even after the concept or skill is apparently learned.

I also have found that structure is an essential classroom element. Everything must be structured so that the child knows what is expected. Discipline must follow from predetermined rules that are applied consistently and fairly. A routine must be established and followed. After several years of trial and error, I have found that structure is the key to a successful year.

It is especially important at the beginning of the year to tolerate no deviation from established rules of behavior. I have found that once the child and I become more familiar with each other as the year progresses, the need for such strictness will naturally diminish. Good behavior simply becomes part of the daily routine. Of course, problems will not disappear altogether, but a little effort spent establishing the teacher's authority at the beginning of the year opens more time later for actual learning.

Structure is important in all areas. When the daily routine becomes established, the children become almost able to direct themselves. A well-structured learning environment reduces the time required for disciplinary matters. It can be as simple as minimizing the time available for mischief by having work ready for students to begin as soon as they enter the room.

I begin each lesson by saying "Feet on the floor, hands on your desk, and eyes on me." This signals to the children that something important is starting and also enforces a rule essential for attention. I never actually begin to teach until I have the attention of all students. The time and patience spent achieving absolute attendance to this one rule will be rewarded with more learning later.

Contrary to what some teachers think, structure does not mean being boring or inflexible. It does involve repetition, but the creative teacher can find so many ways to teach the same lesson that the students will think it is a great adventure in variety. Regardless of what lesson I am teaching, I employ numerous materials such as books, cassettes, filmstrips, cards, albums, different sets of letters and numbers (rubber, wooden, plastic, magnetic, felt), or anything and everything that will foster mastery.

I like to teach through the playing of games. Adapting childhood board games such as "Candy Land," "Checkers," and "Monopoly" can be a fun way to teach reading, math, or any unit. I usually write sight words, math problems, or questions on the cards or on the board itself. The children have fun at the same time they are reinforcing skills they have already learned. I also adapt games such as "Mother May I," "Going on a Bear Hunt," and "Hide and Seek" to teach reading, math, language, or science.

Manipulatives of all kinds—anything students can touch—work both visually and tactually. Activities involving hearing, smelling, and tasting can also be used. I not only try to use a multimedia approach, but also to include all of the disciplines (writing, reading, math, or language) in any lesson that I teach. For instance, while doing a science unit on dinosaurs, I have my students write, read, count, add, subtract, and talk about the "terrible lizards."

Using a multimedia approach and interrelating curricula areas fosters generalization, an aspect of learning in which many students who are retarded are deficient. The more chances the student has to learn the same concept in different ways, the greater the chance the skill will be learned. The student who is retarded often has difficulty recalling learned material in environments where specific cues are missing. I found this to be true in my first year of teaching when I employed a single approach to teach reading. I used a specialized reading program, which was very effective during reading instruction but did not generalize to other situations. The children were mastering the concepts expected by the program, but they could read the words only if they were in the reading book. For instance, the word *is* was *is* to the students only if they saw it in their reading book; if I wrote the word on the board or presented it on a word card, they were unable to read it.

So I completely changed how I taught reading. I immediately started using various teaching methods such as playing games and using different manipulatives such as cut-out letters, word cards, sentence strips, chalkboards, and numerous books, among other items, in addition to the specialized reading program. I was pleased to see a dramatic increase in the students' achievements in reading.

To foster socialization skills, I ask general education teachers about activities in their classroom in which students in my class can participate. I have found that some teachers are very willing to try any type of mainstreaming if it involves no extra work for them. Some of my children attend the general education class during activities such as circle time, center time, outdoor play, or field trips. These activities are very important in fostering desired socialization skills.

I also use general education students in other ways. For instance, I arrange for several students from the program in gifted education to come to my class. My students view it as a special treat to work alone or in a small group with a general education student as a tutor. Usually, the general education student is eager to tutor my students. It is easier than you may think to talk general education teachers into letting you lighten their load by borrowing a few of their students one or two periods a week.

Before I arrange any of these activities, I try to prepare my students. It is important for them to know how to behave and follow the rules. They need to be polite at all times. I expect this and will accept no less from my students, and they generally do not let me down.

Fortunately, my school has a public mall, a park, a grocery store, and several banks within walking distance. I take my class on frequent educational walks. I was surprised to learn that one student in my class had never been to a mall! There can be numerous learning opportunities in taking trips like these. Each year, I also take my class on several big field trips to places such as the zoo, museums of natural history, hands-on museums, and Indian mounds, among other places. I make activities such as these contingent upon good behavior, and those children who choose not to conform to the rules do not participate. However, children who misbehave always have an opportunity to redeem themselves and participate in field trips.

Students who are retarded frequently have difficulties learning self-help skills. I believe that my students need to be totally independent in caring for their personal needs. I usually teach self-help skills as the need arises, which occurs frequently if all situations are viewed as potential learning experiences. I will not assist my students unless they try first. And when I do step in, I do so verbally with as little physical prompting as possible. I slowly will give more prompting as needed.

The daily routine is rich in opportunities to teach these skills. Arrival time presents good opportunities for teaching students to take off and hang up coats and bookbags. My children prepare for lunch independently by passing out the lunch tickets, and washing and drying their hands. Lunchroom routines also have numerous opportunities to teach such self-help skills as serving their own trays (with assistance), opening their milk cartons and ketchup packets, holding their spoons and forks, wiping their mouths, cutting their food, and so on. The students also sweep the floor and clean the table daily.

Transitional goals include preparing my class to be emotionally, behaviorally, and academically ready to learn. I have most of my students for two or three years, which helps tremendously. I try to teach all the basics such as listening and following directions, and other skills needed to be successful in school. Once the foundation or groundwork has been completed, then learning can build on these skills.

The individuals whose perspectives are recorded in this chapter represent only a small sample of the many professionals and family members who, through education and advocacy, are committed to bettering the lives of individuals who are retarded. We hope that their recollections add new meaning to your understanding of individuals who are retarded, and to the diverse and varied purposes of special education.

CHAPTER 2

Historical Perspective

After reading this chapter,
the student should be able to:

- Discuss the underlying dynamics that affect the history of the study of mental retardation.
- Identify major historical eras associated with certain dominant trends.
- Discuss the contributions of persons who have had a significant effect on the development of the field.
- Explain how various sociopolitical events have affected the treatment of people who are mentally retarded.
- Trace the evolutionary development of contemporary issues.

Key Terms

community-based instruction	inclusive environments	normalization
eugenics movement	mental test	pedigree studies
feebleminded	metabolic disturbance	residential facility
homme sauvage	nature–nurture controversy	right to education
		sociopolitical forces
		sterilization

Many events and people have influenced the field of mental retardation, and a look at some of them is a worthwhile venture. From a survey of the history of the field, we can gain a better understanding of the factors that have led to our present state of affairs. However, studying the historical roots of a field is often sacrificed to the study of other topics deemed more important. This slighting of history is unfortunate, because we need to know the contexts that have shaped the field of mental retardation.

While much of the progress made in the field of mental retardation has been due to the unending and dedicated efforts of individuals, strong **sociopolitical forces** have also been at work to influence the development of the field. When studying history, we must appreciate the social climate of a given time, and, in the past, as in the present, much of what happened to people with mental retardation has been determined largely by sociopolitical forces.

Scholars such as Blatt and Sarason have paid much attention to the sociological implications of mental retardation. The conclusion that these professionals reach is that mental retardation is very much a social phenomenon. Blatt (1987) states: "Mental retardation is a concept that developed with history. It has changed through time in its nature and in its significance" (p. 9). Sarason (1985) suggests that mental retardation cannot be understood fully unless one examines the society, culture, and history within which it occurs.

The overall goal of this chapter is to give you an appreciation of how social and political forces have affected our interactions with people who are mentally retarded both in the past and today. In addition, we attempt to establish a case for what we call a "recycling phenomenon." Issues that have received our attention in recent years may not be so new as they seem.

> Many people also think that the issues facing special education today are completely new. But if you read the historical literature of special education, you will see that today's issues and problems are remarkably similar to those of long ago. Issues, problems, and ideas arise, flower, go to seed, and reappear when the conditions are again right for their growth. (Patton, Blackbourn, & Fad, 1996, p. 305)

Throughout this chapter, we mention issues that were discussed and debated long ago. You may feel dismayed by the fact that so much time has elapsed and these issues still remain just that—issues, with few "solutions" forthcoming. Consequently, this chapter has three objectives. First, we focus on the historical context of "mental retardation," giving you a glimpse of both the sociopolitical influences that have determined where we are today and some recurrent themes expressed throughout the short documented history of the field. Second, we present the content of that history, that is, the names, dates, places, and events typically associated with it. Third, we introduce you to the complexities of human services as they relate to programming for people with mental retardation.

A HISTORICAL OVERVIEW

While attitudes toward and treatment of persons who are mentally retarded can actually be traced back to ancient civilizations (including Egypt, Sparta, Rome, China, and the early Christian world), a documented history relating to mental retardation is rather brief, spanning only about the last 200 years. Accordingly, this chapter focuses on the more recent history with some attention given to earlier times. For sake of organization, we have divided history arbitrarily into five periods. These five eras are

These periods are approximations, as no firm markers exist between them.

1. Antiquity: prior to 1700
2. Emergence of and Early Disillusionment of a Field: 1700–1890
3. Facilities-Based Orientation: 1890–1960
4. Services-Based: 1960–1985
5. Supports-Based: 1985–present

Before we proceed through the various periods, we must address the problem of terminology. Throughout this chapter, those to whom we refer as mentally retarded will be described in accordance with current systems. While this usage will help us maintain a consistent standard, we would be remiss if we did not mention that, historically, various terms have been used officially to describe these individuals. Today, however, many professionals find such terms as fool, moron, imbecile, idiot, **feebleminded,** mental defective, and retardate (among others) to be historically accurate but personally offensive.

ANTIQUITY: PRIOR TO 1700

Before the 18th century, the concept of mental retardation, regardless of the term used to describe it, was enigmatic to a world that did not have a sophisticated knowledge base with which to understand it. As a result, people around the world held a wide variety of attitudes and perceptions toward people whose mental abilities and adaptive behaviors varied from the norm.

Basically, there was no consensus among Western societies as to who these deviant people were, why they acted the way they did, and how they should be treated. Different societies' responses to these questions ranged from treating these individuals as buffoons and court jesters to perceiving them as demons or as persons capable of receiving divine revelations. Evidently, throughout ancient history, different patterns of treatment developed.

Throughout this early history and continuing until the early 1900s, when we refer to persons with mental limitations, we are speaking specifically of individuals with more severe involvement. Milder forms of retardation as we perceive them today were neither defined nor recognized. During times when physical skills were most important and when few individuals could read or write, most individuals with mild retardation blended into society without too much difficulty. It was not until the early part of the 20th century that mild retardation became a describable condition.

Before 1700, certain developments resulting from the Renaissance of the 15th and 16th centuries created a new social climate that would eventually have direct implications for persons who were mentally retarded. Although the Renaissance was important to the world in many ways, the fact that it "increased man's willingness to look at himself and his environment more openly, naturally, and empirically (i.e., scientifically)" (Maloney & Ward, 1978, pp. 21–22) is particularly noteworthy. The prevailing social forces tended to refocus man's concept of himself and of the world. The ultimate effects of these changes were reflected in the development of a climate conducive to the philosophy of humanism and to the revolutionary fervor of the 18th century.

Before 1700, if any service (using the word loosely) was provided to individuals with special needs, it was protective in nature (i.e., providing housing and sustenance) and was usually offered in monasteries. Little evidence exists that systematic programs of training or service delivery were available. Although obvious changes were occurring in the world, not much was altering for the 17th-century person with mental retardation.

In America at this time, the family unit was of primary importance, and much responsibility was placed on it to take care of any exceptional member. This same dynamic can be seen in many developing countries throughout the world today. Following European precedents, the colonies enacted laws that "provided for" many individuals who could not care for themselves, by creating almshouses and workhouses. Although looked upon as financial burdens, these individuals, some of whom must have been retarded, were at least taken care of by colonial society.

EMERGENCE OF AND EARLY DISILLUSIONMENT OF A FIELD: 1700–1890

Arguably the most significant features of the 18th century were the advent of "sensationalism" and the revolutionary changes in both Europe and America. Through the efforts of various philosophers, most notably Locke and Rousseau, new ideas stressing the importance of the senses in human development began to take hold. These ideas provided new ways of perceiving the nature of the human mind and ultimately influenced educational reform.

As mentioned earlier, Renaissance thinking encouraged a philosophy of humanism, principally concerned with people's worth as human beings and with their freedom to develop. The idea that all were created equal and had inalienable rights to life, liberty, and the pursuit of happiness were popular. Eventually, these notions came into conflict with the existing philosophies and policies of some established nations, and both Europeans and Americans reacted to these needs for freedom through revolution.

We might wonder what effect these historical events had on people who were mentally retarded. We believe that they had two major implications. First, a new social attitude was established. It held that all "men," even those who were disabled, had rights. Although this attitude was not always evidenced, it helped lead to a climate that would support efforts to assist these individuals. Second, the times were right for idealistic individuals to put the philosophy of humanism and the ideas of Locke and Rousseau into practice.

The first part of the 19th century can be described as a time of enthusiasm for working with people who had various disabilities, an enthusiasm displayed by a number of devoted individuals. Influenced by the events of the previous century, these pioneers were willing to attempt something that had never been tried before: to help less fortunate people through bona fide treatment programs. The mythical birth of special education and systematic services for individuals with disabilities occurred in Europe in the early 1800s.

A movie has been made about Victor, entitled *The Wild Boy.*

Without question, the field of special education was dramatically influenced by Jean-Marc Itard (1774–1838). Early in his career, Itard, a medical doctor who initially was concerned with diseases of the ear and the needs of the deaf, became quite interested in a feral child who was found in a wooded area near Aveyron, France, in 1799. Intrigued by this boy, whom he named Victor, Itard felt that he could transform this ***homme sauvage*** from a state of wildness to a state of civilized behavior (Humphrey & Humphrey, 1962).

Believing that Victor's skill deficiencies were fundamentally due to environmental limitations, Itard thought Victor could develop the skills that were lacking by training in a systematic program. His program included five major objectives:

1. To render social life more congenial to the boy by making it more like the wild life he had recently kept.

2. To excite his nervous sensibility with varied and energetic stimuli and supply his mind with the raw impression of ideas.

3. To extend the range of his ideas by creating new wants and expanding his relations with the world around him.

4. To lead him to the use of speech by making it necessary that he should imitate.

FERAL CHILDREN

The topic of feral children is both fascinating and educational. *Feral* refers to those who have been reared in a nondomestic environment. The most celebrated feral child was Victor, the Wild Boy of Aveyron, whose contact with Jean-Marc Itard led to international attention. Other children have been reared in isolated settings; many of these are described by McNeil, Polloway, and Smith (1984). Some examples are presented here.

The Girl of Cranenburg was found at the age of eighteen living alone in the woods of the Netherlands in 1718. She had to be captured by villagers using ropes and nets. She had been kidnapped from her parents at the age of 16 months, although no one, including the girl, knew at what age she had been abandoned by her abductors. She was mute when found but quickly learned social skills. The last report concerning the Girl of Cranenburg mentioned that she was beginning to speak, had been reclaimed by her mother, and had been taken home (Ogburn, 1959; Zingg, 1966).

The Songi Girl of Champagne (Zingg, 1966) was believed to be 9 or 10 years old when she was found. She walked into a town wearing rags and animal skins and a gourd for a hat. She carried a large stick that she used to kill dogs that bothered her. She swam as well, and caught and ate fish and frogs raw. After capture she cried out if strangers came near her. She eventually was taught social skills, learned to speak and write French, did embroidery, and became a nun. "The Girl of Songi is the only case of this sort [prolonged isolation] . . . who recovered speech . . ." to any significant extent (Zingg, 1940, p. 494).

Tarzancito was captured at five years of age in San Salvador. Immediately after capture, he cried out if anyone came near him. He had lived in treetops, had eaten fruit and fish, and was an excellent swimmer. He was mute when captured but it was noted early that he had good imitative abilities. He learned three words within the first three months of his capture. Seven years after his capture, Tarzancito was in third grade making good progress, and was considered to be completely normal (Zingg, 1966).

Readjustment for these children was easier than for animal-reared children because there was not a competing repertoire of previously imprinted social behavior. While the latter may be considered "antisocial" because they have learned competing animal behaviors, the children reared in wilderness isolation can be thought of as "asocial" because they had no opportunity to learn any system of social behaviors.

5. To apply himself to the satisfaction of his growing physical wants, and from this lead to the application of his intelligence to the objects of instruction. (Kanner, 1964, p. 14)

Itard is often referred to as the "father of special education."

Although Itard worked with Victor for five years, he was disappointed because he felt that Victor had not progressed as much as he had first hoped, particularly in expressive language, and he subsequently terminated the program. From then until Victor's death in 1828, he lived under the care of Madame Guérin, the housekeeper hired to take care of him. Although Itard felt he personally had failed with Victor, he nevertheless received accolades from the French Academy of Science in recognition of his work. Itard's importance rests not so much in his success or failure with Victor but rather in the precedent that he set by systematically working and achieving gains with a child who was considered severely limited. The influence he had on others clearly distinguishes him as one of the most significant pioneers in the field of special education. As Blatt (1987) remarks, "It [Itard's work] was the first of its kind, and all 'firsts' of important movements are especially important" (p. 34).

One person who was affected by Itard's work was Edouard Seguin (1812–1880). Encouraged by Itard to get involved in the treatment of "idiocy," Seguin was motivated by a strong religious influence to help the less fortunate. Like Itard, Seguin also chose to undertake the *éducation de son enfant idiot*. After 18 months of intensive work with an "idot" boy, Seguin was able to demonstrate that the boy had learned a number of skills. Seguin extended his methods to other children, and in 1837 he established a program for "educating the feebleminded" at the Salpetrière in Paris.

Seguin's methods and educational programs, which were even more systematic than Itard's, stressed physiological and moral education. This methodology, as Seguin developed it, incorporated a general training program that integrated muscular, imative, nervous, and reflective physiological functions (Seguin, 1846). Many techniques Seguin used in his programs, such as individualized instruction and behavior management, can be found in current practice.

Seguin emigrated to the United States in 1848, principally because of the political unrest in Paris at that time. While he lived in the United States, he often served as a consultant to those who sought his advice and expertise on programming in institutional settings. In 1866 he published a book entitled *Idiocy and Its Treatment by Physiological Methods,* which became a major reference work for educating individuals with retardation in the latter part of the 19th century. Seguin also served as the first president of the Association of Medical Officers of American Institutions for Idiotic and Feebleminded Persons. Hervey Wilbur (1976), in his eulogy to Seguin, perhaps best summarized the impact this man had on the field:

> He entered upon the work with enthusiasm. There he toiled, till there he grew, little by little, a system—principles and methods—which has been the guide of all later labors in the same direction, the world over.

Chapter 14 provides an in-depth examination of institutions in contemporary society.

Another individual who figured significantly during this time in providing services to those who were mentally retarded was Johann Guggenbühl (1816–1863). Guggenbühl has been acknowledged as establishing the first **residential facility** designed to provide comprehensive treatment for individuals who were mentally retarded. This facility, called the Abendberg, which he founded in 1841, was located in the mountains of Switzerland.

Well publicized, through the efforts of Guggenbühl himself, the Abendberg drew the attention of many prominent people. The real significance of Guggenbühl's facility rests in its impact on the visitors it attracted, many of whom were interested in establishing similar facilities. As Kanner notes, "The Abendberg became the destination of pilgrimages made by physicians, philanthropists, and writers from many lands, who promptly published glowing reports when they went back home" (1964, p. 25).

Unfortunately, the glowing reviews and accolades accorded the Abendberg were short-lived, and eventually the facility came under severe criticism. Although forced to close due to mismanagement and the resulting intolerable conditions, in its heyday, the Abendberg nevertheless served as the model for many other institutions. It can also serve as an example of a program that achieved recognition but was unable to maintain it. Notwithstanding the problems, Guggenbühl created a prototype for institutional care, the effects of which dominated services in the early 20th century and can still be felt today.

Although the discipline of special education was conceived and born in Europe, the field also prospered from the work of important people and from events that occurred in the United States during the mid-1800s. Three individuals who had much to do with promoting the welfare of and developing services for persons with mental retardation in this country were Dorothea Dix, Samuel Howe, and Hervey Wilbur.

During the early 1840s, Dorothea Dix zealously campaigned for better treatment of the less fortunate who were housed in asylums, almshouses, poorhouses, and country homes. At that time, there were no other options for such people. Her efforts are reflected in her own words, directed toward the Massachusetts legislature in 1843:

> I come to present the strong claims of suffering humanity. I come to place before the Legislature of Massachusetts the condition of the miserable, the desolate, the outcast. I come as the advocate of helpless, forgotten, insane, and idiotic men and women; of beings sunk to a condition from which the most unconcerned would start with real horror; of beings wretched in our prisons, and more wretched in our almshouses. And I cannot suppose it needful to employ earnest persuasion, or stubborn argument, in order to arrest and fix attention upon a subject only the more strongly pressing in its claims because it is revolting and disgusting in its details. (Dix, 1843-1976)

Obviously, Dorothea Dix dramatized what advocacy is all about, and through her efforts she was able to focus much attention on those whom she called "suffering humanity," and for whom there were few advocates. A similar plea could be made today for the large number of homeless people in this country.

Samuel Howe (1801–1876) contributed greatly to providing services for people who were mentally retarded through his efforts to establish public support for their training. In 1848, after visiting Guggenbühl's Abendberg and convincing the Massachusetts legislature to appropriate $2,500 per year,

Howe established the first public setting for training individuals who were mentally retarded. This new setting was located in a wing of Boston's Perkins Institution for the Blind, of which Howe was the director. A few months earlier, Hervey Wilbur (1820–1883) had founded the first private setting for treating individuals with mental retardation at his home in Barre, Massachusetts.

What then was the result of the work of pioneers like Itard, Seguin, Guggenbühl, Howe, Dix, and Wilbur? First, an atmosphere of optimism developed. Many of those persons who were mentally retarded, it was thought, could be trained, "cured," and reintegrated into the community as productive citizens. Second, based upon this very same hope and enthusiasm, many promises were made, reflected in the lofty goals that were set. Ironically, it was precisely the enthusiasm prevalent at the time that would be partially responsible for the backlash that was to come.

A similar mood of optimism about inclusion can be felt today.

As any student of United States history knows quite well, the 1860s were a time of national disharmony, inflamed by years of growing sectional conflict. Prior to the Civil War, America was basically an agrarian society characterized by small farms and small towns. After the war, the country began to experience a dramatic change toward urbanization and industrialization. These and other developments had a strong effect on the treatment of persons who were mentally retarded.

This national metamorphosis precipitated many problems, some of which accompanied the increased growth of cities. Correlates of urban life such as crime, poverty, and disease were later to be associated with retardation. In addition, while industrialization provided vocational opportunities for many people, the skills required were often too demanding for many persons with significant limitations.

What happened to the enthusiasm of the mid-1800s? There was a critical change in attitude toward the possibility of reintegrating those with retardation into the community. After initially accepting the grandiose claims of many individuals, who suggested that those less fortunate could be "cured," critics began to realize that these goals, while laudable, were unrealistic. A pronounced climate of pessimism developed. We know today that those individuals who were considered capable of being cured in the 1800s were indeed capable of skill acquisition, but for most of them, attainment of "normalcy" was not possible. That individuals who were more severely disabled had not changed enough to be able to move back into community settings resulted in a negative perception of this group.

Many problems contributed to the disillusionment of this era. Four factors, however, seem to be salient. First, as already mentioned, the population being addressed was not capable of being "cured," or transformed into totally normal functioning members of society. Second, community reintegration demands more than merely providing training and placement. If successful reintegration requires community preparation and development, as we think it does, then we should not be surprised that the neglect of this issue in the 1800s led to failure in attempts at reintegration. Sadly, even today, the provision of community services and supports is glaringly inadequate in many cases. Third, after an atmosphere of hope and excitement had been created, many individuals who were retarded were pitied, resulting in two important developments: (a) dilution of services to individuals who needed systematic, intensive programming, and (b) formation of more institutions. These developments were to have a tragic effect in the late 1800s. Fourth, the previously mentioned demands of the increasingly more complex society created by postwar urbanization and industrialization worked against those who were retarded.

Obviously, these were formidable obstacles to reaching the goals championed by the idealistic pioneers of the early and mid-1800s. While it is easy now to reproach those enthusiasts for creating a no-win situation that ultimately resulted in many regressive developments for those whom they wanted to help, we need to understand that these early advocates (however naive) were most sincere in their zeal, hopes, and efforts. Unfortunately, those individuals on whom the great expectations were based were not being perceived as "incurable." It was bad enough that the early enthusiasm had waned, but even more discouraging was the fact that the worst was yet to come.

FACILITIES-BASED ORIENTATION: 1890–1960

As the 19th century came to a close, disillusionment began to take on a more reactionary tone. A change from concern for caring about individuals who had special needs to one for protecting society from them was evident. Institutions originally designed to serve as training facilities from which individuals would leave to return to community settings now began to assume a new custodial role.

During this period of alarm, a number of events caused a dramatic change in social attitudes, weakening most movements favorable to the needs of this group. Many citizens were now afraid that these people were dangerous to society. Kanner describes the prevailing perceptions during this time:

> The mental defectives were viewed as a menace to civilization, incorrigible at home, burdens to the school, sexually promiscuous, breeders of feebleminded offspring, victims and spreaders of poverty, degeneracy, crime, and disease. Consequently, there was a cry for the segregation of all mental defectives, with the aim of purifying society, of erecting a solid wall between it and its contaminators. (1964, p. 85)

It did not take long for society to develop ways to control people who were mentally defective. The principal means for doing this included various forms of segregation, an extreme example of which was **sterilization.** A committee of the American Breeder's Association, which had been formed in 1911, concluded that "segregation for life or at least during the reproductive years must, in the opinion of the committee, be the principal agent used by society in cutting off its supply of defectives" (cited in Kanner, 1964, p. 136). As an added measure of control, institutions strictly segregated men and women to eliminate their chances of producing offspring who would possibly be feebleminded.

Many contributing factors precipitated repressive events in the late 1800s and early 1900s. Three factors seem to have had a pronounced effect on the creation of this backlash: the eugenics scare, the influx of immigrants to the United States, and the mental test movement.

THE EUGENICS SCARE

Although the thrust of the **eugenics movement** was not felt until the late 1800s and early 1900s, its antecedents can be traced to earlier times. This movement was interested in controlling the number of "feebleminded" persons through selective breeding.

Influenced by the ideas of Charles Darwin, Sir Francis Galton extended Darwin's concept of evolution to humans. In 1869, Galton published *Hereditary Genius,* which espoused the idea that individual traits, most notably genius, were inherited. Galton's work seemed to catalyze the eugenics movement that advocated the genetic control of mental defectives. What Galton established was a theoretical basis for the inheritance of mental defectiveness. Gregor Mendel's discovery of the laws of inheritance in the 19th century lent scientific support to Galton's ideas.

Two publications reinforced society's attitude that mental retardation had genetic implications: *The Jukes, a Study of Crime, Pauperism, Disease and Heredity* (Dugdale, 1877) and *The Kallikak Family* (Goddard, 1912). Each of these works traced the genetic relationships of the families under study. Dugdale's original work actually focused on criminality and its correlates, and only later was the added correlate of mental retardation inferred. Goddard's work, however, had as its central theme the notion that feeblemindedness was inherited; elaborate **pedigree studies** (through five generations) were presented as evidence. Goddard's work was very powerful, and, along with other related events, fueled the movement to control the menace of feeblemindedness genetically. But many years later, Goddard's research on Martin Kallikak's two distinct family lines was called into question. The details of the social myth perpetuated by Goddard are described in J.D. Smith's (1985) book entitled *Minds Made Feeble* (see boxed feature).

MINDS MADE FEEBLE

In 1912 Henry Goddard reported the results of his study of the inheritance of feeblemindedness. His book, *The Kallikak Family: A Study in the Heredity of Feeble-Mindedness,* was influential because it underscored the perceived threat of feeblemindedness to society and helped fuel the eugenics movement. The book was very popular, and to this day the Kallikak story is regularly retold in discussions of mental retardation.

The effects of the study are described well by J. David Smith (1985) in *Minds Made Feeble:*

> Goddard's book on the Kallikak family was received with acclaim by the public and by much of the scientific community. . . . Only gradually was criticism forthcoming which questioned the methods used in the study and the implications and conclusions drawn from the data collected. Even in the light of substantive and knowledgeable criticism, however, the essential message of the Kallikak study persisted for years. Even today its influence, in convoluted forms, continues to have a social and political impact. That message is simple, yet powerful. Ignorance, poverty, and social pathology are in the blood—in the seed. It is not the environment in which people are born and develop that makes the critical difference in human lives. People are born either favored or beyond help.

It was this message and the social myth that accompanied it that compelled Smith to investigate and report the complete story of the Kallikak family and of Goddard's study.

A few highlights of Smith's findings are presented below.

- Serious questions arise as to whether Deborah Kallikak, the woman with whom Goddard came into contact and whose ancestors he studied, was actually feebleminded.
- Goddard's professional acquaintance with influential eugenic leaders seems to have had a great influence on his work.
- The methodology used to study the Kallikak family and the skills of those who collected the information are once again questioned.
- The "real" Kallikaks were not as abhorrent as they were described by Goddard. Smith commented, "The truth of their lives was sacrificed to the effort to prove a point. The Kallikak study is fiction draped in the social science of its time."
- The implications of the study proved to be a very potent indictment against the poor, the uneducated, racial minorities, the foreign born, and those classified as mentally retarded or mentally ill, resulting in such social policies as compulsory sterilization, restricted immigration, and institutionalization, which adversely and unfairly affected these groups.
- Through painstaking investigation, Smith determined the real name of the family Goddard studied (Kallikak was a pseudonym). However, he does not reveal the name.

One of Smith's major contributions is his admonition to be aware of the significance and power of social myths: "Social myths are constantly in the making, compelling in their simplicity, and alluring because we want to believe them. Perhaps understanding the Kallikak story will help in recognizing and resisting them."

Strong evidence that eugenics was being taken seriously can be found in the enactment of sterilization laws during the early 1900s. Indiana holds the dubious distinction of enacting the first such law in 1907. Within 20 years, similar laws were on the books in 23 states. The constitutionality of these laws was challenged in several states and ultimately upheld by the Supreme Court in the famous case of *Buck v. Bell* (1927). As J.D. Smith (1987) highlights, this case "became the precedent for the right of state governments to intervene in the reproductive practices of those citizens deemed defective in some way" (p. 148). The case is noteworthy not only for the precedent it set, but also for two other reasons: (a) Carrie Buck, the woman used to test Virginia's compulsory sterilization law, probably was not mentally retarded; and (b) the prevailing attitude of the time was clearly expressed in the majority opinion given by Justice Oliver Wendell Holmes:

> We have seen more than once that the public welfare may call upon the best citizens for their lives. It would be strange if it could not call upon those who already sap the strength of the State for these lesser sacrifices, often felt to be much by those concerned, in order to prevent our being swamped with incompetence. It is better for all the world, if instead of waiting to execute degenerate offspring for crime, or to let them starve for their imbecility, society can prevent those who are manifestly unfit from continuing their kind. The principle that sustains compulsory vaccination is broad enough to cover cutting the Fallopian tubes. . . . Three generations of imbeciles are enough. (*Buck v. Bell,* 1927, p. 50)

For a thorough discussion of Carrie Buck's life and times, see J. D. Smith and Nelson (1989).

IMMIGRATION

During the second half of the 19th century, the United States experienced a great increase in the number of immigrants, mostly from southern and eastern Europe. As most of these immigrants flocked to the growing urban centers, many problems emerged. Americans of northern and western European origin looked upon these immigrants as inferior; this stance was supported by a study performed by Goddard (1917), which concluded that many of these foreigners were feebleminded. One outcome of this generalized concern was enactment of the Immigration Restriction Act in 1924. This legislation restricted the flow of people of Italian, Russian, Hungarian, and Jewish background into this country until 1965.

THE TESTING MOVEMENT

A third major trend contributing to the alarmist climate of the early 1900s was the introduction of the **mental test.** In 1905, Alfred Binet and Theodore Simon developed an instrument designed to be used in French schools to screen those students who were not benefiting from the regular classroom experience and who might need special services. It is interesting to realize that Binet was concerned that this instrument might be misused. As S.J. Gould (1981) notes, Binet "greatly feared that his practical device . . . could be perverted and used as an indelible label, rather than as a guide for identifying children who needed help" (p. 151). The mental test has had a lasting effect on the field of special education. In essence, in the mental scale of intelligence, Binet and Simon created a mechanism for identifying milder forms of retardation. Before this time, those recognizable as mentally retarded were more severely involved, but now that individuals with less severe mental retardation could be identified, new alarms were being sounded about the magnitude of the problem.

Although Binet and Simon introduced their test in France, before long it was brought to the United States. In 1911, Henry Goddard translated the Binet-Simon scales into English, and in 1916, Lewis Terman of Stanford University refined the mental scales into the instrument known as the Stanford-Binet. (It was W. Stern, a German psychologist, who is given credit for developing the conceptual basis for determining IQ [intelligence quotient].)

The impact of the mental test on the identification of mild mental retardation is still felt today.

Since many more individuals could now be empirically identified as mentally retarded, separate special classes for these students developed and grew in number. In 1896, the first special class in the United States for students who were retarded was established in Providence, Rhode Island. Another event of significance was New Jersey's enactment, in 1911, of legislation mandating education for this type of student. With the beginning of World War I, the military services needed a way to obtain information relatively quickly about large groups of people for use in assigning personnel. Thus, the first group of intelligence scales (the alpha and beta tests) was developed. The results of this testing fed alarmist tendencies by suggesting that mild mental retardation was more widespread than anyone had previously believed. Yerkes's 1921 work on the intellectual capacities of World War I soldiers supported this assumption, further exacerbating negative feelings about retardation.

An alarm had indeed been sounded! Society was frightened by the "menace" of retardation. With the recognition of mental retardation's greater prevalence, with its seeming inheritability, and with its correlation with crime, poverty, incorrigibility, and disease, it is not difficult to understand how restrictive and segregationist attitudes could develop and dominate. Quite strong by the end of the second decade of the 20th century, this aura of fear would begin to fade in the ensuing years. But its impact could be long-lasting.

RELATED SOCIOPOLITICAL INFLUENCES

Social attitudes toward individuals with disabilities changed somewhat after World War I. As in all wars, many veterans returned to their homes with injuries. In 1920, the Vocational Rehabilitation Act (PL 66-236) was enacted to allow civilians to benefit from vocational rehabilitation. This legislation has endured as one of the most important laws enacted to protect the rights of individuals with disabilities. With the end of the war, the need for providing services to veterans had been acknowledged. Now these services were being extended to others who needed them.

Lifestyles changed quickly with the stock market crash of 1929 and the Great Depression that followed. The Great Depression was not a pleasant experience; however, some outcomes were beneficial. The Depression caused the average person, who had been unaware of or uninterested in the problems of human need, to appreciate them, for everyone was needy.

Special education as a bona fide professional field took a tremendous step in 1922, when Elizabeth Farrell established the International Council for the Education of Exceptional Children. Prior to this time, the field had had no unifying organizational structure on a national level. Farrell served as the first president of this new organization, now known as the Council for Exceptional Children (CEC), and it became a new institutional force in special education.

Following a period of great concern about the social menace of mental retardation in the early part of the 20th century, some movement toward greater enlightenment was evident, as Maloney and Ward (1978) state:

1. The view of mental retardation as a unitary, recessive, inherited trait began to fade as the science of genetics grew in scope and precision.
2. New clinical studies demonstrated the significance of other, nonhereditary, sources of mental retardation, such as trauma, infection, and endocrine disturbance.
3. The methodological flaws and biased interpretations of the pedigree studies were becoming more and more apparent.
4. Other surveys of institutional populations indicated that over one-half of them had intellectually normal parents, further weakening the singular heredity view and associated calls for eugenic solutions.
5. The older research studies that had linked mental retardation with every conceivable social ill were critically reanalyzed and found wanting.
6. Newer, better controlled, and more objective studies failed to reveal the dramatic links of the previous era. (p. 57)

During the early 1930s, the United States was trying to regain stability both economically and socially. One notable event occurred when President Herbert Hoover convened the first White House Conference on Child Health and Protection in 1930, drawing national attention, however briefly, to the needs of disabled individuals. Another important trend was the number of classes for special students, which kept increasing.

After the presidential election of 1932, the United States went through many changes. The new president, Franklin D. Roosevelt, influenced this country's attitudes toward the welfare of all its citizens. Roosevelt's New Deal philosophy was responsible for much social change through legislation and the formulation of new programs. One such piece of legislation that affected individuals with special needs was the Social Security Act of 1935. In a nutshell, during the 1930s, two major trends emerged in the treatment of individuals with disabilities: (a) the generation of a new attitude supportive of a public welfare system and (b) the affirmation of responsibility to those in need.

With the direct involvement of the United States in World War II, the attention and behavior of the nation were refocused once again. We can see certain similarities between World War I and World War II vis-à-vis the field of mental retardation. As in World War I, screening of soldiers in the 1940s readjusted the perceived extent of mild retardation. One source that contributed to this changed thinking was a study conducted by Ginzberg and Bray, as described in their book *The Uneducated* (1953). They studied two groups of men being considered for military service. Their primary group consisted of men who were rejected on the basis of mental deficiency; the other group included men who were accepted for service but who experienced major problems in academic skill areas (i.e., literacy).

When the war was over, many families, and the nation as a whole, felt the realities of disability. A heightened sensitivity to the needs of disabled veterans developed. World War II also created increased employment opportunities in war-related industries for individuals who were retarded.

As the 1950s began, the field of special education went through changes that would have notable effects in subsequent years. Foremost among these changes was a new national policy concerned with the problems of special groups of people.

After World War II, the United States experienced a period of renewed prosperity. This created a climate in which "the demands of parents, the enthusiasm of professionals, and federal, state and private funding gave new impetus to progress in the area of mental retardation" (Hewett & Forness, 1977). These three forces, augmented by other factors, highlighted this turning point in the history of special education. Although institutional changes were beginning to occur, at best, these events could be classified only as a "quiet revolution." Individuals were still being institutionalized at an alarming rate; tragically, many persons who should not have been placed in these settings found themselves there. Furthermore, too many had already suffered sterilization, a personal indignity and a violation of their civil rights. By 1938, compulsory sterilizations had been performed on more than 27,000 people in the United States (Marks, cited in J.D. Smith, 1987).

> Since their formation, parent groups have been a major factor influencing policy and practice.

Certainly an important event during this time was the formation in 1950 of the National Association for Retarded Children (NARC)—now known as the Arc. This organization, composed mostly of parents of children who were retarded, became an important advocate for these children. Functioning as lobbyist, service provider, and promoter of research, NARC had a profound impact on individuals who were mentally retarded. Most important, NARC was a coordinated effort of its members to express their attitudes, beliefs, concerns, and desires in politically effective ways.

By the early 1950s, the United States was beginning to adopt a national policy committed to the needs of those who were mentally retarded and a policy willing to give financial support to endeavors that addressed these needs. Over the years, social attitudes toward people with retardation had changed from fear and revulsion to tolerance and compassion. Whether sparked by the troubled times of the 1930s and 1940s that the nation as a whole endured, or influenced by purely economic motives, during the 1950s, the financial backing required to develop more and better programs was provided. If only for economic reasons, the importance of maximizing the potential of persons who were disabled was acknowledged during this time, as was stated by President Eisenhower in a 1954 message to Congress:

> We are spending three times as much in public assistance to care for nonpro-ductive disabled people as it would cost to make them self-sufficient and tax-paying members of their communities. Rehabilitated people as a group pay back in federal income taxes many times the cost of their rehabilitation.

By 1952, 46 of 48 states had enacted legislation for educating students who were identified as mentally retarded. This legislation, however, did not provide programming for all students with mental retardation. Many children in the moderate range and most children in the severe range were still excluded from receiving educational services in public settings.

Not until 1975 and the passage of PL 94-142, the Education for All Handicapped Children Act, was the issue of educating all students with mental retardation formally addressed on a national level. But 1954 is also notable because in that year Congress passed the Cooperative Research Act (PL 83-531), which provided money for research that would focus on mental retardation. In 1958, PL 85-926 was passed, offering incentives to various organizations (state educational agencies and institutions of higher education) in the form of grants to encourage the preparation of teachers of this group of students. Thus, if we look at federal legislation as an index of national commitment to a cause, then we can see that policy supportive of the needs of special people was emerging in the 1950s.

As the decade came to a close, three forces were beginning to shape events. First, a new philosophical view of retardation was forming, as reflected in the 1958 publication of *Mental Subnormality,* published by Masland, Sarason, and Gladwin. This school of thought stressed that certain social and cultural variables have a strong correlation with mental retardation. The influence of this point of view on the field can be observed in the 1959 definition of mental retardation promoted by the American Association on Mental Deficiency (Heber, 1959). This definition associated intellectual deficits with "impairment in one or more of the following: (1) maturation, (2) learning, and (3) social adjustment" (Heber, 1959, p. 3).

Second, educators and advocates became concerned about the segregation in special classes of students who were mentally retarded. Existing research tended to support the special class setting. Nevertheless, this issue would continue to be debated, resulting in some major changes in the 1970s. In addition, the Supreme Court decision in the *Brown v. Board of Education*

(1954) desegregation case also affected thinking and policy making for individuals with mental retardation.

Third, when the Soviet Union launched Sputnik in 1957, the United States responded dramatically; shocked by the event, the country made a commitment to technological development unparalleled in history. The nation's overwhelming desire to grow technologically would focus very sharply on the institution of education. Changes were evidently needed, and many did come about. Both regular and special education were affected by the vigor of the times. The nation was primed for the tumultuous sixties.

RESEARCH AND PROGRAMMATIC INFLUENCES

The importance of scientific discoveries related to etiology is paralleled today by the work of the Human Genome Project.

During this period many important developments took place in both social and physical sciences. In 1934, Fölling, a Norwegian physician, explained the biochemical mechanics related to the **metabolic disturbance** referred to as PKU (phenylketonuria). The importance of this discovery goes beyond this single event:

> This contribution, termed "one of the great discoveries in medical history" by Clemens E. Bonda, at long last made the issue of mental deficiency appear respectable as a legitimate field of research in the biological sciences. Slowly and at first reluctantly, the medical profession began to take an interest. (Kanner, 1964, p. 141)

Two assessment instruments of major importance were developed during this period. In 1935, Edgar Doll published his Vineland Social Maturity Scale (VSMS). Use of this scale allowed professionals to gain additional information about a person's behavior and level of functioning. In 1949, David Wechsler published another intelligence scale, the Wechsler Intelligence Scale for Children (WISC). Like the VSMS, this device became very popular. Ever since their publication, these instruments and their subsequent revisions have had a pronounced effect on the identification and classification of many individuals suspected of being retarded.

Another influence on the public perception of mental retardation was a number of studies that seemed to stress the importance of environment as a cause of mental retardation. As the **nature–nurture controversy** was debated, certain studies, most notably those performed by Skeels and his colleagues, questioned the notion that IQ was fixed or constant. Skeels and Dye (1939) inferred that environmental factors have a critical effect on IQ, or, if you will, on one's classification as mentally retarded.

SERVICES-BASED ORIENTATION: 1960–1985

In the 1960s, a new paradigm was emerging, as described by Polloway, Smith, Patton, and Smith (1996):

> On the heels of the facility-based period came a profound shift toward a "services-based paradigm." Through this model, there was an attempt to provide special services to individuals, as a preparation for their subsequent integration into society. Consequently, programs most typically included self-contained special education classes in regular schools, resource or pull-out programs, transitional workshops, related training programs, and the like. . . . In the services model, the assumption was made that appropriate programming for individuals with disabilities would be followed by successful integrated placement. (p. 5)

If asked to reflect on the decade of the 1960s, one would probably think of the many tragic episodes in a time of rather extreme social change. The violent deaths of national leaders and the widespread opposition and reaction to the Vietnam War are vivid recollections of the 1960s. The early part of this decade was characterized by a generalized enthusiasm, and this enthusiasm was quite evident in the area of special education. For many reasons, special education was on center stage during the sixties.

When President Kennedy assumed office in 1961, he symbolized the energy of our country at that time. Kennedy, who had a sister who was mentally retarded, once again brought national attention to the needs of this group. At the beginning of his administration, he established the President's Panel on Mental Retardation (PPMR), which was to serve as a guide and source for national policy formation. Under the direction of Leonard Mayo, this panel published *A Proposed Program for National Action to Combat Mental Retardation* (Mayo, 1962), which set the tone for policy decisions for the next decade. Many of the principal recommendations found in the report have a contemporary flavor.

1. Research in the causes of retardation and in methods of care, rehabilitation, and learning.

2. Preventive health measures, including (a) a greatly strengthened program of maternal and infant care directed first at the centers of population where prematurity and the rate of "damaged" children are high; (b) protection against such known hazards to pregnancy as radiation and harmful drugs; and (c) extended diagnostic and screening services.

3. Strengthened educational programs generally and extended and enriched programs of special education in public and private schools closely coordinated with vocational guidance, vocational rehabilitation, and specific training and preparation for employment; education for the adult mentally retarded, and workshops geared to their needs.

4. More comprehensive and improved clinical and social services.

5. Improved methods and facilities for care, with emphasis on the development of a wide range of local community facilities.

6. A new legal, as well as social, concept of the retarded, including protection of their civil rights; life guardianship provisions when needed; an enlightened attitude on the part of the law and the courts; and clarification of the theory of responsibility in criminal acts.

7. Helping overcome the serious problems of manpower as they affect the entire field of science and every type of service through extended programs of recruiting with fellowships; and increased opportunities for graduate students, and those preparing for the professions to observe and learn at first hand about the phenomenon of retardation. Because there will never be a fully adequate supply of personnel in this field and for other cogent reasons, the panel has emphasized the need for more volunteers in health, recreation, and welfare activities, and for a domestic Peace Corps to stimulate voluntary service.

8. Programs of education and information to increase public awareness of the problem of mental retardation. (Mayo, 1962, pp. 14–15)

Other recommendations, not unlike some proposed in the 1990s, included the following:

1. That programs for the retarded, including modern day care, recreation, residential services, and ample educational and vocational opportunities, be comprehensive.

2. That they operate in or close to the communities where the retarded live—that is, that they be community centered.

3. That services be so organized as to provide a central or fixed point for the guidance, assistance, and protection of retarded persons if and when needed, and to assure a sufficient array of continuum of services to meet different types of need.

4. That private agencies as well as public agencies at the local, state, and federal levels continue to provide resources and to increase them for this worthy purpose. While the federal government can assist, the principal responsibility for financing and improving services for the mentally retarded must continue to be borne by states and local communities. (Mayo, 1962, pp. 14–15)

Federal legislation relevant to the field of mental retardation continued to be enacted during the sixties. In 1963, Congress passed the Mental Retardation Facilities and Mental Health Centers Construction Act, which provided monies for the construction of Mental Retardation Research Centers (MRRCs). These centers conducted organized multidisciplinary research on various complex facets of mental retardation. In 1965, the Elementary and Secondary Education Act (ESEA) (PL 89-10) was passed. Part of this legislation focused attention on the needs of disadvantaged students. In 1966, ESEA was amended, and as a result the Bureau of Education for the Handicapped (BEH), a subcomponent of the Office of Education (OE), was created.

National policy directed to the needs of the disadvantaged reached its pinnacle with President Johnson's War on Poverty. With the growing interest in social and cultural determinants of behavior, it is not surprising that much attention was given to environmental causes of retardation. Project Head Start did just that. The concept that early intervention could ameliorate some of the negative effects of unfavorable situations was fashionable and encouraged during the mid-sixties.

If nothing else can be said of the 1960s, certainly we can state that it was a time responsive to personal and civil rights. The Civil Rights movement was consummated by passage into law of the Civil Rights Act of 1964; however, this law did not deal directly with people with disabilities. Nevertheless, the achievements and impetus provided by the civil rights movement and the resulting legislation would be realized and extended to people with disabilities in the 1970s through today.

TRENDS IN SERVICE DELIVERY

With continuing support from state and federal governments, programs and services for individuals who were retarded proliferated almost exponentially. But the spotlight was soon to flicker, if not dim. Lloyd Dunn's 1968 questioning of the efficacy of placing students with mild retardation in special classes symbolized some of the reexamination occurring in the late sixties and early seventies.

Wolfensberger prefers the term social valorization to the term normalization.

A new philosophical theme was beginning to take hold. The concept of **normalization,** which originated during the 1950s in Scandinavia, was finding much support in the United States. N. E. Bank-Mikkelsen and Bengt Nirje were eminently responsible for the development and dissemination of this principle in Scandinavia, while Wolf Wolfensberger was instrumental in championing it in the United States.

To a great extent this was due to a single publication that had a great impact on professionals in the United States. Entitled *Changing Patterns in Residential Services for the Mentally Retarded,* this publication included a discussion of the principle of normalization by Nirje (1969), sparking a movement in this country that epitomized the next decade. Nirje defined normalization as "making available to the mentally retarded patterns and conditions of everyday life which are as close as possible to the norms and patterns of the mainstream of society" (p. 181).

As more professionals recognized the needs of people with retardation, there was a new emphasis on community-based services. This trend has continued. To some degree, attention to community issues was a result of parental concern about their now adult children.

During the 1960s, the nature–nurture issue, which had been brewing for many years, seemed to be best answered by those arguing the importance of interaction between heredity and environment. Although supporters of this orientation acknowledged both hereditary and environmental determinants of many types of mild mental retardation, they felt that environmental factors were more influential. In 1969, much attention was drawn to this issue by Arthur Jensen. Jensen (1969) published an article in the *Harvard Educational Review* entitled "How Much Can We Boost IQ and Scholastic Achievement?" He argued that genetic factors are more important than environmental factors in determining IQ (i.e., the high inheritability of intelligence). Where Jensen's article received the most criticism was in his implication that social class and racial variations in intelligence are attributable to genetic differences.

In the changing social climate of the late 1960s, characterized by many forms of reactionary behavior, services to and certain concepts of those with retardation were being challenged. The revolutionary fervor of the sixties would wane as the seventies progressed. For exceptional individuals and those working with them, however, the early seventies were reminiscent of the turbulent sixties in many ways.

Recent times have witnessed the advent of new directions in educating and training students with mental retardation. For instance, there is a definite trend toward providing **community-based instruction** and programming for these students. Great strides have been made in providing services to infants, toddlers, and other young children. Transitional programming is in evidence in various areas of the country where just a few years ago there was none. New models for making these individuals employable have been introduced. Competitive employment options are replacing the former sheltered employment model on a widespread basis.

In the entire history of services to persons who are mentally retarded, there had been no period with more visible gains than the early 1970s. Without a doubt, the pioneers of the early 19th century had made great steps in initiating intervention; however, events of the 1970s were of similar significance. At long last, it was established that Americans who were mentally retarded had certain personal and civil rights guaranteeing services and protection. As can be seen from Figure 2.1, the number of students receiving special education greatly increased during the 1960s and 1970s. (That this number began decreasing toward the end of the 1970s is discussed later.)

FIGURE 2.1

Enrollment of Students with Mental Retardation, 1922-1991

Data are from U.S. Department of the Census and U.S. Department of Education, Office of Special Education.

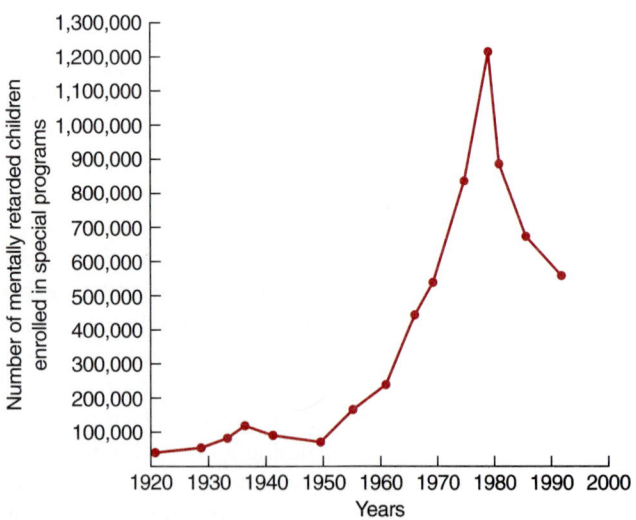

A more detailed discussion of litigation is provided in Chapter 13.

Most notably, the early 1970s were litigious times. A new tactic for ensuring services was beginning to emerge. Previously, courts had been used as a last resort, but now they were used frequently and strategically. Rights afforded the regular citizenry had been denied to many individuals who were mentally retarded, and the courtroom became the forum in which these rights were secured. This policy was supported by parent groups and at least tolerated by a society responsive to human rights infringements, and many issues were brought to the courtroom. Chief among them were rights to education and proper treatment.

The **right to education** issue was sparked in 1971 by a celebrated class action suit, *Pennsylvania Association for Retarded Children [PARC] v. Commonwealth of Pennsylvania*. This litigation resulted in an agreement that established the right to free, appropriate public school education for all children who were mentally retarded within the jurisdiction of this federal court district. However, the impact of the court-ordered agreement extended beyond eastern Pennsylvania, as similar suits dealing with the same issue were filed in many other states in the months following the decision.

Although *PARC v. Pennsylvania* was specifically concerned with the exclusion from public education of children whose primary descriptor was retardation, other students with disabilities were soon to enjoy the same right. In that same year, a suit on behalf of all students with special educational needs, regardless of type and severity, was filed in federal district court in Washington, DC. This case, *Mills v. Board of Education of the District of Columbia* (1972), was decided in favor of the plaintiffs, extending the right to education to all children with disabilities.

During this same period, many individuals living in institutions were receiving very little in the way of services beyond custodial care. In 1971, in the case *Wyatt v. Stickney,* the lack of appropriate treatment provided residents at an institution for the mentally retarded in Alabama was contested. Although aspects of this case are still being reviewed, the original decision declared that the residents of Partlow State School and Hospital were entitled to receive treatment, not just custodial care. The judge enumerated the steps to be taken to comply with this decision.

As can be seen, the courts began to shape certain practices during this time. What may seem strange to the casual observer—and eminently significant to the special education professional—is the critical and influential roles that judges, lawyers, and expert witnesses played during the litigious early seventies. To professionals who were often the main service providers to those who were retarded, it seemed that much policy was being formed by experts in other fields. Although to a certain extent this is true, knowledgeable parents and special educators were the ones who had realized that rights had not been secured or guaranteed through committee or panel action and that, as a result, legal procedures had become necessary.

The judicial activity of the early 1970s culminated in the enactment of federal legislation that affected individuals with disabilities. Two pieces of

COMPONENTS OF THE INDIVIDUALS WITH DISABILITIES EDUCATION ACT (IDEA) OF 1990

IDEA, formerly the Education of the Handicapped Act, is the comprehensive law articulating federal policy concerning the education of and early intervention for infants, toddlers, children, and youth with disabilities. It sets forth requirements regarding the provision of early intervention, special education, and related services and establishes model and demonstration programs, personnel preparation support, research, and information centers. IDEA includes such well-known legislation as PL 94-142, The Education for all Handicapped Children Act of 1975; PL 99-457, the 1986 amendments that support early intervention services; and PL 101-476, the 1990 amendments that include transition services. The name of this act was changed by the 1990 amendments, which also changed its wording to reflect "people first" language and to use the word *disability* rather than *handicap*. Although there is much more to IDEA, we will briefly discuss some of the highlights of the law.

The Eight Parts of IDEA

IDEA consists of the following eight parts:

Part A: states the goals of the Act, provides definition of its terms, and mandates the existence of an Office of Special Education Programs within the U.S. Department of Education. The goals of the Act are as follows:

To assure that the rights of children with disabilities and their parents or guardians are protected.

To assist states and localities to provide for the education of all children with disabilities.

To assess and ensure the effectiveness of efforts to educate children with disabilities.

Part B: authorizes grants to states to help underwrite the costs of educating children with disabilities and sets out the conditions states must meet to qualify for these grants. The Part B program presently provides over $2 billion to state and local educational agencies annually.

Part C: authorizes the federal and regional resource centers that provide technical assistance and training to state education agencies; grants and contracts in the education of children who have severe disabilities, who are deaf and blind, and who have severe emotional disturbances; and grants and contracts in early childhood, secondary, and postsecondary education.

Part D: authorizes grants designed to improve the quality and supply of special education personnel; assist state educational agencies in establishing and maintaining preservice and inservice training programs; and establish training projects, consortia, and partnerships. Grants for clearinghouses on the education of children and youth with disabilities and grants for parent training are also included under Part D.

Part E: authorizes research and related activities for advancing and improving the knowledge base and improving the practice of professionals and others providing early intervention and special education and related services.

Part F: supports the development and distribution of instructional media and captioned films.

Part G: authorizes grants to public and nonprofit agencies to advance the use of new technologies, media, and materials for the education of children with disabilities and for early intervention services.

Part H: sets forth criteria for the provision of early intervention services for infants and toddlers and provides funding to states to develop and expand service delivery systems.

Source: From *Teaching Exceptional Children*, Winter, 1993; p. 85.

legislation stood unparalleled in history at that time for what they mandated. In 1973, amendments to the Vocational Rehabilitation Act (PL 93-112) were passed. Serving as a bill of rights for people with disabilities, Section 504 of this act ensured that "the handicapped of America *should* have access to education and jobs, and *should not* be denied anything that any other citizen is entitled to or already receives" (LaVor, 1977, p. 249). Two years later, the landmark Education for All Handicapped Children Act (EHA) (PL 94-142) was signed into law. The major provisions of this legislation are

- Every child with a disability between the ages of three and twenty-one is entitled to a free, appropriate public education in the least restrictive environment.

- Due process is ensured to protect the rights of students and their parents.

- Students are entitled to special and related services, which are determined as necessary.

- Every student will have a written Individualized Educational Program (IEP) that parents and school personnel agree upon.

- First priority is given to students previously excluded from educational services and second priority to those whose programs were inappropriate.

- No eligible child is to be rejected from receiving services.

Another federal law that had an impact on persons who were mentally retarded was the Developmental Disabilities Assistance and Bill of Rights Act of 1978 (PL 95-602). This legislation provided a functional way of conceptualizing developmental disabilities as well as funding to assist persons who demonstrate problems in major life function areas.

Another very important piece of legislation was passed in 1990. It is the Americans with Disabilities Act (ADA) (PL 101-336) and has been referred to as the most important action related to civil rights since the Civil Rights Act of 1964 (Hardman, Drew, Egan, & Wolf, 1993). Its intent is to provide civil rights protections for and opportunities to individuals who are disabled. It covers both public and private settings and affects employment, public services, transportation, public accommodations (e.g., restaurants, shopping centers), and telecommunications (e.g., relay services). Even though this legislation is not specifically targeted toward persons with mental retardation, its impact on this group is noteworthy.

Many important court cases took place in the 1980s, three of which are featured here. The case of *Larry P. v. Riles* (1972) was heard in the Ninth Circuit Court of Appeals. This court upheld a lower court ruling prohibiting California schools from using intelligence tests to place black students in classes for students who were mentally retarded. In *Pennhurst State School v. Halderman* (1981), the Supreme Court reversed the Third Circuit Court of Appeals' decision that affirmed the right of the residents of Pennhurst State School and Hospital to adequate habilitation under the Developmentally

Small group instruction provides a means of meeting the individual needs of students who are retarded.

Disabled Assistance and Bill of Rights Act. The Supreme Court made it clear that this act does not create any substantive rights to adequate treatment. The third litigative action was the first case relating to PL 94-142 heard by the Supreme Court. At issue in this case, *Board of Education of the Hendrick Hudson Central School District v. Rowley* (1982), was whether a female student with a hearing impairment was entitled to interpreter service to provide her with an appropriate education. Although acknowledging the procedural safeguards and need for individual education programs, the Supreme Court determined that states did not have to provide more than a minimal level of the services designated appropriate. As a result of this decision, schools do not have to be concerned with providing optimal educational programs for students with special needs. This has significant implications in terms of programs for students who are retarded.

During the latter part of the 1980s, a dominant theme in general and special education was the growing number of people "at risk" for any number of pejorative outcomes. At the school level, this includes students who are at risk for school failure (potential dropouts, substance abusers, pregnant teenagers). At the adult level, it includes people who are homeless, those who are unemployed or underemployed, and those who are not able to deal successfully with the demands of daily living. Individuals with mental retardation can be found in all these groups.

SUPPORTS-BASED ORIENTATION: 1985–PRESENT

Significant changes have occurred in the field of mental retardation over the last decade. Polloway and colleagues (1996) highlight the general trend:

> For professionals in the fields of mental retardation and developmental disabilities, the last decade has been particularly momentous. Changes in public attitudes toward persons with disabilities, and the resulting development and provision of services and supports have been truly phenomenal. Consequently the 1990s have become an exciting time to be participating in and/or adapting to the changing perspectives on mental retardation and developmental disabilities. One of the most challenging aspects in the field has been the mixed feelings that accompany these changes as we seek to understand new directions and consider their implications. (p. 3)

This supports-based perspective promotes as a basic tenet the notion of maintaining individuals with mental retardation in inclusive settings, accompanied by appropriate supports when needed. Supports might include personal supports, natural supports, various services, and other technical supports.

SOCIOPOLITICAL INFLUENCES

Beginning in the 1980s and continuing into the 1990s, the data indicate that the school-age population of students with mental retardation has changed. The total number of students identified as mentally retarded has decreased substantially since the late 1970s (see Figure 2.1). Polloway and Smith (1983) have suggested several factors to account for this decrease: (a) definitional changes and changes in professional thinking, which have encouraged caution and conservatism about identification and misdiagnosis, and (b) the effects of early intervention efforts in preventing some cases of mild retardation.

The impact that the various educational reform movements will have on students with mental retardation is difficult to predict. For instance, the six National Educational Goals (see Figure 2.2) put forth in the America 2000 (1991) strategy can portend positive as well as negative scenarios for students with mental retardation. As an example, the intent of Goal 5 is a worthy one; however, for students who may need to concentrate on mastering

FIGURE 2.2
America 2000: The National Education
Goals

By the year 2000:

1. All children in America will start school ready to learn.

2. The high school graduation rate will increase to at least 90 percent.

3. American students will leave grades 4, 8, and 12 having demonstrated competency in challenging subject matter including English, mathematics, science, history, and geography; and every school in America will ensure that all students learn to use their minds well, so they may be prepared for responsible citizenship, further learning, and productive employment in our modern economy.

4. U.S. students will be first in the world in science and mathematics achievement.

5. Every adult American will be literate and will possess the knowledge and skills necessary to compete in a global economy and exercise the rights and responsibilities of citizenship.

6. Every school in America will be free of drugs and violence and will offer a disciplined environment conducive to learning.

the skills needed to be successful in their local communities, the part related to competing in a global economy may not be so important.

Another example of the supports-based, inclusion paradigm is reflected in the most recent definition of mental retardation approved by the American Association on Mental Retardation (Luckasson et al., 1992). Its emphasis on levels of support in the revised classification system in place of the former levels of disability is a strong indication of the concept of supports.

The American Association on Mental Deficiency (AAMD) changed its name in 1987 to the American Association on Mental Retardation (AAMR).

An emerging trend is the concern for empowerment. The notion of creating situations where individuals are more active participants in various aspects of their own lives is a logical outgrowth of a supports-based climate. Polloway and colleagues (1996) note that empowerment includes ideas around which professionals within the field of developmental disabilities "finally can rally because it can embrace considerations related to inclusion, curricular needs, and transitions" (p. 8).

An important element of empowerment is self-determination, a topic that is receiving much professional attention today. Wehmeyer (1993) offers the following explanation of self-determination:

> Self determination refers to the attitudes and abilities necessary to act as the primary causal agent in one's life, and to make choices and decisions regarding one's quality of life free from undue external influence or interference. (p. 16)

Individuals who are afforded the freedom of choice and are more involved in making decisions associated with this choice are likely to enjoy a better quality of life. This is due to the fact that they have had a say in the way it should go.

SERVICE DELIVERY

The supports-based theme has influenced the delivery of service across the lifespan. Infants and toddlers with mental retardation are being provided needed services in their natural environments. A major characteristic of early childhood intervention is the desire to provide parents with the supports to carry out the key pieces of the Individual Family Service Plan (IFSP). The goal of services at the preschool age is to provide education in settings with other children who are not disabled. For this to occur successfully, certain supports will be needed.

Ongoing efforts are being made to teach students with mental retardation in **inclusive environments;** that is, students are being placed in classrooms with peers who are not retarded. Although data suggest many students with mental retardation are still receiving the bulk of their education in separate classes (U.S. Department of Education, 1996a), efforts to increase the opportunities for inclusion are intensifying, and wonderful examples of successful inclusion exist. It is important to remember that the overriding goal is to provide appropriate educational programs so that individuals with mental retardation are fully involved in community activities, including employment.

At the adult level, the supports-based theme can be easily recognized in a number of current initiatives. One of the most successful models of employment training is supported employment. In this arrangement, a job coach or employment specialist works with the individual on site, providing training and addressing other support needs. There has also been an increase in the creation of consumer-owned or rented housing where staff is available as necessary to assist individuals with mental retardation (supported living). For older individuals, specialized approaches have been developed (supported retirement).

Other issues have emerged that are still being discussed. Some of these include the bioethical issues of withholding treatment and the continuing effects of poverty. These and other issues must still be resolved. Cutbacks and restrictions may be the result of economic problems or policy shifts. If a positive national policy supportive of people with special needs is not carefully maintained, our society will be guilty of social neglect, and people who need help will not receive it. Blatt (1987) has poignantly captured the gravity of the situation: "If the business of government isn't charity, and we aren't our brothers' keepers, then some needy people will die before their time, and many needy people will suffer" (p. 83). We must move into the next century with guarded optimism, because what can be done for people needing assistance has been, and will continue to be, grounded in vagaries of the sociopolitical context.

SUMMARY

GENERAL

- Identifiable trends have strongly influenced the field of mental retardation.
- Various sociopolitical factors have had a major impact on the treatment of persons with mental retardation.
- Mental retardation is very much a social phenomenon.
- Many contemporary issues are not new.

ANTIQUITY

- Mental retardation was enigmatic.
- Individuals were treated in a variety of mysterious ways.
- Milder forms of retardation were not recognizable.
- Custodial care was provided in some places.

EMERGENCE/DISILLUSIONMENT

- Jean-Marc Itard worked with Victor (the Wild Boy).
- Seguin developed instructional methodology and educational programs, components of which are still used today.
- Guggenbühl established the Abendberg and set the model for future institutional care.
- In the United States, Dix, Howe, and Wilbur pioneered care for individuals with special needs.

FACILITIES-BASED

- Urbanization and industrialization affected developments in the United States; life was getting more complex.

- Pessimism about what could be done for persons with mental retardation developed.
- Institutions became custodial.
- The eugenics movement began, affecting many persons through sterilization, segregation, and limitations on immigration.
- The mental test was developed, and milder forms of retardation were recognized.
- Vocational rehabilitation was established after World War I.
- Major professional organizations for special education teachers began.
- Landmark medical developments were achieved during this time (e.g., recognition of PKU).
- Important standardized scales for measuring social maturity and intelligence were developed.
- The largest and most powerful parent organization advocating for people with mental retardation was formed.
- Most states established legislation for education of some students who were mentally retarded.
- *Brown v. Board of Education* was litigated.

SERVICES-BASED

- President Kennedy established a national agenda for mental retardation and the President's Panel on Mental Retardation.
- The War on Poverty was initiated.
- The principle of normalization began to take hold.
- The nature versus nurture debate raged.
- A series of major court cases was filed on behalf of individuals with mental retardation, laying the groundwork for later developments.
- The Vocational Rehabilitation Act of 1973 was passed.
- A free, appropriate education became available to all students with disabilities, regardless of severity of the disability, with the passage of the Education of All Handicapped Children Act of 1975.
- The Development Disabilities Assistance and Bill of Rights Act of 1978 passed.
- Community services and placement were advocated.
- The Education of All Handicapped Children Act was amended three times, each time providing innovations. Services to preschoolers were mandated, services to infants and toddlers were encouraged, and plans for transition were required.
- Critical litigation was filed that affected persons with mental retardation.

SUPPORT-BASED

- The number of students identified as mentally retarded kept falling.
- Teaching students in inclusive settings was advocated by parents and professionals.
- Support-based interventions (supported employment, supported living) were encouraged.
- Calls for rethinking students' needs were made.

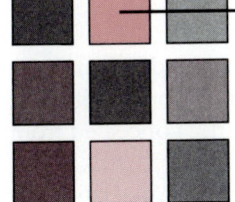

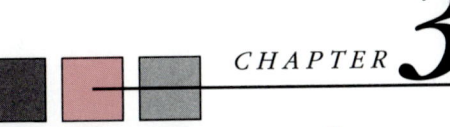

CHAPTER *3*

Definitional Perspectives

After reading this chapter,
the student should be able to:

■ Identify several terms used to describe mental retardation.

■ Discuss the concept of disablism and how it relates to mental retardation.

■ Identify key points of the various definitions that have been developed.

■ Highlight the traditional levels of classification and implications of the AAMR definition.

■ Discuss the issues surrounding the practical implementation of definitions.

■ List and discuss the factors that influence the prevalence of mental retardation.

Key Terms

adaptive behavior
disablism
incidence
mental retardation

prevalence
six-hour retarded
  child
standard deviation

subaverage general
intellectual
functioning

M ental retardation is not a simple phenomenon, and the lives of individuals who are retarded can be complicated. As Edgerton (1984) notes about adults with mild retardation: "In general, their lives are complex, partly concealed from investigation and highly changeable" (p. 32).

In the manual on definition published by the American Association on Mental Retardation (AAMR) (1992), a clear distinction is made between mental retardation as a state and as a trait:

> Mental retardation is not a *trait,* although it is influenced by certain characteristics or capabilities of the individual. . . . Rather, mental retardation is a *state* in which functioning is impaired in certain specific ways. This distinction between *trait* and *state* is central to understanding. (p. 10)

Mental retardation has been defined and will continue to be defined in various and differing ways. This is evident in recent times by the proliferation of discussions related to defining this condition. In addition to the professional debates dealing with conceptualizations, mental retardation has other meanings as well. On the day-to-day level, "For the individual and the family, mental retardation presents very practical concerns. For the community, state, and nation, it presents educational, social, economic, and political challenges" (Grossman & Tarjan, 1987, p. v).

The definition of mental retardation is explored in depth in this chapter. The evolution of how various individuals and organizations perceive the condition is discussed. Ways of dealing with mental retardation on an individual basis are addressed throughout the book. Its challenge to society was underscored from a historical perspective in the previous chapter and will be discussed from a futuristic perspective in the last chapter.

Mental retardation generally refers to substantial limitations in present levels of functioning reflected in delayed intellectual growth and is manifested in inappropriate or immature reactions to one's environment and below-average performance in the academic, psychological, physical, linguistic, and social domains. Such limitations make it difficult for individuals to cope with the demands they encounter each day, those that other people of comparable age and social or cultural background would be expected to deal with successfully on an ongoing basis. For example, in school settings, these individuals display patterns of academic and social performance that are below their chronological peers' level of mastery. Unlike other students who perform below grade level, the principal reason that students with mental retardation

Although by definition individuals who are retarded are different, they have the same needs as individuals who are not retarded.

do so relates to their problems in reasoning, dealing with abstract concepts, and problem solving. Their school-based difficulties are not primarily due to such factors as excessive absences from school or a specific learning disability, although such factors can contribute to the overall picture.

Mental retardation encompasses a heterogeneous group of people with varying needs. It is changeable, as individuals may be asymptomatic at various times of their lives (before formal schooling and later, as adults). Current thinking (AAMR, 1992) suggests that this condition is very much a function of the need for various levels of support. The severity of the condition ranges from mild difficulties to such extreme limitations that the person is dependent upon others for basic skilled nursing care.

People who have fewer needs for support or who are at the border of retardation create problems of identification and eligibility for treatment. Individuals at the borderlines typically create difficulties for service providers. Reschly (1988) has stated that as long as the system perceives mental retardation in terms of dichotomy—one is or is not retarded—rather than a continuum, there will always be a problem classifying individuals at

It is important to underscore the reality that there is not one stereotype for all individuals with mental retardation.

the margins. This is in great part because of (a) the way we conceptualize and measure intellectual abilities and (b) society's definition of acceptable behavior and toleration of behavior that is different.

Alternative ways of thinking about mental retardation exist. One variation is to conceive of mental retardation as solely a social invention, or a reaction to people perceived as different, as some professionals have claimed (Blatt, 1987; Sarason, 1985). Granted, there are biological mani-festations in some individuals who are retarded, but we all have physical differences (e.g., freckles, musculature). Bogdan (1986) describes this orientation:

> The generic term "disabled" and specific disability categories are ways of think-ing about and categorizing others. Whether people are thought of as disabled and the criteria used to determine whether someone is disabled has [sic] to do with how the definers think about these things. (p. 347)

Another perspective that has enjoyed much popularity in recent years is the notion of multiple intelligences. The main message is that professionals' visions of what constitutes intelligent behavior need to be expanded. This notion is examined more closely later in the chapter.

TERMINOLOGY

People who are mentally retarded have been referred to as *dumb, stupid, immature, defective, deficient, subnormal, feebleminded, incompetent,* and *dull,* as well as *idiot* and *fool* in earlier times. Although the word *fool* referred to the mentally ill, and the word *idiot* was directed toward indi-viduals who were severely retarded, the terms were frequently used in-terchangeably (Hilliard & Kirman, 1965). Even today, the conditions of mental illness and mental retardation are regularly confused. For the sake of distinction, mental illness, broadly speaking, is a confused state of thinking involving distorted perceptions of people or one's environment. It may be accompanied by radical changes of mood.

The history of mental retardation is further complicated when we con-sider that retardation has been confused with physical deformity, cerebral palsy, dwarfism, epilepsy, and deafness. The situation is made even more complex because a combination of these conditions sometimes does appear.

One of the first steps in understanding a phenomenon is understanding the terms used to describe it, no matter how crude or limited they may be. In the past, *idiot* was used to refer to people of all levels of mental retardation, from mild to profound. It derives from the Greek *idiotes,* meaning a layman, or unskilled worker. The word used to apply to untrained or ignorant people, and it was used in this sense until the 17th century (Penrose, 1966).

According to Kolstoe (1972), the *de praerogative regis* (prerogative of the king [of England] issued between 1255 and 1290 A.D. defined an idiot as one who "hath no understanding from his nativity" (p. 2). About 200 years later, Sir Anthony Fitzherbert stated that an idiot was "such a person who cannot account or number, nor can tell who his father or mother are, nor how old he is, etc., so as it may appear he has not understanding of reason what shall be his profit or his loss" (Guttmacher & Weihofen, 1952). The key factor in identification as an idiot appears to be lack of understanding.

Idiocy was believed to be inborn and incurable. As mentioned in Chapter 2, one of the first accounts of attempts to cure or at least ameliorate mental retardation was reported by Itard (1801/1962), who worked with a wild boy captured in a forest in 1799. The boy, whom Itard named Victor, did not speak or respond to the sound of gunfire, yet he startled at the sound of a cracking nut. He did not seem to feel differences between hot and cold or smell differences between foul and pleasant odors. Pinel, a well-known physician of the time, diagnosed Victor as an incurable idiot. Itard believed that with proper education Victor could be cured. Seguin, a student of Itard, followed in his footsteps by attempting to cure individuals with severe limitations; Penrose (1966) reports that "Esquirol referred to Seguin's mission as the removal of the mark of the beast from the forehead of the idiot" (pp. 4–5).

The concept *idiot* was elusive and confusing, and it covered conditions with little in common with each other; its primary use was to signify severe mental retardation. Although other terms like *feebleminded* and *mental deficiency* came into vogue, the confusion remained. Only in the 20th century have professionals attempted to systematize the terminology and definitions, although negative repercussions of all labels associated with the concept of mental retardation remain.

Today, the most commonly used terms to refer to this condition are *mental retardation* or *developmental disability*. Mental retardation is one type of developmental disability, as discussed later. However, other terms such as *mental deficiency* and *mental subnormality* are also used. Some advocates like the term *intellectually challenged*.

The continual search for different terms yields diminishing returns. Any word can come to have a negative connotation. For example, one school district, aware of the detrimental effects of labeling children "mentally retarded," began placing these children in an educational program designed to teach language, arithmetic, and reading directly. A series of commercial programs produced by Science Research Associates, DISTAR (Direct Instructional Systems for Teaching Arithmetic and Reading), was used. Before half the year was over, a group of concerned citizens asked that the program be abandoned because DISTAR was for "dumb" kids, and children not enrolled in DISTAR classes were making fun of the DISTAR children by yelling "DISTAR, DISTAR" at them at recess. It may be impossible to find acceptable terms and useful definitions without proper education and increased understanding of persons who are intellectually disabled.

TABLE 3.1

Socially Devalued Groups and the Common Historical Deviancy Roles into Which They Are Most Apt to Be Cast

People who are devalued due to:	Common Deviancy Roles								
	Pity	Charity	Menace	Sick	Sub-human	Ridi-cule	Dread	Childlike	Holy innocent
Mental disorder	X	X	X	X	X	X	X	X	X
Mental retardation	X	X	X	X	X	X		X	X
Old age	X	X		X	X	X		X	
Alcohol habituation	X	X	X	X		X			
Poverty	X	X	X		X		X		
Racial minority membership			X		X	X	X	X	
Epilepsy	X	X		X			X		
Drug addiction	X	X	X	X					
Criminal offenses			X	X	X		X		
Physical handicap	X	X				X			
Deafness/hearing impairment	X	X							
Blindness/visual impairment	X	X							
Illiteracy	X	X							
Political dissidence			X						

Source: From "An Overview of Social Role Valorization and Some Reflections on Elderly Mentally Retarded Persons" by W. Wolfensberger, 1985. In M. P. Janicki & H. M. Wisniewski (Eds.), *Aging and Developmental Disabilities: Issues and Approaches* (pp. 61–76), Baltimore: Paul H. Brookes. Copyright 1985 by Paul H. Brookes. Reprinted by permission.

DISABLISM AND MENTAL RETARDATION

Many groups of people in our society are not perceived favorably by the community at large. As Wolfensberger (1985) points out, "How a person is perceived affects how that person will be treated." If a certain group of people is perceived negatively, then its members will be treated less than favorably. Wolfensberger has identified groups of people that are devalued in our society and listed the major negative social roles into which these groups are typically cast. His analysis of this devaluation is presented in Table 3.1

According to Wolfensberger, only mental disorder evokes more kinds of negative responses than mental retardation. It might be proper to mark the "dread" column in Table 3.1 for mental retardation as well, because there are sufficient examples of this perception (e.g., parents shielding their children from a group of adults who are retarded seated near them on the bus). Wolfensberger's analysis has three major implications: (a) Persons who are considered retarded will be badly treated; (b) this treatment reflects the way society conceptualizes deviancy roles; (c) the perceptions and resultant treatment by others will greatly influence the behavior of people who are retarded.

It is precisely because many individuals with retardation are treated differently from the general population that the concept of disablism is relevant. **Disablism** (formerly referred to as *handicapism*), similarly to racism, sexism, and ageism, results in mistaken beliefs, prejudices, and pejorative actions on the part of individuals or society. Bogdan and Biklen (1977), two professionals who have been interested in this theme, define this concept as "A set of assumptions and practices that promote the differential and unequal treatment of people because of apparent or assumed physical, mental, or behavioral differences" (p. 59). Clearly, disablism affects people who are mentally retarded.

Disablism can be manifested in various ways, most notably through stereotyping, prejudice, and discrimination. Many people view adults with retardation as childlike (stereotyping), which leads to the belief that they are incapable of making decisions for themselves (prejudice), which in turn results in others' making decisions for them without their input or knowledge (discrimination).

A practical example is the situation where a person with mental retardation is not allowed to obtain a library card (discrimination) because it is felt (prejudice) that the person is incapable of being responsible for any books that are borrowed (stereotyping).

There are many other examples of disablism. A very offensive example is the popular "moron" joke ("Why did the moron . . . ?"). These jokes are heard in everyday conversation and can be found in books of "tasteless jokes." Although people with mental retardation are not the only group to suffer from malicious jokes, they certainly are one of the prime targets. Disablism is also evident in media representations of this group. For instance, the character Zero in the comic strip "Beetle Bailey" might be considered retarded, and he is always portrayed in uncomplimentary ways. Bogdan and Biklen also note another common occurrence: newspaper reports associating criminal activity with a specific disability (mental retardation), implying that the disability is somehow responsible for the crime. It is important to be aware of instances of disablism and to strive to eliminate them. Far too often, blatant examples of disablism go unchallenged.

Note that not all media portrayals of individuals with mental retardation are negative. Some media images are laudable: the documentary *Best Boy;* the characters Benny and Corky on the former television shows *L.A. Law* and *Life Goes On;* and the film *Forest Gump.*

Although positive and accurate portrayals are appearing more frequently in various media, many misconceptions are still conveyed through media images.

DEFINING MENTAL RETARDATION

There have been many definitions of mental retardation, all reflecting the different perspectives and perceptions of retardation at different times. Blatt (1987) articulates this notion well:

> Because mental retardation is in the most fundamental and important ways a metaphor (people make of it what they want to, people interpret it in light of their own understandings and prejudices), the definition of "mental retardation" and the terms used to denote the condition represent a hodgepodge of (sometimes irreconcilable) values, words, and ideas. (p. 69)

Whether or not we agree with this, we must deal with the reality that definitions exist and are used to make decisions about persons with retardation.

This section has three major foci: (a) a brief examination of some early definitions, (b) a discussion of the series of definitions developed by the AAMR, and (c) a look at some new definitions that have emerged recently.

EARLY DEFINITIONS

During the first half of the 20th century, two definitions of mental retardation, one developed by Tredgold and the other by Doll, were frequently cited. Tredgold (1937) defined "mental deficiency" as

> a state of incomplete mental development of such a kind and degree that the individual is incapable of adapting himself to the normal environment of his fellows in such a way to maintain existence independently of supervision, control, or external support. (p. 4)

Doll (1941) defined "mental retardation" when he stated,

> We observe that six criteria by statement or implication have been generally considered essential to an adequate definition and concept. These are (1) social incompetence, (2) due to mental subnormality, (3) which has been developmentally arrested, (4) which obtains at maturity, (5) is of constitutional origin, and (6) is essentially incurable. (p. 215)

Without question, the main focus of early conceptualizations of mental retardation was social competence.

Both of these definitions stressed the concept of social competence, a notion that is receiving renewed attention today (see Greenspan, in press). Arguably, Doll's definition is the most important of the early definitions, as it has continued to influence the defining of the condition. The first four elements of his definition can be found in most current definitional perspectives, most notably, the definitions published by the AAMR.

THE AAMR (AAMD) DEFINITIONS

In 1919, the American Association for the Study of the Feebleminded, which would later become the American Association on Mental Deficiency (AAMD),

IOWA'S EFFORT TO
OPERATIONALIZE A DEFINITION

Iowa recently developed technical assistance guidelines for assisting with the identification of students with mental disabilities, the term used in this state. The major objective was to operationalize criteria that are based on the definition used in Iowa. The guidelines presented below are the result of a year-long collaborative effort of a study group composed of a variety of participants, including parents, teachers, administrators, support personnel, and other professionals. Iowa Draft Definition, 1996.

For a student to be classified as mentally disabled, the individual must meet all four criteria.

1. Intellectual Functioning
   a. The assessment of intellectual functioning must include a variety of information sources, and the determination of mental disability is the responsibility of the entire multidisciplinary team
   b. Full scale IQ score of 75 or less
2. Adaptive Behavior
   a. Must include direct measures as well as indirect measures that evaluate the individual's performance in comparison to same-age peers from similar cultural backgrounds
   b. Deficits identified in 2 or more adaptive skill areas

3. Developmental Period
   a. Age 21 and below
   b. Significant discrepancies persist for more than 1 year
4. Educational Performance
   a. Evaluate the individual's performance in the context of his or her current environment
   b. Deficits identified in all core academic areas (math, reading, language arts, science)
   c. Significant deficit means the individual scores at least one standard deviation below the mean of the national standardization sample
   d. Standardized measures must be further validated by in-school data that documents differences between the individual's performance and the performance of same-age peers from the same cultural background
   e. Assessment of academic performance must also include documentation of resistance to general education interventions (p. 192)

Source: Maurer, S. (1997). Struggling with the definition issue: A state level perspective. *Education and Training in Mental Retardation and Developmental Disabilities, 32,* 191–193. Reprinted by permission.

and is now known as the American Association on Mental Retardation (AAMR), appointed a committee on Classification and Uniform Statistics. In 1921, this committee, in collaboration with the National Committee for Mental Hygiene, published the first edition of a manual defining the condition of mental retardation. Revisions of the manual were printed in 1933, 1941, and 1957.

In 1959, a committee of professionals chaired by Rick Heber developed the fifth AAMR definition of mental retardation. That definition was reprinted with minor changes in 1961. The sixth revision was developed by a committee chaired by Herbert Grossman in 1973. Although the definition was similar to that developed by Heber's committee some years earlier, the interpretation was significantly more conservative. Fewer individuals could be identified as mentally retarded under the Grossman definition than under the Heber definition. It is important to mention that the 1973 AAMR definition was incorporated into the Education for All Children Act (EHA) of 1975 (PL 94-142) as the federal definition of mental retardation. Grossman's definition was reaffirmed, with minor revisions, in 1977; the next revision was published in 1983. The 1983 version, which corresponded to definitions developed by the American Psychiatric Association (1980) and the World Health Organization (1978), described important considerations related to interpretation and clinical judgment used in classifying an individual as mentally retarded. This AAMR definition, like its predecessors, is from a clinical perspective, relying on measurements and comparisons. Although the definition has been regularly discussed and often criticized within the field, it remained widely accepted and was used by the federal government. The ninth edition of the manual was published in 1992 (AAMR, 1992) and reflected some major changes, including a shift toward a more functional definition of mental retardation. It is this most recent definition that has led to a splintering of professionals regarding conceptual and practical issues related to mental retardation.

The 1959, 1961 Definitions

It is worthwhile to review the development of the AAMR definitions. The Heber (1959) definition of mental retardation and its subsequent revisions represent major sociopolitical changes and reflect the evolution of the field and changes in thinking about those identified as mentally retarded. The 1961 Heber definition stated:

> Mental retardation refers to subaverage general intellectual functioning which originates during the development period and is associated with impairment in adaptive behavior.

Subaverage general intellectual functioning refers to performance of at least 1 standard deviation below the mean on a standardized intelligence test. The **standard deviation** is a statistic used to describe the degree to which an individual's score varies from the average or mean score for the population. Figure 3.1 illustrates the concepts of the normal curve, standard deviation, and population mean.

In the 1961 AAMR manual (Heber, 1961), the developmental period was recognized as variable, but for purposes of definition, it was judged to range from birth through sixteen years of age. **Adaptive behavior,** a term introduced in the 1961 revision, referred to the individual's adaptation to the demands of his or her environment. Impaired adaptive behavior could be reflected in maturation, learning, or social adjustment (terms used in the 1959 definition). Impaired adaptive behavior was considered in terms of stan-

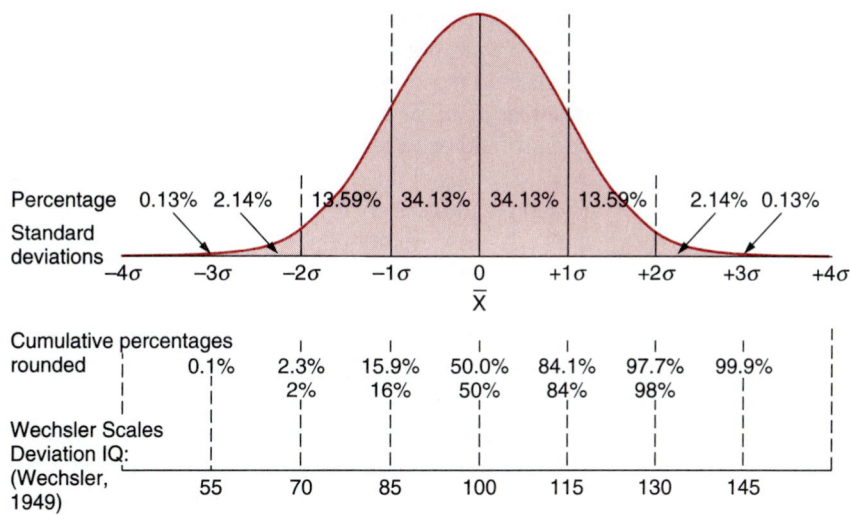

σ = standard deviation
X̄ = population mean—the average score.
The Wechsler Intelligence Scales use a deviation IQ score with a mean of 100 and a standard deviation of 15. In a normal distribution, a person who scores 1σ above the mean receives a Wechsler score of 115. One who scores below 70 on a Wechsler scale (>2σ below the mean) may be classified as mentally retarded if impairments in adaptive behavior are also present.

FIGURE 3.1
The Normal Curve

Source: From "Methods of Expressing Test Scores," 1955, *Test Service Bulletin, 48,* p. 8. Reprinted by permission.

dards and norms of appropriate behavior for the individual's chronological age group. Although deficient adaptive behavior was only loosely defined, its use in the Heber definition represented a major departure from the earlier notions of Tredgold (1937) and Doll (1941) of incurability, for it recognized that an individual might be deficient in one or more aspects of adaptive behavior at one time in life, but not at another. Favorable changes in social demands and environmental conditions, or in the individual's increased ability to meet natural and social demands, could mean that a person would no longer be called mentally retarded. According to Heber (1959, 1961), the definition refers to an individual's current functioning, not to an ultimate or permanent status.

Events Leading to Further Revisions

The 1961 AAMR definition of mental retardation was viewed by many professionals as an improvement over previous definitions, but it was not received without criticism. The concept of adaptive behavior caused considerable debate. Clausen (1972a) argued that the procedures for evaluating adaptive behavior were not adequate for diagnosis. This argument is still waged today, especially in response to the most recent AAMR definition and its suggestion of limitations in adaptive skills areas. He contended that diagnoses of mental retardation should be based solely upon the data from psychometric evaluations. He revealed results of an earlier investigation showing that, in spite of the AAMR's inclusion of the concept of adaptive behavior in the definition, diagnoses of mental retardation were frequently made solely on the basis of intelligence test data (Clausen, 1967). Clausen's proposed psychometric definition was controversial and apparently unpopular. Two basic grounds existed for opposition to a definition based solely on psychometric criteria. First, such a definition could threaten the concept of mental retardation as an alterable or changeable condition. Intelligence test results are quite stable over time; hence, it was possible that important changes in observable behavior would not show on intelligence tests. The second criticism of the psychometric definition was that, on the basis of tests standardized on members of the majority culture, too many children from culturally diverse backgrounds had been misdiagnosed as mentally retarded.

It was generally recognized that the 1961 Heber definition was overinclusive. With that definition as a guide for diagnosis, it was possible to identify statistically almost 16 percent of the general population and perhaps greater proportions of the bilingual/multicultural populations as mentally retarded. Clausen (1972b) suggested that the definition be made more conservative by requiring that an individual IQ score be 2 or more (instead of 1) standard deviations below the mean on an intelligence test. Other professionals suggested that the loose connection between adaptive behavior and intelligence be strengthened. Both positions have been consistently reflected in later revisions of the AAMR definition.

The 1973 Definition

In 1973, the AAMR committee chaired by Grossman was assigned to review the *Manual on Terminology and Classification in Mental Retardation*. The revised definition stated:

> Mental retardation refers to significantly subaverage general intellectual functioning existing concurrently with deficits in adaptive behavior, and manifested during the development period. (Grossman, 1973)

In this version, significantly subaverage intellectual functioning meant performance at least 2 standard deviations below the mean on an intelligence test (i.e., performance comparable to the lower 2.28 percent of the norm statistically). Adaptive behavior was defined in terms of the degree and efficiency with which the individual meets "the standards of personal independence and social responsibility expected of his age and cultural group" (p. 11). Adaptive behavior was thus considered to be relative to the individual's age and sociocultural group. An expanded set of criteria was provided for the assessment of adaptive behavior.

The 1961 Heber definition included both subaverage intellectual functioning and deficits in adaptive behavior as necessary qualifying conditions for diagnosis. The relationship between adaptive behavior and intellectual functioning, however, was not clarified sufficiently. Children were consistently labeled mentally retarded on the basis of IQ alone. The two most important distinctions between the 1961 and the 1973 definitions were that (a) subaverage intelligence was defined as 2 standard deviations below the mean, and (b) the relationship between adaptive behavior and intelligence was emphasized. Instead of simply requiring intellectual functioning and adaptive behavior to be associated, the committee stated that adaptive behavior deficits and subaverage intellectual functioning had to exist concurrently. In addition, the developmental period was extended from birth to eighteen years of age, matching the age when many finish schooling.

In spite of the extension of the developmental period, the 1973 revision was a more conservative definition than those that preceded it. Table 3.2 illustrates this point. According to the 1961 AAMR definition, almost 16 percent of the general population could have been identified as mentally retarded from a purely psychometric perspective. According to the 1973 definition, less than 3 percent of the population could be considered mentally retarded from the same perspective. The 1973 revision of the definition resulted in a reduction by more than 85 percent of the number of individuals who could be identified as mentally retarded. This comparison does not indicate the impact of the required connection between adaptive behavior and intelligence, but the two are imperfectly correlated at all levels of performance. Presumably, a number of individuals who might score 2 or more standard deviations below the mean on an intelligence test would not be referred for evaluation if they demonstrated appropriate adaptive skills.

Two of the most significant documents supporting a more conservative, cautious definition of the mentally retarded were "Special Education for the Mildly Retarded—Is Much of It Justifiable?" by Dunn (1968), and the Report of the President's Committee on Mental Retardation (PCMR) (1970) entitled ***The Six-Hour Retarded Child.*** Dunn, a respected authority in the field of mental retardation and former president of the Council for Exceptional Children, reported that many culturally disadvantaged children were being incorrectly classified as mildly retarded and placed in special classes. The lack of adequate adaptive behavior scales, coupled with the convenient practice of identifying students as mentally retarded on the basis of IQ score alone, probably fostered the mislabeling of nonretarded children as retarded. Dunn stated:

Dunn's (1968) points are similar to those being used to support inclusionary activities today.

I have loyally supported and promoted special classes for the educable mentally retarded for most of the last 20 years, but with growing disaffection. In my view, much of our past and present practices are morally and educationally wrong. We have been living at the mercy of general educators who have referred our problem children to us. And we have been generally ill prepared and ineffective in educating these children. Let us stop being pressured into

TABLE 3.2

Comparison of Heber, Grossman, and Luckasson et al. AAMR Definitions of Mental Retardation

Term	Heber (1959, 1961)	Grossman (1973)	Grossman (1983)	Luckasson et al. (1992)
General Definition	Subaverage general intellectual functioning which originates during the developmental period and is associated with impairment in adaptive behavior.	Significantly subaverage general intellectual functioning existing concurrently with deficits in adaptive behavior and manifested during the developmental period.	Significantly subaverage general intellectual functioning resulting in or associated with concurrent impairments in adaptive behavior and manifested during the developmental period.	Substantial limitations in present functioning. It is characterized by significantly subaverage intellectual functioning, existing concurrently with related limitations in two or more of the following applicable adaptive skill areas: communication, self-care, home living, social skills, community use, self-direction, health and safety, functional academics, leisure, and work. Mental retardation manifests before age 18.
Subaverage	Greater than one standard deviation below the mean.	Significantly subaverage: two or more standard deviations below the mean.	Significantly subaverage: defined as an IQ of 70 or below on standardized measures of intelligence; could be extended upward through IQ 75 or more, depending on the reliability of the intelligence test used.	Similar to Grossman (1983).
Assessment Procedure	General intellectual functioning; may be assessed by one or more of the standardized tests developed for that purpose.	Same as Heber.	Same as Heber for intellectual functioning. Adaptive behavior assessed by clinical assessment and standardized scales.	Governed by a series of steps specifying requisite characteristics.
Developmental period	Approximately 16 years.	Upper age limit 18 years.	Period of time between conception and the 18th birthday.	Similar to Grossman (1983).

continuing and expanding a special education program that we know now to be undesirable for many of the children we are dedicated to serve.

A better education than special class placement is needed for socioculturally deprived children with mild learning problems who have been labeled educable mentally retarded. Over the years, the status of these pupils who come from poverty, broken and inadequate homes, and low status ethnic groups has been a checkered one. (1968, p. 5)

The Six-Hour Retarded Child (PCMR, 1970) corroborated Dunn's charge that a significant number of culturally disadvantaged children, especially in urban areas, had been misclassified as mildly retarded and inappropriately

TABLE 3.2
(continued)

Term	Heber (1959, 1961)	Grossman (1973)	Grossman (1983)	Luckasson et al. (1992)
Adaptive Behavior	*Impairment in adaptive behavior:* Refers to the effectiveness of the individual to adapt to the natural and social demands of his environment. May be reflected in: 1. Maturation 2. Learning 3. Social adjustment	Defined as effectiveness or degree with which the individual meets the standards of personal independence and social responsibility expected of his age and cultural group. May be reflected in the following areas: *During infancy and early childhood:* 1. Sensory-motor skills development 2. Communication skills 3. Self-help skills 4. Socialization *During childhood and early adolescence:* 5. Application of basic academics in daily life activities 6. Application of appropriate reasoning and judgment in mastery of the environment 7. Social skills *During late adolescence and adult life:* 8. Vocational and social responsibilities and performances	Defined as significant limitations in an individual's effectiveness in meeting the standards of maturation, learning, personal independence, or social responsibility that are expected for his or her age level and cultural group.	Movement from conceptualizing adaptive behavior as a global entity to specification of 10 different adaptive skill areas—as presented in the definition.
Levels of Severity	Borderline retardation IQ 68–84 Mild retardation IQ 52–67 Moderate retardation IQ 36–51 Severe retardation IQ 20–35 Profound retardation IQ < 20	— Mild retardation IQ 52–67 Moderate retardation IQ 36–51 Severe retardation IQ 20–35 Profound retardation IQ < 20	— Mild retardation IQ 50–55 to approx. 70 Moderate retardation IQ 35–40 to 50–55 Severe retardation IQ 20–25 to 35–40 Profound retardation IQ below 20 or 25 Cannot be determined	Traditional levels abondoned. System advocates use of intensities of needed support that are subclassified into four levels: • intermittent • limited • extensive • pervasive These levels are applied to the adaptive skill areas.

placed in special education classes. The six-hour retarded children are classified as mentally retarded during the six hours they spend in an academic setting but function normally outside school. The reports by Dunn and the PCMR were emotional, based on systematic observation and a strong philosophical commitment, rather than on rigorous empirical data.

AAMR 1977 Definition

In 1977, the AAMR published its seventh manual on classification and terminology (Grossman, 1977). The wording of the 1977 definition is identical
to that of the 1973 version, but the 1977 manual made a few modifications
in its interpretation. To begin with, the definition of "significantly subaverage" remained 2 standard deviations below the mean, and the definition of
"adaptive behavior" was essentially unchanged. The major change focused
on the issue of clinical judgment. The manual explains in detail the problems of measuring adaptive behavior. Yet its importance was highlighted in
the sentence, "For a person to be diagnosed as being mentally retarded, impairments in intellectual functioning must co-exist with deficits in adaptive
behavior" (p. 12). The manual goes on to state,

> Individuals with [intelligence] scores slightly above these ceilings [two standard
> deviations below the mean] may be diagnosed as mildly retarded during a pe-
> riod when they manifest serious impairments of adaptive behavior. In such
> cases, the burden is on the examiner to avoid misdiagnosis with its potential
> stigmatizing effects. (p. 12)

Later, the committee elaborated, stating,

> A small minority of persons with IQ's up to 10 points above the guideline ceil-
> ings are so impaired in their adaptive behavior that they may be classified as
> having mild mental retardation. (pp. 19–20)

Although the 1977 definition was worded identically to the 1973 definition, the later manual allowed a diagnosis of mental retardation to be extended to individuals who, according to the previous definition, would not
have been so classified.

AAMR 1983 Definition

In 1983, the AAMR published its eighth manual on classification and terminology. The update was:

> Mental retardation refers to significantly subaverage general intellectual func-
> tioning resulting in or associated with concurrent impairments in adaptive be-
> havior and manifested during the developmental period. (Grossman, 1983)

Clinical judgment remained an important issue—so important, that the
appendix cited several short case studies followed by descriptions of the
way decisions were reached from the information presented in the cases.
The tone of the manual emphasized that the content was carefully researched and contemplated before publication, and that the decisions derived
were logical, practical, and consistent with a need to explore a worldwide system of mental retardation. The authors collaborated with representatives of
two other major classification systems so that the different systems would be

as compatible as possible. The two other systems are the World Health Organization's (1978) system of *International Classification of Diseases, Clinical Modification* (9th ed.) (ICD-9) and the American Psychiatric Association's (1980) *Diagnostic and Statistical Manual of Mental Disorders* (3rd ed.) (DSM-III).

The AAMR manual defined "significantly subaverage" as an IQ of 70 or below on a standardized measure of intelligence. Yet this upper limit is intended as a guideline and could be extended to an IQ of 75 or more, providing behavior is impaired and clinically determined to be due to deficits in reasoning and judgment. In this definition, the strict use of standard deviations is discouraged, and the concept of the standard error of measurement inherent in all tests is emphasized.

> Clinicians using the system should be well aware that in determining whether a person is retarded and at what level of intellectual functioning the individual is operating, it is important to understand the concept of standard error of measurement and use it when making a clinical determination of retardation and level of functioning. (AAMR, 1983, p. 7)

No test is perfectly reliable, and some degree of random fluctuation in obtained scores is always expected. The standard error of measurement is an estimate of the degree to which the test scores would be expected to vary because of random error alone. For example, we know that the standard error of measurement on some tests of intelligence is 3 IQ points. If a child received a score of 72 on that test, the examiner should report that the student's true IQ would probably be within the range 69 to 75. The clinician would then decide whether other conditions, such as concurrent deficits in adaptive behavior or cultural difference, were present and associated with the level of performance on the IQ test. According to the 1983 AAMR manual (Grossman, 1983), an individual with an IQ of 75 or higher could be classified as mentally retarded if deficits in adaptive behavior were also present. On the other hand, an IQ of 70 to 67, or perhaps even lower, would not alone provide a sufficient basis for classifying a child from, for example, a minority culture as mentally retarded. The clinician would have to determine to what extent bias affected performance and whether deficits in adaptive behavior were present and associated with the attained level of performance. You cannot measure something precisely unless you can define it precisely. Intelligence, achievement, and adaptive behavior are ready examples of rather imprecisely defined concepts, as Blatt (1987) emphasized. Therefore, it is naive to treat scores as precise when they are obtained by those measures; the standard error of measurement is a concept that allows flexibility in interpretation, yet at the same time provides reasonable structure.

The adaptive behavior component in the 1983 definition remained unchanged, but again, the need for clinical judgment in borderline cases was emphasized. The measurement of adaptive behavior may involve observation, informal interview, or the use of a standardized scale. Adaptive behavior must be compared to norms for the individual's age and cultural group. The manual emphasized throughout that, because of the present state of affairs with adaptive behavior, clinical judgment must be used.

Although the conceptual basis of the developmental period did not change, the range did. The definition stressed that the developmental period begins at conception and extends through age eighteen.

Although the 1983 manual was as up-to-date and definitive as possible, and was supported by other prestigious organizations, the committee recognized that as more data are collected and times change, the definition of mental retardation will also inevitably change:

> The 1983 definition, slightly modified for clarity, was introduced in the 1959 manual; it is intended to represent the current status of scientific knowledge in the field and the current thinking about social issues associated with mental retardation. One may anticipate that as both knowledge and philosophy change, there will be modifications reflecting such changes in future manuals. (Grossman, 1983, p. 10)

This is exactly what happened, as a result of the most recent work of the AAMR's Ad Hoc Committee on Terminology and Classification.

AAMR 1992 Definition

After four years of work, the Ad Hoc Committee on Terminology and Classification, chaired by Ruth Luckasson, published the ninth edition of the manual (AAMR, 1992). The new definition signaled many significant

FIGURE 3.2

General Structure of the Definition of Mental Retardation

Source: From *Mental Retardation: Definition, Classification, and Systems of Supports* (9th ed., p. 10) by the American Association on Mental Retardation, 1992, Washington, DC: American Association on Mental Retardation. Copyright 1992 by the American Association on Mental Retardation. Reprinted by permission.

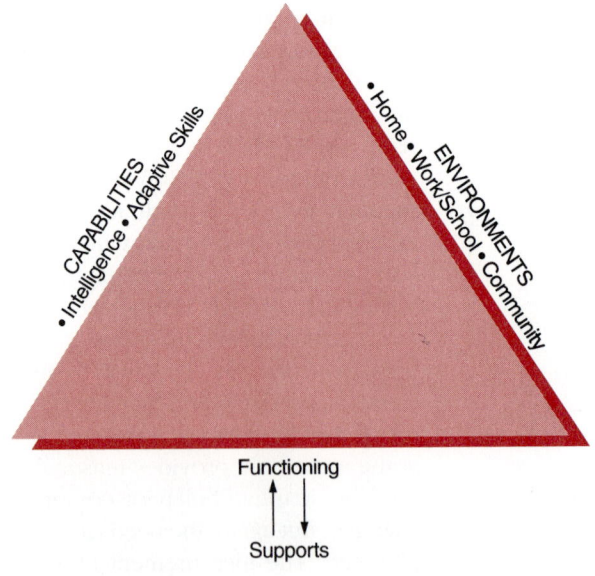

changes from its predecessors, as it is much more functional in nature. It stressed the interaction among three major dimensions: a person's capabilities, the environments in which the person functions, and need for varying levels of support. This interaction and the relationship of these factors to one another are depicted in Figure 3.2.

The wording of the most recent definition differed from that of the 1983 version. Yet, the three major components (intellectual limitations, problems in adaptive areas, and age of onset) of the previous definitions remain. The 1992 definition reads:

> Mental retardation refers to substantial limitations in present functioning. It is characterized by significantly subaverage intellectual functioning, existing concurrently with related limitations in two or more of the following applicable adaptive skill areas: communication, self-care, home living, social skills, community use, self-direction, health and safety, functional academics, leisure and work. Mental retardation manifests before age 18. (AAMR, 1992, p. 1)

The following four assumptions are essential to the application of the definition:

1. Valid assessment considers cultural and linguistic diversity, as well as differences in communication and behavioral factors.

2. The existence of limitations in adaptive skills occurs within the context of community environments typical of the individual's age peers and is indexed to the person's individual needs for supports.

3. Specific adaptive limitations often coexist with strengths in other adaptive skills or other personal capabilities.

4. With appropriate supports over a sustained period, the life functioning of the person with mental retardation will generally improve. (AAMR, 1992, p. 5)

Although some features of the 1983 definition remain (refer to Table 3.2), significant changes are evident in the 1992 definition. In addition to features already discussed, the most notable changes follow:

- Reconceptualization of adaptive behavior by the identification of ten specific adaptive skill areas
- A new three-step procedure for diagnosing, classifying, and identifying systems of support (this process is illustrated in Figure 3.3).
- A new system for classifying individuals in terms of needed levels of support recommended (discussed in the next section of this chapter) accompanied by the recommendation that reference to the former levels of severity (mild, moderate, severe, and profound) be discontinued
- Development of a profile of needed supports based on four dimensions:

- Intellectual functioning and adaptive skills
- Psychological/emotional considerations
- Physical health/etiology considerations
- Environmental considerations

■ Similarity, in some ways, to other functional definitions of disability (e.g., developmental disabilities)

Dimension I: Intellectual Functioning and Adaptive Skills	**STEP 1. Diagnosis of mental retardation** *Determines eligibility for supports* Mental retardation is diagnosed if: 1. The individual's intellectual functioning is approximately 70–75 or below. 2. There are significant disabilities in two or more adaptive skill areas. 3. The age of onset is below 18.
Dimension II: Psychological/ Emotional Considerations Dimension III: Physical Health/ Etiology Considerations Dimension IV: Environmental Considerations	**STEP 2. Classification and description** *Identifies strengths and weaknesses and the need for supports* 1. Describe the individual's strengths and weaknesses in reference to psychological/emotional considerations. 2. Describe the individual's overall physical health and indicate the condition's etiology. 3. Describe the individual's current environmental placement and the optimal environment that would facilitate his/her continued growth and development.
	STEP 3. Profile and intensities of needed supports *Identifies needed supports* Identify the kind and intensities of supports needed for each of the four dimensions. 1. Dimension I: Intellectual Functioning and Adaptive Skills 2. Dimension II: Psychological/Emotional Considerations 3. Dimension III: Physical Health/Etiology Considerations 4. Dimension IV: Environmental Considerations

FIGURE 3.3

The Three-Step Process: Diagnosis, Classification, and Systems of Supports

Source: From *Mental Retardation: Definition, Classification, and Systems of Supports* (9th ed., p. 24) by the American Association on Mental Retardation, 1992, p. 24 by the American Association on Mental Retardation, 1992, Washington, DC: American Association on Mental Retardation. Copyright 1992 by the American Association on Mental Retardation. Reprinted by permission.

Intermittent
Supports on an "as needed basis." Characterized by episodic nature, person not always needing the support(s), or short-term supports needed during life-span transitions (e.g., job loss or an acute medical crisis). Intermittent supports may be high or low intensity when provided.

Limited
An intensity of supports characterized by consistency over time, time-limited but not of an intermittent nature, may require fewer staff members and less cost than more intense levels of support (e.g., time-limited employment training or transitional supports during the school to adult provided period).

Extensive
Supports characterized by regular involvement (e.g., daily) in at least some environments (such as work or home) and not time-limited (e.g., long-term support and long-term home living support).

Pervasive
Supports characterized by their constancy, high intensity; provided across environments; potential life-sustaining nature. Pervasive supports typically involve more staff members and intrusiveness than do extensive or time-limited supports.

FIGURE 3.4
Definition and Examples of Intensities of Supports

Source: From *Mental Retardation: Definition, Classification, and Systems of Supports* (9th ed., p. 26) by the American Association on Mental Retardation, 1992, Washington, DC: American Association on Mental Retardation. Copyright 1992 by the American Association on Mental Retardation. Reprinted by permission.

School districts throughout the United States and Canada are likely to use a variety of definitional perspectives and classification systems.

A constant clamor for changing the classification system has existed for some time. One suggestion has been to move away from classifying individuals toward classifying the services or supports needed. As highlighted earlier, the 1992 AAMR manual suggests a new classification system that abandons the use of IQ levels. Rather, the ninth edition of the AAMR manual suggests adoption of a system describing levels of support as a function of the different adaptive skill areas. The four levels of possible needed supports are shown in Figure 3.4. The intent of this system is to explain a person's functional limitations in terms of the degree of support he or she needs to achieve personal growth and development.

CONTEMPORARY ALTERNATIVE DEFINITIONAL PERSPECTIVES

A number of new definitional efforts has arisen in recent times. In great part, this has occurred because of dissatisfaction with the 1992 AAMR definition and classification guidelines. As Smith (in press) notes, "Even within the AAMR there have been sharp differences of opinion concerning the revised definition." The most critical attacks on the AAMR definition have been waged by Greenspan (1994; in press), Jacobson and Mulick (1996), and MacMillan and his colleagues (Gresham, MacMillan, & Siperstein, 1995; MacMillan, Gresham, & Siperstein, 1993). Concerns have focused on the following aspects of the definition: the IQ cutoff level, the adaptive skills areas, and the levels of needed supports.

Greenspan (in press) remarks that some important signs are present that indicate displeasure with the 1992 definition. These signs include (a) few state departments adopting the definition; (b) publication of a new manual on mental retardation by the American Psychological Association (Jacobson & Mulick, 1996); and (c) refusal of committees working on revisions of the other definitional manuals to include elements of the AAMR definition. Greenspan goes on to suggest that the publication of the 1992 definition has "served to undermine AAMR's credibility as the 'keeper of the MR definition' " (p. X)—a distinction that AAMR was arguably able to claim heretofore.

Two alternative definitional perspectives are discussed next. The first is the 1996 definition published by the American Psychological Association (Jacobson & Mulick, 1996). The second definition reflects the most recent thinking of Stephen Greenspan. Interestingly, it is Greenspan's earlier conceptualizations of social competence upon which the committee working on the 1992 AAMR definition began their discussions. Both definitional perspectives evolved to a great extent as a result of dissatisfaction with the AAMR definition.

The 1996 American Psychological Association Definition

Spearheaded by Jacobson and Mulick, Division 33 of the American Psychological Association published its *Manual of Diagnosis and Professional Practice in Mental Retardation* in 1996. The rationale for developing the manual is reflected in the preface of the work: "a comprehensive statement of what MR is, what it means for the individual and society, and how to serve the needs of affected individuals is specifically called for at the present juncture" (p. xiv). The American Psychological Association's definition reads as follows:

> Mental retardation (MR) refers to (a) significant limitations in general intellectual functioning; (b) significant limitations in adaptive functioning, which exist concurrently; and (c) onset of intellectual and adaptive limitations before the age of 22 years.

TABLE 3.3
Degrees of MR

Degree of Mental Retardation	IQ Score Range	IQ Deviation Cutting Point	Extent of Concurrent Adaptive Limitations
Mild	55–70	−2 *SD*	Two or more domains
Moderate	35–54	−3 *SD*	Two or more domains
Severe	20–34	−4 *SD*	All domains
Profound	Below 20	−5 *SD*	All domains

Note. IQ ranges are approximate due to SE. Limitations in adaptive functioning are relative to expected performance by chronological age and require scores at 22 SD or lower for significance.

Source: From John J. Jacobson and James A. Mulick (Eds.). 1996, *Manual of Diagnosis and Professional Practice in Mental Retardation,* p. 14. Washington: American Psychological Association. Reprinted by permission.

Upon inspection of the American Psychological Association's definition, one realizes that it is essentially a return to the 1983 AAMR definitional constructs with some minor changes. The term *adaptive functioning* is used in place of *adaptive behavior,* and the upper limit of the age of onset has been extended from eighteen to twenty-two. The American Psychological Association manual promotes a classification system that is a return to four ranges of severity: mild, moderate, severe, and profound. As noted in the manual, "Severity is determined by concurrent presence of IQ scores within four ranges and adaptive functioning consistent with each range" (Jacobson & Mulick, 1996, p. 14). Table 3.3 depicts the degrees of mental retardation and the relationship of IQ and adaptive functioning.

Professionals who liked the 1983 AAMR definition of mental retardation will find solace in the American Psychological Association's definition. It represents a return to a system that provides comfortability for those who have clinical and research interests. It avoids much of the psychometric dissonance created by the AAMR definition.

Greenspan's Definition

Initially, some people will find Greenspan's recommendations odious, as they suggest a definitional perspective that attempts to provide a clearer focus on intelligence as the core impairment in mental retardation. However, it is important to recognize that he is proposing a model of intelligence that includes different types of intelligent behavior (i.e., multiple intelligences). Greenspan promotes a tripartite model of intelligence that includes conceptual intelligence (IQ), practical intelligence, and social intelligence. Fundamentally, he notes that "mental retardation clearly is a cognitive disorder, but cognition can be used for many purposes" (Greenspan, in press).

TABLE 3.4
Chronology of Definitional Perspectives of MR

Author	Definition
Tredgold (1937)	Mental deficiency: "A state of incomplete mental development of such a kind and degree that the individual is incapable of adapting himself to the normal environment of his fellows in such a way to maintain existence independently of supervision, control, or external support."
AAMR (Grossman, 1983)	Mental retardation "refers to significantly subaverage general intellectual functioning resulting in or associated with concurrent impairments in adaptive behavior and manifested during the developmental period."
AAMR (Luckasson et al., 1992)	Mental retardation "refers to substantial limitations in present functioning. It is characterized by significantly subaverage intellectual functioning, existing concurrently with related limitations in two or more of the following applicable adaptive skill areas: *communication, self-care, home living, social skills, community use, self-direction, health and safety, functional academics, leisure* and *work.* Mental retardation manifests before age 18."
American Psychological Association (Jacobson & Mulick, 1996)	Mental retardation refers to (a) significant limitations in general intellectual functioning; (b) significant limitations in adaptive functioning, which exist concurrently; and (c) onset of intellectual and adaptive limitations before the age of 22 years.

Greenspan's proposed definition is:

> Persons who are MR are widely perceived to need long-term supports, accommodations or protections due to persistent limitations in social, practical and conceptual intelligence and the resulting inability to meet intellectual demands of a range of settings and roles. These limitations are assumed in most cases to result from abnormalities or events occurring during the development period, and which have permanent effects on brain development and functioning.

This proposed definition of mental retardation contains certain elements of the AAMR orientation (supports, range of settings) while maintaining Greenspan's emphasis on social competence. His classification system includes aspects of the AAMR philosophy and suggests that mental retardation can be divided into three subcategories based on degree of overall disability: limited, extensive, and pervasive. These levels should be based on the need for supports rather than on intellectual dimensions.

After navigating the maze of actual definitions, and the issues and philosophies associated with them (see Table 3.4) regarding definitions and definitional practices, one may be left with solving the problem of determining who is "really" mentally retarded. However, the lesson is not that new definitions are better or more accurate, but that the definition of mental retardation is totally a social and political one that rests with the powers that be, and not in the minds of the people who experience intellectual deficits.

RELATED CONCEPTUALIZATIONS OF MENTAL RETARDATION

The 1983 AAMR definition bears the distinction of being the federal definition of mental retardation. It is also the most frequently cited definition of mental retardation in the professional literature. But in spite of the endorsement and popularity of the Grossman (1973, 1977, 1983) definitions, they have not met with universal approval among professionals. The former AAMR definitions have been criticized because of their clear clinical overtones.

But other definitions and conceptualizations do exist, and selected ones are presented next. Except for the developmental disabilities definition, none of the following points of view enjoys widespread recognition. Yet each presents an orientation important to the field of mental retardation.

DEVELOPMENTAL DISABILITIES

During the last few years, the concept of developmental disabilities has been used more frequently, particularly with adult populations. The meaning of this term overlaps significantly with that of mental retardation. As defined in the Developmental Disabilities Assistance and Bill of Rights Act of 1990 (PL 98-527), the term *developmental disability* means a severe, chronic disability of a person five years of age or older that

1. Is attributable to a mental or physical impairment or combination of mental and physical impairments
2. Is manifested before the person attains age twenty-two
3. Is likely to continue indefinitely
4. Results in substantial functional limitations in three or more of the following areas of major life activity: (a) self-care, (b) receptive and expressive language, (c) learning, (d) mobility, (e) self-direction, (f) capacity for independent living, and (g) economic self-sufficiency
5. Reflects the person's need for a combination and sequence of special, interdisciplinary, or generic care, treatment, or other services that are lifelong or of extended duration and are individually planned and coordinated

The concept of developmental disability is used in some schools in the United States.

The federal definition accentuates functional limitations in major life activities, suggesting problems associated with a more involved population. Nevertheless, it may apply to some persons with milder forms of retardation during some or all of their lives. It is now more similar to the AAMR definition, as both stress functionality. The implication of chronicity and its potential inappropriateness with very young populations make it different from the AAMR definition.

SOCIOLOGICAL PERSPECTIVE

J. R. Mercer (1973a, 1973b) argues that neither the pathological nor the statistical approach to defining mental retardation is adequate for identifying cases of more mild retardation. As an alternative, she offers a social-system perspective, which defines mental retardation as "an achieved social status in a social system."

> The status of mental retardate is associated with a role which persons occupying that status are expected to play. A person's career in acquiring the status of playing the role of mental retardate can be described in the same fashion as the career of a person who acquires any other status such as lawyer, bank president or teacher. (J. R. Mercer, 1973b)

Mercer's research findings (1973a, 1973b) suggest that individuals are labeled mentally retarded as a function of their performance in social situations. She asserts that the social system approach is able to account for the disproportionate numbers of school-age children from lower socioeconomic groups and minority cultures who have been labeled mildly mentally retarded. She advocates a more conservative definition of mental retardation, one that would make the measurement of adaptive behavior more practical. According to her view, multiple norm frameworks must be developed to describe adequately children from different sociocultural settings. That is, children must be described (and labeled if necessary) in relation to their own social and cultural background, without prejudging that background as "deviant" or "deficient." Mercer also recommends that the identification and diagnosis of mental retardation be based upon data that include the children's competencies as well as their deficits. Children whose problems are school-specific should not be labeled mentally retarded.

Gold (1980) developed a different sociological conceptualization of mental retardation. His perspective focuses on the ability or failure of society to provide adequate training and education as the measure of retardation rather than on the failure of the individual. Gold's ideas are reflected in the following statement: "The height of a retarded person's level of functioning is determined by the availability of training technology and the amount of resources society is willing to allocate and not by significant limitations in biological potential" (1980, p. 148).

BEHAVIORAL ANALYSIS PERSPECTIVE

Bijou (1966) has taken the position that mental retardation should be dealt with from a behavioral perspective. He suggests that

> Developmental retardation be treated as observable, objectively defined stimulus–response relationships without recourse to hypothetical mental concepts such as "defective intelligence" and hypothetical biological abnormalities such as "clinically inferred brain injury." From this point of view a retarded individual is one who has a limited repertoire of behavior shaped by events that constitute his history. (p. 2)

According to Bijou, research that concentrates upon "the processes that prevent, reduce, or delay the formation of stimulus–response functions will produce more adequate principles and techniques for dealing with retardation" (1966, p. 2). He regards the development of retarded behavior as a function of the individual's observable interactions with the social, physical, and biological environment.

Repp (1983) has argued that Bijou's approach to mental retardation is the only one that addresses the problem with a solution. Bijou's behavioral definition is based upon two important assumptions. First, all behaviors (adaptive and maladaptive) are acquired and maintained according to the same principles of learning. Persons who are retarded are capable of learning; they may learn more slowly than persons who are not retarded, but they do not learn by a different set of rules. The second basic assumption is that all behavior depends on environmental conditions. In support of that assumption are thousands of demonstrations that systematic manipulations of environmental conditions will produce predictable improvements in the behaviors of persons with retardation.

Like J. R. Mercer (1973a, 1973b), but for different reasons, Bijou (1966) rejects the notion that retardation is a symptom of an underlying condition or pathology. He claims that approaches that have conceptualized retardation as a symptom of more fundamental problems have contributed relatively little knowledge to the field.

It is difficult to determine to what extent this behavioral approach to describe mental retardation has had upon formal definitions of mental retardation. Both the behavioral and the AAMR definitions of mental retardation apply only to present levels of functioning, and they regard the condition of mental retardation as modifiable. Bijou (1966), however, has articulated the most logical basis for considering mental retardation a changeable condition. His definition has had an important impact on the development of educational and therapeutic interventions. Ullman and Krasner (1969) considered that Bijou's behavioral analysis approach was largely responsible for a productive trend during that time in the development of principles and techniques used to teach students who are mentally retarded.

PRACTICAL REALITIES

The relationship between theory and practice in mental retardation is a tenuous one. As the previous sections have focused mainly on conceptual issues of definition, it is useful to look at how definition is put into practice. This section reviews the research that has examined state guidelines in the area of mental retardation, presents some of the current issues concerning the roles of intelligence and adaptive behavior in identification practices, and suggests some possible directions that the field may take in the future.

Studies (Frankenburger, 1984; Huberty, Koller, & Ten Brink, 1980; Patrick & Reschly, 1982; Utley, Lowitzer, & Baumeister, 1987) of various aspects of state departments of education guidelines for defining, identifying, and classifying students with mental retardation have regularly found a great deal of interstate variability. Inconsistency is common in terminology, in the adoption of the federal definition of mental retardation (1983 AAMR definition—Grossman, 1983), and (when adopted) in the implementation of that definition as originally intended. Greenspan (in press) indicates that a negligible number of states have adopted the most recent AAMR definition.

A sense of this interstate variation can be gleaned from the findings of a study of state guidelines in relation to definition, identification criteria, and classification systems that was conducted by Utley et al. (1987). Major findings of this study are highlighted next:

■ Only 56 percent of the states used the term *mental retardation*.

■ 61 percent of the states cited the AAMR definition.

■ 84 percent of the states provided intelligence criteria.

■ Only 61 percent of the states emphasized adaptive behavior.

■ Only 10 percent of the states identified instruments, cutoff points, or deficit areas in adaptive behavior.

■ 74 percent used a classification system of some type (only 14 percent used the AAMR's four-level system).

This information represents state-level reports and does not necessarily tell us what happens on a daily basis. Simply stated, IQ has played and continues to play the dominant role in the decision-making process (Furlong & LeDrew, 1985; Polloway & Smith, 1987). Assessment of adaptive behavior is not being used in the ways that have been suggested. Brady, Manni, and Winikur (1983), in their three-year study of identification practices, state: "There was no trend over the 3 years of this analysis to lead one to believe that evaluation-team members are becoming more aware of the need to consider adaptive behavior as part of their assessment" (p. 298).

For a number of plausible reasons, less importance is given to evaluation of adaptive behavior than to IQ. Zigler, Balla, and Hodapp (1984) contend that the concept is "too elusive and ill-defined to be a criterion of mental retardation" (p. 218). Zucker and Polloway (1987) offer another explanation:

The concept of adaptive behavior has neither the psychometric history of IQ nor the stability across settings expected by diagnosticians for other scores. Although these concerns may actually represent strengths of adaptive behavior measures, their effect has been to prevent full utility of the measures. (p. 71)

Whatever the reason, adaptive behavior takes a back seat to intellectual functioning in the decision-making process. This undermines the value of determining typical behavioral regimens and may be a disservice to many students at the margin of eligibility.

What options does this situation leave us? We offer four different ideas. The first is to abandon the use of adaptive behavior as a criterion, as Zigler et al. (1984) suggest. They argue that mental retardation should be defined and assessed solely in terms of intellectual functioning. Greenspan's (in press) conceptualization of mental retardation fits this orientation, as his model stresses intelligence, albeit multiple intelligences. If, however, only conceptual intelligence is being considered, then problems with this approach are confronted with students whose linguistic, cultural, and economic backgrounds are significantly different from those of the majority population. A second suggestion is that innovative assessment systems be developed. Some of these would incorporate behaviorally or functionally based measures (Zucker & Polloway, 1987). This idea is attractive but not likely to be implemented at the present time. The third view is grounded in the reality that adaptive behavior will continue to be a second-class citizen in the identification process. Instead of being a criterion, it should play a supporting role in (a) justifying eligibility for individuals with IQs above 70; (b) questioning the certification of an individual with an IQ below 70 but with acceptable adaptive behavior skills; and (c) influencing placement and curricular decisions. This may not be the most desirable solution, but it may be the best compromise now available. The fourth and last perspective is more stout-hearted. It argues that we should continue to strive to develop a system in which in-school and out-of-school aspects of adaptive behavior play a key role. One conceptualization of such an idea has been developed by Reschly (1988) and is presented in Figure 3.5. The overriding goal is to identify students in need and provide services to them in the most appropriate manner.

INCIDENCE AND PREVALENCE

It is important to understand the different meanings of the terms *prevalence* and *incidence*.

Prevention and treatment are two of the most pressing issues in the field of mental retardation. To determine causal factors and to deliver services and treatment efficiently, professionals have used estimates of the frequency of mental retardation: incidence and prevalence. Although the words *incidence* and *prevalence* are considered synonymous in some contexts, they refer to different types of frequencies.

TERMINOLOGY DEFINED

Incidence refers to the number of new cases identified within a population over a specific period of time. The data for most estimates of incidence are

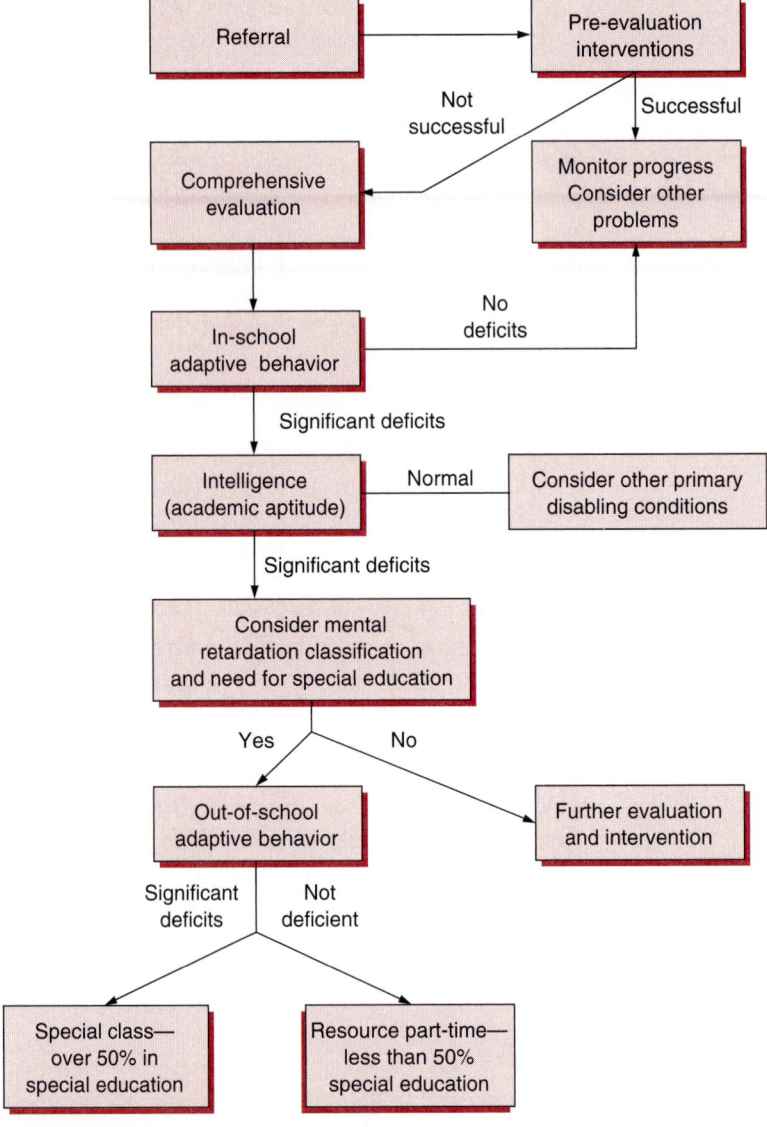

FIGURE 3.5
A Scheme of Use of Adaptive Behavior Information in Mental Retardation Classification

Source: From "*Incorporating Adaptive Behavior Deficits into Instructional Programs*" by D. J. Reschly in *Best Practices in Mental Disabilities* (Vol. 2) edited by J. R. Patton, E. A. Polloway, and L. R. Sargent, 1988, Des Moines, IA: Department of Education. Copyright 1988 by Des Moines, IA, Department of Education. Adapted by permission.

A PERSONAL VIEW OF RETARDATION

Very seldom do we attempt to consider retardation from the eyes and minds of those whom we so label. This approach, referred to as a phenomenological perspective, provides another vantage point from which to understand retardation.

Katie Tager, 29, resides at a semi-independent living apartment building. She is mildly retarded, but that doesn't stop her from keeping her own apartment, contributing to the community, and being actively involved with other people.

She is putting together two books: *Accepting Me,* a collection of her poems and writings, and *Let Special People Be Free,* a collection of essays, poems, personal stories, and artwork by adults and children with disabilities.

The following poem of Katie's was recently published in *Arts Access,* a newsletter of Very Special Arts Hawaii.

Accepting Me

*accepting me for who
I am some people find
it hard to do
They don't see my disability
I tell them I am mildly
retarded but they don't
believe me
I tell them some disabilities
you can't see but its
in my head where it*

*happen to me
I think and do things
slower then you and
sometimes its hard for
me to understand what
you find easy to know
I try and learn the
best I can and accept
what I am not able to
do*

*Try accepting me you
will see how much it
means to me
Its not hard to under
stand and be my friend
then you'll accept me
for who I am*

Source: From an item written by John Oh for *Arts Access.*

obtained from cases that were clinically identified when individuals entered some form of intervention. Incidence figures are valuable for investigating the causes of a disability and developing prevention programs. For example, researchers have found that maternal age at a child's birth and the incidence of the chromosomal aberration that results in Down syndrome are related. That relationship was determined by comparing the incidence rates of Down syndrome births with populations of mothers from different age ranges. For instance, a child born to a mother between the ages of 20 and 30 has a 1 in 1,500 chance of having Down syndrome; to a mother between 35 and 40, a 1 in 300 chance; to a mother between 40 and 45, a 1 in 70 chance; and to a mother over 45, a 1 in 40 chance of having Down syndrome (Bunker et al., 1972). While researchers have not determined why chromosomal aberrations are more frequent among older mothers than younger ones, the relationship between maternal age and the incidence of Down syndrome leads to possibilities for prevention.

Prevalence refers to the total number of cases of some condition existing within a population at a particular place or at a particular time. Unlike incidence, prevalence is not concerned with the number of new cases. Therefore, it is not as useful in determining causal relationships. Prevalence statistics are, however, better than incidence statistics for determining need for services. Prevalence rates are frequently represented as percentages.

There are two ways of conceptualizing prevalence: identifiable and true (Grossman, 1983). *Identifiable prevalence* refers to the cases that have come in contact with some system. *True prevalence,* which is a larger figure, assumes that a number of people who may meet the definitional criteria of mental retardation exist unrecognized by our systems. True prevalence would not include those who once met criteria but no longer do so.

For several reasons, variations in estimates of the incidence and prevalence of mental retardation have been found across studies and populations. Among factors influencing the incidence and prevalence of mental retardation are differences in criteria and methodologies of the researchers, and gender, age, community, race, and sociopolitical factors of the group under investigation. We look at each of these next.

FACTORS ASSOCIATED WITH PREVALENCE RATES

Definitional Perspective

The difficulty defining retardation is reflected by the number of reviews on the prevalence of mental retardation that mention the imprecision in definition and general haziness of the concept. The problem of defining this population was emphasized when G. O. Johnson (1959) criticized one of the most widely quoted surveys (Census of Referred Suspected Mental Retardation, conducted in Onondaga County, New York, in 1953) because it used a broad definition of mental retardation and, therefore, possibly reported more cases of mental retardation than actually existed according to generally accepted definitions.

It is not unusual for prevalence figures to be estimated without a survey's ever being conducted. Hypothetical prevalence statistics can be projected from formal definitions of mental retardation that rely entirely upon psychometric data or depend substantially upon such data (e.g., Grossman, 1973; Heber, 1961).

If IQ were the only criterion for defining mental retardation, approximately 2.3 percent of the population could be considered mentally retarded. In fact, the United States Office of Education reported in 1971–1972 that 2.3 percent of the school-age population was mentally retarded (0.8 percent, moderate or severe; 1.5 percent, mild). The PCMR estimated that approximately 3 percent of the population is mentally retarded. However, the validity of the often-cited figure of 3-percent prevalence has been seriously challenged. J. R. Mercer (1973a) conducted a prevalence survey in a California community that supported a 1-percent prevalence. Most contemporary definitional perspectives of mental retardation suggest a prevalence figure that does not exceed 1 percent.

Gender

In general, more males than females are identified as mentally retarded at all age levels. Three generally accepted explanations account for these sex differences in prevalence. First, biological defects associated with the X chromosome have a greater probability of being manifested by males than by females. Second, it appears that different child-rearing practices and different social demands are associated with sex differences in prevalence. For example, aggressive behavior for males is typically reinforced during child-rearing. An aggressive boy who is mentally retarded may not perceive the differences between appropriate and inappropriate situations for being aggressive. Individuals who exhibit behavior problems have greater chances of being identified as retarded than those who do not. Finally, society's demands for self-sufficiency traditionally have been higher for males than females (Robinson & Robinson, 1976); a lower degree of self-sufficiency is a marker for mental retardation, perhaps leading to males being disproportionately classified.

Communities

Communities vary in their ability to absorb individuals with limited talents. For example, people are more apt to be identified as retarded in urban communities than in rural ones (MacMillan, 1982). That variation has been subject to different interpretations. First, urban communities are generally perceived as more complex than rural communities. It is commonly believed that the social demands of urban communities are, therefore, more difficult to meet. In the past, individuals with borderline retardation from urban districts were more likely to be identified as mentally retarded, because urban districts tend to have better developed referral and diagnostic services. Some marginal cases may never be formally diagnosed in rural districts.

Socioeconomic conditions within communities are also related to differences in prevalence rates. Children who are born and reared in deprived, lower socioeconomic groups are more likely to be labeled mentally retarded than children from suburban settings. Many attempts have been made to account for the much higher rates of mental retardation among children from lower socioeconomic groups and deprived environments. Interestingly, prevalence figures indicate that, as the severity of retardation increases, cultural and socioeconomic factors become less pronounced. In other words, just as many wealthy families as poor families have children with severe retardation.

Prevalence figures also vary according to a country's level of development. In less developed countries, the situation is paradoxical, as the Committee on Terminology and Classification of the AAMR noted (Grossman, 1983):

> In underdeveloped countries lacking mass immunization programs, proper nutrition, hygiene and sanitation, prenatal care for pregnant women, and other public health services, the incidence of mental retardation and other disorders is high. Under these conditions, whereas incidence may be high, prevalence may be comparatively lower because of excessive infant mortality. (p. 75)

It is important that children with mental retardation remain in integrated settings whenever possible.

Another relevant fact is that such characteristics as literacy and cognitive ability, which are highly valued in more developed societies, may not be so important in social settings that are largely subsistence oriented and may thus cause deficiencies in these areas to go unnoticed or deemphasized.

Sociopolitical Factors

Evidence suggests that prevalence is influenced significantly by prevailing attitudes, policy, and practices. For instance, since the implementation of PL 94-142, the number of students classified as mentally retarded by school systems throughout the United States has dropped substantially. Polloway and Smith (1983) noticed this trend early on. They analyzed federal data for the period 1976–1981 and found that the number of students between the ages of three and twenty-one served under PL 94-142 and PL 89-313 dropped approximately 13 percent. An update of these changes indicates an even more dramatic reduction. (Figure 3.6 graphs these changes.) It is important to note that not all states and, for that matter, not all local education

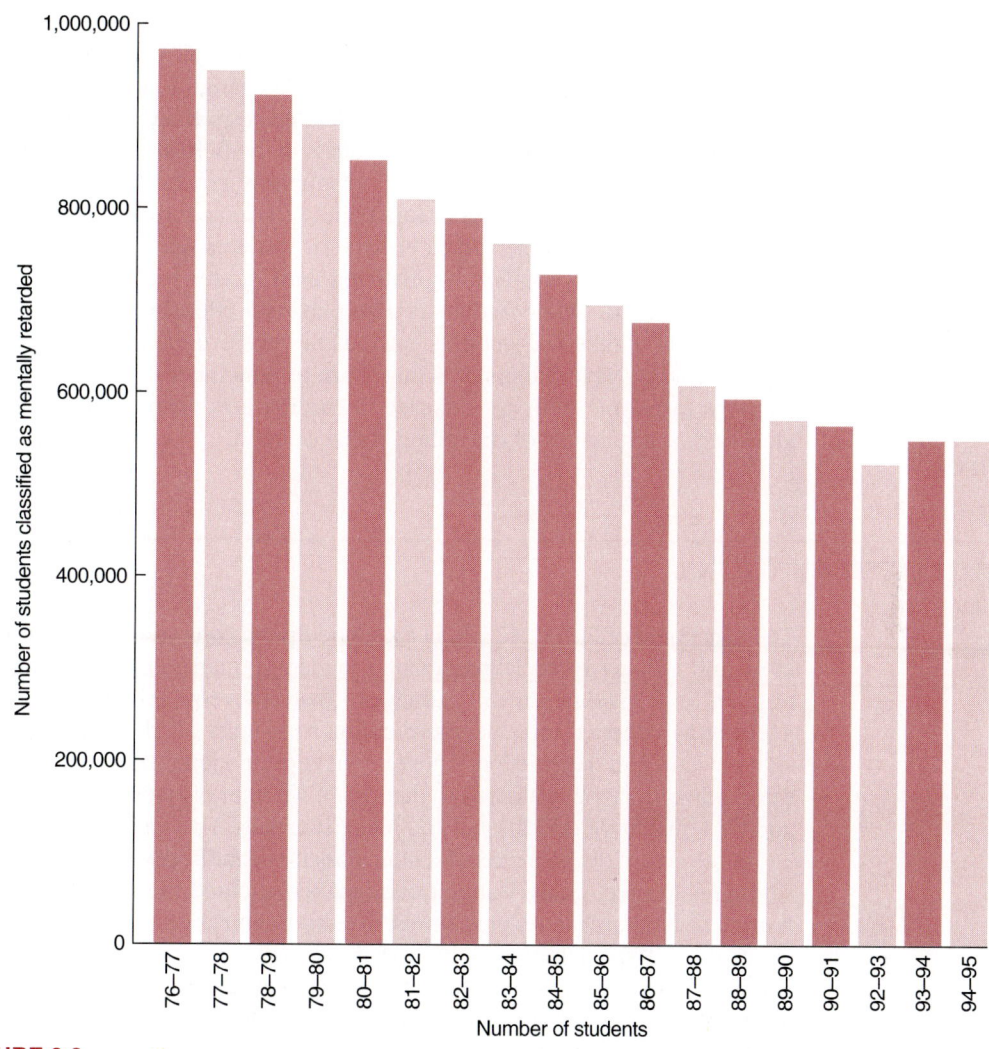

FIGURE 3.6
School-Identified Population (1976–1991)

agencies have experienced decreases; but some areas have seen significant decreases. In the aggregate, however, fewer students are identified as mentally retarded.

The prevalence rates of students with mild forms of retardation have been most affected by a range of sociopolitical factors, which are highlighted next. This issue has become so acute that the viability of the concept of mild mental retardation has been questioned (MacMillan, Gresham, & Siperstein, 1996). MacMillan et al. argue that mild mental retardation "differs markedly from other cases of mental retardation" (p. 357) and recommend that a new term be used to describe this displaced group of students.

The general makeup of classes for students with mild mental retardation in schools today is different from the makeup of these classes fifteen years ago.

Why this dramatic change? In large part it is because of sociopolitical factors that influenced how we identify and serve students who are decidedly below the norm. One important reason for this change is a more conservative posture on identifying students as retarded, especially if they are from culturally diverse backgrounds. Professionals in the field are noticeably wary of the misdiagnosis and misplacement of minority group students. Another reason is that a number of higher functioning students formerly identified as retarded are now being served in classes for students who are learning disabled. These settings are less stigmatizing than classes for students labeled mentally retarded. Other factors are also playing a critical role in the changing numbers of retarded students, such as the positive effects of early intervention efforts. Nevertheless, it is important to remember that much of what happens to people who are retarded, including how many of them are so identified, is a function of prevailing social opinion.

FINAL CONSIDERATIONS

The enactment of PL 94-142 and its expanded provisions as amended in 1983, 1986, and 1990 gave official recognition to the importance of developing case registers of individuals with disabilities. That law required local education agencies to conduct and document efforts to identify all children at risk residing within their jurisdiction. After they have been identified as being at risk, the children must be evaluated to determine whether or not they are disabled and thus qualify for educational and related services. This task was enormous.

Most policy decisions result either directly or indirectly in allocations of resources to meet goals. Public policy makers include the president, members of federal and state legislatures, county commissioners, school administrators, and special-interest groups such as the Council for Exceptional Children. Most persons who make or affect policies related to people who are mentally retarded are not professionals in the field. All of them, however, are involved in making decisions about the relative importance of different goals and deciding the appropriate expenditures of resources to meet each goal. It is important that policy makers identify the most beneficial set of goals and allocate the necessary resources. The prudence and the equity of policy decisions affecting those with mental retardation depend heavily on the decision makers' understanding of the demography of this group.

In 1978, the National Institute of Handicapped Research funded a project to establish a means of providing national estimates of the incidence, prevalence, and other demographic characteristics of disabled Americans. The purpose of this effort was to provide an adequate statistical base for policy. Roistacher, Holstrom, Cantril, and Chase (1982) noted that by 1978 more than eighty federal agencies (plus many more state and local agencies) were providing services to people with disabilities. Many of the agencies collected incidence, prevalence, and demographic data, but most agencies had different legislative mandates, resulting in different purposes for collecting data. Ultimately, the collected data lacked comparability across agencies. Roistacher et al. (1982) noted that different definitions and data collection methodologies made aggregation of data impossible. While definitional and methodological problems can be reduced, Roistacher et al. (1982) stated that developing an adequate statistical base for policy making would be beneficial. Furthermore, while knowing that the numbers of people identified as mentally retarded is important, we are only beginning to learn about their demographic and clinical characteristics, attitudes and aspirations, service experiences, and adult outcomes. Collecting such information is important, but data at the national level reflecting a realistic picture of current events are needed if policy makers are to make informed decisions.

To understand the term *mental retardation,* we must begin by establishing a definition. Historically, a variety of attempts has been made to define concisely the condition implied by this term and its precursors. The AAMR definitions of Heber (1959, 1961) and Grossman (1973, 1977, 1983) have reflected the essential dual dimension of the concept of retardation. The most recent AAMR definition (AAMR, 1992) represents a more functional perspective. Nevertheless, professionals continue to question and suggest alternatives, and further evolution is probable.

Classification involves delineating specific subgroups of persons who are retarded. This task has given rise to a variety of systems and a host of specific terms. Historically, approaches have categorized persons according to level of severity (e.g., the AAMR system). The current AAMR system now recommends that (a) classification be determined on the basis of levels of support across adaptive skill areas; and (b) current systems based on IQ levels be abandoned.

Prevalence figures in mental retardation have proven to be difficult to establish; significantly wide ranges have been reported in the literature. Although 3 percent used to be cited by the government as an estimate of the prevalence of retardation, there is generally no support for this figure today. Most professionals suggest prevalence rates of less than 1 percent. Additional concerns in prevalence relate to variations based on gender, community environment, and sociopolitical factors.

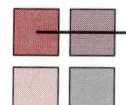

SUMMARY

GENERAL

■ Mental retardation is a complex condition.

■ The condition is characterized by substantial limitations in present levels of functioning.

- Mental retardation encompasses a heterogeneous group of people with varying needs.
- Some professionals suggest that mental retardation be considered a social invention.

TERMINOLOGY

- Various terms have been used formally to refer to mental retardation.
- Many nonprofessionals confuse the concepts of mental retardation and mental illness.

DISABLISM

- Many groups of people are not perceived favorably in today's society.
- *Disablism/handicapism* is a term that refers to stereotyping, prejudice, and discrimination based on apparent or assumed physical, mental, or behavioral differences.
- Media portrayals of individuals with mental retardation provide both negative and positive examples.

DEFINING MENTAL RETARDATION

- Early definitions stressed the concept of social competence.
- The definitions developed by the AAMR have typically included three major components: subaverage general intellectual functioning, deficits in adaptive behavior, and occurrence during the developmental period.
- The most recent AAMR definition (1992) represents a more functional perspective to explaining the condition.
- New definitions have emerged—mostly in response to dissatisfaction with the AAMR definition.

CLASSIFICATION

- Mental retardation can be classified in a number of ways, with the most common being etiological, intellectual, or behavioral.
- Traditional levels of mental retardation include mild, moderate, severe, and profound.
- The AAMR (1992) system advocates the abandonment of levels based on IQ and recommends that classification be determined on the basis of levels of needed support across adaptive skill areas.

ALTERNATIVE CONCEPTUALIZATIONS OF MENTAL RETARDATION

- Alternative definitions exist, and others will be developed.
- The definition of developmental disabilities overlaps significantly with the AAMR (1992) definition of mental retardation.

PRACTICAL REALITIES

- The relationship between what is discussed theoretically and what is put into practice can vary greatly.
- Research suggests that no one definition is used consistently in the United States.
- IQ continues to have more importance in determining whether a student qualifies as being mentally retarded.

INCIDENCE AND PREVALENCE

- The terms *incidence* (i.e., number of new cases) and *prevalence* (i.e., number of existing cases) refer to different types of statistical concepts.
- Prevalence figures have been difficult to determine, with a wide range of figures reported in the literature.
- Most professionals believe prevalence rates to be less than 1 percent.
- Estimates of incidence and prevalence are influenced by definitional perspective, gender, community contexts, and sociopolitical factors.

CHAPTER *4*

Assessment of Mental Retardation

*After reading this chapter,
the student should be able to:*

- Discuss different types of theories of intelligence and intellectual development.
- Identify and describe different instruments used in the practice of intelligence testing today.
- Discuss different types of theories of adaptive functioning.
- Identify and describe different instruments used in the practice of adaptive behavior assessment today.

Key Terms

adaptive behavior
American Association
  on Mental Retardation
assessment

deviation IQ
nature–nurture
  controversy

Stanford-Binet IV
Wechsler scales

Assessment of mental and special abilities covers a wide range of activities. Though **assessment** has been defined in different ways by different people, most agree that it is not so much an activity as a process, dynamic and on-going, and one that changes with the needs of the individual. Salvia and Ysseldyke (1995) suggest that assessment is "more than just the collection of information; it is collection with a purpose" (p. 5).

The importance of testing and assessment is not lost on three of education's most prominent organizations, the American Educational Research Association, the American Psychological Association, and the National Council on Measurement in Education (1985):

> Educational and psychological testing represents one of the most important contributions of behavioral science to our society. It has provided fundamental and significant improvements over previous practices in industry, government, and education. It has provided a tool for broader and more equitable access to education and employment. Although not all tests are well-developed, nor are all testing practices wise and beneficial, available evidence supports the judgement of the Committee on Ability Testing of the National Research Council that the proper use of well-constructed and validated tests provides a better basis for making some important decisions about individuals and programs than would otherwise be available. (p. 1)

Educators are required to provide that children receive individual psychoeducational evaluations prior to classification and placement in special education programs. Policies in most states prescribe that these evaluations include two critical assessment areas, intelligence and adaptive behavior. What follows is an in-depth look at the theories and assessment practices of these important areas.

THEORIES OF INTELLIGENCE

Many of the new models of intelligence developed during the 1980s are now taking a firm foothold in contemporary scientific thought.

Theories of intelligence are useful to the extent that they provide educators with an organizing structure for understanding and evaluating how children learn. For teachers and other service providers in the community, the concept of intelligence is most useful when it helps to formulate instructional strategies.

Assessments of students who are retarded are used to determine appropriate placement and plan effective instructional programs

Theories of intelligence can be evaluated from several points of view. For some people, particularly those who work in the field of education, intelligence can be an intricate and well-defined construct; for others, it may be little more than a generally held notion or idea. According to some theorists, it is the efficiency of the process that is important, for example, how much of a given task one can accomplish in a certain period of time. According to others, it may be the relationships among ideas that really matter. For still others, intellectual theories are best understood in the context of their origin (innate or acquired). While nearly all theories of intelligence contain some of these elements, Wechsler's (1958) definition of intelligence offers one of the most cogent explanations: "The aggregate or global capacity of the individual to act purposefully, to think rationally, and to deal effectively with his environment" (p. 7). A brief description of three very general types of theories of intelligence follows.

Traditional *psychometric theories* have their roots in differential psychology, the study of individual and group differences. Psychometric theorists assume that underlying abilities account for most variations in intellectual functioning. The traditional psychometric theorists range from those who believe that a single trait accounts for all mental abilities (e.g., Spearman, 1927; Vernon, 1950) to multifactored theorists who believe that intelligence is best explained by a multitude of traits or factors (Guilford, 1967; Thorndike, 1927; Thurstone, 1938). Most, however, place these models at two ends of a continuum and believe that reality lies somewhere between the two. Recently, a three-stratum theory of cognitive abilities has been proposed by John Carroll (1993) that allows for a general ability factor similar to Spearman's *g*, second-level factors referred to as broad ability factors (e.g., crystallized intelligence, fluid intelligence), and fifty or more primary (or narrow) abilities, many of which have been previously identified by Thurstone. Carroll's three-stratum theory synthesizes the factor-analytic work of the past century and offers much promise for new developments in the years ahead.

Information processing theories, perhaps better than any others, represent the second and most truly interdisciplinary approach to understanding intelligence. With contributions from anthropology, computer science, education, linguistics, and psychology, information processing theorists focus on the methods by which a person processes information from sensory stimuli to motoric output (Sternberg, 1985). Among the many theories that emanate from an information-processing model, Sternberg's (1985, 1988) triarchic theory of human intelligence is beginning to receive some acclaim. The triarchic theory describes a complex and highly integrated system of mental operations that combines such influential elements as the internal world of the individual, the external world of the individual, and one's life experiences. Sternberg (1997) is careful to point out the underlying components and mechanisms at work in each of these three key areas but cautions that while such operations may be found among people of all cultures, the values placed on specific problem-solving strategies and mechanisms may vary. For example, children of one culture may adapt more quickly to the environmental demands of a new community than other children, based on both past experiences and the social worth of the necessary skills. Consequently, what is deemed intelligent in one culture may not be viewed as intelligent in another. What further distinguishes Sternberg's theory from other contemporary theorists is an explanation of how information is processed within each of the three aforementioned areas. That is, he allows for the presence of higher-order problem-solving skills, performance components that allow for the execution of those problem-solving skills, and knowledge acquisition components that allow one to attend, retrieve, and compare the necessary pieces of information.

Another major theory that is receiving a great deal of attention, is Das, Naglieri, and Kirby's (1994) planning, attention, simultaneous, and successive (PASS) processes model. The PASS model of information processing is an extension and validation of Luria's (1966) turn-of-the-century theory of human cognitive functioning. Luria first reported and others have since verified the presence of three functional units of information processing. The first functional unit allows a person to become aroused by and attend to environmental stimuli. The second functional unit is responsible for acquiring, holding, and then processing the information, of which there are two main approaches, processing multiple pieces of information all at once in an integrated manner (simultaneous) or processing information in a sequential, temporarily organized (successive) manner. The third functional unit is known as the planning unit and provides the individual with the means to analyze cognitive activity, develop a problem-solving strategy, and then evaluate the efficacy of that solution. Das et al. (1994) have suggested that the PASS model offers psychologists and educators a number of options for responding to the special needs of children with disabilities.

The reader is referred to Flanagan, Genshaft, and Harrison's (1997) new text entitled, *Contemporary Intellectual Assessment: Theories, Tests, and Issues,* for further perspectives on these and other works.

The third major category of theories is the most broad, including theories not mentioned in the previous two. Among them is H. Gardner's (1993) theory of multiple intelligences. While reminiscent of the multifactored theories, Gardner's theory allows for multiple definitions of intelligence, including, among others, social and motoric intelligence. Although there appear to be little data in the professional literature to validate Gardner's definition, many educators have embraced it as a new and innovative perspective on intellectual functioning. Whether biological or psychological, developmental or stage specific, more theories and definitions of intelligence will undoubtedly be developed in the coming years. Gardner's theory may hold promise for people who work with persons with mental retardation. The assumption that all individuals are different, and possess their own unique combination of strengths and weaknesses, is in agreement with Gardner's premise that it is possible to be intelligent in specific yet non-traditional ways.

NATURE VERSUS NURTURE

If teachers view intelligence as fixed, biologically based, or predominantly inherited, then they may view their role as disseminators of information rather than cultivators of learning. This position assigns the responsibility of learning and its opposite, nonlearning, primarily to the person receiving instruction. But if teachers view intelligence as something that can be assisted and altered, they may see their job as instrumental in the learning process, thereby allowing them to view a person's learning as an indication of their own effectiveness as teachers.

The many concepts of intelligence and the ways in which individuals learn are very much related to the **nature–nurture controversy,** the question of whether intelligence is innate or acquired. Actually, few authorities claim either the extreme hereditarian or the extreme environmentalist position, believing instead that both factors work together in a sort of duet, to influence one's abilities and patterns of responses (Plomin, 1994).

Piaget referred to such a combination of biological and environmental factors as *epigenetic* in nature.

The bulk of this debate concerns the relative proportions of these two major ingredients that combine to shape one's intelligence. It is generally agreed that a person's upbringing affects cognitive development within the constraints of existing biological potential. But how rigid are those constraints? And how powerful are the environmental forces that influence them? Researchers are divided on these issues. For example, thirty years ago, people probably thought that it was useless to try to assign percentages to the relative influences of heredity and environment. Now, however, given recent and almost daily breakthroughs in molecular genetics, quantitative analysis of genetic structures is rapidly gaining in sophistication. Discoveries are now possible that were not even imaginable a few years ago. Yet, even the most genetically promising minds can have their development retarded if there is no stimulation in the environment. Ingalls (1978) illustrates this with an analogy of plant growth:

> The height of a given plant is a result of the particular gene type of the seed, the quality of the soil, the amount of rain, and numerous other factors. If a given plant grows to be four feet tall, it makes no sense to say that it achieved this height because of the seed variety. It is equally nonsensical to say that 80% of the height was due to the genes. (p. 41)

Though the logic of this approach seems irrefutable, citing research studies, growth figures, and models of intelligence, Jensen (1981) has insisted that genes account for approximately 70 percent of the variance in intelligence, with environment counting for the remaining 30 percent. He objects to theories that cite environmental deprivation and test bias as the reasons for variation in intelligence among cultural groups, claiming instead that the major determinant for intelligence is genetic, not environmental. Bouchard, Lykken, McGue, Segal, and Tellegen (1990) have generated heritability estimates similar to those of Jensen from a sample of 100 sets of twins reared apart. While the authors have hypothesized that the genetic influence on psychological functioning of individuals is indeed strong, they also report that the influence is indirect, and manifests itself through environmental opportunities, thereby enhancing the importance of effective parenting and optimum early learning opportunities.

While environmental influences have been found to have a substantial impact on intelligence, Rushton (1995) suggests that most heritability estimates average out at about 50 percent, lower than those reported by Jensen (1981) and Bouchard et al. (1990), but still quite high. With 50 percent of the variability due to environmental influences, it can be safely said that one's intellectual potential is shaped to a large degree by nonhereditary factors that resonate through all parts of a person's life, into the school, home, and community. Educators and social service delivery personnel must therefore help structure environments in ways that stimulate intellectual growth. In addition, they must accept that changes are both constant and welcome additions where intellectual growth and development are concerned.

INTELLIGENCE QUOTIENT

The notion that one's intellectual capacity can be described with a single value is unsettling to many. While it is still possible to find tests that yield only one score and examiners who define a person's level of academic aptitude in terms of a single value, these tests and examiners are in the minority. The notion of a single IQ score is valid only if one truly believes that a single factor of general ability underlies all problem-solving operations. Since most people today no longer believe in the notion of a lone ability factor, and no major intelligence test is based on a single, underlying dimension, the notion of IQ has changed dramatically from its inception.

Though many of the terms once associated with intelligence and intelligence quotients are no longer accurate, they have remained in the American vocabulary and are worth knowing. The earliest and least sophisticated term for describing a person's level of intellectual functioning is mental age. Mental age is an estimate of one's intellectual level and is different from chronological age. A five-year-old who successfully completes tasks typically performed only by children seven years of age would be considered to have a mental age of seven years. Conversely, a seven-year-old who successfully completes tasks typically performed by five-year-old children would be considered to have a mental age of five years. Louis Terman first introduced the term *intelligence quotient* (IQ) in 1916 as a better scoring index than mental age. While no longer used in practice, the IQ is important in an historical sense and is calculated by dividing one's mental age by one's chronological age and multiplying by 100. The disadvantage of a mental age score as compared with a ratio IQ score, such as that proposed by Terman, is that it provides an index of a child's IQ test performance relative to others in a given age group only. This technique does not, however, work for adults. Beginning in early adulthood, chronological age increases faster than mental age, making adults in general and older adults in particular appear less apt than they really are.

Today, deviation IQs are used in place of intelligence quotients for all age groups. Although many professionals still refer to these scores as IQs, they are not, that is, not in the same way referred to seventy-five years ago when the concept was just originating. A **deviation IQ** is nothing more than a subtest raw score converted to a standard score for the examinee's own age group. The standard score for a particular child is derived by subtracting the mean raw score of all children in the respective age group from the raw score of the child and then dividing that value by the raw score standard deviation for all children in that age group. The advantage of a deviation IQ is that a person's relative standing within a particular reference group can be compared with the scores of many others' including those of differ-ent ages and ability levels. This is the primary reason that most individually administered, norm-referenced intelligence tests used today have a mean (*M*) of 100 and a standard deviation (*SD*) of 15.

ASSESSMENT OF INTELLIGENCE

Although the testing practices of today differ markedly from those of 4,000 years ago when formal testing was first introduced, the premise has re-mained very much the same, to distinguish those who are successful at solv-ing problems from those who are not. According to Ittenbach, Esters, and Wainer (1997), the act of assessment is actually a quest in search of an un-derlying truth or reality. It is a means by which hypotheses are tested and verified using scientifically acceptable methods (Messick, 1988). While the history of testing is virtually 4,000 years old, the history of modern testing is little more than a century old. Sir Francis Galton (1832–1920) is generally considered to be the founder of formal testing. However, it actually was one of his contemporaries, James McKeen Cattell (1860–1944), who is credited with coining the term *mental tests*. What made Galton and Cattell's influence on the mental testing movement so profound was not their shared interests in eugenics and individual differences so much as their particular blend of skills and abilities. Galton, part scientist and part philosopher, was trying to understand better the inheritance of mental abilities through physical traits, whereas Cattell was interested in differences in physiological functioning as evidenced by performances on paper-and-pencil tests.

The critical link between the two investigators was the mathematician Karl Pearson (1857–1936). According to Ittenbach and Lawhead (1997), "Galton had the ideas, but Karl Pearson had the mathematical acumen to sell it to the world" (p. 31). Cattell then applied the new mathematical opera-tions to test scores of his experimental psychology students at the University of Pennsylvania. From there, the union of statistics and experimental psy-chology carried forward to all of American psychology.

As a construct, intelligence is a relatively well-accepted and time-honored notion of problem-solving ability. Yet, the definition of intelligence and the way in which it is measured are open to debate. Many have at-tempted to define intelligence, but few have set out to measure it with any degree of rigor. Those who have attempted to measure intelligence have done so with the understanding that they were attempting to explain one of the most complex and elusive components of human functioning. Test de-velopers have been careful to distinguish the construct of intelligence from its assessment—the manner in which information is obtained. Human ser-vice providers should be careful to do the same.

THE INFLUENCE OF ALFRED BINET

The first effective test of intellectual ability was devised in the early 1900s by French psychologists Alfred Binet, Victor Henri, and Theodore Simon (D. P. Schultz & Schultz, 1996). Although Binet had a wide and varied career within the discipline of psychology, it is in the fields of intelligence and psychometrics that he has "had his most concentrated, enduring, and intellectually powerful influence" (Haywood & Paour, 1992, p. 1). In 1904, the French Minister of Public Instruction appointed Binet to a commission to study the problems of educating children who were not likely to benefit from traditional classroom instruction and who would instead profit from slower-paced educational programs, that is, children with learning problems.

As early as 1895, Binet had already argued in his writings that educational tests were far too narrow in scope and that new tests were needed to understand better the learning process. Thus, Binet and his colleague Theodore Simon devised an instrument to identify children who were considered lacking in mental ability. Their first test, the thirty-item Measuring Scale of Intelligence, was published in 1905, then revised in 1908 and revised again in 1911 (as cited in Haywood & Paour, 1992). Their scale was different from others of the day in that it did not just tap sensory experiences, but instead allowed for the evaluation of such mental abilities as comprehension, memory, and reasoning, intellectual skills deemed critical for scholastic success. In short, the Binet-Simon scale sampled higher-level, complex processes that the authors believed to be essential elements of intelligence.

Binet and Simon went to great lengths to differentiate between the concepts of natural intelligence and acquired intelligence. They were interested in measuring one's *capacity* to learn rather than simply knowledge gained through instruction. Because reading and writing are learned skills, Binet and Simon's tests of intelligence were constructed to avoid measuring reading and writing. In the initial version of their scale, for example, the child's ability to identify pictured objects, repeat a three-digit series, reproduce geometric figure drawings, define abstract words, and perform similar nonacademic tasks were tested.

Among the many versions of the original Binet-Simon scale used in America shortly after the turn of the century, it was actually Terman's Stanford Revision and Extension of the Binet-Simon Scale (1916) that became the template for all subsequent revisions. Terman's version has since been revised in this country three times: in 1937 and 1960 with Maud Merrill and, most recently, in 1986 by Robert Thorndike, Elizabeth Hagen, and Jerome Sattler (1986a). The 1937 and 1960 forms of the Stanford-Binet included such materials as toys and miniature objects (e.g., beads, balls, cars, dolls), which examinees were instructed to manipulate in various ways, and booklets and pictures (animals and household objects, and so on), about which they had to answer questions.

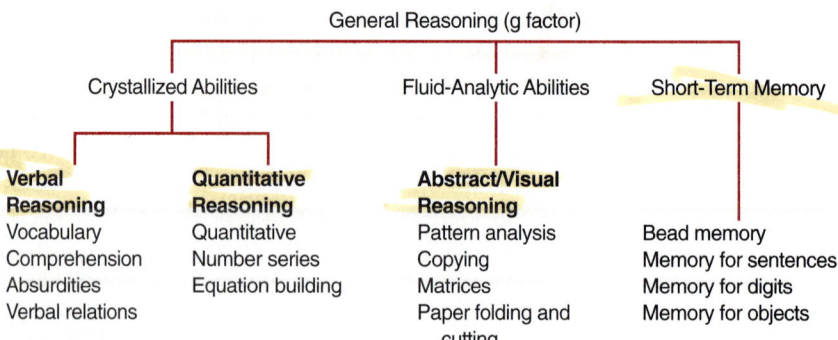

FIGURE 4.1
Stanford-Binet IV Model

The **Stanford-Binet IV** is an individually administered intelligence test based on a three-level hierarchical model of cognitive abilities. At the top of the model is *g,* a general reasoning factor. The next level emanates from the work of J. L. Horn and Cattell (1966) and divides *g* into three secondary factors: crystallized abilities, fluid-analytic abilities, and short-term memory. Crystallized abilities are cognitive factors an individual needs in order to acquire and use information necessary to deal with verbal and quantitative concepts; fluid-analytic abilities are the cognitive skills needed for solving new problems involving nonverbal or figural stimuli; and short-term memory is a measure of the individual's ability to retain information until it can be stored for long-term usage. The third level of the model divides crystallized abilities into verbal reasoning and quantitative reasoning, while fluid-analytic abilities are identified by abstract/visual reasoning alone. Short-term memory has no comparable third-level division. Figure 4.1 illustrates the model and the tests that comprise each of these areas.

In the Stanford-Binet IV, the term *intelligence* has been replaced by the term *cognitive development.* The terms *intelligence, IQ,* and *mental age* are not used in the fourth edition anywhere in the administration or technical manuals (Thorndike, Hagen, & Sattler, 1986b). The term *Standard Age Score* (SAS) serves as a replacement for *IQ.* Five SAS scores are obtainable, one for each of the four areas measured (Verbal Reasoning, Abstract/Visual Reasoning, Quantitative Reasoning, and Short-Term Memory) and the Test Composite. The Composite SAS is a deviation score that is similar, if not identical, to what others consider to be a deviation IQ score. According to Thorndike et al. (1986b), the Stanford-Binet IV has a fourfold purpose:

1. To help differentiate between students who are mentally retarded and those who have specific learning disabilities.

2. To help educators and psychologists understand why a particular student is having difficulty learning in school.

3. To help identify gifted students.

4. To study the development of cognitive skills of individuals from ages 2 to adult. (p. 2)

Each of the items represented in the fifteen tests of the Stanford-Binet IV is arranged in levels of increasing difficulty and designated by letter (A, B, C, etc.). Each level has two items of approximately equal difficulty. For each test, the examiner must establish a basal age and a ceiling age. The multistage format begins with a Vocabulary test, a routing test that determines the entry level for the other tests. From the results of the Vocabulary test, the examiner identifies the subject's appropriate entry level for the remaining tests. No more than thirteen tests are given to any subject, and the authors even recommend several abbreviated versions. The raw scores of each test are converted to SASs. On the Composite SAS, $M=100$ and $SD=16$, while on the individual test, SASs, $M=50$ and $SD=8$.

The Stanford-Binet IV was anxiously anticipated in the hope that it would be a superior instrument, but it has been received with mixed reviews. In its first published form, it contained inaccuracies, and replacement manuals did not appear until a year after the test was released for use. T. F. Hopkins (1988) tried to defend the Stanford-Binet IV by citing the response of Elizabeth Hagen, coauthor of the new Binet: "It reminded her of the words on a tee shirt worn by a burly construction worker: 'I'm Not Perfect, but I Have Many Parts That Are *Very Good*' " (p. 44). Historical significance and personal testimonials notwithstanding, the Stanford-Binet IV has continued to live up to its name, particularly when examiners need a good measure of general intellectual functioning. Additionally, Laurent, Swerdlik, and Ryburn (1992) found the Binet to be effective in discriminating among groups of children with differing intellectual abilities, and a useful predictor of academic achievement. Perhaps Spruill (1988) sums it up best, "In spite of numerous problems, the Fourth Edition will be around for many years—after all, it is still the Binet" (p. 558).

THE INFLUENCE OF DAVID WECHSLER

David Wechsler's (1896–1981) influence on assessment in the schools has been profound. Whereas the Stanford-Binet has served as the standard of intellectual assessment for nearly a century, the Wechsler scales have served as the workhorse (Wechsler, 1949, 1955, 1967, 1974, 1981a, 1989a, 1991a). The **Wechsler scales** are a series of three individually administered intelligence tests, modeled after one another, in which a person's intellectual abilities are described using a verbal/motor framework. The Wechsler scales have provided the preferred vehicle for the identification and classification of countless school-age children for nearly half a century.

Like Binet, Wechsler was trained as a clinician. Though he worked with adults rather than children, he, too, believed that intelligence was a unitary trait and that it was actually only one part of the broader construct of the human personality. Perhaps the most important feature of the Wechsler scales, and very likely the reason their use in the schools has far exceeded that of the Binet, is that the tests are remarkably similar across the preschool-, elementary-, and secondary-age ranges. As opposed to earlier versions of the Binet in which children of different ages were tested using very different tasks, with the Wechsler scales, children of different ages are exposed to different items but to highly similar tasks, thereby adding an element of consistency to evaluations throughout a child's schooling. Sadly, America's educators will never come to know the instrument that Wechsler had intended to complete his battery of intelligence tests across the lifespan, the Wechsler Intelligence Scale for the Elderly (WISE), which was under development at the time of his death in 1981 (Kaufman, 1994).

When they first appeared, the Wechsler scales were distinguished by several other innovative features. For example, every Wechsler test is subdivided into smaller scales and subscales. The Wechsler Intelligence Scale for Children—Third Edition, for example, consists of ten subtests and three supplemental ones: five verbal subtests with one alternate, and five performance (nonverbal) subtests with two alternates. Each subtest theoretically measures a different ability and is treated as a separate entity; combined, all subtests allow the examiner to assess global intellectual capacity. Wechsler (1939) believed that the Binet test of that era did not tap motoric performance, an important facet of intelligence, so he developed a performance scale that complemented the verbal scale in such a way that it offered problem-solving items that required judgment, reasoning, foresight, and planning, but little in the way of verbal ability. Following is a brief description of the three Wechsler tests currently in use today.

Wechsler Preschool and Primary Scale of Intelligence—Revised

The Wechsler Preschool and Primary Scale of Intelligence—Revised (WPPSI-R) (Wechsler, 1989a) is a standardized, individually administered test of intelligence intended for use with children 3 years 0 months (3-0) through 7 years 3 months (7-3) of age. The WPPSI-R is a revision of the original Wechsler Preschool and Primary Scale of Intelligence (WPPSI; Wechsler, 1967). The purpose of the WPPSI-R, as stated in the manual, is to offer assistance with the diagnosis of exceptionalities of young children in educational and private practice settings (Wechsler, 1989b). The WPPSI-R is divided into two major sections, verbal and performance, both of which yield IQ scores, which in turn combine to yield a full-scale IQ ($M = 100$, $SD = 15$). The WPPSI-R has twelve separate subtests ($M = 10$, $SD = 3$), ten of which are required, and two supplemental subtests. The core test may be administered in thirty to sixty minutes with the other two subtests requiring an additional ten minutes. Bonus points are awarded for quick, correct responses. Although the WPPSI-R remains markedly similar to the parent WPPSI, a number of changes were made to keep pace with new developments in clinical assessment. Only one new subtest has been added, Object Assembly, in which the child is asked to assemble puzzles in a specified time period. New items were created to increase the age range of the test, and more attractive materials were used to encourage the young child's participation.

Wechsler Intelligence Scale for Children—Third Edition

The Wechsler Intelligence Scale for Children—Third Edition (WISC-III) (Wechsler, 1991a) is a standardized, individually administered test of intelligence intended for use with children and adolescents 6-0 through 16-11 years of age. The WISC-III is the third in a series of time-honored and clinically tested instruments (i.e., WISC, WISC-R). Although the publication history of WISC-III does not yet equal that of its predecessor, the WISC-R (cf. Kaufman, Harrison, & Ittenbach, 1990), Braden (1995) states in the most recent edition of the *Mental Measurements Yearbook* that the WISC-III meets the needs of researchers and clinicians alike and offers evolutionary progress toward assessment of cognitive abilities.

The purpose of the WISC-III, as stated in its manual, is to offer assistance with educational planning and placement, diagnosis of exceptionality, clinical and neuropsychological assessment, and educational and psychological research (Wechsler, 1991b). The three traditional global scales continue to underscore Wechsler's notion of a broad-based measure of intellectual functioning, but with strong verbal and motor components. The same three principal scores ($M = 100$, $SD = 15$) are obtainable: full-scale IQ, verbal IQ, and performance IQ. In addition to the aforementioned scores, four new scaled scores may also be computed using the existing subtests: Verbal Comprehension, Perceptual Organization, Freedom from Distractibility, and Processing Speed. All four are based on extensive factor analytic research with the WISC and WISC-R. Ten subtests are required; the examiner has the option of using three additional subtests, all with $M = 10$, $SD = 3$ (see Table 4.1). The entire test may be administered in fifty to seventy minutes with the additional three subtests requiring another fifteen minutes. Bonus points are awarded for quick, correct responses.

Wechsler Adult Intelligence Scale—Revised

The Wechsler Adult Intelligence Scale—Revised (WAIS-R) (Wechsler, 1981a) is a standardized, individually administered test of intelligence intended for use with adults 16-0 years of age and older. The WAIS-R is a revision of the original Wechsler Adult Intelligence Scale (WAIS; Wechsler, 1955). The purpose of the WAIS-R differs somewhat from that of the WPPSI-R and WISC-III in that it tends to be used more frequently as a clinical rather than an educational assessment tool (Kaufman, 1990). Like the WPPSI-R and WISC-III, the WAIS-R provides three composite IQ scores ($M = 100$, $SD = 15$): full-scale IQ, verbal IQ, and performance IQ. Eleven subtests comprise the WAIS-R ($M = 10$, $SD = 3$), all of which are required; total administration time is approximately seventy minutes. Eighty percent of the items found on the WAIS were retained for the WAIS-R with no or slight modification (Wechsler, 1981b). As with the other two tests, bonus points are awarded for quick,

TABLE 4.1
WISC-III Subtests

Subtest	Underlying abilities
Verbal Scale	
Information	Long-term memory, fund of information, formal education, richness of early learning experiences.
Similarities	Verbal reasoning, analogic thinking, concept formation.
Arithmetic	Concrete reasoning, numerical reasoning, facility with numbers.
Vocabulary	Fund of information, long-term memory, formal education, richness of early learning experiences.
Comprehension	Verbal reasoning, logical reasoning, social reasoning.
Digit Span[*]	Attention, short-term memory, facility with numbers, ability to copy a model.
Performance Scale	
Picture Completion	Attention to detail, visual organization, logical reasoning.
Coding	Short-term memory, visual-motor speed and coordination, facility with numbers, attention.
Picture Arrangement	Attention to detail, visual organization, logical reasoning, social reasoning.
Block Design	Abstract reasoning, visual-motor coordination, ability to copy a model, planning ability.
Object Assembly	Visual organization, visual-motor coordination, logical reasoning.
Symbol Search[*]	Abstract reasoning, ability to mentally copy a model, visual-motor coordination.
Mazes[*]	Planning ability, visual-motor coordination.

Note. [*]denotes optional subtests.

correct responses. A revision of the WAIS-R, the WAIS-III, is currently under development and should be out in the near future.

OTHER INFLUENTIAL SCALES

Although the Stanford-Binet and Wechsler scales have become very popular with school personnel, there are other individually administered tests of intelligence. While some tests are readily available, inexpensive, easy to administer, and require little in the way of administrator training or time, they may not meet state or local regulations or even provide all the information needed for an in-depth diagnostic evaluation. See Conoley and Impara (1995) for a review of frequently used measures of intelligence. Following are brief discussions of two widely used, well-respected instruments. The

Kaufman Assessment Battery for Children (K-ABC; Kaufman & Kaufman, 1983a) has gained acceptance as a viable instrument for measuring intellectual functioning. It is an individually administered, norm-referenced battery that allows for the measurement of both intelligence and achievement in children 2-6 to 12-6 years of age. The theoretical basis for this instrument is closely tied to concepts of information processing that have been derived from the work of cognitive psychologists. According to this system, two different processing abilities comprise intellectual functioning: sequential processing ability and simultaneous processing ability. Sequential processing involves using bits of information one after another in a step-by-step, sequential manner. In simultaneous processing, however, one uses bits of information all at once, holistically. Besides the two principal scales used, there are two others, Achievement and Nonverbal. The Nonverbal scale provides another way to assess children with atypical abilities by combining certain subtests that can be administered nonverbally and, equally importantly, requires nonverbal responses. The K-ABC has become popular with many psychometrists across the nation, even though it requires them to adjust their diagnostic and interpretive skills. According to Reynolds (1984), although the strong statistical and theoretical underpinnings of the K-ABC have made it a valued measure of intelligence among many child neuropsychologists, it still lacks the name recognition of either the Binet or the WISC-III.

The Differential Ability Scales (DAS; Elliott, 1990) is an American descendant of the well-known British Ability Scales (Elliot, Murray, & Pearson, 1979). The DAS is a standardized, individually administered test of cognitive functioning intended for use with children 2-6 to 17-11 years of age. At the top of the hierarchy of possible scores is a General Conceptual Ability score ($M = 100$, $SD = 15$) similar to an IQ score. Composite standard scores for specific ability areas are also available, depending upon the age and subtests administered (e.g., Verbal Ability, Nonverbal Reasoning Ability, Spatial Ability). The entire battery consists of twenty subtests (seventeen cognitive, three achievement) and takes about one hour to administer. No examinee takes more than twelve subtests. It has been reported by independent reviewers that the instrument was designed "explicitly for use in the schools to identify children with educational problems" (e.g., Sandoval, 1992, p. 89). Of particular note to psychologists and educators testing children are the relatively strong psychometric properties of the DAS and the out-of-level norms (standards for comparison), characteristics that Daniel (1994) believes allow for more accurate and readily interpretable standard scores for individuals performing at the lower end of the distribution.

Concern for children from bilingual and minority backgrounds has sparked the development of a number of "culture-free" measures in which there has been an effort to eliminate all cultural factors that might favor one group over another. One such test is the Matrix Analogies Test (Naglieri, 1985), an instrument that is purported to be a much purer measure of nonverbal

Readers are referred to a special issue of the *Journal of Special Education* (Reynolds, 1984) which is devoted exclusively to the K-ABC.

reasoning ability than other tests. The examinee is shown a matrix of abstract designs with a missing element and is asked to select a design that best completes the picture. Other tests such as the Standard Progressive Matrices (Raven, 1938) and Porteus Mazes (Porteus, 1965) have until recently served as the standards of culture-fair intellectual assessment. While these two instruments minimize verbal ability, they are becoming quite dated, and there is growing evidence that even these tests, which require pattern recognition and basic test-taking skills, may not be as culture-free as once thought.

CRITICISMS OF INTELLIGENCE TESTING

Considerable controversy surrounds the issue of intelligence testing in the schools. Some critics of intelligence testing find fault with the tests, others with the examiners, and still others with the process. They further argue that test scores are subject to various forms of statistical and administrative error and that these scores can vary considerably from one time to another. This point is well taken. The concept of intelligence was introduced at a time when the prevailing belief was that intelligence was hereditary and therefore a constant trait. Laypersons and professionals alike generally think of intelligence as a basic, enduring attribute of an individual. But if intelligence is a constant, why do IQ scores fluctuate? When a child receives an IQ score of 95 at age six, an IQ score of 89 at age thirteen, and an IQ score of 105 at age sixteen, does this mean that the child had average intelligence at first but lost intelligence between ages six and twelve, and became brighter again by sixteen? Obviously not. The most likely explanation is that the child was influenced by emotional, motivational, or experiential factors. Or perhaps the examiner's behaviors and scales used were more or less appropriate on these different occasions. The basic problem is that, although the word *intelligence* is used to refer to the totality of a person's ability and potential, no finite samples of behavior can possibly demonstrate everything that is worth knowing about that person's capabilities. A major premise of most if not all major intelligence instruments is that a score on an IQ test is not synonymous with intelligence. Other nonintellective factors also play a crucial role in both test performance and daily living (Wechsler, 1991b).

The purpose of today's tests, similar to those of Binet's time, is to predict likelihood for success in traditional academic settings. Although never perfect, the tests are indeed able to signal those for whom academic difficulties may be expected. Despite the defensible rationale for the original and continued development of these instruments, many people treat the tests themselves as if they were the offending party. One must wonder if such frustration and anger are really directed toward the tests, toward what the tests predict (academic outcomes), or toward the process of implementing educational interventions. Rather than kill the messenger, why not do as Kaufman (1994) has recommended, and *kill the prediction?* "The fact that most children who score very poorly on the WISC-III will also do poorly in school should not be accepted as a statement of destiny" (p. 7).

Accurate and in-depth assessment followed by verifiable educational interventions can do much to change a child's likelihood for success in a given academic program.

The second major criticism of intelligence testing pertains to the perception by the public and some members of the profession that IQ tests inadequately cover the broad spectrum of abilities defined as intelligence. Much of this criticism stems from the lack of convergence between the theory and structure of existing tests and the current knowledge base of experimental evidence, particularly as it relates to children with special needs (Das et al., 1994). Authors and publishers of tests are quick to point out that the tests do not measure all components of one's cognitive development but rather a sample of abilities in several key areas. The key areas are most often representative of the author's beliefs about intelligence, given the current state of research in the area. Some tests are designed to cover areas that other tests fail to touch. For example, the WISC-III has a strong fine motor component, while the Binet does not. On the K-ABC, the fine motor component is much more subtle, appearing through a combination of other scales. Further, the Stanford-Binet IV has a definable memory scale, while information pertaining to short-term and long-term memory must be teased out on the K-ABC and WISC-III. Though very different tasks are used in the respective tests, all fit into a broader framework for understanding the cognitive functioning of people with and without disabilities.

A third major criticism of IQ tests is that they regulate access to educational opportunities and relegate certain students from minority backgrounds to special education programs. Examined another way, these tests are used by school personnel to help understand why a child is encountering difficulty in traditional academic areas. Whether a child possesses special gifts or has mental retardation, each child is entitled to an environment where full academic growth can be realized. IQ tests are not used to change the academic programs of children who are performing well in the classroom; rather, the tests are used by professionals only after the student, parents, teachers, or other service providers have reason to believe that the child is not successful under normal classroom conditions. When used appropriately and within the context of a multidisciplinary team as mandated by the Individuals with Disabilities Education Act (IDEA), IQ tests serve only to confirm the presence and nature of learning difficulties observed by others. Simply put, IQ tests are intended to reduce, not increase, the number of children qualifying for special education.

THEORIES OF ADAPTIVE BEHAVIOR

The notion of examining what a person does in typical situations is often much more helpful than what a person *can* do or *might* do under the best of circumstances. Recently, increased attention has been directed toward the adaptive skills of persons with mental retardation. The acquisition of adaptive skills for most people is considered to be a continuous and naturally occurring set of events; for persons with mental retardation, however, the process is anything but continuous and very often plagued with difficulty.

Grossman (1983) has defined **adaptive behavior** as the "degree with which individuals meet the standards of personal independence and social responsibility expected for age and cultural group" (p. 1). More recently, the American Association on Mental Retardation (AAMR) (1992) has tended to emphasize definable adaptive skill areas rather than the more abstract term of adaptive behavior. Though some have criticized AAMR's earlier definitions of adaptive behavior as too elusive and ill defined (e.g., Zigler, Balla, & Hodapp, 1984), Kamphaus (1987) has defended the earlier definition as homogenizing, suggesting that it has provided the field with a focus and sense of direction that investigators in other areas have yet to obtain.

Whereas classification of mental retardation has required both an intellective (IQ) and nonintellective (adaptive) component, a new emphasis on adaptive skills has indeed encouraged a more balanced approach to diagnosis, classification, and service delivery where mental retardation is a concern. It is precisely because of the willingness on the part of members of the profession to pursue a deeper understanding of such an elusive construct that service delivery to persons with mental retardation has undergone such vast improvements in recent years. Recent developments notwithstanding, the current benefits of an agreed upon definition have not led to consensus on its theoretical structure. Theories of adaptation appear to be strong and long-standing but have, for the most part, remained outside the interest of most persons in the field of mental retardation. Following is a brief discussion of theories of adaptation from biological, psychological, and sociological points of view.

Adaptation is essentially a biological phenomenon (Gollin, 1985). The capacity of an organism to adjust to changes in the environment depends largely on two types of responses that allow it to remain at equilibrium with itself (homeostasis) and to function over a normal range of biologically acceptable environments (homeokinesis) (Prosser, 1986). While some such changes occur immediately (e.g., reaction to anxiety and fear, or fever in response to an infection), other changes may take days, weeks, months or even years to occur (e.g., muscle development in response to maturation). Still others (such as a species' collective resistance to a disease or its ability to survive in extreme conditions) may take many generations to evolve. Brandon (1990) has defined an organisms's adaptedness in terms of biological properties and its capacity to survive in its own environment.

Contributions from psychology and education to the understanding of adaptation have been many and varied. Individuals, alone or in groups, have their own beliefs, attitudes, and desires. Whereas biologists are interested in the adaptive mechanisms of biological systems, psychologists and educators are interested in the richness of the behaviors and their dependence on various environmental conditions (Staddon, 1983). Well-known to most educators is the work of Piaget (1952), in which the concepts of organization and adaptation are central to the idea of cognitive development. For a child to interpret and adjust to the demands of the external world, new experiences must be understood and modified in the context of preexisting information. Although Piaget limited his work to children, the same principle can be extended across the lifespan. For example, Stewart, Sokol, Healy, Chester, and Weinstock-Savoy (1982) have found that even positive major life events can be stressful and demand a multitude of adaptive responses over time.

Many adaptive behaviors are less a function of the person than of the organization or social unit to which the person belongs. For example, Lumsden and Wilson (1985) have reported that groups of people, like other animals, generate behavioral patterns that fit the social group to the environment. Even characteristics such as loyalty, morality, and altruism exist in groups of people and other animals because of their survival value to the group. A more obvious example of social adaptation may be found in social systems theory, a sociologically based theory often used to explain the structure and function of organized groups (J. R. Gordon, 1991). According to social systems theory, groups that survive over time are those whose development of organizational structures allows them to keep their place of importance in the broader social milieu. Status, roles, norms, and behaviors are as important for the social group as they are for the individuals within the group. Just as "children are born into a world of pre-existing, relatively stable social structures," so are social groups, dictating that they, too, must be "socialized to meet the expectations of the [broader] system" (J. R. Mercer, 1978a, p. 71).

Theoretical work into the construct of adaptive behavior for persons with mental retardation is available but limited. The research that has been conducted has emphasized the characteristics of the instruments instead of furthering the development of the construct itself. Adaptive behavior as a distinct and valued construct is only now receiving the attention that other constructs in psychology and education have known for years. Consequently, debates into the theoretical structure of adaptive behavior are emerging along predictable lines. Similar to the research on human intelligence, there appears to be a growing debate as to whether adaptive behavior is a single or multifaceted construct. C. E. Meyers, Nihira, and Zetlin's (1979) foundational work of twenty years ago identified two main factors present in the construct of adaptive behavior, responsibility and self-sufficiency. Since that time, investigators have reported everything from a single underlying dimension (e.g., McGrew & Bruininks, 1989; Millsap, Thackrey, & Cook, 1987) to as many as four to six stable factors (e.g., Widaman, Reise, & Clatfelter, 1994; Widaman, Stacy, & Borthwick-Duffy, 1993), depending upon whether items or scales were used in the analysis. In their review of research on adaptive behavior, Widaman and McGrew (1996) suggest and even provide evidence for the presence of a higher-order factor structure with one or perhaps two broad factors with several underlying dimensions. An example of a model that illustrates the hierarchical nature of adaptive behavior rather nicely is Greenspan's (1997) model of personal competence. According to Greenspan, "competent individuals can be defined both in terms of the qualities they bring to various goals and challenges, as well as by their relative degree of success in meeting those goals and challenges" (p. 131). In his model, there are four broad domains of competence: physical competence, affective competence, everyday competence, and academic competence. Greenspan posits a number of lower-order factors that are contained in each of the aforementioned domains, factors that all have relevance for persons with mental retardation and that offer a range of response options for persons of all ability levels. (See Figure 4.2 for a depiction of this model.)

Adaptive behaviors are the behavioral skills that are demonstrated in response to environmental demands (Widaman & McGrew, 1996). With the AAMR's shift toward a more functional definition of mental retardation, references to the more vague term of "adaptive behavior" have been replaced by ten very specific adaptive skill areas: "communication, self-care, home living, social skills, community use, self-direction, health and safety, functional academic, leisure, and work" (AAMR, 1992, p. 1). The change to the more easily definable adaptive skills areas "is not intended as a refutation of the term *adaptive behavior*" (AAMR, 1992, p. 38) but as a response to the many limitations and criticisms of the adaptive behavior measurement process. It is believed that by emphasizing the ten aforementioned skill areas, specifically, the potential for agreement on identification and remediation of abilities is enhanced.

ADAPTIVE BEHAVIOR VERSUS INTELLIGENCE

Before intelligence tests were developed, social incompetence was the standard for identifying persons with mental retardation (Nihira, 1969). Recent definitions of mental retardation now allow for an individual's ability to function adequately within the individual's principal environment. According to Leland (1978), the ability to cope with the more social demands of one's environment is "the reversible aspect of mental retardation, and it reflects primarily those behaviors which are most likely to be modified through appropriate treatment or training methods" (p. 28).

Beginning with the 1961 AAMR definition of mental retardation (Heber, 1961), and most certainly since the 1973 definition (Grossman, 1973), the relationship between the constructs of adaptive behavior and intelligence took on a new sense of importance in the diagnosis and classification of persons with mental retardation. Although the two constructs share much in common, they also stand apart in several substantive ways. First, examiners using measures of adaptive behavior attempt to obtain an index of a person's *usual* actions, whereas intelligence tests are designed to obtain estimates of *maximal* performance. Second, adaptive behavior measures tap a number of different everyday living areas, while intelligence tests typically focus on higher-order reasoning abilities. Third, intelligence tests are administered under very controlled conditions, while adaptive behavior information is

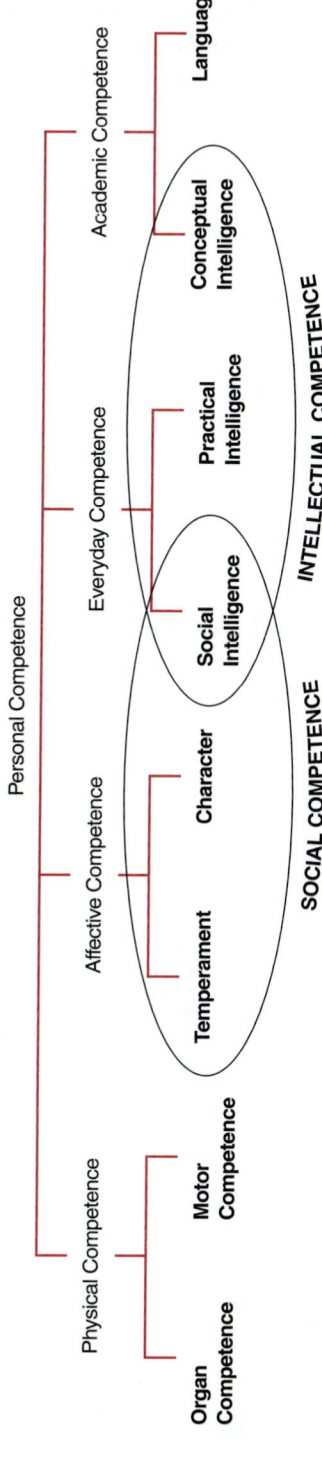

FIGURE 4.2
Greenspan's Model of Personal Competence

Source: From "The Role of Intelligence in a Broad Model of Personal Competence" by S. Greenspan and J. Driscoll in *Contemporary Intellectual Assessment: Theories, Tests, and Issues* (p. 133) edited by D. P. Flanagan, J. O. Genshaft, and P. L. Harrison, 1997, New York: Guilford. Copyright 1997 by Guilford. Reprinted by permission.

usually obtained through semistructured interviews with third-party respondents (people who know the person well).

Because of the importance of both adaptive behavior and intelligence, and the notion on the part of many that one may serve as a stand-in for the other, researchers have investigated the relationship between the two constructs. In a comprehensive review of forty-two studies documenting the relationship between measures of intelligence and of adaptive behavior, Harrison (1987) found a moderate relationship between the two constructs. Others, using more sophisticated statistical techniques, have found that the two constructs represent separate but related entities (i.e., Ittenbach, Spiegel, McGrew, & Bruininks, 1992; Keith, Fehrman, Harrison, & Pottebaum, 1987; McGrew, Bruininks, & Johnson, 1996).

Individuals are considered normal when they develop and function as their peers do. Only when a person's behavior lags behind that of age-mates is mental retardation considered. Persons with extensive to pervasive support needs are usually identified during infancy and early childhood because of the severity of the disability. The slower the development in areas of communication and sensorimotor functioning, the greater the need for early supports in these critical life-skill areas. During childhood and early adolescence, mental retardation is suspected when the child fails to keep pace with age-mates in school, or when there is an apparent deficiency in basic areas of learning such as reasoning, judgment, or social functioning. The greatest incidence of mental retardation occurs during the developmental period.

A dilemma of classification develops when children are seen as mentally retarded at school but appear to function normally with family and friends outside of school. Such is the problem of the six-hour retarded child (President's Committee on Mental Retardation, 1970). In late adolescence and adulthood, people are looked upon as mentally retarded when they repeatedly prove incompetent in handling social and vocational responsibilities. Yet social and vocational problems need not grow directly out of ineptitude; it is very common to find adults who were identified as mentally retarded during their school years and who later function quite well in their postschool environments. In fact, most adults with mental retardation, including those with multiple disabilities, adjust very nicely to community living (Conroy, 1996; Larson & Lakin, 1991).

ASSESSMENT OF ADAPTIVE BEHAVIOR

The term *adaptive behavior* represents a relatively new name for an old concept (Reschly, 1985). Prior to the Middle Ages, references to one's adaptive skills were informal, and care was provided based on behavioral deviance and physical deformity (E. Horn & Fuchs, 1987). In light of the long-standing recognition of the relationship between adaptive behavior and mental retar-

Advocates believe that a child's adaptive behavior must be evaluated in the context of his or her social and ethnic background

dation, assessment of adaptive functioning is much more focused and quantifiable than ever before. Much progress has been made in the name of adaptive behavior in the fifty years since Doll's (1947) first Social Maturity Scale, but more work remains.

While experts in the field appear to have reached relative agreement on the definition of adaptive behavior, and perhaps even on the skills that are believed to comprise it, the actual components of effective adaptive functioning remain much more puzzling. For example, in a content analysis of adaptive behavior measures, Bruininks, Thurlow, and Gilman (1987) found ten different categories of behaviors composed of forty-five different skills (see Figure 4.3). Complicating the measurement process are the realizations that adaptive behavior is a dynamic, ever-changing construct and that it is influenced by such factors as cultural norms, age-related expectations, and a combination of anticipated and idiosyncratic behaviors (E. Horn & Fuchs, 1987). Whether one is interested in the construct of adaptive behavior or the operationally defined skills that undergird it, attention to tasks that are developmentally appropriate and contextually relevant are important considerations for people whose quests toward personal independence and social responsibility are not to be taken for granted.

Self-help, Personal Appearance

    Feeding, eating, drinking
    Dressing
    Toileting
    Grooming, hygiene

Physical Development

    Gross motor skills
    Fine motor skills

Communication

    Receptive language
    Expressive language

Personal, Social Skills

    Play skills
    Interaction skills
    Group participation
    Social amenities
    Sexual behavior
    Self-direction, responsibility
    Leisure activities
    Expression of emotions

Cognitive Functioning

    Pre-academics
    (e.g., colors)
    Reading
    Writing
    Numeric functions
    Time
    Money
    Measurement

Health Care, Personal Welfare

    Treatment of injuries, health problems
    Prevention of health problems
    Personal safety
    Child-care practices

Consumer Skills

    Money handling
    Purchasing
    Banking
    Budgeting

Domestic Skills

    Household cleaning
    Property maintenance, repair
    Clothing care
    Kitchen skills
    Household safety

Community Orientation

    Travel Skills
    Utilization of community resources
    Telephone usage
    Community safety

Vocational Skills

    Work habits and attitudes
    Job search skills
    Work performance
    Social vocational behavior
    Work safety

FIGURE 4.3

Clusters and Specific Adaptive Behavior Areas

Source: From "Adaptive Behavior and Mental Retardation" by R. H. Bruininks, M. L. Thurlow, and C. J. Gilman, 1987, *The Journal of Special Education, 21*(1), p. 74. Copyright 1987 by PRO-ED. Reprinted by permission.

Best practice in the assessment of adaptive behaviors requires several key considerations (Harrison & Robinson, 1995). First, the examiner should incorporate adaptive behavior assessment into a broad-based model of assessment and intervention. Failure to link the assessment to the probable forms of intervention, at the outset, is to deny the very reason for which the

Information gained from learning activities in the classroom can provide valuable insight about students' adaptive behaviors

assessment was conducted. Second, the examiner should be able to match the reasons for assessment with the *specific* needs of the child so as to answer important questions relevant to both the referral and to the most likely means of intervention. Third, the examiner should use a combination of both norm-referenced and non-norm-referenced measures of performance and adaptive skill functioning when possible. Non-norm-referenced measures such as clinical interviews and observations, sociometric status, and various self-report inventories can provide this valuable function. Finally, the examiner should always include information about adaptive skill functioning in both school and nonschool (home) settings. To use one at the exclusion of the other overlooks an important piece of information relative to everyday living skills.

THE INFLUENCE OF THE AMERICAN ASSOCIATION ON MENTAL RETARDATION

From the early work of the AAMR's first president, Edward Seguin, to the contributions of today's leaders, the **American Association on Mental Retardation** (AAMR) has served as the scientific leader in the field of mental retardation. As noted in Chapter 2, Seguin's work on the physiology of mental retardation is well-known. Less well-known are the contributions of Goddard (1907), who challenged Seguin's early work, saying that while individuals who are mentally retarded were limited cognitively, they could still

REACTION TO 1992 AAMR DEFINITION OF MENTAL RETARDATION

The American Association on Mental Retardation's (1992) most recent published manual on definition, classification, and systems of supports has generated much discussion. The substance of the definition was discussed in Chapter 3.

Certain members of the American Psychological Association's (APA's) Division 33 (Mental Retardation and Developmental Disabilities) have expressed serious concerns about the latest definition. There is such dissatisfaction on the part of some members of this division that a proposal to develop an alternative manual on definition, tentatively entitled a "Manual of Diagnosis and Professional Practice in Mental Retardation," has been submitted to the American Psychological Assoc-iation.

Major criticisms raised by psychologists involve various aspects of the definition, but most of their concerns focus on assessment issues. These concerns include

- Conceptual basis for choosing the ten adaptive skill areas was arbitrary.
- Certain adaptive skill areas (e.g., leisure skills) are not necessarily part of a diagnosis of mental retardation.
- Technically sound measures do not exist for relating some adaptive skill areas to mental retardation.

- Individually administered, norm-referenced instruments do not exist for certain areas.
- The term "substantial limitations in present functioning" was not defined clearly.
- Criterion of "performance at the 6th percentile or below in at least two of ten areas of life activity" was arbitrarily chosen.
- Great variability across the country in diagnosing mental retardation is likely due to the ambiguities noted above.
- Role of psychologist changes to that of a psychometrist only.
- Age range for age of onset should be raised to include twenty-one-year-olds.

It should be noted that counter arguments have been made in reaction to the concerns listed above and that efforts to address some of these concerns are occurring. However, the debate surrounding the new AAMR definition will continue, as other groups attempt to understand the implications of this definition and recognize that it differs from other recognized definitions (i.e., World Health Organization, American Psychiatric Association). It is inevitable that other professional and parent organizations will generate position statements on this topic.

function quite well with adequate preparation and support. The problem, Goddard said, was with the instruction, not with the person; the pace of instruction needed to be slower and conducted with more patience.

Little more than a decade later, the organization's members felt a pressing need to define, diagnose, delineate, and otherwise specify the nature of the "defective delinquent," a term coined by Doll to represent individuals having trouble adapting to society. C. E. Meyers et al. (1979) cite Doll's (1947) work as the formal beginning of adaptive behavior assessment. Believing that individual differences occurred in social competence just as in intelligence, Doll (1953) assumed that these differences represented a unitary trait, were developmental in nature, and were essential for an accurate diagnosis of mental retardation.

In 1965, the AAMR initiated a study of the broad dimensions of adaptive behavior. The study produced two adaptive behavior scales, one designed for children three through twelve years of age, and the other for adolescents and adults. The two scales were then combined into one; a second formal scale was then modified and standardized for use in the schools. Two recently revised scales now comprise the family of AAMR Adaptive Behavior Scales, one for residential and community settings and one for school settings. Following is a brief description of each.

AAMR Adaptive Behavior Scale—Residential and Community, 2nd ed.

The AAMR Adaptive Behavior Scale—Residential and Community, 2nd ed. (ABS-RC:2) (Nihira, Leland, & Lambert, 1993a) represents the AAMR's latest revision of a project begun in 1965 to study the broad dimensions of adaptive behavior. The ABS-RC:2 is a norm-referenced, individually administered, comprehensive measure of adaptive and maladaptive behavior intended for use with persons living in residential and community settings. The authors of the ABS-RC:2 report that the scale has a fourfold purpose: to determine strengths and weaknesses in a person's adaptive skills, to identify persons whose adaptive behavior is substantially and significantly different from those of same-age peers, to gauge the progress of persons receiving intervention services, and to serve as a valid measure of adaptive behavior in research studies (Nihira, Leland, & Lambert, 1993b).

Although the ABS-RC:2 has a companion scale, the AAMR Adaptive Behavior Scales—School (ABS-S:2, see following section), the two scales are completely independent of one another and have their own unique features. The ABS-RC:2 consists of two principal sections: Personal Independence (Part I) and Social Adaptation (Part II). Following is a breakdown of the domains comprising each of the two sections:

Part I	Part II
Independent functioning	Social behavior
Physical development	Conformity
Economic activity	Trustworthiness
Language development	Stereotyped/hyperactive behavior
Numbers and time	Sexual behavior
Domestic activity	Self-abusive behavior
Prevocational/vocational activity	Social engagement
Self-direction	Disturbing interpersonal behavior
Responsibility	
Socialization	

Information is obtained through a standardized interview format conducted by an examiner trained in psychodiagnostic methods. Item types vary; some take a Likert-type format with scores ranging from *behavior not present*

(0) to *behavior present in highest form* (3), as, for example, when the examiner wishes to know how well a person is able to function when visiting a restaurant. For other items, the examiner may wish to know only whether a behavior is present. Examples of this type of behavior are: taking food off other's plates, eating too fast or too slow, or swallowing food without chewing. In each of these cases, the response would be scored as either *yes* (1) or *no* (0). Five types of profile scores are available through the ABS-RC:2: raw scores, percentiles, domain standard scores, factor quotients, and age equivalents. The ABS-RC:2 was standardized on 4,103 persons from forty-six states and is reported in the manual to be representative of all persons with mental retardation nationwide using major demographic variables (Nihira et al., 1993b).

According to the authors, a convenient feature of the ABS-RC:2 is that the scale and the information it provides fit nicely into the three-step model of diagnosis, classification, and support now encouraged for all formal evaluations of persons with mental retardation (see AAMR, 1992). Software is available from the publisher to help with scoring and report writing.

AAMR Adaptive Behavior Scale—School, 2nd ed.

The AAMR Adaptive Behavior Scale—School, 2nd ed. (ABS-S:2) (Lambert, Nihira, & Leland, 1993a) is a norm-referenced, individually administered, comprehensive measure of adaptive and maladaptive behavior intended for use with school-age children. The instrument consists of two parts: Part I is divided into ten behavior domains important for personal responsibility and independent living (independent functioning, physical development, economic activity, language development, numbers and time, domestic activity, prevocational/vocational activity, self-direction, responsibility, and socialization). Part II assesses social adaptation and maladaptive behavior, and consists of seven domains (social behavior, conformity, trustworthiness, stereotyped and hyperactive behavior, self-abusive behavior, social engagement, and disturbing interpersonal behavior).

Like its residential and community counterpart, the school version offers a standardized interview format. The standardization sample appears to be relatively strong, with over 1,000 children with and without disabilities from thirty-one states serving as the normative base. Percentiles, standard scores, and age equivalents are available to the examiner. Five factor scores are also available. Internal consistency estimates for all scores reportedly exceed .80 (Lambert, Nihira, & Leland, 1993b). Software designed to help with scoring and report writing is available from the publisher at an additional cost.

THE INFLUENCE OF EDGAR DOLL

The Vineland Social Maturity Scale was developed in 1935 by Edgar A. Doll at the Vineland Training School in Vineland, New Jersey. It has undergone three revisions, the most recent in 1964 (Doll, 1965). It has since been translated into German, Italian, Japanese, Spanish, and Swedish and has been adapted for use with such diverse English-speaking cultures as those found

Edgar A. Doll constructed the Vineland Social Maturity Scale, one of the first attempts to measure what we now call "adaptive behavior."

in Hawaii and Australia. The most comprehensive presentation of the Vineland scale can be found in the manual Measurement of Social Competence (Doll, 1953).

The author's original purpose in constructing the scale was to provide a means of measuring social competence, or "social maturity," which would help diagnose mental deficiency. Recognizing the need for an adaptive behavior component in the classification of persons as mentally subnormal, Doll sought to devise a measure "distinguishing between mental retardation with social incompetence (feeblemindedness) and mental retardation without social incompetence (which is often confused with feeblemindedness)" (Doll, 1965, p. 2). He defined mental deficiency as the demonstration of intellectual inadequacy, social inadequacy, and arrested mental development.

The Vineland scales have been revised and renamed the Vineland Adaptive Behavior Scales. There are currently three versions of the scale: interview edition, expanded form (Sparrow, Balla, & Cicchetti, 1984a); interview edition, survey form (Sparrow, Balla, & Cicchetti, 1984b); and classroom edition (Sparrow, Balla, & Cicchetti, 1985). Of these three, the survey form is most similar to the original Vineland scales. The purpose of each of these newer versions is indicated in its title. The first two scales are administered to individuals who know the person being assessed, usually parents or caregivers. The classroom scale is typically completed by the teacher. These scales assess five major domains of adaptive behavior: communication, daily living skills, socialization, motor skills, and maladaptive behavior (assessment of the last domain is optional).

Administration and scoring of the scales follow a structure in which items are organized according to domain. Raw scores are converted to standard

See Chapter 3 for a
more complete
discussion of the
evolution of the
construct of adaptive
behavior.

scores, percentiles (both national and supplementary, which include norms of different groups of people with disabilities), stanines, age equivalents, and an estimated adaptive level. A sum of all domain standard scores can be converted to an adaptive behavior composite ($M = 100$, $SD = 15$). By using standard scores for each of the domain areas, the investigator can produce a graphic representation of performance in profile form. The Vineland continues to be a popular measure of social competency, and many now place it among the best measures of adaptive behavior.

OTHER INFLUENTIAL SCALES

Contributions to the development of adaptive behavior assessment are not limited to the AAMR and Edgar Doll. Following is a brief discussion of several other instruments that have helped influence the means by which adaptive behavior is measured and explained.

Scales of Independent Behavior—Revised

The Scales of Independent Behavior—Revised (SIB-R; Bruininks, Woodcock, Weatherman, & Hill, 1996a) were developed by Robert Bruininks and his colleagues at the University of Minnesota's Institute on Community Integration. The SIB-R is a norm-referenced, individually administered measure of adaptive and maladaptive behavior "designed to measure functional independence and adaptive functioning in school, home, employment and community settings" (Bruininks, Woodcock, Weatherman, & Hill, 1996b, p. 1). The instrument yields two composite indices, a Broad Independence (adaptive) score and a General Problem Behaviors score. Within the adaptive behavior portion of the instrument are four broad skill areas (Motor Skills, Social Interaction Skills/Communication Skills, Personal Living Skills, Community Living Skills). Within the problem behavior portion are three areas (Internalized Maladaptive Behavior, Asocial Maladaptive Behavior, Externalized Maladaptive Behavior). Each area, or cluster as it is called in the SIB-R, consists of a number of subscales that allow the examiner to evaluate a person's level of performance in areas of typical daily living (see Figure 4.4)

Although the SIB-R is technically part of the Woodcock-Johnson Psychoeducational Battery—Revised (Woodcock & Johnson, 1989), its use is not dependent upon the rest of the battery and is considered by persons in the field to be a strong and stable instrument in its own right. The advantage of being linked with a broad-based measure of intelligence and achievement such as the Woodcock-Johnson is that it allows for a better understanding of one's adaptive functioning in the context of cognitive and school-related development. The scoring procedures for the SIB-R are straightforward. When administering adaptive behavior items, the examiner simply asks parents or care providers to rate how well and how often a person performs a given task, ranging from *never* or *rarely* (0), to *very well, always or almost always* (3). For the Problem Behavior scales, the parent or

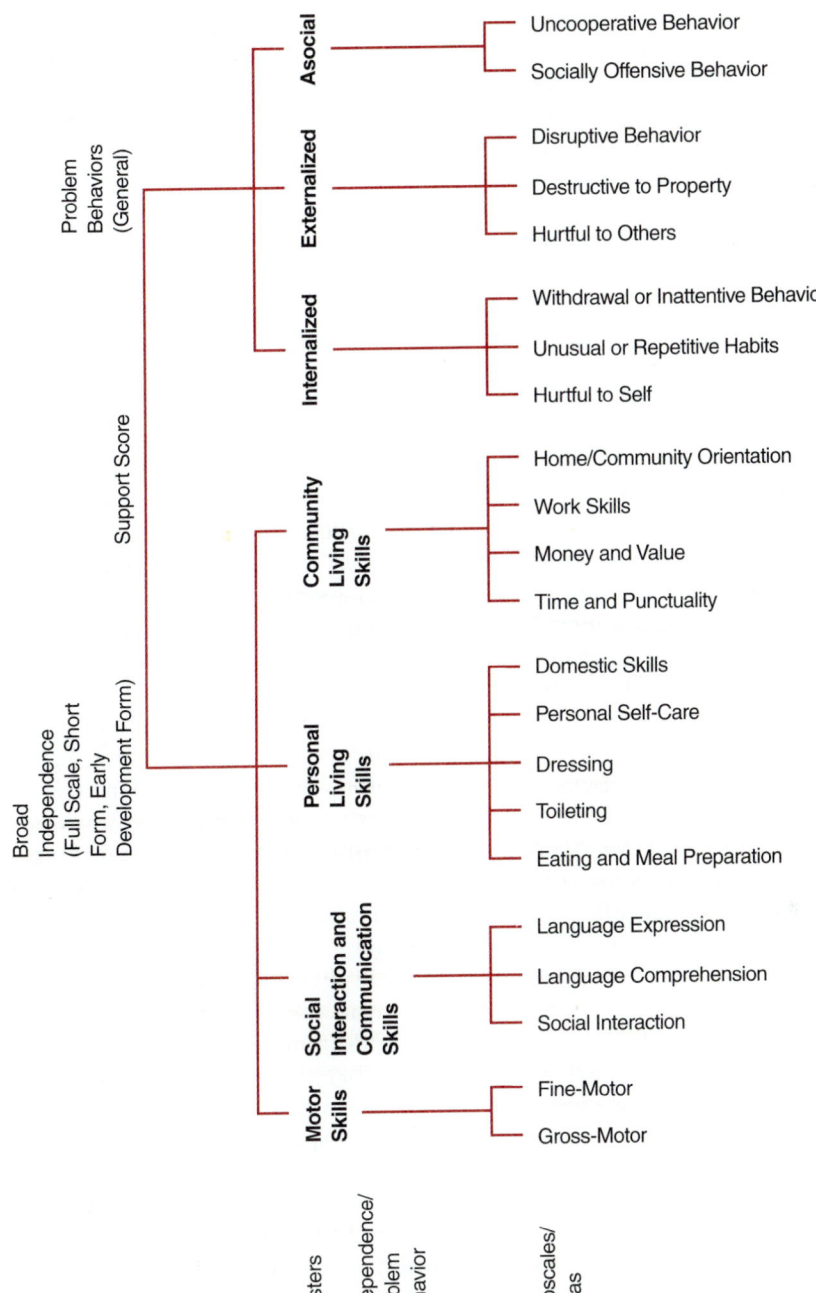

FIGURE 4.4
Structure of the SIB-R

care provider is provided with the description of a series of behaviors and is asked to rate the frequency and severity of occurrence. For example, when asking about disruptive behaviors, the examiner may ask if the person interferes with the activities of others by "clinging, arguing, picking fights, or screaming." Response options for frequency of occurrence range from *less than once a month* (1) to *one or more times an hour* (5); severity response options range from *not serious* (0) to *extremely serious* (4).

What makes the SIB-R different from other norm-referenced measures of adaptive behavior is its systems-level approach to assessment and intervention. While the SIB-R is part of the Woodcock-Johnson battery, it is also part of a broader adaptive behavior assessment program. For example, the SIB-R is linked to the Checklist of Adaptive Living Skills (Morreau & Bruininks, 1992), a criterion-referenced assessment device that focuses directly on a person's instructional needs and training objectives, which are in turn linked to a curriculum-based program containing more than 800 specific and measurable instructional objectives organized into 24 separate life-skill teaching units. According to Cheri Gilman, one of the developers of the Adaptive Living Skills Curriculum (Bruininks, Morreau, Gilman, & Anderson, 1992), even such instructional models as meal planning and preparation, sexuality, home safety, and job search skills are traceable to information obtained with the SIB-R (personal communication, December 16, 1992).

A host of other instruments have been introduced into the adaptive behavior market lately, with varying degrees of success. One such instrument is the Adaptive Behavior Inventory for Children (J. R. Mercer & Lewis, 1982). The ABIC is designed to assess adaptive functioning of children from five to eleven years of age and measures a child's adaptive functioning through a questionnaire completed by the child's mother or other primary caretaker. The ABIC attempts to minimize cultural bias by offering information about a child's adaptive behavior in the appropriate sociocultural context. The Adaptive Behavior Evaluation Scale: Revised (ABES; McCarney, 1995), obtains information in the ten adaptive skill areas put forth in the 1992 diagnosis and classification manual. As with the AAMR scales, there are two versions of the ABES, home and school, appropriate for children in grades K–12. The ABES is one of Hawthorne's growing armada of diagnostic instruments that links special needs with service delivery in a practical, user-friendly manner. Different from the other adaptive scales just mentioned, there is a new instrument that focuses on the needs of adults, specifically. The Independent Living Scales (ILS; Loeb, 1996) consists of five principal scales: memory and orientation, managing money, managing home and transportation, health and safety, and social adjustment. The ILS was designed in such a way as to distinguish among those who can identify and respond to environmental needs, those who can identify problem areas but who need help in addressing them, and, finally, those who are not capable of identifying and meeting even their basic needs. The ILS must be given by a trained examiner and takes approximately forty-five minutes to administer.

CRITICISMS OF ADAPTIVE BEHAVIOR ASSESSMENT

No single assessment instrument, either intelligence or adaptive behavior, can adequately cover the broad range of abilities underlying each construct. All tests, no matter how complete, represent an author's perspective on a given construct.

In theory, adaptive behavior has emerged as an important index in the identification of mental retardation; in practice, its usage has been limited because of its imprecision (Patrick & Reschly, 1982). As indicated previously, the use of adaptive behavior measures has been and will likely continue to be controversial. Some of the debate focuses on conceptual issues, while other concerns center around practical matters. Many of the conceptual problems derive from the multiple dimensions of the concept, suggesting that the "term 'adaptive behavior' actually encompasses more than one concept" (Coulter & Morrow, 1978, p. 216). One criticism pertains to the ambiguity of the construct itself. The more recent, functional definition of mental retardation now defines very explicitly the areas of adaptive functioning that must be considered in service delivery. Prior to the new AAMR definition, however, adaptive behavior was defined by what published tests measured rather than what *should* be measured. The new definition provides direction based on both empirical research and logical reasoning and should continue to reduce some of the ambiguity surrounding the construct of adaptive behavior.

A second major criticism pertains to the school-age population and the degree to which intellectual factors play a part in the determination of adaptive skills. While J. R. Mercer (1978a) sees intelligence as an unnecessary part of adaptive functioning, Reschly (1985) sees intellectual functioning as a crucial component of environmental adaptation. Problem-solving skills carry over from one environment to the next whether in school, home, play, or otherwise. Evidence is mounting that intelligence and adaptive behavior are two separate but related constructs, necessitating that the two be included in all diagnostic evaluations regardless of the level of supports required for everyday living.

A third major criticism of adaptive behavior scales pertains to their use. While some contend that adaptive behavior scales favor certain groups over others, this usually is not the case. That is, some believe that because these scales are often used with intelligence tests, the adaptive behavior scales are also plagued by many of the same limitations associated with intelligence tests in years past. The deeper issue here (as with most tests) is probably appropriateness of use. Any instrument that is not used by trained examiners, that is not used according to guidelines set forth by the test publisher, or that is administered without allowances for cultural and linguistic variations, is very likely being used outside the bounds of good assessment practice. The best instrument in the wrong (poorly trained) hands is no better than a poorly designed instrument in the best of hands.

SUMMARY

THEORIES OF INTELLIGENCE

- Theories of intelligence may be evaluated along a number of dimensions such as the source of one's knowledge, the amount of one's knowledge, or the pattern of one's mental processing ability.

- Most professionals and laypersons believe that intelligence is epigenetic in nature, a combination of both biological and environmental factors.

- Deviation IQs are considered to be the best index of intellectual ability because they allow an examiner to compare a person's score with others of markedly different ages and ability levels.

ASSESSMENT OF INTELLIGENCE

- The first effective test of intellectual ability was the thirty-item Measuring Scale of Intelligence designed by Alfred Binet and Theodore Simon in 1905.

- The Wechsler scales are a series of three individually administered intelligence tests, modeled after one another, in which a person's intellectual abilities are described using a verbal/motor framework.

- A number of quick and easily administered intelligence tests are available to school personnel but may not provide the information needed for a meaningful in-depth diagnostic evaluation.

- Criticisms of intelligence tests take several different forms: some are directed at the tests themselves, others are directed at the examiners who conduct the evaluations, and still others are directed at the assessment process.

THEORIES OF ADAPTIVE BEHAVIOR

- Adaptive behavior refers to a person's ability to meet age-appropriate standards of independence and personal responsibility.

- Adaptive behavior is considered to be a construct separate from but related to the construct of intelligence.

- The AAMR continues to serve as the scientific leader in the field of mental retardation.

ASSESSMENT OF ADAPTIVE BEHAVIOR

- The first formal measure of adaptive behavior was Doll's (1935) Vineland Social Maturity Scale, developed at the Vineland Training School in Vineland, New Jersey.

- Several different measures of adaptive behavior have been developed over the years, ranging from simple behavioral checklists to in-depth diagnostic interviews.

- When measures of adaptive behavior are criticized, objections are usually directed at such things as the psychometric integrity of the instrument, the role of intelligence in adaptive functioning, and the appropriateness of the measure's use.

CHAPTER **5**

Etiology and Preventive Efforts

Edward A. Polloway, Ed.D.
Lynchburg College

J. David Smith, Ed.D.
Longwood College

After reading this chapter,
the student should be able to:

- Discuss the basic principles of genetics.
- Identify and discuss the major causes of mental retardation.
- Discuss the environmental, hereditary, and interactionist positions regarding causation.
- Suggest various ways that mental retardation can be prevented.
- Identify selected ethical issues facing the field.

Key Terms

amniocentesis	homozygous	nondisjunction
anoxia	Human Genome	phenylketonuria
autosomes	Project	(PKU)
chromosomes	hydrocephalus	polygenetic
deletion	innate	inheritance
dominant inheritance	karyotypes	recessive inheritance
genes	meiosis	teratogens
genetics	mosaicism	translocation
heterozygous	myelomeningocele	

The task of sorting out the many causes of mental retardation is a formidable one. From the primitive beginnings of the study of retardation in the earliest centuries of history to the more advanced efforts at the dawning of the 21st century, the search for causation has been complex and challenging. The goal of this chapter is to provide a foundation for an understanding of the many complexities in the causes of retardation.

Causes of retardation and related developmental disabilities have traditionally been divided into two categories: biological (or physiological) and environmental (or psychological and sociological). Consequently, a taxonomic grouping of causes might create an apparently clear dichotomy of specific causes into either biological or environmental cases. In this chapter, however, the inclusion of both biological and psychological causes in a single discussion should reinforce the fact that most often, factors from both these domains are relevant in individual cases of mental retardation.

While hundreds of specific factors have been identified as causative agents of mental retardation, the number of unknown or at least unspecifiable causes of retardation still dwarfs those that are known and specifiable. The fact is that in only about 50 percent of cases of retardation can a cause be specified. A key problem in the study of retardation is that causes are often undetermined for that large category of people diagnosed as having mental retardation.

Known and specifiable biological causes are often classified as either pathological, organic, or clinical. Although such causes may result in cases at all levels of retardation, most attention in the past was drawn to their etiological roles in the more severe cases. Pathological factors can be identified in from 60 to 75 percent of cases where the individual's IQ falls below 50 (McLaren & Bryson, 1987). But the traditional association of a single, organic cause with severe retardation is too simplistic; many individuals with mild retardation may also be affected because of such etiological factors. The other traditional assumption—that mild retardation is the result of multiple, unspecifiable environmental events—has given way to the fact that from 25 to 40 percent of all cases of mild retardation have a specific identifiable cause (see McLaren & Bryson, 1987). Thus, it is important to recognize that many individuals with mild disabilities are also frequently affected by genetic and other biological causes and that psychological and social influences are equally important in cases of severe retardation.

Given this confounding complexity, why should educators, psychologists, and other behavioral scientists spend time studying the causation of

Even before conception, the health of the prospective mother has significant implications for the developing child.

It is important for nonmedical professionals such as teachers to know about the causes of mental retardation.

mental retardation? Kolstoe (1972), in his classic work, noted that familiarity with etiological factors in mental retardation facilitates multidisciplinary communication, is an essential element of professionalism, and is important in giving professionals the ability to make accurate information available to parents. In certain situations, etiological information can contribute to a more accurate diagnosis. Such information can also assist in identifying high-risk and low-risk individuals; in prescribing treatment through biomedical and, in some instances, educational intervention; and in conveying to family members data on the possible hereditary or nonhereditary transmission of specific disorders (Chaney & Eyman, 1982). The role of teachers, for example, may include monitoring the effects of ongoing or progressive disorders that may hinder daily performance, preventing future occurrences through parent counseling, or facilitating immediate change, such as intervention in cases of child abuse.

While a general awareness of causative factors is necessary for any professional in the field of mental retardation, the mechanisms of specific causes require multidisciplinary involvement. Input from various disciplines is essential to determine whether a cause can be specified or is even relevant to treatment and/or education. That many etiologies cannot be currently identified should also serve as a stimulus for future research.

Finally, while considering information on causation, it is important that the reader not lose sight of the fact that behind these data are persons affected by the various causative agents. As Burton Blatt (1987) cautioned, "Treatises that deal with etiological conditions rarely recognize the human being [in] the superficially unattractive trappings of the condition" (p. 128). Readers must not overlook the fact that we are talking about real people who happen to have a given condition.

This discussion of causes begins with attention to terminology and then focuses on genetics, other biological causes, and environmental influences. It concludes with attention to the prevention of mental retardation and related ethical issues.

TERMINOLOGY

For a student, understanding the causes of mental retardation and developmental disabilities and translating specific names for known causes into useful information can be difficult. This section offers ways to understand some of the labels ascribed to representative syndromes associated with retardation.

The terminology used to identify various syndromes comes primarily from three sources: conventional wisdom or practices related to a specific historical era; names of persons who initially identified or described the condition; and biomedical terms describing the cause or the resultant disabilities.

Several examples illustrate historical names for syndromes. Perhaps best known is the term *mongolism,* which was coined by J. Langdon Down in 1866, two decades after Seguin's discovery of the condition (Menolascino & Egger, 1978). For 100 years, this term, which was assigned simply because of Down's inaccurate observation that one frequent characteristic of the syndrome was facial similarity to Asians, prevailed in medical and psychological circles. Jordan (1976) has suggested that the term's popularity can be traced to Rudyard Kipling's 19th-century idea of the "white man's burden." This concept assumed the genetic inferiority, including mental inferiority, of non-Caucasian races. Realization that the syndrome is found in all racial groups (including persons from Mongolia) eventually aided in the withdrawal of the term from the vocabulary of most professionals, although its use persists in the general public and in some popular media.

Another example of a term with a history is *cretinism,* an unfortunate referent for hypothyroidism. Its source has been variously attributed to a

TABLE 5.1
Biomedical Terminology

Stems and Affixes	Meaning	Example(s)
ab-, abs-	from, away	abnormal, abscess
amnio-	pertaining to embryonic sac	amniocentesis
anomalo-	irregular	chromosomal anomaly
auto-	self, same	autism, autosomes
-cele, -coele	sac, cavity	meningocele
-cephalo-	head, brain	hydrocephalus
-encephalo-	head, brain	encephalitis
endo-	inner, inside	endogenous
ex-, extra-	outside, away from	exogenous
fibro-	connective tissues	neurofibromatosis
galacto-	milk	galactosemia
glyco-, gluco-	sweet, sugar	glycogen, hyperglycemia
hydro-	water	hydrocephalus
hyper-	over, more than usual	hyperkinetic
hypo-	under, less than usual, lowered	hypothyroidism
-lepsy	seizure	epilepsy, narcolepsy
lipo-	fat	lipids
macro-, mega-	large	macrocephaly, acromegaly
meningo-	central nervous system membranes	meningitis
micro-	small	microcephaly
myelo-	marrow, spinal cord	myelomeningocele
neuro-	nerve	neurofibromatosis
-osis	condition of	toxoplasmosis
-plasia	cellular growth	skeletal dysplasia
-plasma	blood	toxoplasmosis
-plegia	paralysis	monoplegia, paraplegia
-semia	sign, symptom	galactosemia
-somy, -some, soma-	body	chromosome, trisomy
toxo-	poisonous	toxemia
-trophy	nutrition, nourishment	atrophy, dystrophy

Source: From *Introduction to Military Medicine and Surgery,* Study Guide 6, 1975, Fort Sam Houston, TX, Academy of Health Sciences, U.S. Army.

Teutonic word for chalky, to the French word *chrétien* (from the church's care for those affected), and to the island of Crete (Jordan, 1976). In spite of its colorful past, *cretinism* has fortunately joined mongolism on the shelf of retired, stigmatizing labels.

A second, more direct way to identify a clinical syndrome is to attach to it the name of the researcher who contributed in a major way to its understanding. For instance, professionals now identify as Down syndrome the chromosomal condition formerly called mongolism. Other relatively well-known syndromes so named include Tay-Sachs disease, after the British and American physicians who described the characteristics in the late 1880s, and Lesch-Nyhan syndrome, named for the researchers who identified this disorder in 1964.

The third source of syndrome labels is biomedical terminology. Although some of these terms are frequently used by laypersons, their meanings often seem obscure. Many of the labels, however, do convey some of the primary features of the disorder, causal or characteristic. Table 5.1 lists some of the more common terms used to identify clinical disorders. For each entry, the specific derivatives are noted, along with their usual meaning and examples of their use.

Although labels are only an attempt to refer to complex medical, biological, or behavioral phenomena, simply being familiar with the derivatives can be of assistance in understanding the nature of these disorders and terms related to them. Several specific terms illustrate the system. For example, toxoplasmosis indicates a condition (-osis) of poisonous (toxo-) blood (-plasm). Although the clinical definition of toxoplasmosis is much more specific, the word, when analyzed, gives a fair suggestion of what the condition is about. Another example is **hydrocephalus.** The term refers to a disorder resulting from a blockage of cerebrospinal fluid, but breaking the word down into water (hydro-) and head or brain (cephalo-) provides a descriptive picture of the condition. A third example is the disorder called **myelomeningocele.** As the term suggests, this condition is characterized by a saclike mass (-cele) on the spinal cord (myelo-) containing membrane tissue of the central nervous system (-meningo-).

GENETIC DISORDERS

Genetics can be defined as the study of heredity and its variations. As such, its scope is enormous and its complexities great. Advances in genetics over the past fifty years rival those in any area of science. The contributions of geneticists to understanding the causes of developmental disabilities are particularly noteworthy. Currently, this knowledge base is mushrooming due to research on gene mapping and DNA sequencing under the auspices of the **Human Genome Project.**

An understanding of heredity begins with the study of **genes.** Genes are the basic biological units carrying inherited physical, mental, or personality traits. Between 50,000 and 100,000 genes are present in each human cell. Genes occupy specific positions on **chromosomes,** the threadlike or rodlike bodies that contain genetic information and material.

Chromosomes vary widely in size and shape, but for human cells, the normal pattern is consistent. Each cell contains twenty-three pairs of chromosomes. The embryo initially receives one member of each pair from each parent. There are two types of chromosomes—**autosomes** and *sex chromosomes*. Autosomes are matching pairs and constitute 44 of the 46 chromosomes within the usual human complement (i.e., 22 of the 23 pairs). Sex chromosomes make up the other pair. The letter X is used to represent the female sex chromosome, and Y to represent the male sex chromosome. While the X chromosome contains a substantial amount of genetic information, the Y functions primarily as a determinant of male sex. At conception, an X chromosome is contributed by the mother, while either an X or a Y is contributed by the father. The XX combination creates a female, and the XY a male.

The precise and rather fragile roles of genes and chromosomes as building blocks of development are dramatically represented in mental retardation research. The most prevalent general groups of biological causes of retardation are *genetic transmission of traits* (i.e., genetic disorders) and *chromosomal abnormalities*. But even in these seemingly clear-cut cases of genetic disorders, it is important to keep in mind that development is still shaped significantly by environmental influences.

GENETIC TRANSMISSION

Many traits are transmitted from one generation to the next according to the makeup of a specific gene pair. We thus can trace many specific characteristics to the presence or absence of a single gene. Transmission can occur through autosomal dominant or recessive inheritance and through sex-linked inheritance. **Dominant inheritance** means that an individual gene can assume "control" over, or mask, its partner and will operate whether the two elements of an individual gene pair are similar or dissimilar to each other. **Recessive inheritance** refers to genes that cannot control their partners. In a sense they "recede" when paired with a dissimilar mate and become influential only when matched with another recessive gene. Pairs of genes carrying the same trait are called **homozygous;** pairs carrying different traits are **heterozygous.**

The dynamics of dominant and recessive inheritance are illustrated in Figure 5.1. Capital letters indicate dominant traits, while lowercase letters denote recessive traits. In the typical case of dominant inheritance (Example A), only one parent would have the specific dominant trait in question, which is transmitted, theoretically, to two of their four children. In the common case of recessive inheritance (Example B), probability suggests that at each conception, chances are one in four that the child will be homozygous and will manifest the recessive trait (hh), two in four that he or she will be a heterozygous carrier for the succeeding generation (Hh, hH), and one in four that he or she will be homozygous, therefore lacking the recessive gene altogether (HH).

Dominant Transmission

Dominant inheritance determines a variety of common traits, including brown eyes and prematurely white hair. Several rare physical disorders are carried as dominant traits. Frequently these disorders are *structural,* that is, they occur with visible signs. Examples include Marfan's syndrome, which manifests itself through tall stature, loose joints of the limbs, and heart disorders, and achrondoplasia (dwarfism). Neurofibromatosis and tuberous

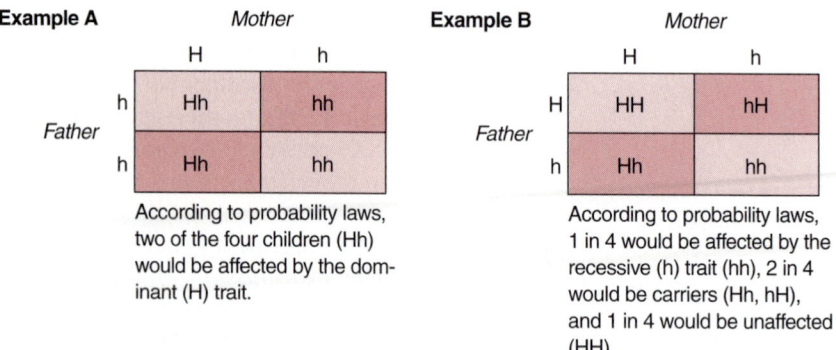

FIGURE 5.1
Dominant and Recessive Inheritance

sclerosis (which are discussed next) are examples of dominant gene disorders that may involve mental retardation. The incidence of this type of disease may be affected by reduced penetrance, variable expressivity, and late age at onset of the dominant trait. Some cases may also be the result of genetic mutation.

Neurofibromatosis is also known as von Recklinghausen's disease, named for the man who first described the disorder in 1882. The gene for neurofibromatosis has been identified as occupying a site on chromosome 17. It affects 1 in 3,000 newborns (Polloway & Rucker, 1997), with about 50 percent of the cases being inherited and the remainder caused by mutations occurring spontaneously. It is identifiable by light brown patches (called *café-au-lait*) on the skin, and multiple, soft, fibrous swellings or tumors (neurofibromas) that grow on nerves or appear elsewhere on the body (Clayman, 1989) and can result in severe physical deformities. It has been hypothesized that neurofibromatosis was the affliction from which both John Merrick (the "Elephant Man") and Quasimodo (the Hunchback of Notre Dame) suffered (Blatt, 1987). Surgical procedures for tumors may be recommended (i.e., when the growths cause complications or have a major effect on comfort or appearance), although the tumors may recur.

Neurofibromatosis varies greatly in how it is expressed (i.e., variable expressivity) from case to case. The café-au-lait patches are primarily a cosmetic concern, but the locations of the tumors have an effect on mental development, which may be severe if they appear on the brain. Otherwise, the individual may be in the normal range of intelligence, as the story of John Merrick illustrates, since his wisdom eventually became far more significant for many people than his physical characteristics. An estimated 40 percent may have learning disabilities (Nativio & Belz, 1990). A continuing concern is for the psychological development of individuals who see themselves as deformed and question whether they should have children.

Tuberous sclerosis is another skin disease carried by a dominant gene. The two words derive from the Latin and Greek for "root-like" and "hardening," respectively. Its tumors are similar to potatoes in density and destroy the cells in the organs where they are found (Menolascino & Egger, 1978). As with neurofibromatosis, the changes resulting from tuberous sclerosis are primarily structural rather than biochemical, a common finding in autosomal disorders. The degree of expressivity of the gene can result in great variation in characteristics of the people who have the disease. In the mild form, no retardation or serious health problems occur; in the severe variety, tumors can result in dysfunction of a number of organs (e.g., brain, lungs, kidneys), followed by mental deterioration, epilepsy, and early death.

Recessive Transmission

Recessive inheritance is commonly associated with, for example, blue eyes and a variety of other common traits. But other recessive traits involve disorders capable of producing severe disabilities. Examples include sickle cell anemia and cystic fibrosis, while examples in the field of mental retardation include phenylketonuria, Tay-Sachs disease, and galactosemia. Since transmission of recessive traits is a function of the union of two carriers (see Figure 5.1), controlling these disorders entails using genetic screening measures to identify unknowing carriers. The greatest number of specified causes of retardation is due to recessive genetic disorders that are associated with metabolic factors. This category includes those disorders that can be traced to dysfunction in the body's mechanisms for the processing of food—so-called inborn errors of metabolism. In particular, imbalances related to fats, carbohydrates, and amino acids have been well established as causative agents of retardation.

Metabolic disorders resulting from an increase in lipids, or fats, in the body's tissues are frequently progressive, degenerative diseases. The developmental profile is typically that of a normal progression until onset of the disorder, from which point the condition rapidly worsens. *Tay-Sachs* disease is inherited as an autosomal recessive trait. It is disproportionately prevalent among persons of Ashkenazic Jewish backgrounds, although recent findings have shown that it occurs more frequently among the general population than originally thought. Infants with Tay-Sachs disease appear normal at birth. The disease is typically manifested late in the child's first year, followed by a course of severe retardation, convulsions, blindness, paralysis, and death by the age of four. There is no cure for Tay-Sachs disease.

An example of a carbohydrate disorder is *galactosemia,* a recessive condition characterized by the inability to metabolize galactose, a form of sugar found in milk, into glucose (Widerstrom, Mowder, & Sandall, 1991). The physiological changes occurring in galactosemia are biochemical rather than structural, a feature common in recessive disorders. Manifestations of the syndrome may include retardation, liver and kidney dysfunction, and cataracts. Following identification of the disorder, the removal of dairy products from the child's diet has proved successful in interrupting the process of deterioration. Koch and colleagues (1988) reported on longitudinal research indicating that early treatment generally leads to satisfactory

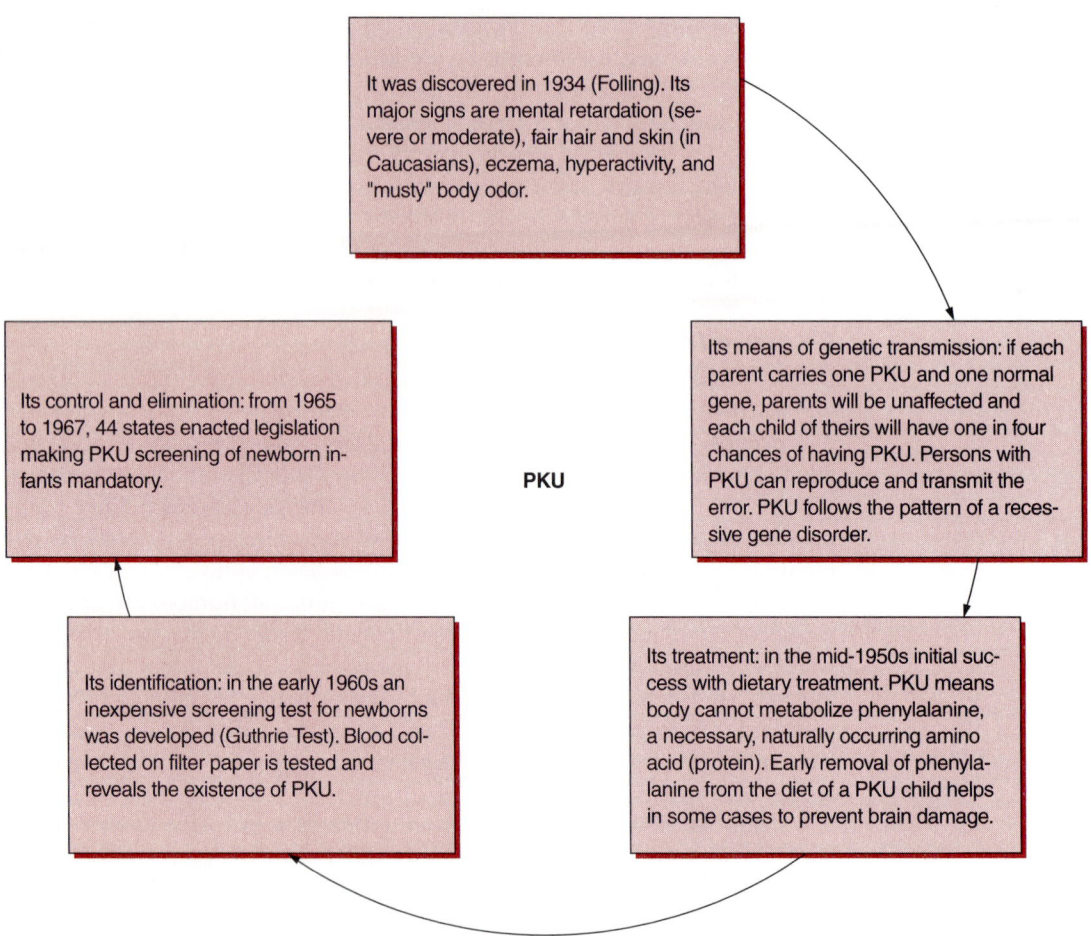

It was discovered in 1934 (Folling). Its major signs are mental retardation (severe or moderate), fair hair and skin (in Caucasians), eczema, hyperactivity, and "musty" body odor.

Its control and elimination: from 1965 to 1967, 44 states enacted legislation making PKU screening of newborn infants mandatory.

PKU

Its means of genetic transmission: if each parent carries one PKU and one normal gene, parents will be unaffected and each child of theirs will have one in four chances of having PKU. Persons with PKU can reproduce and transmit the error. PKU follows the pattern of a recessive gene disorder.

Its identification: in the early 1960s an inexpensive screening test for newborns was developed (Guthrie Test). Blood collected on filter paper is tested and reveals the existence of PKU.

Its treatment: in the mid-1950s initial success with dietary treatment. PKU means body cannot metabolize phenylalanine, a necessary, naturally occurring amino acid (protein). Early removal of phenylalanine from the diet of a PKU child helps in some cases to prevent brain damage.

FIGURE 5.2
Phenylketonuria (PKU)

Source: From *Mental Retardation: The Known and the Unknown* (p. 25) by President's Committee on Mental Retardation, 1976, Washington, DC: U.S. Government Printing Office.

intellectual development. The IQs of children treated early (prior to four months of age) are virtually normal.

Diet control can also mediate the effects of genetic transmission of the amino acid disorder **phenylketonuria (PKU),** the most common of the genetic disorders. PKU is caused by an autosomal recessive gene and, if left untreated, produces retardation. It is frequently associated with aggressiveness, hyperactivity, destructiveness, and other disruptive behaviors. Since it was first described by Folling in 1934, PKU has been virtually eliminated as a causative factor in severe retardation, despite its incidence of 1 in every 12,000 to 15,000 births. Menolascino and Egger (1978) noted that PKU played a significant role in the field because it was the first inborn metabolic anomaly proven to cause retardation. Its discovery led to both increased research into etiology and a pronounced change in the aura of hopelessness that once surrounded retardation. Figure 5.2 illustrates the historical discovery process for PKU.

The early results of diet treatment for PKU were most encouraging. Johnson and his colleagues (Johnson, Koch, Peterson, & Friedman, 1978) reported that a group of 148 treated PKU children did not significantly differ from the general population in the prevalence of congenital anomalies or major neurological defects. Intellectual development near or within the normal range was considered achievable. Children treated very early—before they were a month old—had significantly higher IQs than those whose treatment began in the second month (Koch et al., 1988); continued adherence to the diet had positive results as well.

Two major problems remained, however. The diet prescribed for children with PKU can be unappealing and hard to follow, and it may be difficult to balance protein control against the protein needs of developing children. For years, the special diet was generally discontinued by approximately school age, but this practice has caused concern. For example, Matthews, Barabas, Cusack, and Ferrari (1986) reported decreases in social quotients for individuals for whom the diet was discontinued at age five and a half years. In children who maintained their diets to the age of ten, Fishler, Azen, Henderson, Friedman, and Koch (1987) found higher school achievement, intellectual level, language, and perceptual skills. Clarke, Gates, Hogan, Barrett, and MacDonald (1987) concluded:

> The bulk of evidence appears . . . to indicate that older children with PKU allowed access to unrestricted diets do experience some deterioration in intelligence, that this is associated with specific neuropsychological deficits that are not attributable simply to their intellectual handicap, and that this deficit is at least partly reversible by a return to carefully regulated dietary . . . restriction. On the other hand, although the effects of a return to the diet are statistically significant, they are apparently not clinically significant in the short term. Therefore, although the data would support efforts to maintain older children with PKU on . . . restricted diets for as long as possible, the meager short-term clinical benefits, along with the well-known difficulty of re-introducing the therapeutic diet in older children . . . suggest that long-term return to dietary treatment is unlikely to succeed except in unusually highly motivated patients. (p. 260)

A second problem concerns women who were treated in childhood for PKU. As adults, these women's metabolic imbalances can harm their unborn children. Consequences can include retardation, heart disease, and microcephaly (Schultz, 1983). Berg and Emanuel (1987) have stated that such women should reinstate their restricted diet during pregnancy, although it is not clear how successful reinstatement will be in alleviating risk. Evidence of this concern, however, can be noted in common product warnings, for example on diet sodas or some low-fat foods, that these items contain phenylalanine. Unless pregnancy is avoided, Koch et al. (1988) indicated that the effect of maternal PKU could offset the preventive benefits of screening programs and dietary treatment interventions.

Sex-Linked Inheritance

A third type of genetic transmission is through sex-linked (or X-linked) inheritance. This name derives from a variety of recessive traits carried on the X chromosome. The female has two X chromosomes, and a specific gene carrying a disorder can be dominated by its mate. But the male (XY) will inevitably be affected by a single recessive gene carried on the X chromosome, because there is no additional X whose genes could dominate the pathology-producing recessive trait. Instead, he has a Y chromosome, which does not carry genes that will counterbalance the X-linked gene. A female can be affected only if her father is affected and her mother is a carrier. Thus, the problem of sex-linked inheritance is particularly significant for males. X-linked recessive traits include color blindness, hemophilia, Duchenne type muscular dystrophy, Lesch-Nyhan syndrome (discussed next), and a variety of other conditions that may be as much as ten times more common in males than in females. The unique nature of sex-linked recessive inheritance is perhaps best illustrated by the presence of the disorder of hemophilia within the royal families of Europe.

Lesch-Nyhan syndrome, a disorder first identified in 1964 (Lesch & Nyhan, 1964), is inherited as an X-linked recessive and thus is much more common among males. According to Nyhan (1976), this syndrome is the second most common metabolic disorder (after PKU). The most striking manifestation of Lesch-Nyhan syndrome is an apparently uncontrollable urge to cause injury to oneself and, to a lesser extent, to others.

Typically, children with Lesch-Nyhan syndrome will begin displaying extreme self-injurious behavior (SIB), when acquiring teeth. They may bite ferociously and, in their frenzy, rip and tear tissue (Libby, Polloway, & Smith, 1983; Nyhan, Johnson, Kaufman, & Jones, 1980). Aside from SIB, they may hit, pinch, and bite others, use obscene language, spit, and engage in a variety of disruptive actions because of their inability to control their impulses (Hoefnagel, Andrew, Mireault, & Berndt, 1965). When unrestrained, they may scream as if terrified of the pain they might inflict on themselves, while when restrained they seem more tractable.

Both biomedical and educational interventions have been attempted with children who have Lesch-Nyhan syndrome. Drug treatment to alter the metabolism has proven efficacious on a short-term basis. Continued work on biochemical processes in the brain also offer great promise. Educational interventions with children with Lesch-Nyhan historically have included a variety of attempts at behavioral change, with differing levels of success (see Anderson, Dancis, & Alpert, 1978; Bull & LaVecchio, 1978; Duker, 1975).

Polygenic Inheritance

The preceding discussion has focused on single-gene anomalies, reflecting the mechanism of one gene controlling one trait. Many traits, however, do not fit simple rules but are transmitted through **polygenetic inheritance.** Polygenic or multigenic inheritance has particular importance in the consideration of psychosocial retardation. Unlike the one-gene/one-trait pattern of numerous disorders associated with retardation (e.g., PKU), in polygenic inheritance, the interaction of multiple genes and networks influences the individual level of intellectual functioning. Since the complexity of this phenomenon makes precise evaluation difficult in single cases, researchers depend on statistical data from population samples in seeking to understand polygenetic inheritance. That is, "genetic predictions . . . have to be based on empirical data from population statistics. Simple genetic models just do not apply" (Scarr & Carter-Saltzman, 1982, p. 804). The concept of heritability and the data base on inheritance (i.e., twin studies) are discussed later in this chapter in the section entitled, "Heredity Position."

CHROMOSOMAL DEVIATIONS

A second major source of biological causes of disabilities are chromosomal anomalies. Although these disorders are rare in the general population, their numbers are significant among those cases of developmental disabilities where cause can be specified.

The intensive research on chromosomes that began in the late 1950s and early 1960s has provided an increasingly detailed portrait of both typical and atypical chromosomal patterns. These patterns are clarified through the use of **karyotypes.** The process of karyotyping includes taking a picture of the chromosomes in a human cell, enlarging it, cutting out the pictures of individual chromosomes, and then arranging them from the largest (pair 1) to the smallest (pair 22), followed by the sex chromosomes.

Approximately 10 percent of pregnancies begin with some chromosomal imbalance, but most of these abort spontaneously during the first three months of pregnancy. A small number of these pregnancies do go to term, and the children born illustrate the potential effects of irregularities in the arrangement or alignment of autosomes or sex chromosomes. Chromosomal errors can be identified in approximately 1 in 200 live births.

While genetic disorders are classified as hereditary, chromosomal problems are more accurately termed **innate,** since an abnormal chromosome arrangement is present from the moment of conception but most often is not the product of hereditary exchange. Disorders of this type usually result from abnormalities occurring during the stage of cell division called **meiosis.** During meiosis, individual reproductive cells divide

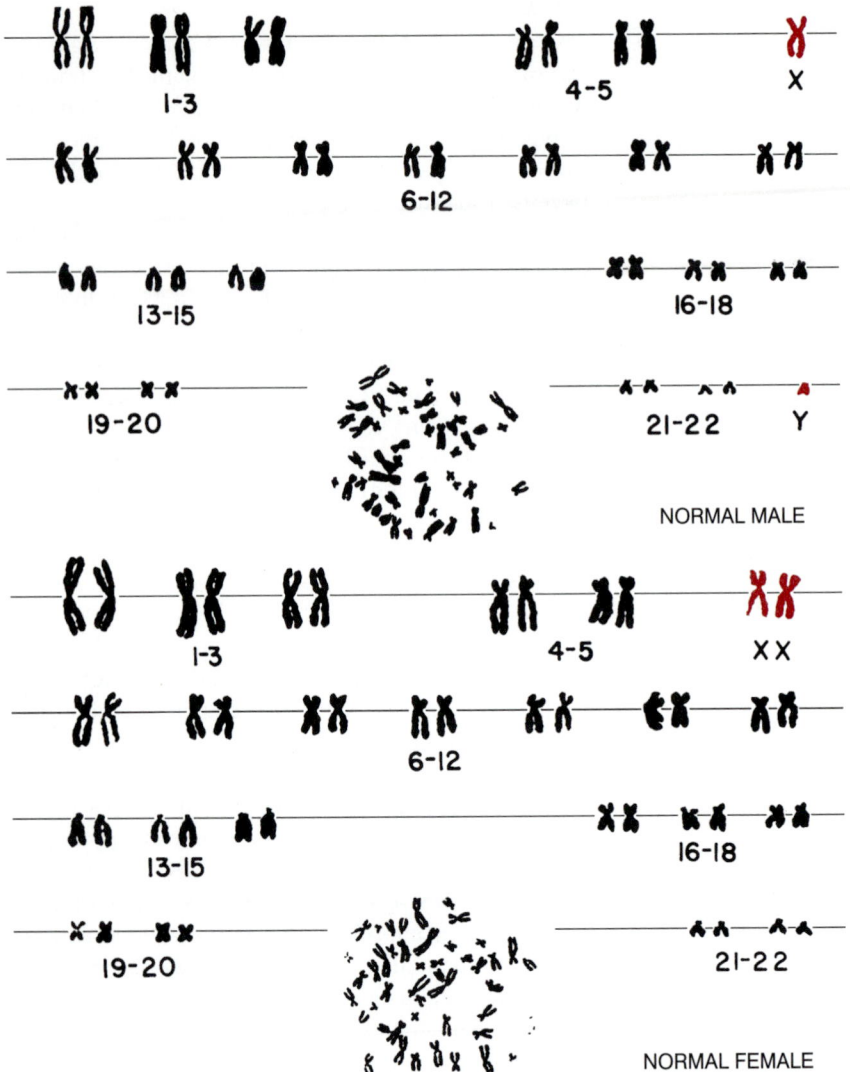

FIGURE 5.3
Normal Chromosomal Karyotypes

Source: From *Handbook of Mental Retardation Syndromes* (pp. 33–34) by C. H. Carter, 1975, Springfield, IL: Charles C. Thomas. Reprinted by permission of Charles C. Thomas, Publisher.

and then pair up to form the genetic foundation of the embryo. The normal process includes 23 chromosomes from each parent, which are paired to form the new organism's complement of 46 chromosomes. Figure 5.3 illustrates the karyotypes for a male and a female with normal chromosomal patterns.

Several specific abnormalities that can occur during the process of chromosomal arrangement and alignment result in either too much or too little chromosomal material being present. In **nondisjunction,** a given parental pair of chromosomes fails to split at conception, causing the formation of a group of three chromosomes (a *trisomy*) in lieu of the normal pair. A trisomy on chromosome 21 is the most common cause of Down syndrome. In **translocation,** a fragment of chromosomal material is located across from or exchanged with another chromosomal pair. For example, a translocation that results in Down syndrome occurs when a fragment broken off from chromosome pair 21 attaches to a chromosome from group 15. In **deletion,** a portion of the original genetic material is absent from a specific chromosome pair. Finally, **mosaicism** is an uneven pattern of dissimilar cells of 46 or 47 chromosomes.

Before the 1950s, causes of the disorders now classified under chromosomal anomalies were unknown. Research published by Lejeune and his colleagues (Lejeune, Gautier, & Turpin, 1959) and other cytogeneticists then led to a much clearer understanding of the nature of chromosomal abnormalities. As mentioned earlier, aberrations in the number or arrangement of chromosomes are likely to damage the developing organism. Down syndrome and cri-du-chat syndrome are examples of autosomal disorders; Klinefelter and Turner syndromes come from sex chromosome abnormalities. Chromosomal errors may account for approximately one third of severe retardation. Persons with chromosomal disorders often may function in the mild retardation range or may be nonretarded.

DOWN SYNDROME

For many laypeople, Down syndrome represents the physical stereotype of mental retardation.

Down syndrome is by far the best known, most prevalent, and most frequently researched type of biologically caused retardation. For many laypersons, the concept of a person with mental retardation is virtually synonymous with a Down syndrome child. A reasonable estimate of the prevalence of the syndrome is 5 to 6 percent of all persons identified as retarded.

Study of the disorder has revealed three separate chromosomal causes. The first and most common, trisomy 21, is due to the failure of one pair of parental chromosomes to separate at conception, resulting in the child's having 47 chromosomes (see Figure 5.3). This abnormality has historically been found more often in children born to older mothers, and researchers have suggested a variety of possible reasons.

Specific deleterious factors that have been suspected of causing trisomy 21 include medication and drugs, exposure to radiation, chemicals, or hepatitis viruses, and the possible absence of a mechanism in the mother to abort the fetus spontaneously. It is important to realize that, although risk is related to age and increases to approximately one in thirty at forty-five years old, age per se is not the cause. There has also been an assumption of linkage of paternal age with Down syndrome in an estimated 20 to 25 percent of cases of trisomy 21 (Abroms & Bennett, 1980). With the increased public awareness of the correlation between age and risk of occurrence, many older parents undergo prenatal screening for Down syndrome and may then consider abortion. This fact plus the fact that births to parents over forty are relatively rare, results in the large majority of births of children with Down syndrome to younger parents.

A second form of Down syndrome is caused by a translocation transmitted hereditarily by carriers. Although this translocation is usually to chromosome pairs 13 or 15, the extra material comes from pair 21 and forms, in a sense, a partial trisomy. Mosaicism, the uneven division that creates cells varying in chromosome numbers (47 and 46), is the third and rarest form.

Down syndrome is frequently associated with specific physical traits. A list of characteristics that *may be* associated with it are listed below:

- Short stature
- Flat, broad face with small ears and nose
- Short, broad hands with incurving fingers
- Upward slanting of the eyes with folds of skins (epicanthic folds) at the inside corner of the eye
- Small mouth and short roof, which may cause the tongue to protrude and may contribute to articulation problems
- Single crease across the palm
- Reduced muscle tone (hypotonia) and hyperflexibility of joints
- Heart defects (in about one third of instances)
- Increased susceptibility to upper respiratory infections
- Incomplete or delayed sexual development

These traits vary greatly from one individual to another. Contrary to popular opinion, the number of physical characteristics present does not predict the level of intelligence (Belmont, 1971).

A relatively recent change in the syndrome picture concerns life expectancy. Patterson (1987) indicated that while in 1929, expectancy for individuals with Down syndrome was only nine years; by 1980, that average had increased to over thirty years, with 25 percent of individuals living past fifty years. As age increases, association of the syndrome with Alzheimer's disease has also increased. Individuals with Down syndrome apparently run a much greater risk of developing Alzheimer's disease (Patterson, 1987; Stark, Menolascino, & Goldsbury, 1988; Zigman, Schupf, Lubin, & Silverman, 1987). The association is not unexpected, given the identified locus for Alzheimer's on chromosome pair 21. Epstein (1988) has pointed out that the loss of intellectual functioning associated with advanced age will be seen more often now that life expectancies have increased.

Life expectancy issues have also been explored by Eyman, Call, and White (1991). These researchers noted that life expectancy has increased from the commonly accepted age of under twenty years to contemporary views of above fifty. Interestingly, they found that mobility and feeding ability were more predictive of longer life span than, for example, the presence of congenital heart disease.

Many of the behavioral characteristics traditionally associated with Down syndrome have generally not been documented in research. In particular, the stereotype of the child with Down syndrome who is cheerful, affectionate, rhythmic, and unusually dexterous has not been empirically established.

Most significant have been the data collected on the intellectual functioning of children with Down syndrome. Traditionally, the syndrome had been assumed to result most often in moderate retardation, with rare cases reaching a ceiling IQ of 70. Occasional anecdotal reports of ability and special talents (Hunt, 1967) were considered more interesting or unusual than typical.

The first comprehensive study that altered people's views was reported by Rynders, Spiker, and Horrobin (1978). Their review of fifteen studies provided data on the intelligence test scores of children with Down syndrome that indicated a significant range in level of functioning and refuted the alleged ceiling IQ of 70.

Optimistic data on the abilities of children with Down syndrome continue to accumulate. Early intervention seems to be the key to the future. Rynders and Horrobin (1990) provided further support for this premise in their updated review on expectations for academic achievement. Research consistently supports higher expectations for academic achievement in students with Down syndrome. However, they caution that IQs frequently diminish over time, and therefore achievement levels should be stressed in assessing level of functioning and designing educational programs.

Individual case histories add further fuel to the excitement building around Down syndrome. For example, an illustration of the range of effects of the mosaic form of Down syndrome was offered by Turkington (1987), who described the life of Paige Barton, a thirty-five-year-old woman with Down syndrome who had completed an associate arts degree in early childhood education and hoped to become certified as a teacher.

In addition to the encouraging data on intellectual development, recent efforts in plastic surgery should be mentioned. Such efforts, most notably in Israel in the work of Reuven Feuerstein and his colleagues, have demonstrated that the physical stigmata of Down syndrome can be reduced. May (1988) provides a good discussion of the rationales, benefits, and cautions of plastic surgery for people with Down syndrome. According to research reported by May and Turnbull (1992), the majority (88 percent) of plastic surgeons were familiar with the procedures, and 24 percent had performed it. Reasons given for the surgery included (in rank order): to normalize appearance, to improve speech and eating abilities, to improve breathing, and as a response to parental request.

Two overriding points must be made clear. First, individuals with Down syndrome are first and foremost people who have needs, desires, and rights similar to those of other people. Second, the effects of intensive interventions with young children who have Down syndrome have only been evaluated since the late 1970s, and thus, historical descriptions of the syndrome are no longer accurate. For example, as reported in the popular press, Charles de Gaulle had a child with Down syndrome. At the time of her early death in 1948, he reflected the sentiments of parents at an earlier historical era when he comforted his wife by saying "Come, . . . now she is like everybody else."

FRAGILE X SYNDROME

New information regarding the fragile X is emerging on a regular basis.

A chromosomal anomaly that was first noted in 1943 but began to receive significant attention after its formal discovery in 1979 is *fragile X syndrome*. After Down syndrome, this syndrome is likely to be the most common clinical type of retardation. Further, it is now seen as the most common hereditary cause of retardation (Lachiewicz, Harrison, Spiridigliozzi, Callanan, & Livermore, 1988).

The disorder is caused by a deficiency in the formation of the X chromosome. Figure 5.4 shows a karyotype of fragile X syndrome. The fragile site appears as a pinched or restricted location on the lower arm of the X chromosome (Barker, 1990). Recently, the region containing the gene for fragile X has been isolated. The gene occurs in about 1 in 1,500 males and about 1 in 1,000 females in the general population (Clayman, 1989). Diagnosis can be made prenatally, although most often is made clinically during the early childhood period and is performed after observation of developmental delays and/or the appearance of large ears (Buyse, 1990).

The majority of males with fragile X are likely to have mild-to-moderate retardation.

According to Rogers and Simensen (1987) and Barker (1990), common physical characteristics of fragile X include prominent jaws, macro-orchidism (large testes), long and thin faces, long and soft ears and hands, prominent foreheads, and enlarged heads. The syndrome has been associated in males with severe retardation, although reports of its occurrence in individuals with various levels of retardation (and also with normal intelligence) suggest the need for caution and for careful consideration of environmental experience (Rogers & Simensen, 1987). Behavioral manifestations may include attentional difficulties, repetitive behaviors, and gaze avoidance, while speech and language patterns may include echolalia, perseverative use of given utterances, and palilalia (i.e., repeating statements at increasing rates of speed and loudness) (Bellinger, Rucker, & Polloway, 1997). Although males with fragile X are typically thought to be infertile, several instances exist where this has not been the case.

Women who have the fragile X chromosome are frequently clinically viewed as carriers and may not be identified because of low expressivity (Barker, 1990); however, an estimated one third may also be partially affected and may have mild disabilities (Rogers & Simensen, 1987). A pattern of varied strengths and weaknesses is particularly apparent in girls who have fragile X. Although not frequently mentally retarded, such girls may be learning disabled (Neely, 1991).

FIGURE 5.4
Karyotype of Fragile-X Syndrome

Source: Courtesy of M. C. Phelan, Director, Cytogenetics Laboratory, Greenwood Genetics Center, Greenwood, S.C.

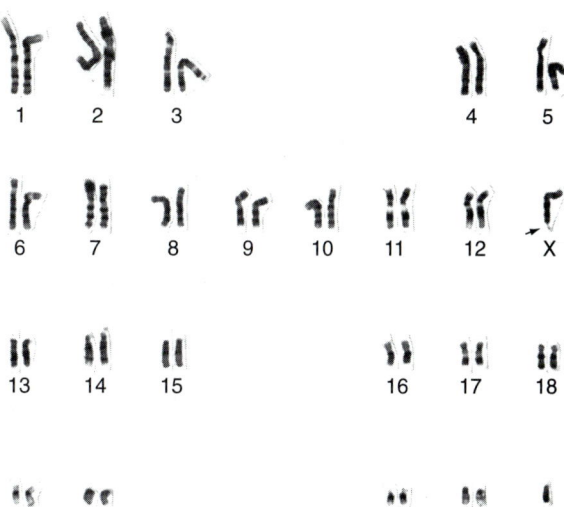

A consistent relationship between fragile X and autism has been reported in the literature, with males with fragile X having a 5 to 46 percent prevalence of autism or autistic-like behaviors. On the other hand, children with autism have fragile X in around 15 percent of cases.

Although similarities in behavior exist between fragile X syndrome and autism, there is no conclusive evidence that a relationship between the two conditions exists. While males with fragile X often exhibit autistic-type behaviors, they are usually less significant than the behaviors seen in persons who are clinically diagnosed as autistic. However, the similarity in behavior patterns does lead to difficulty in making a diagnosis of typical autistic-like behaviors versus clinical autism (Bellinger et al., 1997; Cantu, Stone, Wing, Langee, & Williams, 1990).

The discovery and initial decade of research on the syndrome provide an exciting direction for further development. It seems quite likely that a number of individuals who had retardation for which no cause was previously specifiable may have had fragile X.

OTHER CHROMOSOMAL ANOMALIES

Abnormalities in the sex chromosomes have also been found to affect development adversely. Two such conditions are discussed next; their karyotypes are shown in Figure 5.5.

Klinefelter syndrome is a condition in which males receive an extra X chromosome, so that they have an XXY arrangement. The clinical pattern of the syndrome includes frequent social retardation, sterility and underdevelopment of the male sex organs, and the acquisition of female secondary sex characteristics. The syndrome is often associated with borderline or mild levels of intellectual retardation. Deficits increase with the number of X chromosomes

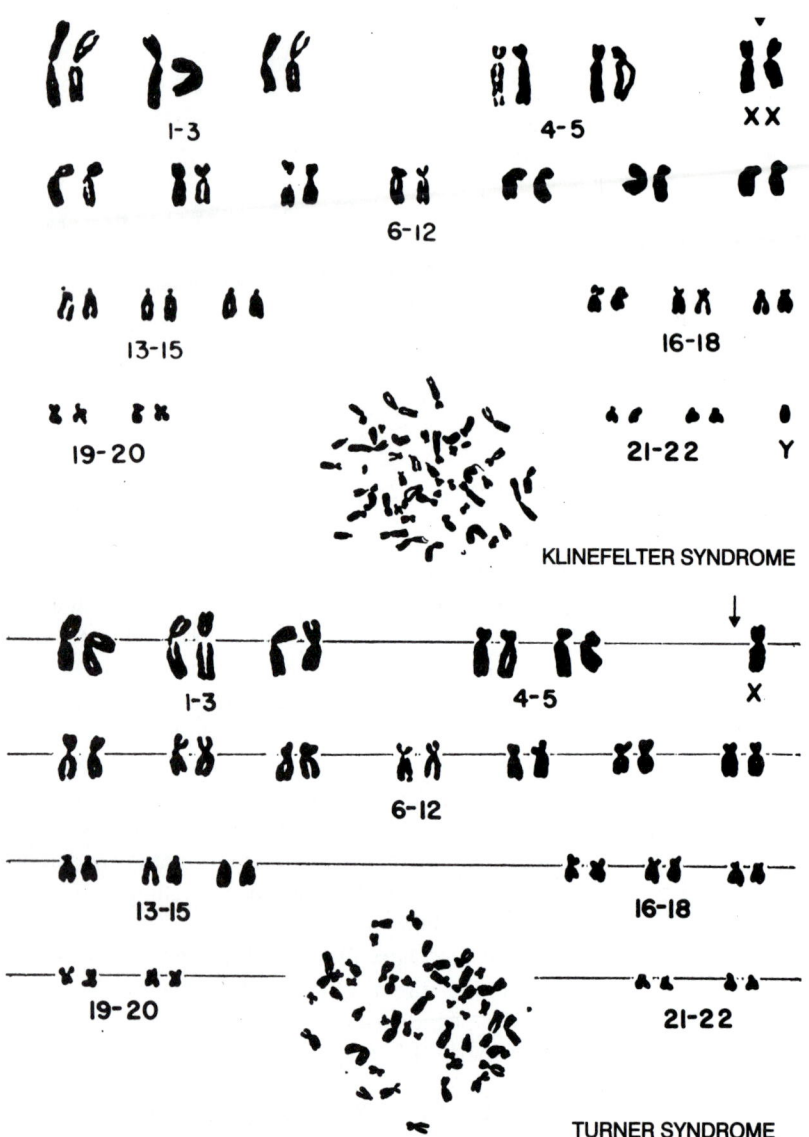

FIGURE 5.5
Sex Chromosomal Abnormalities

Source: From *Handbook of Mental Retardation Syndromes* (pp. 39, 43, 45) by C. H. Carter, 1975, Springfield, IL: Charles C. Thomas. Reprinted by permission of Charles C. Thomas, Publisher.

(XXXY, XXXXY). Incidence is relatively high: 1 in 500 male births. Although no specific cure exists, physical aspects of the condition can be alleviated through surgery and hormonal treatment. XXY boys can have problems with auditory perception, receptive and expressive language, and a general deficit in processing linguistic information (Bender, Fry, Pennington, Puck, Salonblatt, &

Robinson, 1983). Although often discussed in relation to mental retardation, Klinefelter syndrome is more commonly associated with learning disabilities. This reflects a general pattern in which autosomal anomalies are more often associated with mental retardation, while sex chromosomal disorders are more often associated with learning disabilities (Bender, Puck, Salbenblatt, & Robinson, 1986; Polloway & Rucker, 1997).

A sex chromosomal disorder in females, *Turner syndrome,* results from an absence of one of the X chromosomes (XO). It is the only syndrome with a true monosomy and thus the only one where individuals with the syndrome show fewer than 46 chromosomes. Its rarity (1 in 2,500 female births; Rovet, 1993) is underscored by the fact that over 95 percent of fetuses conceived with the XO pattern are spontaneously aborted. Although Turner syndrome is not usually a cause of mental retardation, it is worthy of mention because it is often associated with learning disabilities. Some data indicate that the pattern of females with XO syndrome includes lower performance scale and full-scale IQ scores (but not lower verbal scores) and with somewhat lower educational and occupational attainments than their peers. Common problems are in spatial relations and hence mathematical abilities, memory, attention, and social competence (Downey et al., 1991; Rovet, 1993). As with Klinefelter syndrome, Turner syndrome produces deviations from normal development, with lack of secondary sex characteristics, sterility, and short stature as common features.

Prader-Willi is an example of a condition that requires a thorough understanding of how to manage individuals who have it.

Finally, one other condition that has been linked to chromosomal abnormality is *Prader-Willi syndrome.* Specifically, it is most often related to a partial deletion of chromosome 15 (Holm et al., 1993; Widerstrom et al., 1991). The most significant characteristics are delay in motor and mental development, hypogenital development, insatiable appetite (and hence obesity), small features and stature. It has been associated with mild-to-moderate retardation and with learning disabilities. The biological mechanism underlying the syndrome brings about a preoccupation with eating that has prompted observers to suggest that, for a Prader-Willi child, "life is one endless meal." The characteristics associated with Prader-Willi syndrome generally present in two stages, an infantile hypotonic phase and a childhood/adulthood obesity phase (Donaldson et al., 1994). Initially, a major paradox is their failure-to-thrive condition, given that failure to thrive subsequently turns into excessive eating and obesity as the child increases in age. In addition, infants with Prader-Willi generally experience hypotonia, and thus the term "floppy baby" has frequently been used to describe these children during infancy. Between the ages of one and three years, the characteristics of the second phase of the syndrome begin to become apparent. This phase may include hyperphagia (i.e., an insatiable appetite) and constant preoccupation with food with uncontrollable eating often leading to life-threatening obesity. Also noted during this phase are delayed psychomotor development, signs of cognitive impairment, and delayed and/or abnormal pubertal development (Scott et al., 1997, p. 4).

Goldman (1988) noted that the association of Prader-Willi syndrome with obesity has led to the assumption that the expected life span for individuals with the disorder is limited, at least in part because of the physical complications of being grossly overweight. In contrast, her research indicates that older individuals with the syndrome do exist but may be unidentified. Since the disorder was first described only in 1956, obviously, some older persons could have escaped detection. Goldman (1988) described two adult women for whom the desire to overeat continued with no evidence of their understanding the need to manage intake. Goldman's two subjects obtained food through their own devices. "Even when the environment is believed to be controlled, these persons evidently engage in some variety of successful covert foraging" (p. 101).

Additional information on the mechanics of the disorder and the effectiveness of various treatment options continue to be available as research develops. Intervention strategies that involve early intervention, exercise, monitoring of caloric intake, environmental controls, and specialized transition planning (Scott et al., 1997) are indicated.

CRANIAL MALFORMATIONS

Several conditions associated with retardation manifest as cranial malformations. The most dramatic is anencephaly, literally, the absence of major portions of the brain. More common, however, are microcephaly and hydrocephalus.

Children who have *microcephaly* are characterized by a small, conical skull, a curved spine that leads to a stooping posture, and severe retardation. In rare cases, the condition can be transmitted genetically, probably as an autosomal recessive trait, but it is more commonly a secondary consequence of such conditions as congenital rubella or fetal alcohol syndrome (see later), or it may be the result of radiation exposure. Individuals affected by microcephaly have been characterized as imitative, good-natured, and lively. There is no known cure.

Hydrocephalus consists of at least six types of problems associated with interference in the flow of cerebrospinal fluid within the skull. The most common type of blockage results in progressive enlargement of the cranium and subsequent brain damage. Physical manifestations of this condition differ widely; however, an enlarged skull is not present in all cases. Hydrocephalus may result from polygenic inheritance or as a secondary effect of maternal infections or intoxications. The effects of this condition can be reduced in many infants by draining off the fluid, using shunts to decrease the cranial pressure. *Shunts* are valves or tubes surgically inserted under the child's skin to pump the fluid away from the brain and maintain proper flow. The results of early shunt treatment have been very encouraging in preventing head enlargement, the symptom most often associated with an increase in the probability of retardation. Wolraich (1983) indicated that proper treatment can ensure the survival of affected children, although significant disabilities remain a possibility. Milder cases may escape detection, with no ill effects noted. For example, some observers think that Einstein may have had a mild, nonprogressive case of hydrocephalus (Beck, 1972).

CONGENITAL FACTORS

The category of congenital factors includes a variety of harmful factors called **teratogens** that can significantly affect prenatal (and in some cases, postnatal) development. The first widespread public exposure to the awesome power of teratogenic agents came from the thalidomide tragedy of the 1960s. Intended as a relaxant during pregnancy, this drug caused severe physical deformities (e.g., missing and/or shortened limbs) in many unborn children. This discussion focuses on some of the specific forces that have been identified as having teratogenic effects.

MATERNAL DISEASE

The brain is especially susceptible to damage through maternal disease during the first three months of pregnancy. Infection of the mother by rubella (German measles) early in pregnancy has been found to result in fetal defects in up to 50 percent of cases. This is particularly significant because rubella has historically been a disease of epidemic occurrence. Recently developed immunization procedures help to limit its incidence, but trends in the 1990s indicate increases in the disease. In addition to retardation, congenital rubella can result in heart disease, blindness, and deafness. It has been one of the primary causes of severe multiple disabilities among children.

Congenital syphilis (as well as other venereal diseases) is another maternal disease that can damage the central nervous system and result in severe effects in developing fetuses. Perhaps the most alarming feature of this disorder has been its increasing prevalence in recent years—after it had nearly been eradicated. This may be due in part to antibiotic-resistant strains of the disease. Research has also addressed the possible effects of maternal acquired immune deficiency syndrome (AIDS) as an agent of congenital disabilities.

One other significant possible cause of retardation that, though not a disease, may function as an insult to the fetus, is *blood-group incompatibility* between mother and unborn child. Most commonly, the condition occurs as a result of the Rh factor, a protein on the surface of red blood cells. Rh-positive blood cells contain this protein; Rh-negative cells do not. When an Rh-positive male and an Rh-negative female conceive an Rh-positive child, neither mother nor fetus is adversely affected. At birth, however, the mother's immune system will react to the fetus's Rh-positive blood by forming antibodies to the Rh factor. These antibodies remain in the mother's system and will enter the bloodstream of the next Rh-positive baby conceived, attacking its central nervous system and possibly resulting in retardation, epilepsy, and cerebral palsy. Treatment of this immune response focuses on preventing the destructive antibodies from forming. One technique is to vaccinate the mother with Rh immunoglobulin serum midway through each suspected Rh-positive pregnancy and within seventy-two hours of its termination (whether by birth, miscarriage, or abortion). This serum destroys the Rh-positive cells that pass from the infant's to the mother's bloodstream, inhibiting the development of antibodies that would otherwise attack the next fetus carried. This procedure does not alter the mother's immune response mechanism but can remove the stimuli that engage it.

SUBSTANCE EXPOSURE

A great deal of research has addressed the effects of drugs and industrial chemicals on the fetus. Particular attention has been given to nicotine, caffeine, lysergic acid (LSD), and other related drugs. The results of exposure to these substances are clear, and we should assume that any other powerful chemical substance should also be avoided by pregnant women.

The first significant breakthrough of understanding in this domain was with alcohol consumption. Problems associated with alcohol have been generally acknowledged for years. For example, Haggard and Jellinek (1942) noted that "infants born to alcoholic mothers sometimes had a starved, shriveled and imperfect look" (p. 165). But despite this long-standing suspicion of teratogenic effects, only since the 1970s has the nature of fetal alcohol syndrome (FAS) been documented. Jones, Smith, Ulleland and Streissguth (1973) coined the term *fetal alcohol syndrome* after studies of eight unrelated offspring born to chronically alcoholic mothers showed a recognizable pattern of major and minor malformations, growth deficiencies, and developmental disabilities.

The best estimates of FAS occurrence are between 1 and 3 cases per 1,000 births (Warren & Bast, 1988). Other studies have also reinforced this approximate rate of occurrence, placing the figure at 1 in 650 births (Webb, Hochberg, & Sher, 1988). At this rate, FAS may be the first or second leading known cause of mental retardation along with Down syndrome (Abel & Sokol, 1986). While the precise prevalence is not clear, there is little question that FAS is one of the major causes of retardation in the United States, with conservative estimates standing at 5,000 children born with FAS each year (Stark, Menolascino, & Goldsbury, 1988).

It is useful to note that not all children whose mothers drank during pregnancy will have FAS/FAE and not all children with FAS/FAE will have mental retardation.

In FAS, the mother's heavy alcohol consumption has direct toxic effects on the fetus. Exact levels of consumption that cause FAS are not known, but those mothers who are alcoholic, who have several drinks per day, or who engage in binge drinking run a confirmed, significant risk of damaging their unborn children. Risk rates are particularly high during the first trimester of pregnancy. Research continues on the risks of light or moderate drinking. An important area of study has been *fetal alcohol effects* (FAE), a more subtle disorder associated with learning and attentional problems. Given the risk of FAE, a common recommendation is for total abstinence (Ouellette, 1984).

The characteristics of FAS can be separated into three primary features: central nervous system dysfunction (e.g., mild-to-moderate retardation), craniofacial malformations (e.g., cleft palate microcephaly), and prenatal and postnatal growth development (e.g., low birth weight). A diagnosis of FAS is warranted when a child has a cluster of disorders within these three areas (Griesbach & Polloway, 1991).

While research on the nature and effects of FAS has progressed in the last twenty-five years, the commitment to its prevention has been somewhat less dramatic. Baumeister and Hamlett (1986), reporting on a national survey, concluded:

> Of all of the major known specific causes of severe mental retardation, FAS is, in principle, preventable with knowledge currently at our disposal. The most direct course of action would appear to be abstinence or, at least, reduction of alcohol consumption during pregnancy. Even though there are some workable ways to approach this problem, we do not have a national program to prevent this preventable disease. A coordinated prevention and evaluation program should be initiated that involves federal and state government. (p. 173)

In recent years, attention has broadened to other drugs, most notably cocaine. The number of children exposed to drugs prenatally has climbed exponentially in some cities in the United States, with estimates in the late 1980s indicating that 10 to 11 percent of all births were thought to be to drug-exposed mothers (Sontag, 1989; Stoddard, 1992). However, significant problems persist in determining the actual number.

The concerns that have been raised by this increase in substance abuse among pregnant women has often generated more heat than light in the media. Vincent, Poulsen, Cole, Woodruff, and Griffith (1991) make two key points about the knowledge base:

1. The media have painted a dire picture of infants who were exposed to alcohol and other drugs in utero. This picture is not fully supported by research or clinical experience with these children: We do not know the incidence of prenatal exposure to alcohol and other drugs, nor do we know the long-term effects of such exposure.

2. Many women who abuse alcohol and other drugs during pregnancy also experience other psychological, social, and medical events that can affect the health of their children. Thus, the risks of substance exposure are often compounded by other difficulties, such as inadequate housing, medical care, child care, and nutrition, that place these children at risk for developmental delays. (pp. 1–2)

These cautions are useful in considering directions for the future and in planning intervention strategies. It is with these in mind that the following possible characteristics are noted for children who are at risk due to prenatal exposure to drugs. Poulsen (1991, cited by Vincent et al., 1991) indicated that problem areas could include

- Exhibition of behavioral extremes
- Being easily overstimulated
- Low tolerance for changes
- Constant testing of limits set by adults
- Difficulty in reading social cues
- Difficulty in establishing and maintaining relationships with peers
- Language delays
- Sporadic mastery of skills
- Inconsistent problem-solving strategies
- Auditory processing and word retrieval difficulties
- Decreased capacity to initiate and organize play
- Decrease in focused attention and concentration (p. 14)

PREMATURITY AND PERINATAL CONCERNS

Potential correlates of prematurity and low birth weight are illustrated in Figure 5.6, although no simple, cause–effect relationship exists for any of these factors. Perhaps most notable in light of recent demographic trends is teenage pregnancy, a phenomenon that clearly increases risks of prematurity and low birth weight (Berg & Emanuel, 1987; Rucker & Polloway, 1997).

Determining the effects of prematurity has been a difficult task. Full-term infants are born between thirty-seven and forty-one weeks, and normal birth weight is above 5.5 pounds (Widerstrom et al., 1991). Extremely short pregnancies (less than twenty-eight weeks) or very low birth weights (below 1,500 grams, or 3.5 pounds) frequently present problems. For less substantial deviations from the norm in term or weight, the results are not so clear. Data indicate that the relationship between prematurity, birth weight, and mental retardation is most significant for very low birth weight (C. Berg & Emanuel, 1987).

Menolascino and Egger (1978) further discussed the relationship between preterm birth and retardation when they noted a combination of conditions that could produce retardation. They stated:

> A complex, but not unusual, example would be an infant born at 32 weeks gestation, weighing 4 pounds (1,800 grams), and displaying cyanosis and respiratory distress at birth, whose mother is an . . . unmarried 17-year-old female from a low socioeconomic class. So many variables are present, and many of them are so difficult to quantify, that it is no wonder that consistent answers regarding prematurity and mental retardation are difficult to derive. (p. 230)

In addition to low IQ, prematurity has also been linked to increased occurrence of cerebral palsy, attentional deficits, and other neurological and medical complications. The exciting technological efforts exhibited in neonatal intensive care units (NICUs) represent the promise for assistance for these

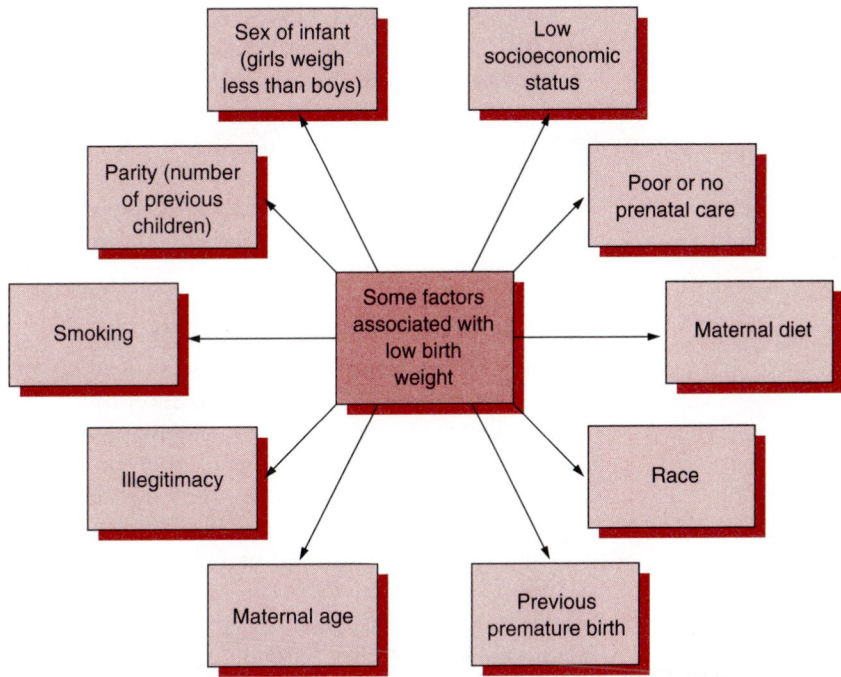

Prematurity: Gestation time of less than 37 weeks.
Low Birth Weight: Weight at birth equal to or less than 2,500 grams.

FIGURE 5.6
Low Birth Weight and Prematurity

Source: From *Mental Retardation: The Known and the Unknown* (p. 31) by President's Committee on Mental Retardation, 1976, Washington, DC: U.S. Government Printing Office.

special infants. The challenge is to provide a medically responsive facility that coincidentally offers the neonate a psychologically supportive environment. Widerstrom et al. (1991, p. 114) cite the recommendations of Bennett (1987) for NICU practical guidelines:

■ Recognize the unusual physiological stresses being endured by the premature infant.

■ Modify the environment to decrease overstimulation (specifically screen out grossly bombarding and unnecessary sensory stimuli such as handling during periods of quiet sleep).

■ Introduce diurnal rhythms to promote behavioral organization.

■ Gradually facilitate reciprocal visual, auditory, tactile, vestibular-kinesthetic, and social feedback during alert periods.

■ Immediately terminate or alter approaches that produce avoidance responses.

■ Educate and assist parents in reading, anticipating, and appropriately responding to their own infant's cues and signals, thus fostering and reinforcing parents' feelings of competence.

Oxygen deprivation, often referred to as *hypoxia* or **anoxia,** can result from such birth difficulties as knotted umbilical cord, extremely short or long labor, or breech birth. Anoxia has long been associated with pronounced deficiencies in the affected infant, including lower IQ scores (Graham, Ernhart, Thurston, & Craft, 1962; McLaren & Bryson, 1987). The deficiencies it produces may vary greatly and are often unstable, so it is difficult to give an accurate prognosis for a child who experiences anoxia. Other problems at birth that can be traumatic include the delivery itself and the specific anesthetic procedures used.

POSTNATAL BIOLOGICAL CONCERNS

A variety of postnatal traumatic events leading to disabilities can occur throughout early childhood. McLaren and Bryson (1987) have estimated that the prevalence of mild retardation stemming from trauma and neglect is as high as 15 percent. *Head injuries* account for the greater part of such cases. It has been estimated that one in thirty newborns will experience a serious brain injury before the teen years are completed (Allison, 1992). Eighty-nine percent of injuries are caused by falls, bicycle and motor vehicle accidents, and sports-related activities. The highest risk years are between fifteen and twenty-five, with boys being twice as likely to be affected as girls, and with motor vehicle accidents being the most common cause of injury (Pipitone, 1992; Vernon-Levett, 1991). The relationship of auto accidents to brain injury has spurred the passage by all states of mandatory child-restraint laws.

Child abuse is a special concern, particularly because of the relationship between children's disability and their abuse. Child abuse can result from and aggravate primary disabilities (Zantal-Weiner, 1987; Zirpoli, 1986). Zantal-Weiner (1987) noted in her review that children with disabilities are less able to defend themselves from abuse, have greater difficulty determining appropriate and inappropriate contact and telling anyone of the abuse once it has occurred, are more dependent on those who abuse them, are less likely to report abuse, and are seen as less credible when they do report it. In addition to striking, other negative disciplinary actions like violent shaking can potentially play a role in brain hemorrhage and retardation.

Traditional notions held that traumatic brain injury in young children may be less serious than in adults because another area of the brain would pick up the functions for a damaged brain region. Current views suggest, however, that the problems associated with brain injury may be manifested later in life, especially when cognitive demands have increased (Allison, 1992).

Lead poisoning, which may lead to encephalitis, is permanently and progressively toxic to the central nervous system. It can cause seizures, cerebral palsy, and retardation. Other effects of lead poisoning include gastrointestinal disturbances (e.g., anorexia, vomiting) and central nervous system manifestations (e.g., convulsions, drowsiness, irritability). Although commercial paints no longer contain lead, poisoning is still a factor in residences where a child has access to old, peeling paint. Conscious urban renewal is reducing the scope of this problem through repainting with unleaded paints. In older homes, lead paint can also enter the body through inhalation of dust or fumes, such as during renovation work (Marino et al., 1990) or from the soil around the houses. The existence of high lead levels remains most serious in inner-city areas where abatement efforts have not been fully implemented. Elevated lead blood levels can also be caused by water from lead waterpipes, by prolonged breathing of polluted air, as in towns with lead smelters and heavy traffic congestion, and by the young child's mouthing and eating objects containing lead. Analysis of metal concentrations for lead and other elements has indicated higher levels for children with mild disabilities than for their peers without disabilities (Marlowe, Errera, & Jacobs, 1983). There may be no such thing as a safe level for heavy metals in the body (Stark et al., 1988).

Nutritional deficiencies are noted here, although these are obviously both prenatal and postnatal concerns. Developmental deficiencies can occur when either the mother or child has an inadequate diet. Malnutrition during gestation or the first six months of life hinders the development of brain cells and can lead to as much as a 40 percent deficit in their number. Resnick (1988) stated that the first two trimesters may be most critical to the prevention of such lacks, although he also indicated that maternal nutrition before pregnancy may be even more important. Since later brain growth is in weight rather than in number of cells, the effects of early malnutrition have long been viewed as irreversible (Cravioto, DeLicardie, & Birch, 1966). As Cravioto et al. (1966) and Crnic (1984) have pointed out, however, it is difficult to assess the true detrimental effect of poor nutrition because it tends to accompany other unfavorable circumstances—inadequate housing, substandard living conditions, poor hygiene, and poor prenatal care, as wells as diets high in calories but low in important nutrients.

PSYCHOSOCIAL CONCERNS AND ENVIRONMENTAL FACTORS

Although the categories discussed so far are representative of hundreds of specific causes of retardation, most cases are classified as having psychosocial or environmental causes. Environmental causes have most often been associated with mild mental retardation, but it is important that we keep two things in mind as we discuss these factors. First, people with mild mental retardation are also frequently affected by genetic and other biological factors, and second, environmental influences are important factors in the lives of people with more severe disabilities. The following discussion focuses on environmental, hereditary, and interactional perspectives.

ENVIRONMENTAL PERSPECTIVE

Historically, the environmental view of intellect and personality derives from the philosopher John Locke's concept of the *tabula rasa,* which suggests that children are born with a mind that is a "blank slate" on which the environment "writes" experiences and thus develops traits. Complete acceptance of this position places a heavy responsibility on parents, educators, and other agents of society, because it implies that a child's mental development is molded almost exclusively by home training, other family and community influences, and educational programs.

The strict environmental position holds that the primary determinant of a child's current level of intellectual functioning is that child's experiential background. Pasamanick (1959) clearly stated this position:

> Except for a few hereditary clinical deficiencies . . . and for exogenous injury to neural integration, behavior variation does not seem to be the result of genetically determined structural origin. It is now possible to entertain a new tabula rasa theory [hypothesizing] that at conception individuals are quite alike in intellectual endowment except for these quite rare hereditary neurological defects. It appears to us that it is life experience and the sociocultural milieu influencing biological and psychosocial function which, in the absence of organic brain damage, makes human beings significantly different behaviorally from each other. (p. 318)

The radical behavioral position is consistent with the environmental perspective. From this view, all behavior (including responses on an IQ test) is learned through interaction with the environment, so that individuals become "retarded" when, because of inadequate or deficient experiences, they fail to learn appropriate behaviors—or succeed in learning inappropriate ones.

Watson (1930), the "father of behaviorism," framed a controversial yet eloquent description of this point of view:

> Our conclusion, then, is that we have no real evidence of the inheritance of traits. I would feel perfectly confident in the ultimate favorable outcome of careful upbringing of a healthy well-formed baby born of a long line of crooks, murderers and thieves, and prostitutes. Who has any evidence to the contrary?
>
> I should like to go one step further now and say, "Give me a dozen healthy infants, well-formed, and my own specific world to bring them up in and I'll guarantee to take anyone at random and train him to become any type of specialist I might select—doctor, lawyer, artist, merchant-chief and yes, even beggar-man and thief, regardless of his talents, penchants, tendencies, abilities, vocations, and race of his ancestors." I am going beyond my facts and I admit it, but so have the advocates of the contrary and they have been doing it for many thousands of years. . . .
>
> The truth is society does not like to face facts. Pride of race has been strong, hence our Mayflower ancestry—our Daughters of the Revolution. We like to boast of our ancestry. It sets us apart. . . . Again, on the other hand, the belief in the inheritance of tendencies and traits saves us from blame in the training of our young. (p. 103)

If an environmental position is to be scientifically supported, rather than simply philosophically advanced as in the preceding comments, then that position's adherents must supply a model for understanding the influence of sociocultural effects on the development of the young child. Coulter (1988b) provides an insightful hypothesis for considering such effects:

> How can one understand the neurological basis of mental retardation result- ing from adverse sociocultural influences? When one considers that neuronal connections form and are maintained as a result of appropriate input or stim- ulation, and that this process continues throughout childhood, one can hy- pothesize that inadequate or inappropriate input during childhood could result in abnormal connections in the brain. This structural defect in connec- tivity could then result in the functional defect of mental retardation. The clearest example of this process is in the visual system, where lack of visual stimulation during the critical period of early infancy results in defective de- velopment of the visual cortex. A similar process may occur in the auditory cortex when children are born deaf or suffer from prolonged hearing impair- ment due to chronic otitis in infancy. It is interesting to note that children raised in the wild, deprived of exposure to human speech and communication during early childhood, are seldom able to learn to communicate effectively through speech. These experiences suggest that there are critical periods in childhood during which effective sensory input must occur in order for the appropriate connections in the brain to develop. Deprivation of these envi- ronmental inputs would then result in inadequate connectivity. Specifically, sociocultural influences that result in diffuse environmental deprivation might cause a deficiency of connections throughout the brain. Mental retardation attributable to sociocultural influences could thus be considered as a *hypocon- nection* syndrome. (pp. 121–123)

This hypothesis is quite consistent with the ongoing research on the de- velopment of infants and toddlers.

ENVIRONMENTAL CORRELATES

Concern over the role of environment in promoting or retarding the devel- opment of children emerged as a national, social, and political concern dur- ing the administration of President Kennedy and in President Johnson's "War on Poverty." The Head Start program for economically disadvantaged chil- dren was one manifestation of this focus on the environment as a source of retarded development. Psychosocial retardation has been closely linked to a number of variables that can occur in an environment of poverty. The common estimate that approximately 25 percent of all American preschool- ers belong to families with incomes below the poverty level highlights the immensity of the problem.

Three cautions are critical when we consider poverty environments. First, as Chan and Rueda (1979) have stressed, since minority groups are overrepresented among the poor, we must separate the effects of poverty from the essence of cultural differences. This distinction allows us to assess the negative effects of poverty without making judgments about cultural

TABLE 5.2
High-Risk Index

Factor	Weight	Factor	Weight
Mother's educational level (Last grade completed)		Father's educational level (Last grade completed)	
6	8	6	8
7	7	7	7
8	6	8	6
9	3	9	3
10	2	10	2
11	1	11	1
12	0	12	0

Family income indexed by family size (e.g., if a family of 2 has an income of $5,010, they receive a score of *1*.)

			Weights		
Size	8	7	6	4	1
1–2	≥2,000	3,000	4,000	5,000	6,000
3–4	≥4,000	5,500	6,500	7,500	9,000
5–6	≥7,000	8,000	9,000	10,000	12,000
7–8	≥7,500	8,500	9,500	10,500	12,500
9–10	≥8,000	9,000	10,000	11,000	13,000
11–12	≥8,500	9,500	10,500	11,500	13,500

Factor	Weight	Factor	Weight
Father absent	2	Any member of mother's or father's immediate family required special services in school (special class placement or repeated school failure).	3
Any member of mother's or father's immediate family required special community services provided for the mentally disabled (ranging from disability payments to institutionalization).	3	Relevant social agencies in the community indicate that the family is in need of assistance.	3
School-aged siblings have repeated one or more grades or scored one or more grade levels below the norm on school-administered achievement tests.	3	One or more members of the family has sought counseling or professional.help in the past five years.	1
Payments received from welfare agencies within past five years.	3	Existence of special circumstances not included in any of the above which are likely contributors to cultural or social disadvantage.	2
Record of father's work indicates unstable job history or unskilled labor.	3		
Records of mother's or father's IQ indicate scores of 85 or below.	3		

Source: From "Project CARE: A Comparison of Two Early Intervention Strategies to Prevent Retarded Development" by C. T. Ramey et al., 1985, *Topics in Early Childhood Special Education, 5*(2), pp. 15–16. Reprinted by permission.

variance between these groups and the majority culture. Second, while research has attempted to identify specific environmental factors that relate to retardation, factors usually act in combination. Although these variables appear more frequently in lower social class environments, we must avoid presuming that they will be present in every economically poor home situation.

Table 5.2 lists some correlates of poverty that may place children at risk for school failure, and its weighting system suggests the additive effect of the variables. Third, the "vast majority of individuals who are considered poor function well within normal intellectual levels, and yet they remain poor" (Garber, 1988, p. 2). The ability to identify causative factors does not necessarily imply that we can also simply correct them and improve an individual's situation.

Within poverty environments, *parenting practices* are as varied as they are within the general population. Authoritarianism and inconsistency, however, are perhaps more prevalent in these environments. Parents may emphasize external controls that inadvertently stress, for example, the problems of getting caught for stealing over ethical reasons for avoiding stealing. Parents' reliance on punishment for control can lead children to imitate their aggressive models. Lack of structure and disorganization can also interfere with the child's need for stability. A lack of stimulation or excessive or inappropriate stimulation (e.g., bombardment of noise) may also interfere with cognitive development.

Kagan (1970) focused on several key psychological differences between children of lower socioeconomic class and those more privileged. He asserted that these differences emerge during the first three years of life and remain stable over time. He identified seven major psychological differences between the two groups: language, mental set, attachment, inhibition, sense of effectiveness, motivation, and expectancy of failure. Garber (1988) draws attention to the poverty-bound mother with low IQ and limited verbal skills who cannot effectively mediate the environment for her child, a case that directly evokes the concept of hypoconnection as hypothesized by Coulter (1988b). All these variables may directly or indirectly influence school performance, and deficits in them can also limit a child's problem-solving skills.

Inappropriate patterns of parenting and child guidance, however, are clearly not inherent in the lower-class home. As Chan and Rueda (1979) point out, these deficiencies are likely to reflect the parent's lack of access to information on techniques for enhancing psychosocial development.

In a lower-class environment, one parent, frequently the father, is often absent, and the burden of child-rearing falls more heavily on the mother. The large number of children in many of these families aggravates the problem, and the potential result is a decrease in each child's direct, individual contact with adult models.

The *practical problems* of making ends meet for persons living in poverty are often overlooked and must be considered. The time and effort that middle-class parents spend to motivate and stimulate children may, in a lower-class home, need to be devoted to finding a job, finding suitable housing, and arranging child care. Where poverty is the overriding concern, parents do not have the luxury of planning for the future. The difficulties of daily living can make people feel fatalistic about their environment and reject the value of even trying to improve their situation. A parent who is worried about finding money for daily meals may not set high priority for getting a child to a preschool program on time or of following through with a home training program.

This sense of fatalism is shockingly portrayed in *There Are No Children Here* by Kotlowitz (1991). His book is an account of his observations and involvement in the lives of two young boys living in the poverty and danger of a public housing project in Chicago. Kotlowitz derived his title from the comment made by the boys' mother when asked what life was like for children living in an environment of poverty, crime, drugs, and death. Her response was, "Mister, there are no children here." Kotlowitz found moving and disheartening attitudes among the children in the projects when asked about their hopes for the future. He found that these children, who had seen many of their playmates shot and killed by gang leaders, drug dealers, and the police, spoke in terms of "if I grow up" rather than "when I grow up." It is not surprising that educational concerns may be neglected or, at least, fail to take precedence, in such an environment.

Children born to *teenage mothers* form one increasingly researched subgroup that runs an especially high risk of subsequent difficulties. As Berg and Emanuel (1987) noted in their review:

> Teenage mothers as a group are at elevated risk for producing low birth weight babies: the younger the mother, the higher the risk. . . . A number of studies have found lower IQs among the offspring of teenage mothers and have attributed this association primarily to social disadvantages. . . . While it is not clear whether problems of adolescent pregnancies are primarily due to biological or social factors, the fact remains that pregnant teenagers as a group are at high social risk, are more apt to be unmarried and poorly educated, and as a group have poorer pregnancy outcomes than older women. . . . Even if there is no biological hazard, the multiple social and personal problems associated with teenage pregnancy indicate the need to discourage reproduction in this age group. (pp. 50–51)

Whitman, Borkowski, Schellenbach, and Nath (1987) underscored the numerous variables affecting parenting behavior when they developed the model presented in Figure 5.7. Although their focus was on teenage parents, the model's components give an excellent idea of the constellation of factors affecting child development. As they noted:

> It is our contention that in order to parent effectively, adolescent mothers must be cognitively and emotionally prepared. The cognitive readiness of adolescent mothers depends upon the formal and informal education they receive from the social support systems and their ability to assimilate and utilize this information in specific parenting situations. In addition, their ability to cope emotionally with the stresses associated with parenting depend upon whether their children display deviant biological characteristics that complicate their parenting task, the type of physical and emotional assistance they receive from their social support systems and their own personal coping resources. Ineffective

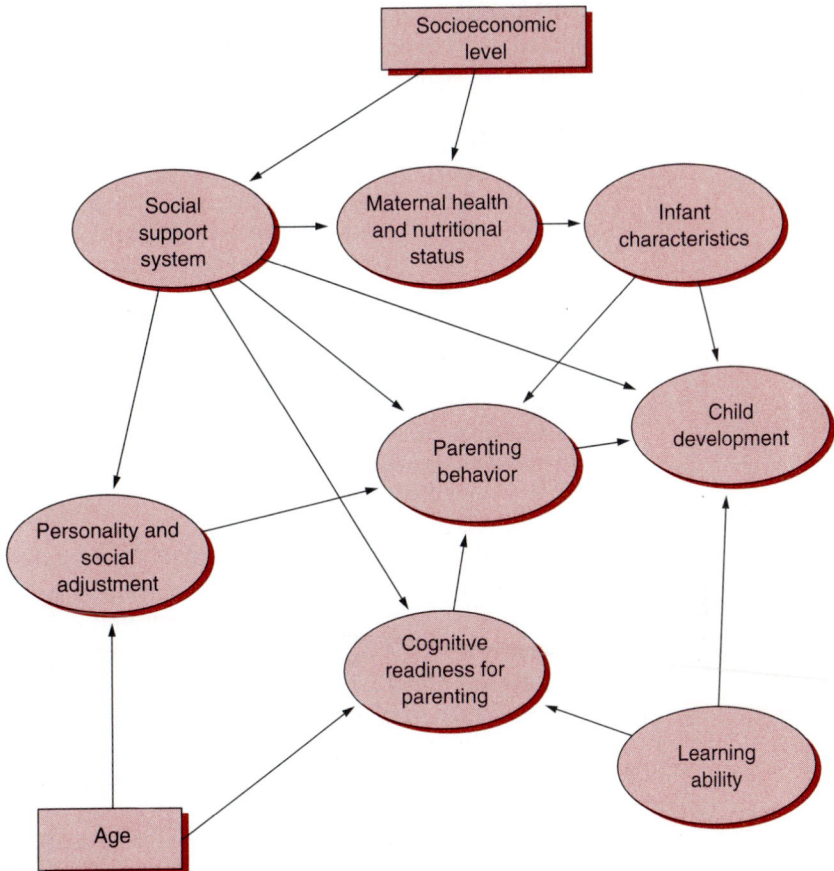

FIGURE 5.7

A Model of Teenage Parenting and Child Development

Source: From "Predicting and Understanding Developmental Delay of Adolescent Mothers: A Multidimensional Approach" by T. L. Whitman, J. G. Borkowski, C. J. Schellenbach, and P. S. Nath, 1987, *American Journal of Mental Deficiency, 92,* p. 51. Reprinted by permission.

parenting results if external stressors are great, cognitive preparation is insufficient, and/or personal-emotional problems are overwhelming. (p. 51)

Health problems can compound the detrimental effects of poverty. Particular concerns include nutritional deficiencies, lack of resistance to disease, exposure to toxic substances, and inadequate medical care. Although these are biological concerns, they tend to appear with a host of psychosocial factors and may, with them, jeopardize mental development. Nowhere is this reality more evident than with the increasing numbers of homeless families. In his book *Rachel and Her Children,* Kozol

(1988) describes the realities of homelessness through interviews he conducted with people he describes as "ordinary people" who have no homes. He makes it clear that most of these people are more like the rest of us than they are different. He also portrays in stark terms the dimensions of the problem for children and their families:

> By the time these words are printed there will be almost 500,000 homeless children in America. If all of them were gathered in one city, they would represent a larger population than that of Atlanta, Denver, or St. Louis. Because they are scattered in a thousand cities, they are easily unseen. And because so many die in infancy or lose the strength to struggle and prevail in early years, some will never live to tell their stories.
>
> Not all homeless children will be lost to early death or taken from their parents by the state. Some of their parents will do better. . . . Some will be able to keep their children, their stability, their sense of worth. Some will get back their vanished dreams. A few will find jobs again and some may even find a home they can afford. Many will not. (p. 3)

Probably the clearest documentation of health problems in high-risk lower-class children was Kugel's classic study (1967; Kugel & Parsons, 1967). Kugel studied thirty-five children and found substantial evidence of short pregnancies and long labor, infectious toxemia, anoxia, prematurity, and neurological abnormalities. Those results were interpreted as a negation of the idea of inherited factors as the basis for mild retardation, and an indication that psychosocial and pre- and postnatal biological factors combine as specific causative agents. Kugel (1967) concludes his report by stating that:

> By working diligently with this group of individuals when they are no older than 3 or 4 years of age, some of the pernicious factors can be ameliorated so that these persons need not be condemned to lifelong mental subnormality. (p. 61)

Educational opportunity is another key consideration. Kozol (1991) examined the unequal educational opportunities that exist for children and adolescents in the poorest communities of our country and contrasts these with the wealth of educational resources and opportunities in the nation's most affluent communities. His book, *Savage Inequalities: Children in America's Schools,* profiles specific schools and illustrates the differences in resources, talent, and support for students in rich and poor schools and school districts. In speaking of the odds against success for students in Chicago's South Side, Kozol (1991) states:

> In strictly pedagogic terms, the odds of failure for a student who starts out at Woodson Elementary School, and then continues at a nonselective high school, are approximately ten to one. The odds of learning math and reading on the street are probably as good or even better. The odds of finding a few moments of delight, or maybe even happiness, outside these dreary schools are better still. For many, many students at Chicago's nonselective high schools, it is hard

to know if the decision to drop out of school, no matter how much we discourage it, is not, in fact, a logical decision. (p. 59)

This enumeration of problems suggests a linkage between poverty and retardation, but since the overwhelming majority of individuals reared in lower-class homes are *not* functionally retarded, the equation is far from exact. A critical continuing need in research is the attempt to determine if specific factors or clusters of factors are most significant in their negative effect on a child's development and, if so, which these are. Several classic longitudinal research projects have illustrated how psychosocial variables can influence early experience so that retardation becomes likely; two such projects are discussed next.

INFLUENTIAL RESEARCH ON ENVIRONMENTAL FACTORS

The foremost name in research into early environmental experiences is that of Harold Skeels. His work, begun in the 1930s (when most people believed IQ was stable and genetically determined), helped lay the foundation for the massive intervention efforts that began in the 1960s. The importance and even the romance of this research leads us to discuss it in some detail.

The first research effort by Skeels and Dye (1939) investigated the reversibility of the effects of nonstimulating orphanage environments upon children. Skeels and Dye based their program, unusual in its inception and implementation, on the observation of two female infants. Describing the children, Skeels (1966) later wrote:

> The youngsters were pitiful little creatures. They were tearful, had runny noses, and coarse, stringy, and colorless hair; they were emaciated, undersized, and lacked muscle tone or responsiveness. Sad and inactive, the two spent their days rocking and whining. (p. 5)

Though their chronological ages were 13 and 16 months, their development levels were 6 and 7 months, respectively.

It was impractical to place these children with foster parents or an adoption agency, so they were transferred to an institution for persons with mental retardation—not as residents, but as "house guests." Each girl was "adopted" by an older woman, who, under staff supervision, acted as a surrogate mother. The babies received the parental care and attention necessary for normal development, as well as appropriate levels of enrichment and stimulation. Six months after the transfer, Skeels rediscovered the two children (Bricker, 1986). He described them as "alert, smiling, running about, responding to the playful attention of adults, and generally behaving and looking like any other toddlers" (Skeels, 1966, p. 6).

Excited by this discovery, Skeels and Dye (1939) established an experimental group of thirteen children by selecting eleven more from the same orphanage. The mean IQ for the group was 64, and all but two of the children were classified as within the retarded range and thus by state law unsuitable for adoption. A contrast group of twelve orphanage children under three years of age was later selected for comparison. This contrast group comprised four girls and eight boys with an average IQ of 86. Only two of these children were classified as having mental retardation.

While the contrast group remained in the orphanage and received minimal health and medical services, each experimental subject received care on a one-to-one basis. Each "mother" (all were adolescents) was given instructions on how to care for "her" child. They were instructed and trained in how to hold, feed, change, talk to, and stimulate the young child. No other direct educational experiences were provided for the children.

Two years later (Skeels, 1942) the groups were retested, and the thirteen experimental children showed an average gain of 28 IQ points. Of the thirteen experimental children, eleven had IQs high enough to make them eligible for adoption, and they were placed in good homes.

In 1965, more than twenty-five years after the original study had begun, Skeels again located the subjects. His follow-up study reported that eleven of the thirteen had married, and apparently all but one of the marriages were still intact. These adults' mean level of education was twelfth grade; four had completed one or more years of college. All were either self-supporting or functioning as homemakers. Their occupations ranged from professional work and business to domestic service (the two who had not been adopted), and their income was consistent with national and state averages.

The contrast group showed an initial drop in mean IQ of 26 points and as a result were generally not eligible for adoption. When he located them in 1965, Skeels found that these eleven subjects (one had died) had a mean educational level of the third to fourth grade. Four of the subjects in the contrast group were institutionalized and unemployed and were costing the state approximately $200 per month each. Those who were employed, with one exception, were categorized as "hewers of wood and drawers of water." Peterson's (1987) summary of vocational outcomes for experimental and contrast subjects is presented in Table 5.3.

Skeels (1966) concludes his follow-up report with the following statement, which has served as the philosophical basis for many subsequent early intervention programs:

> It seems obvious that under present-day conditions there are still countless infants with sound biological constitutions and potentialities for development well within the normal range who will become retarded and noncontributing members of society unless appropriate intervention occurs. It is suggested by the findings of this study and others published in the past 20 years that sufficient knowledge is available to design programs of intervention to counteract the devastating effects of poverty, sociocultural, and maternal deprivation. . . . The unanswered questions of this study could form the basis for many life-long research projects. If the tragic fate of the twelve contrast group children provokes even a single crucial study that will help prevent such a fate for others, their lives will not have been in vain. (pp. 54–55)

TABLE 5.3

Occupational Achievements of Skeels and Dye (1939) Subjects

Experimental Group Subjects	Contrast Group Subjects
1 elementary school teacher	3 residents of institutions
1 registered nurse	3 dishwashers
1 licensed practical nurse	1 unskilled laborer
1 beautician	1 cafeteria worker
1 clerk	1 worked for institution where he had been a resident
1 airline stewardess	1 typesetter for a newspaper
2 domestics in a private home	1 had been in and out of one institution; during out one time lived
1 vocational counselor	with grandmother doing odd jobs for her
1 sales manager for estate agent	1 died in adolescence
1 staff-sergeant—Air Force	

Source: From *Early Intervention for Handicapped and At-Risk Children* (p. 34) by N. L. Peterson, 1986, Denver: Love Publishing Company. Reprinted by permission.

In the late 1960s, at the height of support for the environmental position, Skeels received a Kennedy Scientific Award for his research contribution (Dunn, 1973a). Participation in the ceremony by one of Skeels' experimental group subjects who had completed college was an impressive testimony to the potential of modifications in early childhood experiences.

Another research and intervention program concerning the question of environmentally caused mental retardation is the Milwaukee Project. It received much attention in professional journals as well as in the popular media (Garber, 1988; Garber & Heber, 1973; Heber & Garber, 1971). Garber and Heber (1973) referred to the project as a habilitative effort aimed at preventing intellectual deficiencies in children identified as at high risk. The project used an intensive educational program for very young children, beginning during the first few months of life. After a survey of inner-city living environments, Garber and Heber concluded that poverty conditions create a high risk of mental retardation by virtue of the mother's lower intelligence, socioeconomic status, and community of residence. According to Garber (1988), the project

> was a longitudinal study concerned with understanding the influence of family and/or home environments on the intellectual development of normal newborns for whom the survey data indicated high risk of declining intelligence test performance and who therefore were increasingly likely to be identified as mentally retarded by school age. (p. 5)

The intervention's design included two components: maternal rehabilitation and infant stimulation. Maternal rehabilitation was an attempt to enable the women to provide for their families better, and infant stimulation worked toward enhancing the psychosocial and intellectual environment in the home. Mothers with an IQ below 80 were the initial focus of the project, since the researchers found that 45.5 percent of the mothers studied who came under this heading accounted for more than 78 percent of the children with similarly low IQs. The groups ultimately participating in the full project included 17 experimental and 18 control subjects whose mothers had IQs below 75 (Garber, 1988).

The infant stimulation program began before the child reached the age of six months. Typically, a child and a teacher stayed in a one-to-one relationship until the infant reached ten months of age; at that time, the pair joined a second teacher–infant pair. At around fifteen months, the two children began instruction with only one teacher. At eighteen months, small groups were formed for teaching. The curriculum design focused on the major language, perceptive, motor, and cognitive needs that research had established for this group of children.

A detailed program of measurement included comparison on physical and developmental measures, intelligence scores, learning tasks, and language tests. When the children reached the age of seventy-two months, the mean IQs of the experimental children were reported to be about 32 points higher than those of the control children (119 vs. 87). Also encouraging was the fact that their IQs were about 11 points above those of a contrast group whose mothers had IQs above 100. In concluding their interim report, Garber and Heber (1973) noted:

> Infant testing difficulties notwithstanding, the present standardized test data, when considered along with performance on learning tasks and language tests, indicate an unquestionably superior present level of cognitive development on the part of the experimental group. (p. 10)

To affirm this finding, Garber (1988) noted that 39 percent of the control children had IQs below 75, while none of the experimental children did. Similar benefits accrued in problem-solving behaviors and language acquisition.

Garber's (1988) subsequent data analyses, however, were not as encouraging in several areas. Both experimental children and control children tended to do poorly later in school; the majority of both groups were below-average achievers in reading and mathematics by fourth grade. Fewer experimental children repeated grades or needed special assistance, but more of them had problems with "school deportment" (documented on report cards) than did the control group, and reports on both groups indicate continued evidence of poor self-concept and negative attitudes toward school. Nevertheless, the alluring results that Garber and Heber (1973) reported have supported the hypothesis that the declines in cognitive functioning typically prevalent in low socioeconomic populations can be reversed through early intervention.

Without question, the "Miracle in Milwaukee," as this project became known, was very influential in resurrecting the concept of compensatory ed-

BURTON BLATT: ON THE ACADEMICS OF NATURE–NURTURE

Just before his death, Burton Blatt, in his book *The Conquest of Mental Retardation* (1987), shared his thoughts about the field. One subject to which he returned several times was that of the academic warriors in the nature–nurture battle:

> Much has been written, and much has been ignored, concerning the work of scholars who have assumed polarized positions on the nature/nurture controversy. Burt was disgraced for alleged fudging and presenting nonexisting data. Heber apparently committed more financially oriented indiscretions. Skeels was once castigated and made the pariah, and years later Arthur Jensen found himself in similar circumstances. It almost appears as if those who insist on engaging in IQ controversy will get dirty—at least on the outside, and, so it seems, once in a while on the inside. The Harvard Psychologist R. J. Herrnstein (1982) has claimed that the press and other media distort the controversy entirely in favor of the environmentalists. He has plaintively recounted the rigorous manner in which every unseemly element of Cyril Burt's life, time and time again, came out in the magazines and newspapers; on the other hand, he found it less than amusing that hardly a word was mentioned in those same journals and newspapers concerning Heber's fall from grace. Herrnstein has expressed concern about why *The New York Times* never asks a psychometrist to review books on the nature/nurture controversy, warning us that an antitesting bias has infected the media and many leftist organizations and their contributors. He has claimed that powerful pressure groups in politics, education, and the judiciary seek to contain the knowledge that science could bring to this controversy. There are anti-psychologists, egalitarians, sociologists, and other citizens who do not like testing—who do not like pitting white capability against black capability, the socially disadvantaged against the affluent. Of course, while Herrnstein's view must be examined seriously, environmentalists might make the same case of media neglect and distortion of their work. And so the controversy continues—fueled not only by the prejudices sustaining the principals engaged in battle, but also by the prejudices of those who observe it, those who write about it, those who influence the larger society.

Source: From *The Conquest of Mental Retardation* (p. 314) by B. Blatt, 1987, Austin, TX: PRO-ED. Copyright 1987 by PRO-ED. Reprinted by permission.

ucation. But over the years, questions arose that tarnished the miraculous appearance of the program. Even in the afterglow of the initial publicity, Page (1972) raised concerns about several aspects of the program. He questioned in particular the possible bias in sampling of the population under study, the testing procedures, and the inaccessibility of the project data to external review by professionals. Page and Grandon (1981) noted:

> The Milwaukee Project . . . seems seldom to have appeared in referred science journals, and details remain clouded. Yet its fame has been remarkable, particularly for its central claim: Working with available materials and intensive personal attention, we may raise children 30 IQ points; indeed, we may move them from dull normal to superior in intelligence.

If this claim is true then the Milwaukee Project deserves its apparent image as the high-water mark of environmentalist accomplishment. And, repeatedly, writers advocating interventions have cited this project as such, even though it only had, as it in effect still has, the status of press releases supported with occasional brief, undetailed addresses to uncritical professional audiences. An event of this kind, whether or not properly understood, can take on a mythic quality and become a pillar in one's ideology about the origins of human nature and the proper directions for social reform. (p. 240)

While the Milwaukee Project stands as a symbolic representation of the value of environmental intervention, the research underlying it is only now emerging from a host of methodological and legal issues. Burton Blatt (1987) eloquently responded to the controversies that have been associated with the work of Rick Heber on this project as well as with other researchers in the area of the inheritance of intelligence. He stated:

Nowhere in the social sciences has there been more controversy, more battle, more acrimony, more scandal than in the mental retardation research connected with intelligence, its meaning, and its modifiability. In a sense, the concept of intelligence is the quintessential social science battlefield, and the IQ is the battle cry that goads people who otherwise know better to assume extreme and untenable positions as well as to engage in foolish, unseemly, and sometimes dishonest behavior. It's a commentary on the unfortunate state of affairs, as well as a reflection of the general pessimism concerning the possibility that capability is educable, that there exists a shadow upon the work and the persons—unfortunately, also the many honest and competent persons—involved in efforts to enhance educability. (p. 53)

HEREDITY POSITION

The study of the role of heredity in causing mental retardation has a long and somewhat tortuous history. Family pedigree studies at the turn of the century (e.g., Goddard, 1912) fueled the fire of the eugenics scare by applying Mendel's theories of the simple genetic transmission of traits to the infinitely more complex issue of human intelligence. Despite obvious flaws (see Kanner, 1964; Smith, 1985), studies of mental retardation and genetics became inexorably joined. The early 20th-century assumption that intelligence is a fixed, stable trait merged comfortably with this perspective (Smith, 1985).

A number of prominent scholars have continued to advocate the genetic determinism position. They include Arthur Jensen, Sir Cyril Burt, Richard Herrnstein, and Charles Murray. When we review the hypotheses of these powerful advocates, however, we must not lose sight of the researchers and theoreticians who take a more moderate position. The assumption underlying most genetic models is the polygenic inheritance of intelligence as discussed earlier in the chapter. Some bases for this position are discussed next.

Social Class Differences in Intelligence

A strong genetic position has direct implications for the social class differences that have been noted in intelligence testing results. Social classes thus become perceived as "breeding populations" that produce an inevitable correlation between intelligence and the genetic base for each class (Jensen, 1969). Social mobility could theoretically increase this correlation, because the more able individuals would rise in class level, while the least able would drop to, or remain within, the lower class. The hypothetical outcome of this mobility is gene pools within the social classes. In theory, gene pools would determine the genetic makeup of future generations.

In a highly mobile society, advocates of genetic determinism suggest, variance in intelligence within groups is constantly being transformed to variance between groups. Given equal opportunity, the classes should increasingly reflect differences in biologically determined ability, as opposed to arbitrary social discrimination (Herrnstein & Murray, 1994).

If one accepts genetic determinism, the higher prevalence of mild retardation among lower-class children becomes perceived as a direct function of inheritance within the social group. This conclusion is seemingly compatible with the oft-cited study of Reed and Reed (1965), who researched family histories and concluded that approximately 1 to 2 percent of the fertile family members with retardation in one generation are responsible for 30 to 40 percent of the persons in the next generation who are retarded.

The strong genetic stance is highly controversial. In a society dedicated to a belief in equality, adopting this position has powerful implications. Underlying any biological intervention to promote equality would be prevention of the birth of children with retardation through birth control or genetic engineering. While genetic engineering offers exciting challenges for the near future, the idea of socially mandated birth control and sterilization is only a new segment in the continuing saga of the eugenics movement. Sterilization is hardly a new idea; it has historically been the treatment of choice in tens of thousands of cases of people with retardation throughout the country. Revelations in the 1970s in Virginia, for example, indicate that as many as 8,000 persons were, without their knowledge, legally sterilized in state institutions between the height of the eugenics scare in the 1920s and the early 1970s (Smith, 1989b, Smith & Polloway, 1993). Although more recent proposals advocate voluntary sterilization, the history of sterilization and the nebulous zone between informed consent and involuntary treatment cast doubt on whether any such programs could be truly voluntary.

Although legislatures have revoked many of the laws enacted during the eugenics scare, the specter of sterilization is bound to haunt us as long as the strongly deterministic genetic perspective receives serious attention. Informed consent is not emphasized with such procedures among this population, since parental approval can often supersede individual consent. It is critical that anyone discussing so-called eugenic measures distinguish between disorders clearly associated with genetic transmission (e.g., PKU, Tay-Sachs disease) and those whose causes remain uncertain, such as psychosocial retardation.

The Sterilization of Carrie Buck

In 1927, a young woman named Carrie Buck was sexually sterilized. Without understanding or agreeing to what was being done to her, Buck's ability to bear children was taken away from her. *The Sterilization of Carrie Buck* by J. David Smith (1989b) tells her story.

Carrie Buck was the first person to be sterilized under Virginia's law that allowed the state to impose the surgery on people judged incompetent and likely to pass their deficiency on to offspring. The unwed Buck had a child, was diagnosed as being "feeble-minded," and was placed in an institution when she was eighteen years old. She was then chosen as the test case of the constitutionality of the law. Carrie Buck's mother had been institutionalized before her, and it was claimed that her infant daughter also showed signs of mental deficiency. To the physicians, lawyers, and politicians who wished to see the validity of the law upheld, she seemed the perfect test case. Their judgment proved sound. The Supreme Court, in *Buck v. Bell* (1927), supported the constitutionality of the law under which Virginia sterilized Carrie Buck and thousands of others. The same law became the model for sterilization statutes in other states and in European countries, including Nazi Germany.

Justice Oliver Wendell Holmes wrote the majority opinion in Carrie Buck's case. His opinion included the famous phrase, "three generations of imbeciles are enough." His reasoning was consistent with the view that mental retardation is most often hereditary and that people who are mentally retarded are a primary source of crime and social problems. The argument was made that sterilization would help stem this flood of incompetence.

After institutionalization and separation from her infant daughter, Buck never saw her again. The child, Vivian, the "third generation of imbeciles," grew up to be an attractive child and an honor roll student. Her mother, the "second generation of imbeciles," was "paroled" to a mountain village, where she soon married the deputy sheriff. Later in her life she was entrusted with the care and comforting of elderly and chronically ill people. Friends and employers attest to the fact that she was never mentally retarded.

Carrie Buck's story is a tragic example of an injured life, but it is also a warning, for it illustrates that mental retardation is a social phenomenon that involves arbitrary definitions and value judgments. Her story embodies a particularly important lesson for people working in the field of mental retardation, who most need to be sensitive to the social and political implications of their work.

Data Base

A key concern in terms of the hereditary position is the validity of the data base. For example, some have raised objections to the use of the figure of 0.80 for the heritability of intelligence. No trait's heritability is fixed; heritability is always bound to a distinct population, period of time, and developmental situation (Scarr-Salapatek, 1971a, 1971b). Any trait can change greatly over generations from the influence of environment. Establishing heritability figures within a specific group does not permit assumptions to be made between groups (Gage, 1972).

Second, we must ask: How valid is the use of several of the identical twin studies (i.e., Burt, 1966; Juel-Nielsen, 1965; Newman, Freeman, & Holzinger, 1937; Shields, 1962) as a data base for generating hypotheses on the importance of genetic inheritance? In one of the most scathing attacks on the foundations of the genetic position, Kamin (1974) questions whether many of the identical twins studied had in fact been reared apart. For example, after reviewing the original case studies from the reports of Newman et al. (1937), Kamin offers the following analysis of this specific twin pair, allegedly reared apart:

> Ed and Fred's separation is at one point in the text described as "complete until their first meeting at 24 years of age." Further, "they lived without knowledge of each other's existence for twenty-five years." Their genes, during this period, appear to have impelled them to remarkably similar experiences. They each worked as electrical repair men for the telephone company, and each owned a fox terrier named Trixie. The case study, however, reports that "they even went to the same school for a time, but never knew that they were twin brothers. They had even noticed the remarkable resemblance between them, but they were not close companions. When the twins were about eight years old, their families were permanently separated." This simply does not square with the earlier account of no knowledge of each other's existence for 25 years. . . .
>
> The case study includes a photograph of the twins side-by-side "at the time of their first meeting. . . ." The twins are remarkably alike in appearance. They are wearing identical pinstriped suits, and identical striped ties. These, of course, might have been bought "at the time of their first meeting." (1974, pp. 53–54)*

Kamin (1974) further elaborates on the possible sources of bias within the selections of subjects for the Newman et al. (1937) study.

> The twins were rewarded with considerable newspaper and magazine publicity; one threatened a legal suit because a magazine had described her as intellectually inferior to her twin. There was also a very tangible inducement offered to all twins. . . . "Pair after pair, who had previously been unmoved by appeals to the effect that they owed it to science and society to permit us to study them, could not resist the offer of a free, all-expenses paid trip to the Chicago Fair." To qualify for this reward, the twins had to attest to the fact that they had been separated, and that they were remarkably alike.
>
> This raises a very serious issue. The facts about separation, in all the twin studies, depend heavily upon the verbal account of the twins themselves. When there are not tangible inducements, the twins are exhorted to make themselves available in the name of science. They receive free medical examinations, and enormous amounts of detailed individual attention from distinguished scientists. They could scarcely be blamed if, in a misguided effort to cooperate with science, or to bolster a sense of their unique worth, they were to stretch a fact or two. (p. 54)*

The other twin studies have been criticized along similar lines. Kamin (1974) describes several of the twins, again supposedly reared apart, who participated in the Shields (1962) study:

> Bertram and Christopher were separated at birth. "The paternal aunts decided to take one twin each and have brought them up amicably, living next door to one another in the same Midlands colliery village. . . . They are constantly in and out of each other's houses" (p. 50). Odette and Fanny were separated from birth until the age of 12. The conditions of their separation seem to have been worked out by a specialist in experimental design. From the age of 3 until the age of 8 the twins were rotated every 6 months, one going to the maternal grandmother and the other to the mother.*

Given these interesting revelations, we must remember that such research can be considered valid only if the data support the fact that the twins were reared in significantly different environments. Professionals have, unfortunately, often trivialized or even ignored this critical point (Smith, 1988b). The question of different environments in twin studies is very complex. Aldous (1992), in a discussion of this issue, has pointed out that researchers studying twins can divide the total variance in a psychological trait into three compartments, one genetic and the other two environmental: the shared and nonshared environments. He argues that twin studies have revealed that the shared family environment exerts little influence on traits like IQ and personality. Differences between individuals in one family are generally larger than would be predicted by environmental theories, he observes, and the nonshared environments of these individuals may account for much more of the variance between them.

Finally, critics have also raised questions about the data from the studies by Cyril Burt (1966), who had been the most respected authority in this field. The most damning assertion has been that Burt's data are fictional. His official biographer, Hearnshaw (1979), suggests that Burt invented many of the twins in his study, along with his two mysterious research collaborators, who may or may not have existed. As Hawkes (1979) concludes, this biography confirms the suspicion that Burt "engaged in deliberate deception, fabricated research data and invented nonexistent 'colleagues' to support his theories about intelligence" (p. 673). Gould (1981) explains that Burt's ruse was a way to circumvent the problem of the extreme rarity of identical twins reared apart.

Difficulties and deception notwithstanding, professionals continue to give considerable attention to these data bases and their implications. Scarr and Carter-Saltzman (1982) have provided a comprehensive review of the relation between genetics and intelligence. They noted that, although removing Burt's flawed research from collections of research on kinship groups reduced the magnitude of the heritability of intelligence (correlations for identical twins reared apart dropped from 0.84 to 0.74), both older and newer studies attest to a moderate genetic component. They concluded that the available data on both twin studies and adoption studies support the theory that heredity plays a major role in determining differences in intelligence between individuals.

As a less serious conclusion, consider the comments of Gould (1981) in his classic work, *The Mismeasure of Man:*

> If I had any desire to lead a life of indolent ease, I would wish to be an identical twin, separated at birth from my brother and raised in a different social class. We could hire ourselves out to a host of social scientists and practically name our fee. For we would be an exceedingly rare representative of the only really adequate natural experiment for separating genetic from environmental effects in humans— genetically identical individuals raised in disparate environments. (p. 234)

INTERACTIONAL POSITION

The interactional position holds that intellectual development cannot be attributed solely to either genetic or environmental determinants and admits the importance of both variables to intelligence—and, possibly, to retardation as well. A child functions at a certain level because of the interaction of inherited abilities and biological characteristics, as modified by environmental experiences. Thus, the position concedes genetic limitations but maintains that environmental variables can enhance or reduce the individual's development (Bricker, 1986). By stressing the influence of both variables, interaction avoids the oversimplification that occurs when individuals are reduced either to their genetic endowment or to the influences of their environment (J. D. Smith, 1988a).

Dobzhansky (1955) originally proposed the most commonly accepted model for examining the interaction of genetic and environmental components. He theorized that inherited characteristics and constitutional restrictions (genotype) create a *range of reaction* within which a human trait develops. The behavior pattern that a person develops within this genetically endowed range is a function of the environment. The behavior that results from the interaction is called the *phenotype.*

Gottesman (1963) translated Dobzhansky's (1955) concepts into a schematic paradigm, presented in Figure 5.8. Gottesman's hypothesized range for phenotypic development greatly increases as a function of genotype. Individuals with poor genetic endowment (genotype A), such as victims of recessive trait disorders or chromosomal abnormalities, may have a smaller range for phenotypic development regardless of environment. Those blessed with a richer genetic endowment (genotype D) have an extensive range for potential development.

The actual magnitude of range of reaction cannot be established, particularly for an individual case, and to reduce human development to an arithmetical equation is scarcely reasonable (Lewontin, Rose, & Kamin, 1984; Smith, 1988a). Nevertheless, estimates have placed the general range of reaction in the vicinity of 20 to 25 IQ points (Begab, 1981; Zigler & Balla, 1981). Accepting such a figure certainly encourages us to develop effective

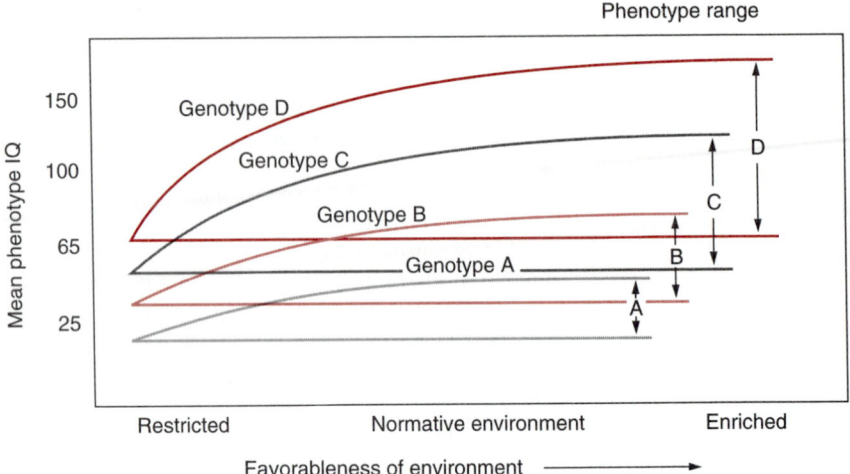

FIGURE 5.8
Estimates of Reaction Range for Hypothetical Genotypes

Source: From *Handbook of Mental Deficiency* (p. 255) edited by N. R. Ellis, 1963, New York: McGraw-Hill. Copyright 1963 by McGraw-Hill. Reprinted by permission.

intervention programs, but at the same time it falls short of promising total prevention of mild retardation. As Zigler and Seitz (1982) noted, such a middle ground between a dogmatic genetic or environment position has "the advantage of generating energetic willingness to attempt interventions without unrealistic expectations about what they can accomplish" (p. 615).

Although there are still "genetic radicals" and "blank slate extremists" who are plying their trades, most scientists and practitioners have come to believe that heredity and environment cannot be separated. As most people have embraced the interactional perspective, the idea that the nature–nurture controversy is waning has become quite popular; some feel that the debate is dead. However, a cursory look at the literature reveals that strong genetic arguments are still being made (Smith, 1994). Equally true is that environmental determinism is still quite pervasive both in the sciences and in social sciences. The nature–nurture controversy has not been resolved. The concepts of determinism and reductionism, of reducing human beings to simple organisms that are programmed in all of their actions, still reign in the arenas of both heredity and environment.

In their book, *Not In Our Genes,* Lewontin et al. (1984) explain that the relationships between heredity and environment are complex in ways that have never been adequately encompassed by simple reductionist arguments. In the same way that hereditarian reductionism has misportrayed human beings as the mere products of genes, extreme cultural determinism has inaccurately portrayed people as simply the product of family circumstances, social class, and the random environmental events they have encountered. They feel that environmental determinism is just as wrong, indeed, just as absurd, as biological determinism. Lewontin and his colleagues argue that both of these reductionistic approaches share an arithmetical fallacy: that the life of a human being can be partitioned neatly into a biological proportion and an environmental proportion.

Lewontin et al. (1984) observe that a move in the right direction was made by those who advocate the interactionist model of human nature. However, they see interactionism as an insufficient model for understanding the human condition. A major flaw that they perceive in the interactional model is that it actually supposes an alienation between the individual and the environment. This alienation draws a clean line of demarcation between the person and the environment and portrays the environment as acting upon the human being (and in this sense "interacting") while forgetting that the person acts on the environment.

Lewontin et al. (1984) offer a different model, which they call "interpenetration," for human development. From this perspective, people do not simply adapt to previously existing conditions, but themselves define their environments. They are viewed as creating and transforming the world by their own actions. Lewontin and his colleagues believe that, "just as there is no organism without an environment, there is no environment without an organism" (1984, p. 273). From this perspective, neither the human being nor the environment is a closed system. The person is open to the environment and the environment is open to the person.

The major theme of their discussion is that all human beings are not simply the results of, but are also the creators of, their own environments. From this perspective, development is viewed as a process of codevelopment between the organism and its environment. Thus, at every juncture, the developing mind, which is partially the consequence of past events and biological conditions, is also engaged in an active re-creation of the world in which it exists. Therefore, any serious account of psychological development must specify not only the influence of heredity and environment, but also the way in which the individual penetrates these factors, how he or she creates environments. From this perspective, we see the individual human being as actively interpreting the world, making choices, and therefore, altering his or her own reality. It is an interesting challenge to think of retardation in the terms presented by Lewontin and his colleagues (1984), and to consider whether the real challenge for those who work with children and adults with mental retardation is to equip them not only to adapt to the environment but to change it in ways that will make them truly active in defining their own lives.

PREVENTION

The purpose of this section is to survey the tools, techniques, and procedures that assist in the process of preventing retardation. Progress has been particularly significant during the last forty years. Inspired by a government

FIGURE 5.9

The Developmental Continuum of Risk

Source: From "The Impact of Definitions of Higher Risk on Services to Infants and Toddlers" by M. Graham and K. G. Scott, 1988, *Topics in Early Childhood Special Education, 8*(3), p. 25. Adapted by permission.

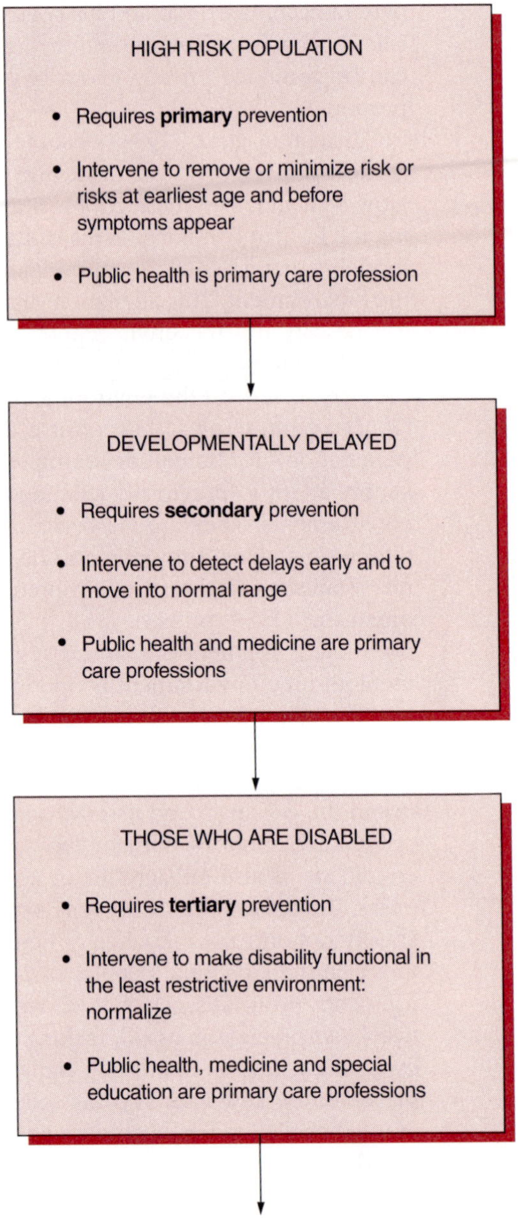

HIGH RISK POPULATION

- Requires **primary** prevention

- Intervene to remove or minimize risk or risks at earliest age and before symptoms appear

- Public health is primary care profession

DEVELOPMENTALLY DELAYED

- Requires **secondary** prevention

- Intervene to detect delays early and to move into normal range

- Public health and medicine are primary care professions

THOSE WHO ARE DISABLED

- Requires **tertiary** prevention

- Intervene to make disability functional in the least restrictive environment: normalize

- Public health, medicine and special education are primary care professions

commitment to prevent the occurrence of 50 percent of all cases of retardation by the end of the century (President's Committee on Mental Retardation, 1976b), researchers have tackled virtually all causes of retardation. In every *known* case, a specific preventive measure has been identified.

Graham and Scott (1988) developed a comprehensive model for conceptualizing prevention (Figure 5.9). They distinguish three levels of prevention:

TABLE 5.4

Elements of a Comprehensive Prevention Program

Prenatal Strategies
Ensure family planning and timing of pregnancies.
Provide genetic counseling.
Test for genetic carriers.
Provide adequate prenatal care and diagnostics.
Reduce teenage pregnancy rates.
Reduce births out of wedlock.
Avoid alcohol and other teratogenic substances during pregnancy.

Perinatal Strategies
Screen newborns for disorders.
Screen newborns for diseases (e.g., HIV).
Provide early intervention for at-risk infants (e.g., those born prematurely).

Preschool Strategies
Enroll children in early intervention programs.
Provide parental education and support.
Avoid lead in environment.
Avoid hazards associated with brain injury.
Reduce occurrences of child abuse and neglect.
Use safety restraints in vehicles.
Immunize for diseases.
Provide proper medical care and treatment.
Plan for appropriate transition to school.

School Preventive Strategies
Provide effective instruction and relevant curriculum.
Involve parents in education.
Provide a family life curriculum to future parents.

Federal and State Policy Strategies
Commit to a reduction in poverty.
Reduce the prevalence of homelessness.
Provide public information about prevention.
Support comprehensive prevention programs.
Develop and provide universal health-care programs.

primary—risk conditions can be eliminated so that a condition never comes into existence; *secondary* preventive efforts reduce or eliminate the effects of an existing risk factor; and *tertiary* intervention assists a child who has a disability. Further, Crocker (1992) has identified the specific activities associated with a comprehensive prevention program. These are adapted for Table 5.4. These considerations are implicit in the discussions that follow.

PRECONCEPTION

Preventive measures taken before conception can avert hereditary, innate, congenital, and other constitutional disorders. One basic tool is genetic counseling, an attempt to determine risks of occurrence or recurrence of specific genetic or chromosomal disorders. The tools of the genetic counselor include the family history and personal screening. Study of the persons' genetic and general medical history is particularly concerned with evidence of spontaneous abortions or stillbirths, relatives' age at death and causes of death, and the existence of any intrafamily marriages that might bear on the presence of specific genetic disorders. Screening is primarily for carriers of recessive trait disorders. Blood samples can be analyzed rather easily and inexpensively. Based on an understanding of the mathematical probabilities associated with recessive, dominant, or sex-linked inheritance, prospective parents can make an informed decision about the risks of having a child who may be developmentally disabled.

Other specific means of prevention are also available during this period. Immunization for maternal rubella can prevent women from contracting this disease during pregnancy. Blood tests can identify the presence of venereal diseases. Adequate maternal nutrition can lay a sound metabolic foundation for later childbearing. Family planning in terms of size, appropriate spacing, and age of parents can also affect a variety of specific causal agents.

DURING GESTATION

Two general approaches to prevention during pregnancy are prenatal care and analysis for possible genetic disorders. Numerous prenatal precautions can be taken to avert congenital problems. Adequate nutrition, fetal monitoring, and protection from disease are certainly the foundations of prenatal care. Avoidance of teratogenic substances resulting both from exposure (e.g., radiation) and from personal consumption (e.g., alcohol and drugs) also relate specifically to this period.

Analysis of the fetus for the possible presence of genetic or chromosomal disorders is a key component of genetic counseling. This analysis includes amniocentesis, chorionic villi sampling (CVS), fetoscopy, fetal biopsy, and ultrasound. **Amniocentesis** involves drawing amniotic (embryonic sac) fluid for biochemical analysis of fetal cells. It is usually performed during the fourteenth to sixteenth week of pregnancy. This procedure is depicted in Figure 5.10. In the majority of cases where amniocentesis is used, its primary purpose has been the detection of such chromosomal errors as Down syndrome.

Generally, the technique is safe. However, the patient should be informed of certain considerations including the risk of about 0.5 percent or less of a miscarriage, the possibility of an unsuccessful culture of fetal cells, and the possibility of disorders remaining undiagnosed by the procedure. More recently, the procedure has been used earlier in gestation, but the risks are slightly increased.

A more recent technique for prenatal diagnosis is CVS, which can also provide information on chromosomal and biochemical anomalies. In CVS, chorionic tissue (fluffy material that forms the placenta) is withdrawn. The test can be performed after approximately nine weeks of gestation with initial results (chromosomal analysis) within two days, and a full culture two weeks after sampling. The most significant advantage of the process is that it allows an earlier analysis of fetal status. It has been estimated that CVS is associated with a risk rate for miscarriage and other complications only slightly higher than that for amniocentesis (about 1 percent or less).

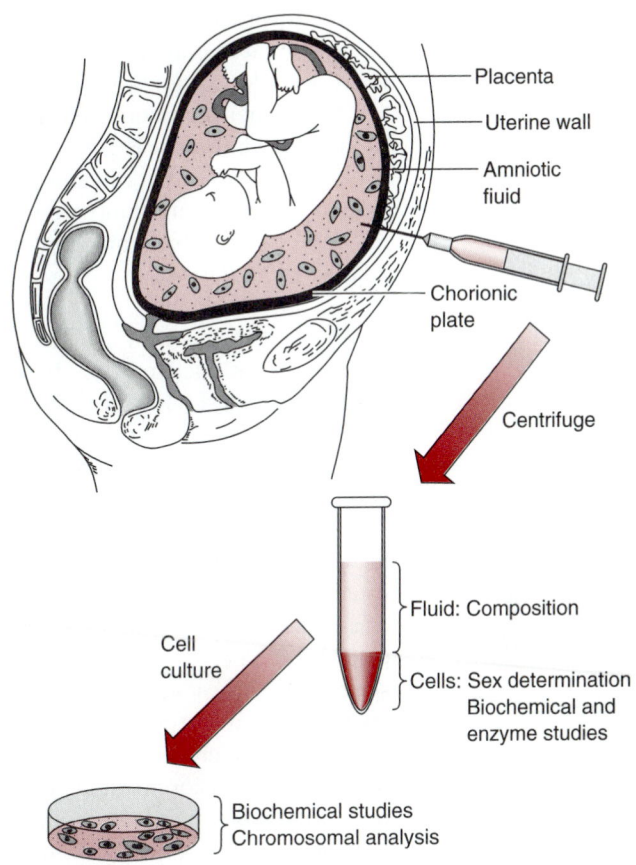

FIGURE 5.10
Amniocentesis

Source: From *Fetal Monitoring and Fetal Assessment in High-Risk Pregnancy* by S. M. Tucker, 1978, St. Louis: C. V. Mosby. Copyright 1978 by C. V. Mosby. Reprinted by permission.

These two analytical techniques have three purposes. Most encouraging, of course, is that negative tests assuage parental fears or anxieties. Second, the result can confirm suspicions of disorders and give the parents a chance to determine what to expect. They also may alert the physician to the need for careful monitoring prenatally, perinatally, and postnatally. Finally, the information can be used as a basis for decisions about abortion. The use of these techniques along with elective abortion has significantly reduced the occurrence of a number of specific disorders, although obviously it has also generated much controversy.

Pueschel (1991) stresses that genetic counseling never results in value-free messages to parents. Professionals should not advocate a particular action but must transmit factual data and present alternatives. In the case of a genetic disorder, he notes that this could include termination of pregnancy or allowing it to continue to term and, in the latter case, either caring for the child or seeking adoption.

One other technique that has contributed to an understanding of the prenatal environment is *ultrasound,* or *sonography.* This technique can be used for possible determination of hydrocephalus, some central nervous system disorders, and limb anomalies. The technique is also used to determine the location for amniocentesis, to assist in delivery, and as a common adjunct to *fetal therapy,* which seeks to correct conditions existing in utero.

AT DELIVERY

Prevention at delivery is based on anticipating possible problems. Pregnancies deserving of special attention include those involving very young or older mothers, mother's low socioeconomic status, inconsistent prenatal care, closely spaced pregnancies, drug exposure during pregnancy, and a history of previous children with genetic disorders.

Several specific measures are associated with the perinatal period. The most common is the Apgar test of vital signs (Apgar, 1953), an evaluation routinely given in American hospitals at one and five minutes after the birth of a child. The physician rates each of the following factors on a scale of 0 to 2: heart rate, respiratory effort, muscle tone, skin color, and reflex response. An Apgar score of 8 to 10 suggests the newborn is healthy and responsive; scores of 5 to 7 and 0 to 4 indicate moderate and severe depression, respectively. Initial screening using such a scale can assist in preliminary decision making about children who may be at risk for specific disorders, and a more comprehensive assessment then follows. Intensive intervention can begin almost immediately for premature and other infants identified as having a particular difficulty.

Computer-assisted obstetric measures assist in the close monitoring of both mother and child, and another helpful measure during the first three days after birth is injection of Rh immunoglobulin serum, as described earlier (see section entitled, "Maternal Disease"). If a child is born to a mother who did not have the necessary series of injections in the course of a previous pregnancy, a complete transfusion of the newborn's blood can prevent the destruction of its blood cells by the mother's antibodies.

EARLY CHILDHOOD

Several types of intervention are important during early childhood. Proper nutrition is critical throughout development, but particularly so during the first six months. Dietary restrictions for specific metabolic disorders should be maintained until no longer required. Avoidance of hazards in the child's environment can prevent brain injury, and avoidance of exposure to substances such as lead are mandatory to proper development.

An exciting area of activity has been the use of early intervention programs as a basis for the primary or secondary prevention of psychosocial

Developmental deficiencies may result from improper nutrition.

problems associated with retardation and other disabilities. Because mild disabilities are most often diagnosed after the child begins school, these efforts generally concentrate not solely on previously identified children but on children living in poverty who are "high risk" for later school-related difficulties. Programs of note and validated procedures for early intervention are discussed in detail in Chapter 8.

PERSPECTIVE

The preceding discussion has highlighted a variety of preventive measures that target the various causes of retardation discussed earlier. For biological causes, the advances of the last forty years have been breathtaking. In terms of psychosocial causes, the successes that have been achieved are tempered by the obvious need for greater commitment. Whether our society is willing to devote the necessary resources to breaking the poverty cycle and altering the effects of psychosocial causes, with the goal of reducing the prevalence of retardation, is still an unanswered question. Governmental commitment, especially at the federal level, is very important.

It is clear that, regardless of whether or not a child already has a disability, growing up in restricting conditions interferes with a child's opportunity to develop and mature as well as his or her more privileged peers. The negative consequences of an unstimulating environment must be diminished through the most promising intervention strategies. As Baroff (1974) wrote twenty-five years ago, "Equality of opportunity is a ghastly charade if individuals are so stunted by early experiences as to be unable to take advantage of the opportunities our society offers" (p. 116). By facilitating children's cognitive, academic, social, and emotional development, we increase the chances of having a future population of healthy, self-sufficient, mature adults. Intervention strategies with a preventive aim must work to identify children at risk and establish strategies designed to facilitate the development of each one of them.

ETHICAL ISSUES

The incredible advances in the medical technology of the past several decades have enabled doctors and other professionals to sustain the lives of many people with disabilities who in an earlier time would have died prematurely. As a by-product of these medical advances, however, both the medical profession and society in general have been confronted with the need to evaluate the active and passive measures now available. It is critical to consider carefully the actions that can be taken before and after birth, once a specific disability has been identified.

Our earlier discussion of amniocentesis focused on its use to detect specific genetic disorders, especially Down syndrome. Gradually, this practice has come under increased scrutiny. Public encouragement to screen for the disorder has led to an increase in the number of abortions of fetuses found to be affected. As Smith (1981) noted,

> The ease with which the abortion of Down syndrome fetuses is accepted as the best alternative, even by people who otherwise oppose abortion, may be related to the conventional wisdom or popular misunderstanding of the level of mental retardation or other disabilities associated with this condition. (p. 9)

Smith questioned whether children with Down syndrome had become defined as an out-group, something less than human, through the process of *pseudospeciation,* that is, placing certain human beings in a separate "species" on the basis of group characteristics like race or disability.

The question of selective abortion of individuals with disabilities concerns more than just Down syndrome. Lehr and Brown (1984) summarized the arguments in favor of the practice as including the possible need for intensive medical surgery, the potentially negative effects on the family (e.g., financial difficulty of caring for the child), and the drain of valuable resources from society. Included in the reasons against the practice are opposition to

Some children will always be recognized as being different. However this fact should not interfere with their being accepted.

abortion in general, presumed devaluation of the humanness of persons who are disabled, and possible spillover effects into services for young children (if the fetus does not have the right to life, why should the child be entitled to support?). Ultimately, as Lehr and Brown (1984) noted, the resolution of the issue has come down to the legal question of the parents' right to make the decision about whether or not to give birth to the child.

A second major ethical concern is the question of the right to life after birth of children who are disabled. Newspaper accounts of the cases of Baby Doe in Indiana; Baby Jane Doe in New York; Phillip Becker, a California teenager with Down syndrome; and Baby Gabriel in Canada sensitized the public to issues that for years were quietly debated in professional circles. In most cases, the argument is whether a child's disability should be a primary factor in the decision to provide maximum medical care. In addition to the important legal questions involved, philosophical issues are also significant in this arena.

Orelove and Sobsey (1984) summarized the debates surrounding ethics and moral values as reflecting several positions in reference to individuals with severe disabilities. These positions include the following:

- Treat all nondying newborns, with focus only on medical indications for treatment.
- Terminate the lives of selected nonpersons, with the justification that non-treatment is appropriate if an infant is defective and thus not counted as a person.
- Withhold treatment according to parental discretion, on the assumption that care could be withheld as an act of mercy to the infant and for relief to the suffering parents.
- Withhold treatment according to quality of life, with decisions based on the potential for so-called meaningful life.
- Withhold treatment judged not in the child's best interests, under the presumption that the treatment would maintain a burden of existence for the infant. (pp. 341–343)

A third ethical issue receiving attention is that of using the organs of infants born with anencephaly—a condition of absence of the cranial vault and virtual absence of the brain except for the brain stem—for transplantation to young children with heart or kidney disorders. Coulter (1988a) discusses the unique issues that surround the practice of transplanting organs from infants who are virtually but not technically brain dead. Again the ethical and legal dilemmas stemming from medical advances are well illustrated.

A fourth ethical issue is that of "Do Not Resuscitate Orders" for persons with special needs. Given the complexity of the medical needs of some individuals, this area promises to be of great concern in the future. Smith's (1995) discussion of John Lovelace, an adult with mental retardation who was deinstitutionalized, provides a vivid discussion of this issue.

The increased attention to ethical issues demands the scrutiny and advocacy of professional educators. In fact, as Smith (1989a) has noted, special educators may often be better informed than physicians concerning the possibilities and potentialities for the lives of children with disabilities. They are in a unique position to act as advocates. In this vein, the Division on Mental Retardation of the Council for Exceptional Children (CEC-MR) promulgated a position statement (Smith, 1988b) that supports the right to life for persons with mental retardation and encourages professional advocacy (see the accompanying box).

It is not the purpose of this brief discussion to conclude with a specific recommendation. Rather, we conclude by stressing that professionals must carefully evaluate their positions on these issues and be prepared to express and defend them.

A Position Statement on the Right of Children with Mental Retardation to Life Sustaining Medical Care and Treatment

Position Statement

The Board of Directors of the Division on Mental Retardation of the Council for Exceptional Children resolves that the fact that a person is born with mental retardation or acquires mental retardation during development is not a justifiable reason, in and of itself, for terminating the life of that person. Mental retardation alone is not a nullification of quality or worth in an individual's life and should not be used as a rationale for the termination of life through direct means nor the withholding of nourishment or life sustaining procedures.

Background

The issue of pediatric euthanasia is complex and troubling to professionals in the field of mental retardation. A most basic question posed by this dilemma is that of who is to make the decision to deny treatment or nourishment to a child who has mental retardation. Most often involved in this decision are parents, physicians, and, in most cases which become public, the courts. Arguments have been made for and against the role of each of these parties in making such a decision.

Support for parents as decision makers derives from the concept that children are the property of their parents and that they have the final voice in any crucial matter concerning their offspring. Critics of this view believe that parents are often emotionally distraught and lack adequate information on which to base their decision when faced with such a dilemma. Their decision may be unduly influenced by fears concerning raising the child or of institutional placement.

Physicians often feel that they are in the best position to make an objective decision. It has been observed, however, that they often are motivated by their perception of what will prevent suffering in the family. It is argued that physicians should not be the decision makers because their duty is to preserve life, not to judge which lives deserve preservation.

Parents of newborns and physicians have rarely had the opportunity to experience living or working with individuals having mental retardation across the course of their lives. As special educators serving children with disabilities from infancy through adulthood, the Board of Directors of CEC-MR observes that mental retardation alone does not necessarily cause a life of pain, suffering or absence of life quality for the affected persons, and that it should not imply a justification for the termination of life. Research and experience with persons having mental retardation demonstrate that all people can learn, all can participate (at least partially) in the wide range of human experiences and most become productive citizens and are valued human beings by persons who truly know them. It is with these factors in mind that CEC-MR takes a public position on this issue.

FINAL THOUGHTS

Hundreds of specific factors have been identified as causes of mental retardation and developmental disabilities. Nevertheless, in the vast majority of individual cases, a specific cause cannot be identified.

To understand etiology, we must first understand the principles of genetics, since a large percentage of biological causes stem from recessive, dominant, and sex-linked inheritance and from chromosomal abnormalities. Other causes include prenatal infections and intoxications, brain injury, malnutrition, cranial malformations, disorders related to pregnancy, and environmental influence.

The environmental position claims that a number of specific external factors, especially as related to poverty, may negatively affect development. Such classical environmental intervention studies as the longitudinal research of Harold Skeels have given this position an empirical grounding. The heredity position is based on assumptions about the frequency of retardation found in families from lower social class backgrounds. Support for this viewpoint has come from family pedigree studies and twins research. This position carries implications for controversial, biologically oriented intervention measures. Accepting either the environmental position or the concept of the interaction position between heredity and environment demands a commitment to intensive intervention with young children.

Prevention of retardation requires an intensive program that begins before conception and continues throughout the developmental period. Every specifiable cause of retardation has a preventive measure of one type or another.

Advances in medical technology have created ethical problems that society must face. Each person must accept the responsibility of becoming informed on these issues and developing her or his own position.

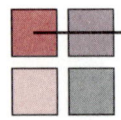

SUMMARY

INTRODUCTION

■ The cause of mental retardation is often a complex issue.

■ Professionals in the field of mental retardation need to have a general awareness of causes.

■ Terminology used to describe various etiologies comes from three sources: conventional wisdom, names of specific people, biomedical vocabulary.

GENETIC AND CHROMOSOMAL DEVIATIONS

- Genetics is the study of heredity with a particular focus on genes.
- Mental retardation can result from problems with genetic material on either autosomes or sex chromosomes.
- Karyotypes are the resultant charting of chromosomes.
- The most recognizable condition associated with chromosomal anomalies is Down syndrome.
- Fragile X syndrome is another type of anomaly.

OTHER ETIOLOGICAL DOMAINS

- Cranial malformations involve conditions such as hydrocephaly.
- Many different toxic substances can significantly affect prenatal and postnatal development.
- Prematurity and other perinatal factors are related to a number of birth defects, including limited intellectual capacity.
- Events such as head injuries and child abuse can also contribute to mental retardation.

PSYCHOSOCIAL CONCERNS AND ENVIRONMENTAL FACTORS

- Environmental factors are often associated with mental retardation and encompass a host of variables related to poverty, from parenting practices to health problems and daily living difficulties.
- A heredity perspective of explaining mental retardation is based on assumptions about the frequency of this condition found in families from lower social class backgrounds.
- An interaction position holds that intellectual development cannot be attributed solely to either genetic or environmental determinants and admits the importance of both variables.

PREVENTION

- Prevention of retardation requires an intensive program that begins before conception and continues throughout the developmental period.
- Every specifiable cause of retardation has a preventive measure of one type or another.

ETHICAL ISSUES

- Advances in medical technology have created ethical problems that society must face.

PART 2

Introduction to the Different Levels of Mental Retardation

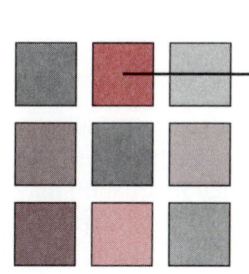

Characteristics of Individuals with Milder Forms of Mental Retardation

*After reading this chapter,
the student should be able to:*

- ■ Discuss the general descriptors and caveats that apply to this group.

- ■ Identify the demographic characteristics that describe this group.

- ■ Discuss those characteristics that affect performance in school and community: motivation, sociobehavioral, learning, speech and language, and physical and health characteristics.

- ■ Provide a description of educational placement, services received, and graduation rates.

Key Terms

educable mental retardation (EMR)	learned helplessness locus of control	trainable mental retardation (TMR)
grouping	mediation	

he best way to gain an understanding of individuals who are mildly mentally retarded is to spend time with those so labeled. We recognize, however, that many students enrolled in an introductory course in mental retardation may not have this opportunity. With this in mind, we designed this chapter to give the reader an understanding of the characteristics of this group.

CHARACTERISTICS OF MILDER RETARDATION

By definition, individuals who are mentally retarded are distinguished from people who are not retarded on the basis of intellectual functioning and adaptive skills. Significantly subaverage intellectual functioning has traditionally been described along a continuum of mild, moderate, severe, and profound, according to the degree to which a person's measured general intelligence deviates from the normal range. The term *adaptive behavior* historically has been used to convey the nature of one's personal independence and social responsibility.

In both of these domains, the amount or degree of deficit is of prime importance. According to the manual on definition offered by the American Association on Mental Retardation (AAMR, 1992), importance is given to the interaction of (a) the capabilities of the individual, (b) the various personal and social environments that one encounters on a daily or regular basis, and (c) the actual functional performance of the individual. Based on this interaction, persons who are mentally retarded will display different needs and require varying levels of assistance across adaptive skills areas.

In this chapter, we examine the characteristics and needs of individuals who require little or no support systems in most adaptive skills areas. In the next chapter, we take a closer look at individuals who require more intensive levels of support.

One erroneous generalization commonly applied to people who are mentally retarded is that they are "childlike." In numerous instances, adults who are mentally retarded have been treated like children. Referring to thirty-year-old adults as "kids" is not appropriate. Langness and Levine (1986) pointed out that this misguided perception allows us to consider persons with retardation "to be irresponsible[,] . . . to categorize them as incompetent[,] . . . to assume they inevitably have bad judgment, do not know what they want, and cannot be trusted[,] . . . to overprotect them and on the other hand to ignore them" (p. xi).

A discussion of stereotyping and its effects is presented in Chapter 3. See Chapter 3 for a discussion of the decrease in students classified as mentally retarded.

The characteristic behaviors discussed in this section are frequently observed among people who have various levels of retardation at different stages of life. As previously mentioned, many factors influence individual functioning and behavior. Some of these variables are organic involvement, disabling conditions such as sensory or orthopedic impairments, problems relating to health, the nature of environmental demands, the concern and resources of the family, the availability of services (both medical and educational), and the age at which the retardation was diagnosed and intervention was begun.

Individuals who are mildly retarded demonstrate adaptive behavior and intellectual functioning at the upper end of the retardation continuum. According to the most recent AAMR definition (1992), the assessed intellectual functioning of individuals who are retarded is an IQ standard score of approximately 70 to 75 or below, with concurrent deficits in adaptive skill areas.

Evidence suggests that the number of individuals who are mildly mentally retarded varies greatly from one locality to another. As discussed at length in Chapter 3, there has been an appreciable decrease in the number of students classified as mentally retarded since 1977, when PL 94-142 went into effect. This change has affected the group of individuals who are mildly retarded most dramatically.

Those who have been studying this phenomenon (MacMillan & Borthwick, 1980; Polloway & Smith, 1983) suggest that a "new" group of students is being identified as mildly mentally retarded and that people now classified in this group are lower functioning than those called "mildly mentally retarded" a decade ago. For this reason, it is not advisable to compare research results of ten or more years ago with more recent findings, as the subjects are likely to differ in many important independent variables. Similarly, many conclusions made about the "traditional" group may not hold for this "new" group of students.

While the slower rate at which children who are retarded develop motor, social, and language skills may be noticeably different from their peers, milder forms of retardation have often not been suspected until the children enter school. Frequently, a combination of difficulty with academic subjects and behavioral problems generates concern. Learning problems sometimes appear to be specific to one subject, such as reading, but more often they are recognized across subjects.

Children who do not have the verbal and communication skills of their age mates may withdraw from interpersonal relationships or seek attention in inappropriate ways. Inappropriate social behavior can result from any number of factors. These children may misbehave because they cannot clearly distinguish between acceptable and unacceptable standards of behavior. Problem behavior can also result from the frustrations of scholastic failure or as an attempt to gain acceptance from other children, who might encourage deviant behavior.

Mental and physical limitations do not imply that children cannot participate in exciting activities.

Some individuals who are retarded also have significant psychiatric disorders, resulting in a dual diagnosis. Reber (1992) remarked that there is a higher prevalence of these problems with children who are mentally retarded than with those who are not retarded. We present a more detailed discussion of this topic later in the chapter.

A number of terms have been used to describe individuals who have been identified formally as mentally retarded and subsequently provided with special education and related services. Even though the use of traditional labels for levels of retardation (mild, moderate, severe, and profound) is discouraged in the latest AAMR manual on definition, classification, and systems of supports, it is likely that many existing terms will continue to be used. This will happen because many states and provinces have established certain terminology, and it will take some time for this to change, even given the desire to do so.

Other terminology is used in certain states and provinces.

Two terms that have a long history of usage in school settings are **educable mental retardation (EMR)** and **trainable mental retardation (TMR).** Lately, these terms have fallen into disfavor with most professionals in the field; however, they are still used in certain locations. The term *EMR* referred to students whose abilities were adequate for them to profit from an academically oriented curriculum; *TMR* referred to students whose programs emphasized the "training" of basic functional skills (e.g., self-help skills). The underlying thinking associated with these terms and the programmatic decisions based on them have changed dramatically in recent years. As a result, their usage has declined drastically as well.

While some data support the contention that individuals who are mildly retarded display more secondary problems than the population as a whole (Barlow & Durand, 1995; Borthwick-Duffy, & Eyman, 1990; Forness & Polloway, 1987; Polloway, Epstein, Patton, Cullinan, & Luebke, 1986), the vast majority of these individuals can lead satisfying and productive lives, as attested to in such biographical works as *Like Normal People* (R. Meyers, 1980). Adults who are mildly mentally retarded are capable of securing and maintaining employment and becoming economically self-sufficient. However, adult outcome data (e.g., the large amount of unemployment and underemployment) provide a chilling realization that much work must still be done. With increased knowledge about how individuals who are retarded learn, and with more effective methodology for improving their performance, we should be able to provide even better programs, sensitive to both current and future needs.

DEMOGRAPHIC CHARACTERISTICS

Information about the characteristics and background of a given population enables us better to understand, prepare for, and serve the needs of that group. For two reasons, the following discussion focuses primarily on the demographics of individuals who are mildly mentally retarded. First, this segment of the population appears to have changed the most in the past few years. Second, individuals who need more intensive systems of support are generally not overrepresented in any given socioeconomic or racial group; they are fairly evenly distributed throughout the general population.

GENDER

More boys than girls are labeled "mentally retarded." In Dunn's (1973a) review of the literature on persons who are mildly retarded and his subsequent description of that population, he stated that students labeled EMR were more likely to be male. This apparently still holds true, if figures in recent studies characterizing individuals who are mildly retarded are indicative of the population as a whole (M. H. Epstein, Polloway, Patton, & Foley, 1989; Polloway et al., 1986; Wagner, Newman, & Shaver, 1989).

Reasons given for a preponderance of males include greater role expectations placed on males; aggressive behavior more often exhibited by males, leading to referral and subsequent labeling; and a higher probability of such biological factors as gender-linked influences affecting male children (Robinson & Robinson, 1976). A possibility also exists that gender bias in the diagnostic/classification process may affect disproportionately the number of males categorized as mentally retarded (U.S. Department of Education, 1996).

ETHNICITY

Reviewers of demographic data historically have reported a disproportionate number of racial and ethnic minority children being labeled as mildly mentally retarded (Doll, 1962; Dunn, 1973a). During the 1960s and 1970s, the racial imbalance in the makeup of EMR classes became the focus of much litigation, which in part led to changes in the procedures for identifying and labeling children as mentally retarded. But even with definitional changes and more stringent identification procedures, the same trend continues in evidence today.

A study conducted by the New Jersey State Department of Education (Manni, Winikur, & Keller, 1980) reported that 43 percent of the public school population labeled EMR were African American and 13.3 percent were Hispanic, although they accounted for only 17.8 and 7.4 percent of the school population, respectively.

Polloway and colleagues (1986) reviewed information on elementary and secondary students labeled EMR who were receiving services in several medium-sized cities in northern Illinois. They, too, found a disproportionate number of racial minority students in EMR programs. A follow-up study, also in Illinois but with different subjects, utilized data from Individual Educational Programs (IEPs) of 107 elementary school students labeled EMR (M. H. Epstein et al., 1989). The authors found that the representation of racial minorities was approximately twice that of the total school population. While these studies represent only a limited geographic area, they fuel the continuing concern about racial overrepresentation in programs for students who are mildly retarded. Additional study is needed to evaluate compliance with identification procedures and definitional requirements designed to limit discrimination (Brady, Manni, & Winikur, 1983).

According to data reported in the *Eighteenth Annual Report to Congress on the Implementation of the Individuals with Disabilities Education Act (IDEA)* (U.S. Department of Education, 1996), the percentage of African American students placed in special education programs is high relative to the percentage of these students in the general school population. In some disability categories and in some states, Hispanic students are over- and underrepresented relative to their proportion of the total school population. The disproportionate representation of African American students in special education programs may, in part, be attributed to relatively low income and the disabilities associated with poverty. When income is accounted for, however, there is still a disproportionate representation of African American students in programs for students who are mentally retarded.

SOCIOECONOMIC AND FAMILY PATTERNS

Information available on secondary school level youth who are disabled (U.S. Department of Education, 1994) indicates that these youth, when compared to the general population of youth, are more likely to

- Live in single parent families
- Come from families characterized by lower socioeconomic status
- Live in a family that has a lower household income

The implication drawn from this information is that these factors may affect the educational performance, physical and health status, and adult outcomes of these youth. It is also important to recognize that these findings are related to all youth with disabilities—not just those who are mentally retarded.

Environmental deprivation as a variable in the etiology of mental retardation is recognized by the AAMR in its inclusion of "psychosocial disadvantage" as an etiological classification. The description associated with this category implies that individuals experience impoverished environmental conditions involving poor housing, inadequate nutrition, and inadequate medical care. In at least one study describing this population (M. H. Epstein et al., 1989), factors sometimes associated with low socioeconomic status, such as a preponderance of single-parent homes, children raised by people other than their natural parents, and family involvement with one or more community agencies for support services, have been substantiated as contributing elements.

The higher prevalence of milder forms of mental retardation among low-income families has been acknowledged for some time (Westling, 1986). This disproportionate representation, however, appears to be almost entirely limited to those needing less intensive systems of supports. Socioeconomic conditions do not seem to affect the prevalence of those with more extensive and intensive needs (Conley, 1973).

MOTIVATIONAL AND SOCIOBEHAVIORAL CHARACTERISTICS

Children who are mentally retarded have the same basic physiological, social, and emotional needs as children who are not. Because of their experiences in dealing with environments in which they are less able to display appropriate adaptive skills, however, they often develop patterns of behavior that serve further to distinguish them from those who are not retarded. For example, members of this group show a higher prevalence of emotional and behavioral problems (Barlow & Durand, 1995; Polloway, Epstein, & Cullinan, 1985). The motivational and behavioral characteristics presented in this section are generalizations supported by studies of groups of people who are retarded. Because individuals are unique, and there is at least as much variability among those who are retarded as among persons who are not retarded, the following generalizations will not fit every individual.

MOTIVATIONAL

Many early investigations came from research in the field of social learning theory and concentrated on distinctions between individuals who were mildly retarded and those who were not retarded. This discussion, however, has relevance for those with slightly more intensive needs as well.

External Locus of Control

Locus of control refers to how one perceives the consequences of one's behavior. Individuals who operate primarily from an internal locus of control see events—both positive and negative—as results of their own actions. Those who see positive and negative events as primarily controlled by such outside forces as fate, chance, or other people have an external locus of control.

Young children tend to be externally oriented, perceiving many circumstances and events in their lives as being beyond their control. As children mature, however, they become more aware of the influence of their own actions. As a result, they gradually shift to a more internal locus of control (Lawrence & Winschel, 1975). External control, therefore, is considered a more debilitating orientation, as it keeps individuals from accepting responsibility for their own successes and failures and from developing self-reliance and self-regulatory behaviors. **Learned helplessness** is another term sometimes used to reflect the belief that failure will crown even the most extraordinary efforts (Seligman, 1975).

C. D. Mercer and Snell (1977) reviewed the results of locus of control studies that involved subjects who were retarded. The results of the studies indicated that such subjects are more externally oriented than their peers who were not retarded. Mercer and Snell recommend that professionals identify and encourage techniques that promote internal orientations.

Expectancy of Failure

Expectancy refers to the reinforcement that is anticipated as a result of a given behavior. Rotter (1954) postulated two types of expectancies. The first is the expectation of a particular type of reinforcement, such as a tangible reward or social approval. The second involves expectations generalized from the results of past experiences with particular types of problem-solving activities. In other words, new situations are approached with either the expectation of success or the expectation of failure, based on what the individual has experienced in the past.

Studies by Cromwell (1963) that involved subjects who were retarded found them to have a high expectancy of failure. Zigler (1973) and Balla and Zigler (1979) noted that an individual who has accumulated experiences of failure sets lower aspirations and goals in an effort to avoid additional disappointment. Heber (1964) pointed out that this fear of failure may become circular: The expectation of lack of success lowers the amount of effort put into a task, performance of the task is thus below what might be anticipated from the capabilities of the individual, and the expected failure becomes a reality.

Those working with individuals who demonstrate the debilitating attitude of expecting to fail must create situations that encourage and reward effort. It is important for these individuals to experience success and to recognize it when it occurs. However, it is equally important to teach them how to deal with failure and how to persevere.

Outerdirectedness

Another result of attempts to avoid failure is a style of problem-solving called *outerdirectedness*. Instead of being self-reliant in problem solving, the outerdirected individual relies on situational or external cues for guidance (Bybee & Zigler, 1992).

While this type of behavior is certainly not limited to those who are retarded, Zigler (1966) suggested that it prevails among this group because they have learned to distrust their own abilities, again because of the frequency with which they have failed in the past. Efficient problem solving necessarily involves using both external cues and one's own cognitive resources. The use of external cues may be an appropriate adaptation to one's limitations (Bybee & Zigler, 1992). However, relying too heavily on external cues could result in a dependence upon them, even for a task well within one's own capabilities (Balla & Zigler, 1979).

In the three motivational orientations discussed (locus of control, expectancy for failure, and outerdirectedness), one recurring factor is the

POSITIVE SUPPORTS

A Definition of Positive Supports

Positive supports are actions and beliefs that reflect respectful interpersonal relationships, choice, communication, inclusive communities, and self determination to assist a person to become a more independent, contributing member of the community. They encompass a variety of strategies that are considered unconditionally for a person who may be exhibiting behaviors that challenge family members, educational staff, service providers, and/or the community. People also require positive supports during other times in their lives. A committed group of diverse people collaborate to identify, develop, and secure the needed supports, while acknowledging a person's individuality. Positive supports recognize people's rights to make informed choices, take risks, and contribute in the decision-making process.

Foundations of Positive Supports

- Community
- Being heard
- Individualized supports
- Ongoing support
- Enhanced quality of life

Core Elements of Positive Supports

- Active member of an inclusive community
- Person centered planning
- Communication
- Choice
- Friendship
- Collaborative team
- Control resides with person
- Support during crises
- Teaching/building competencies

Positive Supports Questions to Ask

Is the support you provide to individuals with disabilities positive in its approach? Take a moment to answer the questions below to find out.

1. Does the person have the opportunity to make informed choices that impact his/her life (e.g., real life choices such as who, or what agency will provide support, hiring and firing staff, where to live/work, what/how much to eat)?

2. Does the person have a way to communicate his/her needs and wants throughout the entire day?

3. Does the person have reciprocal relationships in his/her life? (While paid staff at times develop reciprocal relationships with a person, these paid relationships should not be the only ones a person has.)

4. Is the person an active member of the community, participating in events of his/her choice on an individual basis? (This does not include activities designed exclusively for individuals with disabilities.)

5. Is person centered planning used to identify supports based upon the person's dreams, goals, strengths, and needs ensuring that the supports are unique to him/her?

6. Do supporters reevaluate what is needed when identified supports do not appear beneficial?

7. Do supporters listen to and acknowledge the concerns and requests that a person may have no matter how he/she makes that request (e.g., talking, use of behavior)?

8. Do supporters acknowledge that their own values, behavior, and needs may influence their interactions with and the behavior of others?

9. Do supporters respect the person's right to take risks after he/she has obtained relevant information and the support needed to evaluate the information?

10. Does the person advocate for him/her self to determine his/her own life?

11. Are identified supports flexible to meet the everchanging needs a person may have?

12. Do we recognize and accept the diversity of the people we work with and support?

Source: From "Positive Supports" and "Positive Supports Questions to Ask," 1996, *Centerpoint, 1*(2), pp. 3–4. Copyright 1996 by the Center for Community Inclusion, University of Maine at Orono. Reprinted by permission.

detrimental effect of repeated failures. Perhaps the most important implication for those working in the field, then, is the necessity of providing children who are retarded with tasks at which they can succeed. This holds true for both social and academic settings. Allowing the child to be successful is an invaluable motivational tool. Yet all children, disabled and otherwise, need to learn to deal with failure as well. A sensitive teacher can shape classroom experiences in such a way that the child gains enough self-confidence through repeated successes to be able to rebound from an occasional inevitable failure. Parents and teachers need to be sensitive to their own expectations for the child, so that they do not inadvertently reinforce the child's negative expectations. They must take care to avoid conveying the idea that they think the child is not competent to handle simple tasks. Rather, parents and teachers should require all children to assume the responsibilities that are within their grasp, make it clear to them exactly what is expected of them, and allow them the opportunities to try.

Other ways to increase the chances of success are setting specific, realistic goals, providing immediate feedback for specific behavior, and rewarding accomplishments. If the child has repeatedly failed at a certain task, the situation should be restructured to present a novel approach that makes success possible. Finally, while it is desirable to help children who are retarded become more innerdirected and self-reliant, their tendency to rely heavily on external cues should be used to advantage. Teachers and parents should provide appropriate behavior models for children (Kauffman & Payne, 1975; C. D. Mercer & Snell, 1977).

SELF-REGULATORY BEHAVIORS

More attention is being given to developing self-regulatory behaviors due to their importance for an individual's inclusion in regular education settings and successful integration into the community.

Ultimately, we would like all individuals to exert control over their lives. For them to do so, it is essential that they develop self-regulation of many behaviors across different settings and maintain the behaviors over time. Despite the desirability of developing self-regulation in persons with mental retardation, Whitman (1990) warns that they are likely to be delayed in acquiring this skill. This admonition is based on the fact that self-regulation is a linguistically guided process, and this group displays linguistic limitations. Nevertheless, the goal of developing self-regulatory behaviors is warranted and attainable. A strong rationale for achieving self-regulation with persons who are mentally retarded is offered by Whitman (1990):

> By exercising self-control, persons with retardation can increase the probability that they will act effectively without external direction, maintain what they have learned, and generalize learned responses to situations where training contingencies have not been applied. Moreover, by self-regulation of their behavior, they are more likely to be able to live in more normalized settings where close supervision is not possible. Finally, because independent action is valued by our society, individuals with retardation who become more autonomous are also more likely to be reacted to more positively by others, which in turn will increase their feeling of self-efficacy. (p. 348)

SOCIOBEHAVIORAL

Children and adolescents who are more severely mentally retarded histori-cally have been described as displaying more social and behavioral prob-lems than their peers who are not disabled (Balthazar & Stevens, 1975; Robinson & Robinson, 1976). According to Guralnick and Weinhouse (1984), for example, in play settings, young children who are severely de-velopmentally delayed interact less frequently with their peers and engage more frequently in solitary or unoccupied activities. Similarly, in work set-tings, adults who are more severely retarded demonstrate difficulty in ac-cepting criticism, resolving conflicts, following instructions, and engaging in conversation (Sherman, Sheldon, Harchik, Edwards, & Quinn, 1992). Studies focusing on students who are mildly retarded confirm similiar problems in this population as well (M. H. Epstein, Cullinan, & Polloway, 1986; Polloway et al., 1985; Russell & Forness, 1985). Some of the specific problem areas in-clude disruptiveness, attention deficits, low self-esteem (Polloway et al., 1985), overactivity (Polloway et al., 1986), distractibility and other attention-related problems (M. H. Epstein et al., 1989), and difficulty in interpersonal cognitive problem solving (Healey & Masterpasqua, 1992).

Individuals whose needs for supports are minimal often have difficulty in establishing and maintaining interpersonal relationships. They may, for example, have trouble developing close personal friends, as there is evi-dence that they are more often rejected than accepted by their peers (Polloway et al., 1986). This frequency of rejection is associated with the de-gree of inappropriateness of behavior they display. Further, inappropriate behavior and peer rejection may be apparent as early as preschool. Kopp, Baker, and Brown (1992), for example, found that preschoolers who were developmentally delayed demonstrated less positive affect and more dis-ruptive and regressive behaviors that interrupted play than did their peers who were not developmentally delayed. Findings from such studies as these have important implications for the social acceptance and subsequent friendship formation of these students.

Some educators have implied that the lower the intellectual level, the more pronounced the behavioral deviations. This suggests that individuals with greater needs for supports would exhibit more behavioral problems than those with fewer needs for supports. There does appear to be a higher incidence of behavioral and psychiatric disorders in individuals referred to as moderately retarded, particularly among persons whose retardation is as-sociated with central nervous system dysfunction (Robinson & Robinson, 1976; Russell & Forness, 1985). A wide range of behaviors may be evidenced in such individuals, including distractibility, hyperactivity, mood distur-bances, and stereotypic behaviors. Health-related problems as well as the effects of medication may affect attention and concentration, leading both to a slower, more limited acquisition of social skills, and to an increase in inappropriate behaviors.

TABLE 6.1
Psychiatric Conditions that Accompany Dual Diagnosis

Psychiatric disorders

        Bipolar disorders (e.g., mania and depression)

        Schizophrenia

        Major depression with psychotic features

        Obsessive-compulsive disorders

        Delirium and dementia

        Attention deficit hyperactivity disorder

        Anxiety disorders

        Psychoactive substance use disorders

Genetic syndromes associated with mental retardation and abnormal behavior

        Fragile X syndrome

        Rett syndrome

        Prader-Willi syndrome

        Lesch-Nyhan syndrome

Source: Reber (1992).

A growing area of concern focuses on the mental health needs of individuals who are retarded. The extent of the problem is evidenced in data reported by Borthwick-Duffy and Eyman (1990) showing that approximately 10 percent of the clients served by the state of California have been dually diagnosed (i.e., given both a mental retardation and a psychiatric diagnosis). There are numerous patterns of behavior that might result in a dual diagnosis. Table 6.1 provides some examples of psychiatric disorders that some individuals with milder forms of mental retardation might display, based on a discussion by Reber (1992).

Since being able to meet more normal behavioral expectations is often a consideration in the decision to integrate special students into general education programs, social skill problems may contribute to more restrictive placements. Also, a great many variables influence the learning process. Better social, motivational, and behavioral adjustment is likely to relate to better academic functioning. Another major consideration is that successful adult adjustment requires competence in many social and behavioral areas (Cronin & Patton, 1993). Curricular attention to this area would enable a more successful integration into community life.

Further implications extend into higher education, where professionals are trained to work with exceptional students. In the area of mental retardation, teachers need to prepare themselves for a diversity of social and behavioral problems and receive training in appropriate intervention and management techniques for dealing with them (M. H. Epstein et al., 1986). Training is also needed in ways to incorporate social skills into the curriculum and in methods and materials by which such skills may be taught.

LEARNING CHARACTERISTICS

We may think of learning as the process whereby practice or experience produces a change in behavior that is not due to maturation, growth, or aging. The definition implies (a) that the changed behavior is relatively permanent, as distinguished from responses to, for example, drugs or fatigue, and (b) that the learner is involved and participating, not just changing because of physical growth or deterioration (Bower, 1978).

Learning is a hypothetical construct and, as such, cannot be measured directly. How much or how little learning has actually taken place can be inferred only from performance. If a student points to the object that the teacher has just named or spells a word correctly, we assume that learning has taken place. If the student performs the task incorrectly or does not attempt the task at all, we assume that learning has not occurred. Since learning can be measured only indirectly, we must be cautious in interpreting performance levels as direct indicators of learning. A great many factors influence whether and how a pupil responds in any given situation.

We have implied that physical maturity can result in behavioral changes. The development of such motor skills as walking appears not to be influenced by training or experience until the child has the necessary physical maturity. Delayed development, however, is a characteristic of people who are retarded, and the degree of delay is generally related to the severity of the retardation and the presence of other inhibiting conditions. People who expect a person with disabilities to acquire skills at the normal rate may end up frustrated and may fail in their attempts to teach new skills. Training and practice will not supplant the maturation process, but studies of infant stimulation provide enough encouragement to justify training and practice to enhance development.

COGNITIVE DEVELOPMENT

Quantitative Versus Qualitative Perspectives

Use of the concept of mental age (MA) to express the level of cognitive functioning of a given individual has given rise to differing orientations from which to view the cognitive development of persons who are retarded. For example, cognitive development may be viewed as quantitative and comparable among individuals of similar MA, regardless of chronological age.

This perspective, the developmental position, assumes that cognitive development, at least for the youngster who is mildly retarded, is similar to that of a younger child who is not retarded. According to Zigler (1969), such children progress through the same developmental levels in the same sequence as do children who are not retarded, although at a slower rate and lower level of ultimate functioning.

Proponents of this point of view believe that children who are retarded fail because they are presented with tasks beyond their current ability level. Educational programs based on a developmental model would, therefore, use traditional teaching strategies but be geared primarily to the MA of the individual. The developmental view of cognitive growth can be thought of as a series of steps or stages in which new tasks are presented only when the child reaches the level of mental ability appropriate to that task.

Proponents of the difference position, however, view the cognitive development of persons who are retarded as being qualitatively different from that of those who are not retarded. Ellis (1969) contended that there are differences in the ways in which this group processes information and that the main task of research is to describe these areas of difference. The implications for teaching are that unique teaching methods and materials are needed to overcome or lessen the effects of the deficiency.

Research favoring one orientation over the other is plentiful. Firm conclusions, however, are difficult to reach because of the many variables that affect cognitive development (e.g., etiology of the retardation, motivational differences, problems associated with matching individuals based on MA). Regardless of one's position on this issue, the research in this area adds to our larger understanding of the learning process of individuals who are retarded.

Since much of the developmentally oriented research is based upon Piaget's theory of carefully sequenced stages of development, we briefly present this theory along with its application for learners who are retarded. In this section, we describe some learning processes where distinctions between learners who are retarded and learners who are not have been noted.

Cognitive-Developmental Theory

The original tenets of cognitive-developmental theory were formulated by Jean Piaget, based on observations of his own ("normal") children. He viewed mental development as a result of the continuous interaction with and adaptation to the environment, or the child's perception of it. According to Piaget (1969), each child progresses through stages of development where various cognitive skills are acquired. The main stages of development, along with approximate age norms, are

1. Sensorimotor stage—birth to two years
2. Preoperational stage—two to seven years
3. Concrete operations—seven to eleven years
4. Formal, or abstract, operations—eleven years and older

The sensorimotor stage is characterized by sensory experiences and motor activity. As young children become more aware of the surrounding environment, they begin to distinguish between themselves and other persons and objects. The second stage, preoperational, involves more than purely physical operations. Children begin to use symbols for the people and objects around them, to assimilate customs, and to acquire new experiences by imitating the actions of others. During the concrete operations stage, children develop further abilities to order and classify objects. While mental operations are more highly developed, children are usually limited to solving problems with which they have had direct or concrete experience. The ability to perform abstract thinking and reason by hypothesis is said to develop around the age of eleven or twelve and characterizes the formal operations, or abstract, stage.

Piagetian theory has been related to children who are mentally retarded by Inhelder (1968) and Woodward (1963, 1979), who viewed the child who is retarded as progressing through the same stages of cognitive development as his peers who are not retarded, with the major differences being in rate and highest level achieved. The age at which a child who is retarded will reach each stage will be later, and the more severe the retardation, the slower the progression through the stages. In addition, individuals who are mentally retarded may not achieve all stages of development. According to Inhelder, children who are mildly mentally retarded may reach the concrete operations level, but individuals who have been called moderately retarded will go no further than the preoperational stage. Those who are severely or profoundly retarded will remain at the sensorimotor level.

According to Piagetian theory, mental development progresses as a result of children's interactions with their surroundings. The role of the educator, therefore, is that of a provider of materials and opportunities appropriate to children's stage of development, with which they can interact. Teachers of students who are retarded need to be aware of the developmental sequences in order to determine a child's readiness for a particular task and to consider the slow rate and the expected optimal level of functioning when planning curricula for children with varying levels of retardation.

PROCESSES INVOLVED IN LEARNING

Individuals who are mentally retarded, by definition, perform below average on tests of intelligence and are slow and inefficient learners. Whether one subscribes to the developmental or difference model of the cognitive functioning of people who are retarded, the practical issue of providing an optimum learning environment remains. Toward this end, a vast amount of research has been conducted in the area of learning and applied to individuals who are retarded. Most researchers have concentrated their efforts on one aspect of learning, such as attention or memory. In generalizing the findings to educational programming, however, we must emphasize that implications from various theories relating to separate aspects of learning should be used in combination to offer learners who are retarded the best opportunities for realizing their potential.

The major processes that are discussed in this section include attention variables, mediational strategies, memory, and transfer/generalization. Table 6.2 summarizes the major features of each of these along with select references that are associated with each process. The discussion that follows details some of the seminal research in these areas.

Attention Variables

In any learning situation, attention to the task at hand is critical for successful learning. Zeaman and House (1963) did much of the early work in the area of attention. Their experiments involved two-choice visual discrimination tasks where subjects were rewarded for choosing the dimension (color, shape, size) that the investigator had previously selected as the correct choice. Responses were recorded and translated into learning curves or graphs illustrating the percentage of correct responses upon each trial. Analysis of the curves revealed that learning the discrimination tasks had two stages. In the first, subjects responded correctly about 50 percent of the time, or at about chance level. During the second stage, however, correct responses increased dramatically, resulting in a sharp rise on the learning curve. Zeaman and House have suggested that the first stage is an attention phase, where the subject randomly attends to various aspects of the task. Once the subject has focused on the key features of the task, or selectively attends to the critical stimuli, the second phase begins (see Figure 6.1).

Zeaman and House (1963) compared the learning curves obtained from performances of children who were or were not retarded whose MAs varied. They found the two stages in the curves of all groups, as well as the sharp rise in performance at the beginning of the second stage. The difference between the groups was the number of trials composing the first stage. Children with lower MAs required more trials in the attention phase than did children with higher MAs. Zeaman and House therefore concluded that subjects who were retarded needed more time to learn to attend to the relevant dimensions of the stimuli.

In updating their theory, Zeaman and House (1979) also noted a relationship between MA and the number of dimensions that a subject could attend to simultaneously. Learners who were retarded could not attend to as many dimensions simultaneously as could those who were not retarded. In addition, some learners who were retarded seemed to prefer some dimensions over others, which also may have affected their response. This is particularly relevant if, as Brooks and McCauley (1984) maintained, such learners have less attention to allocate, and "attentional allocation is a problem in general for mentally retarded people that may extend to all domains of information processing" (p. 482).

The initial research by Zeaman and House continues to generate investigations, but from it we can draw implications for teaching students who are retarded. For example, teachers should (a) present initial stimuli that vary in only a few dimensions, (b) direct the child's attention to these criti-

TABLE 6.2
Learning-Related Characteristics

Characteristic	Description	Reference
Attention Variables	• Difficulty in the three major components of attention: attention span (length of time on task), focus (inhibition of distracting stimuli), and selective attention (discrimination of important stimulus characteristics). • Key concern is to train students to be aware of the importance of attention and to learn how to actively monitor its occurrence.	Alabiso (1977) Zeaman & House (1963, 1979) Connis (1979) Howell, Rueda, & Rutherford (1983) Kneedler & Hallahan (1981)
Mediational Strategies	• Less likely than normal learners to employ effective techniques for organizing information for later recall. • Typical techniques of mature learners include verbal rehearsal and repetition, labeling, classification, association, and imagery. • Research indicates that students who are retarded have difficulty producing mediational strategies. • Tend to be "inactive learners"	Spitz (1966) Bray (1979) Robinson & Robinson (1976) Strichart & Gottlieb (1983)
Memory	• Difficulty in the area of short-term memory (STM) but retain information over the long term. • Long-term memory (LTM) is usually similar to that of persons who are not disabled. • Certain STM problems involving nonsensical tasks have been associated with deficits in the spontaneous use of mediational strategies. • As noted above, strategy production is difficult for students with mild retardation, but improvements in recall can be achieved when they are shown how to proceed in an organized, well-planned fashion.	Belmont (1966) R.C. Cohen (1982) Baumeister & Brooks (1981) Borkowski & Cavanaugh (1979)
Transfer/Generalization	• Tend to show deficiencies in the ability to apply knowledge or skills to new tasks, problems, or stimulus situations. • Such difficulties relate to the inability to form learning sets. • In particular, they may fail to use previous experience to formulate rules that will help solve future problems of a similar nature.	Stephens (1972) Stevenson (1972) Robinson & Robinson (1976)

Source: Reprinted with the permission of Merrill, an imprint of Prentice Hall, from EXCEPTIONAL CHILDREN AND YOUTH, Sixth Edition by Norris G. Haring, Linda McCormick, and Thomas G. Haring. Copyright © 1994 by Prentice Hall.

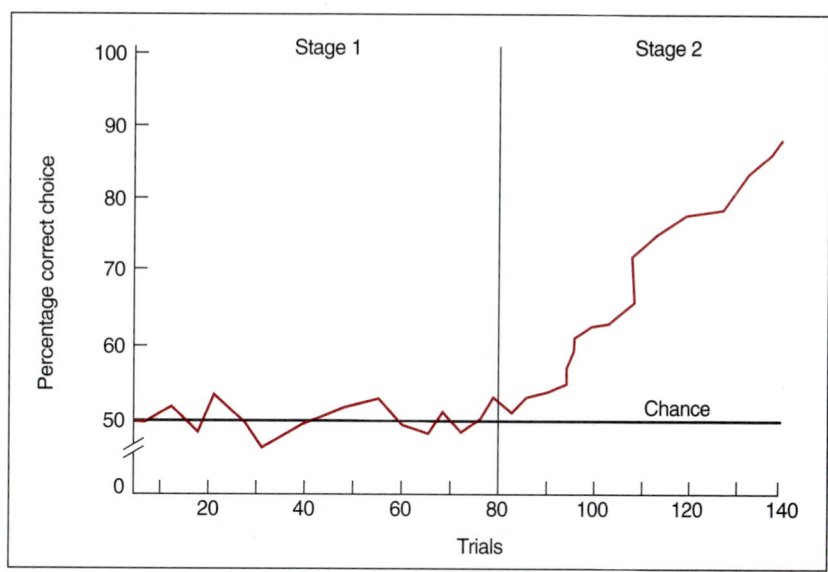

FIGURE 6.1

Typical Learning Curve Generated by Persons with Retardation on Discrimination Task in Zeaman and House (1963) Study

cal dimensions, (c) initially remove extraneous stimuli that may distract the child from attending to the task at hand, (d) reward the child for attending to the task, and (e) increase the difficulty of the task over time.

Mediational Strategies

After attending to a specific stimulus, an individual must organize and store it so that it can be recalled when needed. Spitz (1966) referred to this process as "input organization" and has conducted research to determine the functioning in this area of persons who are mentally retarded.

Spitz's (1966) research led him to theorize that the input step in the learning process was more difficult for subjects who were retarded than for other subjects, because of a deficiency in their ability to organize the input stimuli for storage and recall. This finding has generated a great deal of research into strategies that teachers may use to enhance a student's ability to categorize incoming data. Two such methods are grouping and mediation.

Grouping, or clustering material prior to its presentation, is seen by Spitz (1973, 1979) as more beneficial to the learner who is retarded than presenting material in random order. Restructuring the perceptual field for individuals who characteristically have difficulty at this stage of the learning process should facilitate memory and recall. Grouping is perhaps the simplest method of organizing information. Material may be grouped spatially, in different visual arrangements; temporally, with a pause or time lapse between items;

perceptually, with certain items enclosed in a shape or configuration; or categorically, by content or commonality of items.

Stephens (1966) has further broken down the categories of grouping by content into physical similarity (e.g., items of the same color), function (e.g., articles of clothing), concepts (e.g., plants, animals), and sequential equivalence (e.g., subjects and objects as used in grammatical arrangements). Work by Stephens (1972) in presenting stimuli according to types of grouping indicates that the most basic type of grouping is that of physical similarity. As a child increases in MA, more advanced grouping strategies are used. This same progression was reported for subjects who were not retarded as well as for subjects who were mildly retarded.

A mediator is something that goes between or connects. In verbal learning, **mediation** refers to the process by which an individual connects a stimulus and a response. One approach to the study of verbal learning, *paired associate learning,* focuses on verbal mediation as a means of learning responses to stimulus words or elements. In this technique, the subject is generally presented with pairs of words. Then only the first word in each pair is repeated, and the subject tries to recall the second. Verbalizing the connection between the two stimulus words seems to enhance performance. In studies reviewed by C. E. Meyers and MacMillan (1976), researchers noted marked improvements in tasks of this type, even by subjects who were retarded, when the subjects were instructed in mediation strategies or provided with such mediators as sentences relating the stimulus to the response. The meaningfulness of the material and the use of stimulus words or objects familiar to the subject (Estes, 1970) also facilitated learning in paired associate tasks.

Several implications for teaching can be drawn from this research. First, materials presented to learners who are retarded should be familiar or have some relevance for them. Second, information should be grouped or organized into meaningful parts. Finally, such learners should be instructed in mediational strategies.

Memory

Memory, the ability to retrieve information that has been stored, is one of the most heavily researched components of the learning process. As one would expect, individuals who are retarded tend to perform less well on tasks of memory than do their age- or grade-level peers. Moreover, the more severely retarded the individual, the greater the deficit in memory displayed.

Researchers have hypothesized that the root of memory problems in individuals who are retarded may be related to a lack of selective attention (Payne, Polloway, Smith, & Payne, 1981), inefficient or nonexistent rehearsal strategies (Brooks & McCauley, 1984; Ellis, 1970), delay in developing learning sets (Hallahan & Reeve, 1980), or an inability to generalize learned skills to new settings, with different people, or in different ways (Stevens, 1972). Polloway and Patton (1993) stated that an inability to generalize skills hampers the ability of individuals who are retarded to be more independent and reduce their needs for external supports.

Early researchers of memory processes usually made a distinction between short-term memory (STM) and long-term memory (LTM). Information recalled after a period of days or months or longer is usually referred to as being in LTM, while data stored from a few seconds to a few hours are in STM (Ellis, 1970). Most early researchers contended that once learned, information is retained over the long term about as well by those who are retarded as by those who are not (Belmont, 1966; Ellis, 1963). In the area of STM, however, early researchers concluded that learners who are retarded appeared to have considerable difficulty (Borkowski, Peck, & Damberg, 1983; Ellis, 1963).

Belmont and Butterfield (1971) and A. L. Brown, Campione, and Murphy (1974) reported success in efforts to improve STM performance among these learners, by direct teaching or by rehearsal or practice procedures, although the effects of the training appeared to be specific to the training task at hand and not readily transferable to other situations (Belmont & Butterfield, 1977). The major rehearsal strategies noted by C. D. Mercer and Snell (1977) in their review of studies of STM were verbal rehearsal and image rehearsal. Verbal rehearsal relates to the concept of self-instruction and refers to labeling aspects of a task and verbalizing these labels aloud or silently while the task is being performed. In image rehearsal, a form of visualization, the individual is taught to associate aspects of a task with pictures of events that will help to recall them.

Dunn (1973a) criticized the early research on memory problems in individuals who were retarded as plagued with methodological problems that made interpretation difficult and noted that currently, researchers of memory processes had moved toward an information processing model.

Executive control and *metacognition* are components of an information processing model. These two terms apply to the process one consciously goes through to analyze a problem, anticipate outcomes of various actions, decide how the problem should be solved, and monitor progress toward the solution (Campione, Brown, & Ferrara, 1982). Researchers have noted that learners who are retarded generally do not spontaneously employ executive control processes (A. L. Brown, 1974; Sternberg & Spear, 1985), but that they can be taught to use them effectively (Borkowski et al., 1983). Other teaching techniques to facilitate recall include (a) organizing material into meaningful segments, (b) using reinforcement and incentives for remembering, (c) using repetition and drill, (d) reminding and encouraging the learner to use rehearsal strategies, and (e) using reconstructive elaborations.

OBSERVATIONAL LEARNING

Modeling, imitation, and learning through observation are the terms most often associated with *observational learning,* which refers to learning from

Children who are retarded often learn by watching others demonstrate how to perform tasks.

demonstrations by others. Much of the research in this area has been done by Bandura (1969) and his associates. It substantiates the important role that observational learning plays in acquiring social behaviors, gender roles, language, and religious and political practices. In addition, modeling and imitation are involved in the development of new behaviors and the modification of existing ones and may result in the learning of inappropriate as well as appropriate responses.

Certain characteristics of individuals who are retarded give support to the use of this tool to teach new behaviors. The tendency of these learners to be outerdirected or to look to others for cues or guidance in problem solving (Turnure & Zigler, 1964), and their suggestibility (Zigler, 1973), indicate that modeling can be effectively used for acquiring or changing behavior. Suggestions for using observational learning as a teaching tool include (a) being aware that any behavior may serve as a model, (b) using prompts or cues to direct students' attention, (c) calling attention to students exhibiting desirable behavior, (d) ignoring undesirable behavior so that others do not model it in an attempt to gain attention, and (e) rewarding imitation of appropriate behavior.

SPEECH AND LANGUAGE CHARACTERISTICS

Speech and language problems occur with greater frequency among individuals identified as mentally retarded than among those not so identified (Bernstein & Tiegerman, 1993; S. F. Warren & Abbeduto, 1992). This is not unexpected, since cognitive ability and language development are closely related. The speech problems most often seen are difficulties in articulation, voice, and stuttering (Hardman, Drew, & Egan, 1996). Common articulation errors include the substitution, omission, addition, or distortion of sounds, which make speech less intelligible. Language disorders that commonly accompany mental retardation include delayed language development and a restricted or limited active vocabulary (Spradlin, 1968). Language is so important to independent functioning that prospective parents, parents of high-risk children, and day care personnel should be trained in various means of encouraging language development.

As corroboration of the evidence that students who are mildly retarded display lower overall functioning than those classified similarly before the passage of PL 94-142, we see an increasing occurrence of secondary handicapping conditions (MacMillan, 1989; MacMillan & Borthwick, 1980). For example, M. H. Epstein et al. (1989) gathered information from the Individualized Education Programs (IEPs) of 107 children identified as mildly retarded and receiving special education in northern Illinois. Speech and language problems were the most frequent secondary disability; well over half the students were eligible for and receiving speech and language therapy. Language deficits may be related to such factors as absence of or limited adequate speech and language models and less encouragement to use language. A disproportionate number of students who are mildly retarded are also members of cultural or ethnic minorities (U.S. Department of Education, 1996), which may also play a role in the language deficiencies found in this population.

Recent research on the language abilities of individuals who are retarded offers some interesting findings. Abbeduto and Nuccio (1991) studied the receptive language abilities of this group and found that students who were retarded focused on the formal, sequential aspects of spoken language rather than on its semantic, conceptual aspects. Individuals who were not retarded demonstrated the latter abilities. In a study on the use of repair behaviors (i.e, speaker's effort to make an utterance understood when listener indicates a problem in understanding), Scudder and Tremain (1992) found that students who were retarded displayed appropriate repair behaviors. However, as situations became more demanding, students who were retarded did not reuse effective strategies and became more frustrated.

Among those whose needs are more pronounced, speech and language disorders are even more common, not only because of their decreased intellectual development, but also from the increased possibility of concomitant disabling conditions. The motor dysfunction accompanying cerebral

CHANGING THE LOOK OF MENTAL RETARDATION

Plastic surgeons can straighten the slanted eyes, build up the cheekbones and minimize the protruding tongue commonly found in children with Down syndrome. But should they? Plastic surgery remains the most controversial treatment offered Down syndrome children.

The 1½ to 2½-hour operation is fairly straightforward. Surgeons can build up the bridge of the nose, cheekbone, and chin with bone grafts or synthetics, change the slant of the eyes and cut fat from the lower eyelids. There are usually no facial scars because the work is done through the mouth or by cutting skin flaps behind the hairline. The tongue, which appears too large and protrudes from an unusually small mouth, is reduced by about one-fifth.

Advocates of surgery believe that children with Down syndrome are rejected partly because of their physical features, and that improving their appearance may result in greater social acceptance. Critics respond that there is little hard evidence that the surgery has these effects. In fact, it has to be admitted that even the most gifted plastic surgeons can't make a child with Down syndrome look entirely normal. After surgery, the gait, neck and body proportions are still unusual. Even the face remains clearly different. "I've yet to see a child after the operation," says Diane Crutcher of the National Down Syndrome Congress, "who doesn't look like a child with Down syndrome." Moreover, say some critics, the surgery is itself a kind of rejection, a message that the children are not acceptable as themselves. It is society's preoccupation with "good looks" that should change, these critics argue, not the faces of children with Down syndrome.

Even those who advocate the operation admit that not every child with Down syndrome is a good candidate for surgery, and both parents and child must go through an intensive screening process before their surgeon lifts a scalpel. "The surgery should only be performed in children whose quality of life can be improved by the procedures," cautions Garry S. Brody, clinical professor of plastic surgery at the University of Southern California. Surgery is immediately ruled out if the child is profoundly retarded or has life-threatening physical problems. In addition, parents must be realistic about what the surgery will and won't do. "If you think the child is going to roll out of the operating room with 20 more IQ points," says Crutcher, "you're going to be disappointed."

While controversial, plastic surgery remains an option for those willing to try every avenue. The American Society of Plastic and Reconstructive Surgeons operates a toll-free number (800/635-0635) for information on reconstructive and cosmetic surgery for Down syndrome, and offers a referral list of board-certified plastic surgeons qualified to perform the operation.

Source: From "Special Talents" by C. Turkington, 1987, *Psychology Today,* September, p. 45. REPRINTED WITH PERMISSION FROM PSYCHOLOGY TODAY MAGAZINE, Copyright © 1987 (Sussex Publishers, Inc.).

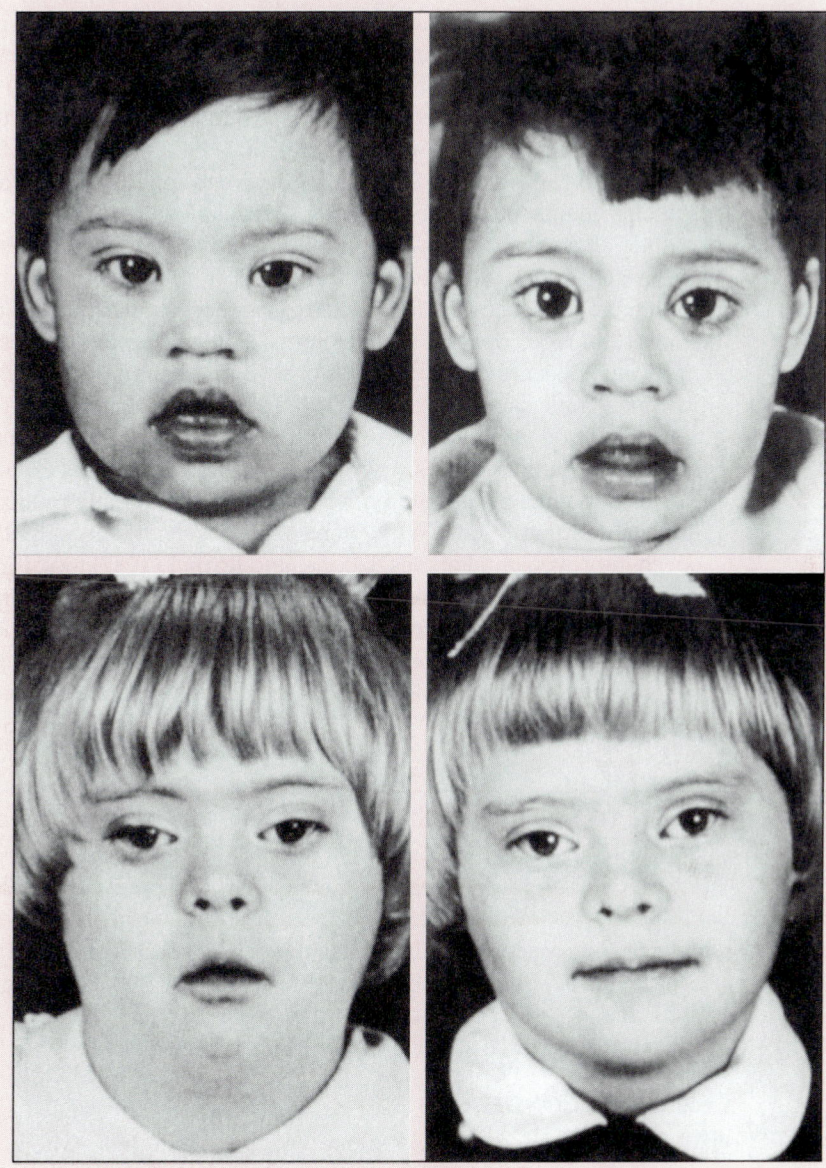

Before and after: Advocates of surgery say it reduces the stigma often associated with Down syndrome. Critics say it sends the message that the children are unacceptable in appearance as they are.

Photos courtesy of Dr. Kenneth Salyer, Dallas, TX

palsy, for example, can seriously impede the ability to produce intelligible speech. A higher prevalence of hearing impairment also exists in this population, and poor hearing affects articulation and may contribute to a further delay in the acquisition of language. Many students, especially those with Down syndrome, have frequent bouts of middle ear infections during their childhood years (Brooks, Wooley, & Kanjilal, 1972). The conductive hearing loss these infections can cause also delays language and creates speech problems (Balkany, Downs, Jafek, & Krajicek, 1979).

One of the features typically found in the child with Down syndrome is a protruding tongue. Tongue-reduction surgery, often in combination with facial surgery, has become increasingly common as a means of diminishing some of the more obvious characteristics. The usefulness of such surgery in improving speech, however, is dubious. Lemperle and Rada (1980) reported more intelligible speech for a majority of sixty-three children with Down syndrome after undergoing surgery, although no formal speech evaluations were conducted. In other studies, Olbrisch (1982) and Lemperle (1985) sent questionnaires to families of children who had received tongue-reduction surgery and reported that 88 and 68 percent, respectively, of the parents perceived speech improvement. Parsons, Iacone, and Rozner (1987) took formal speech assessment measures before surgery, four weeks after surgery, and again six months after surgery with twenty-seven children with Down syndrome. The number of articulation errors did not differ significantly across time, although the parents were almost unanimous in perceiving speech improvement.

PHYSICAL HEALTH CHARACTERISTICS

In general, the physical health characteristics and needs of persons who are mildly retarded do not differ dramatically from those of other individuals. More pronounced physical and health concerns, however, tend to co-occur in individuals who are more severely retarded. The following discussion highlights selected conditions of retardation as well as general health considerations that have specific implications for this population.

SELECTED CONDITIONS

We begin with motor development, which even in those who are mildly retarded may be delayed and markedly less accomplished than in the child who is not retarded. Motor deficits include problems of balance, locomotion, and manipulative dexterity (Bruininks, 1974). The growth rate may be slower, and these individuals are generally shorter and lighter than children who are not retarded (Bruininks, 1974; Mosier, Grossman, & Dingman, 1965). Reschly, Robinson, Volmer, and Wilson (1988) demonstrated that, as the severity of retardation increases, so do problems in motor skills areas; this relationship is depicted in Table 6.3.

TABLE 6.3
Analysis of Motor Skills across IQ Levels

IQ	N	$\overline{X}$[a]	s.d.	Total with Weaknesses[b]	
				N	%
<50	39	2.10	1.07	29	74
50–54	33	2.18	1.10	23	70
55–59	35	2.46	1.07	17	49
60–64	52	2.48	0.96	25	48
65–69	59	2.53	0.95	24	41
70–74	121	3.08	0.91	26	21
75–79	155	2.95	0.88	40	26
80–84	118	2.97	0.85	30	25

[a]Mean scores were derived from a Likert rating scale that used the anchor points of 1 = Significant Weakness, 2 = Weakness, 4 = Strength, and 5 = Significant Strength.

[b]Total was formed by the sum of the Significant Weakness and Weakness ratings.

Source: From *Iowa Mental Disabilities Research Project: Final Report and Executive Summary* by D. Reschly, G. Robinson, L. Volmer, and L. Wilson, 1988. Des Moines, IA: State of Iowa, Department of Education. Copyright 1988 by State of Iowa, Department of Education. Reprinted by permission.

Sensory defects are also more common among individuals who are retarded, with visual and auditory problems frequently noted (Barlow, 1978). Color blindness appears to be more prevalent among individuals who are moderately retarded than among those who are more mildly retarded or normal (O'Connor, 1975). Early screening for sensory defects is essential, as specific correctional devices or types of intervention may be indicated. In fact, early identification of any health problems may be critical to the total development of the child. While the retardation itself may obscure problems or impede efforts to diagnose them, early intervention and treatment may lessen the effects of the disability and influence the rate and level of development the child may attain.

Down Syndrome

See Dmitriev and Oelwein (1990) for a comprehensive discussion of Down syndrome.

A child who is retarded may be classified as a clinical type. To be regarded as a specific clinical type, an individual must show certain facial, body, and disorder characteristics relating to a particular syndrome associated with mental retardation. While there are a number of these syndromes, the one most frequently associated with mental retardation is Down syndrome.

Besides their distinct physical appearance, children with Down syndrome frequently have specific health-related problems. Many have structural defects of the heart that may threaten their survival, although surgical procedures can be successful in correcting the defect. Lung abnormalities are also frequent in children with Down syndrome, resulting in susceptibility to upper respiratory infections. The incidence of leukemia is higher than in the normal population. Other common health problems of Down syndrome are eye and ear infections, obesity, skin problems (primarily due to their characteristically rough and dry skin), problems of the teeth and gums, and hearing impairments (D. W. Smith & Wilson, 1973).

Individuals who work with children with Down syndrome should be alert to signs of infection, particularly ear and upper respiratory infections, so that early medical treatment can prevent more serious problems. Physical education and exercise programs should also be provided, although the type and amount of activity required of a particular child should be planned with the guidance of medical personnel.

Cerebral Palsy

Not all children with cerebral palsy are mentally retarded; however, a child who does have this condition presents a number of health-related problems. Cerebral palsy is a neuromuscular disability that may result from damage to the brain at birth or during the first 4 years of life. While the condition may include any number of intellectual, sensory, and behavioral disorders, the motor disability presents several potential problems. Because of fluctuating muscle tone, hypertonicity, or hypotonicity, children with cerebral palsy may exhibit atypical posture and movements that limit their participation in learning activities. Limbs that are not exercised may lose their usefulness altogether. Children with cerebral palsy, therefore, usually require professional assistance in handling and positioning. Some children may be in movement or exercise programs that need to be repeated at certain intervals during the day. According to Rainforth and York (1991), the goals of positioning assistance include stabilizing the body, maintaining proper body alignment, and increasing participation in learning activities. If a child wears a cast or a brace, those working with that child should be alert to such signs of circulation problems as swelling, coldness, change of color, and evidence of infection, as well as other skin problems (Robinault & Denhoff, 1973).

Individuals working with youngsters who have both retardation and cerebral palsy should be aware of a number of other problems that sometimes accompany the disorder. Speech difficulties complicated by lack of muscle control are common and often require speech therapy or other special educational measures. Visual and auditory problems are also seen more frequently in the child with cerebral palsy, and corrective measures to improve vision or hearing may be warranted. Difficulties with chewing and swallowing may present real hazards if the child is given such foods as hard candy, popcorn, and chewing gum. Teachers should consult the parents for specific instructions about eating and drinking. As with other disabilities, upper respiratory infections are common, and early symptoms should be reported, since the consequences of such infections may be severe.

Seizure Disorders

Another health problem often associated with cerebral palsy, but also characteristic of other conditions that may accompany mental retardation, is seizures (Neisworth & Smith, 1978). Since convulsive disorders are significantly more common among those who are retarded than among those who are not, teachers working with these individuals should be trained to respond appropriately and to be aware of the possible side effects of seizure control medication (M. H. Epstein et al., 1989).

Seizures vary from momentary disturbances, which may go unnoticed (absence, or petit mal), to episodes involving jerking of the muscles and loss of consciousness (tonic-clonic seizure, or grand mal). Some children experience an aura of sensation just before a seizure begins and may be able to give some indication that it is imminent. In some children, the likelihood of a seizure is increased by external factors, such as flickering lights or loud sounds, or the child's physical condition, such as being highly excited, ill, or fatigued. By being aware of these cues, teachers can be alert to circumstances that might precede or precipitate seizures. Once a seizure occurs, it should not be interrupted. The major concern is to keep the child from injuring himself. During a tonic-clonic (grand mal) seizure, the child should be eased to the floor, furniture and other objects pushed away, and if possible, restrictive clothing loosened and the child turned on his or her side to aid breathing. Someone should remain with the child until the seizure ends, and then allow the child to rest.

Substance Abuse

Until recently, little was written on this topic as it pertains to individuals who are retarded, and the common perception was that this group was less likely to have problems than those without retardation (Ferrara, 1992). Although some studies support this perception (D. Delaney & Poling, 1990), there is still reason for concern. Other sources suggest that problems associated with substance abuse, when it does occur, may arise more quickly and at lower levels of drug use for this group (Resource Center on Substance Abuse and Prevention and Disabilities, 1992). This finding is extremely disturbing, given the fact that more individuals who are retarded live in communities where this threat is widespread.

GENERAL HEALTH CONSIDERATIONS

Nutrition

Proper kinds and amounts of food are necessary for the general well-being of all children. Poor diet not only arrests biological development and diminishes resistance to disease and illness but is also a negative factor in social adjustment and academic learning (Paige, 1975). Inadequate or unbalanced diets may be a result of insufficient food, poor supervision of meals and snacks, or lack of understanding of the importance of proper nutrition and how to provide it.

Illness and Disease

As might be expected, children who are retarded are more susceptible to disease and illness than are children who are not. Poor nutrition and lack of adequate health care (including immunizations) appear to be major factors in promoting problems among children from lower socioeconomic classes. Children who are mildly retarded often have additional disabling conditions or health problems that account for their relatively poor health. The frequency of heart and lung disorders among Down syndrome children is just one example.

Several specific problems are commonly noted among children who are retarded. Colds and upper respiratory infections are more frequent and often last longer than in other children. The seriousness of the symptoms can be compounded by the presence of other disorders such as cardiac conditions.

The incidence of dental problems is also relatively high among children who are retarded. Dental problems are often due to poor nutrition, failure to brush teeth regularly, or absence of routine dental checkups.

Accidents and Injury

Children who are developmentally delayed, as indicated, can be poorly coordinated and awkward. Add to this the poor judgment and impaired reasoning that may come with subaverage intellectual ability, and a higher than average accident rate can be predicted. Conditions accompanying the retardation—limited vision, muscle weakness, motor disabilities, and seizures—may also contribute to increased injuries. This group can also suffer physical injury due to abuse (Zirpoli, 1986).

Physical Activity

A certain amount of exercise and activity is necessary to the total well-being of any individual. For the child who is mentally retarded, a planned program of physical activity is essential for a number of reasons. Individuals who are mildly retarded may not differ appreciably in physical and motor skills from those who are not retarded, and sports and other physical activities may provide an opportunity for expression and achievements as well as an outlet for tension. Gains in physical strength and motor coordination as well as feelings of accomplishment often enhance social and personal adjustment.

For those individuals who deviate more markedly from their nondisabled peers both mentally and physically, planned physical education and recreation programs offer enjoyment and a productive use of leisure time as well as the typical benefits associated with physical activity. Adaptive equipment and materials enable individuals with certain conditions to participate in a wide variety of games and activities.

While opportunities for physical education and recreation historically have represented an area of neglect with respect to people who are mentally retarded (Chinn, Drew, & Logan, 1979), the outlook for the future is far more encouraging (Beasley, 1982; Halle, Silverman, & Regan, 1983). Provisions of the Individuals with Disabilities Education Act include not only physical education but also recreation and leisure education as related services that must be extended to all students. Community agencies and citizens' groups are becoming more actively involved in providing opportunities for recreation. The Special Olympics program remains a viable source of physical activity as well. Programs offered by colleges and universities designed to train professionals in techniques for working with students with disabilities in the area of physical education and recreation are increasing in number and scope.

EDUCATIONAL CHARACTERISTICS

This section examines various facets of the educational programs of students with mild-to-moderate retardation. Specifically, we focus on placement options, curricular and service issues, and performance characteristics.

The diagnosis of milder forms of retardation and any subsequent delivery of special services typically take place after a student has encountered difficulty with the academic, social, or behavioral requirements of general education. As evidence accumulates that this population is less able and has more accompanying disabilities than similarly labeled students of a decade ago (MacMillan, 1989), we can expect earlier diagnosis. Support for this is evidenced by the results of a study by Polloway et al. (1986) of the IEPs of 234 public school students who were identified as EMR. The average age at the time of placement for the younger students in the study (ages six to eleven) was five and one-half years, as opposed to seven and one-half years for the older students (ages twelve to eighteen). In addition, the U.S. Department of Education (1996a) reported an increase of 7 percent in the number of infants and toddlers receiving early intervention services during the 1993–1994 school year and an increase of 6.7 percent in the number of eligible preschoolers receiving services in the fiscal year 1995. The earlier diagnoses imply that special education and related services are being provided earlier in the school careers of children who are mildly retarded than was the case in the past.

Some students who are mildly retarded have been placed in general education for the majority of the school day, with a smaller proportion of time being spent in a special education setting. Data from the U.S. Department of Education (1996), however, continue to paint a picture of limited inclusion in general education classes. While students who are learning disabled or emotionally disturbed are spread across general education classrooms, resource rooms, and separate special education classrooms, students who are retarded are most often placed in separate special education classrooms. Predictably, students who are mildly retarded are more often served in general education classes than are students who are moderately or severely retarded. At the junior and senior high level, students who are mildly retarded may be assigned to resource sections of academic subjects. Special educators usually teach these classes and focus on the academic goals specified in the IEPs. Other periods in the school day may be spent in such classes as health, physical education, athletics, vocational classes, or any one of a number of elective subjects if these are considered appropriate for the individual student. Additional research, however, is necessary to confirm that limited integration of pupils who are mildly retarded into general education programs is a trend.

Retardation and its accompanying problems are recognized earlier in a child with more limited intellectual abilities and adaptive functioning. The more exaggerated developmental delays in motor and language skills and/or physical and health problems are usually responsible for early contacts with medical personnel and community agencies (Bricker & Dow, 1980). With early identification comes a greater chance for eligibility for services now available for preschool-age children as well as for infants and toddlers.

PROGRAMMATIC REALITIES

Preparing students to deal successfully with the demands of adulthood and to live as independently as possible should be the primary goals of any program. The particular demands of adulthood for which one needs to be prepared will vary somewhat depending on probable subsequent environments. Moreover, the nature of the program will also be influenced by the individual's level of schooling (e.g., elementary vs. secondary). The emphasis of curriculum will change as a function of school level and needs of the individual. Figure 6.2 illustrates a two-dimensional (curricular approach and level of schooling) model for deciding the nature of instructional programs. Fundamentally, programs must develop a student's competence in the following areas: employment or further education, home and family, leisure pursuits, community involvement, physical and emotional health, personal responsibility, and interpersonal relationships (Cronin & Patton, 1993).

It is interesting to note, however, that while the literature favors a broad-based curriculum, recent studies of IEP goals for students who are mildly retarded indicate a strong emphasis on academic goals (M. H. Epstein et al., 1989; McBride & Forgnone, 1985). In light of the more recent descriptions of this population, it is not surprising that professionals in the field are calling for a more comprehensive approach to the education of these students, one that includes life skills preparation (D. E. Brolin, 1989; Cronin & Patton, 1993), social skills training (Gresham, 1982; Polloway et al., 1986), and vocational training (J. C. Brolin & Brolin, 1979; Edgar, 1987; Jaquish & Stella, 1986).

Related services are provided to students who have been identified as disabled to enable them to benefit fully from their educational program. It is

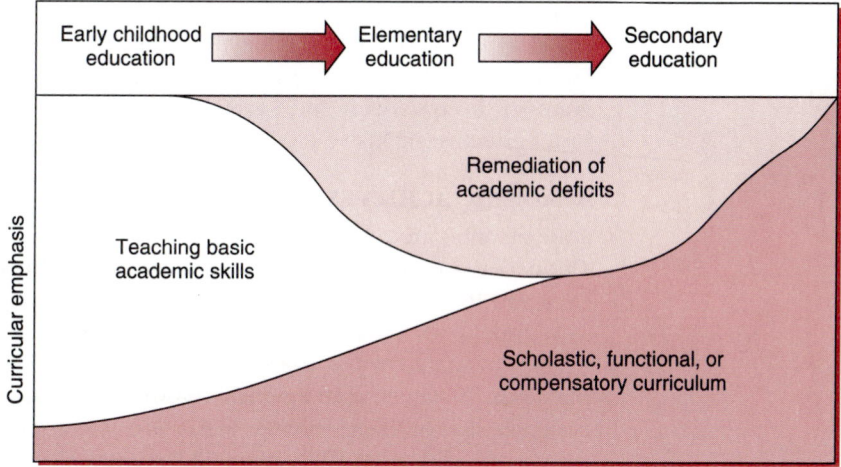

FIGURE 6.2

Curricular Emphasis across Levels of Schooling

Source: Adapted from Michael L. Hardman, Clifford J. Drew, M. Winston Egan, & Barbara Wolf, HUMAN EXCEPTIONALITY: SOCIETY, SCHOOL AND FAMILY, Fourth Edition. Copyright © 1993 by Allyn and Bacon. Reprinted by permission.

likely that many individuals may have secondary impairments and will need additional related services. In the study by M. H. Epstein et al. (1989), the majority of the IEPs for students with mild retardation listed some type of secondary problem. Nearly 90 percent of the students had speech and language disorders; and sensory disorders (particularly visual impairment), convulsive disorders, and emotional and behavioral disorders were more common than in the general population. This study is consistent with other research (MacMillan, 1982; MacMillan & Borthwick, 1980) that characterizes many individuals who are mildly retarded as displaying multiple disabilities and therefore being in need of more related services and support personnel.

School programs for those who need more supports deviate markedly from the general school program in the past. Programs are designed to reflect both the developmental age (level of ability) and the chronological age of the student in selecting goals leading to self-sufficiency (L. F. Brown, Nietupski, & Hamre-Nietupski, 1976). The curriculum for this group typically includes self-help, basic readiness, independent living, communication, socialization, recreation, leisure skills, and cognitive development (Geiger, Brownsmith, & Forgnone, 1978; Snell & Renzaglia, 1986). Researchers advocate the use of age-appropriate materials to teach functional skills that relate to the present or anticipated environmental needs (L. F. Brown, Branston, Hamre-Nietupski, Pumpian, Certo, & Gruenewald, 1979).

As the inclusion movement grows, we anticipate that more students whose needs for supports are greater will be provided services in general education settings. Much work needs to be done to accomplish this goal. For this goal to become a reality, changes to current systems are required. Furthermore, changes must be made within the personnel preparation programs of both general and special educators to create the conditions that foster effective inclusive environments.

ACADEMIC ACHIEVEMENT

Students who are retarded are likely to show deficits in all academic areas. The majority of students who are mildly retarded read at levels lower than expected for their MA, and of the various aspects of reading, comprehension appears to be the most difficult for them (J. L. Carter, 1975; Dunn, 1973a). In mathematics, the majority of students can learn the basic computations; however, mathematical reasoning and appropriate application of concepts to problem-solving tasks are more difficult for this group. Functional arithmetic skills involving money, time, and measurement, because they are important for community living, are an integral part of the curriculum (Westling, 1986).

The school exit rate for students who are mentally retarded has remained fairly stable over the past five years. According to the U.S. Department of Education (1996), results of research studies on students with disabilities leaving school indicate that students who received vocational training during their secondary school years have achieved positive long-term results in terms of greater success at independent living, higher rates of employment, and greater community participation.

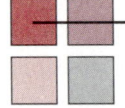

SUMMARY

GENERAL

- Not every person who is mentally retarded may display all the characteristics discussed in this chapter.
- This chapter focuses on individuals who require few or no supports systems in most adaptive skills areas.
- Those considered mentally retarded are part of a heterogeneous group.
- Individuals who are mildly retarded have been referred to as educable or trainable in the past.

DEMOGRAPHIC CHARACTERISTICS

- More males than females are identified.
- There has historically been a disproportionate number of racially different and ethnic minority children being labeled as mildly mentally retarded.

■ Some data support the description that many youth who are mentally retarded live in single-parent families and come from families characterized by lower socioeconomic status.

MOTIVATIONAL AND SOCIOBEHAVIORAL CHARACTERISTICS

■ Motivational characteristics include external locus of control, expectancy for failure, outerdirectedness, and more limited self-regulatory behaviors.

■ Social and behavioral problems are more likely, with some students displaying psychiatric problems as well.

LEARNING CHARACTERISTICS

■ By definition, this group has problems in cognitive areas; however, there is some difference of opinion whether cognitive development is qualitatively or quantitatively different from that of children who are not retarded.

■ Various processes (attention, mediation strategies, memory, generalization) associated with learning can be problematic for this group.

SPEECH AND LANGUAGE CHARACTERISTICS

■ Speech and language problems occur with great frequency among this population.

■ Delayed language development is expected.

PHYSICAL HEALTH CHARACTERISTICS

■ Motor development may be delayed.

■ Sensory deficits are more common among persons who are mentally retarded.

■ Individuals with Down syndrome have a number of physical features common to this condition.

■ Cerebral palsy and seizure disorders occur more frequently in persons who are retarded.

■ The data on the extent of substance abuse in this group are equivocal at this time.

EDUCATIONAL CHARACTERISTICS

■ Students who are mentally retarded enjoy limited inclusion in general education settings.

■ Studies of IEP goals indicate a predominance of academic goals.

■ Many students qualify for related services.

■ The school exit rate for students who are retarded has remained fairly stable over the past five years.

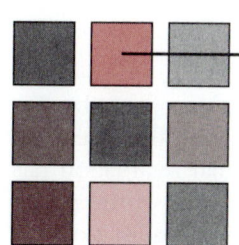

CHAPTER 7

Characteristics of Persons with Severe Mental Retardation

Shannon H. Kim, M.Ed.
The University of Mississippi

Mitylene B. Arnold, Ed.D.
The University of Mississippi

After reading this chapter, the student should be able to

- Discuss ways in which severe mental retardation is defined and how persons with this diagnosis are perceived.
- Describe appropriate curricula and methods of instruction for persons with severe mental retardation, and explain the philosophical model on which these ideas are based.
- Identify and describe suitable outcomes for persons with severe mental retardation.
- Discuss the various types of supports accessed by persons with severe mental retardation.

Key Terms

community-referenced
  instruction
ecological model

extensive supports
natural supports

normalization
pervasive supports

I n Chapter 6, you were introduced to the group of people who comprise the majority of individuals with mental retardation. But what about the rest? Who are they? What are they like? As the definition of mental retardation has changed throughout the years, so has society's perceptions of the group known as persons with severe mental retardation. They are quite possibly our most vulnerable population. Easily observed to be different, they encounter prejudice and fear throughout their lives. Despite such legislative efforts as the Education of the Handicapped Act Amendments of 1990 (PL 101-476, 20 U.S.C. 1400), commonly known as the Individuals with Disabilities Education Act (IDEA), and the Americans with Disabilities Act of 1990 (ADA; PL 101-336, 42 U.S.C. 12101), they are still very often excluded from school and community activities. This chapter describes persons with severe mental retardation, first by exploring various definitional perspectives and then by considering important aspects of this traditionally underserved segment of the population. An expanded focus on educational practices, outcome goals, and support functions follows.

Various implications of the IDEA and the ADA for persons with severe forms of mental retardation are described later in this chapter.

DEFINING THE POPULATION

Generally speaking, individuals who require more extensive supports than those described in Chapter 6 are referred to as persons with severe mental retardation. The "severe" label encompasses the groups specifically designated as having moderate, severe, and profound levels of mental retardation. The lives of these persons have always been greatly impacted by the practice of labeling. Such things as living arrangements, educational practices, and general social acceptance have been influenced by the definition of the day. This section discusses the current demographic descriptors of individuals with severe mental retardation and the various ways in which the construct has been defined.

CURRENT DEMOGRAPHICS

Chapter 3 introduced the idea that the definitions of mental retardation are a reflection of the times in which they are drafted; that "people make of it what they want to, people interpret it in light of their own understandings and prejudices" (Blatt, 1987). People with more severe forms of mental retardation have often suffered in the face of such perceptions. Miscalculation

Life skills instruction is critically important for these students.

of their potential is documented throughout history. One must only look to such descriptions as provided by Goddard in 1920:

> Yet they are the persons who make for us our social problems. The emphasis here is on the word *"incapable."* This is the thing that we have heretofore ignored. We have known that these people *did not* compete successfully and that they *did not* manage their affairs with ordinary prudence, but we have not recognized that they were fundamentally *incapable* of so doing. (p. 5)

Unfortunately, the winds of change were slow to come. Nearly a half-century later, the same sentiment is reflected by another author. "The profoundly retarded individual is considered, on the basis of current knowledge and practices, incapable of profiting from any type of training or education" (Stevens, 1964, p. 4).

Why is the road to understanding the needs, capabilities, and *humanity* of these individuals so long? One reason may well be that it is difficult to understand that which we do not see. Besides the fact that individuals with severe forms of mental retardation have known little community integration until recent times, our understanding is hampered by their status as a relatively rare segment of the population. According to data from the American Psychiatric Association (1994), of the approximately 3 percent of the total population who have mental retardation, only about 15 percent need extensive supports. Specifically, about 10 percent are within the moderate range, with 3 percent in the severe range, and only about 2 percent in the profound range (Figure 7.1).

FIGURE 7.1

Percentages of Population with Mental Retardation

Source: From *Diagnostic and Statistical Manual of Mental Disorders* (4th ed., p. 41) by the American Psychiatric Association, 1994, Washington, DC: American Psychiatric Association. Copyright 1994 by the American Psychiatric Association.

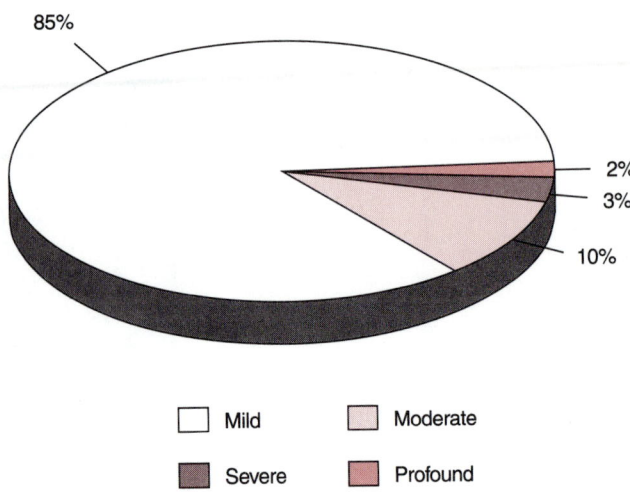

Levels of Mental Retardation

Percentages of Total Population with Mental Retardation

Severe forms of mental retardation are generally recognized earlier in life than are the milder cases. More pronounced developmental delays and additional related medical conditions make this earlier diagnosis possible. Unlike the milder forms of mental retardation, environmental deprivation is not usually an associated factor. Although certain prenatal factors such as premature births are more common in impoverished areas, the prevalence of the condition is relatively stable across all socioeconomic classes (American Psychiatric Association, 1994).

TODAY'S DEFINITIONS

The definition of mental retardation offered by the latest American Association on Mental Retardation (AAMR) manual (1992) discontinued the use of the distinguishing terms *mild, moderate, severe,* and *profound.* For the purposes of this chapter, persons with severe forms of mental retardation are those who generally require extensive and/or pervasive supports to function with maximal success. More extensive support needs are differentiated from more limited support needs in frequency, duration, and urgency. We return to the discussion of supports later in this chapter. Specifically, **extensive supports** are provided regularly, in at least some environments, and on a long-term basis. **Pervasive supports** are provided on a constant basis, across all environments, and are of a potentially life-sustaining nature (AAMR, 1992). Supports may be provided to assist with basic and/or complex tasks of daily life, with management of emotional or psychological concerns, or with physical health needs.

Though the AAMR definition has been considered the definitive one in the field of mental retardation, the *Diagnostic and Statistical Manual of Mental Disorders: Fourth Edition* (DSM-IV; American Psychiatric Association, 1994) has been the generally accepted authority for diagnosing psychological disorders that may require services. At the present time, the DSM-IV is used primarily by professionals in the fields of psychology and psychiatry and still adheres to the levels of severity used in Grossman's 1983 AAMR definition for diagnostic purposes. The manual gives in-depth descriptions of the various levels of mental retardation. For example, people with moderate retardation are described as profiting from vocational services and training in social skills. People with severe mental retardation are presented as usually able to learn sight words and function well in the community. People with profound mental retardation are described as needing the most intensive supports with respect to self-help, vocational, and communication skills.

The definitions provided by the AAMR and the DSM-IV are designed for diagnostic purposes and specialized knowledge is required to apply them to individual cases. The sociopolitical climate of the past thirty years has generated a number of special interest groups and service providers to ensure that persons with mental retardation and other disabilities are afforded the opportunities that all citizens of the United States have come to expect. Such organizations are not generally responsible for diagnosing disabilities but do need to expressly define the populations they are designed to serve. The rarity of severe and profound levels of disabilities such as mental retardation and autism has led to the development of inclusive definitions such as "severe disabilities" or "developmental disabilities."

The Association for Persons with Severe Handicaps (TASH), the advocacy leader for persons with severe disabilities, offers a person-centered perspective through the following definition:

> . . . individuals of all ages who require extensive ongoing support in more than one major life activity in order to participate in integrated community settings and to enjoy a quality of life that is available to citizens with fewer or no disabilities. Support may be required for life activities such as mobility, communication, self-care, and learning, and necessary for independent living, employment and self-sufficiency. (Lindley, 1990, p. 1)

These definitions present an image of individuals who need varying but intensive levels of support to participate in society. Definitions that define supports needed for participation in the community facilitate the processes of needs assessment, goal setting, and quality of life evaluation. Definitions are important for accessing the service delivery system, but due to the highly individualistic, complex nature of these individuals, the specification of each individual's educational goals and support needs provides the most meaningful information.

NATURE AND NEEDS OF PERSONS WITH SEVERE MENTAL RETARDATION

As alluded to previously, our perceptions of persons with severe mental retardation and the types of services they may require have vast implications for the persons and families of persons with more extensive support needs. In this section, we discuss the four dimensions of mental retardation identified in the 1992 AAMR manual as they apply to persons with severe mental retardation. The dimensions are: intellectual functioning and adaptive skills, psychological/emotional aspects, physical and other health considerations, and environmental considerations.

INTELLECTUAL FUNCTIONING AND ADAPTIVE SKILLS

Although one's IQ score no longer dictates any specific range of mental retardation in the most recent AAMR definition, one would generally expect that as IQ decreases, the intensity of needed supports increases. This is often a valid assumption, but it does not hold true in every case. For example, it is possible for an individual who has an IQ below 50 to function with limited or intermittent supports, just as it is possible for an individual with an IQ above 55 to need extensive or pervasive supports. Though IQ is an integral part of the definition of mental retardation, it is generally not the most useful source of information about a person's needs and abilities.

A more salient information source for identifying an individual who requires extensive supports is adaptive skill assessment. The AAMR (1992) has provided ten areas of adaptive skill used to generate a profile of a person's strengths and weaknesses. Some of these skill areas, such as communication, home living, and self-care, have been the focus of education in treatment plans for years. Others, such as social and leisure skills, are being brought to the fore as more persons with greater degrees of disability move into the community. Table 7.1 lists some common attributes of persons with severe mental retardation. The educational concerns section addresses adaptive skills in more depth.

PSYCHOLOGICAL/EMOTIONAL ASPECTS

The issue of dual diagnosis, as discussed in Chapter 6, has implications for individuals with severe mental retardation as well as those with milder forms of mental retardation. Mental illness has been estimated to occur about 5 to 15 percent more often among persons with mental retardation residing outside institutions than among the general population (Parsons, May, & Menolascino, 1984). These rates increase if individuals living in institutions are also considered (Spreat, Telles, Conroy, Feinstein, & Colombatto, 1987). Impulse control disorders, anxiety disorders, and mood disorders are cited as having a high rate of diagnosis in the severe to profound ranges (King, DeAntonio, McCracken, & Forness, 1994).

TABLE 7.1

Characteristics of Persons with Severe Mental Retardation

Persons with severe mental retardation frequently have multiple disabilities, including physical problems, and usually look and act differently from persons of the same age without disabilities.

Slow rates of acquisition of new skills

Difficulty in maintenance and generalization of newly learned skills

Deficits in communication skills

Impaired physical and motor development

Deficits in self-help skills

Frequent maladaptive behavior

Display warmth, humor, sociability, and persistence

Can (and do!) learn

Source: From *Exceptional Children: An Introduction to Special Education* (5th ed., p. 525) by W. Heward, 1996, Upper Saddle River, NJ: Merrill/Prentice Hall. Copyright 1996 by Merrill/Prentice Hall. Adapted by permission.

Few instruments exist for the assessment of psychological disorders among persons with severe mental retardation. Test developers face the challenges of overcoming such barriers as physical limitations, speech impairments, sensory impairments, and communication skills. Table 7.2 provides a list of instruments designed for use with this population.

Diagnosing psychological disorders may be problematic in that the symptoms can be misinterpreted or altogether unnoticed for persons with severe or profound mental retardation. For example, a study by Meins (1995) indicated that depressive symptoms are more likely to mimic acting out behavior (e.g., psychomotor agitation and irritable mood) than typical sadness. Issues such as these have led to the questioning of the applicability of the DSM-IV definitions of psychiatric disorders to individuals with severe and profound mental retardation. However, the DSM-IV is the definitive diagnostic source for such disorders, and its classification system is recommended for use by the AAMR (1992). DSM-IV advises that information should be garnished from several sources to guard against misdiagnosis. Behavioral observations, interviews with the individual and his or her significant others, medical examinations, and psychometric evaluations are some examples of valuable sources of information for the diagnostic process (Table 7.2).

PHYSICAL AND OTHER HEALTH CONSIDERATIONS

The need for extensive and pervasive supports for persons with severe mental retardation is, in many cases, directly related to physical or health-related concerns. Many of the etiological conditions known to cause mental retardation, especially the more severe forms, are also associated with physical impairments. The risk of sensory, neuromuscular, cardiovascular, neurological, and other biologically based conditions increases with the severity of mental retardation (American Psychiatric Association, 1994).

"OH, WHAT A BEAUTIFUL MOURNING"

The poem printed below was written by Marc Gold, a respected leader in the area of vocational training and a strong champion for the rights of people with mental retardation. This poem, read at the end of a speech that Gold gave in 1973, has been cited often since then and is used in the opening sound track of the film *Try Another Way*. Embedded in the poem is commentary about expectations, perceptions, testing, opportunities, and capabilities. The message of this poem is as relevant today as it was in 1973 or when its author reflected back on it (Gold, 1980).

An End to the Concept of Mental Retardation

Oh, What a Beautiful Mourning

If you could only know me for who I am
Instead of for who I am not,
There would be so much more to see
'cause there's so much more that I've got.
So long as you see me as mentally retarded,
Which supposedly means something, I guess,
There is nothing that you or I could ever do
To make me a human success.
Someday you'll know that tests aren't built

To let me stand next to you.
By the way you test me, all they can do
Is make me look bad through and through.
And someday soon I'll get my chance,
When some of you finally adapt.
You'll be delighted to know that though I'm MR,
I'm not all handicapped.

Source: From "An End to the Concept of Mental Retardation: Oh, What a Beautiful Mourning" by M. W. Gold in *Did I Say That? Articles and Commentary on the Try Another Way System* (pp. 143–144), 1982, Champaign, IL: Research Press. Reprinted by permission.

The range of functional abilities for persons with severe mental retardation ranges from very athletic to virtually immobile. Whereas some persons may be able to climb mountains, others may be unable to chew their food. Even the healthiest of individuals may have physical limitations that warrant extensive supports. For example, a person born without a right hand may require a prosthetic device, specially constructed tools and utensils, and extended time allowances for tasks requiring the use of two hands. But for those persons for whom health and physical concerns are paramount, the intensity of needed supports is much greater. Not only must they overcome such obstacles as obtaining adequate nutrition, exercise, and hydration, but their lives may also be complicated by a heightened susceptibility to common ailments and infections.

Health concerns are compounded by the difficulties of diagnosing injuries and illnesses as they arise. Persons with severe mental retardation are often unable to communicate their feelings of discomfort and may be even less able to vocalize the sources of their pain. Additionally, persons with extensive and pervasive support needs represent such a small segment of the

TABLE 7.2

Psychiatric Assessment Tools for Persons with Severe Disabilities

Assessment Tool	Purpose
Aberrant Behavior Checklist (ABC) Aman (1986)	For persons with mental retardation in residential settings; may indicate areas for further exploration
The Maladaptive Behavior Rating Subscale of the AAMD Adaptive Behavior Scale—Revised. American Association on Mental Deficiency (1974)	A component of adaptive behavior assessment that may indicate areas for further exploration
The Psychopathology Instrument for Mentally Retarded Adults (PIMRA) Matson (1988)	Diagnostic screening instrument for persons with mental retardation; although the PIMRA is largely a self-report measure, there is an informant interview as well
The Reiss Screen for Maladaptive Behavior Reiss (1987)	Diagnostic screening instrument for persons aged 12 and up who have mild, moderate, or severe mental retardation

References: Matson, J. L. (1988). *The Psychopathology Inventory for Mentally Retarded Adults.* Orland Park, IL: International Diagnostic Systems.

American Association on Mental Deficiency. (1974). *AAMD Adaptive Behavior Scale-Revised.* Washington, DC: Author.

Aman, M. (1986). *Aberrant Behavior Checklist.* East Aurora, NY: Slosson Educational Publications.

Reiss, S. P. (1987). *Reiss Screen for Maladaptive Behavior.* Worthington, OH: International Diagnostic Systems.

population that their complex, specialized needs may not be especially well understood by community health-care providers.

ENVIRONMENTAL CONSIDERATIONS

A diagnosis of mental retardation reflects the characteristics of an individual relative to society as a whole. The constructs of intelligence, adaptiveness, psychological well-being, emotional stability, and even physical health exist as continua with no precise dividing line between the haves and the have-nots. It stands to reason that persons who lack a sense of comfort and familiarity with the society in which they live, or who lack the tools necessary for success in that environment, are likely to demonstrate skill deficits and aberrant behaviors. An American taking an intelligence test designed for an unfamiliar society could easily score in the below-average range. She may have difficulty with skills deemed very simple, her natural emotional reactions may be seen as abnormal, and her physical dexterity and skills could be interpreted to be underdeveloped. She could easily be considered to have "extensive support needs." However, the longer she lives in the new society, the more comfortable they try to make her. The more they teach her about their culture, the more independent she will become and the less support she will require.

We cannot expect persons with severe mental retardation to advance in adaptivity unless they are involved with the community to which they are expected to conform. As with all human beings, the relationship between persons with severe mental retardation and the community is a reciprocal one. The more society is willing to invest in providing supports, the higher the likelihood that the individual will learn to function without them. This is not to say that we can "cure" mental retardation. However, we can and should expect that "with appropriate supports over a sustained period of time, the life functioning of individuals with mental retardation will generally improve" (AAMR, 1992, p. 109). Studies of skill acquisition of persons with severe mental retardation who have increased interactions with the community verify this expectation. Kennedy and Itkonen (1994) indicate social gains under such conditions. Several authors, including Snell (1993) and Wilcox and Bellamy (1982), have noted over the years that students with more severe mental retardation who participate in a community-based curriculum find and retain jobs at a greater rate than do those who participate in self-contained educational programs.

On the topic of increased interactions between persons who have disabilities and those who do not, questions about the impact on society at large naturally arise. Research has indicated that authority figures and nondisabled peers develop helpful, accepting, positive attitudes toward persons with severe mental retardation after inclusive experiences (Strully & Strully, 1989). Block and Rizzo (1995) discuss the development of facilitative attitudes of nondisabled peers and authority figures after inclusive experiences. Additionally, Bernabe and Block (1994) report a case of designing supports that allowed a young girl with multiple and severe disabilities, including moderate mental retardation, to play on a softball team. They indicate that her participation not only helped the girl to make gains in attention, coordination, and social skills, but also showed that the other girls in the league were ready and willing to provide encouragement, support, and friendship—all without any adverse effect on the performance or standing of the team. So, it would seem that community involvement with persons who have extensive support needs offers positive outcomes for all.

EDUCATIONAL CONCERNS

Little historical information about the education of persons with severe mental retardation is known. Education of such persons simply was not a subject of great concern in centuries past. The contributions of 19th-century re-

Communication is one of the most important skills addressed in special education settings.

formists (e.g., Eduoard Seguin, Samuel G. Howe) laid the groundwork for subsequent models of instruction for persons with mental retardation (Safford & Safford, 1996). A. McDonnell, McDonnell, Hardman, and McCune (1991) provide an excellent description of the three major educational models used since 1900: the institutional model, developmental model, and ecological model. In this section, we discuss each of these models as well as curriculum development and teaching strategy.

INSTITUTIONAL MODEL

During the early 1900s, it was commonly believed that persons with severe mental retardation were incapable of learning. Institutions were built to separate and protect such people from society and to protect society from them. Unfortunately, persons with disabilities were even held responsible for an array of societal problems including crime, immorality, venereal disease, and prostitution (Wolfensberger, 1972).

During this period, the institutional model defined the provision of educational services to persons with severe mental retardation. This model was based on the belief that persons with severe disabilities were "sick," unable to learn, and a menace to society (A. McDonnell et al., 1991). Institutions were structured on a medical model of service delivery. Services were based

Work by Sayegh and Dennis (1965), Skeels (1966), and Sloan and Harmon (1947) document the negative influences of institutional placement on the educational development of their residents.

on a diagnosis of the individual's pathology and a treatment plan to return to a "healthy" state. This philosophy offered little hope for persons with the most extensive needs. Many professionals believed that to try to teach basic skills to individuals with severe mental retardation was unkind, since there was no hope of mastery (J. McDonnell & Hardman, 1995). As early as the 1940s, empirical evidence began to show that institutions limited the development of their residents (Kaplan, 1943).

DEVELOPMENTAL MODEL

America's behind-the-scenes look at institutional life triggered social, judicial, and legislative mandates for change. One consequence was a shift to a developmental model of education, a model that encompassed the principle of **normalization**—the idea that persons with severe disabilities should live *as much as possible* like their peers without disabilities (Nirje, 1969; Wolfensberger, 1972). The developmental model conceives of persons with disabilities as those who can benefit from training and educational instruction. This model is based on two primary assumptions: persons with severe disabilities learn in the same way as their peers without disabilities but require more time to master skills; and persons with disabilities have the right to participate in the normal routines of life and to establish a lifestyle comparable to their peers without disabilities.

The developmental model of education was a remarkable improvement over its predecessor. It is a great step to move from the belief that certain individuals are incapable of learning to one that encourages the notion of treating them as normally as possible. Unfortunately, the notion of being developmentally similar was based on the statistical concept of "mental age." Individuals who scored below 30 on an intelligence test were considered to have a "mental age" similar to that of a very young child. The developmental philosophy led to educational programming in which adults with severe mental retardation were playing with toys designed to develop skills in preschool children. This happened when practitioners assumed that a person with a "mental age" of two should play with two-year-old toys until they had reached the "developmental age" of three. This type of educational programming led to few positive outcomes for persons with severe mental retardation.

Furthermore, the principle of normalization led to environments that were "work-like," "home-like," and "classroom-like." Far from including persons with severe mental retardation in meaningful educational experiences, the developmental model forced persons with disabilities to "prepare" to enter school, and to "get ready" for more time in the classroom and cafeteria. The achievement of predetermined developmental goals and objectives would indicate a person was ready to move to a less restrictive environment. The ultimate goal was for the student to move through the channels to full-time regular class placement. Figure 7.2 visually represents this continuum of services (S. J. Taylor, 1988).

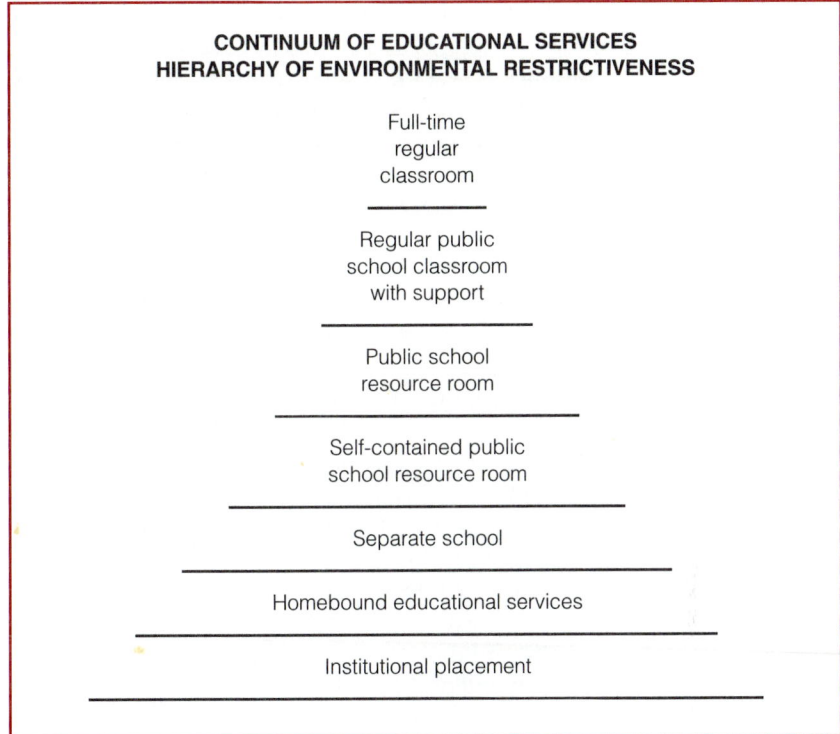

FIGURE 7.2

Continuum of Educational Services: Hierarchy of Environmental Restrictiveness Information

Source: From "Caught in the Continuum: A Critical Analysis of the Principles of the Least Restrictive Environment" by S. J. Taylor, 1988, *Journal of the Association for Persons with Severe Handicaps, 13,* p. 43. Copyright 1988 by JASH. Adapted by permission.

Unfortunately, tenets put forth by the developmental model were based on a faulty premise. Persons with severe mental retardation do not follow a slowed-down version of normal learning. The characteristics of the individual's disability prevented the achievement of developmental milestones and accordingly diminished his or her chances of moving to less restrictive environments. Research in the early 1980s documented that significant numbers of adults with severe disabilities were unemployed (Wehman, Kregel, & Seyfarth, 1985), had little interaction with peers without disabilities (L. Harris et al., 1986), had no friends outside their residential programs (Bercovici, 1983), and had little independence or autonomy in making lifestyle choices (Scheerenberger & Felsenthal, 1977). Again, research indicated the need to move to a more effective educational model to ensure that persons with severe mental retardation could become fully participating members of society.

ECOLOGICAL MODEL

More recently, best practices in educational services have been based on the **ecological model.** The ecological model includes the beliefs that people with disabilities have a right to participate in educational, economic, and social aspects of the community, and that educational programs should be designed to enable persons with severe disabilities to select supports that will enable them to participate fully in a broad range of school and community activities.

The ecological model is based on a philosophy of "place then train." This enables persons with severe mental retardation to learn in the environment in which the particular skills will be used, rather than learning the skill in a segregated setting and attempting to generalize it to a second setting. The ecological model of instruction is meant to achieve the maximum level of societal participation possible for each individual rather than attempting to replicate "normal" functioning in non-normal environments. Educational programming, in this model, must be highly individualized. Some individuals may achieve total independence, while others will be involved in partial participation, depending upon the levels of support each needs and receives (cf. Snell, 1993).

Schalock (1986) defines a three-phase process to maximize the fit between individuals and their environment. First, the specific demands of the activity and the environment are evaluated in relation to each person's behavioral abilities. Second, the "goodness of fit" between each person's capabilities and the environmental demands is assessed. Assessment, in this case, centers on barriers that prevent the person's achievement in the particular setting. Third is the development of supports designed to overcome the barriers to success.

Proponents of the ecological model have paved the way for innovations in supported living, employment, and education. These developments have led to new avenues of inclusion for persons with severe mental retardation. Programs based on the ecological model identify life options that meet personalized needs, then assist the student to attain those goals through very specific supports. Rusch, Chadsey-Rusch, and Johnson (1991) provide research data suggesting that the ecological model provides more positive outcomes for individuals with severe disabilities than those in the developmental model.

CURRICULUM AND TEACHING STRATEGIES

Educational programming for persons with severe mental retardation has made great strides since the late 1970s. Teaching methods relate directly to traditional learning theory and the methods developed in education and psychology (and referred to in that discipline as applied behavior analysis). Systematic instruction of students with severe mental retardation has provided empirical data to illustrate that learning actually occurs (Snell, 1993). The information generated from systematic instruction has provided a large body of data from which to draw conclusions. These data indicate that teaching persons with severe mental retardation is often considered to be the most exciting and rewarding instruction in public education.

What should these persons be taught? The determination of curriculum is overwhelmingly important for learners with severe mental retardation. These learners must be given choices in the selection of instructional goals and objectives. Choice and autonomy are considered integral to a best practice approach to education. Skills that are selected are typically found in the domains of self-help, domestic, leisure, communication, vocational, community, and social/friendship. These areas reflect the ten adaptive skill areas examined in the AAMR's diagnostic process. Table 7.3 provides brief descriptions of these important skill areas. The evaluation of school success is determined by the relative independence, productivity, and social integration of the person completing the public school process.

Educational programming has several other issues worth investigating. Optimal educational programs are generally **community-referenced instruction,** or are related to actual incidents that naturally occur in the environment. Instructional time is too valuable to waste learning unnecessary skills. The most useful learning activities are both functional and age appropriate. For example, a seventeen-year-old will probably derive more benefit from learning to recognize words and symbols that warn of danger than from learning the alphabet song. Not only are such activities more likely to promote autonomy, but they are also more naturally incorporated into the regular curriculum.

Since education is designed to enhance the student's ability to function successfully in a world inhabited largely by people without disabilities, it is important that instruction be delivered in integrated settings. Consider the difference between a person from Iowa who took a class in Spanish as a high school sophomore, and a person from Iowa who spent his sophomore year as an exchange student to Spain. While it is possible to learn about another culture without experiencing it first-hand, opportunities for learning are greatly enhanced through direct experience. L. Brown et al. (1989) list four reasons why all school-age children should be educated in the same settings. First, students without disabilities who are educated alongside students with disabilities are more likely to function as responsible adults in a pluralistic society. Second, integrated schools provide more meaningful instructional environments. Third, families have greater access to activities in neighborhood schools. Finally, there are more opportunities to develop a wide range of social relationships in integrated schools. If a child associates exclusively with persons who have severe disabilities, chances are very good that he or she will assume at least some of the maladaptive behaviors they display. Likewise, the child has a better chance of acquiring more adaptive behaviors if these are displayed by classmates without disabilities on a daily basis.

Integrated learning settings are as important for adults as they are for children. If anyone has ever tried to tell you how to ride a bicycle, then

TABLE 7.3

Curriculum Components: Skills Commonly Addressed through Education

Communication skills are of particular concern to such individuals. Learners should be encouraged to express themselves, whether verbally or augmentatively.

Community living skills are those such as accessing public transportation, shopping, banking, and other similar activities.

Domestic skills are related to housekeeping-type chores. These skills include such things as making beds, the preparation of meals, appropriate use of household appliances such as microwave ovens, clothes washers, and dryers.

Friendship and socialization skills are central to both instruction and long-term outcomes.

Leisure activities are an integral part of all people's lives. Without suitable leisure skills, all individuals risk mental and physical health problems.

Self-help skills include tasks that promote personal independence (dressing, feeding, toileting, and bathing) and are of varying levels of importance to the individuals who do not have such skills.

Vocational skills are critical to all students. Persons with severe mental retardation are capable of working in competitive employment with support. The school years can do much to facilitate competitive employment outcomes. Financial independence and productivity are central to our society's concept of an individual and must be included in preparing students with severe mental retardation for the transition from school to work.

you understand that it is not always easy to apply information you've learned *about* a skill to actually *performing* that skill. When teaching a person who has pronounced difficulties learning new information, it is very important to give the person every advantage. For adults, this means that job skills are taught on the job and domestic skills are taught in the person's home.

APPROPRIATE OUTCOMES

Perhaps no one has been more influential in the design, implementation, and evaluation of appropriate outcomes than Professor Lou Brown and his students at the University of Wisconsin at Madison.

In the previous section, we made several allusions to the concept of outcomes. Desirable educational outcomes for students with disabilities are identical to those outcomes for their age mates without disabilities. John Dewey (1966) told us that good schools should work to develop good citizens. Good citizens are personally responsible (independent), work hard (productive), and have networks of support through their families, neighbors, friends, and associates (an integral part of the community in which they live). All educational goals and support plans should have a clear and positive relationship to fulfilling that purpose. In this section, we explore outcomes of independence, productivity, and community integration, which are currently considered to be the standard by which all goals should be set.

INDEPENDENCE

To obtain a level of personal independence, an individual must be allowed to experiment and make mistakes. Overprotection is a common injustice inflicted upon persons with severe mental retardation. Independence is fostered when a person is encouraged to make choices and to take part in collective decision-making processes. Making choices must be something an individual does every day so that he or she has a better chance of becoming self-reliant and self-assured. If one has never learned to make such basic decisions as what cereal to eat for breakfast, how can that person be expected to function successfully in the community?

For persons with severe mental retardation, life plans are tangible entities. For much of society, life plans are vague concepts that are in a continual stage of revision. Each person may consider the input of others, but final decisions are generally made in the minds of each individual. Imagine if your life was planned *for* you by a group of professionals for whom planning the lives of others was only one part of a very demanding occupation. The desires of persons with mental retardation must be sought, regardless of level of disability. Parents, family members, and significant others can be very helpful in assisting each individual to express his or her likes and dislikes. Persons with severe mental retardation and their parents can and should make decisions regarding all aspects of life, including their educational goals, objectives, and activities. Teachers should serve to facilitate these choices (Arnold & Serpas, 1992).

PRODUCTIVITY

In our society, *productivity* is generally defined as holding a job and being economically self-sustaining. Therefore, the most desirable outcome for all individuals, including those with severe mental retardation, is competitive employment. For this to occur, education and training must focus on vocational instruction and on-the-job skill development. Research generated since the early 1980s demonstrates that competitive employment is a viable outcome for persons with severe mental retardation (M. L. Hill, Wehman, Kregel, Banks, & Metzler, 1987).

Job placement is rarely the final chapter in an adult's education. Like the rest of society, persons with severe mental retardation must be able to adjust to the world of work, maintain employment, and recuperate from job loss. Rusch, Enchelmaier, and Kohler (1994) identified the following as outcome components for successful school-to-work transition: development of individual transition plans; demonstration of improved work opportunities; job placement in competitive, integrated settings; and documentation of progress in employment-related skills. These outcomes must continue to be documented

TRAVEL TRAINING FOR PERSONS WITH COGNITIVE OR PHYSICAL DISABILITIES

Traveling independently on public transportation is one occasion when a person with a cognitive impairment must perform with absolutely no assistance. Training a person with a cognitive impairment to use public transportation requires a comprehensive and individualized instructional program. Before a person with a cognitive disability can safely use public transportation, she or he must demonstrate 100 percent consistency in many functional skill areas, beyond simply learning the travel route to and from a destination.

Before travel training begins, a travel trainer determines a student's strengths and weaknesses, assesses how much support the student can expect from her or his parents or guardians, and reviews the travel route to determine the feasibility of traveling to a specific destination. Travel training begins only when the student is ready to learn the travel route and has support from parents or guardians. It's notable that a student with a cognitive disability does not necessarily have to know how to read a clock, make change, or understand survival signs to succeed in a travel training program, though these skills certainly are assets.

A comprehensive travel training program for people with a cognitive disability should consist of the following:

Phase 1:   Detailed instruction in specific travel routes, fare costs, boarding and deboarding sites, and the demonstration of pedestrian skills necessary for this travel route, as well as constant practice in life skills such as appropriate interaction with community workers and with strangers, use of public telephone, and appropriate behavior in public places.

Phase 2:   Direct observation of the student by the travel trainer to verify that the student has learned all necessary travel skills taught in Phase 1.

Phase 3:   Instruction in emergency procedures. Emergencies can include boarding the wrong transit

throughout life. Occupational change is by no means unusual in the United States. It is therefore unreasonable to expect that an individual with severe mental retardation would retain one job throughout adulthood. As normal life transitions and fluctuations in the labor market occur, individuals will need different supports in different jobs to maintain consistent employment.

COMMUNITY INTEGRATION

Community integration implies that the individual is not only situated in a place with his or her nondisabled peers but is actually involved to the extent that he or she cares to be involved. Early efforts to enhance the lives of persons with mental retardation through deinstitutionalization were criticized as too often subjecting individuals to even more social isolation than they had experienced in the institution (Bercovici, 1983). Placement in the vehicle, missing a stop, or losing one's fare or transfer pass.

Phase 4: Assessment of the student's interactive skills with strangers. Travel training programs may use plainclothes police officers or travel trainers (whom the student has not met) to approach the traveling student and try to extract personal information from him or her. Students pass this assessment procedure if they do not impart personal information to or leave with a stranger.

Phase 5: Indirect observation of the student. As the student walks to and from the transit stop and rides the transit vehicle independently, her or his performance is assessed at a distance by a travel trainer, who follows in a car. The student is aware that she or he is being observed.

Phase 6: Covert observation and assessment. The student is not aware that she or he is being observed.

Phase 7: Follow-up observations. Periodically, a student who successfully completes a travel training program should be covertly observed to verify that she or he is still practicing safe travel skills.

While different travel training programs may vary the order in which they teach travel skills, the teaching methods of travel training programs should be the same. The average length of a quality travel training program is fifteen sessions, though training time will vary according to the complexity of the travel route and the nature of the student's disability.

Once a person with a cognitive impairment begins to travel independently along one travel route, typically, she or he learns other travel routes with relative ease. Sometimes intense instruction is required to travel to a new destination, especially if reaching the new destination requires new or more advanced pedestrian skills or different modes of transportation.

Source: From "Travel Training for Persons with Cognitive or Physical Disabilities: An Overview" by P. J. Voorhees, 1996, *NICHCY Transition Summary, 9,* pp. 7–9.

community is not enough. The support systems must extend to foster a sense of belonging in that community. Amado (1996) reminds us that we sometimes lose sight of the true purpose of inclusion:

> Sometimes the service system seems to be based on an assumption that people with disabilities are different from those without disabilities—that for persons with disabilities, the more skills they learn or programs they pass the more satisfying their lives will be. The truth is that for all of us the main ingredient of happiness and satisfaction is how much love we have in our lives. (p. 8)

Common services that the majority of the population can take for granted are sometimes difficult for a person with severe mental retardation to obtain. Barriers to accessing such community resources may include lack of knowledge of such resources (Schleien, Ray, & Green, 1996), deficits in social skills

A statement of transition services must be included in the IEP of all students no later than age 16 identified as disabled under IDEA.

Questions regarding the ability of persons with severe mental retardation to participate effectively in religious practice have been addressed through guidelines by Hoeksema (1995).

(Gaylord-Ross & Chadsey-Rusch, 1991), and social self-consciousness (Zetlin & Turner, 1985). Elective participation in religious activities is an example of a commonly overlooked element of true community membership. A study by Riordan and Vasa (1991) indicated that clergy were aware of few persons with disabilities in their congregations, so provisions for their education and participation in rites of passage have been infrequent. Inclusion in traditional religious practice may not only allow them the opportunity to worship but also provide them with a sense of community (Hoeksema, 1995). Peer groups are important sources of social support for all people; persons with severe mental retardation are no different. We all share the need for human interaction.

One group that can sometimes become particularly isolated is the over sixty-five age group. The Administration on Aging works to ensure that elderly Americans have access to several types of community programs. Within the administration, Area Agencies on Aging offer such services as congregate meal sites and often coordinate activities for members of this age group. However, May and Morazas (1994) found avenues of community involvement among seniors with mental retardation to be very limited. Community integration as a measure of outcome should reflect equal access for all people to all social opportunities. It is toward that end that best practice efforts are currently being directed.

SUPPORTS

Throughout this chapter, we have utilized the concept of supports. By now you have probably gathered that a support is a resource that enhances a person's ability to live, learn, and work with greater independence. Persons with severe mental retardation will vary in the number and intensity of supports needed. Some may be able to function successfully with less extensive supports in one or more areas but will very likely need increased levels of individually designed supports in the majority of areas. The AAMR (1992) sought to explicitly define different kinds of supports and the functions they serve. Table 7.4 lists some of these supports and will be referred to throughout this section as we discuss the planning and implementation of supports.

SUPPORTS PLANNING

For persons with severe mental retardation to achieve maximal independence, the necessary supports must be accessible in all domains of life. Coordinating the various supports needed in different environments can be an exceptionally difficult task. Input should be sought not only from professionals involved in such areas as education, psychology, and medicine, but also from family members and the person with severe mental retardation. The involvement of family members is valuable not only for their ideas but because they can assist others in understanding the many ways their loved one expresses any preferences, needs, and opinions. The AAMR's position is that "the intensities of supports can be determined at least in part by the person with mental retardation . . ." (1992, p. 105). Every person can justifiably expect to be treated with respect and dignity; this includes participation in his or her own life planning. According to the Americans with Disabilities Act of 1990:

> Individuals with disabilities are a discrete and insular minority who have been faced with restrictions and limitations, subjected to a history of purposeful unequal treatment, and relegated to a position of political powerlessness in our society, based on characteristics that are beyond the control of such individuals and resulting from stereotypic assumptions not truly indicative of the individual ability of such individuals to participate in, and contribute to, society; the Nation's proper goals regarding individuals with disabilities are to assure equality of opportunity, full participation, independent living, and economic self-sufficiency for such individuals. (U.S. Code 12101, § 2.a.7, 2.a.8)

Beyond legality, the principles of motivation and goal attainment demonstrate the importance of including the person with mental retardation in the assessment and decision-making process. There is value inherent in the person's input; namely, who would have better insight into what is needed or wanted? Research shows that people who participate in planning their course of action have a greater likelihood of follow-through than those whose course is planned for them (Berkman & Meyer, 1988; Egan, 1994). Additionally, if the overarching goal of support is to promote independence through choice and self-advocacy, would it not be hypocritical to disallow the person's participation in the planning process?

TABLE 7.4
Support Functions and Representative Activities

Support Function[a]	Representative Activities		
Befriending	Advocating Car pooling Supervising Instructing	Evaluating Communicating Training Giving feedback	Befriending Associating Collecting data Socializing
Financial planning	Working with SSI-Medicaid Advocating for benefits	Assisting with money management Protection and legal assistance	Budgeting Income assistance and planning/considerations

Employee assistance	Counseling
	Procuring/using assistive
	  technology devices
		Supervisory training
		Job performance enhancement
			Crisis intervention/assistance
			Job/task accommodation and
			  redesigning job/work duties

Behavioral support	Functional analysis
	Multicomponent instruction
	Emphasis on antecedent
	  manipulation
		Manipulation of ecological and
		  setting events
		Teaching adaptive behavior
			Building environment with effective
			  consequences and minimizing
			  the use of punishers

In-Home living assistance	Personal maintenance/care Transfer and mobility Dressing and clothing care Architectural modifications	Communication devices Behavioral support Eating & food management Housekeeping	Respite care Attendant care Homehealth aides Homemaker services and med alert devices

Community access and use	Carpooling/rides program
	Transportation training
		Recreation/leisure involvement
		Community awareness
		  opportunities
		Vehicle modification
			Community use opportunities and
			  interacting with generic agencies

Health assistance	Medical appointments Medical interventions Supervision	Emergency procedures Mobility (assistive devices) Counseling appointments	Hazard awareness Safety training Physical therapy and related activities and
	Med Alert devices	Medication taking	Counseling interventions

Source: From *Mental Retardation: Definition, Classifications, and Systems of Support* (9th ed., p. 104) by the American Association on Mental Retardation, 1992, Washington, DC: American Association on Mental Retardation. Copyright 1992 by the American Association on Mental Retardation. Reprinted by permission.

Note: Adaped from Googins (1989); Horner et al. (1990); Hughes et al. (1990); Koehler, Schalock, and Ballard (1989); Kiernan and McGaughey (1991); Meador, Osborn, Owens, Smith, and Taylor (1991); Nisbet and Hagner (1988); Powell et al. (1991); Roberts et al. (1991); Schalock and Kiernan (1990); Schalock and Koehler (1988); and Temple University (1990).

[a]The support functions and activities may need to be modified slightly to accommodate individuals of different ages.

NATURAL SUPPORTS

Many support activities can be performed by the person who uses the support or by significant others. Support activities that are provided without the aid of technology or service agencies are termed **natural supports.** If the individual implements the activity independently, it is considered to be a personal support. This should not be confused with skills learned through education and treatment. Boggs (cited in AAMR, 1992) explains this difference as follows:

> Capacity or competence, if developed or restored through training or treatment, belongs to the individual and may in fact reduce disability . . . personal support services facilitate function while present but do not reduce the intrinsic disability. This fact should not be obscured as long as the individual can/will once more experience the consequences of his functional disability if he . . . loses the personal support. (p. 107)

Personal resources make excellent supports for independent thinking and self-determination. They can be useful as schedule reminders, troubleshooters, or for helping individuals navigate multistep tasks. For example, a person may have a guide for grocery shopping that facilitates memory and decision making and eliminates the need for reading skills. Personal supports may be utilized by persons with severe mental retardation to control intense emotional reactions or to monitor their physical well-being for signs of threat to safety or health. For example, a person with a lifelong health concern, such as Lesch-Nyhan syndrome (characterized by intense compulsions to self-abuse), might provide personal support by self-restraining when the compulsion arises. Though supports such as these are implemented entirely by the person, they serve to compensate for specific skill deficits. Grocery guides do not enhance the memory of the person using them; they replace the need for memory. Likewise, individuals with Lesch-Nyhan syndrome will still feel a compulsion to self-abuse. Self-restraint is a way they can provide themselves with support until the compulsion passes.

Many forms of support enlist the participation of other people. Employees, friends, and volunteers may provide support in areas such as transportation, accessing community stores and facilities, handling household repairs, and completing daily living tasks (Heyne, Storley, Rone, Levine, & Denelle, 1996). The involvement of others is likely to be necessary for any individual with more extensive support needs but may be of primary or of tertiary importance. Pervasive support resources are likely to be more intrusive and involve more people than limited or even extensive supports. It may be necessary for others to assist these individuals with tasks basic to survival. Examples include providing medical care, preparing meals the person can swallow and digest, assisting with personal hygiene needs, monitoring health and safety, and representing the person's interests to others outside the home.

Other people can function as support resources in an extensive, but not pervasive manner, as well. Possibilities for involving others exist in every activity listed in Table 7.4. Support may be given overtly, such as providing job training, assisting with money management, intervening in crisis situations, or active teaching of skills. Alternatively, more subtle ways of providing support also exist in such forms as interacting socially, offering advice, providing information, and making introductions. None of us, whether we have a severe disability or not, can get along in the world without receiving support from others.

When others provide assistance to an individual with severe mental retardation, they must remember that a *support* becomes a *hindrance* the moment it is no longer necessary. Supports should enhance each person's sense of confidence, self-esteem, and independence (Abery, 1994). The implementation of appropriate supports is expected to facilitate advancement and decrease the intensity, frequency, or duration of that support need. Individuals whose supports are faded or withdrawn should provide feedback about their success without the support, and service providers and significant others should continue to monitor the person's needs for such support (AAMR, 1992).

SUPPLEMENTARY SUPPORTS

Several support functions and activities can be accessed through service delivery if they cannot be obtained in the person's natural environment (see Table 7.4). Of particular relevance to persons with severe mental retardation are such activities as advocating, supervising, financial management, in-home assistance, accessing transportation, and health assistance. Persons with extensive or pervasive support needs are less apt to become totally independent in these areas than individuals with less intensive needs. Over the years, family members may not be able to provide as much support. Also, the intensity of required involvement may be so great that primary caregivers need relief or even specialized help (M. F. Hayden & DePaepe, 1994; G. C. Smith, Majeski, & McClenny, 1996). For example, a person who has a psychological disorder such as schizophrenia requires the services of a psychiatrist. Or, family members of a person who cannot assist with mobility may find they are no longer able to provide the necessary physical assistance. Consequently, it is very important to have outside services available.

Sometimes the greatest service support is information about other resources or about legislation that protects and promotes the welfare of persons with disabilities. The U.S. Department of Education, Office of Special Education and Rehabilitative Services funds Parent Information Centers in each state to address parent concerns. Similarly, within the Department of Health and Human Services, the Administration on Developmental Disabilities and the Administration on Children and Families maintain family preservation/family support initiatives. These initiatives provide funding vouchers to families whose relatives are deemed "institution eligible," and living at home. The provisions make access to such services as behavioral training, respite care, social work, psychological, and nutritional services financially feasible.

As helpful as all of the supports provided by significant others and service agencies can be, sometimes persons with extensive support needs wish to further their independence by, in essence, eliminating the middle man. For example, a student who has a speech impairment may have friends who are able to interpret for unfamiliar listeners. This is one example of a natural support provided by others. However, occasions may arise when the student really wants to express herself without the assistance of her friends. Persons living today have a very distinct advantage over previous generations in this area—technology. As our scientific knowledge base continues to grow at an astounding rate, opportunities are presented to meet the needs of persons with severe mental retardation. In fact, Meyer, Eichinger, and Park-Lee (1987) found technological supports to be among the highest rated items in their analysis of quality indicators in educational services for students with severe disabilities.

In addition to the devises that are available to provide a voice to the expressions of persons with speech impairments, persons with multiple severe disabilities are being presented with opportunities to communicate in ways that require no voice and no hands. Computerized technology is another commonly seen technological support in place for those with extensive and pervasive needs. We can expect even more inventive, independence-promoting concepts to be unveiled as time goes by.

The movement toward greater community involvement and independent living arrangements has also furthered the cause of technological support development. By mandating equal access to community facilities, public transportation, and job opportunities, the ADA has forced human ingenuity (Bleyer, 1992). This legislation includes everything from architectural accommodations to job task reconceptualization (D. R. Johnson & Lewis, 1994). Individuals need homes that they can navigate: lower counters for persons who use wheelchairs, safety measures in bathrooms for persons with less developed grip, muscle tone, or seizure disorders. Safety precautions are not limited to the bathroom, either. Also available are stoves and irons that turn themselves off, water temperature regulators, and telephone security systems that automatically call for help if the person does not "check in" as scheduled.

Although none of these types of supports are intrinsically tied to persons with severe mental retardation, their existence makes it more feasible for persons with such extensive needs to live independently than has ever been thought before. While some supports (e.g., hearing aids) have been addressing needs for many years, the newer developments are instilling hope in a wide range of individuals. Bellamy (1990) reminds us, however, that extensive architectural and state-of-the-art technological supports will not be useful if they are not cost-effective. In the same spirit as their initiatives to ensure access to services, the Department of Health and Human Services now makes funding available to persons with disabilities for such architectural essentials as widening doorways, building ramps, and making bathrooms and kitchens wheelchair accessible.

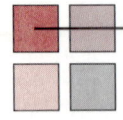

SUMMARY

DEFINING THE POPULATION

- Of the 3 percent of the population estimated to have mental retardation, only 15 percent have greater than mild disabilities.

- Various definitions have generated terms of reference, such as severe/profound levels of retardation, persons with extensive support needs, and individuals with severe disabilities.

- Definitions that define supports needed for participation in the community facilitate the processes of needs assessment, goal setting, and quality of life evaluation.

NATURE AND NEEDS

- Assessments of adaptive skills will generally provide a better indication of a person's support needs than will assessments of intellectual functioning.

- Mental illness is suspected to occur at greater rates among persons with mental retardation than in the general population, but diagnosis is complicated by a lack of formalized assessment measures, barriers in communication, and atypical demonstration of symptoms.

- The need for extensive and pervasive supports for persons with severe mental retardation is in many cases directly related to physical or health-related concerns.

- The extent of support a person requires is influenced by the environment. Environments that encourage independence, productivity, and social interaction can enhance the development of a person with severe mental retardation.

EDUCATIONAL CONCERNS

- Historically, gross underestimates of the potential of persons with severe mental retardation resulted in prejudice, fear, and mistreatment of persons with severe mental retardation.

- Persons with severe mental retardation do not follow a slowed version of normal cognitive development.

- Educational programming for persons with severe mental retardation should be functional, individualized, and age appropriate.
- Instruction works best when it is community-referenced and delivered in the setting where the skill will be used.

APPROPRIATE OUTCOMES

- Independence is fostered when persons are encouraged to make choices.
- Supported employment is a viable alternative for persons with severe mental retardation.
- Community integration is not complete until persons with severe mental retardation have equal access to all privileges of society, including friendship and a sense of belonging.

SUPPORTS

- Persons with severe mental retardation and their families can and should be consulted in the construction of educational and support plans.
- Extensive and pervasive supports differ from less intensive levels of support in frequency, duration, and urgency.
- Supplemental support services are particularly important for individuals with severe mental retardation because they are more likely than persons with mild mental retardation to continue to need supports over time.

PART 3

Programming and Issues Across the Lifespan

CHAPTER **8**

Infancy and Early Childhood

After reading this chapter,
the student should be able to:

- State the rationale for early childhood special education.
- Discuss the legislation and implementation affecting early childhood special education programs.
- Describe assessment procedures used with infants, toddlers, and young children who are disabled.
- Discuss considerations in programming for young children.

Key Terms

at risk
criterion-referenced
 testing (CRT)
curriculum
curriculum-based
 assessment (CBA)
early childhood special
 education
early intervention

family-directed
 assessment
Individual Family
 Service Plan (IFSP)
Individualized
 Education Program
 (IEP)
informed clinical
 opinion

judgment-based
 assessment
mastery learning
norm-referenced
 testing
precision teaching
transition

RATIONALE FOR EARLY CHILDHOOD
SPECIAL EDUCATION

Early childhood special education is a system of services for children from birth to five years of age who are disabled, developmentally delayed, or at risk of developing developmental delay. The system of services that are usually provided free of charge for these children and their families is known as **early intervention.**

Educational programs for infants and children with disabilities were virtually nonexistent twenty-five years ago. In recent years, due to legislation and effective early intervention techniques, early childhood special education has experienced phenomenal growth. Today, the focus is on early intervention and programming for children in the birth to five-year age range who are disabled, developmentally delayed, or at risk of developing developmental delay.

Among the first to draw attention to the importance of the early years were Marie Montessori, Friedrich Foebel, and G. Stanley Hall. Other researchers have added their support. For example, Bloom (1964) found that children develop 50 percent of their total intellectual capacity by age four and 80 percent by age eight. B. L. White (1975) concluded that the period between eight months and three years is of utmost importance in the development of intellectual and social skills. In addition, Hayden and Pious (1979), McDaniel (1977), B. J. Smith and Strain (1984), and Weissman and Littman (1996) have argued that for children with physical, social, emotional, or mental disabilities, educational programming should begin shortly after birth.

See Chapter 5 for a discussion of early intervention in the prevention of mental retardation.

The rationale for early childhood special education has been built on research and scholarly writing that clearly demonstrates the importance of the early experiences of children to their later growth and development. Bricker and colleagues (Bricker & Cripe, 1992; Bricker & Veltman, 1990) defined the theoretical underpinnings of early intervention programs:

1. Children with developmental disabilities require more and/or different early experience than children without disabilities.
2. Formal programs with trained personnel are necessary to provide the required early experience to compensate for developmental difficulties.
3. Developmental progress is enhanced in children with disabilities who participate in early intervention programs. (Bricker & Cripe, 1992, p. 9)

Bailey and Wolery (1984) provided a knowledgeable argument for early childhood education. According to these authors, early intervention can successfully detect problems when they are distinct and remedial, change the behavior of children in different areas of development, prevent the secondary consequences of primary disability, reduce the cost of serving these children at a later age, and provide assistance and training to families in need.

In testifying before the U.S. House of Representatives Committee on Education and Labor in 1986, Dr. Lisbeth Vincent indicated that the hope of early intervention is to improve, or even eliminate, disabling conditions in young children so that the children can have a better chance at education in the K–12 years. According to Vincent, with early intervention, children may need less intensive and expensive services in the elementary and secondary schools which, in the long run, becomes a cost-saving measure.

Families of children who are developmentally delayed or at risk for developing developmental delay form the other side of the rationale for early childhood special education (Vincent, 1986). With early intervention, families learn how to be better parents and thus are able to provide additional experiences on a continual basis for the young child in the home. Learning about their child's condition and how to help reduces the parenting stress level, which enables parents to make more positive contributions to their child's future.

In a review of early intervention findings from the Abecedarian Project, Project CARE, and the Infant Health and Development Program, Ramey and Ramey (1992) found that the benefits of daily early educational intervention in the first five years of a child's life can improve a child's intellectual performance and academic achievement at least until early adolescence. Daily intervention activities considered essential to such outcomes are (a) to be encouraged to explore the environment; (b) to be guided toward basic thinking skills, such as sorting and sequencing; (c) to celebrate and reinforce accomplishments; (d) to practice the skills learned and to expand upon these skills; (e) to avoid negative consequences during the trial-and-error process of learning; and (f) to provide a full verbal and written language experience for the child.

LEGISLATION AFFECTING EARLY CHILDHOOD SPECIAL EDUCATION PROGRAMS

On October 8, 1986, Congress passed PL 99-457, the Education of the Handicapped Amendments, which extended to three- and five-year old children who are disabled the rights and privileges that had been afforded individuals in the six- to twenty-one-year old category. In July of 1997, Congress amended the IDEA by PL 105-17 to extend the developmental delay state option for children aged six to nine. The purpose of the extension is to promote services that are not driven by a particular label. PL 99-457 also provided for the voluntary development of programs for children from birth to two years of age who had disabilities, were developmentally delayed, or at risk for developing developmental delay.

To meet its objectives of serving the educational needs of preschool children with disabilities, PL 99-457 is structured around two components.

Incentive grants are awarded with the expectation that at the end of the funding period the project will secure support to continue operation.

The *preschool component* was mandatory; it required that by the school year 1990 to 1991 any state receiving funds under the law must have provided free appropriate preschool education with related services to all children with disabilities aged three to five. The *infant component* of the law was voluntary; it provided individual states with incentive grants to assist in the development of an interagency council whose purpose was to ensure planned, coordinated services for children with disabilities aged birth to two years of age. A unique feature of the law was the recognition of the need for parental involvement in the education of their children. Under PL 99-457, parents must be given assistance in determining the needs of their child and in obtaining services for their child.

While the purpose of PL 99-457 was to extend the parameters of PL 94-142 to younger children with disabilities, the regulations for its implementation differed substantially from those of PL 94-142. In addition, regulations for implementing the law's preschool component differed from the requirements for the infant component.

PRESCHOOL COMPONENTS

The preschool component of the law was mandatory. Regulations accompanying PL 99-457 that differed from those of PL 94-142 follow:

1. Individual states serving three- to five-year-old children (now six- to nine-year-old children) with disabilities were not required to report child count figures by existing disabilities categories.

2. Each Individualized Education Program (IEP) for children in the three- to five-age group (now six-to-nine age group) had to include instructions for parents.

3. To allow local education agencies to use a variety of service delivery options (including full- or part-day, center-based, home-based, and combination programs), the length of the school day and school year can vary.

4. Preschool education programs for children three to five years (now six to nine years) are administered through the state education agency; local education agencies, however, can contract services from other programs (e.g., Head Start) or other agencies (e.g., Department of Social Services) to meet the requirement for provision of a full range of services.

5. Failure to comply with the new law resulted in the loss of federal funds generated by the Preschool Grant, funds generated under the larger PL 94-142 formula for children three- to five-years-old (now six- to nine-years-old), and federal grants and contracts for preschool education programs.

INFANT COMPONENT (PART H)

Requirements accompanying the voluntary component of PL 99-457 differ from those of PL 94-142 and from the mandatory component of PL 99-457 in the following ways:

1. Policy makers in states applying for grants to serve infants and toddlers with disabilities aged birth to two years of age had to establish an Interagency

Coordinating Council to assist parents in determining needs and obtaining services. This Council had to be composed of service providers and agencies that routinely served children in this age range.

2. Criteria for classification of infants and toddlers with disabilities aged birth to two years had to be established by the individual state. Eligible children included those who (a) were developmentally delayed, (b) had conditions that typically resulted in developmental delays, or (c) were considered at risk for substantial developmental delay (from poor prenatal care, low socioeconomic status, or other potential risk factors).

3. Every eligible child and family was assigned a service coordinator whose responsibility was to ensure that the child and family received appropriate services.

4. Except where federal or state law set a schedule of adjusted fees, services were free.

5. Services included (a) multidisciplinary assessment, (b) a design to address the child's developmental needs, and (c) a written **Individual Family Service Plan (IFSP)** developed by a multidisciplinary team with assistance from parents. Figure 8.1 shows the content of the IFSP.

6. PL 105-17 requires policies and procedures to ensure that, to the maximum extent possible, early intervention services are provided in natural environments and requires that the IFSP justify services outside natural environments.

PL 94-142 (1975) was reauthorized and amended in 1990 and 1997. In 1990, the law changed its name from the Education of All Handicapped Children Act to the Individuals with Disabilities Education Act (IDEA), PL 101-476. Both PL 101-476 and its recent amendment PL 105-17 require that children with disabilities age birth to two years be served by the states.

Early childhood special education now provides services for children with disabilities from birth through nine years of age and their families under Part B and Part H of IDEA. In accordance with other policies in IDEA, the services are free of charge to the children and their families. The laws now support what educators, researchers, and scholars have long believed: Appropriate early intervention has a significant impact on a child's intellectual capacity and potential to learn.

IDEA (1990) established new priorities for meeting the needs of infants and toddlers with disabilities. Under the demonstration and outreach programs, new priorities included

1. Facilitating and improving early identification of children with disabilities or at risk for developing developmental delays

2. Facilitating the transition of infants at risk or with disabilities from medical care to early intervention services and from early intervention services to special or general education preschool services

3. Promoting the use of assistive technology services and devices

4. Increasing the understanding and addressing the early intervention and preschool needs of children exposed prenatally to maternal substance abuse

(1) a statement of the infant's or toddler's present levels of physical development, cognitive development, and adaptive development, based on acceptable objective criteria,

(2) a statement of the family's resources, priorities, and concerns relating to enhancing the development of the family's infant or toddler with a disability,

(3) a statement of major outcomes expected to be achieved for the infant or toddler and the family, and the criteria, procedures, and timelines used to determine the degree to which progress toward achieving the outcomes is being made and whether modifications or revisions of the outcomes or services are necessary,

(4) a statement of specific early intervention services necessary to meet the unique needs of the infant or toddler and the family, including the frequency, intensity, and the method of delivering services,

(5) a statement of the natural environments in which early intervention services shall appropriately be provided,

(6) the projected dates for initiation of services and the anticipated duration of such services,

(7) the name of the case manager (hereafter in this part referred to as the 'service coordinator') from the profession most immediately relevant to the infant's or toddler's or family's needs (or who is otherwise qualified to carry out all applicable responsibilities under this plan) who will be responsible for the implementation of the plan and coordination with other agencies and persons, and

(8) the steps to be taken supporting the transition of the toddler with a disability to services provided under Part B of this Act to the extent such services are considered appropriate (section 677).

FIGURE 8.1
Individualized Family Service Plan Defined: Part H of PL 99-457 (IDEA)

Source: From *United States Code Congressional and Administrative News,* Vol. 1 (1986), 99th Congress, 2nd Session. St. Paul: MN, West 100 Stat. 1145–1177.

Part H ("Handicapped Infants and Toddlers") of the existing law has been expanded to require that the state agency responsible for administering the early intervention program prepare and disseminate to all primary referral agencies (e.g., hospitals, physicians) information for parents on the availability of early intervention services and determine the extent to which the primary sources disseminate information on the availability of services to parents of infants with disabilities. Part H also requires that the state agency provide training to primary referral agencies on the basic components of early intervention services available in the state. Figure 8.2 gives the statutory definition of infants and toddlers as defined in Part H, which grants flexibility to the states in deciding which disabilities qualify for services.

One of the major dilemmas in implementing the "at risk" early intervention programs lies in the definition of at risk. One definition of **at risk** is "A risk factor is any ascertainable characteristic or circumstance of a person or group of persons that is known to be associated with increased prob-

More programs are now available to young children who are retarded.

ability of having, developing, or being adversely affected by the process producing a handicapping condition" (Garber & McInerney, 1982, p. 134). Common examples of risk factors include the socioeconomic status of the family, the intellectual abilities of the parents (especially the mother), and the number of children in the family.

---

(1) The term "infants and toddlers with disabilities" means individuals from birth to age 2, inclusive, who need early intervention services because they—

  (A) are experiencing developmental delays, as measured by appropriate diagnostic instruments and procedures in one or more of the following areas: cognitive development, physical development, communication development, social or emotional development, or adaptive developments, or

  (B) have a diagnosed physical or mental condition which has a high probability of resulting in developmental delay. Such term may also include, at a state's discretion, individuals from birth to age 2, inclusive, who are at risk of having substantial developmental delays if early intervention services are not provided (section 672(1); 34 CFR 303.16).

FIGURE 8.2
Infants and Toddlers with Disabilities: Part H of PL 99-457 (IDEA)

Source: From *United States Code Congressional and Administrative News,* Vol. 1 (1986), 99th Congress, 2nd Session. St. Paul, MN: West, 100 Stat. 1145–1177.

MAGGIE AND IDA

Maggie Erickson, a preschool student, and Ida Singer, an 87-year-old elder who volunteers in the Intergenerational Inclusive Preschool Program, have become important parts of each others' lives. Just how important can be seen in the following excerpts from conversations with Cathy Erickson, who is Maggie's mother, and with Ida.

Maggie's mother says: My daughter, Maggie, attends the JCC preschool for two days each week. Ida comes in every morning that Maggie is at school to help her. During the evenings, Maggie and I talk about everyone at the JCC preschool and Maggie always speaks of Ida with fondness. Like any child, Maggie is sometimes slow about getting ready to go to school. When that happens, I remind her, "You will get to see Ida today!" and before I know it she is out the door. Last year, Maggie had to have a cast put on her leg and she needed to stay home from school.

She was thrilled when Ida made a special trip to visit her at our home.

Elders such as Ida provide love and acceptance to the children with disabilities and their classmates, and the children provide the same to the elders. Elders also contribute a wealth of life experience to the children and to the classroom curriculum. Too often families who have children with disabilities tend to become isolated. It is nice to know that there is another adult in Maggie's life who can provide her with support and acceptance.

"Grandma" Ida says: I have always had a very wonderful feeling about grandparents. I never knew my own grandparents, but I've always thought they are very special—you can learn them. I'm a different kind of grandma for the preschool children. Their grandmas are all young—busy and socializing. I'm the spoiling grandma.

When Maggie first came to the preschool

Keogh and Daley (1983) concluded that three types of children are at risk. Their categorization highlights the point that there are important differences in the ways in which we should conceptualize at-risk children. The categories are as follows:

1. *Established risk:* Children in this category have known medical conditions that affect their lives.
2. *Suspect risk:* These children have developmental histories that suggest the presence of a biological problem, but the problem is not apparent.
3. *Environmental risk:* Children who fit this group have no known medical or biological problem, but they do experience life situations (e.g., family, school) that can give rise to problems.

When considering whether children are at risk, it is important not only to evaluate the children but also to investigate such external factors as their homes and life events. If efforts to identify and provide services to children who are at risk and their families are well designed and systematically implemented, then fewer children should fail at school, and consequently fewer will be identified as in need of special services.

she used to play mostly by herself, with the dolls. At first she really needed me there. I tried not to hover over her or "smother" her with attention. I'm sure it is easy to do that, but I thought if I gave her too much attention, she couldn't grow. So I try to take a back seat. I keep an eye on what Maggie is doing, in case she needs my help, but also interact with all of the kids. Now Maggie is mixing well with the children. She is benefiting on her own because she is doing a lot on her own. She likes everybody.

I never realized that three-year-olds were so smart. You can carry on a conversation with a child and learn a lot from them. For instance, even though I have a disability—I walk with a cane—the children learn to handle it. They realize that I can't pick them up readily. They learn that people have limitations. Like with my glasses. They would ask, "Why do you have to wear glasses, Ida?" They said, "Take them off!" I took them off

and asked, "So how do I look?" "You still look like a grandma!" It keeps me young—keeps me younger—knowing that the children accept me for who I am.

I think it is important to get the different generations together. I think it is beneficial to the kids to have an overall picture of what people are—of what older people are, of what younger people are, of the different ways there are to live. If kids see an older person who can help themselves, it leaves an impression.

Working with the children makes a difference in how I feel about myself. I feel capable. It gives me a challenge, something to look forward to. If the children respond to something I do or say, then I feel good. I have a good feeling when I leave the classroom.

Source: From "Maggie and Ida" by L. A. Heyne, 1996, *Impact,* 9(4), p. 11. Copyright 1996 by Institute on Community Integration, University of Minnesota, Minneapolis. Reprinted by permission.

In Section 602 (a) (1) of IDEA, children in the three- to five-year age (now six to nine) range must "need special education and related services" and qualify by fitting within the definition of "children with disabilities," which "means children with mental retardation; hearing impairments, including deafness; speech or language impairments; visual impairments, including blindness; serious emotional disturbance; orthopedic impairments; autism; traumatic brain injury; other health impairments; or specific learning disabilities." States have the option of extending the developmental delay category required for children in the birth to two-year range to the children in the three- to five-year range. These free services are provided by the local education agencies (LEAs), and, like provisions for children beyond the age of five, the children and families have a due-process right in disputes between LEAs and themselves.

Children in the three- to five-year (now six to nine) range who qualify under Section 602 (a)(1) of IDEA are served through the **Individualized Education Program (IEP),** which is an individually written plan of instruction composed by a team specifying a child's present level of functioning, annual goals, short-term objectives, special education and related services required, extent of participation in the general education classroom, if appropriate, time line of initiation and duration of services, objective criteria, and evaluation procedures.

Services to children who are retarded are well designed and systematically implemented.

There are some notable differences between the IFSP used for children from birth to age two and the IEP used for children from three to nine years. One of the main differences between a child who is birth to age two served under the IFSP and the child who is three to nine years of age served under the IEP is the categorical approach used for the IEP. Also included in the IFSP are a statement of the family's strengths and needs as well as a case manager; these are not included in the IEP.

As of December 1, 1994, 154,065 eligible infants and toddlers were served under IDEA according to the *Eighteenth Annual Report to Congress on the Implementation of the Individual with Disabilities Education Act* (1996). This represented 1.3 percent of the total birth through two population.

Finally, IDEA authorizes that grants be awarded for developing and operating extended school year demonstration programs for infants and toddlers with severe disabilities and for developing appropriate criteria to identify, evaluate, and serve infants and toddlers from minority backgrounds. In 1994, $339 million was appropriated by Congress for preschool grants; this figure represents a 4-percent increase from 1994 (U.S. Department of Education, 1996).

The system of birth through the age of 21 presently in place for children who are disabled, developmentally delayed, or at risk as presented in IDEA represents a seamless system of service both to these children and their parents. The intent of the law is to meet the needs of both the child and the parent through individual planning and systematic implementation of the plan.

DEC-RECOMMENDED PRACTICES

In 1993, the Division of Early Childhood (DEC), a part of the Council for Exceptional Children (CEC), issued a set of recommended practices for infants and young children with disabilities and their families. Since no one practice is necessarily the best practice for all young children with disabilities, DEC addressed recommended practices across a broad spectrum. All practices fulfill the following obligations:

1. *Research-based or value-based.* The practices are supported through research indicating a positive impact or through practices that are supported as deemed valuable by a consensus in the field of early childhood.
2. *Family-centered.* The needs of the family as well as the child are considered as opposed to strictly child-centered approaches.
3. *Multicultural emphasis.* Benefits to the child and the child's family are viewed and adapted to support cultures and values that are different from the mainstream population of the United States.
4. *Cross-disciplinary participation.* This requires members of the various disciplines to work together as a team for the benefit of the child and the family and to share information and expertise.
5. *Developmentally/chronologically age appropriate.* This is a match between what the child is capable of doing, the learning needs of the child, and the environment that is most natural to the age of the child.

The components of these practices are to be observed throughout contact with the child or the child's parents. In the referral or evaluation phase of contact, for example, the instruments used should be multicultural in emphasis, developmentally and chronologically age appropriate, and family centered with cross-disciplinary participation.

REFERRAL

Under Part H of IDEA, each state is required to have an early intervention system in place. A *lead agency* is to be selected by the state to be responsible for the implementation of Part H in the state to carry out the state plan, to coordinate the work of the public and private agencies within the state, to create a statewide comprehensive directory of services available, and to create a statewide database containing numbers of children who have disabilities, are developmentally delayed, or are at risk. The states are responsible for creating a State Interagency Coordinating Council in the role of advisement to the lead agency (see Figure 8.3).

The early intervention system within the state must also support child find efforts to identify and locate families and their children who have disabilities,

As part of the *House Report 102-198* (1991), a lead agency must be established by the governor to carry out the following six areas:

1. the administration, supervision, and monitoring of programs and activities involved with families and children with special needs whether or not these programs receive federal assistance;
2. the compilation of a central directory listing early intervention services, resources, and personnel available to aid parents of children with disabilities;
3. the assignment of financial responsibility to the various agencies;
4. the development of procedures ensuring that children with special needs and their families receive assistance and services in a timely fashion;
5. the resolution of disputes between agencies and service providers; and,
6. the agreement between agencies and service providers regarding responsibility, assignments, and finances.

The lead agency assigned by the governor assumes the role of leadership in the interagency collaboration process. This Interagency Coordinating Council (ICC) is comprised of "families, service providers, legislators, persons in personnel preparation, and agency representatives" (R. Miller, 1996).

FIGURE 8.3
Interagency Collaboration: Part H of PL 99-457 (IDEA)

Source: From *United States Code Congressional and Administrative News,* Vol. 1 (1986), 99th Congress, 2nd Session. St. Paul: MN, West, 100 State 1145–1177.

are developmentally delayed, or at risk. The system has further responsibility in arranging for evaluations for all referred children, preparing IFSPs and IEPs for all eligible children, and serving all eligible children and their families. Procedural safeguards are still in place for all children and for children under Part H referral for early intervention services may not be made without the written consent of parents.

EVALUATION AND ASSESSMENT

The terms *evaluation* and *assessment* are often used interchangeably, yet in Part H of the IDEA the terms are considered different. An *evaluation* is a formal process conducted by qualified, licensed personnel who administer standardized tests for initial placement and continued eligibility, whereas an *assessment* is an ongoing, often informal, process in which workers from many disciplines contribute information and participate in an ongoing process to determine specific strengths and weaknesses. The IDEA further emphasizes **informed clinical opinion,** which utilizes at least 50 percent of a clinician's expertise in addition to the formal testing results to aid in determining eligibility.

Testing of young children who are believed to have disabilities or delays, or who are considered at risk requires prior parental consent. The

IDEA, Part B, section 615(b)(1)(C), and Part H, section 680(6), requires that parents or guardians receive prior written notice of any proposal to test a child in the parent's native language.

Based on DEC-recommended practices (DEC, 1993), assessments and evaluations should incorporate the following principles:

1. Use multiple sources and multiple measures gathered on multiple occasions in multiple settings.

2. Use approaches that are culturally and developmentally appropriate to determine the strengths and weaknesses of the child, capitalizing on the child's known interests and the family's sensitivities.

3. Use of the collaborative decision-making process to determine assessment and evaluation results to determine the current status of the child and family, eligibility for services, and plan of action, should services be needed.

The quality of information obtained in psychoeducational evaluations is, to a large extent, dependent on the integrity of both the instruments and the methods used to obtain that information. Two basic approaches to the assessment of early childhood abilities have predominated in recent years, formal and informal methods. Although both dimensions are necessary for a comprehensive approach to service delivery, neither one alone can provide all the information necessary for effective intervention. While formal measures continue to serve as the standard means of assessment, teachers are increasingly turning to informal measure to assist with program planning and evaluation.

EVALUATION

Formal assessment procedures are those with specific guidelines for administration, scoring, and interpretation (McLoughlin & Lewis, 1990). Formal assessment procedures generally include such norm-referenced tests as intelligence tests, achievement tests, and interest inventories. The term *standardized* refers as much to the rigors of administration and scoring as to the scores themselves. In standardized or **norm-referenced testing,** each child's test performance is compared to that of other children using a standardized score. The standardization sample serves as the basis for all comparisons in norm-referenced testing. While norm-referenced tests do not generally provide the classroom teacher with specific guidelines for instruction, they do allow a teacher to compare a child's test performance to that of other children of similar age and under similar conditions.

Neisworth and Bagnato (1988) identified three principal purposes for norm-based assessment: (a) to describe a child's level of development, (b) to place a child in a diagnostic category, and (c) to predict a child's future level of development. Well-designed tests with representative reference groups (age, race, sex, residence, geographic region, and socioeconomic status) allow educators to do more than just compare a child to other children on general measures of aptitude or ability; such tests also allow educators to estimate the child's unique skills and abilities.

Under IDEA, Part H and Part B, evaluation is to be comprehensive and multidisciplinary. A multidisciplinary approach synthesizes the expertise of specialists in various areas and the expertise of parents and teachers who know the child well into a comprehensive plan for the child that includes intervention, preschool and elementary special education, and related services. Both Part H and Part B of the law are explicit against the use of any single test or procedure as the sole basis of placement. Figure 8.4 gives the statutory definition of the evaluation of infants and toddlers as based on IDEA, Part H.

IDEA, Part H, requires that the evaluation be conducted in a timely manner. Based on the Department of Education's regulation, *timely* means "within 45 days after . . . referral" (34 Code of Federal Regulations [CFR] 303.321[e], 303.322[e]).

IDEA, Part B, further clarifies evaluation materials. The materials are provided and administered in the child's native language or preferred mode of communication.

Tests are to be appropriate by both validity and reliability for use with preschool populations. The validity and reliability of any tests rest upon using the same kinds of children used to establish the original validity and reliability scores. In most instances, preschool children who are disabled, developmentally delayed, or at risk were not included in the original sam-

---

"[A] timely, comprehensive, multidisciplinary evaluation of the functioning of each infant and toddler with a disability in the state and the needs of the families to appropriately assist in the development of the infant or toddler with a disability (section 676(b)(3).

The department's Part H regulation explains that evaluation is to:

(1) Be conducted by personnel trained to utilize appropriate methods and procedures
(2) Be based on informed clinical option; and
(3) Include the following:
    (i) A review of pertinent records related to the child's current health status and medical history
    (ii) An evaluation of the child's level of functioning in each of the following developmental areas:
        (A) Cognitive development
        (B) Physical development, including vision and hearing
        (C) Communication development
        (D) Social or emotional development
        (E) Adaptive development

FIGURE 8.4

Statutory Definition of Infant and Toddler Evaluation: Part H of PL 99-457 (IDEA)

Source: From *United States Code Congressional and Administrative News,* Vol. 1, (1986), 99th Congress, 2nd Session. St. Paul, MN: West, 100 Stat. 1145–1177.

pling of children. Limited meaning, therefore, can be gleaned from the results of standardized measures. Concurring, D. Fuchs, Fuchs, Benowitz, and Barringer (1987), in their evaluation of twenty-seven widely used aptitude and achievement tests, reported little support toward the appropriateness of such tests for the preschool population.

If describing a child's skills and abilities well enough to meet the qualifying criteria for placement is the letter of the law, then describing a child's strengths and weaknesses well enough to design effective interventions represents the spirit of the law. School-age children must have a diagnostic label before they can receive services, but preschoolers, infants, and toddlers need only be at risk for substantial delay in order to qualify. Early childhood educators are required to meet both the spirit and the letter of the law by designing interventions based more on needs of the child than on the stereotypical description of a label. Well-designed standardized tests can help educators assess the child's needs accurately.

ASSESSMENT

IDEA, Part H, requires assessment in five areas of development and outlines the process to be used. Figure 8.5 provides the definition and procedures as set forth in Part H.

Informal assessment methods are similar to formal methods in that they are designed to elicit educationally relevant information, but dissimilar in that they allow the examiner to obtain information under less stringent conditions. Because external criteria are absent, the teacher is free to design techniques and methods of assessment based on hypotheses about the particular preschool child's learning pattern. What these techniques lack in normative data they make up for in relevance to instruction. Using informal methods has several advantages: Test items may be designed and administered by the teacher; test

---

An assessment of the unique needs of the child [shall be conducted] in terms of each of the developmental areas [cognitive, physical, communication, social or emotional, adaptive], including the identification of services appropriate to meet those needs.

Assessment means the ongoing procedures used by appropriate qualified personnel throughout the period of a child's eligibility under this part to identify
  (i) The child's unique strengths and needs and the services appropriate to meet those needs; and
  (ii) The resources, priorities, and concerns of the family and the supports and services necessary to enhance the family's capacity to meet the developmental needs of their infant or toddler with a disability (34 CFR 303.322)

FIGURE 8.5
Definition and Procedures for Assessment: Part H of PL 99-457 (IDEA)

Source: From *United States Code Congressional and Administrative News,* Vol. 1 (1986), 99th Congress, 2nd Session. St. Paul, MN: West, 100 Stat. 1145–1177.

Classroom teaching materials are often used in curriculum-based assessment.

items may coincide with instruction; the teacher can revise the items and the format as testing progresses; and the teacher can assess the child before, during, and after each lesson, depending on the type of information needed.

Although many different types of informal assessment exist (interviews, observations, task analyses, work samples), a frequently used in-class method is **criterion-referenced testing (CRT),** which is when the teacher attempts to measure the child's skills against preestablished levels of mastery (Salvia & Yssledyke, 1991). CRT is based on the premise that a child's performance may be best understood in the context of what a child can do within a given content area, instead of simply how well a child performs relative to other children (Anastasi, 1988). A fundamental prerequisite to CRT is defining a content area well enough to represent it with prespecified questions. CRT is versatile enough to be appropriate for everything from school readiness to self-help skills.

Curriculum-based assessment (CBA) is one type of CRT in which test items are drawn directly from the teaching materials. This is a highly effective way of monitoring and modifying methods of instruction. L. S. Fuchs and Fuchs (1990) have identified two specific forms of CBA: precision teaching and mastery learning. In **precision teaching,** a lesson is broken down into a hierarchy of skills. Measurement procedures allow the teacher to analyze the child's performance at each step in the skills hierarchy. In **mastery learning,** the teacher tests a concept, gives feedback, and then tests the concept again until the child has completely mastered the task. Precision teaching and mastery learning share a number of elements in common: teacher-designed assessment tasks, assessment through short-term objectives, and measurement focus shift upon mastery.

Judgment-based assessment (JBA) provides a structured framework within which a teacher may include and quantify the opinions and impressions of primary caregivers (Neisworth & Bagnato, 1988). In JBA, the examiner constructs a scale or checklist designed to measure abilities not typically covered in standardized tests. The individual is the sole referent for each analysis. The principle advantage of JBA is that it provides a type of social validity (Wolf, 1978), a means of linking a child's traits and behaviors with results from other, more formalized tests.

Family-directed assessment is a special kind of assessment to study "the resources, priorities, and concerns of the family and the identification of the supports and services necessary to enhance the family's capacity to meet the developmental needs of their infant or toddler with a disability" (IDEA, section 677[a][2]). This assessment comes under Part H and not Part B of IDEA. The inclusion of the family-directed assessment is especially critical for infants and toddlers, as they cannot be understood apart from their family. The assessment, however, is a voluntary component on the part of the family. The family has the right to determine whether and to what extent they will participate, knowing that the results of the family-directed assessment become part of the IFSP.

MEASURES OF EARLY CHILDHOOD DEVELOPMENT

Delays in and limitations in the domains of socioemotional, cognitive, speech and language, motor, and adaptive behavior development are important in early childhood education. Screening for educational and psychological delays, therefore, is a routine part of assessment at all levels of education. Cohn (1992) has suggested that a good preschool screening instrument is one that is easy to administer and score, allows for multidimensional assessment of different developmental areas, is valid and reliable across all ages for which it was designed, and is cost-effective given budgetary, time, and staff constraints.

SOCIOEMOTIONAL ASSESSMENT

Delays in and limitations of social or emotional development in young children who are retarded are no less important than delays and limitations in young children who are not retarded. The child's socioemotional development represents two major components, social (interpersonal) and emotional (intrapersonal) (Brooks-Gunn & Luciano, 1985). During the early childhood years, early childhood professionals work more closely with the family than is possible during the elementary and secondary school years. This family focus gives professionals an opportunity to intervene in order to prevent, extinguish, or improve behaviors by the child.

Unfortunately, and because of the limited cognitive and verbal abilities of young children who are retarded, assessment and intervention are often extremely difficult. Assessment of socioemotional development requires that comparisons be made with reference to normal development (R. P. Martin, 1991). Generally, the decision regarding the socioemotional development is made based on one of two principal avenues: (a) assessment of personality through the use of projectives, drawing, dialogue, play therapy, or open-ended questions, and (b) assessment of observable behavior in structured and unstructured settings. Aydlett (1993) expressed concern over the number of standardized tests available for use in the socioemotional development assessment of young children. R. P. Martin (1991) reported that as much as 90 percent of the information on socioemotional functioning in young children is derived from behavior-rating scales. The *Personality Inventory for Children* (Lachar, 1990), the *Behavioral Evaluation Scale—II* (McCarney & Leigh, 1990), the *Child Behavior Checklist* (CBCL; Achenbach, 1992), and the *Test of Early Socio-Emotional Development* (Hresko & Brown, 1984) are examples of frequently used measures of socioemotional development (see Table 8.1).

COGNITIVE ASSESSMENT

Intellectual assessment is addressed in greater detail in Chapter 4.

Understanding and explaining how young children obtain, modify, and use their cognitive abilities remains an extremely difficult task. Whether one conceptualizes a young child's intelligence as general ability or as a set of separate but related abilities, the capacity to solve problems for everyday living is paramount. Until recently, most definitions of intelligence were restricted to the quantity of one's knowledge rather than the quality of one's ability to process information. In an effort to keep pace with new developments in clinical, cognitive, and developmental psychology, however, researchers have proposed theories and tests that define intelligence in terms of one's ability to solve new and unfamiliar problems rather than simply in terms of how much a child has learned (Kaufman & Kaufman, 1983a). Newly constructed or revised measures of intellectual functioning such as the *Kaufman Assessment Battery for Children* (Kaufman & Kaufman, 1983a), the *Stanford-Binet Intelligence Scale: Fourth Edition* (Thorndike, Hagen, & Sattler, 1986a), and the *Wechsler Preschool and Primary Scale of Intelligence—Revised* (Wechsler,

TABLE 8.1
Measures of Socioemotional Development

Instrument	Age Range	Domains/Areas	Scores Provided	Standardization Sample Size and Model	Median Scale Reliability Estimate
Behavior Evaluation Scale II (McCarney & Leigh, 1990)	K–12th grade	Learning problems Interpersonal difficulties Inappropriate behavior Unhappiness/depression Physical symptoms/fears	Behavior quotient scores (M=100, SD=15) Scaled scores (M=10, SD=3)	Not reported (N=2,278)	Not available
Burks' Behavioral Rating Scales: Preschool and Kindergarten Edition (Burks, 1977)	3.9–6.11	18 scales	Raw scores	Not reported (N=464)	Not reported
Child Behavior Checklist (CBCL) (Achenbach, 1994)	2.0–18.11	Parent rating scale Teacher rating scale Student rating scale Direct observation form Semistructured clinical interview		N=1,100 children nonreferred & 1,700 children referred N=665 teachers	0.89
Personality Inventory for Children (PIC); Revised Format (Lachar, 1990)	3.0–16.0	16 scales	Scaled scores (M=50, SD=10)	Not reported (N=2,380)	0.74
Test of Early Socioemotional Development (Hresko & Brown, 1984)	3.0–7.11	Parent rating scale Sociogram Student rating scale Teacher rating scale	Scaled scores (M=10, SD=3) Percentile ranks Deviation quotients (M=100, SD=15)	1983 statistical abstract (N=1,006 children and teachers) (N=1,773 parents)	0.89*

*Asterisk denotes values calculated from standardization data for preschool ages only.

Abbreviations: M, mean; SD, standard deviation, N, sample size.

TABLE 8.2
Measures of Cognitive Development

Instrument	Age Range	Domains/Areas	Scores Provided	Standardization Sample Size and Model	Median Scale Reliability Estimate
Kaufman Assessment Battery for Children (Kaufman & Kaufman, 1983a)	2.6 to 12.6	Sequential processing Simultaneous processing Achievement Nonverbal	Standard scores (*M* = 100, *SD* = 15) Subtest scores (*M* = 10, *SD* = 3) Age equivalents Percentile ranks Stanines	1980 census (*N* = 2,000)	0.90[*]
Stanford-Binet Intelligence Scale: Fourth Edition (Thorndike, Hagen, & Sattler, 1986a)	2.0 to 23.11	Verbal reasoning Abstract/visual reasoning Quantitative reasoning Short-term memory	Standard scores (*M* = 100, *SD* = 16) Subtest scores (*M* = 50, *SD* = 8) Percentile ranks	1980 census (*N* = 5,013)	0.91[*]
Wechsler Preschool and Primary Scale of Intelligence— Revised (Wechsler, 1989a)	3.0 to 7.3	Verbal Performance	Standard scores (*M* = 100, *SD* = 15) Subtest scores (*M* = 10, *SD* = 3) Percentile ranks	1986 census (*N* = 1,700)	0.95[*]

[*]Asterisk denotes values calculated from standardization data for preschool ages only.

1989a) continue to serve as the foundation for routine psychoeducational evaluations. See Table 8.2 for a brief description of these instruments.

SPEECH AND LANGUAGE ASSESSMENT

The ability to communicate is closely linked to other aspects of development in young children. Children vary in terms of the age at which spoken language is acquired and in terms of development of both receptive and expressive language. Many young children enter preschool unable to communicate effectively. While the term *speech and language development* reflects the fact that speech and language are important components of communication, they are not synonymous with one another. *Speech* refers to the neuromuscular coordination of the lips, tongue, jaw, and vocal cord movement, while *language* refers to the knowledge of rules allowing for the exchange of information between a speaker and listener (Seymour & Wyatt, 1992). Both are important parts of the communication process.

Investigators have failed to identify consistent patterns among different categories of specific language-related disabilities for young children who are mentally retarded; research in linguistic development of young children has "provided the foundation for the creation of theoretically sound language assessment procedures" (Olswang & Bain, 1988, p. 286). Well-designed assessment instruments are able to help identify the source of the difficulty and thereby guide the way for intervention. Standardized instruments commonly used by early childhood service providers are the *Peabody Picture Vocabulary Test—Revised* (Dunn & Dunn, 1981), *Preschool Language Scales—3* (Zimmerman, Steiner, & Pond, 1992), the *Receptive-Expressive Emergent Language Test* (Bzoch & League, 1991), the *Test of Early Language Development* (Hresko, Reid, & Hammill, 1991), and the *Utah Test of Language Development—III* (Mecham, 1989). See Table 8.3 for a brief description of these instruments.

ADAPTIVE BEHAVIOR ASSESSMENT

See Chapter 4 for a detailed discussion of adaptive behavior.

Responding appropriately to the social and environmental demands of life varies from child to child and culture to culture (Leland, 1983). Measures of self-help skills, or in this case, adaptive behavior, allow service providers to identify small but important patterns in atypical early childhood development (Ittenbach, 1989). The assessment for adaptive behavior evaluates activities that are both age-appropriate and situation-appropriate. Young children who fail to develop basic adaptive skills run the risk of developing maladaptive behaviors that decrease further the likelihood of adjustment to other environmental conditions. Tests designed to assist with diagnosis and intervention of adaptive behavior skills include the *AAMR Adaptive Behavior Scale—School Edition* (2nd ed.; Lambert, Nihira, & Leland, 1993a), the *Normative Adaptive Behavior Checklist* (Adams, 1984), the *Vineland Adaptive Behavior Scales* (Sparrow, Balla, & Cicchetti, 1984a, 1984b, 1985), and the *Scales of Independent Behavior* (Bruininks, Woodcock, Weatherman, & Hill, 1985b). See Table 8.4 for a brief description of these instruments.

TABLE 8.3

Measures of Speech and Language Development

Instrument	Age Range	Domains/Areas	Scores Provided	Standardization Sample Size and Model	Median Scale Reliability Estimate
Peabody Picture Vocabulary Test—Revised (Dunn & Dunn, 1981)	2.6 to 18.0	Receptive language	Standard scores ($M = 100$, $SD = 15$) Age equivalents Percentile ranks Stanines	1970 census ($N = 4,200$)	0.76[*]
Preschool Language Scale—3 (Zimmerman, Steiner, & Pond, 1992)	Birth to 6.11	Auditory Comprehension Expressive Communication Total language	Standard scores ($M = 100$, $SD = 15$) Percentiles Age equivalents	1980 census ($N = 1,200$)	0.84
Receptive-Expressive Emergent Language Test (Bzoch & League, 1991)	Birth to 3.0	Expressive language Receptive language	Standard scores ($M = 100$)	Not available	0.96
Test of Early Language Development (2nd Ed.) (Hresko, Reid, & Hammill, 1991)	2.0 to 7.11	Expressive language Receptive language Syntax semantics	Language quotient ($M = 100$, $SD = 15$) Age equivalents Percentiles	1979 census ($N = 1,329$)	0.97
Utah Test of Language Development—3 (Mecham, 1989)	3.0 to 9.11	Language comprehension Language expression	Percentiles Standard scores	1985 abstract ($N = 1,708$)	0.84

[*]Asterisk denotes values calculated from standardization data for preschool ages only.

TABLE 8.4
Measures of Self-Help Skills

Instrument	Age Range	Domains/Areas	Scores Provided	Standardization Sample Size and Model	Median Scale Reliability Estimate

AAMR Adaptive Behavior Scale—School (Lambert, Nihira, & Leland, 1993a)	3.0 to 16.0	Part One
		  Independent functioning
		  Economic activity
		  Language development
		  Numbers and time
		  Prevocational/vocational activity
		  Responsibility
		  Self-direction
		  Socialization
		Part two
		  Violent and antisocial behavior
		  Rebellious behavior
		  Untrustworthy behavior
		  Stereotyped and hyperactive behavior
		  Eccentric behavior
		  Withdrawal
		  Disturbed behavior
			Standard scores, quotients, percentiles	not available
				(N = 1,000)
				1,000 students with no disabilities
					0.80

Normative Adaptive Behavior Checklist (Adams, 1984)	Birth to 21.0	Self-help skills Home skills Independent living skills Social skills Sensory-motor skills Language concepts	Standard scores (M = 100, SD = 15) Age equivalents Percentile ranks Performance rankings	1980 census (N = 6,014)	0.94[*]

Vineland Adaptive Behavior Scales: Survey (Sparrow, Balla, & Cicchetti, 1984b)	Birth to 18.11	Communication
		Daily living skills
		Socialization
		Motor skills
			Standard scores
			  (M = 100, SD = 15)
			Age equivalents
			Adaptive level norms
			  Composite and domains
			Percentile ranks
			Stanines
				1980 census
				(N = 3,000)
					0.89[*]

Scales of Independent Behavior (Bruininks, Woodcock, Weatherman, & Hill, 1985b)	0.3 to 29≤	Motor skills Social and communication skills Personal living skills Broad independence	Standard scores (M = 100, SD = 15) Age equivalents Functional performance level Instructional range Normal curve equivalents Percentile ranks Relative performance index Stanines	1980 census (N = 1,764)	0.90[*]

[*]Asterisk denotes values calculated from standardization data for preschool ages only.

TABLE 8.5
Measures of Motor Development

Instrument	Age Range	Domains/Areas	Scores Provided	Standardization Sample Size and Model	Median Scale Reliability Estimate

Bruininks-Oseretsky Test of Motor Proficiency (Bruininks, 1978)	4.6 to 14.6	Fine motor
		Gross motor
			Standard scores
			($M = 50$, $SD = 10$)
			    Battery composite
			    Gross motor composite
			    Fine motor composite
			Subtest scores
			($M = 15$, $SD = 5$)
			Age equivalents
			Percentile ranks
			Stanines
				1970 census
				($N = 765$)
					Not available

Peabody Developmental Motor Scales and Activity Cards (Folio & Fewel, 1983)	Birth to 6.11	Fine motor Gross motor	Standard scores ($M = 100$, $SD = 15$) Developmental motor quotient Gross motor composite Fine motor composite Age equivalents Percentile ranks	1976 census ($N = 617$)	Not available
Test of Gross Motor Development (Ulrich, 1985)	3.0 to 10.0	Gross motor	Composite quotient ($M = 100$, $SD = 15$) Subtest standard scores ($M = 10$, $SD = 3$) Percentile ranks	1980 census ($N = 908$)	0.86[*]

[*]Asterisk denotes values calculated from standardization data for preschool ages only.

MOTOR ASSESSMENT

Unlike other, more elusive constructs such as cognitive and adaptive behavior, there appears to be relative agreement as to the general definition of motor development. H. G. Williams (1991) has defined *motor development* as the "gradual acquisition of control and/or use of the large and small muscle masses of the body" (p. 284). Although motor functioning and development are important at all ages, years two to six are considered to be the golden years of one's motor development (H. G. Williams, 1991). A child's level of development in all critical areas is dependent upon success in the motor domain, as it is motor functioning that allows the young child to interact with and learn about the environment. Disabilities that negatively affect this interactive process increase the likelihood of delay in this and other areas of development affecting the child in both his or her daily life and in assessment results. Early childhood service providers have typically been interested in one of two types of motor development, fine motor development and gross motor development. While most standardized tests intended for use at the early childhood level have fine or gross motor components, only a few standardized tests focus on motor development exclusively. Tests commonly used by early childhood service providers to provide information as to one's level of motor development are the *Bruininks-Oseretsky Test of Motor Proficiency* (Bruininks, 1978), the *Peabody Developmental Motor Scales and Activity Cards* (Folio & Fewell, 1983), and the *Test of Gross Motor Development* (Ulrich, 1985). See Table 8.5 for a brief description of these instruments.

ISSUES IN EARLY CHILDHOOD ASSESSMENT

The assessment and evaluation of young children with disabilities are crucial components to service delivery. School districts have policies and approaches that guide and assist service providers and that comply with the laws regulating special education. Yet this is an area of difficulty, since there is a wide range of acceptability within the developmental process. The process is further compounded by factors relating to personnel and procedures.

At the preassessment level, professionals and families should meet to share information and concerns regarding the assessment procedures. All questions regarding the choice of the assessment materials, procedures, and personnel should be fully explained. The assessment should be multidimensional with information gathered on multiple occasions. These informed participants can then design an individual assessment that conforms to the needs of the child and the family (Division for Early Childhood Task Force, 1993).

PERSONAL

Each child is unique, regardless of disability or classifying condition. Factors such as age, place of residence, socioeconomic status, genetic factors, environmental factors, personality, cultural heritage, and gender all shape the developmental and educational status of the child and must be considered within the unique components of the child's development. Researchers have found that while some developmental patterns signal the possibility of difficulties later on, others do not, making early identification of certain disabilities extremely difficult. Logically, then, the occurrence of such a disability as mental retardation only serves to complicate a procedure that is already delicate and fragile. Early childhood service providers must assess these abilities using methods and instruments that fairly yet appropriately identify the disability and its related areas. Understanding how children grow and develop relative to their own unique conditions and abilities is essential to designing sound intervention strategies (Drew, Hardman & Logan, 1996; C. R. Reynolds & Clark, 1983).

Variables also exist in terms of time of day of alertness with each child, in particular with infants. Results can be affected if the child is not rested, fed, comfortable, and attentive. This means that only a few hours per day may be available for optimal testing.

The child's stage of development will also impact the test results. During particular developmental stages, children are strongly attached to the primary caregiver, which means that the primary caregiver must be present with the child for assessments to occur.

Children who are delayed in development may not comprehend the testing process and may need repeated prompts and encouragement as well as repeated explanations. This extra time required then impacts the physical and mental endurance of the child to attend to the task at hand, which, at times, requires extra sessions to complete the assessment.

PROFESSIONAL

Few components are as important to successful assessment, evaluation, and intervention as the training of early childhood service providers. Although recommendations for best practice vary from school to school and district to district, adequate preparation of professionals should be a constant. Unfortunately, and as alluded to previously, evidence suggests that traditional methods of early childhood assessment are less than optimal and that many examiners lack the necessary skills and training to provide high-quality services (L. J. Johnson & Beauchamp, 1987; Schakel, 1987). Examiners may be required to modify test instructions and physically guide a child through the explanation process in order for the child to comprehend the requirements of the task. This requires a great deal of flexibility and understanding on the part of the examiner. To increase the quality of services provided, examiners should have formal education in such areas as child development, assessment of mental and special abilities, and educational interventions, in addition to formal, supervised, field-based training experiences.

Equally important is the psychometric integrity of the respective instruments. While the reliability and validity of preschool instruments have been criticized in recent years (e.g., Bracken, 1987; Ittenbach, Harrison, & Deck, 1989), their vulnerability appears to be diminishing as users have been demanding and test publishers have begun providing instruments with the same level of sophistication as those used with school-age populations. Standardized instruments with large, nationally representative normative samples, theoretically valid content areas, published validity information, and user-qualification criteria are all hallmarks of a good instrument.

PROCEDURAL

Local educational agencies have little flexibility in the decision to provide service to three- to five-year-old children who are disabled. They do, however, have a great deal of flexibility in the process by which children with special needs are identified for service. For example, in some states, a delay of 25 percent or more is all that is required for service; in other states a delay of 25 percent in two or more areas is required; and, in still others, a 35 percent delay in a single area is necessary for qualification. As with other exceptionalities, state guidelines allow for such multiple criteria as standardized test scores, discrepancy formulas, or percentile ranks. For state and local agencies offering services to infants and toddlers, a case manager must be assigned to the child's family to coordinate educational services. The mechanics of evaluation also vary. For example, while most school districts require a multidisciplinary team approach to assessment, some bring the teams together only as referrals are made; therefore, some teams assist one child at a time. Other districts require that teams assemble on a routine basis to assess children in large numbers. Equally broad is the spectrum of settings used to offer such services (Thurlow, 1992). Understandably, school district personnel offering screening services to children individually after school in a quiet room will likely elicit very different results than will a team consisting of professionals and volunteers conducting a mass screening in a gymnasium on a Saturday morning with parents and peers watching. Professionals should make decisions based on the unique needs of the child using sound logic and valid reasoning and not simply to meet the needs of the group making the decision or because it is the most cost-efficient and expedient route to take.

PROGRAMMING FOR YOUNG CHILDREN

An individual plan of action determines the framework for each young child. Such a plan becomes the group consensus on what is appropriate for each child. Programmatic issues addressed are "how to arrange environments, how teachers should interact, how programs should be monitored, and how data describing programs must be used to inform parents about their effectiveness

TABLE 8.6
Service Delivery Models for Young Children with Disabilities

Model	Advantages	Disadvantages
Home-based	Rapport with family is more easily established.	Parents who may lack skills are responsible for implementing much of the intervention.
	Family routines are less likely to be disrupted.	Teachers spend potential planning and instructional time traveling from site to site.
	Children are more at ease, less frightened in familiar surroundings.	No opportunity exists for peer interaction and socialization.
	Materials can be designed to meet the needs of the natural setting.	
	Building and maintenance costs are unnecessary.	
Center-based	All primary and support services are housed in one location.	Cost of providing facilities and range of services is high.
	Teachers have more time for planning and instruction.	Center may need to provide transportation and bus aides, which increases cost.
	Situation promotes peer interaction and socialization.	Families may move and time may be lost in reorganizing bus routes or locating the family.
Combination	Greater flexibility in delivering services is possible.	Same as with home- and center-based models.
	Same as with home- and center-based models.	
Consultation	More efficient use of staff time.	Parents are responsible for implementation of the intervention.
		Imposes on parents to transport children.
		Limited amount of service can be provided to child or family.

in meeting children's needs" (Carta, Atwater, Schwartz, & McConnell, 1993, p. 243). Table 8.6 details the advantages and disadvantages of the various models.

SERVICE DELIVERY MODELS

The educational needs of young children with disabilities differ from those of their school-age counterparts. To meet the diverse needs of younger children, greater flexibility and variety in service delivery options are needed in a coordinated plan. Educators responsible for planning and implementing appropriate early intervention services must identify current resources, coordinate existing programs, and develop innovative service delivery models

TABLE 8.7

HCEEP Projects Approved for National Dissemination by the Joint Dissemination Review Panel

Project	Primary handicap of children	Ages served	Sample size	Duration (weeks)
Home-based				
Macomb 0–3 Project, IL	Combination	0–3	34	77
Peoria 0–3 Project, IL	Combination	0–3	77	52
UNISTAPS Project, MN	Hearing-impaired	0–5	25	39
Central Institute Project, MO	Hearing-impaired	0–4	29	154
DEBT Project, TX	Combination	0–2	103	65
PEECH Project, IL	Combination	.5–6	98	189
SKI*HI Project, UT	Hearing-impaired	0–6	40	43
C.P. Project, WI	Orthopedically impaired	0–3	36	39
Portage Project, W	Combination	0–6	57	39
Center-based				
Rutland Canter, GA	Emotionally	2–8	49	22
PEECH Project, IL	Combination	3–5	37	30
High/Scope Project, MI	Combination	4–6	16	39
Regional Demo. Project, NY	Combination	3–5		
Chapel Hill Project, NC	Combination	4–6	90	34
Good Samaritan Hospital	Multiple handicapped	0–6	28	39
Down Syndrome Project, WA	Mentally retarded	0–6	66	39
Combined Home-Center				
ERIN Project, MA	Combination	2–7	25	26
Preschool/Families Project, ND	Combination	0–6	35	30
Teaching Research Project, OR	Combination	1–8	20	—
MAPPS Project, UT	Combination	0–5	120	77
Communication Project, WA	Speech/language	0–6	39	43

Source: From "What Is Known about Early Intervention" by K. R. White and G. Casto in *Implementing Early Intervention* (pp. 3–20) edited by G. Tingey, 1989, Baltimore: Brookes. Copyright 1989 by Brookes Publishing Co.

with the informed consent of the family. This information should be presented in the family's preferred language. Personnel within the programs should be schooled in the services, strategies, and interventions for children in the particular age group with whom they are working (Division for Early Childhood Task Force, 1993). Table 8.7 provides descriptions of selected early intervention projects sponsored by the Handicapped Children's Early Education Program of 1968 (HCEEP) and approved by the Joint Dissemination Review Panel.

Hospital-Based Services

Due to the emphasis on early detection among the medical and educational communities, newborns who are high risk may be placed in neonatal intensive care units for specialized care. These units provide specialists in neonatology to care for the child and to provide education, guidance, and support for the parents. Referrals are made based on the individual children and their families (Division for Early Childhood Task Force, 1993; Flynn & McCollum, 1989).

Home-Based Services

The goal of home-based intervention, which is where the majority of infants and toddlers receive services, is to assist families in setting goals and acquiring the skills needed to meet them (U.S. Department of Education, 1996). Family training and cooperation are the keystones in service delivery. A teacher, consultant, or paraprofessional visits the home on a regular basis and helps the family to develop an appropriate home intervention program for the child who is retarded. Depending on the needs of the child and the family, visits may occur as often as several times weekly or as infrequently as once monthly. During visits, the teacher, consultant, or paraprofessional may assess the child and/or family situation, review the child's progress since the last visit, observe parent–child or family–child interactions and offer suggestions, demonstrate activities, or aid the parent in designing materials or developing activities.

Advantages to the home-based services are many. The home is the natural environment for the child. Parents, other family members, and friends become the first instructors for the child, and with the services of the professionals, these first lessons are designed for the individual child. This early intervention and training actively involve and educate the family so that they can participate at a higher level in planning later in the child's life when the learning environment shifts away from being primarily in the home. From a monetary viewpoint, home-based services are less expensive, as facilities do not need to be provided for education, and transportation costs are incurred only by the professionals.

With all the advantages of home-based service, the program is not without disadvantages. Not all families are willing or able to participate in services in their home. With the provision of a professional coming to the home, families are denied the services of the variety of professionals available in a center-based program; thus, the number of services provided is decreased. Finally, families and children are denied social interaction and support with others in similar circumstances.

Center-Based Services

Services in center-based programs take place in a single location outside the home. Professionals consider center-based programs most appropriate for preschool age children who require services from a team of specialists, for children who need peer models or peer interaction, and for children whose parents are not always available to participate in their education. Some programs accommodate only children who are disabled, and others include children who are disabled with those who are not. Usually, the children attend the center for three to five hours per day, four to five days per week. Effective center-based programs have curricula that are unbiased and nondiscriminatory and are housed in buildings that are physically accessible to the children and their parents. Family participation in center-based programs varies and may include observation or classroom participation, scheduled meetings to review progress or to receive instruction for home implementation of center activities, and parent support groups.

The advantages of center-based programs include the availability of a wide variety of specialists, increased opportunity for contact with children who are developing at a normal rate, and a support group for parents. Disadvantages of such programs include the expense of transportation for each family, the cost and maintenance of the facility, and reduced individual contact for the family with a center professional.

Combined Home–Center Programs

Combination service models offer various configurations of home- and center-based services. This allows the child and the family to receive the intensive help of the professionals in a center-based program along with the peer interaction and family support while maintaining the home atmosphere of attention and family interaction. Family training is conducted on multidimensional levels within the home and the center.

Consultation Services

In the consultation service model, parents bring the child to the center, and professionals provide instruction for training. Unlike home-based parent training programs, however, consultation usually involves only one or two sessions. As with home-based programs, this method of service delivery relies on parents to implement the recommendations of professionals.

CURRICULUM

Curriculum is the planned sequence of content and methods of instruction for an individual student or groups of students to modify behavior. Most early childhood special education programs employ a variety of approaches in teaching infants and young children. Generally, the curriculum is derived from one of three theoretical perspectives on learning: developmental, behavioral, or functional.

Developmental Curriculum

This curriculum is based largely on the work of the Swiss psychologist Jean Piaget. Piaget considered the child an active agent in the learning process of trial-and-error experiments. According to Piaget, skills develop hierarchically, and children pass through developmental stages in a highly predictable fashion. Development of high-level skills is inextricably bound to development of lower level skills. The teacher following the developmental curriculum matches tasks to normal developmental milestones, identifies deficits, and gears instruction to accelerating the rate of development of the child or infant who is disabled to the rate of peers who are not disabled. Fewell and Kelly (1983) pointed out that an advantage of developmental curricula is the use of clusters of interrelated behaviors, which encourages generalization of skills. The disadvantages, however, are that developmental tasks are based on normal development that presupposes all senses intact and that children are to be guided through their current developmental level without instruction in higher developmental levels (Piaget & Inhelder, 1969). Berkeley and

Ludlow (1989) also cited the limited sample of developmental indicators at each age, a lack of empirical support that children with disabilities follow the same course of development as children without disabilities, the possibility that curricular objectives may discourage individual program planning as children are moved through a standard curriculum at a slower rate, and the uncertainty that curricular objectives identify critical skills for present and projected future environments.

Behavioral Curriculum

B. F. Skinner (1953) gave us the approach of operant conditioning in which behavior is related to consequences or reinforcements. Behaviors that have pleasant consequences or reinforcements tend to be repeated while behaviors that have negative consequences or reinforcements tend to be avoided; consequences, therefore, shape behavior. This is the principle of positive and negative reinforcement. Contained within the principle of reinforcements is the concept of successive approximations in which the child is rewarded for steps toward the behavioral goal. Proponents of behavioral curricula believe that children learn best by experiencing repeated reinforcement for responses to environmental stimuli. Skills are taught in the behavioral curriculum according to the child's or infant's needs in the present or projected future environment. The model defines skills precisely in behavioral terms and states criteria for performance clearly and quantitatively. Supporters of this approach maintain that children who lack essential skills require a highly structured approach to learning and that the structure can be relaxed and skills integrated as learning progresses. Wolery, Bailey, and Sugai (1988) reported that experimental evidence indicates that the behavioral curricula help children with disabilities but the method remains controversial. Fewell and Kelly (1983) pointed out that opponents of the behavioral approach argue that the use of such an approach inhibits the cognitive and emotional development of young children with disabilities by prohibiting interaction with the environment.

Functional Curriculum

The functional curriculum approach is a hybrid of the developmental and the behavioral curricula. Functional curricula attempt to incorporate the best features of the two. Insofar as they emphasize teaching interrelated classes of behavior and generalization within task classes, they are developmental; in their emphasis on teaching skills that the infant or child needs now or will need later, they are behavioral.

To date, no single curricular approach has been demonstrated to be superior to the others with all children. Curriculum should be chosen based on the individual needs of the child and the family.

PROGRAM IMPLEMENTATION

Programs for infants and preschoolers differ from programs for school-age children in the amount of time spent in school and in the goals and objectives for learning. Yet teachers of young children face similar challenges in arranging the classroom and scheduling the school day. Workable classroom arrangements and effective scheduling are crucial to the success of infant and preschool programs.

CLASSROOM ACCOMMODATIONS AND ADAPTATIONS

Within a teacher's classroom is the culture of power where teachers exercise power over the students in terms of determining curriculum, presenting world views, and establishing rules and regulations. Students enter the classroom with the culture of the home. If the teacher's culture and the student's home culture are similar, then students enter knowing how to perform in the culture of the teacher's classroom. If, however, a student's home culture differs from the teacher's culture, then student's must be instructed in the culture of the classroom in order to perform adequately (Delpit, 1988). The learning environment provided by the teacher influences and, in some cases, determines the development of the child. Designing the optimal classroom, therefore, requires careful planning. Among the factors teachers must consider are the following:

1. *The space available.* State education agencies usually dictate the minimum allowable space for infant and preschool classrooms. But the shape of the room and the presence of fixed features like windows, sinks, and toilets sometimes inhibit optimal classroom arrangements. Polloway and Patton (1997) suggest that teachers begin planning room arrangement by drawing a rough sketch of the room, then adding in basic equipment like tables, desks, and chairs. In designing classroom space, the placement of materials in the classroom should be designed to facilitate student learning and involvement. Teachers should be mindful of their schedule and create a traffic flowchart to and from activities in the classroom with discernible boundaries that separate areas of instruction.

2. *The physical needs of the students.* The physical needs of preschool children who are disabled often differ from those of their peers who are not disabled. Children in wheelchairs or walkers or on portable stretchers, for example, require carefully planned room arrangements. At the very least, the teacher must consider fixed barriers (e.g., doorways) and movable barriers (e.g., tables). For children who are not toilet trained or who are incontinent, the teacher must consider the need for privacy of changing tables. Finally, as with all children, the size of the furniture must match the size of the child. These types of physical accommodations should be reflected in the room arrangement and traffic pattern of the classroom to increase the comfort level of all children within the classroom.

3. *Group arrangements.* Infant and preschool programs use a variety of group arrangements during the school day. Individual work areas should be located together in a quiet area of the classroom to encourage attending to task. Group work areas should be away from the individual work area. The group area should be flexible and fluid to allow for configuration and reconfiguration of small, medium, and large group activities. The various areas should be plainly labeled to facilitate flow within the classroom, to enable students to identify their assigned area, and to promote student involvement.

4. *The purpose of instruction.* Lesson objectives frequently suggest the location and type of space needed. Activities that involve direct teacher instruction

(e.g., language learning) require a more structured, quieter setting than activities that involve only teacher supervision (e.g., free play). Consideration must also be given as to how the students will interact socially. Peer interactions may involve individual activities, parallel activities, or cooperative activities. In an inclusive classroom, each child as well as the group must be considered in determining how instruction will be delivered.

5. *Material accessibility*. Searching for materials stored in out-of-the-way places can waste valuable teaching time, and materials that are not readily available are less likely to be used. Also, because fostering independence is an important goal of early childhood special education programs, teachers should avoid making materials difficult for children to locate and secure on their own. Lund and Bos (1981) suggest placing instructional areas close to material storage places, keeping frequently used materials close together to facilitate accessibility, and labeling or color coding storage areas.

6. *Personal territory*. Like their school-age counterparts, children in preschool arrive with a variety of personal possessions. A safe and accessible space is needed in the classroom to store outerwear, storybooks, toys, and so on. Gray (1975) points out that personal space in the classroom contributes to the child's sense of belonging. Lund and Bos (1981) suggest using cubbies or lockers for children's personal belongings and picture cues to assist students in identifying their personal space.

In considering the six points listed, the teacher is viewing the individual child from various perspectives that will enable the teacher to determine not only what is best for the child but also to what extent the child can be included in a general education classroom for meaningful participation with children who are not disabled. One way to help teachers arrive at the proper balance for children with special needs is to use the preschool checklist presented in Figure 8.6 (Drinkwater & Demchak, 1995). The checklist covers the areas of scheduling and instructional arrangements, socialization and communication, alternative communication, and appearance of the child to aid teachers not only in including children with special needs in a general education classroom but also to aid the teachers in creating goals to enable the inclusion to be successful. Benefits that can be gained from including students with special needs into the general education classroom are as follows: "(a) enhanced skill generalization, (b) increased self-initiations in social situations, (c) equivalent development gains to nondisabled peers, (d) preparation for dealing with the real world, (e) increased communication skills with peers and family members, and (f) increased number of nondisabled friends" (Drinkwater & Demchak, 1995, p. 7).

TECHNOLOGY

Schools in many instances have been relatively unaffected by the technological advances in society. Basically, textbooks remain the dominant source of information delivered by teachers to students (Mehlinger, 1988). IDEA, however, provides for assistive technology devices or services to be delivered free to a student who qualifies. This inclusion of assistive technology

Teacher: _____ Student: _____
Date: _____

SCHEDULING AND INSTRUCTIONAL ARRANGEMENTS

yes   no   1. Is the child positioned so that he or she can see and participate in the activity?

yes   no   2. Is the child positioned so that other children and teachers may easily interact with her or him (e.g., without an adult between the child and other children, not isolated from other children)?

yes   no   3. Is the child involved in the same activities as other children?

yes   no   4. Does the child engage in activities at the same time as other children?

yes   no   5. Is the child actively involved in activities (e.g., plays a role in group activities, asks/answers questions)?

yes   no   6. Is the child given assistance only as necessary?

yes   no   7. Does the child use the same or similar types of materials during activities as other children?

yes   no   8. Are the least intrusive, natural prompts and contingencies used, if needed, to help the child to participate in the activity?

yes   no   9. Are the materials appropriate for the chronological age of the child?

yes   no   10. Does the child participate in activities that are appropriate for his/her chronological age?

SOCIALIZATION AND COMMUNICATION

yes   no   1. Does the child have a way to communicate (e.g., signs, gestures, pictures, speech) with other children?

yes   no   2. Do the other children know how to communicate with the child (e.g., use gestures, understand simple signs, respond to pictures)?

yes   no   3. Does the child socialize with other children (e.g., playing at free time, using playground equipment)?

yes   no   4. Is the socialization/interaction with other children facilitated (e.g., children are prompted and reinforced for initiations and interactions)?

yes   no   5. Do teachers interact in the same way with the child as with other children (e.g., praise, hugs)?

yes   no   6. Is the child given opportunities to demonstrate competence (e.g., line leader, passing out snacks, helper of the day)?

FIGURE 8.6

Preschool Checklist: Integration of Children with Disabilities

Source: From "The Preschool Checklist: Integration of Children with Severe Disabilities" by S. Drinkwater and M. Demchak, 1995, *Teaching Exceptional Children, 28*(1), pp. 4–8. Copyright 1995 by the Council for Exceptional Children. Reprinted by permission.

in the classroom has the power to transform the general education classroom as well as to provide for the inclusion of students with special needs who have been excluded previously from such settings. Examples of technology in the classroom may be as simple as television or as complex as computer-assisted instruction with expanded devices to facilitate communication (Morsink & Lenk, 1992; Todis & Walker, 1993).

Current advances in technology that could have an immediate impact on education are video-on-demand, the electronic panning camera, and the delivery of electronic multimedia over the network (DEMON). This technology has the potential of increasing a teacher's effectiveness for children with special needs and their families in various localities (Karpinski, 1993).

ALTERNATIVE COMMUNICATION (If this section is not applicable to the child, please skip to the next section.)

yes   no   1. If the child uses an alternative communication system (e.g., signing, picture cards), do other children know how to use it?

yes   no   2. Do teachers know how to use the alternative communication system?

yes   no   3. Is the alternative communication system always available to the child?

APPEARANCE OF THE CHILD

yes   no   1. Does the child have accessories that are similar to those of other children (e.g., small back-pack, hair clips)?

yes   no   2. Is the child's dress age appropriate?

yes   no   3. Is clothing for activities appropriate (e.g., paint shirts, napkins not bibs)?

yes   no   4. Are personal belongings (e.g., change of clothing, diapers) carried discreetly?

yes   no   5. If the child has special equipment, is it kept clean?

yes   no   6. Is the child's hair combed and kept neat?

yes   no   7. Are the child's hands clean and dry?

yes   no   8. Is the child's clothing changed as necessary to maintain a neat appearance?

SUMMARY OF THE PRESCHOOL CHECKLIST

Scheduling and Instructional Arrangements: _____/10

Socialization and Communication: _____/6

   Alternative Communication: _____/3 (if applicable)

Appearance of the Child: _____/8

Total Score: _____/24 (or 27 if Alternative Communication is applicable)

GOAL AREAS

Please feel free to use this section to set goals for yourself and your assistant(s) on ways that you can more fully include the targeted student in preschool activities and routines.

Goals areas to lead to fuller inclusion:

_____

_____

FIGURE 8.6
(continued)

The video-on-demand has been called a "real-time scheduler," since the system can be programmed to arrange information packets in a priority manner. Packets that are not top priority can be held through e-mail at a "packet rest station," while top priority packets are sent directly to the computer. For the hospital–home-based child and family, these packets arranged in a top priority fashion not only can aid compacted learning but also can conserve a child's strength for learning (Karpinski, 1993).

The electronic panning camera offers more effective implementation of live video classes by affording the instructor the ability to view the class(es) addressed or by allowing the hospital–home-based child and family to feel

POSITION STATEMENT REGARDING ASSISTIVE TECHNOLOGY DEVICES AND SERVICES

The Board of Directors of the Division on Mental Retardation and Developmental Disabilities (CEC-MRDD) acknowledges the critical importance of appropriate assistive technology devices and services in the lives of individuals with disabilities across cultures. It recognizes that a wide range of assistive technology devices, ranging from "low tech" to "high tech" in design, is currently available to potentially enable persons with mental retardation and developmental disabilities to acquire important skills that may enhance their quality of life and result in greater independence in family and community settings. It also recognizes that assistive technology services articulated in the *Individuals with Disabilities Education Act* should be used to support the use of assistive technology devices. These include training, leasing, purchasing, maintenance, repair, and other necessary services. The Board also recognizes that though persons with mental retardation and developmental disabilities at all age levels and across cultures may benefit from assistive technology devices and services many individuals remain unserved.

For persons with mental retardation and developmental disabilities and for professionals to achieve optimal benefits from assistive technology devices and services, the Board recommends that:

- the identification of appropriate assistive technology devices and services for persons with mental retardation and developmental disabil-

ities involve consideration of multiple domains of influence, including individual, device/service, service system, family, and cultural factors; therefore:

- a family and culturally sensitive multidisciplinary team process should be used to identify and recommend appropriate assistive technology devices and services that may be needed for individuals with mental retardation and developmental disabilities;
- assistive technology devices and services should be written into service plans when appropriate to ensure their delivery to those individuals who can benefit from them;
- appropriate funding mechanisms necessary to pay for assistive technology devices and services should be identified and utilized efficiently by individuals with mental retardation and developmental disabilities, families, and service systems;
- creative solutions for funding a full range of assistive technology devices and services across the age span should be cooperatively developed when existing mechanisms are insufficient to meet such needs; and
- greater collaboration should be encouraged between persons with mental retardation and developmental disabilities, family members, and professionals to examine and document perceptions and impact of assistive technology devices and services.

more like participants in the classroom rather than just observers. The individual user chooses the camera angle for viewing without affecting any other viewer. Five different cameras assemble a composite 150-degree picture of an event. The viewer, through the use of a remote control, can scan an entire scene or zoom in or out. These options can also be utilized by the teacher to more effectively include hospital–home-based students and their families into the general education classroom (Karpinski, 1993).

The meeting logger records classes on video for later recall. Users can review entire classes or scan rapidly, starting and stopping at any point. For students or families needing review or for those who missed an entire class, the meeting logger enables learning to continue at the best pace for the students and their families. This technology also enables students and families to view classes at a time of the day that is most convenient for them (Karpinski, 1993).

DEMON enables multimedia information to be held in storage for later editing or viewing. The system anticipates user need and speed of delivery. Once again, children with special needs and their families have options for review (Karpinski, 1993).

SCHEDULING

In arranging a schedule for a classroom, teachers should take into account the abilities, disabilities, personalities, mobility, and so on of the various children enrolled in the class and the instructional objectives to be reached. While teachers may not know ahead of time the exact needs of each child, they can plan a schedule with all options included. Polloway and Patton (1997) point out that the first step is to determine how many hours the child is in school and how much of that time is available for instruction. Such events as snack or lunch, related services (e.g., physical therapy), sharing time, and so forth must be scheduled in and deducted from instructional time. Once these factors are accounted for, the teacher should consider high- and low-probability activities. Low-probability activities require direct teacher instruction in a skill or concept (e.g., classifying words into categories like food, animals, transportation). The most difficult low-probability

8:30–8:50	Interaction with children and parents, hang up coats, etc.
8:50–9:10	Circle time (days of the week, months, colors, etc.; varies with need).
9:10–9:20	Group 1 with teacher for direct instruction. Groups 2 and 3 with aide for activities.
9:20–9:30	Group 2 with teacher for direct instruction. Groups 1 and 3 with aide for activities.
9:30–9:40	Group 3 with teacher for direct instruction. Groups 1 and 2 with aide for activities.
9:40–10:10	Free play or outdoor play.
10:10–10:20	Transition, bathroom, etc.
10:20–10:40	Snack.
10:40–11:00	Circle time (language, cognitive development, etc.).
11:10–11:20	Story time.
11:20–11:30	Interact with children and parents, put on coats, etc.
11:30	Dismissal.

FIGURE 8.7
Half-Day Preschool Schedule with Direct Instruction

activities should be taught early in the day when children are most alert and, for variety, interspersed with such high-probability activities as story time or work centers designed to develop different skills. Next, the teacher must consider whether and how to schedule small group or one-on-one instruction. The schedule will direct the flow of the day, and each day, each child should find an area of joy in the schedule.

Many preschool programs provide for a half-day of direct instruction services. The teacher may spend the rest of the day in planning, case management, consulting with other professionals, or meeting with parents. Other programs provide for a full day of services. Regardless of the length of the

8:30–8:45	Interaction with children and parents, hang up coats, etc.
8:45–9:05	Circle time (days of the week, months, colors, etc.; varies with need).
9:05–9:35	Free play (activities designed to develop various areas—cognitive, motor, etc.).
9:35–9:50	Story time.
9:50–10:00	Transition, bathroom, etc.
10:00–10:20	Snack.
10:20–10:45	Outdoor play.
10:45–11:00	Circle time (language, cognitive development, etc.).
11:00–11:20	Free play (as above).
11:20–11:30	Interaction with children and parents, put on coats, etc.
11:30	Dismissal.

FIGURE 8.8
Half-Day Preschool Schedule Without Direct Instruction

8:00–8:30	Teacher planning.
8:30–9:00	Arrival, self-help (undressing).
9:00–11:00	Individual activities: physical management, gross motor, fine motor, cognition.
9:30–10:00	Language group 1 (augmentative).
10:00–10:30	Language group 2 (3–4 word utterances).
10:30–11:00	Language group 3 (imitation).
11:00–12:00	Lunch; self-help (eating, brushing teeth, toileting).
12:00–1:00	Nap.
	Arrival of nonhandicapped students.
1:00–1:30	Self-help (dressing), self-directed activities.
1:30–2:00	Individual language activities (groups 1, 2, 3).
	Language group 4 (integrated).
2:00–2:30	Snack and socialization groups (integrated).
2:30	Departure.
2:30–4:00	Teacher planning.

FIGURE 8.9
Full-Day Preschool Schedule

8:00–8:30	Teacher planning.[*]
8:30–9:00	Arrival and interaction with families.
9:00–11:00	Individual activities.[**]
	Physical management.
	Motor development.
	Language development.
	Cognition.
11:00–12:00	Lunch; oral motor skills, self-help (eating, brushing teeth, toileting).
12:00–1:00	Nap.
1:00–1:30	Self-help (dressing, toileting).
1:30–2:00	Sensory activities, individualized within group setting to enhance social skills.
2:00–2:30	Interaction with families.
2:30–4:00	Teacher planning; case management activities, home visits.

[*]The infant schedule must be flexible to take into consideration each child's schedule of eating and sleeping.

[**]These activities match the overlap between domains during infancy. Emphasis is placed on developing skills across domains to encourage the infant to interact with all facets of the environment.

FIGURE 8.10
Full-Day Infant Schedule

school day, the daily schedule is an important ingredient in the effectiveness of the service and sets the tone for learning. Figures 8.7 to 8.10 on pp 302–304 provide examples of possible schedules for the preschool years.

FAMILY INVOLVEMENT

With the enactment of PL 99-457, families participate on the IFSP and IEP committees as collaborators. The law requires that family needs and re- sources be assessed and that parents be counseled about their child's needs and be assisted in the acquisition of services for the child. Family members have the opportunity to participate in an active manner in the writing of the IFSP and IEP and in the instruction of the child. The definition of family was not provided in the law, but the definition used in this chapter refers to

> two or more people who regard themselves as a family and who perform some of the functions that families typically perform. These people may or may not be related by blood or marriage and may or may not usually live together. (Turnbull, Turnbull, Shank, & Leal, 1995, pp. 24–25)

When professionals gain information about the family in an individual and personal way, then the professional is in harmony with the family's strengths, weaknesses, desires, expectations, priorities, and needs. By using the Family

Systems Conceptual Framework (Turnbull, Summers, & Brotherson, 1984) illustrated in Figure 8.11, the professional gains valuable facts about the interrelatedness of the family unit. This personalized knowledge aids the professional in the collaboration process by examining four components of the family unit: family characteristics, family interaction, family functions, and family life cycle.

Heward (1996) outlines seven roles that parents of children with special needs fulfill.

1. *Teaching*. Many children learn skills in an incidental fashion, but children with special needs must be directly instructed in order to learn many tasks. Since families are in day-to-day contact with these children, the family becomes the first teacher in early childhood. Some families must further learn to use special equipment and devices in order for their children to function in society.

2. *Counseling*. In addition to the normal counseling role that parents deal with in addressing emotions, feelings, and attitudes, the parents of the child with special needs must also deal with greater intensity of these areas due to the disability. The disability itself must be addressed with the child, the siblings, and the greater society. The parents must guide the child through the day-to-day life with a disability.

3. *Managing behavior*. This again is in addition to the normal role of parenting in training children toward the behavioral expectations of society. Many times these parents must first be taught how to handle behavior so that they in turn can teach the child and then the society at large.

4. *Parenting siblings without disabilities*. No two children without disabilities are identical, but the difference is magnified when there is a disability present. Parents must learn to parent both types of children so that all children reach their full potential. In the course of their parenting, parents must also teach siblings without a disability about the disability itself and how this disability impacts the sibling with the disability, the family, and the siblings without the disability.

5. *Maintaining the parent-to-parent relationship*. Having children decreases the time that parents have for themselves as a couple, but when a child with a disability is born, the time decreases even further. To find time for themselves as a couple, the parent must leave the child with a disability in a competent care situation. This requires additional time for the parent in an already stressful situation, as the caretaker must be educated in the role of the parent. In addition to time is the factor of money. Many disabilities require additional funds to care for the child who is disabled, which decreases the funds available for parent time as a couple.

6. *Educating significant others*. Just as parents must educate caretakers of their child with a disability, the parent must educate those in the family and the community who come in contact with their child. Children with disabilities require consistency in their lives, and this happens only when the family and the community as a whole can be educated and react in a single-minded fashion toward the child with a disability.

7. *Relating to the school and community*. The parents' role is that of an advocate for their child. No one knows the child as intimately as the parent. The

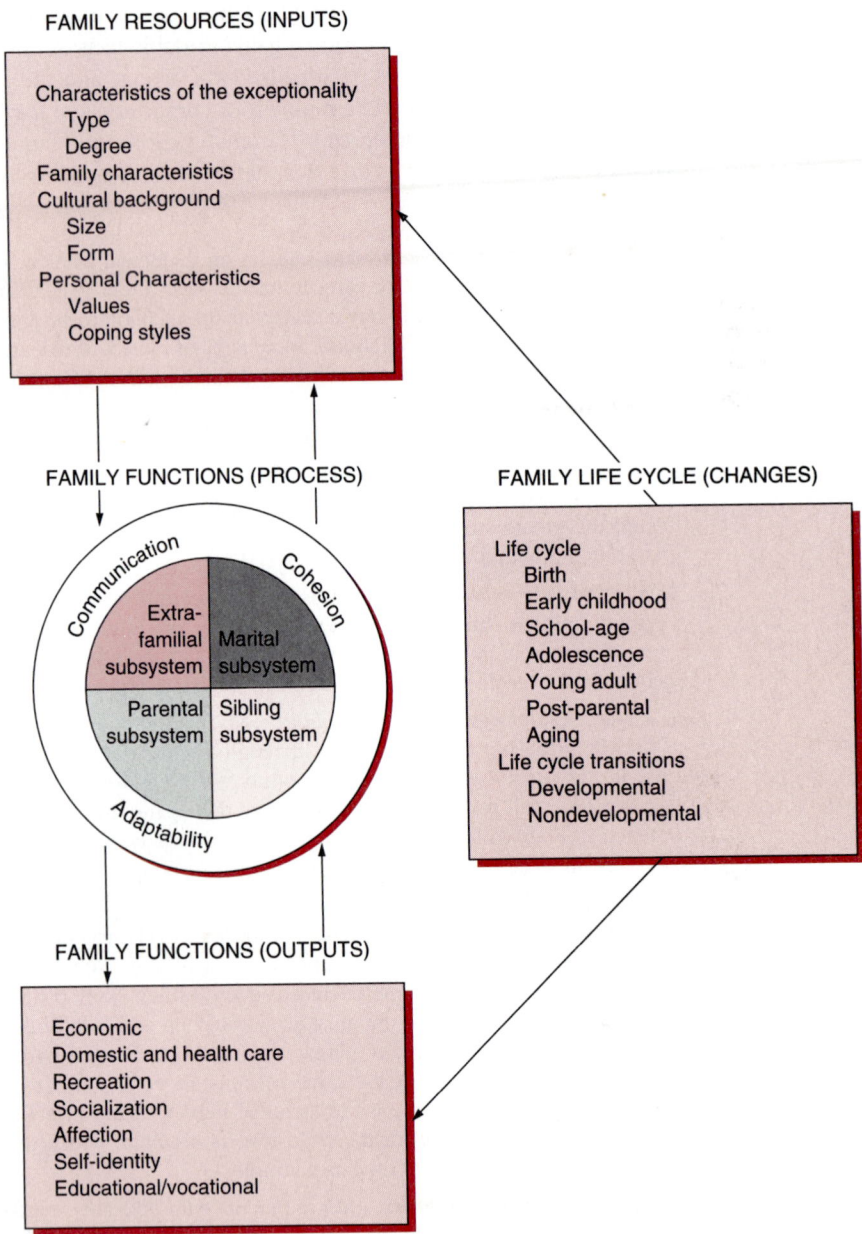

FAMILY RESOURCES (INPUTS)

Characteristics of the exceptionality
  Type
  Degree
Family characteristics
Cultural background
  Size
  Form
Personal Characteristics
  Values
  Coping styles

FAMILY FUNCTIONS (PROCESS)

Communication
Cohesion
Adaptability

Extra-familial subsystem | Marital subsystem
Parental subsystem | Sibling subsystem

FAMILY LIFE CYCLE (CHANGES)

Life cycle
  Birth
  Early childhood
  School-age
  Adolescence
  Young adult
  Post-parental
  Aging
Life cycle transitions
  Developmental
  Nondevelopmental

FAMILY FUNCTIONS (OUTPUTS)

Economic
Domestic and health care
Recreation
Socialization
Affection
Self-identity
Educational/vocational

FIGURE 8.11
Family Systems Conceptual Framework

Source: From *Working with Families with Disabled Members: A Family Systems Approach* (p. 60) by A. P. Turnbull, J. A. Summers, and M. J. Brotherson, 1984. Lawrence, KS: Kansas University Affiliated Facility. Copyright 1984 by the University of Kansas.

school and community, therefore, should seek to include the parents in an active collaboration role for the benefit of the child with a disability and for the benefit of the school and community. When all who work with the child are acting in a manner that is consistent, then the child with a disability benefits.

TRANSITION

In early childhood special education, **transition** is the passage or change from one stage or level to the next. Changes in programming needs may result in a number of transitions within the service delivery system for young children with disabilities and their families. Children often move from home-based to center-based programs or from programs sponsored by health-care agencies to those sponsored by local education agencies. Families and children must adjust to new locations, to new teachers and staff, and to changes in program format, curriculum, and emphasis. The level of parental involvement, intensity of parental contact, or availability of services for parents change in each location and at the various age levels of the child. The necessary changes as a child grows may affect adversely the child's ability to adjust to new settings or to acquire new skills. These transitions and the concerns of the family must be addressed in both the IFSPs and the IEPs.

SUMMARY

RATIONALE FOR EARLY CHILDHOOD SPECIAL EDUCATION

- Research supports the importance of early childhood special education in growth and development of infants, toddlers, and young children with disabilities or who are at risk.

- The focus of early childhood special education is on early intervention and programming.

LEGISLATION AFFECTING EARLY CHILDHOOD SPECIAL EDUCATION PROGRAMS

- Recently passed laws recognize the need for special education early intervention services for infants, toddlers, and young children with disabilities or at risk for disabilities and their families.

- Public Law 99-457 extended the rights and privileges of PL 94-142 to infants, toddlers, and preschoolers and their families.

- Public Law 101-476 established new priorities for meeting the needs of infants and toddlers with disabilities and their families.

DEC-RECOMMENDED PRACTICES

■ The DEC issued a set of broad-spectrum recommended practices for infants and young children with disabilities and their families.

REFERRAL

■ Each state is required to establish a lead agency for the implementation of IDEA, Part H.

■ Within each state there is to be an early intervention system to identify and locate children who have disabilities, are developmentally delayed, or at risk and their families.

EVALUATION AND ASSESSMENT

■ Evaluation is a formal process conducted by qualified, licensed personnel who administer standardized tests for initial placement and continued eligibility, whereas assessment is an ongoing, often informal, process in which workers from many disciplines contribute information and participate in an ongoing process to determine specific strengths and weaknesses.

■ Evaluation and assessment use multiple sources and multiple measures gathered on multiple occasions in multiple settings.

MEASURES OF EARLY CHILDHOOD DEVELOPMENT

■ According to PL 99-457, assessment of preschool abilities must occur in each of five developmental areas: cognitive, socioemotional, motor, speech and language, and self-help skills.

ISSUES IN EARLY CHILDHOOD ASSESSMENT

■ Each child is unique regardless of disability or classifying condition.

■ Professionals should be adequately prepared to perform evaluation and assessment, while the instrument used should possess a high degree of psychometric integrity.

■ A multidisciplinary team approach should be used for evaluation, assessment, and placement.

PROGRAMMING FOR YOUNG CHILDREN

■ Educators responsible for planning and implementing appropriate early intervention services must identify current resources, coordinate existing programs, and develop innovative service delivery models with the informed consent of the family.

■ A variety of approaches should be used based on one of the following curricula: developmental, behavioral, or functional.

■ Professionals must make classroom accommodations and adaptions based on space available, physical needs of the students, group arrangements needed, purpose of instruction, material accessibility, and personal territory.

■ Scheduling should take into account the varied children enrolled and the instructional objectives to be reached.

FAMILY INVOLVEMENT

■ With the enactment of PL 99-457, families participate on the IFSP and IEP committees as collaborators.

■ Parents of children with special needs fulfill the following roles for their children: teaching, counseling, managing behavior, parenting siblings without disabilities, maintaining the parent-to-parent relationship, educating significant others, and relating to the school and community.

TRANSITION

■ As children with special needs and their families move through the various service options in special education, planned transition services are necessary.

CHAPTER 9

Educational Programming— School Years

After reading this chapter,
the student should be able to:

- Discuss the educational placement alternatives available under IDEA for students who are disabled.
- Discuss educational assessment procedures used with students who are retarded.
- Describe the uses of assessment procedures in making placement decisions and planning educational programming.
- Discuss considerations in programming for school-age learners.

Key Terms

annual goals
behavioral objectives
categorical programs
collaborative
  consultation
collaborative teaming
cross-categorical
  programs

curriculum
inclusion
Individualized
  Education Program
  (IEP)
interdisciplinary team
mainstreaming

noncategorical
  programs
parity
reciprocity
Regular Education
  Initiative (REI)
related services
short-term objectives

e have already dealt with the causes, characteristics, and assessment of individuals who are mentally retarded. Now it is time to go a step further and focus on the critical task of developing and implementing educational programs that give all individuals who are mentally retarded, regardless of their limitations, the opportunity to participate in the activities of their daily environment as much as possible.

In this chapter, we look at a number of key aspects in the process of educational programming for school-age learners. We begin our discussion with a review of placement alternatives available under the Individuals with Disabilities Education Act (IDEA, PL 105-17) for students who are disabled, and we consider the appropriateness of these placement alternatives. Next, we discuss the role of assessment in the educational programming process. In this section, we focus on the various types of educational assessments typically used with students who are mentally retarded. We examine the uses of assessment procedures in developing Individualized Education Programs (IEPs) and planning sound educational programs. Finally, we address programming for school-age learners. In the last section of this chapter, we focus on important aspects of curricular planning and the basic principles of effective teaching.

PLACEMENT ALTERNATIVES

The trend today toward providing appropriate, beneficial, humanistic services to persons in our society who are retarded has led to changes in the structure of American schools as well as to the development of entirely new educational alternatives. The goal is no longer to hide individuals who are disabled from view, but to habilitate them. A guiding principle is normalization—the idea that people who are mentally retarded should lead lives as much like yours and mine as possible. For children and youth, this principle is reflected in part by the mandate of the IDEA, PL 105-17 for appropriate education in the least restrictive environment.

In this section we deal with various program alternatives for individuals who are mentally retarded. We look at placement choices for school-age children and youth, and also at the statements of proponents and opponents of the Regular Education Initiative (REI) about the issues surrounding proposals for more integrated systems of education for students with disabilities.

Many students who are retarded benefit from the same services as their peers who are not disabled.

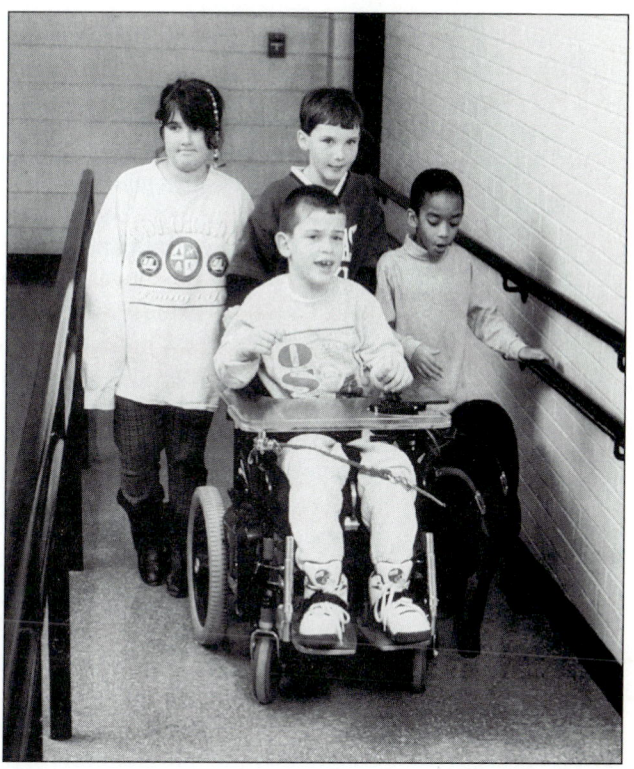

PROGRAMS FOR CHILDREN AND YOUTH WITH DISABILITIES

The free public school system in the New World was established in 1642 (Spring, 1986). Before that time, education was mostly limited to church-sponsored programs for which the provision of equal education for all children was not a concern. During the early part of the nineteenth century, states enacted laws that required communities to offer educational opportunities but did not make attendance mandatory. These efforts at mass education emphasized the importance of curricular content and not the needs of individual children. For the most part, children with mental and physical disabilities were excluded from school. The advent of compulsory attendance, which began in Massachusetts in 1852, with all states following suit by 1919, forced schools to provide a greater array of services, and residential and special self-contained classes were established. The "two-box" arrangement (M. C. Reynolds, 1989), with students with disabilities served in special education settings and students without disabilities served in general education settings, persisted until pressure from parents, professional concerns, and passage of PL 94-142, The Education for All Handicapped Children Act of 1975, with its requirement for education in the least restrictive environment, resulted in a full continuum of placement alternatives.

As Reynolds (1989) has noted, the history of special education is one of progressive inclusion. Over time, we have moved from exclusion to inclusion in school settings of students with disabilities. In the past few years, there has been a trend toward serving students with disabilities in integrated school settings. This trend, which encompasses integration and mainstreaming, envisions teaching all students who are disabled, including those who are mentally retarded, in the general education classroom or integrating them into general education settings whenever possible.

The goal of the movement toward more inclusive education for all students with disabilities is to provide them with educational opportunities that will maximize their potential and allow them to function fully in society. How best to accomplish this goal is the subject of ongoing debate in the field of special education. Some special educators support full integration and the dissolution of our current special education service delivery system while others maintain that a full range of placement alternatives is necessary to meet the special needs of students with disabilities.

MacMillan (1982), for example, has stated that the student who is retarded should be placed in the program closest to the general education class that the student's needs and characteristics will allow and that arrangements for instruction should be flexible enough to allow as much integration of the student into mainstream education as possible. From our perspective, educators responsible for determining the initial level of placement for any student who is retarded should make only a tentative commitment to program level; placement in any program should not be considered permanent or terminal. Further, opportunities for moving students who are retarded from more segregated to more integrated settings should be evaluated constantly and changes made whenever feasible. Finally, the requirements of the law that governs the placement of students in special education programs must be considered. We discuss these requirements in the following section.

THE INDIVIDUALS WITH DISABILITIES EDUCATION ACT

As mentioned in earlier chapters, the Individuals with Disabilities Education Act (IDEA, PL 105-17) is the 1997 amendment to PL 101-476. As such, it includes PL 94-142, The Education for All Handicapped Children Act of 1975, and PL 99-457, the 1986 early intervention amendments. The IDEA governs the provision of educational services to all children and youth with disabilities. Two of its legal guarantees are relevant to the educational placement of individuals with disabilities:

1. Assurance of the availability of an appropriate public education at no cost to parents for all children and youth who are disabled.
2. Assurance that special education will be provided in the least restrictive environment (LRE) to all children and youth who are disabled.

TABLE 9.1

Models for Educating Retarded Pupils According to Level of Program Segregation and Degree of Retardation

Children with intermittent or limited support needs	*Regular class-based programs* Special materials and equipment Special materials, equipment, and consultation Itinerant services Resource room with special education teacher Diagnostic-prescriptive teaching center
Children with limited or extensive support needs	*Special class-based programs* Special education class Part-time in regular class Full-time in special class
Children with extensive or pervasive support needs	*Special school-based programs* Special day school Special residential school
Unless temporary, children with pervasive support needs	*Nonschool-based programs* Hospital instruction Homebound instruction

These assurances compel educators to ensure that no child or youth is denied services on the basis of a disability, and that each child or youth is integrated, to the maximum extent possible, with peers who are not disabled. A number of placement alternatives are available for students who are disabled. We can group the program alternatives currently used with school-age youngsters who are disabled, including those who are mentally retarded, into sixteen types. These programs are divided into four major categories: those based in general education classrooms, in special education classrooms, in special schools, and in other settings (see Table 9.1).

GENERAL EDUCATION CLASS PROGRAMS

When placement decisions are made judiciously and reviewed routinely, the goal of providing the most beneficial services to students who are disabled with minimal segregation from their peers is attainable. Some students who are mentally retarded can reach this goal in the general education classroom with only minor adaptations in instructional procedures or the learning environment. Problems in accommodating the needs of students who are retarded in the general education classroom tend to arise when the student/teacher ratio is too high, the student's problems are not easily correctable, or the teacher lacks motivation, experience, or skill.

Instructing students who are retarded in the general education classroom requires teachers who are highly skilled and sensitive to the needs of these learners. According to Keogh (1990), such teachers must be able to maintain

CEC POLICY ON INCLUSIVE SCHOOLS AND COMMUNITY SETTINGS

At the 1993 Annual Convention of the Council for Exceptional Children, the following policy was approved by the Delegate Assembly.

The Council for Exceptional Children (CEC) believes all children, youth, and young adults with disabilities are entitled to a free and appropriate education and/or services that leads to an adult life characterized by satisfying relations with others, independent living, productive engagement in the community, and participation in society at large. To achieve such outcomes, there must exist for all children, youth, and young adults a rich variety of early intervention, educational and vocational program options and experiences. Access to these programs and experiences should be based on individual education need and desired outcomes. Furthermore, students and their families or guardian, as members of the planning team may recommend the placement, curriculum option, and the exit document to be pursued.

CEC believes that a continuum of services must be available for all children, youth and young adults. CEC also believes that the concept of inclusion is a meaningful goal to be pursued in our schools and communities. In addition, CEC believes children, youth, and young adults with disabilities should be served whenever possible in general education classrooms in inclusive neighborhood schools and community settings. Such settings should be strengthened and supported by an infusion of specially trained personnel and other appropriate supportive practices according to the individual needs of the child.

Policy Implication

Schools. In inclusive schools, the building administrator and staff with assistance from the special education administration should be primarily responsible for the education of children, youth, and young adults with disabilities. The administrator(s) and other school personnel must have available to them appropriate support and technical assistance to enable them to fulfill their responsibilities. Leaders in state/provincial and local governments must redefine rules and regulations as necessary,

a reasonable balance between the special needs of students who are disabled and other students in the classroom. These teachers must demonstrate a willingness to teach students who are disabled in their classrooms, be able to judge the capacity of these students to learn and adjust instructions accordingly, be able to predict and intervene when problems arise among peers, and know how to handle the insecurities of students who are disabled who cannot compete with their peers in all areas.

Special Materials and Equipment

Occasionally, general education teachers are able to teach pupils who are retarded in their classrooms with the help of some special education materials. The material may be a high-interest, low-vocabulary reading series, a programmed reader, a job-related mathematics book, or any material or hardware that allows the teacher to individualize instruction. This level of special and grant school personnel greater authority to make decisions regarding curriculum, materials, instructional practice, and staffing patterns. In return for greater autonomy, the school administrator and staff should establish high standards for each child and youth, and should be held accountable for his or her progress toward outcomes.

Communities. Inclusive schools must be located in inclusive communities; therefore, CEC invites all educators, other professionals, and family members to work together to create early intervention, educational and vocational programs and experiences that are collegial, inclusive, and responsive to the diversity of children, youth, and young adults. Policymakers at the highest levels of state/provincial and local government, as well as school administration also must support inclusion in the educational reforms they espouse. Further, the policymakers should fund programs in nutrition, early intervention, health care, parent education, and other social support programs that prepare all children, youth, and young adults to do well in school. There can be no meaningful school reform, no inclusive schools, without funding of these key prerequisites. As important, there must be interagency agreements and collaboration with local governments and business to help prepare students to assume a constructive role in an inclusive community.

Professional Development. And finally, state/provincial departments of education, local educational districts, and colleges and universities must provide high-quality preservice and continuing professional development experiences that prepare all general educators to work effectively with children, youth, and young adults representing a wide range of abilities and disabilities, experiences, cultural and linguistic backgrounds, attitudes, and expectations. Moreover, special educators should be trained with an emphasis on their roles in inclusive schools and community settings. They also must learn the importance of establishing ambitious goals for their students and of using appropriate means of monitoring the progress of children, youth, and young adults.

Source: From "CEC Policy on Inclusive Schools and Community Settings" by the Council for Exceptional Children, 1993, Annual Convention of the Council for Exceptional Children, San Antonio, Texas. Copyright 1993 by the Council for Exceptional Children.

education support requires a highly skilled general education teacher who is willing to adjust instruction to meet the needs of learners who are retarded.

Special Materials, Equipment, and Consultation

In this plan, limited consultation from a special education teacher supplements the general education teacher's special materials and equipment. Consultation may consist of demonstrating materials or equipment, assessing the child's needs, developing teaching strategies, or providing an inservice training program. This level of support also requires that the general education teacher be willing to adapt instruction to meet the needs of learners who are retarded.

The success of either of these two plans depends on a reasonable student/teacher ratio. When classrooms are overcrowded, teachers become frustrated; frustrated teachers are less likely to attempt to accommodate the special needs of students who are disabled. Mueller, Chase, and Walden (1988) recommend class sizes in the mid-twenties and note that reasonable class sizes are particularly important in the earlier grades.

Itinerant Services

An itinerant services program supplies general education teachers with consultative and instructional services for their pupils who are retarded. Itinerant teachers travel from school to school and visit each of their assigned schools periodically, usually working in individualized or small group instruction with students who have special needs that hamper their scholastic progress. This option is especially popular for students who have vision or language disorders. Since these services are limited (visits are typically weekly or biweekly), responsibility for the children's education rests with the general education teacher. Occasionally, school-based tutors, who are either volunteers or teacher aides, bolster the itinerant services. Student tutoring helps teachers to individualize instruction; it is gaining popularity as a technique for assisting general education teachers with learners who are retarded. Peer tutoring has also been successfully used to improve academic skills, foster self-esteem, help the shy youngster, help students who have difficulty with authority figures, improve race relations, and promote positive relationships and cooperation among peers (Beirne-Smith, 1991; C. D. Mercer & Mercer, 1993).

Resource Room with Special Education Teacher

The purpose of the resource room is to provide educational support to students who are disabled and their teachers. In this plan, students who are disabled remain in the general education classroom for the majority of the school day and receive supplemental instruction on a regularly scheduled basis in the resource room.

The role of the resource teacher is to instruct students and to consult or collaborate with the general education teacher, other service providers, and parents or guardians (see Figure 9.1). In a finely tuned resource program, there is consistency between what occurs in the resource room and what occurs in the general education classroom. Goals and objectives are similar, and methods of teaching and procedures for evaluating students and programs are coordinated and compatible. Such a program requires general and special education teachers who are attuned to the needs of the students and are highly skilled in both teaching technologies and collaborative consultation.

Models of resource room programs vary substantially from school district to school district. Regulatory requirements and preferences of school administrators usually dictate the form the resource program takes. According to Wiederholt and Chamberlain (1989), most students with disabilities are served in one of three types of resource programs: categorical, cross-categorical, or noncategorical.

Categorical programs serve only students who are diagnosed with a specific disability (e.g., mental retardation) and officially placed in a special education program. The purported advantage of the categorical program is that these programs are staffed with teachers certified in the disability area and thus presumably knowledgeable about the unique needs and characteristics

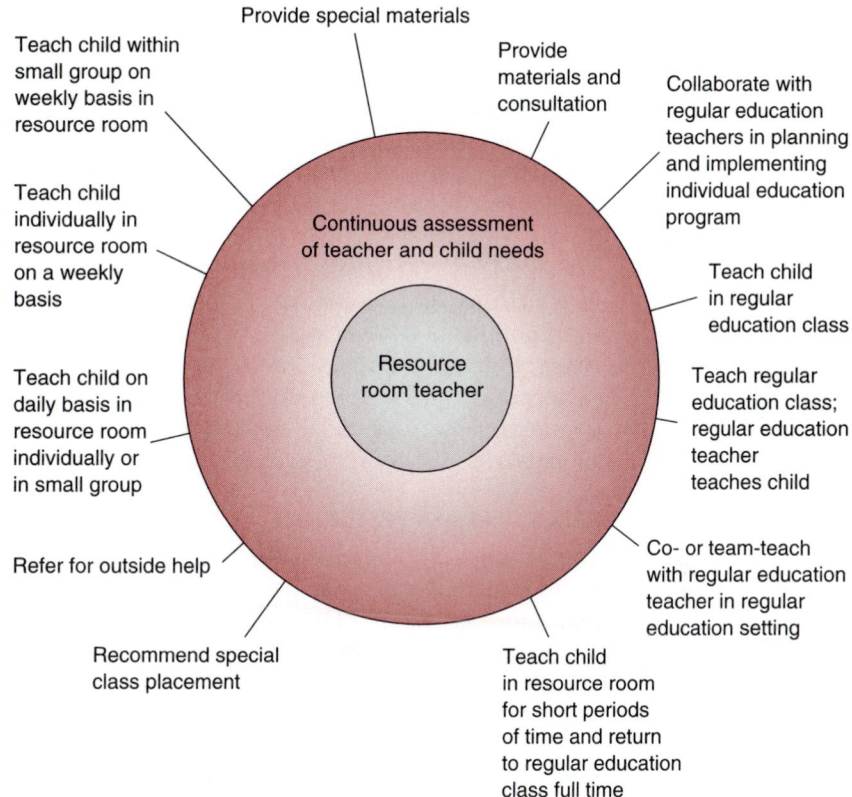

FIGURE 9.1

Service Alternatives for the Resource Room Teacher

of the particular group of students served by the program. **Cross-categorical programs** are also reserved for students who are officially placed in a special education program, but cross-categorical programs may serve students from more than one disability area (e.g., mental retardation and learning disabilities). The purported advantage of the cross-categorical program is that students can be grouped according to their instructional needs rather than by disability. **Noncategorical programs** serve both students who are disabled and students who are not disabled but are in need of supplemental instruction. Noncategorical programs have the purported advantage of eliminating the need to label and place students in special education programs.

Although the resource room is the most frequently used model for serving students with mild learning-related disabilities (U.S. Department of Education, 1996), its efficacy is presumed rather than documented. In their analysis of studies of resource rooms, Wiederholt and Chamberlain (1989) concluded that methodological problems so confounded the results that no firm conclusions about the efficacy of the models could be drawn. They state: "Given the complexities and difficulties inherent in the efficacy research, it is likely that this line of research will not provide an answer in the near future on the appropriateness of resource rooms as a viable service delivery system" (p. 22). Nonetheless, the increased emphasis on serving students with disabilities in inclusive settings and the advantage of the resource room in allowing the needs of these students to be addressed while facilitating maximum integration with peers who are not disabled suggest that the demise of the resource room in the foreseeable future is unlikely.

Diagnostic-Prescriptive Teaching Center

In the diagnostic-prescriptive teaching center plan, students are taken for short periods of time to in-school centers staffed by a team of special educators and diagnosticians. The center's staff members assess the student's performance and develop an individualized educational strategy. The student returns to the general education class, but instruction is based on the program that the center's staff recommends.

SPECIAL CLASS PROGRAMS

Special class programs provide a self-contained instructional environment for the student who is unable to profit fully from education in the general education classroom. Classes of this kind usually serve no more than ten to fifteen students and often have an aide to assist the teacher. The duties of the aide may vary from preparing materials (e.g., photocopying worksheets) to instructing small groups under teacher supervision.

Special Education Class

Self-contained special classes are designed for children who cannot keep up with the pace of instruction in a regular education classroom. Generally, the special education class consists of a group of children identified as disabled and in need of extraordinary treatment (for instance, students who are mentally retarded, emotionally disturbed, or learning disabled). Students may receive all their academic instruction in the self-contained class, or they may divide their academic day between self-contained class instruction in some subjects and general education class instruction in others. Although special class students usually participate in general physical education, art, and music classes, they are largely segregated from the larger school environment. According to U.S. Department of Education (1996) statistics, the self-contained class is the most frequently used placement for students who are retarded.

Segregation in self-contained special classes can be debilitating in its potential to stigmatize the student or discourage the development of social relationships with peers. Every effort must be made to determine the types and intensities of supports needed for the student to succeed in the larger school environment. At the same time, we must recognize that for some students the self-contained special class may be the only public school setting that is educationally appropriate.

In other words, when used to educate those students who require it, the self-contained program is a viable service delivery model. C. D. Mercer (1991) has set the following criteria for times when the special class is deemed appropriate:

1. The special class teacher should be trained to teach the types of students in the class.

2. The students should be selected on the basis of learning or social-emotional problems, not on the basis of socioeconomic status or race.

3. Each child should receive intensive and systematic instruction tailored to his unique needs.

4. A wide variety of teaching materials and resources should be available to the teacher.

5. The class size should be considerably smaller than a regular class.

6. A variety of teaching styles is needed to accommodate the different needs of the pupils.

7. Each pupil's progress should be constantly monitored. Reintegration into the mainstream should be considered when it appears feasible.

8. The class should have administrative support. (p. 185)

SPECIAL SCHOOL PROGRAMS

In the past, school districts placed the majority of their students who were mentally retarded in special schools. Under this arrangement, students were bused to a day school whose sole purpose was to serve students with disabilities. The chief advantage of special schools is that they exert complete control over the student's curriculum and daily life. In this setting it is possible to arrange all the variables in the learning environment—scheduling, physical facilities, instructional climate, and so forth—to provide the maximum benefit to the individual student.

The disadvantage of special schools is that the absence of contact with peers who are not disabled presents an unrealistic picture of the world and eliminates the benefits that students who are disabled gain through modeling and socialization with their peers. Such gains can be substantial, and as a result, few school districts today use special schools.

Special Day School

A student whose disability is so severe as to prevent functioning in a general education school may attend a special day school on either a part-time or a full-time basis. In systems combining general and special day schools, students with the most severe disabilities are bused to a central school for part of the day for essential educational services not provided in their home schools. In systems where services for students who are retarded are not available in the general education school, they may receive their entire educational program in a special day school. In sparsely populated regions, it may be economically impractical to set up special classes in each local school, and district administrators may perceive that it is necessary to use a special school instead.

Special Residential School

In cases where a student who is retarded has educational and social disabilities so pronounced as to warrant round-the-clock attention, the student might attend a special residential school. Facilities of this kind have very low pupil/staff ratios, which benefit the students by allowing intensive instruction. Such segregated schools, however, deny pupils who are retarded the opportunity to interact with peers who are not disabled, and in so doing contradict the principles of normalization and least restrictive environment of IDEA. Nonetheless, there are, and will continue to be, certain persons with disabilities so severe that they require the highly specialized treatment offered in residential facilities. Many of these individuals have physical or multiple disabilities that demand close attention. The environment of a residential school may, then, for some individuals, be the least restrictive environment in which they can function effectively. Even then, according to IDEA, educators must monitor the progress of each individual in case a move to a less restrictive environment becomes possible.

OTHER PROGRAMS

Hospital tutelage and homebound instruction are the two most common alternatives for school-age children and youth who are unable physically to be transported to school.

Hospital Instruction

Hospital instruction is usually temporary and limited to students who are recovering from an illness or accident. For students confined to a hospital or convalescent home for serious, chronic afflictions, however, hospital instruction is a continuing process. Itinerant or general education teachers often teach such students, although some children's hospitals have fully developed educational programs. Such programs usually employ a multidisciplinary approach to the treatment of the individual's illness or injury and often include certified special education teachers who work with other team members in designing and implementing the educational component of the treatment plan.

Homebound Instruction

Homebound instruction is similar to hospital instruction in that it is provided for students who are temporarily unable to attend school. Itinerant or general education teachers usually furnish the instruction. Since it is costly, segregates the child from peers, and provides limited time for instruction, homebound instruction should be a last resort.

Students who are retarded profit from being in an education environment that is as normal a setting as possible.

The characteristics of the individual, the philosophy and mission of the school, the parents, and the community influence the individual's assignment to an educational program. Child-related variables include the nature of the disability, motivation, academic skills, and behavioral characteristics. School variables include the nature of the general education class program, the availability of appropriate special education facilities, and the competence of educators. Parental and community factors include parental support, home environment, and community services.

Although these factors influence placement decisions, the strongest determinant in keeping with the prevailing trend toward inclusion should be the attempt to educate students who are disabled in as normal a setting as is feasible. The student should be integrated as much as possible within the school, the home, and the local community. In essence, programs that segregate students with disabilities from the normal environment are the least desirable placement alternative.

INCLUSION

As previously mentioned, researchers and educators have long questioned the efficacy of special class placement for students with disabilities. Recently, the entire system of delivering services to students with disabilities has come under fire. Under the auspices of the U.S. Department of Education, Office of Special Education and Rehabilitation Services (Will, 1984) advanced a proposal called the **Regular Education Initiative (REI).** In this proposal, Will recommended fundamental changes in the ways in which we educate students with disabilities, including those categorized as mentally retarded. The REI proposed a merger of special and general education services that would result in providing educational services to students with disabilities within the framework of the general education system. As a result of the REI, professionals in special education have begun to make distinctions between the traditional special education practice of mainstreaming and the newer reform-based practice of inclusion. Generally, the term **mainstreaming** refers to the practice of placing students who are disabled in the general education classroom to the extent appropriate to their needs. Some mainstreamed students may spend the entire school day in the general education classroom but most spend part of the day in a special education setting, usually a resource room. The special educator assumes primary responsibility for the education of students who are mainstreamed. The term **inclusion** refers to the practice of placing all students who are disabled, regardless of the degree or severity of their disability, in their home school in a general education classroom for the entire school day. The general educator assumes primary responsibility for the education of students who are included.

Inclusionists view mainstreaming as an irresolute attempt to integrate students who are disabled in general education settings. Most inclusionists, therefore, advocate eliminating the full continuum of services for students who are disabled. In the words of Laski (1991), "In terms of placement, the home-school focus renders the LRE irrelevant and the continuum moot" (p. 413). Further, inclusionists argue that current special education practices, particularly identification, categorization, and separation of services, have proven ineffective in meeting the needs of large numbers of students with disabilities. Specifically, proponents of inclusion state that the number of children identified as disabled is increasing at an alarming rate (M. C. Reynolds, Wang, & Walberg, 1987); that data are accumulating to indicate that methods used to classify students are questionable, arbitrary, and discriminatory (Algozzine & Ysseldyke, 1981; Lakin, 1983; Stainback & Stainback, 1992); that teaching technologies and methodologies used by special educators are becoming less "special" and more like those of general educators (Lilly, 1986); and that placement in a special education class is no more effective than placement in a general education class (Glass, 1983; Skrtic, 1991).

Opponents of inclusion argue that diluting or eliminating hard-won services for students who had been poorly served in or excluded from general education programs without analysis of what will happen is dangerous (Keogh, 1988); that parents, students, and general and special education teachers are, for the most part, satisfied with the continuum of services (Guterman, 1995; Semmel, Abernathy, Butera, & Lesat, 1991); that the potential of the general education system to serve students with disabilities is untested; and that the resources to serve these students in general education settings are not now available (Baker & Zigmond, 1995; McKinney & Hocutt, 1988). They also point out that charges that special education programs serving students with mild disabilities are inefficient and have failed to increase skills and achievement significantly in these students are based on research that is less than substantial and methodologically flawed (Hallahan, Keller, McKinney, Lloyd, & Bryan, 1988; Kauffman, 1987; Schumaker & Deshler, 1988).

Efforts are currently under way to test the limits of the movement toward inclusion. A number of research projects and experimental programs that focus on expanding the role of the regular education teacher in educating students with disabilities are being developed and implemented. Such innovations as *teacher assistance teams* (Chalfant & Pysh, 1989) and *mainstream assistance teams* (D. Fuchs, Fuchs, & Bahr, 1990) are designed to restructure referral procedures to include a prereferral component intended to limit the number of students referred to and subsequently placed in special education programs. Such approaches as *collaborative consultation* (Idol, Paolucci-Whitcomb, & Nevin, 1986), *collaborative problem solving* (Knackendofel, Robinson, Deshler, & Schumaker, 1992), *peer collaboration* (Pugach & Johnson, 1989), and *peer coaching* (Showers, 1985) are designed to deliver technical assistance to aid general education teachers in accommodating the needs of students with disabilities in their classrooms. Collaboration (discussed in the next section of this chapter) is a common element in each of these innovative approaches.

The results of the research on attempts to meet the needs of students with disabilities in general education classrooms are equivocal; the long-term impact of the movement toward inclusion on the delivery of services to students with disabilities is, as yet, unknown. While educators have not reached a consensus, much is being written about the inclusion of students with disabilities in general education programs, and trial programs are being implemented. We believe that while we should work to increase the numbers of students with disabilities served successfully in general education classrooms, a select group of these students, particularly those whose needs are pervasive and not easily correctable, will continue to be best served in special education settings.

COLLABORATIVE APPROACHES

As evidenced by the number of approaches mentioned in the previous section, collaboration is referred to by a variety of terms (e.g., peer collaboration, collaborative problem solving, collaborative consultation). Each of these approaches differs in how the collaborative process is implemented. There are, however, some commonalities among the approaches. First, all approaches view collaboration as a *process* rather than as a service delivery model. Knackendofel, Robinson, Deshler, and Schumaker (1992), for example, define **collaborative teaming** as "an ongoing process whereby educators with different areas of expertise voluntarily work together to create solutions to problems that are impeding students' success, as well as to carefully monitor and refine these solutions" (p. 1). The definition of collaboration formulated by Idol et al. (1986) states, in part, that "**Collaborative consultation** is an interactive process which enables people with diverse expertise to generate creative solutions to mutually defined problems" (p. 1). Second, collaborative approaches are built on the principles of parity and reciprocity. Parity and reciprocity refer to the *mutuality* of the process. **Parity** means that all members are accorded equal status; no single individual is viewed as the expert, and all contributions are judged solely on their merit as a feasible solution to the problem. **Reciprocity,** as defined by West, Idol, and Cannon (1989) "means allowing all parties to have equal access to information and the opportunity to participate in problem identification, discussion, decision making and all final outcomes" (p. 1).

The collaborative process involves a number of steps. Most collaborative approaches include a variation of the steps specified by Idol et al. (1986):

1. *Entry/goal setting.* Participants define their roles and responsibilities and set the purpose of the meeting.

2. *Problem identification.* Participants define the problem and discuss it until they reach a mutual understanding of the problem.

3. *Intervention recommendations.* Participants generate possible interventions; select those that appear workable; use these in the expected order of implementation; develop written, measurable objectives; specify criteria to determine if the problem is solved; delineate the roles of the participants and the student; and identify resources needed to implement the solution.

4. *Implementation of recommendations.* Recommendations are implemented according to established time lines.

5. *Evaluation.* Interventions are evaluated according to the criteria established in step 3.

6. *Follow-up/redesign.* Participants decide to continue, modify, or discontinue the interventions based on data collected.

ASSESSMENT

Comprehensive, accurate assessment is critical to the delivery of appropriate educational services to students with disabilities. As one of the mandated components in the assessment process, educational assessment has three general purposes:

1. To provide data that are usable by the interdisciplinary team in determining eligibility for special education services.
2. To determine the student's present level of performance and future instructional needs.
3. To evaluate the outcomes of educational programs.

For students who are retarded, educational assessment has two additional purposes:

4. To identify the supports needed to further the learner's independence, productivity, and community integration.
5. To evaluate the effects of the supports. (American Association on Mental Retardation. [AAMR], 1992)

The first step in conducting a comprehensive educational assessment is to evaluate referral information and the accompanying documents (e.g., school records, work samples) to determine the areas for testing. Tests and observation procedures should be multifaceted and tailored to the needs of the individual student. Further, observations should be conducted across settings and over time. Once the initial test battery has been selected and administered, the resulting data should be analyzed to determine areas in need of further testing. The process of testing and analyzing data should continue until the tester is satisfied that all necessary information has been collected.

A comprehensive educational assessment should have several outcomes. First, it should give an overall picture of the student's present level of performance. Second, it should pinpoint the specific strengths and weaknesses in the student's behavioral repertoire. Third, it should clarify the logical next steps in the student's development—often the next steps on the assessment scale. Instead of coming up with a single score or label, the assessment process should yield many individual items of information and point to many different areas where instruction would be beneficial in moving the student toward more independent functioning.

See Wallace, Larsen, and Elksin (1992) for information on assessing students with disabilities.

Norm-referenced and criterion-referenced assessments provide the assessor with different kinds of information. In norm-referenced assessment, a student's performance is compared to the performance of age- or grade-level peers. Norm-referenced measures provide a global picture of the student's level of functioning. Many standardized achievement or intelligence tests are norm-referenced. Such measures are useful in obtaining information for placement decisions. Criterion-referenced or curriculum-referenced assessments measure a student's mastery of specific, observable behavior and are more program oriented. In criterion-referenced assessment, the student's performance is measured against a preset criterion (e.g., 80 percent) or the student's previous performance on the task, skill, or concept. Curriculum-referenced assessment is one type of criterion-referenced assessment. In curriculum-referenced assessment, the student is tested on what was taught. Both criterion-referenced and curriculum-referenced assessment are useful in determining instructional objectives. Curriculum-referenced assessment, however, is more easily incorporated in daily lessons and thus provides the teacher with a clearer picture of the student's ongoing progress.

Hundreds of behavioral criterion-referenced assessment tools are available. They either include a range of skill areas or focus on one or two discrete areas (e.g., sight-word vocabulary, mathematical facts, and dressing behavior). Several disciplines (e.g., language therapy and physical therapy) have highly specialized but useful tools. Tools vary in usefulness and objectivity, and prospective users must examine them carefully. In selecting one or more assessment tools, the professional must take care to match their complexity and difficulty level with the functioning level of the student. Special care, for instance, must be taken when selecting an assessment instrument for use with individuals whose cognitive functioning falls at the lower end of the scale. Testers must take care to select instruments that give credit to individuals who are lower functioning for rudimentary behaviors and slight improvements in skill levels. For this reason, many teachers choose to develop their own assessment tools. Teacher-developed assessment tools often reflect what is being taught in the classroom and thus are useful in guiding the teacher in planning instruction and measuring student progress. Whatever the assessment tools selected, testers must ensure that the data collected are usable for the purposes of the assessment—making placement decisions, formulating goals and objectives for the IEP, planning instruction, or evaluating student learning and the instructional program. Finally, testers must be aware that "testing conducted for the purposes of making a diagnosis and developing or evaluating educational programs measures an individual student's *functioning level or ability at a given point in time, not the actual potential of that student*" (AAMR, 1992, p. 113). Assessment should be an ongoing process. Table 9.2 lists the types of school assessment procedures that are relevant to students who are retarded.

THE INTERDISCIPLINARY TEAM

The **interdisciplinary team** is charged with the task of providing comprehensive, appropriate educational programs for all students with disabilities. To meet the challenges of this task and fulfill their responsibilities of making placement decisions and formulating IEPs, team members rely heavily on assessment data. Usable assessment data, therefore, are critical to the effective functioning of the interdisciplinary team. The team itself is composed of a group of individuals who have expertise in areas related to the student's suspected disability (e.g., a school psychologist) or who have a vested interest in the student's educational program (e.g., a parent). The rationale behind the use of an interdisciplinary team is that students who are retarded (as well as students with any disability) have a wide variety of needs that can best be met through input from people with a broad range of training, experience, skills, insights, and perspectives. Team members can be, for example, teachers, psychologists, school administrators, parents, student advocates, nurses, social workers, physical, occupational, language therapists,

TABLE 9.2

Types of School Assessment Relevant to Students with Mental Retardation

Assessment function	Assessment method
1. To establish priority skill and students' activity needs for IEP in relevant skill domain	**Ecological inventory**: interview student, family, teachers, relevant community members, peers; observation in relevant home, school, work, leisure, and other community settings
Relevant to: Students of all ages *Frequency:* Roughly every 3 years unless student moves, then repeat following move	
2. To plan for school-to-work transition following graduation(ITP)[a]	**Transitional and vocational planning assessment**: interview and observation **Alternate methods**: work sampling, income and benefits, increased integrated activities, etc.
Relevant to: Students ages 14 to 16 through school completion *Frequency:* Update annually or as needed	
3. To evaluate IEP[b] objectives	**Observation in natural settings**: Probe and training data **Alternate methods**: family report, schedule changes, peer comments, self-assessment, etc.
Relevant to: All students *Frequency:* Roughly each week for performance data	
4. To evaluate behavioral problems	**Functional analyses**: interviews and program development observation **Direct observation**: mastery of replacement skills, reduction in excess behavior, increases in social interactions, etc. **Alternate methods**: interview and observation
Relevant to: Students whose behavior interferes with their health, with school and community acceptance, and/or with learning *Frequency:* Multiple times per day to less often	
5. To determine student and family satisfaction	**Satisfaction measures**: interview, questionnaire, observation **Alternate methods**: monthly pay, happiness self-report, emergency room visits and days of illness, number social activities, choices and peer contacts, etc.
Relevant to: All students *Frequency:* Annually or more often	

[a]Individualized Transitional Program   [b]Individualized Education Program

Source: From *Mental Retardation: Definition, Classification, and Systems of Supports* (9th ed., p. 118) by the American Association on Mental Retardation, 1992, Washington, DC: The American Association on Mental Retardation. Copyright 1992 by the American Association on Mental Retardation.

and even the student. Each has an important contribution to make to the team effort. The needs of the individual student determine the exact composition of the team. Typically, the size of the team increases proportionally to the degree or intensity of the student's suspected disability. The team must make a coordinated effort to decide about such critical areas as assessment procedures, instructional objectives, educational placement, instructional strategies, and evaluation. To maximize effects and avoid duplication of efforts, the team should meet regularly to plan and review programs and should carefully delineate each person's responsibilities.

THE INDIVIDUALIZED EDUCATION PROGRAM

An **Individualized Education Program (IEP)** is a written plan of action that specifies an individual's progress toward specific educational goals and objectives. The purpose of the IEP is to organize and integrate the total educational program to maximize instructional benefits for the learner. Usable assessment data are necessary to fulfill this purpose. The IEP provides a measure of accountability for teachers and schools, but it is not a legally binding contract. The intent of IDEA is that the IEP be used by teachers as a functional guide to confer with other service providers and parents about the educational program, to develop instructional plans, and to record student progress.

Historically, IEP committees have used levels of intellectual functioning to make placement decisions and design educational programs for students who are retarded. Students who are more severely retarded, for example, have been placed in more restrictive settings and provided instruction in such basic areas as self-care, communication, and socialization. The recently proposed supports-based definition of mental retardation (AAMR, 1992; see Chapter 3) extends the responsibilities of the IEP committee for students who are retarded beyond merely "matching" the student with a particular setting or set curriculum to an IEP committee that

1. Collects and analyzes a broader set of assessment information (adaptive skills and limitations; physical, medical, and psychological characteristics and needs; and environmental strengths and limitations).

2. Translates these assessment data into a profile of needed supports to compensate for, improve, or overcome the student's current performance in specific areas of weakness.

3. Develops plans (i.e., [Individual Family Service Plans] IFSPs, IEPs, [Individual Transition Plans] ITPs) to address how the educational services and other needed supports will be delivered to the individual, involving agencies beyond the school when appropriate.

4. Designs programs that include the student, to the greatest extent possible, in educational, social, and leisure activities with peers who do not have disabilities and supplies the educational supports to enable successful inclusion and prevent segregated programs.

5. Evaluates the individual's progress under these plans and makes improvements on at least an annual basis considering assessment data, diagnosis, actual services and supports delivered, location of placement, the individual's progress, and the family's and student's degree of satisfaction. (AAMR, 1992, p. 116)

As mentioned in the previous section, the IEP is developed by the interdisciplinary team or a subset of its members, who form the IEP committee. As with the interdisciplinary team, the size of the IEP committee tends to correspond to the degree or intensity of the student's disability. That is, as the severity or intensity of the disability increases, so does the size of the IEP committee. Under the law, the IEP committee must, at a minimum, include

1. A representative of the local education agency (LEA) who is knowledgeable about special education and the student's disability (e.g., a special education supervisor or teacher)
2. The student's teacher
3. The student's parents or guardians
4. When appropriate, the student
5. Other individuals at the request of the LEA or the parents who have information about the student's disability or educational needs or who can act as an advocate for the student

The law also requires that one member of the team be qualified to administer and interpret the results of the assessment instruments and procedures used to assess the student. Finally, the law specifies the components but not the form of the IEP, so formats vary widely by locality.

IEPs contain eight major components:

1. *Statement of present levels of functions.* PL 105-17 requires a statement of present levels of educational performance, including how the disability affects the progress of the student in the general education curriculum.

2. *Annual goals and short-term objectives.* Annual goals and short-term objectives are derived from assessment data. **Annual goals** are statements of what the student can reasonably be expected to achieve in the course of one calendar year. **Short-term objectives** are behaviorally stated objectives, based on the annual goals, that provide a clear direction for instruction and ongoing evaluation of student progress. (Examples of behaviorally stated objectives are provided later in this chapter.) PL 105-17 links annual goals to the general education curriculum and drops mandatory short term objectives, making short-term objectives alternatively permissible with shorter, more usable benchmarks.

3. *Special education and related services.* Each IEP must contain a statement of the type (e.g., resource) of special education services provided and who is responsible for providing those services. **Related services** refer to additional services (e.g., special transportation, speech or language therapy, or occupational or physical therapy) needed to ensure that the program meets all of

the student's educational needs, including supports needed for the child to be involved in and progress in the general education curriculum and to participate in extracurricular and other nonacademic activities. Related services may be delivered directly to the student, or they may take the form of family services (e.g., parent training).

4. *A statement describing the extent of the student's participation in the general education program.* The extent of participation varies according to the individual's unique needs and is determined by the expected benefits on a case-by-case basis. Some students may benefit from full integration in the general education program, while the needs of others may prohibit any participation in the general education program at the time in question.

5. *Time line of initiation and duration of services.* Each IEP must contain a statement of the date on which special education services will begin and their anticipated duration. Services must occur as frequently as and in the order that the interdisciplinary team schedules.

6. *Objective criteria and evaluation procedures.* PL 105-17 requires that a student's IEP contain a statement of how the parents will be regularly informed at least as often as parents of students who are not disabled are informed and how a student's progress toward annual goals will be measured.

See Chapter 10 for a discussion of transitional planning for students who are retarded.

7. *Transition services.* Each IEP must contain a statement of transition services needed by students who are sixteen or over and annually thereafter; and beginning at age fourteen, a statement of transition service needs focusing on a child's course of study.

8. *Age of majority.* Beginning at least one year before the child reaches the age of majority, each IEP must contain a statement of information regarding rights transferred on reaching the age of majority.

Developing, writing, and monitoring IEPs is quite time-consuming, and some teachers report that the burden of the paperwork outweighs the usefulness of the document (Deno & Mirkin, 1980; Morgan, 1981; Morgan & Rhode, 1983; S. W. Smith, 1990; Sugai, 1985). Recently, microcomputers have proven useful as a time-saving device for interdisciplinary team members and teachers. Microcomputers enable team members and teachers to collect and store student data efficiently, analyze these data rapidly, and produce multiple, legible copies of reports for educational planning (D. W. Smith & Wells, 1983; Nolley & Nolley, 1984). Some special educators have expressed concern that computer-generated IEPs foster a "cookbook mentality" and do not reflect a truly individualized program; M. W. Jenkins (1987), however, found that computer-generated IEPs were of higher quality than handwritten IEPs.

Goals and Objectives

Determining goals and objectives is an important aspect of developing the IEP. Team members and teachers who write IEP goals and objectives must attend carefully to the results of assessment data. Teachers can draw on a number of sources to determine appropriate educational goals and objectives, remembering that a goal is relevant only to the degree to which it is functional for each individual. Goals and objectives can be drawn from curriculum guides or from assessment tools that measure important adaptive behaviors or can be developed through careful observation of a learner's needs in everyday settings.

As mentioned previously, goals refer to the broader, long-term purposes of educational programs. Examples of functional areas addressed by long-term goals are improving self-care skills, such as clothing selection; learning a trade, say, furniture refinishing; or learning to make a weekly home budget. Examples of academic areas addressed by long-term goals are increasing mathematics skills in counting money, increasing sight vocabulary skills, or improving handwriting skills. Instructional or behavioral objectives are derived from long-term goals and refer to logically arranged sequences of specific, short-term steps toward meeting a program's goals. These objectives are important so that educational programs can be not only planned but also evaluated later on the basis of learner progress toward meeting specific criteria. **Behavioral objectives** are statements that specify an observable behavior, the conditions under which it will occur, and the acceptable standard for accuracy against which to measure performance. Listed below are examples of behavioral objectives that are appropriate for teaching academic and functional skills to students who are retarded:

- Given ten high-frequency sight vocabulary words, the student will read each word within 5 seconds of presentation with 100 percent accuracy over three consecutive days.

- Given five coins of different denominations, the student will arrange the coins in order from most valuable to least valuable and state the value of each coin at least four of five times.

- Given a help-wanted newspaper ad, the student will say the meanings of four abbreviations with 100 percent accuracy.

- Given a toothbrush, toothpaste, and a cup of water, the student will brush his teeth, moving the brush along all surfaces and using a circular brushing pattern for at least two minutes.

- When his name is called, the student will maintain eye contact with the teacher for at least two seconds within five seconds of the cue.

Often, teachers of students who are retarded concentrate instruction on discrete skill areas and fail to teach the student to generalize the use of the skill to similar tasks, to other settings, or with other people. Generalization is discussed in greater detail later in this chapter. For now, at the planning stage, it is important for teachers to remember that when they write a behavioral objective for teaching a skill in isolation they must also write a corresponding objective for teaching the skill in context. For the first objective above, the teacher might write an objective that requires the student to use the skill on another task. For example,

■ Given a five-sentence paragraph composed of known and recently introduced high-frequency sight vocabulary words, the student will read the paragraph with 100 percent accuracy over three consecutive days.

Sometimes it is possible to include generalization of the skill in a single
objective. For the last behavioral objective above, for example, the teacher
might write an objective that requires the student to use the skill with various people. For example,

■ When his name is called, the student will maintain eye contact with the teacher,
the aide, or a peer for at least two seconds within five seconds of the cue.

Methods, Materials, and Activities

Some IEP formats include space for the teacher to specify methods, materials,
and activities that will be used to meet IEP goals and objectives. Specifying
methods, materials, and activities at the planning stage assists teachers in
thinking through how they will instruct the student in the classroom.

Methods.   Instructional methods involve actively structuring the learning environment to promote learning of targeted objectives. Specifically, the
teacher is concerned with choosing instructional methods that facilitate effective, efficient learning. These variables and corresponding instructional
strategies and techniques are discussed later in this chapter.

Materials.   The teacher should choose instructional materials that help
promote active learning of targeted skills. Materials can run the gamut from
texts and other print materials, workbooks, dittos, audio- and videotapes,
records, films, models, realia, and games and toys, to teaching machines,
computers, programmed learning materials, and prosthetic equipment.
Teachers should use materials that add interest to the lesson, that are age-
appropriate, that closely match the student's ability level, and that lead directly to skill acquisition. Materials geared for general education classrooms
can often be used or adapted, particularly for students whose learning-
related needs are intermittent to limited. A number of materials checklists
are available to assist teachers in evaluating materials for use in their classrooms (see Figure 9.2 for an example of a materials evaluation checklist).
Many teachers and other specialists develop their own instructional materials, which are usually less expensive than commercially produced materials
and often motivate their students more because they can be personalized.

Activities.   Teachers also plan individual and small- and large-group activities that help in the acquisition of target behaviors. Activities can involve
performing motor behaviors, talking, gesturing, writing, role playing, classifying, counting, and so on. Activities should be varied to add interest to the
curriculum and should provide many opportunities for learners to make active responses. When appropriate, they should take place in the real-life environment (such as a store or laundromat), so that the transition from the
simulated to the real-life environment is easier.

EDUCATIONAL MATERIALS EVALUATION CHECKLIST

Title: _____   Subject/Skill Area: _____

Publisher: _____   Brief Description: _____

Address: _____

Yes/No   INSTRUCTIONAL SCOPE AND SEQUENCE

1. Are the scope and sequence of the material clearly specified?
2. Are behavioral objectives or learner outcomes specified?
3. Are student prerequisite skills specified in a hierarchical order?
4. Are skills, concepts, and facts ordered in a logical manner from simple to complex?
5. Does the instructional sequence proceed in small steps appropriate for difficult-to-reach students?

Comment: _____

CONTENT

6. Do the concepts and skills included adequately represent the content area?
7. Is the content consistent with the stated objectives?
8. Is the information presented in the material accurate?
9. Is the information presented in the material current?
10. Are various points of view concerning treatment of minorities, persons with handicapping conditions, ideologies, social values, sex roles, socioeconomic status, and so forth, objectively presented?
11. Are the content and topic of the material relevant to the needs of difficult-to-teach students as well as to other students in the general classroom?
12. Is the content appropriate to the
    a. chronological age of the targeted student(s)?
    b. mental age of the targeted student(s)?

Comment: _____

INITIAL ASSESSMENT/PLACEMENT

13. Does the material specify and provide a method for determining initial placement into the material?
14. Does the initial placement tool contain enough items to accurately assess and place the learner into the material?

Comment: _____

ONGOING ASSESSMENT/EVALUATIONS

15. Does the material specify and provide a method for determining ongoing progress in the material?
16. Are there sufficient evaluation items to accurately measure student progress?
17. Are procedures and/or materials for ongoing record-keeping provided that are useful to the student and teacher?
18. Is student progress monitoring possible by self-recording or charting?

Comment: _____

INSTRUCTION

19. Are instructional procedures for each lesson clearly specified?
20. Does the material provide for a maximum amount of direct teacher instruction on the skills/concepts presented?
21. Does the direct teacher instruction provide for active student involvement and response?
22. Are the direct instructional lessons adaptable to small-group/individual instruction?
23. Are a variety of cuing and prompting techniques used to elicit correct student responses?
24. When using verbal instruction, does the instruction proceed in a clear, logical manner?
25. Does the material provide for teacher modeling and demonstration when appropriate to the skills and concepts being taught?
26. Does the material specify correction and feedback procedures for use during instruction?

Comment: _____

PRACTICE

27. Does the material contain appropriate practice activities that contribute to mastery of the skills/concepts?
28. Are the practice activities directly related to the desired outcome skills/behaviors?

Comment: _____

REVIEW/MAINTENANCE

29. Are practice and review of content material provided?
30. Are review and maintenance activities systematically and appropriately spaced?
31. Are adequate review and maintenance activities provided for the difficult-to-teach student?

Comment: _____

FIGURE 9.2

Educational Materials Evaluation Checklist

Source: From *Effective Instruction of Difficult to Teach Students* (pp. 82–85) by L. Idol and J. F. West, 1993, Austin, TX: PRO-ED. Copyright 1993 by PRO-ED. Reprinted by permission. Adapted from *Teaching the Mildly Handicapped in the Regular Classroom* (2nd ed., pp. 125–127) by J. Q. Affleck, S. Lowenbraum, and A. Archer, 1980, Upper Saddler River, NJ: Merrill/Prentice Hall. Copyright 1980 by Merrill/Prentice Hall. Adapted by permission.

MOTIVATION/INTEREST

____ 32. Are reinforcement procedures built in or suggested for use in the material?

____ 33. Are procedures specified for providing feedback to the student on his or her progress?

____ 34. Has the material been designed to motivate and appeal to students?

Comment: _____

ADAPTABILITY TO INDIVIDUAL DIFFERENCES

____ 35. Has the material been adequately field-tested with students with learning difficulties?

____ 36. Can the pace be adapted to variations in student rate of mastery?

____ 37. Can the method of response be adapted to the individual needs of the student?

____ 38. Can the method of instruction be adapted to the individual needs of the student?

____ 39. Can the student advance to subsequent tasks after demonstrating proficiency?

____ 40. Can the student be placed in the material at the learner's own level?

____ 41. Does the material offer alternative teaching strategies for students who are failing to master an objective?

Comment: _____

GENERAL USE CHARACTERISTICS OF THE MATERIAL

____ 42. Is a teacher's manual or set of teacher guidelines for use provided?

____ 43. Are teacher instructions clear, complete, and precise?

____ 44. Are teacher skills needed for appropriate use of the material with students specified?

____ 45. Is the amount of teacher preparation time for intial and daily use of the material specified?

____ 46. Is the estimated amount of daily or weekly time required of the student for effective use of the material specified?

____ 47. Are instructional grouping strategies provided for appropriate use of the material?

____ 48. Are the types of student responses needed for effective use of the material clearly specified for both instruction and practice situations?

____ 49. Is there a simple procedure for verifying correct responses and detecting errors in response?

____ 50. Are correction procedures specified when a student makes an error?

____ 51. Are other materials/media required for effective use of this material?

Comment: _____

PHYSICAL CHARACTERISTICS AND COSTS

____ 52. Is the initial cost per student reasonable?

____ 53. Is the replacement cost per student reasonable?

____ 54. Are there extra costs involved in effective use of the material (e.g., duplication, extra materials, equipment, etc.)?

____ 55. Is the material consumable?

____ 56. Is the material durable?

____ 57. Is the material warranted?

____ 58. Is the material safe?

____ 59. Can the materials be easily stored and organized for classroom use?

____ 60. Is the format of the material clear, attractive, and in a type size and style appropriate for targeted students?

____ 61. Are the directions and illustrations for use by the student clear?

____ 62. Are the auditory components of the material clear and adequate?

Comment: _____

EVALUATION SUMMARY

APPROPRIATE USE(S) WITH TARGETED STUDENT(S)   Comment: _____

____ Initial Assessment

____ Monitoring Progress/Mastery

____ Instruction

____ Practice

____ Reteach

____ Motivation

____ Not Appropriate

FIGURE 9.2
(continued)

Evaluation

According to the IDEA, the learners' progress toward targeted objectives must be measured regularly. Highly effective teachers measure learner progress on a daily basis and use the results of the evaluation to make teaching decisions. These teachers test what is taught and use the results of the evaluation to determine what to teach next. Progress—or lack of progress—signals the teacher when to move on to more complex objectives, when to repeat instruction, or when to change instructional objectives, methods, materials, and activities to avoid failure situations and facilitate success. Progress data to guide educators in the decision-making process may be obtained in many different ways. Often, the simplest procedures (e.g., recording the number of correct and incorrect oral responses) provide the teacher with the most accurate indication of learner progress.

The educational programming process we have described helps achieve an integrated educational program based on individual students' needs. It is closely related to the process and requirements that the IDEA mandates for the IEP.

PROGRAMMING FOR SCHOOL-AGE LEARNERS

EDUCATIONAL PROGRAMMING

Educational programming for school-age learners who are retarded involves a number of interrelated and mutually influencing components. Educational programs must be designed, implemented, and evaluated systematically so that educators make decisions that have an optimal effect on the development of each learner. Such programming requires that educators consider variables related to the student, the teacher, and the environment.

The programming process we describe next can work for all educational programs regardless of the learner's age, placement, or level of support needed. Based on the assessment process described earlier in the chapter, the teacher first determines the learner's current level of performance and instructional needs and then arranges the teaching/learning environment to facilitate the acquisition and maintenance of adaptive behaviors. Instructional variables are largely under the direct control of the teacher. Other variables such as learner aptitude or characteristics may be influenced by the decisions the teacher makes but are not under the direct control of the teacher.

CHARACTERISTICS OF STUDENTS WHO ARE RETARDED

Students who are retarded often have characteristics that teachers must address in order to make learning profitable for the student. The first characteristic is the tendency to have an external locus of control; that is, individuals who are retarded may think they have little control over the environment

COMPONENTS OF EFFECTIVE INSTRUCTION

Much time is spent discussing the effectiveness of programs, materials, and people. Most programs implemented today, educational or other, include mechanisms for evaluating effectiveness. However, what does "effective" instruction mean? On a general level, responding to this query is relatively easy. An answer to the question would probably imply that some type of progress or learning takes place. Reflection obscures the meaning of this question, making it difficult to answer.

Other related but more specific questions—To what specific skills are we referring: academic, social, or what? Does time come into play here; is rate of learning important?—are critical to any analysis of effective instruction. Moreover, effective instruction implies the most facile acquisition of a wide range of knowledge or skills in a psychologically healthy, appropriately structured learning environment. Furthermore, effective teachers consider the components of effective instruction.

The figure below highlights a number of significant facets of effective instruction (from a teacher's orientation) that helps learning occur. The essential components are divided into three phases, although some overlapping exists. For a more extensive discussion of this model, see Polloway and Patton (1997).

Source: From *Strategies for Teaching Learners with Special Needs* (6th ed., p. 16) by E. A. Polloway & J. R. Patton 1997, Upper Saddle River, NJ: Prentice Hall. Copyright 1997 by Prentice Hall. Reprinted by permission.

Precursors to Teaching	Teaching Behaviors	Follow-ups to Teaching

Physical dimension
Classroom arrangements
Environments factors
 	
Psychosocial dimension
Teacher variables
Student variables
Classroom/school variables
Parent variables
Peer variables
 	
Management dimension
Classroom rules and procedures
Scheduling
Record-keeping
Grouping
Behavior management
Time management
 	
Instructional dimension
Selection of curricular orientation
Interpretation of diagnostic
   information
Program planning
Acquisition of materials
Modification of materials
	Effective instructional practices
	Appropriate for learning stage
	Individualized
	Teacher-directed
	Demonstration-guided practice-
	   independent practice paradigm
	Clear communication
	
	Active engagement of students
	
	**Appropriate utilization of specialized
	   techniques**
	Equipment
	Materials
	Methodologies
	
	Self-regulated instruction
	
	**Consistent curricular-based
	   monitoring of progress**
		Feedback to students
		Motivational
		Informational
		
		**Data management and
		decision making**
		Data entry
		Data analysis
		Future planning
		
		Grading
		
		**Communication to profes-
		sionals and parents**
		
		**Analysis of instructional
		environment**

or the consequences of their actions. The teacher can use several strategies to help students become more internally oriented. First, students must acquire skills that are adaptive and functional, so that they actually achieve a measure of control over their environment. Second, instruction should teach the students to associate their actions with their consequences, and then to anticipate probable consequences so that they can choose appropriate behaviors. An effective strategy for teaching this type of skill is role playing, which allows the student to practice repeatedly, in a nonthreatening situation, choosing and using suitable adaptive behaviors. Another strategy involves the use of a social learning contract that spells out, in writing or in pictures, the environmental factors linking various situation-specific behaviors and their possible positive, negative, and neutral results.

A second characteristic that teachers must address is the high expectancy for failure shown by many learners who are retarded. This negative orientation is readily understandable, as many people who are retarded have long histories of failing to learn new skills, often as a result of poor (or nonexistent) educational programming. Not only may these individuals anticipate failure when trying to learn new tasks; they may even refuse to attempt new tasks.

Teachers can counteract this nonproductive trait in several ways. First, they should look closely at the results of their assessments and set reasonable, achievable goals and objectives based on the student's demonstrated level of functioning in each skill area. Second, they should structure the instructional program for success by breaking down objectives into small learning steps (via task analysis) and using a rich schedule of positive reinforcements. Third, they can reward effort and improvement as well as perfect performance. Fourth, they can teach students to use overt (i.e., spoken aloud) or covert (i.e., progressive whispers, mouthings, or thoughts) self-talk to monitor or reinforce their own behavior. These and similar strategies can help make students more willing to try new tasks and may lead to positive comments—"I can do it"—that indicate that they expect to succeed, not fail.

A third characteristic of learners who are mentally retarded is outerdirectedness, or a tendency to rely on external cues or instructions for behavior. For example, a student who needs help with work may always wait for the teacher to notice the problem and give advice and instructions. Teachers can reward more innerdirected behaviors such as actively asking the teacher for help or independently identifying several possible solutions to the problem and then trying each one until the solution is reached. In every case, teachers must look beyond general characteristics to plan programs based on each individual's characteristics.

THE ROLES OF THE TEACHER AND THE LEARNER

The educator's goal in teaching is to identify adaptive behaviors for each individual and to structure the educational environment carefully so that students will learn. Meeting this goal involves making sound decisions about placement, assessment, the learner, curriculum, instruction, and evaluation so that the student who is retarded (a) acquires a wide variety of adaptive skills, (b) learns when and where to use them, (c) generalizes specific skills to other settings, and (d) maintains the skills over time. The educator must keep these four objectives for the learner in mind. In this way, the tasks of teacher and learner will be complementary.

Acquiring a Wide Variety of Adaptive Behaviors

Persons who are retarded must function successfully in school, home, job, and community settings. To do so, they need skills in many areas, including self-care, mobility, communication, social interaction, academics, health and safety, leisure, and vocational pursuits. While the teacher must target useful learning objectives in each of these areas (with the possible exception of academics for students functioning at the lower end of the scale), the degree to which each area is taught and the instructional procedures selected will vary, of course, according to the individual needs of the student.

Learning When and Where to Use the Skills

Students who are retarded must learn to observe and respond to environmental cues that signal that a particular behavior is adaptive and appropriate in that setting. Along with being able to perform a skill to a certain level of mastery, students must recognize the proper conditions for its performance. For example, when is it appropriate to approach, shake hands with, and introduce oneself to another person? At a party when a new person arrives, on the street to a complete stranger, or in a work setting while in the midst of completing a task? Or when is it appropriate to add numbers? When making a withdrawal from a checking account, when estimating the total cost of groceries to be purchased, or when asked to find the product of two numbers? Or when should one reach and grasp an object? When handed a soft toy, when given a bowl of hot cereal, or when within reach of another person's hair or eyeglasses? Discrimination tasks like these require learners who are retarded to observe each setting to determine relevant cues and then quickly and reliably decide which behavior from their repertoire is appropriate. The teacher must structure the educational program so that students learn to attend to relevant cues, make adaptive responses, and receive positive reinforcement for their efforts.

Generalizing Adaptive Behaviors to Other Appropriate Settings

Generalizing behaviors is a corollary of learning skills. The person who is retarded must be able to identify similar tasks for which a behavior is appropriate and respond correctly in those instances. For example, obtaining lunch in a variety of fast-food restaurants, repotting several types of plants and flowers, and filling out job applications for different clerical jobs all have similar but not identical elements that a person should recognize as cues for a particular set of adaptive behaviors. Also, the person must be able to generalize responses from the training situation to the real-life environment in which the behavior should occur. Whenever possible, skills trained in the school environment should also be trained in an authentic environment. Teachers should not assume that teaching a student to count change in a classroom store, for example, will result in the student's being able to count change at a fast-food restaurant or a grocery store.

Maintaining the Performance of New Behaviors over Time

Behaviors must continue in the person's repertoire past formal training into future environments and situations that occur throughout life. Here again, the structure of programs can facilitate generalization, maintenance, and adaptation of new behaviors through systematic manipulation of such program variables as training materials, instructors, practice, and reinforcement schedules.

Selecting Functional Behaviors

One key to successful educational programming is the selection of functional behaviors. A functional skill or behavior is one that is useful to students and that gives them some control over their environment in terms of obtaining positive and consistent results. A student will probably not maintain a nonfunctional behavior over time. When selecting functional skills, teachers must ask if the skill is likely to be useful in the student's present or projected future environments. Is it age-appropriate? Will the student retain the skills over time? If the answer is no, then teachers must choose more useful behaviors on which to focus the student's time and attention.

Regardless of the student's level of functioning, the educator should ask the following questions when selecting each target skill for an individual's educational program:

1. What skill clusters or activities does the person need to function in the environment in the same way as do their same age peers (e.g., in home, school, leisure, community, work)?

2. What skill clusters of activities will the person need to learn in the near future to function like peers in targeted environments (e.g., home, school, leisure, community, work)?

3. What skill clusters or activities, either present or needed by the student, are highly preferred by the student?

4. Which of these skill clusters are critical, essential, or of high priority to this student (or family) in the domestic, personal management, leisure, community, and vocational domains?

5. Which of these skill clusters, if any, are critical to the student's health and safety? (more needed activity/skills)

6. Which of these activities are highly preferred by the student? (more needed activity/skills)

7. Which activities will promote increased independence and interdependence in integrated community settings? (more needed activities/skills)

8. Which activities will contribute to the student's happiness, acceptance by others, and personal life satisfaction? (more needed activities/skills)

9. Which activities either cannot be taught or can only be taught with great difficulty (performed very infrequently, require great travel, necessitate simulation to teach)? (less easily taught activities/skills)

10. Which activities (a) are or will be *age inappropriate,* or (b) are highly time-limited (not valuable beyond the student's near future), or (c) have questionable future value? (less needed activities/skills) (AAMR, 1992, pp. 130–131)

CURRICULUM

So far in this chapter, we have discussed placement alternatives and the laws and procedures that guarantee access to educational services for all school-age learners who are disabled, including those who are retarded. Access alone, however, does not guarantee success. It is time now to turn our attention to two areas concerned with the outcomes of the educational process. Teacher decisions about what and how to teach are critical to the success of students who are retarded. In this section, we discuss the curriculum and curricular alternatives for students who are retarded. In the next section, we focus on variables that are important in designing an effective, efficient instructional program.

School-age learners who are retarded have diverse learning needs based on their level of intellectual functioning, their individual characteristics, their age, their present and projected future environments, their previous educational experiences, their family, their cultural and socioeconomic background, and the community in which they live. To accommodate the diverse learning needs of these students, educators must first address what is taught in school. A primary concern in programming for students who are retarded is the curriculum.

The curriculum has been defined in various ways. Hoover (1988) defines the **curriculum** as planned learning experiences that have intended educational outcomes. Armstrong (1990) defines it as a "master plan for selecting content and organizing learning experiences for the purpose of changing and developing learners' behavior and insights" (p. 4).

School-age learners who are retarded have a wide range of skill levels and needs. Therefore, curricula designed for students who are retarded must be individualized, functional, and comprehensive. Such curricula are built around the assessed needs of the student and work from cradle to grave, not just during the typical school age period of five to eighteen years. Comprehensive curricula cover a wide range of content areas and levels of difficulty. Polloway, Patton, Epstein, and Smith (1989) describe a comprehensive curriculum as one that is

TABLE 9.3
Decision-Making Variables

1. Student Variables
   - cognitive-intellectual level
   - academic skills preparedness
   - academic achievement
   - grade placement
   - motivation and responsibility
   - social interactions with peers and adults
   - behavioral self-control

2. Parent Variables
   - short- and long-term parental expectations
   - degree of support provided (e.g., financial, emotional, academic)
   - parental values vis-á-vis education
   - cultural influence (e.g., language, life values)

3. Regular Class Variables
   - teacher and peer acceptance of diversity (classroom climate)
   - administrative support for integration
   - availability of curricular variance
   - accommodative capacity of the classroom
   - flexibility of daily class schedules and units earned toward graduation
   - options for vocational programs

4. Special Education Variables
   - size of caseload
   - availability of paraprofessionals or tutors
   - access to curricular materials (for specific curriculum models)
   - focus of teacher's training
   - consultative and materials support available
   - related services available to students

Source: From "Comprehensive Curriculum for Students with Mild Handicaps" by E. A. Polloway, J. R. Patton, M. H. Epstein, and T. E. C. Smith, 1989, *Focus on Exceptional Children, 21*(8), p. 8. Copyright 1989 by Love Publishing. Reprinted by permission.

- Responsive to the needs of the individual student at the current time
- Reflective of the need to balance maximum interaction with nondisabled peers against critical curricular needs
- Related to service delivery alternatives (i.e., resource programs, self-contained classes, and modified models)
- Derived from a realistic appraisal of potential adult outcomes of individual students
- Consistent with transitional needs across the life span
- Sensitive to graduation goals and specific diploma track requirements

Table 9.3 describes decision-making variables involved in designing a comprehensive curriculum for learners who are disabled.

Curricular Orientations

Polloway and Patton (1993) identified four general curricular orientations: remedial (i.e., basic skills and social skills), regular class support (i.e., tutorial instruction, learning strategies, and cooperative teaching), academic content mastery, and adult learning outcomes (i.e., vocational training).

Remedial Approaches

The basic skills remedial approach is most often used in elementary special education programs. In this approach, the student's skill deficits are identified and remedial instruction in deficit areas is provided. The advantage of the basic skills approach is that it directly addresses the identified needs of the student. Disadvantages of this approach are that the clear focus on academic deficits often results in teachers' overlooking the student's areas of strength, it may fail to include training in generalization of skills learned, and it may be inappropriate for secondary students who, at this point in their schooling, need instruction in life skills.

The social skills remedial model is characterized by its concentration on developing social competence in students. The advantage of this approach is that social competence is necessary to the student's success in the regular education program and in life. The disadvantage of this approach is that few social skills curricula have demonstrated meaningful, observable change in students' behavior or generalization to other settings.

General Class Support

Approaches that provide support to students enrolled in general education classrooms have employed tutorial instruction, learning strategies, or cooperative teaching.

Tutorial approaches instruct the student in class content. The advantages of tutorial instruction are that students, parents, and teachers tend to view this approach as less stigmatizing than remedial instruction, students may be motivated by instruction that corresponds to instruction in the general education classroom, and it allows the student to be maintained in the general education classroom. The disadvantage of this approach is that it is a short-term response that usually does not address the long-term needs of the student. That is, it may assist the student in succeeding in the class for which tutoring is provided but it will not necessarily teach the student skills needed to succeed in subsequent classes.

Learning strategies approaches focus on teaching the student *how* to learn rather than *what* to learn. Such approaches emphasize the learner's role as an active participant in the learning process. The advantage of learning strategies approaches is that they emphasize generalization of skills and concepts. Disadvantages of these approaches are that many students who are retarded lack the entry-level skills necessary to succeed with learning strategies, such approaches may result in limited attention to other curricu-

FIGURE 9.3
Adult Outcome Domains
Source: From *Major Areas of Transition* by the Hawaii Transition Project, 1987, Honolulu: Hawaii Transition Project. Copyright 1987 by the Hawaii Transition Project. Reprinted by permission.

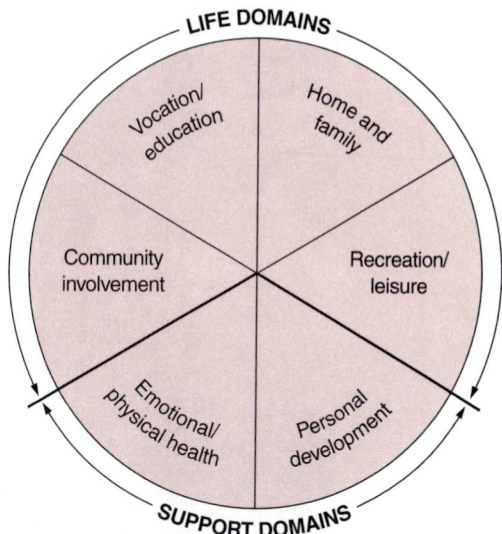

lar needs (e.g., life skills), and it may be difficult to motivate students to learn a strategy that has long-term rather than short-term benefits.

Cooperative teaching is based on collaboration between the general education and special education teachers and is designed to provide the support needed to maintain students with disabilities in the general education classroom. The advantages of cooperative teaching are that it draws on the combined expertise and knowledge base of the general education and special education teachers, and it provides a way to promote content learning and integration. The disadvantages of cooperative teaching are that it is a relatively new approach that lacks support for its efficacy, and it requires skill in collaboration that few teachers have developed.

Academic Content Mastery

Academic content mastery approaches are based on the idea that students with disabilities need instruction in the same content areas as their peers who are not disabled. The advantages of the academic content approach are that it provides support for students with disabilities in the regular education classroom and it allows for instruction in academic survival skills (e.g., study skills). Concerns related to this approach include the ability of the special education teacher to deliver academic content and the functionality of the content to the student's needs.

Adult Outcomes

Adult outcomes curricula focus on concerns related to the demands of adulthood and adult adjustment. This approach emphasizes knowledge acquisition and skill development that fall within two major domains (six

The best learning environment for students who are retarded is one in which learners reach their highest level of potential..

topical areas; see Figure 9.3). The advantages of this approach are that adolescents often have positive perceptions about curricula that emphasize adult outcomes and therefore may be motivated by such an approach. The disadvantage of this approach is that, without systematic attention to adult outcomes, the curriculum may provide limited long- or short-term benefits.

INSTRUCTIONAL PROGRAMS

The goal of instructional programming for students who are retarded is to create a learning environment in which all learners reach their highest possible level of potential in the shortest possible time. Designing an instructional program that is both effective and efficient requires teachers to act as responsible, reflective decision makers and to exploit the knowledge that has been gained about practices that constitute effective teaching.

Over the past two decades, researchers in education have investigated the relationship between teaching and learning in an effort to identify instructional factors that influence academic outcomes for students who are disabled, including those who are mentally retarded. Initially, this research focused on factors that were intrinsic to the learner. More recently, these studies have looked at environmental variables that affect learning. A series of systematic studies now provides us with a knowledge base from which we can describe effective instruction for students with disabilities.

The results of this research confirm what we have long suspected, that teaching and learning are complex processes that involve both unique contributions from and interactions among the teacher, the learner, and the environment. Some variables that affect learning (e.g., learner aptitude) are influenced by but are not under the direct control of the teacher. There are, however, other variables that the teacher can manipulate to make learning a more efficient and successful experience for learners who are retarded. Christenson, Ysseldyke, and Thurlow (1989) identified ten instructional factors that affect student achievement. Each of these factors is discussed next:

1. *The degree to which classroom management is effective and efficient.* Effective classroom teachers are proactive in their management of time, class routines, and student behavior. They anticipate and plan for potential problems in the classroom. They make students aware of goals and expectations. They establish class rules and routines, routinely monitor student behavior and progress, and are fair and consistent in their application of rewards and punishment. Effective teachers protect instructional time. They secure administrative support to minimize interruptions in their classrooms and arrange the class schedule and activities to limit time lost during transition and instruction.

2. *The degree to which there is a sense of "positiveness" in the school environment.* Student achievement is higher in classrooms in which teachers foster positive attitudes toward learning. Effective teachers demonstrate their belief that all students can learn by setting high but realistic goals for student performance, actively monitoring and rewarding student progress, and stating explicitly that they expect all students to succeed.

3. *The degree to which there is an appropriate instructional match.* Effective teachers adapt instruction to meet the particular needs of each student. They use assessment data to determine each student's current level of performance, interests, motivation, use of strategies, processing skills, and persistence for learning and match these to the student's stage of learning and task difficulty. They also assess the appropriateness of environmental conditions in the classroom to determine if the time allocated for instruction is sufficient to ensure learning.

4. *The degree to which teaching goals and teacher expectations for student performance and success are stated clearly and understood by the student.* Skilled teachers communicate goals effectively and frequently. They inform students of the quantity and quality of work needed for acceptable performance on a task. They preset criteria for mastery and provide students with task-specific feedback and correction. They provide equal opportunity for all students to respond and to participate in learning activities and they reinforce or correct responses in a manner that facilitates student improvement on the task.

5. *The degree to which lessons are presented clearly and follow specific instructional procedures*. Effective teachers demonstrate concern for the quality of instruction in their classrooms. They encourage active student participation by using a demonstration–prompt–practice sequence and actively monitor student responses. They tie old knowledge to new learning by beginning each lesson with a review of previously learned material, and they include an overview of the lesson in their introduction. They use step-by-step presentation of instructional material to make explicit *what* skill is to be learned, *why* the skill is important, *when* the skill is useful, and *how* to apply it. They check student understanding of task demands frequently. They use positive reinforcement, spaced and repeated practice, and varied activities to gain and maintain student attention and to promote generalization.

6. *The degree to which instructional support is provided for the individual student*. Effective teachers use diagnosis, prescription, monitoring, interactive teaching, and record keeping to adjust instruction to meet the particular needs of individual students. They provide varied types and degrees of practice based on the student's ability or level of functioning. They adjust the amount of time devoted to learning certain tasks, skills, or concepts. They instruct the student in *how* to learn, in addition to *what* to learn.

7. *The degree to which sufficient time is allocated to academics, and instructional time is used efficiently*. Effective teachers recognize that time is a valuable teaching resource over which they exercise considerable control. These teachers work to increase student achievement by increasing the amount of time students are actively engaged in learning or by decreasing the amount of time students need to learn. They allocate sufficient time to instruction, use effective instructional procedures, and ensure that students are successfully engaged in academically relevant tasks.

8. *The degree to which the student's opportunity to learn is high*. Effective teachers provide frequent opportunities for students to respond. They interact frequently with students. They provide prompts or cues that lead the student to a correct response. They carefully sequence instruction to maintain high rates of accuracy. They use such teaching procedures as choral response, peer tutoring, and cooperative learning to increase students' opportunities to respond. Finally, they ensure that all students have an equal opportunity to participate.

9. *The degree to which the teacher actively monitors student progress and understanding*. Effective teachers use frequent and active monitoring of student progress. In addition to asking for a response to questions, they ask the students to demonstrate and describe how they perform the task. They scan the classroom frequently to monitor students' attention to task.

10. *The degree to which student performance is evaluated appropriately and frequently*. Effective teachers use frequent evaluation and ensure that the evaluation is congruent with what is taught. These teachers use data from their evaluations to make teaching decisions about the needs of individual students and what to teach next.

SUMMARY

PLACEMENT ALTERNATIVES

■ Over time, special education has moved from exclusion to inclusion of students with disabilities in school settings.

■ The IDEA ensures that free appropriate public education will be provided to all students with disabilities and that this education will be in the least restrictive environment.

■ Placement alternatives for students who are retarded include those based in regular education classrooms, in special education classrooms, in special schools, and in other settings.

■ The REI is a movement to alter ways in which services are provided to students with disabilities.

■ Collaborative approaches to teaching are being implemented as a way of meeting the needs of students with disabilities in the regular education classroom.

ASSESSMENT

■ Comprehensive assessment is critical to the delivery of appropriate special education services.

■ The interdisciplinary team is responsible for ensuring that students with disabilities are provided appropriate educational services.

■ The IEP is designed to organize and integrate the educational program of students with disabilities.

PROGRAMMING FOR SCHOOL-AGE LEARNERS

■ Educational programs for students who are retarded involve a number of interrelated and mutually influencing factors.

■ The curriculum—what to teach—is an important consideration in planning educational programs for students who are retarded.

■ Curricular alternatives for students who are retarded include remedial learning, regular class support, academic content mastery, and adult learning outcomes.

INSTRUCTIONAL PROGRAMS

■ Instructional programs for students who are retarded are influenced by many variables under the control of the teacher.

■ Research has identified ten instructional variables that can have a positive effect on student learning.

CHAPTER 10

Transitional Years: Preparing for Adulthood

After reading this chapter, the student should be able to:

- List the goals of transitional planning.
- Compare and contrast career education and vocational education.
- Define transition services.
- List the models of transition programs.
- Identify the types of vocational options available to students with disabilities.

Key Terms

career education	supported	transition services
job coach	employment	vocational education
life skills	transition education	

H uman beings experience different types of transitions throughout life. These changes from one stage of life to another may involve education, work, and personal relationships (Ysseldyke, Algozzine, & Thurlow, 1992). In this chapter, we explore the concept of transition as related to the preparation for work and other aspects of adulthood. Some are normative and predictable; others are time or situation specific and may not apply to everyone. These transitions typically involve a number of changes. Comprehensive transition planning, which involves assessing needs, developing individual plans, and carrying out the plans, is necessary to best prepare individuals for the next environment in which they will find themselves (Patton & Dunn, 1998). Transition planning and services are needed to help students with disabilities reach their fullest potential as adults. Halpern (1994), in a position paper approved by the Division on Career Development and Transition (DCDT) of the Council for Exceptional Children, refers to transition as

> . . . a change in status from behaving primarily as a student to assuming emergent adult roles in the community. These roles include employment, participating in post-secondary education, maintaining a home, becoming appropriately involved in the commmunity, and experiencing satisfactory personal and social relationships. The process of enhancing transition involves the participation and coordination of school programs, adult agency services, and natural supports within the community. The foundations for transition should be laid during the elementary and middle school years, guided by the broad concept of career development. Transition planning should begin no later than age 14, and students should be encouraged, to the full extent of their capabilities, to assume a minimum amount of responsibility for such planning. (p. 117)

A number of critical points are evident in this definitional perspective. First, individuals must be prepared for a number of different adult roles—of which employment is only one. Second, cooperation and communication are essential for this process to work. Third, transition efforts (instruction and planning) need to begin at an early age. The instructional aspect of this point, discussed thoroughly by Clark, Carlson, Fisher, Cook, and D'Alonzo (1991), suggests that the precursors of transition planning and services should start at the elementary level. The planning piece must begin many years before the student exits the school system. Fourth, a major effort is being made to empower students to become key players in the transition planning process.

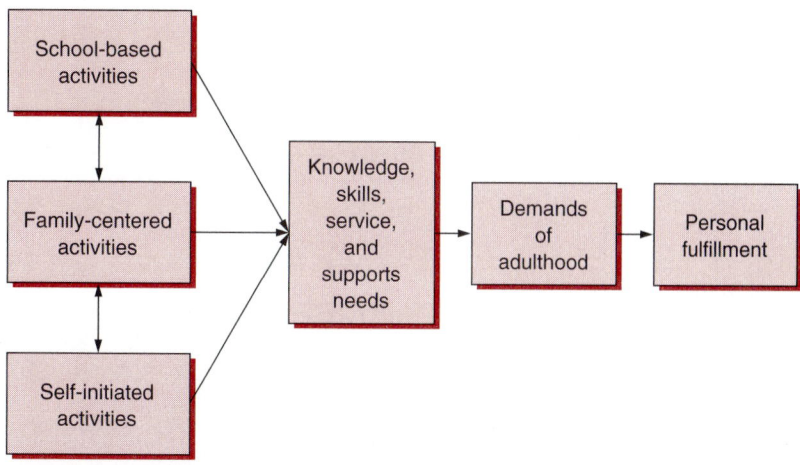

FIGURE 10.1

Adulthood Implications of the Transition Process

Source: From *Transition from School to Young Adulthood: Basic Concepts and Recommended Practices* by J. R. Patton and C. Dunn, 1998, Austin, TX: PRO-ED. Copyright 1998 by PRO-ED. Reprinted by permission.

Much emphasis is being placed on the active involvement of the student in determining transition needs and goals.

The transition planning process is, at its core, a shared responsibility of the school, the home, the student, and adult service providers. The process, if implemented appropriately, should lead to (a) the acquisition of important knowledge and skills and (b) connections with essential supports and services in the community—all of which contribute to assisting the individual to deal with the challenges and the demands of everyday life. Ultimately, if this outcome is achieved, the individual is likely to experience some sense of personal fulfillment. This process is graphically represented in Figure 10.1.

The concept of transition planning and services continues to evolve. The early transition initiatives, as promulgated by the Office of Special Education and Rehabilitative Services (OSERS) in Will's (1984) document, focused mainly on moving students from school to employment. Halpern (1985) brought professional attention to a more expanded notion of transition that included consideration of one's living environment and the adequacy of one's social and interpersonal networks. More recently, the critical areas of transition have broadened even further, as evidenced by the major transition planning domains of select states depicted in Table 10.1.

The 1990 Individual with Disabilities Act (IDEA, PL 101-476) mandated that a statement of transition services be included on a student's Individualized Education Program (IEP) beginning no later than age sixteen. IDEA defined transition services as

TABLE 10.1
Transition Planning Areas

Major domain	AL	AR	CA	CO	CT	FL	HI	IA	ID	IL	KS	KY	LA	MN	NJ	TX	UT
												State					
Adult services				X	X	X				X		X			X		
Advocacy/legal	X								X				X				
Assistive technology												X					
Career planning options									X								
Communication												X					X
Community participation	X			X	X	X	X		X	X	X	X	X	X	X		X
Daily living (including domestic areas)		X		X	X		X	X	X			X	X	X			X
Employment (including workplace readiness and specific job skills)	X	X	X	X	X	X			X	X	X	X	X		X	X	X
Financial/income/money management	X		X		X			X	X			X	X	X			
Functional academics															X		
Health (including medical services)	X			X	X			X	X			X	X	X	X		X
Independent living (including living arrangements)	X	X	X		X	X			X	X	X	X	X	X	X	X	X
Insurance									X		X						
Leisure/recreation		X	X	X	X		X	X	X			X	X	X	X	X	X
Lifelong learning								X									
Personal management	X																
Postsecondary education		X	X	X	X	X	X		X	X	X	X	X	X	X	X	X
Relationships/social skills		X	X	X				X	X			X	X	X			X
Self-determination/self-advocacy					X			X	X			X	X	X			X
Transportation/mobility	X	X		X	X			X	X			X	X	X	X		
Vocational evaluation	X																
Vocational training		X			X	X	X	X		X					X	X	X

Source: From *Transition Planning Inventory* by G. M. Clark and J. R. Patton, 1997, Austin, TX: PRO-ED, Inc., Copyright 1997 by PRO-ED, Inc. Reprinted with permission.

A coordinated set of activities for a student, designed within an outcome-oriented process, which promotes movement from school to post-school activities, including post-secondary education, vocational training, integrated employment (including supported employment), continuing and adult education, adult services, independent living, or community participation. The coordinated set of activities shall be based upon the individual student's needs, taking into account the student's preferences and interests, and shall include instruction, community experiences, the development of employment and other post-school adult living objectives, and, when appropriate, acquisition of daily living skills and functional vocational evaluation. (20 U.S.C. 1401 [a] [19])

IDEA was reauthorized in 1997 by the 105th Congress (PL 105-17). While maintaining the basic tenets of the 1990 mandates, the law now re-

These new aspects of IDEA underscore the reality that the transition process must begin early.

quires inclusion of a statement of transition needs of the student under the applicable components of the student's IEP that focus on the student's courses of study. This statement must be in place by age fourteen and updated annually. The purpose of this statement is to focus attention on the student's educational needs. This statement precedes the statement of needed transition services, which must be in place by age sixteen.

From Edouard Seguin in the 1850s, to Richard Hungerford in the 1940s, to the present concern over transition to adulthood, workers in the field of mental retardation have recognized the need to prepare each person with retardation to be a contributing member of society. In the 1850s, Edouard Seguin firmly stated that occupational preparation should have a place in educational programs. A century later, Richard Hungerford outlined a comprehensive program of **vocational education.** His program, entitled "Occupational Education," was designed to build vocational and social competence skills. The program included occupational education, vocational training, and vocational placements (Hungerford, DeProspo, & Rosenzweig, 1948). Today, practitioners are seeking to provide more realistic vocational training for students who are retarded, to integrate them into regular education vocational training programs, and to assist them in making a successful transition from school to work. Whether they are optimistic or pessimistic about career programming for individuals who are mentally retarded, professionals in this area need to move forward in the development of stronger career preparation programs that prepare such individuals to be gainfully employed and to fit naturally into their communities.

In this chapter, we focus on those transitional issues pertinent to the career and vocational education of individuals with disabilities, with a specific focus on individuals who are mentally retarded. The first section takes a look at the development of the concept of career development, various career development models, and issues in career education. The second section of this chapter discusses specifics aspects of the transition planning process. Its primary emphasis is on assessing transition needs and developing transition plans. The third section of the chapter deals with various aspects of vocational training.

CAREER DEVELOPMENT

The term career development is often used in place of the term career education.

Career education for all students became a national priority in 1971, when U.S. Commissioner of Education Sidney P. Marland called attention to the insufficient preparation of our nation's youth for careers after completion of high school. Marland (1971) made three basic points: (a) career education is needed by all students, whether they will work immediately after school ends, or whether they go to college; (b) career education should occur throughout the individual's educational career, starting in kindergarten and continuing into adulthood; and (c) career education is meant to give the individual a start

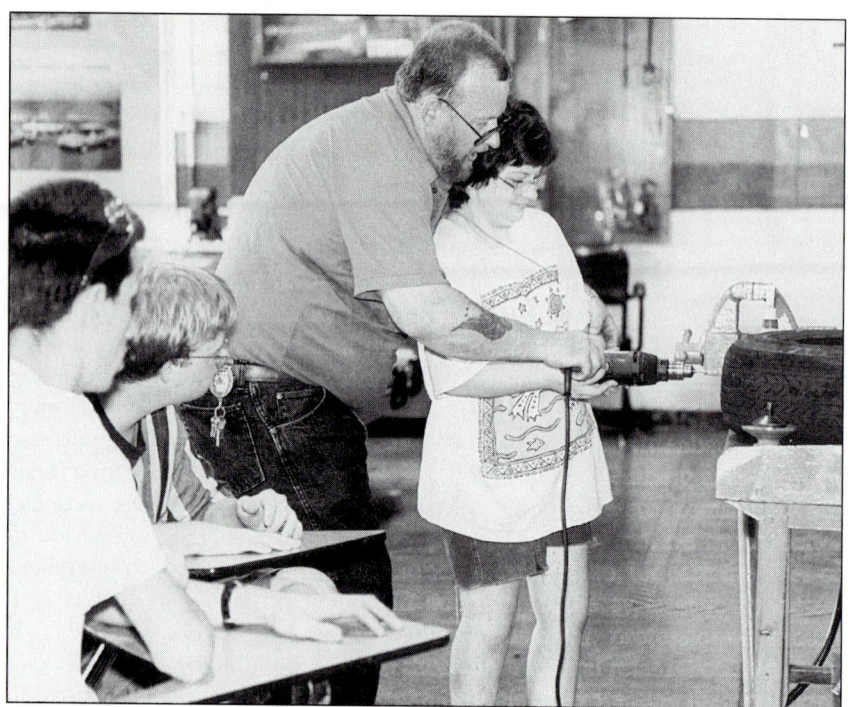

Individual Transition Plans for students who are retarded should include provisions for employment in competitive settings.

in making a living. Marland's postulates about career education seem to have the following implications for students who are mentally retarded:

1. Since a person assumes varying roles throughout life, and these roles are a function of both the social system and the person's experiences, it is imperative that the educational opportunities of students who are retarded prepare them for the different roles in which they will find themselves.

2. It is essential to view the person as a whole. Only by considering the varied aspects of a person's present circumstances and probable future circumstances can effective education be implemented. Thus, career education for students who are mentally retarded requires a knowledge of each individual's interests, preferences, and needs.

3. Great knowledge and experience are necessary to reach specific career education goals. These goals are often complex and can be realized only through the cumulative effect of an educational program that proceeds from kindergarten through grade 12 and beyond.

4. Placement in real work situations is a vital part of education for each student. This situation is no less necessary for students who are mentally retarded.

5. All persons, including individuals who are mentally retarded, have a right to an education suited to their needs and capabilities.

DEFINING CAREER DEVELOPMENT

Career development and vocational education are not synonymous; career development has a broader meaning. According to the Division on Career Development and Transition of the Council for Exceptional Children, career development involves the preparation of the individual for the roles of student, worker, family member, and citizen. Another way to conceptualize career development in relation to ongoing transition efforts is to consider it **transition education** (Patton, Cronin, & Jairrels, 1997). A multifaceted approach, which includes teaching, counseling, and community intervention, is used to facilitate career development. Career development and vocational education both accept the idea that schools are supposed to prepare students for participation in the larger society, but they differ in their interpretation of this idea. Vocational educators attempt to prepare students to enter the job market as competent, employable wage earners. To this end, vocational education focuses on the high school student who will soon be seeking full-time employment. Vocational educators perform such functions as assessing students' work potential, helping the workers-to-be explore different work possibilities in their community, and arranging a number of trial work experiences through which to identify their preferences. Career educators, on the other hand, see preparing students for participation in adult life as their mission and emphasize that career development extends from the elementary grades through secondary school level. Vocational education is actually a subcategory of career education or transition education. We can see that other aspects of the school curriculum—reading, writing, science, mathematics, family life education, consumer education, and sex education—could also be subsumed under these broad headings because they are components of an educational program whose purpose is to prepare students for future life.

The concept of transition education has been promoted by Clark and Kolstoe (1995).

Transition education is even more than the sum of these elements, because it is the unifying vehicle for ensuring that an individual has more than an even chance to become a contributing member of society. For example, in the past, although most elementary pupils at some point would discuss different kinds of jobs and the workers who did them, these discussions were usually a matter of happenstance instead of a part of the educational plan. However, these discussions—at whatever school level—can become a required part of the curriculum. Thus, students can be continually exposed to different careers as they move up to higher grades. Career education also helps youngsters see how such basic subjects as reading and mathematics will enable them to succeed at certain jobs or functions in their communities.

MODELS OF CAREER DEVELOPMENT

Clark and Kolstoe (1995) have devised a School-Based Career Development and Transition Education Model for Adolescents with Disabilities, based on an earlier work of Clark (1979). The four elements of (a) values, attitudes, and habits; (b) human relationships; (c) occupational information; and

AAMR Policy Position
on Self-Determination

The issue of "self-determination" is attracting much professional attention. Including persons with mental retardation in making important decisions about their lives is essential from a personal dignity perspective. The following policy position of the American Association on Mental Retardation underscores the importance of this topic.

Call for Action

The international, national, state and local development and support of groups that provide opportunities for individuals with disabilities to advocate for themselves.

Background

In the mid-1970s, people with developmental disabilities began to advocate for recognition and acceptance of their ability to speak for themselves when making decisions affecting their lives. The self-advocacy movement is now an international movement.

The definition of self-advocacy is speaking for oneself, making decisions about one's life, participating on decision-making bodies, learning and exercising the full rights and responsibilities of citizenship, and participating in and contributing to the community.

Self-advocates continue to struggle with the low expectations of professionals, parents, and the public.

Principles

People with disabilities must be present and involved when decisions are being made about their lives.

Instrumental assistance may be needed before and during meetings.

Training and support in how the system works are needed for people who are not members of a self-advocacy organization.

Independent thinking must be encouraged.

Professionals must raise their expectations of people with disabilities.

Actions Proposed

- Publish information on effective efforts to support individual choice and decision making.
- Encourage individuals with disabilities to participate in presentations at conferences, including the soliciting presentations from self-advocates.
- Plan to include and support the participation of people with disabilities in decision-making bodies of the Association.
- Explore establishing an affordable membership fee for people with disabilities and reach out to self-advocacy organizations to facilitate membership recruitment.
- Encourage research concerning self-advocacy and self-determination.
- Explore the possibility of people with disabilities developing an oral history.
- Support developing self-advocacy groups that provide opportunities for individuals with disabilities to speak for themselves.
- Support forming a national network of self-advocacy organizations.

(d) acquisition of job and daily living skills are the basis for instruction and learning experiences throughout the school years. Clark and Kolstoe maintain that school personnel and parents should teach career-related values and that values, attitudes, and habits are interdependent. Clark and Kolstoe emphasize the importance of attitudes in job retention. Students must

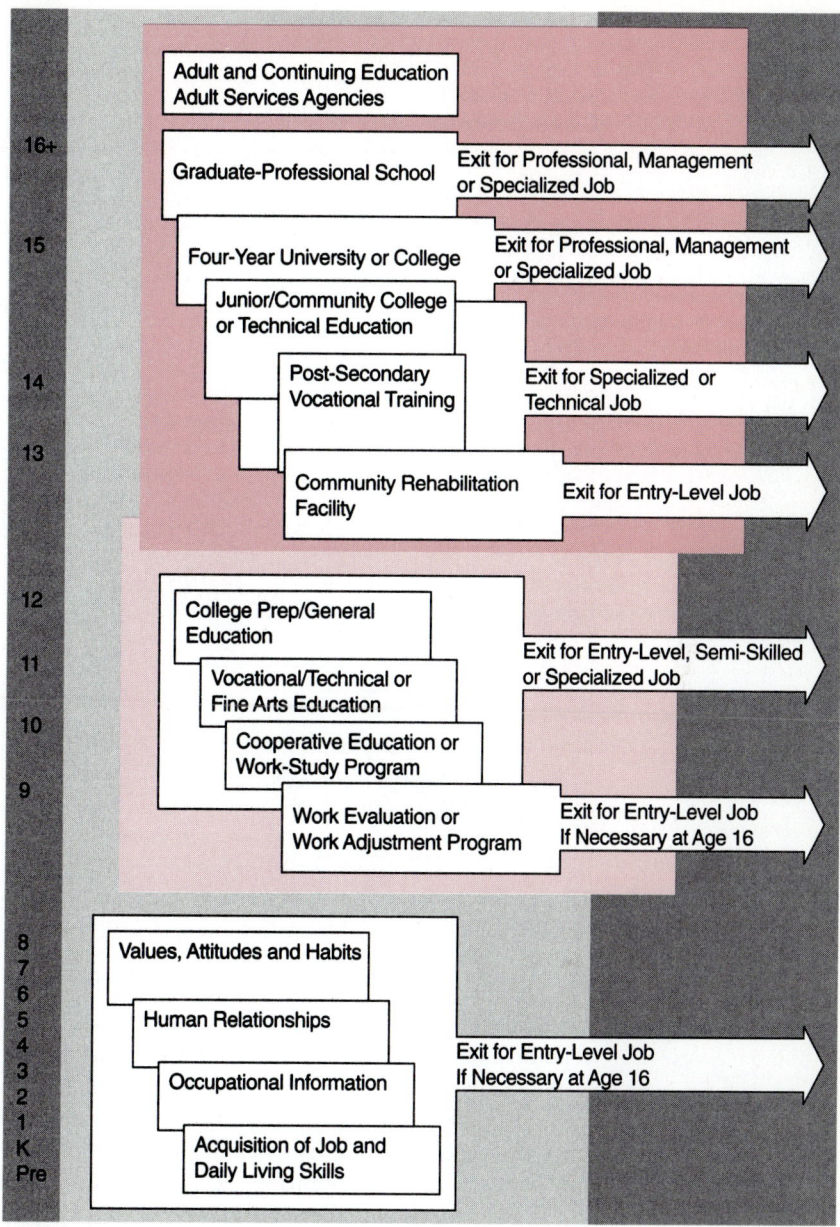

FIGURE 10.2

A School-Based Career Development and Transition Education Model for Adolescents with Disabilities

Source: From Gary M. Clark and Oliver P. Kolstoe, CAREER DEVELOPMENT AND TRANSITION EDUCATION FOR ADOLESCENTS WITH DISABILITIES. Copyright © 1990 by Allyn & Bacon, p. 45. Reprinted with permission.

TABLE 10.2
Career Education and Life Skills Education Models

Source	Major components
Life-Centered Career Education (LCCE) (Brolin, 1991)	Three major areas: • Daily living • Personal-social • Occupational guidance and preparation
School-Based Career Development and Transition Education Model (Clark & Kolstoe, 1990)	Four major areas: • Values, attitudes, and habits • Human relationships • Occupational information • Acquisition of job and daily living skills
Hawaii Transition Project (1987)	Four major areas: • Vocation/education • Home and family • Recreation/leisure • Community/citizenship
Community-Referenced Curriculum (Smith & Schloss, 1988)	Five major areas: • Work • Leisure and play • Consumer • Education and rehabilitation • Transportation
Community Living Skills Taxonomy (Dever, 1988)	Five major areas: • Personal maintenance and development • Homemaking and community life • Vocational • Leisure • Travel

develop their interpersonal skills so that they can maintain positive human relationships as teenagers and as adults. Transition programming must include occupational information about the practical aspects of employment, and occupational roles, vocabulary, and occupational alternatives. Students must also acquire competencies in job and daily living skills for a successful transition from school to work. Figure 10.2 illustrates this model.

A number of other models that address successful adult functioning are highlighted in Table 10.2. All of these models stress that career development (i.e., transition education) must include instruction that prepares students for a range of adult roles and situations for which a host of competencies are needed.

CAREER DEVELOPMENT FOR PERSONS WHO ARE MENTALLY RETARDED

Since the goals of career development are appropriate for all students, career goals for people who are mentally retarded should be similar to goals

TABLE 10.2
(continued)

Source	Major components
Life Problems of Adulthood (Knowles, 1990)	Six major areas: • Vocation and career • Home and family living • Enjoyment of leisure • Community living • Health • Personal development
Domains of Adulthood (Cronin & Patton, 1993)	Six major areas: • Employment/education • Home and family • Leisure pursuits • Community involvement • Physical/emotional health • Personal responsibility and relationships
Post-School Outcomes Model (National Center on Educational Outcomes, 1993)	Seven major areas • Presence and participation • Physical health • Responsibility and independence • Contribution and citizenship • Academic and functional literacy • Personal and social adjustment • Satisfaction
Quality of Life Domains (Halpern, 1993)	Three major areas: • Physical and material well-being • Performance of adult roles • Personal fulfillment

Source: From "Transition to Living: The Neglected Components of Transition Programming for Individuals with Learning Disabilities" by P. L. Sitlington, 1996, *Journal of Learning Disabilities, 29,* p. 35. Reprinted by permission.

for those who are not. However, the nature of these goals may vary as a function of each individual's general and specific characteristics. Individuals whose need for support is minor or nonexistent should be capable of independent living as adults. Those individuals who have greater needs for support in school and into adulthood may have more select options and may be dependent upon support from others to achieve appropriate levels of success. However, the major goals remain operative.

Research on the community and postschool adjustment of individuals who are mentally retarded strongly supports the need for career development for these students. The data for postschool adjustment come from studies employing different sampling techniques, different definitions of adjustment, and different statistical techniques. Consequently, inconsistencies of interpretation are common among these studies. Results show that persons with mental retardation have varying degrees of success in adjusting to life following school.

Career goals are appropriate for all students.

Generally, though, most studies indicate that adults, even those recently released from institutions, can adapt to community life if given proper training supports and services. Following is a synopsis of information derived from reviews and studies of workers with retardation conducted by Goldberg, McLean, LaVigne, Fratolillo, and Sullivan (1990); E. Gordon (1990a, 1990b); Heal, Copher, DeStefano, and Rusch (1988); Lagomarcino and Rusch (1990); and Stark and Goldsbury (1988).

1. Attitude plays a more significant role in job success than does IQ.
2. Employment rates are tied to the economy. In good economic times, adults who are mentally retarded are able to obtain and keep more jobs.
3. Employees who are mentally retarded sometimes cannot afford better than substandard housing.
4. Individuals with mental retardation are often underemployed.
5. Individuals who have participated in supported employment tend to fare better in competitive employment than those who have not.

Some of these findings clearly indicate that adults who are mentally retarded are capable of being successful workers and making successful community adjustments. They also suggest that being a successful worker and adapting in the community are consequences of learned behaviors. We can analyze these learned behaviors in terms of the skills and knowledge needed for successful functioning and teach them as part of a comprehensive career education program.

Individuals who are more severely retarded can likewise make successful adjustments to society and become contributing members of their communities. Recently, for example, workers with moderate and severe retardation have been successfully placed in competitive employment, performing such jobs as kitchen utility worker, porter, elevator operator, dishwasher, groundskeeper, janitor, and assembly-line worker.

The key to the success of competitive employment for individuals who need significant levels of support appears to be appropriate training and ongoing job assistance. Rusch (1983) recommends that training include a survey-train-place-train model. Using this model, the job counselor would "(a) survey potential employers to determine important skills that need to be trained, (b) train students to perform these skills, (c) place trained clients in nonsheltered settings, and (d) provide long-term follow-up training" (p. 503). Although programs differ in the type of ongoing work support provided, Bellamy and Horner (1987) note that successful programs usually have four common elements: They (a) use systematic approaches to training and maintaining work behaviors; (b) focus on work opportunity over work preparation; (c) emphasize social integration with co-workers, customers, and others in the workplace; and (d) define program success in terms of wages and work benefits. These authors also note that ongoing support in the form of retraining, contingency management (management based on behavior), and crisis intervention may be needed for workers who are severely disabled for as long as they are employed.

ISSUES IN CAREER DEVELOPMENT

We have now looked at our conceptions of the nature of career development, its current status, and its value for people who are mentally retarded. While many other educators share these views, agreement is far from universal and debate continues. The following issues, originally raised by D. E. Brolin and D'Alonzo (1979), remain of interest today.

Obviously, we do not have the last word on any of these issues, but we do have some reasoned opinions:

- *Should career development/transition education be primarily job-centered or life-centered?* Career education, in our opinion, should be life-centered, with employment as a key area of focus. Past and present evidence indicates that too heavy a reliance on a job-centered perspective to the exclusion of such aspects as attitude training has caused many of the problems (such as underemployment and unemployment) that adults who are mentally retarded or otherwise disabled presently face.

- *Should career development be infused into all levels of the curriculum, or should it be a separate program?* One of the problems with current school curricula is that they contain few mechanisms to prepare each student for life. Most students in our schools learn to read, write, and compute. Some learn marketable vocational skills. We believe that career education can provide the comprehensive framework to bring all these educational elements together so that the individual can more easily move through different life experiences. To do so means infusing career education and transition concepts throughout the curriculum; if students see the functional uses of the skills they learn, then they will get a more integrated, realistic view of their skills.

■ *Who should be responsible for ensuring that students who are disabled are included in transition education?* The IDEA stipulates inclusion of a transition needs statement and a transition services statement on a student's IEP. Consequently, special education teachers, general education teachers, and parents must play critical roles in providing students with educational programs that they need. As special education teachers may be moving away from providing direct services to all students with disabilities, career education opens an avenue to them for making certain that those students receive an appropriate education.

■ *Can the goals of inclusion and career development be accomplished at the same time?* Inclusion and career education can enhance the chances of success for all students with disabilities by providing them with more lifelike experiences and by relating instruction to real-life existence (Cronin & Patton, 1993).

■ *How will teacher preparation programs give new teachers career/transition education skills?* Ensuring that career/transition education concepts are systematically included in teacher preparation programs can be difficult and is compounded by the fact that many teacher preparation programs are still struggling with the task of teaching general educators to deal with students who are disabled. Teacher educators must inform preservice teachers of the requirements of IDEA, provide them with instruction about the various career development models, and incorporate career education strategies into all methods courses.

TRANSITION PLANNING

EVOLUTION OF TRANSITION PROGRAMS

In the mid-1980s, many transition-related projects were funded by the federal government.

Prior to the enactment of IDEA, local educational agency personnel had begun to recognize the need to prepare students who are retarded more comprehensively for life after high school. The literature had documented this need (Rusch & Phelps, 1987), and according to Will (1984), planning for the postschool adjustment of students with disabilities had already been targeted nationally as a top priority. It should be noted that in 1991 six national goals for education were published. One of these goals is focused on such postschool outcomes as adult literacy and the ability of an individual to function successfully and to assume the responsibilities of citizenship. The goals of transitional planning are to help individuals with disabilities to develop the skills necessary to live productive lives within the community.

The process of planning for the transition from school to adult life has three major phases: (a) secondary level curricula, IEP management, and career development; (b) transitional management; and (c) availability and appropriateness of postsecondary supports and services.

The prospect of adjustment by adolescents who are retarded to the world of work and community living depends greatly on how well various transition activities occur. The cooperative efforts of local education personnel, vocational rehabilitation counselors, postsecondary education staff, other adult service providers, and various community agencies that assist such young adults are vital to this transition process.

LIFE SKILLS PREPARATION

To prepare students for the challenges that will face them when they leave school, efforts must be focused on teaching them **life skills** that will facilitate their inclusion as contributing members of their communities and their successful adjustment to adulthood. The major functional domains of adulthood in which all of us must demonstrate some level of competence are represented in Figure 10.3.

Two important elements are crucial to providing life skills content to students: (a) identification of appropriate life skills that are locally referenced and culturally appropriate and (b) provisions for covering appropriate skills within existing curricular options.

Cronin and Patton (1993) suggest the use of a "top-down" strategy for identifying appropriate life skills, as indicated in Figure 10.4. This system requires that the process of curriculum development begin by examining

FIGURE 10.3

Functional Domains of Adulthood

Source: From *Life Skills Instruction for Students with Special Needs: A Practical Guide for Integrating Real Life Content into the Curriculum* (p. 13) by M. E. Cronin and J. R. Patton, 1993, Austin, TX: PRO-ED. Copyright 1993 by PRO-ED. Reprinted by permission.

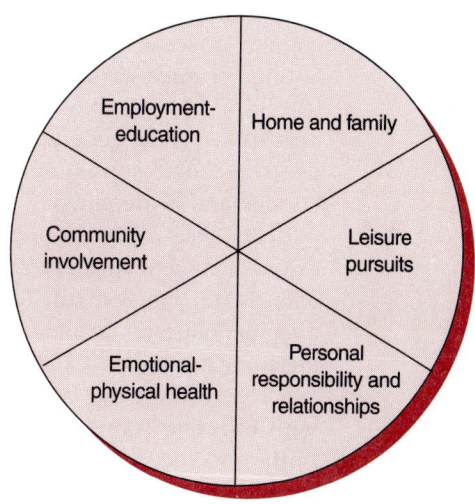

FIGURE 10.4

Top-Down Approach to Curriculum Development

Source: From *Life Skills Instruction for Students with Special Needs: A Practical Guide for Integrating Real Life Content into the Curriculum* (p. 10) by M. E. Cronin and J. R. Patton, 1993, Austin, TX: PRO-ED. Copyright 1993 by PRO-ED. Reprinted by permission.

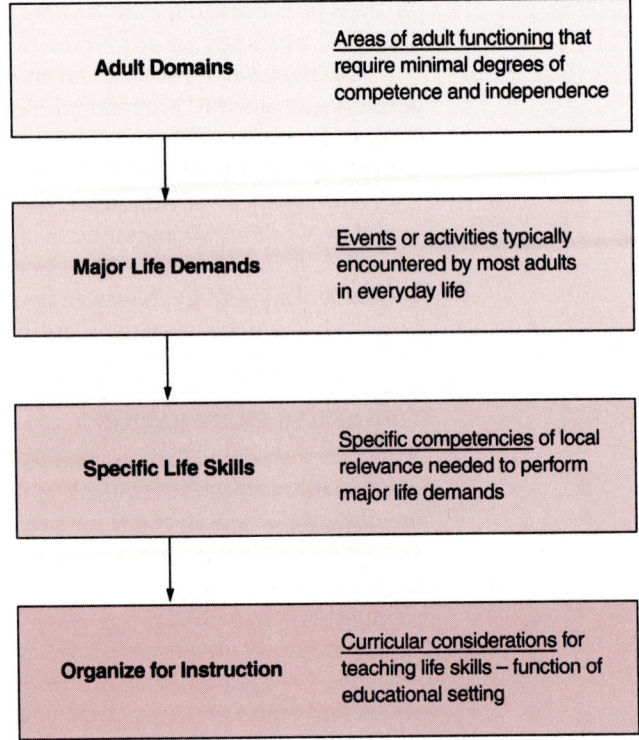

likely adult outcomes and then working down to specific life skills that are needed to deal successfully with these adult demands. Ultimately, these life skills must be covered through instruction.

Major life demands represent those events that most adults will encounter at some time in their lives, depending on location and lifestyle. Listings of such demands have been developed by various professionals (Brolin, 1993; Cronin & Patton, 1993). The critical step from an educational perspective is the generation of all relevant life skills that are specific to students' probable subsequent living and working environments once a major life demand is identified.

Life skills instruction can occur in any educational placement. The extent of content coverage can vary from the development of a set of life skills courses to infusion of life skills topics into the content covered in a regular education course. Examples of how to integrate life skills into existing curricular content can be found elsewhere (Patton, Cronin, & Wood, 1998).

The relationship between the skills/competencies that are associated with effective schooling and the adult domains presented earlier is important to recognize. As can be seen in Table 10.3, these scholastic and social skills can relate closely to the demands of community living. For example, under the domain of emotional and physical health, reading

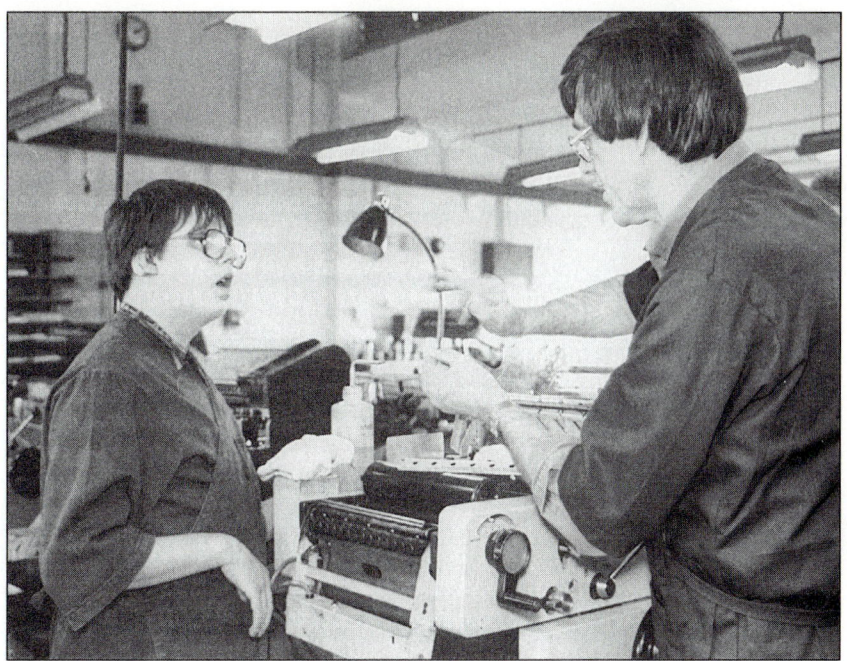

Giving students exposure to experiences with jobs that are available in their communities is a key element in good programs.

skills are needed to comprehend directions for taking medications. All the scholastic/social skill areas (reading, writing, listening, speaking, math applications, problem solving, survival skills, and personal-social skills) have practical applications and are fundamentally a part of life skills preparation.

INDIVIDUALIZED TRANSITION PLANNING

As mentioned earlier, the IDEA requires that every IEP contain a statement of transition needs (by age 14) and a statement of transition services (by age 16). As expected, there is great variability across states in terms of the quality and comprehensiveness of assessing needs and generating transition goals.

The transition planning process involves a progression of activities beginning with an assessment of the student's transition needs, including the development of transition goals (instructional and linkage), and ending with action being taken on these goals. A graphic representation of this process is shown in Figure 10.5.

Assessing Transition Needs

A variety of techniques yield information that can be useful for transition planning. Certain instruments, however, have been developed specifically for assessing transition-related areas. Some of these include the *Enderle-Severson Transition Rating Scales* (Enderle-Severson, 1991), *LCC Knowledge Battery* (Brolin, 1992), *Life Skills Inventory* (Brigance, 1995), and *Transition*

TABLE 10.3
Secondary Matrix: Relationship of Scholastic/Social Skills to Adult Domains

	Employment education	Home and family	Leisure pursuits	Community involvement	Emotional–physical health	Personal responsibility relationships
Reading	Reading classified ads for jobs	Interpreting bills	Locating and understanding movie information in a newspaper	Following directions on tax forms	Comprehending directions on medication	Reading letters from friends
Writing	Writing a letter of application for a job	Writing checks	Writing for information on a city to visit	Filling in a voter registration form	Filling in your medical history on forms	Sending thank you notes
Listening	Understanding oral directions of a procedure change	Comprehending directions	Listening to a weather forecast to plan an outdoor activity	Understanding campaign ads	Attending lectures on stress	Taking turns in a conversation
Speaking	Asking your boss for a raise	Discussing morning routines with family	Inquiring about tickets for a concert	Stating your opinion at the school board meeting	Describing symptoms to a doctor	Giving feedback to a friend
Math applications	Understanding difference between net and gross pay	Computing the cost of doing laundry in a laundromat versus home	Calculating the cost of a dinner out versus eating at home	Obtaining information for a building permit	Using a thermometer	Planning the costs of a date
Problem-solving	Settling a dispute with a co-worker	Deciding how much to budget for rent	Role-playing appropriate behaviors for various places	Knowing what to do if you are the victim of fraud	Selecting a doctor	Deciding how to ask someone for a date
Survival skills	Using a prepared career-planning packet	Listing emergency phone numbers	Using a shopping-center directory	Marking a calendar for important dates (e.g., recycling, garbage collection)	Using a system to remember to take vitamins	Developing a system to remember birthdays
Personal-social	Applying appropriate interview skills	Helping a child with homework	Knowing the rules of a neighborhood pool	Locating self-improvement classes	Getting a yearly physical exam	Discussing how to negotiate a price at the flea market

Source: From *Life Skills Instruction for Students with Special Needs: A Practical Guide for Integrating Real Life Topics into the Curriculum* (p. 33) by M. E. Cronin and J. R. Patton, 1993, Austin, TX: PRO-ED. Copyright 1993 by PRO-ED. Reprinted by permission.

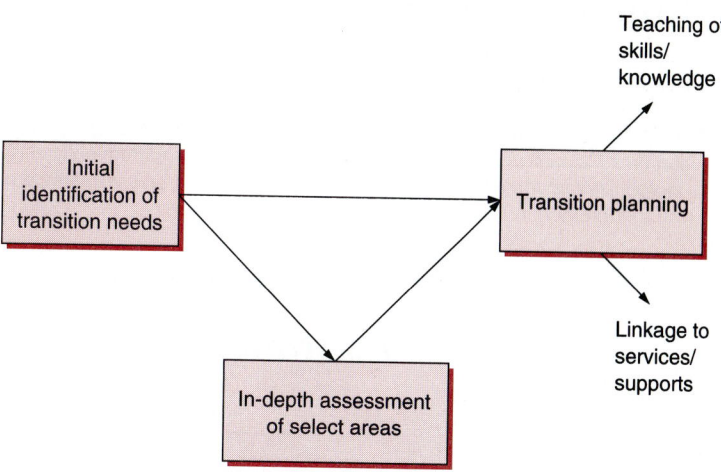

FIGURE 10.5

Transition Planning Process

Source: From *Transition Planning Inventory* (p. 26) by G. M. Clark and J. R. Patton, 1997, Austin, TX: PRO-ED. Copyright 1997 by PRO-ED. Reprinted by permission.

Planning Inventory (Clark & Patton, 1997). For a more in-depth discussion of transition assessment, see Clark (1998) and Sitlington, Neubert, Begun, Lombard, and Leconte (1996).

Given that the transition process should be predicated on the student's preferences, interests, and needs, it is worthwhile soliciting information about the various transition domains from the student. For this reason, many of the transition instruments noted here request information from the student as well as from school-based personnel and the family.

Comprehensive assessment of transition needs should lead to appropriate planning.

Transition Planning

Assessment should lead to planning. Some states require a separate document called an Individual Transition Plan (ITP); other states incorporate all transition goals within the IEP. The ideal ITP includes the following components: goal statements, present levels of performance, activities that need to be undertaken, time lines for accomplishing the goals, and the individuals who are responsible for carrying out the goal. An example of an ITP, which contains this information, can be found in Figure 10.6.

The IEP must include a transition needs statement for the student no later than age fourteen. This is extremely important so that there is sufficient time to prepare students to move successfully from school to community living. It is equally important to consider all adult domains and not just the employment/education area.

Student Profile

Garland is a 21-year-old student with mental retardation. He is verbal and ambulatory. Garland can read approximately 30 sight words and complete simple written math problems with a calculator. He knows coin values but cannot count change. Garland can print his name and copy other words. He is strong and frequently engages in unorganized sports with classmates and family. Garland lives with his parents and younger brother and sister in a low-middle income suburb.

Individual Transition Plan

Student's Name ___Garland_____
                First   M.I.   Last

Birthdate _____ School ___Turner High_____

Student's ID No. _____ ITP Conference Date _____

Participants

Name	Position
Garland	student
Sam and Susan	parents
Mary	teacher
Miller	case manager
Laurence	vocational rehabilitation (VR) counselor

FIGURE 10.6
Individual Transition Plan

Source: From *Individual Transition Plans: The Teacher's Curriculum Guide for Helping Youth with Special Needs* (pp. 65–70) by P. Wehman, 1995, Austin, TX: PRO-ED. Copyright 1995 by PRO-ED. Reprinted by permission.

I. Career and Economic Self-Sufficiency

1. Employment Goal	Garland will work full time in the deli department of a local grocery store with supported employment.
Level of present performance	Garland has been employed by school enclaves at two sites and has taken a vocational food preparation course at school.
Steps needed to accomplish goal	(1) Assist Garland with applying for jobs at local groceries; (2) arrange for transportation by carpool; and (3) provide job training assistance and support as needed.
Date of completion	6/98
Person(s) responsible for implementation	VR counselor
2. Vocational Education/Training Goal	Garland will work part time with supported employment prior to graduation
Level of present performance	Garland has received vocational situational assessment at two grocery stores and has been assigned a Department of Rehabilitative Services (DRS) counselor.
Steps needed to accomplish goal	(1) Meet with DRS counselor and assist in job application as needed; (2) arrange Garland's school schedule to accommodate work schedule; (3) provide staff for job-site training; (4) provide transportation; and (5) share information and responsibilities with DRS counselor.

FIGURE 10.6
(continued)

Date of completion	12/97
Person(s) responsible for implementation	teacher
3. Postsecondary Education Goal	Garland will attend classes of interest offered by Parks and Recreation.
Level of present performance	Garland can follow modeled instructions and is interested in working on cars, with wood, and other manual activities.
Steps needed to accomplish goal	(1) Seasonally obtain brochures of classes; (2) budget for classes; (3) complete applications; and (4) arrange for transportation.
Date of completion	3/98
Person(s) responsible for implementation	case manager
4. Financial/Income Needs Goal	Garland will be independent of his parents for basic financial needs.
Level of present performance	Garland receives a paycheck and SSI. He has a savings account. His parents provide basic needs and make deposits for him.
Steps needed to accomplish goal	(1) Assist Garland in planning budget for basic needs; (2) initiate payment of rent to parents until alternative residence is secured; and (3) assist Garland in budgeting for and purchasing food and clothing.
Date of completion	5/98
Person(s) responsible for implementation	parents

FIGURE 10.6
(continued)

II. Community Integration and Participation

5. *Independent Living Goal*	Garland will live in a supervised apartment with one to two roommates close to his parents.
Level of present performance	Garland is close to his family but wants to be independent. Garland is independent in personal hygiene and basic household chores.
Steps needed to accomplish goal	(1) Apply for residential services; and (2) provide instruction in responding to emergencies.
Date of completion	8/98
Person(s) responsible for implementation	case manager, Garland, and parents
6. *Transportation/Mobility Goal*	Garland will use a taxi to travel to destinations nearby but not within walking distance.
Level of present performance	Buses are not available in Garland's area. He can ride a bike, use a telephone (given a written number), and cross streets safely.
Steps needed to accomplish goal	(1) Teach Garland to access taxi service by phone; (2) teach Garland to identify list of usual destinations by name and street; and (3) teach Garland to use "Dollar-move" strategy to pay for taxi.
Date of completion	3/98
Person(s) responsible for implementation	VR counselor and teacher
7. *Social Relationships Goal*	Garland will enjoy safe social/sexual relationships with female peers.

FIGURE 10.6
(continued)

Level of present performance	Garland likes the company of girls and has several "girlfriends" among his disabled peers.
Steps needed to accomplish goal	(1) Provide family life instruction; and (2) access appropriate co-ed recreational group activities.
Date of completion	12/97
Person(s) responsible for implementation	teacher and parents
8. *Recreation/Leisure Goal*	Garland will join a Saturday bowling league.
Level of present performance	Garland's parents have been on bowling teams. Garland is a good bowler but cannot keep score.
Steps needed to accomplish goal	(1) Assist Garland in joining a team; (2) obtain a teammate mentor for Garland; and (3) assist Garland in budgeting for leagues and obtaining transportation.
Date of completion	3/98
Person(s) responsible for implementation	parents

III. Personal Competence

9. *Health/Safety Goal*	Garland will maintain control over seizures.
Level of present performance	Garland had infrequent grand mal seizures as a young child. He has remained seizure-free since age 15 but still takes low doses of Dilantin.

FIGURE 10.6
(continued)

Steps needed to accomplish goal	(1) Assist Garland in taking daily medications as recommended; and (2) continue regular checkups with family physician
Date of completion	12/97
Person(s) responsible for implementation	family
10. Self-Advocacy/Future Planning	Garland will benefit from family estate planning. He will assume his own guardianship and his siblings will act as future trustees.
Level of present performance	Garland's parents are his guardians. His siblings are 2 and 4 years younger than Garland. Garland stands to share the inheritance of property.
Steps needed to accomplish goal	Obtain legal counsel to advise and prepare plan
Date of completion	6/98
Person(s) responsible for implementation	parents

Student Career Preference

Working at a grocery store

Student's Major Transition Needs

1. Employment

2. Residential Services

3. Transportation

FIGURE 10.6
(continued)

4. _Financial Management_

5. _Social Relationships_

6. _____

7. _____

8. _____

9. _____

Additional Notes

FIGURE 10.6
(continued)

Professionals have stressed that individuals with disabilities should be empowered to make decisions about their futures and that transition planning should include the students themselves along with their families. A variety of curricular materials have been published with the specified purpose of enabling students to be more involved in the transition process (see Field & Hoffman, 1996; Halpern et al., 1997; Martin & Marshall, 1996).

An Example

The Marshall County School System (Alabama) established the Marshall County Transition School during the 1991–1992 school year ("Marshall County Transition," 1992). Six faculty members provide daily instruction to approximately 150 students, some of whom do not have disabilities. Students with disabilities served in the program include those with mild retardation and those who are learning disabled. The students receive on-the-job training, job coaching, and vocational counseling. The instructors also discuss issues related to independent living. Local employers provide training assistance and jobs.

The Montgomery County (Maryland) Public Schools System operates a School/Community Based Program for students ages five through twenty-one who have greater needs for support (Foley, 1988). Instruction is received concerning the domestic (e.g., personal hygiene), community (e.g., routine activities in stores), recreation/leisure, and vocational aspects of life. Students spend approximately 50 percent of the week in community training activities while they are in elementary school. This time eventually increases to as much as 85 percent in high school.

In high school, students experience different vocational training activities and try different jobs. Interagency collaboration between school services and adult service agencies is begun while the students are still in school. The goal of this early collaboration is to enable students to move directly from school to work.

VOCATIONAL PREPARATION

In this section, we discuss topics concerned with the relationship of career development and vocational preparation, identifying job opportunities for students who are mentally retarded, traditional vocational options, program evaluation, and issues related to vocational education.

RELATIONSHIP OF CAREER DEVELOPMENT AND VOCATIONAL PREPARATION

Regardless of the model one follows for developing a systematic view of how ultimately to prepare students who are mentally retarded for the world of work, your model must contain several crucial elements. Among those elements are adequate program objectives, provision of counseling services, and a distinct stage for developing specific vocational skills. These three elements are not the only ones that can cause a career preparation program to succeed or fail, but if one or any combination of them is missing, then the program will be less than optimal. Without clear program objectives, it will lack direction; without counseling services, program participants will not always make the best choices when confronted with career decisions; and unless they learn some specific vocational skills, many participants will leave the program without skills that they can put to use.

Developing Program Objectives

Analyses of comprehensive career preparation programs reveal that program objectives are delineated clearly. While not all programs will have the same objectives, because of differences in students' characteristics, jobs available in the community, and so on, certain objectives should be almost universal. The objective that should lead off any preparation program is the development of a continuing career profile of the student's skills and interests. Since students enter a program with different skill and interest levels, the program coordinator must assess these skills and interests to determine the appropriate beginning training level for each student. For example, if a student is interested in auto mechanics and has already been working in this area, she would probably be placed ahead of others just beginning an auto mechanics training program. As the student moves through the program, the instructor should gather and record additional information that reflects the trainee's changing or developing skills and interests. This information can then be used to motivate the student, as well as to convince employers that she is a desirable job candidate.

A second program objective should be to engage each student in actual or direct job experiences and activities. This objective is important because, as the ARC-U.S. has stated, many programs that attempt to train persons who are retarded for different kinds of work have been too academically oriented. Although academic skills are important, they should not be emphasized to the neglect of life skills (Polloway & Patton, 1997). This oversight can be corrected by allowing the student on-the-job training opportunities, with support services, in any reasonably safe environment, whether it is a typical school or factory. A third, related objective for all career preparation is the development of entry-level job skills for every student. For this, students work on actual job sites both to learn how to adjust to the demands of the job and to fellow workers and to begin building a repertoire of the requisite skills for employment in the particular area of work. For instance, the best way for aspiring cement masons to learn the latest mortaring techniques is to apprentice with a skilled craftsman under whose direction they can handle genuine masonry tools and do the actual cementing. Experiences of this kind are particularly crucial for students who are mentally retarded.

The fourth important objective of all programs is to provide job placement and follow-up services for students who have completed or will complete the preparation program. Since many of the persons we are concerned with will qualify for services from vocational rehabilitation or other agencies, personnel from those agencies can often provide placement and follow-up services. In other instances, schools may have their own vocational placement facilities. What is important here is to make placement and follow-up one of the goals of the career preparation program.

Providing Counseling Services

Counseling is another essential ingredient in a career preparation program. Rehabilitation counseling is a related service that students with disabilities are entitled to receive under IDEA. A rehabilitation counseling professional should be knowledgeable about career development, employment preparation, and methods to help the student achieve independence and integration in the community (56 *Federal Register,* 41, 266, 1991).

Developing Vocational Skills

The culminating phase in the career education process involves the development of some specific vocational skills. We explore this topic more extensively in the next section, but we give here an overall view of what should take place at this time. First, job availability in the community should be studied, and present and projected jobs should be analyzed to determine what skills are necessary to perform these jobs. Next, all students' skills should be assessed. Once this is done, students should be trained on the basis of their present skill level, their interests, and projected job availability. Following training, students should be placed on permanent job sites. Worker and employer should receive follow-up services that identify potential problem areas and provide interventions to ameliorate or minimize the consequences of these problems. Finally, professionals should evaluate the program for how well it has prepared the student for employment and for how well community employment needs have been met.

IDENTIFYING JOB OPPORTUNITIES

It is important to understand that the success of any vocational preparation program depends to a great extent on the accurate identification of available and appropriate jobs in the community. To meet the goal of job placement, personnel involved in preparing individuals who are retarded for employment should first conduct annual surveys of available community employment options. Information from this survey should then be used to conduct job analyses. "A job analysis is . . . a structured way of determining the specific demands of any job" (Clark & Kolstoe, 1995). Survey data should also be used to assess student skills and to develop goals and objectives for the vocational preparation program. Omitting this critical step may result in preparing students for jobs that are scarce or in mismatching students with jobs that are inappropriate for their skills or interests.

TRADITIONAL AND EMERGING VOCATIONAL TRAINING OPTIONS

High School Work-Study Programs

The high school work-study program has been a frequently used model for teaching vocational and occupational skills to students who have few needs for support. In many cases, the high school work-study program usually runs over a three-year period encompassing grades 10 to 12. In the first year of the program, lessons emphasize areas like transportation, budgeting, peer relationships, personal hygiene, and measurement. Units are usually part of the academic portion of the program, which covers half of the school day. The student spends approximately half the day in the formal classroom setting and half in more practical instruction. In this part of the program, job analysis and job explorations, as well as specific assessment of the student's vocational skills and interests, begin. During the second year of the program, students refine their skills by learning how to complete a job application and how to behave in a job interview. At this time, they should develop some rudimentary skills in a number of areas, such as clerical work, food service, carpentry, or automobile repair. During the third year of the program, students begin to concentrate on work skill refinement in one or two specific areas, spending part of the day on an actual job and the remaining time in school. As the third year draws to a close, students spend more time on the job and less in school.

There are five phases in the special education and work program: vocational exploration, vocational evaluation, vocational training, vocational placement, and follow-up. These phases are incorporated into a work-oriented special education curriculum of skill training experiences and job-related classroom instruction. In the first phase, vocational exploration, the instructor familiarizes the student with various occupations and their skill requirements. During this prevocational stage, two separate sets of assessment take place. One evaluation determines students' vocational capabilities and the types of jobs that may interest them. Simultaneously, a job analysis is performed within the community. Vocational evaluation, the second step, involves experiences with different job skills prescribed in order to determine the student's vocational abilities and preferences. The vocational training stage is designed to develop job skills in the pupil's general area of preference. To help prepare for a variety of occupations, training covers a wide range of job skills, usually at the semiskilled level. The choice of such specific job skills as word processing or bricklaying is based on the previous assessments. In the next stage of the program, the person is exposed to a variety of actual on-the-job experiences under the supervision of the special education faculty. An individual who has tried out several jobs for brief periods will then begin to seek permanent employment. Vocational placement consists of locating a job for the student upon graduation from high school. Follow-up entails counseling to help the newly employed person deal with any difficulties encountered on the job. This phase may also involve further training or replacement if the student is unable to adjust to the assignment.

Due to requirements and constraints resulting from legislation passed in the 1970s, work-study programs are not present in public schools to the extent that they were in the 1960s (Halpern, 1992). Elements of the work-study program, however, are found in various other career education models and transition programs.

Sheltered Employment

The sheltered workshop has been traditionally used as a setting to train individuals who need significant levels of support. In these workshops, clients work on contract jobs. These contract jobs are of short duration, and a staff person is needed to bring in new ones. The facility may or may not provide vocational assessment and training for persons outside the center.

With recent emphasis on transition planning and integration of individuals who are severely disabled into competitive work settings, the concept of the sheltered workshop has come under fire. Criticism centers around its segregated approach to employment, low wages, and general failure to move clients effectively into competitive work environments (Schuster, 1990). The trend is to use nonsheltered employment options.

Competitive Nonsupported Employment

More adults who are mentally retarded are taking their places in independent, competitive employment settings. Unfortunately, some of these jobs involve only unskilled or semiskilled labor, and many of them are only part time. Some individuals are self-employed and hire themselves out as yard workers or housekeepers. These persons obtain positions through their vocational programs or, more often, locate jobs independently through friends, family, or their own efforts. Numerous variables dictate whether competitive employment is feasible for a particular client: individual abilities, personality, and preparation; employer attitude and willingness to consider the person a capable worker; and flexibility within the work environment.

Competitive Supported Employment

Supported employment is paid employment for those with disabilities who need ongoing support on the job. Most professionals consider the use of supported employment to employ individuals with disabilities preferable to the sheltered workshop (Wright, King, & National Conference of State Legislatures Task Force on Developmental Disabilities, 1991). According to McLaughlin and Wehman (1996), there are four types of supported employment models:

1. *Individual Placement Model.* A **job coach** or employment specialist provides on-the-job training to individuals with disabilities. The job coach provides services and gradually decreases the time spent with an employee. At any point, however, the job coach can continue to provide services to the employee as needed. The job coach tries to make a successful match between the employee and the job.

2. *Mobile Work Crew Model.* Individuals with disabilities work in groups that travel from one work site to another. The supervisor is usually an employee of a supported employment agency. The work crew performs jobs such as custodial work on contracts negotiated by the supported employment agency with the business. One advantage, according to McLaughlin and Wehman (1996), is that individuals can have different job experiences by changing work crews.

3. *Enclave Model.* Employees with disabilities work in an integrated setting at a business or industry. They are allowed to compete for all job opportunities. Their supervisors are human service workers who remain on site permanently.

4. *Entrepreneurial Model.* Workers with and without disabilities work at a not-for-profit job site. Their supervisors are human service workers who serve permanently in those positions.

A key player in the supported employment model is the employment specialist or job coach. According to Winking, DeStefano, and Rusch (1988), the job coach helps to make the match between the employee and the job and learns the job that will be taught to the individual with the disability. Winking et al. add that in a survey of program coordinators at supported employment agencies, program coordinators stated that the competencies needed by job coaches are flexibility, good oral and written communication skills, the ability to cope and manage stress, confidence, and the ability to take the initiative. Some of the duties of the job coach are to write task analyses, provide social skills training, maintain regular contact with parents, and provide job safety instruction. Winking et al. have stated that the work of a job coach can be quite varied. In one minute, he or she might have to perform manual labor, and then in the next minute, attend an important meeting with a company representative.

Individuals with mental retardation who are trained through a supported employment model may fare better in competitive employment than those who have worked only in a sheltered workshop (Goldberg et al., 1990; Wehman. et al., 1989). The benefits of a supported employment model accrue to taxpayers and also to the employees with disabilities. The Rehabilitation Research and Training Center (1988) completed benefit–cost analyses over an eight-year period for taxpayers and consumers (employed individuals with disabilities). The results of the cost analysis indicated that both groups benefitted from the supported employment model as opposed to the sheltered workshop model. Taxpayers benefitted because of the lower costs associated with the supported employment model, a decreased consumer reliance on governmental financial aid, and an increase in revenue generated by the consumers. All the consumers had more income as a result of supported employment. The savings from supported employment, however, did not occur until the third year of the program.

Some state officials have shown a willingness to use the supported employment model. Virginia awards grants to sheltered workshops that convert to the supported employment model. Maryland set a goal that at least 65 percent of those with disabilities would be provided training through a supported employment model.

VOCATIONAL ASSESSMENT

A number of methods can be used in vocational assessment, including personality tests, self-report devices, and rating devices (Clark & Kolstoe, 1995). The most commonly used and perhaps the most useful are written tests, observation of work samples, and interviews. We can group written assessment devices into at least two categories: aptitude tests and interest inventories. Aptitude tests measure the abilities and traits of an individual in a certain area. For example, an aptitude test that measures word processing abilities should indicate whether or not a person can word process or learn how to word process. Educators most often use results of these tests to predict an individual's chances for success in a stated field. An example of an aptitude test is the OASIS-2 Aptitude Survey (Parker, 1991a). Interest inventories assess the student's feelings and preferences about types of occupations rather than measure potential proficiency. The Harrington-O'Shea Career Decision-Making (CDM) System, Revised Edition (Harrington & O'Shea, 1992), and the OASIS-2 Interest Survey (Parker, 1991b) are two such devices. The CDM-revised has two levels. Level One is written at a fourth-grade reading level and is designed for those with lower reading skills, including students in special education. Level Two is designed for high school and college students. Both levels address abilities, job values, school subject preferences, and interests. The OASIS-2 Interest Schedule measures artistic, scientific, nature, protective, mechanical, industrial, business detail, selling, accommodating, humanitarian, leading–influencing, and physical performing interest factors.

Another way to assess work skills is through a work sample or job simulation. This procedure evaluates each individual's rate of production and general job-related behaviors. Brolin (1982) has offered the following suggestions for making the most of this procedure: The job sample or work sample should be written up and organized with the requisite tasks in rank order from the least to the most demanding. The students should be allowed to practice each task and learn it completely before proceeding to the next one; in this way, they can master each task necessary for the production of a particular good or service.

One example of a job simulation device is the Jewish Employment and Vocational Service Work Samples (JEVS) package. Brolin (1982, 1986) has described these work samples as being composed of twenty-eight tasks that measure worker skills in fourteen general industrial categories. During the evaluation, which covers a two-week period, the person being evaluated is required to perform work-related tasks that vary from simple (lettering signs) to complex (disassembling and rebuilding equipment).

See Clark (1998) for additional information about vocational assessment.

Another procedure recommended for determining an individual's transition needs is curriculum-based vocational assessment. This assessment derives from an evaluation of a student's performance within the vocational curriculum (Ianacone & Leconte, 1986). The data collected can be used to guide efforts to improve curriculum and to assist program personnel in decision making (Porter & Stodden, 1986).

Interviewing can also be used as a method to obtain as much information as possible. According to Clark and Kolstoe (1995), the interviewee should understand the purpose of the interview. Some of the information obtained should include the interviewee's likes, interests, and future goals. The interviewer should attempt to verify the interviewee's statements through the use of follow-up and parent interviews, or rating scales, with special attention given to any discrepancies in the data from the various sources.

While these instruments and procedures do yield valuable information about students' vocational capabilities, they have frequently been criticized for several reasons. First, the reading level for many of the paper-and-pencil tests is too high for many students who are retarded (reading levels for these instruments are usually at or around a sixth-grade level). Second, few if any items relate directly to women. Third, socioeconomic differences are ignored (the preponderance of items reflects a middle-class orientation). Finally, U.S. racial and cultural diversity are not taken into account. Work sample evaluations are criticized because they are expensive and time-consuming, often requiring extensive travel to and from the work site. The question of accuracy of the interview method is a problem. The information may be biased or limited in value as a result of misinformation or insufficient information (Clark & Kolstoe, 1995). This is why the interviewer must attempt to verify statements made during the interview.

VOCATIONAL PLACEMENT

Once a student has acquired some vocational skills, either the school or some other organization such as a vocational rehabilitation agency seeks to place the student on a permanent job site. Smith and Payne (1980), Clark and Kolstoe (1995), and Wehman (1990) suggest a number of procedures to aid the placement specialist. The following list summarizes these procedures:

1. Make as many personal contacts with local employers as possible.
2. Use local clubs to advertise your program, as well as to secure information concerning placement sites.
3. Become more selective in the use of job sites as the program grows.
4. Consider employers an integral part of the program. Use them at different levels of the program; for example, the prevocational as well as the vocational level.
5. Obtain information from such resources as state job service centers, the state division of vocational rehabilitation, and the local Chamber of Commerce and job training partnership act program.
6. Program personnel should review the budget to ensure that job placement concerns are receiving the most favorable level of funding.

FOLLOW-UP AND EVALUATION

In the more desirable employment models, the individual receives follow-up services, as needed, on a continuous basis (McLaughlin & Wehman, 1996). Information gained during the follow-up period can be used to assess program effectiveness. The relationship between follow-up and evaluation makes it possible for future as well as present program participants to benefit.

PROGRAMMING ISSUES

Vocational preparation of students who are retarded has come a long way, but we do not have all the answers yet. Two problem areas still demand special attention.

The first, as mentioned, is the difficulty of the written material used in vocational programs for students who are mentally retarded. The reading level of much of this material is too high. Vocational and special educators have struggled with this problem for some time without being able to reach a workable solution.

The second problem relates to what to do when a person who is mentally retarded resigns or is fired from a job. A similar event causes some concern with a person who is not retarded, but it seems to occasion greater consternation on the part of family, friends, and professionals who work with people who have disabilities. Should a job termination be more of an issue for workers who are retarded than for the rest of the labor force? We believe that an employee who is mentally retarded has as much right as the next person to like or dislike a job or co-workers and to leave an unpleasant or unproductive situation if necessary. To deny this is to deny equal rights (and responsibilities) to the adult who is mentally retarded, and it runs wholly contrary to the idea of inclusion, self-determination, and empowerment.

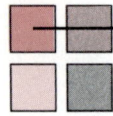

SUMMARY

CAREER EDUCATION

- Marland (1971, 1972) is credited with calling attention to the need for career education.

- *Career development* is a broad term that can be equated with the term *transition education,* indicating a program aimed at helping students prepare for life as well as for a job.

- Vocational education is an aspect of career education that focuses on employment.

- Career development should be infused into all levels of the curriculum.

TRANSITION PLANNING

- PL 101-476 mandated that, beginning no later than age sixteen, a student's IEP must include a statement of transition services.

- PL 105-17 now requires that a statement of transition needs to be in place by age fourteen.

- A comprehensive assessment of transition needs is essential.

- Transition plans should include the development of life skills.

VOCATIONAL PREPARATION

- A career preparation program should include specific program objectives, counseling services, and the development of specific vocational skills.

- Studies have shown that with systematic training and ongoing support, many individuals with greater needs can succeed in integrated, competitive work settings.

CHAPTER 11

Adult Years

After reading this chapter,
the student should be able to:

- Discuss important factors influencing the lives of adults as they transition from school into the community.
- Identify and describe the three major developmental periods of adulthood.
- Discuss factors that contribute to a person's likelihood for success in community residential environments.
- Identify and describe key issues affecting the lives of adults with mental retardation today.

Key Terms

advocacy

community acceptance

community adjustment

economic integration

employment integration

recreational/leisure integration

residential integration

social integration

hile most professionals in the field of mental retardation advocate programs that allow for the complete involvement of individuals with mental retardation into all aspects of community living, others have argued that this perspective is far too shortsighted and that it ignores the complexity of the community adjustment process. **Community adjustment** implies more than just physical location in mainstream surroundings, it is the "adjustment and integration of the whole person into community life" (Ittenbach, Larson, Spiegel, Abery, & Prouty, 1993, p. 19). According to Kleinberg and Galligan (1983), programmatic interventions are critical to successful community adjustment, and without it, community placements may not be much better than institutional placements. Adulthood *is* complex; so, too, are the lives of persons with mental retardation. In addition to the systematically determined criteria for successful community adjustment, professionals should consider what adjustment means to those with mental retardation. Not only are adults with mental retardation quite capable of expressing their opinions about issues that are important to them, but their concerns are sometimes very different from those of their primary care providers (Foxx, Faw, Taylor, Davis, & Fulia, 1993). This chapter highlights many of the key issues that are typically considered to be a part of the adult years.

TRANSITION FROM SCHOOL TO COMMUNITY

The transition of young adults from home and school to life in the community continues to be a pressing concern of parents, professionals, and policy makers. Despite long-standing agreement on the essential components of a successful transition program, there is evidence to suggest that the greater the support needs, the greater the level of difficulty in adjusting to community living (Thurlow, Bruininks, & Lange, 1989; Thurlow, Bruininks, Wolman, & Steffens, 1989).

The importance of monitoring and improving transition services to adults with mental retardation is underscored by the substantial number of young adults receiving special education services annually. For example, from 1982 through 1994, there was a 66-percent increase of eighteen- to twenty-one-year-olds served under PL 94–142's Part B (federal funds provided to states for special education services), now called the Individuals

Program interventions are critical to successful transition from school to community.

with Disabilities Education Act (IDEA) (U.S. Department of Education, 1983, 1995). Not all young adults with mental retardation currently served in secondary settings remain in school, however, as one in three drop out prior to graduation (National Institute on Disability and Rehabilitation Research, 1994), well before needed transition programs can be completed. More than ever before, family members to service providers to state and federal policy makers are expressing an interest in meeting the wide range of educational, occupational, and community living needs of adults with disabilities transitioning into new environments (DeStefano & Wagner, 1990).

Of the many skills and content areas introduced to young adults in secondary-school settings, vocational preparation often receives the greatest attention. In contrast to their peers without disabilities, the vocational and transitioning needs of adolescents with disabilities ranks among the priorities for improved service delivery. However, legislation and school-to-work incentive programs constitute only part of the mechanism by which the movement from school to community can be facilitated. Krieg, Brown, and Ballard (1995) put the role of transition services into a broader framework with three precise objectives: first, to gather and use as much information about the person as possible; second, to design an organized and integrated

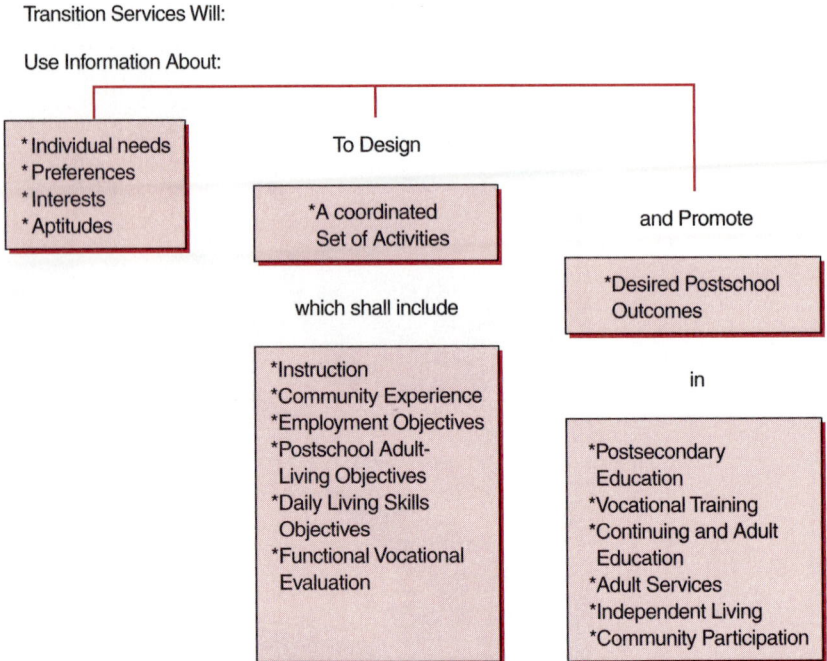

Transition Services Will:

Use Information About:

* Individual needs
* Preferences
* Interests
* Aptitudes

To Design

*A coordinated
Set of Activities

which shall include

*Instruction
*Community Experience
*Employment Objectives
*Postschool Adult-
Living Objectives
*Daily Living Skills
Objectives
*Functional Vocational
Evaluation

and Promote

*Desired Postschool
Outcomes

in

*Postsecondary
Education
*Vocational Training
*Continuing and Adult
Education
*Adult Services
*Independent Living
*Community Participation

FIGURE 11.1
The Role of Transition Services

Source: From *Transition: School to Work* (p. 23) by F. J. Krieg, P. Brown, and J. Ballard, 1995, Bethesda, MD: National Association of School Psychologists. Copyright 1995 by the National Association of School Psychologists. Reprinted by permission of the publisher.

set of services; and third, to promote achievable post-school outcomes (see Figure 11.1). Though the list is not exhaustive, it does emphasize the notion that adulthood is a time of many complex and interrelated demands. Given the rather extensive nature of the domains presented here, it is certainly understandable that as the need for supports increases, so, too will the need for more complex transition planning.

Much of what is currently known about the adjustment of adults with mental retardation comes from postschool follow-up studies such as those just mentioned. Heal and Rusch (1994) conducted one of the most extensive studies on the postschool adjustment status of special education youth exiting high school between 1985 and 1987. Two of their findings are worth mentioning here. First, key factors such as levels of intelligence, adaptive living skills, and maladaptive behaviors "appear to be better predictors of post-school living arrangement status than are school characteristics such as training for community living and employment" (p. 238). Second, persons with milder forms of disabilities performed relatively better in the community than young adults with more serious disabilities. For adults with mental retardation, specifically, Thurlow, Bruininks, Wolman, and Steffens (1989) found significant differences in adjustment according to one's level of disability. That is, persons with more severe levels of mental retardation reported greater difficulty adjusting to community living than persons with milder levels of mental retardation, one to five years after leaving high school. In a related study by Thurlow, Bruininks, and Lange (1989), young adults with mild-to-severe levels of mental retardation two to ten years out of school were examined for differences in a number of quality of life variables (e.g., degree of independence, adaptive and maladaptive behaviors). While persons with moderate-to-severe levels of mental retardation were able to find limited success in employment, social integration, and community functioning following the school years, they did *not* find the same degree of postschool improvement observed in persons with mild mental retardation.

Although there are few formally agreed-upon guidelines with which to evaluate a person's overall level of adjustment to community living following the school years, consensus appears to have been reached on three major points: First, differences exist among adults with mental retardation just as they do among adults without mental retardation; second, certain factors are crucial to the community adjustment process (e.g., level of intelligence, adaptive behavior, social skill development); and third, one's likelihood for success in the transition process is shaped by many factors such as the person's characteristics, the environment, and an interaction of the two. It is now abundantly clear to most service providers that when the community adjustment experience is not successful and a return to a more restrictive residential facility is required, it is much more of an indictment of the service delivery system than an indictment of the person attempting to live in the community.

ADULT DEVELOPMENT

Adulthood is a time of many changes. For some people, these changes may be eagerly anticipated; for others, however, they may represent anything from an untimely predicament to an insurmountable crisis. Though much is known about the developmental patterns of children and adolescents, only a modest amount of information is available about the adult years. For adults with mental retardation, the literature base is even scantier. When one considers adult development specifically, one must keep in mind that normative and nonnormative stages of progression will vary from one period to the next. Following is a brief description of the three major developmental periods of adulthood.

YOUNG ADULTHOOD

Young adults with mental retardation enter the adult world with many of the same expectations as young adults without mental retardation. Levinson

Young adults with mental retardation share the same concerns about the adult world as young adults without mental retardation.

(1978) cites young adulthood as the most dramatic time of one's life. For many, young adulthood represents the biological and intellectual peak of development; it is a time when decisions are made relative to major life events (Blalock, 1988). Establishing and maintaining friendships, a career, and a residence are life tasks faced by most young adults, regardless of intellectual or adaptive level of functioning. Though the transition for persons with mental retardation is often much more difficult, just the opportunity to strive for normative young adult milestones is what is valued and appreciated. Very few adults have accomplishments that match their expectations, particularly young adults. For the young adult with mental retardation, special occasions may take on an enhanced sense of importance, given the rather restricted nature of social opportunities. For example, promotions at work, major birthdays, and major family events (e.g., becoming a mother, father, aunt, or uncle) offer occasions of great personal significance that can help define one's role as an adult. Kail and Cavanaugh (1996) have suggested that cultural rituals signifying entrance into adulthood are often the most important rituals within a culture and very often have the greatest effect on the quality of one's early adult life.

MIDDLE ADULTHOOD

There is no formally agreed-upon range that corresponds to middle adult-hood, though many consider it to be roughly 40 to 60 years of age. Opinions differ as to the nature of middle adulthood. Some consider it to be just an-other stage in one's life, others consider it to be the prime of one's life where personal and professional achievements are at their maximum; and still oth-ers consider it to be a time of diminished demands and the beginning of a period of introspection. Erikson (1950) described this portion of the lifespan continuum as "Generativity vs. Stagnation," the point at which the middle adult makes the decision to live for oneself or for others. All middle adults must begin adjusting to the limits of the aging process. For many adults with mental retardation, this is a difficult task, especially for those who have al-ready had to make many accommodations. Readjusting to a life without par-ents or to a life with aging parents, finding a niche in the local community that one can count on, and finding new and enjoyable recreational/leisure activities are all hallmarks of the middle adult years (Rice, 1986).

OLDER ADULTHOOD

Few trends characterize America more than the graying of its population. In 1900, older adults accounted for only 4 percent of the U.S. population. By the year 2030, it is expected that adults sixty-five years and older will ac-count for approximately 20 percent of the population. More noteworthy per-haps is that people eighty-five years of age and older now constitute the fastest growing segment of the older adult population, a segment that is ex-pected to double in size by the year 2030, with a fivefold increase expected by the year 2050 (U.S. Department of Commerce, 1996). While numbers alone do not make the aging process any easier, they do increase the like-lihood that more services will be available for persons in need. Older adult-hood is often characterized by a turning inward and withdrawing from so-ciety. Establishing and accepting new roles in the family, adjusting to lowered social expectations, and adjusting to continued limitations of the aging process are all considered to be developmental tasks of older adult-hood (Levinson, 1978).

For the older adult with mental retardation, creating a new lifestyle pat-tern that allows one to deal with the onset of illness and the general sense of loss of one's abilities and youth are all factors that must be addressed to assure the highest quality of life possible. The developmental work of the-orists such as Erikson and Levinson has much to offer persons who work with adults with mental retardation. Despite the increasing amount of infor-mation on normative life events for adults in general, there continues to be a void of information on the development of adults with mental retardation. Some predict that lifespan issues pertaining to persons with mental retarda-tion will become a paramount theme of the next few decades (Glidden & Zetlin, 1992; Ittenbach, Larson, et al., 1994).

ADJUSTING TO LIFE IN THE COMMUNITY

Community adjustment research typically pertains to one of two transitional processes, home/school to community, dealt with in this chapter, and institution to community, which will be addressed in Chapter 14.

The complexity of each person's life, variety of experiences, and opportunity to assume responsibility for one's own and others' behaviors all depend on such things as the availability of community resources, public and private attitudes, and the unique characteristics of the individuals involved. While Schalock and Kiernan (1990) identified home, work, and recreational/leisure environments as the three major environments in which people operate, they contend that it is actually the community environment that unites all three. Until recently, the results of research on the construct of community adjustment have not supported any one combination of variables that predicts successful adjustment. Though the literature base is modest, results of early studies appear promising. Researchers at the University of Minnesota's Institute on Community Integration and the University of Oregon's Rehabilitation and Training Center in Mental Retardation have sought to identify and measure outcomes of the community adjustment process (e.g., Bruininks, Chen, Lakin, & McGrew, 1992; Halpern, Nave, Close, & Nelson, 1986; Ittenbach, Bruininks, Thurlow, & McGrew, 1993; McGrew, Bruininks, Thurlow, & Lewis, 1992). In a review of this research, McGrew, Johnson, and Bruininks (1994) found as many as eight possible factors that characterize one's likelihood for success in community living (see Figure 11.2). Following is a brief description of research pertaining to these factors.

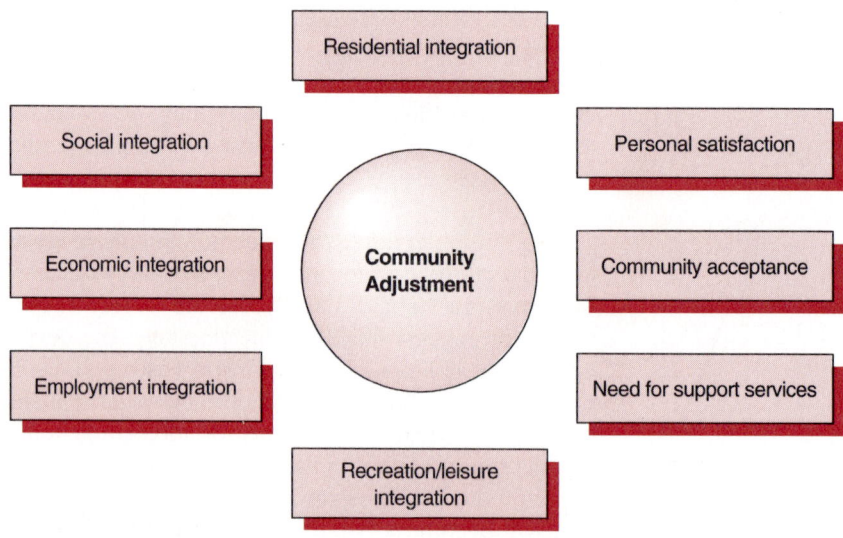

FIGURE 11.2
Life in the Community

INDEPENDENT LIVING

Timmy and Carol Savage presently live in an apartment, on their own and as independent as any couple could possibly be. Tim spent thirty-seven years of his life in the state's institution for those who are mentally retarded, after which he lived in a group home. Tim now works full time sanding picture frames for ACME Industries, while Carol performs routine maid services for the Best Western Inn. According to Tim, and incidentally confirmed by the landlord, "We pay on time, every time. We don't get behind."

Tom Houston, housing developer for the handicapped with Mental Retardation Services, explains it has been a long process of educating landlords and neighbors alike that those who are mentally retarded are more similar to than different from those pegged as normal. "Many landlords have very legitimate concerns about disabled individuals, because if a tenant is impeded in his performance of his duties as a tenant, it could result in a loss to the landlord."

The Savages have access to a Citizens Advocacy program that matches a volunteer from the community with a "special-friend," a process by which the program hopes to develop lasting friendships. The layperson acts as an advocate for the human and legal rights of the person with retardation. It is simply one more way that differences can be diminished; volunteers grow in their understanding of the handicapped.

Houston feels compelled to assure a prospective landlord that when a tenant who is handicapped has inadequacies, there will be a professional, or a layperson like a Citizen Advocate, to compensate. Some people like the Savages need little supervision. They have demonstrated a consistency of behavior that assures a landlord of their ability to handle most of their duties as tenants with little guidance from others.

When a client is deemed ready for independent living, Houston helps him work out an agreement for monthly rent payments, including utilities, which are not to exceed one quarter of the individual's gross income.

Once an apartment is found to suit everyone's purposes, a one-year lease is signed. The client is guaranteed that his rent subsidy will be renewed annually for the next five years.

"Some landlords are very responsive," says Houston. They call him up when they have a vacancy because they like the program and go out of their way to help the tenant. For our landlords, "It's just a cut-and-dried agreement, strictly business. He wants to know, 'Am I going to get my checks on time? Is my lease going to be violated?' "

Houston says over and over again that these tenants are turning out to be reliable. They like structure and adhere rather consistently to a routine once good habits are taught them. But Houston is quick to point out that "it's not a humanitarian thing. It's a good business deal."

"I wouldn't be on the phone to you," he tells a landlord, "if I didn't feel it was a good business."

SOCIAL INTEGRATION

Social relationships constitute the heart and soul of community integration (C. H. Kennedy, Horner, & Newton, 1989). Few will argue the importance of family, friends, and significant others to one's overall well-being. Fewer still will argue the importance of a strong and stable support network for persons experiencing difficulty with the community adjustment process. It seems ironic, then, that so little attention has been paid to the study of **social integration,** a person's general level of intra- and interpersonal functioning, particularly as it relates to persons with mental retardation (Ittenbach, Abery, Larson, Spiegel, & Prouty, 1994).

A major finding within social integration research is that persons with mental retardation tend to be accepted less often and rejected more often than persons without mental retardation, leading to less satisfaction with personal relations (A. R. Taylor, Asher, & Williams, 1987). Fewer friends, less intimacy, and less empathy among peers with disabilities were reported by adolescents with mental retardation than by adolescents without mental retardation (Zetlin & Murtaugh, 1988). Abery and others (Abery, Thurlow, Bruininks, & Johnson, 1990; Abery, Thurlow, Johnson, & Bruininks, 1989) found the social lives of persons with mental retardation to be highly restrictive, making transitions through key developmental stages more difficult and detracting substantially from overall quality of living. Though many adults with mental retardation report a substantial number of friends, C. H. Kennedy et al. (1989) found a limited number of "companions who remained a part of a participant's social sphere for more than a few months" (p. 195).

Contributing to this lack of meaningful social relationships is a tendency toward a rather shy and reticent temperament, particularly in mainstreamed settings. Though researchers have contested the notion that people with mental retardation lack essential social skills, there appears to be agreement on the need for peers and confidants who can model effective social behaviors in community settings. Peers without mental retardation offer opportunities for social involvement not always available to peers with mental retardation (Abery et al., 1990; Brinker, 1985). For example, in a study involving 245 children, adolescents, and young adults from nine states, Brinker (1985) found that students without mental retardation extended more social bids to students with mental retardation than did peers with mental retardation; equally important, students without mental retardation responded to more social bids from students with mental retardation than did peers with mental retardation.

Offsetting the difficulties inherent in the adjustment process is the finding that adults with mental retardation tend to make greater use of their rather limited social support networks than do adults without mental retardation (J. W. Rosen & Burchard, 1990). The many benefits to others of investing in social relationships with persons with mental retardation (such as an increased tolerance of others, a reduced fear of persons with disabilities, and added friendships) cannot be overlooked (Peck, Donaldson, & Pezzoli, 1990).

ECONOMIC INTEGRATION

The extent to which a person is able to earn and spend money, hereafter referred to as **economic integration,** is a crucial component of life in the community. Though many if not most adults with mental retardation benefit from entitlements that guarantee supports for their essential needs, there

FIGURE 11.3
Matrix of Entitlement Programs

Source: From *How to Provide for Their Future* (p. 26) by the Association of Retarded Citizens of the United States, 1984, Arlington, TX: Association of Retarded Citizens of the United States. Copyright 1984 by the Association of Retarded Citizens of the United States. Reprinted by permission.

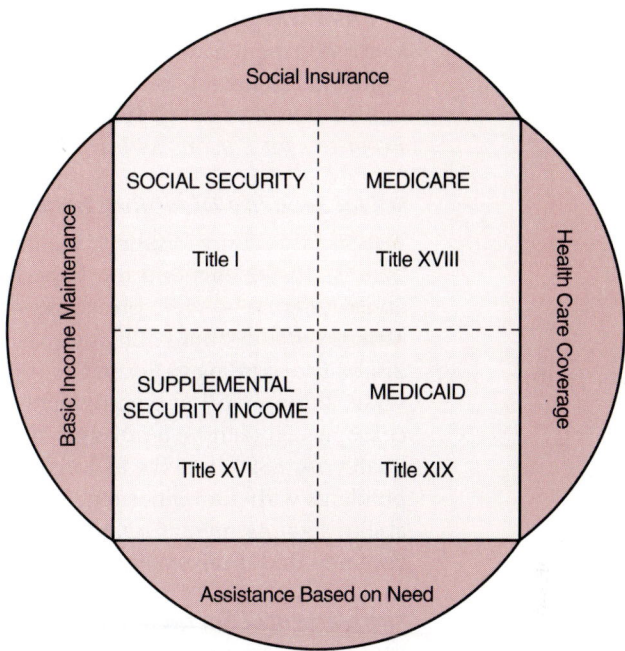

Matrix representing relationships among Social Security (SSDI, ADC). Medicare, Supplemental Security Income (SSI), and Medicaid for persons with disabilities. The criteria for eligibility based on disability are uniform for all programs in all states. The economic criteria differ. Social Security and Medicare are federally administered according to uniform rules in all states. SSI basic entitlements are federally administered according to uniform rules; most states provide state supplementation under state-specific criteria. Medicaid is a federally assisted, state-administered program. In most states, SSI-eligible persons are also eligible for Medicaid. In addition, some persons who meet the disability criteria may meet the economic criteria (means tests) for Medicaid even if ineligible for SSI. Children with disabilities may be eligible for SSI, Medicaid, or both.

is more to community living than simply meeting basic financial obligations. It is the depth to which the person with mental retardation exercises the right to make decisions as to how one's own money is earned and spent.

Adults with mental retardation do not have the same income and financial independence as adults without mental retardation. As financial dependence increases, lack of access to other community-based programs increases. Lack of discretionary income affects more than just one's ability to purchase desired goods and services, it makes one less likely to participate in certain social, recreational, and vocational activities, missing out on many of the benefits of community living. At a time when other adults are assuming direct control over their financial lives, adults with mental retardation continue to be dependent upon the wishes and preferences of others around them, their own income notwithstanding. Equally important is the fact that as consumers their voices are not heard, and they therefore miss the opportunity to influence manufacturers' habits.

As a way to provide regular income and health service coverage to persons with mental retardation, a number of federally funded programs are available. Following is a brief discussion of four programs as described in the U.S. Department of Health and Human Service's (1990) *Task II: Federal Programs for Persons with Disabilities* (see also Figure 11.3).

Social Security Disability Insurance Program

Staying abreast of new developments in health service coverage means staying abreast of the ever-changing legislation pertaining to persons with disabilities and their families.

The Social Security Disability Insurance (SSDI) program offers monthly cash benefits to persons and the dependents of persons sixty-five years of age and younger who were previously insured and who have left the workforce because of a disability. Eligibility is based on two factors: the presence of a disability according to Social Security Administration guidelines, and insured status through prior employment. Although childhood benefits typically cease at eighteen years of age, dependents who are disabled continue to qualify for SSDI benefits as long as the disability continues. Most adult dependents with disabilities receiving such services have a developmental disability such as mental retardation, autism, or cerebral palsy; cash benefits continue under this category as long as the person is a dependent.

Supplemental Social Security Income Program

The Supplemental Social Security Income (SSI) program offers monthly cash benefits to persons and dependents of persons who are aged or disabled and whose income falls below a certain level. The SSI program is a federally funded program supplemented by state funds to meet the basic living needs of its recipients. All but seven states provide funds to supplement federal benefits. The benefits are designed to reach those not previously employed and, thus, not covered by the SSDI program. As a group, SSI recipients are younger than SSDI recipients because of no requirement for prior insurance coverage and work history. Approximately 27 percent of all SSI recipients under the age of sixty-five have mental retardation; approximately 42 percent of the children with disabilities covered by these benefits have mental retardation. According to Castellani (1987), SSI's importance is twofold: it directly assists individuals and is a source of funding to community-based services through its recipients.

Medicare

Medicare is a federally funded program that provides health insurance coverage (e.g., hospice, hospital, home health care) to persons with and without disabilities over the age of sixty-five and to persons who have left the workforce due to a disability prior to age sixty-five. Disability criteria are identical to those in the previous two categories; eligibility requirements are closely aligned with SSDI requirements. Dependents of SSDI recipients are not covered until age twenty. Of the nearly three million persons with disabilities receiving Medicare benefits in 1987, approximately 17 percent were adult dependents with disabilities.

Medicaid

Medicaid is a jointly operated federal and state health-care program for people who cannot afford private insurance or medical services. Originally commissioned to serve the acute health-care needs of persons with low incomes, "it has now become the nation's primary program for financing long term care services to elderly and disabled individuals" (U.S. Department of Health and Human Services, 1990, p. 102). Adults with mental retardation typically qualify for Medicaid. Though states are required to operate within federal guidelines, services vary widely from state to state. Disability criteria for the federal portion of the program are the same as for the other three previously mentioned programs; however, state eligibility criteria may vary. Under Medicaid, the federal government reimburses states for 50 to 77 percent of the costs incurred.

EMPLOYMENT INTEGRATION

The routines, rhythms, and responsibilities of work are all part of **employment integration.** For instance, it is common for people to commute to work each morning, punch in, work through the morning, take coffee breaks, talk with co-workers, have lunch, work through the afternoon, and then return home, another day passed and another dollar earned (Wolfensberger, 1972).

Work is no less significant for the person with mental retardation than for the person without mental retardation. Changes in legislation, social policy, and public attitudes have allowed more such people to enter the workforce and share in the benefits of gainful employment than ever before. Whereas people with disabilities were once thought to possess little potential for gainful employment, even individuals with the most pervasive support needs are now considered by employers to be quite capable of performing complex vocational tasks (Chamberlain, 1988; D. E. Craig, & Boyd, 1990; Tilson, Luecking, & Donovan, 1994).

The ultimate goal of habilitation is placement in a regular, competitive job, yet some adults with mental retardation cannot meet this goal. Today a number of employment options are available for adults with mental retardation (see Table 11.1). Economic conditions, extent and adequacy of systematic training, flexibility of employment sites to facilitate adjustment, and individual characteristics all interact to determine which option is most appropriate for a specific person at a given time. Following is a brief description of three general categories of employment:

Nonemployment

This category is appropriate for three groups of people. The first group comprises those whose need for supports is so pervasive or whose skills are so minimal that it is unlikely that vocational training can be undertaken and employment secured. The second group consists of those who are capable of working but who choose not to work. This group includes people who are influenced by disincentives that create compelling reasons for

TABLE 11.1

Breakdown of Employment Options

Employment option	Dimension			
	Financial reimbursement	Employment supports	Community integration	Production of valued goods
Nonemployment	none	none	none	none
Unpaid	none	varies	likely	possible
Sheltered	below minimum	continual	none	unlikely
Supported	minimum+	continual/faded	yes	yes
Competitive	minimum+	varies	yes	yes

Source: From "New Directions and Strategies in Habilitation Services: Toward Meaningful Employment Outcomes" by R. P. Schutz, 1988, in L. W. Heal, J. I. Haney, and A. R. Novak Amado (Eds.), *Integration of Developmentally Disabled Individuals into the Community* (2nd ed., p. 201), Baltimore: Paul H. Brookes; and from "Establishing Community Employment Programs for Persons with Severe Disabilities: Systems Designs and Resolutions" by R. T. Vogelsberg and R. P. Schutz, 1988, in M. D. Powers (Ed.), *Expanding Systems of Service Delivery for Persons with Developmental Disabilities* (p. 131), Baltimore: Paul H. Brookes. Adapted by permission.

not seeking employment. The third group comprises those who want to work but cannot find employment, including workers who have been temporarily laid off.

Unpaid Employment

Some adults with mental retardation may have opportunities to work but for whatever reason do not receive pay. In some instances, this situation is positive, as in the case of volunteer work, where income is neither necessary nor expected. In other situations, this option may reflect unfair treatment, as when a person is not paid for work that usually generates income. Many have argued that persons with mental retardation, including persons with extensive support needs, should have access to the same vocational training and employment opportunities as persons without mental retardation. For some individuals, that means the right to forego paid employment in restrictive settings in favor of nonpaid employment in nonrestrictive settings (L. F. Brown et al., 1984).

Paid Employment

Few things are as important to employees as compensation. For most that usually means a paycheck, but for others it often means payment through other types of goods or services. The range of paid employment options varies from highly protected to highly competitive settings. A brief breakdown of three types of settings follows:

■ *Sheltered employment*. Sheltered workshops consist of programs that provide daytime activities for persons who require continuous supervision. These workshops provide both long-term and short-term placements, they stress self-sufficiency over employability, and serve persons with intermittent to pervasive support needs. Most workshops provide basic rehabilitation services, including screening, evaluation, training, placement, and follow-up services.

■ *Supported employment*. For persons for whom competitive employment is not an option, supported employment is often used. Supported employment exemplifies the movement away from sheltered settings toward integrative ones. These programs allow for decreased supervision and segregation and increased autonomy and integration through structured support (job coaches), paid employment, and the opportunity to work in competitive settings.

■ *Competitive employment*. This category represents employment on the open market, usually alongside persons without mental retardation. More adults with mental retardation are obtaining placements in independent, competitive settings than ever before. Adults seeking this form of employment are as likely to obtain jobs through family, friends, or their own efforts as through organized vocational programs.

Chapter 10 contains a more complete discussion of sheltered, supported, and competitive employment.

Forces still act against job attainment. Castellani (1987) has noted that employment is often at odds with certain community services, particularly income support and health-care programs, which many adults with mental retardation receive. Conley, Noble, and Elder (1986) have identified three major obstacles: (a) reduction of net gain from work, (b) development of dependency and negative attitudes toward work, and (c) greater income security for those who continue to receive the services than their working peers. In the first case, employment for some individuals may result in a net loss of income and an additional tax burden. Next, a person who qualifies as being unable to earn above the substantial gainful activity (SGA) level and therefore receives monthly benefits has little incentive to disprove this determination. The third factor works on a simple principle—it's better to be safe than sorry—a check in hand each month is worth more than all of the untested job initiatives in the world. Bowe (1993) offered this analysis on the 20th anniversary of the SSI program:

> [T]he disability employment figures from the Census Bureau loom large. They suggest, indirectly but provocatively, that the fall-off in employment by males with disabilities since 1970 is at least in part a function of the attractiveness they find in the SSI program (and in the SSDI program, as well). . . . Women with disabilities, for their part, might have made more gains during the 1970–1990 period if they, too, did not have the options offered by SSDI and SSI. (p. 85)

RECREATIONAL/LEISURE INTEGRATION

Like all people, adults with mental retardation need recreational and leisure activities to balance the rigors of daily living. Unfortunately, far too many

It is important for people with retardation to have a variety of friends and leisure activities.

individuals with mental retardation remain outside the mainstream of community life in these areas. According to the *National Consumer Survey* (Temple University Developmental Disabilities Center, 1990), one of every three persons with mental retardation in the United States has an expressed need for **recreational/leisure integration** but is unable to acquire it.

Though many persons with mental retardation have an interest in a wide range of leisure-time activities, the activities consist primarily of passive rather than active pastimes (e.g., watching TV, listening to the radio or CDs, reading magazines) (Aveno, 1987; Kregel, Wehman, Seyfarth, & Marshall, 1986). Recreational programs have been a part of institutional life for many years; however, they have generally been more concerned with keeping residents occupied and providing relief for staff than with developing lifetime skills. Schleien, Meyer, Heyne, and Brandt (1995) provide an extensive review of the literature related to leisure skills and leisure education for persons with mental retardation and conclude that the benefits are many. For example, skills learned during play extend across the curriculum (e.g., language, problem solving), increases in socially appropriate free-time activities decrease the likelihood of socially inappropriate free-time behaviors, and a well-developed repertoire of free-time activities increases the quality of the relationships with family and friends.

Advocates have begun demanding that community recreational opportunities available to persons without mental retardation be extended to persons with mental retardation. The demands have been heard. Programs ranging from special skill-building programs to competitive international competition are now underway. While most human service providers are aware of the Special Olympics, less well-known but potentially more important for encouraging community acceptance is the Special Olympics' Unified Sports program in which athletes with and without mental retardation participate in equal numbers on the same teams in local, regional, national, and international competitions. The growth of the Unified program remains unparalleled among organized athletic programs for persons with disabilities. According to Ms. Annette Lynch of Special Olympics International, 39,827 athletes in the United States participated in the program in 1996, representing a sixfold increase from the 6,636 participants who participated in 1990 (personal communication, December 18, 1996). Park and recreation clubs, drama groups, day camps, craft guilds, jogging clubs, cooking groups, and other special organizations for combined involvement of persons with and without mental retardation are being formed with increasing frequency. The continued development of special equipment like modified bowling balls and walkers for ice skating has broadened opportunities for participation in sports in ways not imagined even a few years ago. Instructions for home-centered hobbies such as card games, board games, stamp collecting, and other leisure projects are also being included in curriculum plans (e.g., Schleien, Ray, & Green, 1996).

If programs are so plentiful and efforts so numerous, why does one in three persons report an unmet need for recreational/leisure services? According to Ittenbach, Abery et al. (1994), adults with mental retardation face three major barriers to recreational/leisure integration. First is the issue of lack of a friend or companion with whom to share the activity. No matter how enjoyable an activity is, it is more fun when it can be shared with someone else. Second is the general lack of guidelines for planning and implementing integrated programs available to recreational specialists. New guidelines have been developed in recent years, but more are needed. Third is a lack of skills necessary to take advantage of such programs. A willingness to try and pursue new activities is in part dependent upon success in other, related areas.

RESIDENTIAL INTEGRATION

The actual location of a person's place of residence in a community, often referred to as **residential integration,** exerts a profound influence on that person's likelihood for acceptance in the broader community. That is, *where* people live determines to a great extent *how* they live. This seems obvious when one thinks of persons in institutions, but it is also true of those living in the community. For some people with mental retardation, that may mean an active life that includes interacting with neighbors, catching a bus to work, and planning for a party; for others, it may mean spending hours alone in a room, not knowing where to go or whom to visit. The shift in placement patterns from residential to community settings over the past twenty years has been substantial (Prouty & Lakin, 1996). It is interesting to recognize, as Lakin, Hill, and Bruininks (1988) have pointed out, that this movement has occurred in the absence of any national program aimed at increasing residential services.

Good homes are those in which the individual is allowed to balance an active community life with individually determined alone time. Residences that are placed in neighborhood communities are generally referred to as community residential settings. The orientation of these settings is usually a function of the characteristics and needs of their residents. Community residential settings vary in size, location, number of residents, staffing patterns, and degree of handicapping conditions of residents. The level of mental retardation does not determine the most appropriate residential setting. The match between an individual's needs and those of the setting defines the quality of the living arrangement. Areas in which community settings may differ include residents' role in facility policy, degree of residents' privacy, staff philosophy of community involvement, residents' responsibilities within the facility, and decor and furnishings.

Residential options represent a continuum of sorts; unfortunately, their availability in some locations, particularly rural settings, may be very limited, and quality may vary markedly from one setting to another. Following is a breakdown of the classes of residential facilities using the nine categories described by Amado et al. (1990, p. 8):

Protected Settings

Certain community living arrangements afford adults with mental retardation protected settings with varying degrees of support and supervision. The most notable in this category are the foster homes and semi-independent living homes. The goal, in each case, is to allow individuals to live as completely and independently as possible in a family-oriented setting.

Generic foster homes. A licensed foster care home providing services to persons with and without mental retardation.

Specialized foster care homes. A licensed foster care home providing services to persons with mental retardation and other developmental disabilities, exclusively.

Semi-independent/supported living homes. Personal homes or apartments occupied by persons with mental retardation who require less than full-time supervision or support.

Group Homes

The group home is the most common community living arrangement available to adults with mental retardation and developmental disabilities. In these homes, a group of persons with mental retardation or other developmental disabilities lives within a residential neighborhood and receives support and supervision from live-in counselors. Some homes are transitional, others serve as long-term residences. Many evoke images of comfortable family settings with decorations and personal belongings of the residents to encourage a sense of ownership and responsibility among household members.

State-operated small group residences.   Fully staffed, public residential facilities equipped to provide services to fifteen or fewer people.

Nonstate-operated group residences.   Fully staffed, privately (or local government) operated residential facilities equipped to provide services to fifteen or fewer people.

Large Group Facilities

Although the number of people with disabilities living in large group facilities has dropped in recent decades, institutional living remains an option for many persons and families of persons with mental retardation. Following is a breakdown of three such types:

State-supported institutions.   Fully staffed residential facilities equipped to provide services to sixteen or more people at a time. There are two different kinds of large, state-operated institutions: (a) those that provide services to persons with mental retardation and developmental disabilities exclusively and (b) those that provide services to persons with mental illness primarily but who also have mental retardation.

Nonstate-supported institutions.   Fully staffed, privately (or local government) operated residential facilities to provide services to sixteen or more people with mental retardation and developmental disabilities.

Nursing homes.   Large group facilities offering medical, nursing, and personal care to persons with and without mental retardation.

PERSONAL SATISFACTION

Why do so many people without mental retardation try so desperately to distinguish themselves from others when persons with retardation try so hard to be like everyone else? This phenomenon has two different interpretations. In 1967, Edgerton used the phrase "cloak of competence" to describe the lives of fifty-three persons recently released from institutions who, he believed, attempted to cloak themselves in an air of normalcy. He was referring to their efforts to assume roles, behaviors, and life stories that essentially denied to themselves and others the reality of the label and previous years in an institution. In contrast to this is the more recent trend toward self-affirmation and self-determination in which adults with disabilities acknowledge their limitations but fail to let them stand in the way of optimum daily living.

While some see personal satisfaction as synonymous with overall quality of life, others see the two constructs as somewhat different (e.g., Edgerton, 1990; Heal, Borthwick-Duffy, & Saunders, 1996; Stark & Goldsbury, 1990). A major point of difference in the positions is the amount of control people have over the parts of their lives that bring them satisfaction. Without getting caught up in the philosophical nature of the debate, adults with mental retardation are indeed entitled to a life that is both satisfying and of the highest quality possible. Whether or not one's life in the community meets these criteria is up to the individual. More difficult, perhaps, is their proficiency in keeping society's mores and standards from inappropriately affecting their own sense of self-worth and self-determination.

The terms used by members of society to define adulthood—*independence* and *productivity*—and the roles adults are expected to assume (worker, partner, parent, household manager, etc.) contrast sharply with the images often evoked by the term *mental retardation*. In fact, the expression "adults with mental retardation" often seems contradictory to many people who do not consider adults with mental retardation to be adults at all. Instead they may view them as childlike, dependent, and unable to make the necessary decisions. They are not children; they are adults attempting to establish themselves in their own communities in the best way possible. If having a job, meaningful relationships, a home, and personal possessions are the hallmarks of adulthood and normalcy, then many if not most adults with mental retardation living in the community have very likely achieved both.

Most adults with mental retardation want very much to be part of a system that is often hesitant to welcome them. Whether it is more accurate to see these adults resisting exposure for who they are, or as simply not considering themselves mentally retarded, it is safe to say that the label of mental retardation is not a comfortable one. The development of a positive sense of self is a lifelong endeavor for adults without mental retardation; why should it be any different for adults with mental retardation? The answer is quite simple: For adults with mental retardation, the stakes are higher and the cards are often stacked against them.

COMMUNITY ACCEPTANCE

Few things are more important to the success of the community adjustment process than the goodwill, acceptance, and support of the public. Known simply as **community acceptance,** the public's knowledge and attitudes are key components in the psychological health and well-being of the environment in which persons with mental retardation live. Zoning laws, program proposals, and mandates of elected officials are essential and formal means of acceptance. Less formal but equally important are the subtle, day-to-day gestures of acceptance and support put forth by one's neighbors each day.

Although the public in general and communities in particular support the idea of community acceptance, there are substantial barriers yet to overcome. It is now coming to light that the public's understanding of mental retardation is deeply rooted in the structure of society. The roles and status people with mental retardation are allowed to achieve are tied firmly to the extent to which people in the community believe the new members are different from themselves (e.g., appearances, behaviors, values) (Calvez, 1993; J. M. Quinn, Sherman, Sheldon, L. M. Quinn, & Harchik, 1992). Simply stated, the more "normal" people appear, the more rights, privileges, and autonomy they are afforded in day-to-day living. Cnaan, Adler, and Ramot (1986) offer a New Jersey Department of Health study in which 50 percent of all planned community residential settings in that state were not opened due to community resistance. Specific fears have ranged from a decrease in property values to concerns for the health and well-being of neighborhood children (Lubin, Schwartz, Zigmond, & Janicki, 1982; C. S. Ryan & Coyne, 1985).

Fortunately, fears and reactions such as those just mentioned can generally be changed or averted altogether. Most people view those with mental retardation as unable to live independently and in need of close and constant supervision. These low expectations and the fears associated with them often dissipate when individuals get to know persons with mental retardation and recognize their abilities and potential. Seltzer (1984) found that efforts to educate the public about mental retardation and group homes correlated positively with community opposition and that "opposition is less likely when the community becomes aware either after the residence begins operations or more than 6 months before it opens" (p. 7). The implication of these findings is that it might be better to adopt a low-profile entry strategy rather than a high-profile one when establishing a community residential setting.

To facilitate acceptance of persons with mental retardation and their community residential facilities, professionals must address the need for public education. Efforts must be made to inform the public about the nature, causes, and implications of mental retardation and even how to respond to people with mental retardation. These educational efforts must provide opportunities for interaction that are both positive and progressive. The deinstitutionalization project of New York state serves as a model of comprehensive community education and involvement. Public media reports providing information on the needs and nature of mental retardation, task forces comprising community members who locate appropriate group home sites, and speakers' bureaus to address community concerns form the basis of this campaign to obtain community support. Not surprisingly, evidence in the literature suggests that positive outcomes are likely when planned and cooperative opportunities are created.

Readers are referred to Hayden and Abery's (1994) book linking current research concerning outcomes and supports for persons with mental retardation to particular and pressing challenges inherent in our present service delivery system.

NEED FOR SUPPORT SERVICES

All adults require services for community living. Whether working, shopping, banking, or pursuing recreational pastimes, very few people are able to live successfully without the services and supports of others in the community. Some adults, like those with mental retardation, require more support services than others, services that are specific, costly, and critical to the community living status of the person requesting the services.

Several studies have been conducted to determine the service needs of persons with mental retardation living in the community. In their review of research on supports required by residents of foster homes, group homes, and institutions, Ittenbach, Larson et al. (1993) found medical services, social and recreational services, case management services, and income assistance to be the major support services needed for daily living (see Table 11.2). Of the 13,000 persons who participated in the *National Consumer Survey* (Temple University Developmental Disabilities Center, 1990), well over half reported needing recreational and leisure time activities, and another 50 percent reported needing transportation to access these services. In the areas of economic and employment integration, 55 percent of all respondents reported a need in income assistance, and 28 percent required vocational and other employment-related services. Thirty-four percent reported needing a friend, companion, or advocate to assist with the adjustment process.

If full participation in all aspects of community living is the goal of the community adjustment process, then full access to community supports should be a requisite to residential placement. Such is not always the case. Communities vary in their services available and services rendered. Complicating the person–environment match further are the unique needs of the person, the family, and the community, all of which must be considered when planning and seeking support services.

ISSUES RELATED TO COMMUNITY LIVING

Frustration, puzzlement, jubilation, and boredom are many of the feelings felt by adults with mental retardation as they venture out into community life. These feelings, and others like them, are a very typical part of everyday living for adults with and without mental retardation. Adequate resolution of these feelings and the predicaments that bring them about are the testing grounds for continued adult development. Following is a brief discussion of several key issues affecting the lives of adults with mental retardation today.

SEXUALITY

Sexual development and sexual activity may comprise the most controversial issues pertaining to adults with mental retardation. Although the sexual de-

TABLE 11.2

Support Services Needed and Used by Persons with Mental Retardation

Types of Support	Supports Needed[a]	Supports Used in	
		Small Communities[b]	Public Institutions[c]
Financial			
Health Insurance	46		
Income Assistance	55		
Payment or Provision of Medical Equipment/Supplies	37		
Payment or Provision of Medication	52		
Medical			
Dentist	66	95	96
Medical Specialists		49	
Nurse	12	38	
Nutritional/Dietician		19	
Occupational Therapist	32	15	16
Physical Therapist	33	20	19
Physician	67	99	100
Psychologist		32	
Professional Counselor	24	10	15
Speech/Communication	40	33	17
Other			
Advocacy	34		5
Social/Recreational	55		35
Social Worker/Case Manager	60	62	
Transportation	50	62	16

Note. All values reported here are percentages. Small community facilities housed 1 to 6 persons with mental retardation. National Consumer Survey results include responses identified by 30% or more of the respondents. The absence of a value in any category means that the use of this type of support was not evaluated in the study. [a]N = 13,075, Temple University Developmental Disabilities Center, 1990; [b]N = 336, B. K. Hill et al. 1989; [c]N = 997, B. K. Hill, Lakin, Sigford, Hauber, & Bruininks, 1982.

velopment of persons with mental retardation is, for the most part, no different from that of persons without mental retardation, many misconceptions remain. Parents, peers, and professionals continue to hold on to a number of misconceptions ranging from a lack of interest in sex on the part of the person with mental retardation to a fear that they will reproduce "their kind."

For many, the movement toward less restrictive living arrangements brings with it a number of opportunities not previously encountered in more restrictive settings. Many professionals argue that sexual development and sexual activity are a normal part of daily living and that the right to sexual expression should not be prohibited. Others disagree, citing a number of unfortunate and even life-threatening consequences of sexual activity as possible outcomes. Unwanted pregnancies and sexually transmitted diseases are examples of such consequences (Monat-Hallar, 1992).

A number of factors make the right to socially appropriate sexual activity and sexual expression a bit more difficult. These include the heightened supervision and supports in comparison with individuals without mental retardation; lack of accurate information typically provided by service providers about sexual development and functioning; and fewer socialization opportunities in which to try out new behaviors, roles, and expectations. Increased independence and current patterns of social interaction now evidenced in the community necessitate, in practical terms, that the issue of sexuality no longer be ignored (Sundram & Stavis, 1994).

LIFELONG LEARNING

Continuing education, whether formal or informal, is receiving growing emphasis as a means of achieving professional advancement, recreational outlets, and personal enrichment for persons with and without mental retardation. Institutions of higher learning (e.g., junior colleges, colleges, universities) have begun offering credit and noncredit courses to the general public to promote and further stimulate interest in continued educational development. Continued lifelong learning is essential for people to reach maximum levels of independence and to adapt to an ever changing world. Consequently, lifelong learning is a logical endeavor for adults with mental retardation to undertake.

Instruction may occur in a number of different settings. Often, it takes place at the employment site or training center. The place of residence can also provide nontraditional educational opportunities; educational programs are often part of the weekly schedules of many if not most group homes. Another setting sometimes used for continuing education for adults with mental retardation is the community college. McAfee and Sheeler (1987) found that one third of the community colleges surveyed had students with mild mental retardation on their campuses. Some colleges and universities have established programs for adults with mental retardation, while others meet the needs of this group by providing counseling, remedial coursework, and other supplemental services. Adult education programs for students with mental retardation, specifically, have also been established. Many of them follow programs developed at the Metro College for Living in Denver, Colorado, and the Night College in Austin, Texas. Although most programs are still coordinated and funded by special services, the impetus for their adoption by regular continuing education facilities is rapidly growing.

In addition to the information provided, these colleges often furnish meaningful leisure time activity for adults with mental retardation. Courses offered through the University of Virginia's Night College emphasize daily living skills and functional academics (see Table 11.3). They also provide opportunities for socialization not routinely found through other secondary and postsecondary training programs for adults with mental retar-

TABLE 11.3
Course Offerings: Night College, Charlottesville, Virginia

I. Communication	**IV. Community Education**
Talk and Say a Lot	Riding the City Bus
Keep On Talking	How to Find and Keep a Job
Community Checklist	Know Your Community I
For Your Own Writing	Know Your Community II
Using the Telephone	Living on Your Own
The Communication Workshop	First Aid and Home Safety
II. Money and Money Management	Driver's Education
Money Skills Assessment	What's Cooking: The Basics in
Simple Money	Good Eating
Money I	**V. Leisure Time**
Money II	Fun in Your Free Time
Using Your Money	Bicycle Safety
Community Checklist	Swimming and Water Safety
Budgeting	Art and Nature
Opening a Checking Account	Photography
III. Sex Education, Hygiene, and Personal Adjustment	
Looking Good	
You and Others I	
You and Others II	
Understanding Yourself	

dation. Programs such as the College for Living and Night College programs have broadened the opportunities for these adults to expand their behavioral repertoires and to participate in activities that foster dignity, responsibility, and contributions to others. They are a source of pride for the participants and also provide firsthand experiences for persons interested in pursuing careers in the human services field. Because they use regular college campuses and community resources, they also help educate those without mental retardation about the skills and abilities of those with mental retardation.

ADVOCACY

Advocacy is the formal representation of one's interests in an effort to bring about changes in the broader social order. For persons with mental retardation, that means the elimination of barriers to full community living and inclusion. The true spirit of advocacy, however, extends well beyond simple legal rights to include the more basic rights of autonomy, independence, and self-determination. Further, it also includes such things as the freedom to live and move in the least restrictive environment, to gainful and productive employment, and to marry and have a family (Schalock & Kiernan, 1990, p. 163). Over the past several decades, the advocacy movement has become a very popular and potent consumer force.

TABLE 11.4
Types of Advocacy

Type	Advocate	Purpose
Systems (corporate) advocacy	An independent collective of citizens	Represent the rights and interests of groups of people with similar needs Pursue human service system quality and progressive change
Legal advocacy	Attorneys-at-law	Represent individuals or groups of individuals in the litigation or legal negotiation process
Self-advocacy	Individuals whose rights are at risk of being violated or diminished	Represent one's own rights and interests; speak on one's own behalf
Citizen advocacy	A mature, competent, volunteer citizen	Represent, as if they were his or her own, the rights and interests of another citizen

Despite the fact that most adults with mental retardation find mere survival sufficiently complex, many communities are still raising legal and social obstacles to the notion of full community living. Consequently, persons with mental retardation continue to be represented by many local, state, and national advocacy organizations. The President's Committee on Mental Retardation, the Council for Exceptional Children, the Association for Persons with Severe Handicaps, and the ARC (formerly known as the Association for Retarded Citizens), are examples of such organizations. Additionally, legislation such as the Vocational Rehabilitation Act, the Developmental Disabilities and Bill of Rights Act, and the Americans with Disabilities Act have helped tremendously. But it is only through the patience and persistence of persons with mental retardation, their parents, professionals, and friends of persons with mental retardation that community initiatives, formal advocacy organizations, and recent legislation have grown from simple ideas into participatory reality.

At a less formal level, advocates have helped by evaluating the availability and appropriateness of services at the local or community level and then serving as catalysts for change. Friends, relatives, and interested others have assisted with such things as helping people with mental retardation get jobs, stay in school, negotiate public transportation, and move about one's environment in a humane, respectful way. More important, advocates have also helped by providing companionship to individuals who often have few friends. The role of advocates as models of acceptance cannot be underestimated and cannot be replaced by paid service delivery personnel.

See Chapter 1 for personal perspectives on advocacy.

Several types of advocacy now exist (see Table 11.4). The third type, self-advocacy, is a relatively new and highly effective movement that is increasing in popularity nationwide. One excellent example of an organized effort of self-advocacy is People First, a movement in which individuals with mental retardation have organized themselves at the local, state, and national levels to identify common needs and develop lobbying power. Systems advocacy is another type of advocacy in which a group of individuals with and without mental retardation forms to better serve the needs of persons with mental retardation. ARC is one such example. Though a relatively new social movement, advocacy has been heralded as a major force that can and will ensure success for persons with mental retardation in the coming years.

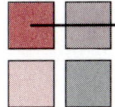

SUMMARY

TRANSITION FROM SCHOOL TO COMMUNITY LIVING

- Adjustment to community living is a complex and multiply determined concept.
- Results obtained from follow-up studies have revealed certain common themes: Differences in the adjustment capability of persons with mental retardation exist just as they do for persons without mental retardation; certain factors are crucial to the adjustment process; and likelihood for success in the community is shaped by many factors such as the characteristics of the person, the characteristics of the environment, and the interaction of the two.

ADULT DEVELOPMENT

- Young adults with mental retardation enter the adult world with many of the same expectations as young adults without mental retardation.
- Adjusting to a life with aging parents, finding a niche in the local community, and finding new and enjoyable recreational/leisure activities are hallmarks of the middle adult years.
- Establishing and accepting new family roles, lowered social expectations, and adjusting to continued limitations of the aging process are characteristics of the later adult years.

ADJUSTING TO LIFE IN THE COMMUNITY

- Adults with mental retardation generally have less extensive social networks than adults without mental retardation.
- Economic integration depends on the degree to which adults with mental retardation experience the right to make decisions as to how their money is earned and spent.
- Nonemployment, unpaid employment, and paid employment are three general categories of employment options one must consider when evaluating a person's economic integration.

- According to the *National Consumer Survey* (Temple University, 1990), one in three persons with mental retardation in the United States surveyed reported a need in the area of recreational/leisure integration activities.
- Residential living options for persons with mental retardation range from generic, small-group foster homes to public and private large-group institutions.
- The development of a positive sense of self is a lifelong process; for adults with mental retardation, however, the stakes are often higher and the cards are usually stacked against them.
- For full community acceptance of persons and residences of persons with mental retardation, efforts must be made to inform the public about the nature, causes, and implications of mental retardation.
- Adults with mental retardation are similar to other adults in that they require support services for daily living, and they are different from others in the sense that their supports are generally specific, costly, and critical to the community living status of the person requesting the services.

ISSUES RELATED TO COMMUNITY LIVING

- Sexual development and sexual activity may comprise the most controversial issues pertaining to the lives of adults with mental retardation.
- Formal educational opportunities at the postsecondary levels broaden opportunities by expanding individuals' behavioral repertoires and by allowing access to activities that foster dignity, responsibility, and contributions to others.
- Over the past several decades, the advocacy movement has become a popular and very potent consumer force.

PART **4**

Continuing Concerns

CHAPTER 12

Family Considerations

*After reading this chapter,
the student should be able to:*

- Identify and describe several different models of family functioning.
- Discuss the major forces influencing family functioning.
- Identify and describe many of the factors influencing relationships between families and practicing professionals.
- Discuss key issues faced by families during daily living.

Key Terms

centrifugal forces
centripetal forces

family
family support services

natural homes
wraparound services

E veryone is a member of a family, whether biological or social, organizational or spiritual, permanent or temporary; everyone has a family of one sort or another. For most people, however, the concept of **family** implies a combination of immediate and distant relatives who, through birth, adoption, or marriage, come to live together for extended periods of time. Goldenberg and Goldenberg (1996) have maintained that these naturally occurring units have their own rules, roles, and methods of communication; they maintain their membership through good times and bad by such factors as affection, loyalty, and concern for one another. The family, then, represents the most basic and critical unit of a culture, the one with the strongest and most enduring influences.

Several years ago, the traditional family unit consisted of a mother, father, and two or more children; however, the typical American family of the 1950s now represents more of an ideal than a reality. Despite a population that has increased by 39 percent from 1970 (53 million families) to 1994 (to 73.5 million families), the size of the average family has fallen approximately 11 percent, from an average of 3.6 persons in 1970 to 3.2 persons in 1994. Like families in other countries throughout the world, an increasing number of American children are growing up in single-parent households or no households at all (see Figure 12.1). For example, the number of families headed by single men and single women has more than doubled in the past twenty-five years, from 1.3 million to 3.2 million headed by men, and from 5.8 million to 13.6 million headed by women (Bureau of the Census, 1995). A divorce rate that has also doubled in the same period is one explanation.

While it may come as no surprise that children raised in a one-parent household receive less "parental attention, affection, and supervision than children raised in two-parent households," children raised in one-parent households have also been found to be at greater risk for accidents (20 to 30 percent), grade retention (40 to 75 percent), and expulsion from school (70 percent) (Family Research Council, 1992, p. 29). Based on data for the last three decades, there is no reason to expect these trends to change anytime soon. The range of children's living accommodations goes well beyond what it was only a few decades ago. Extended families, step-families, common-law families, communal families, serial families, or some combination thereof may be the only reference point a child has (see Table 12.1). These new types of living arrangements often introduce their own unique sets of

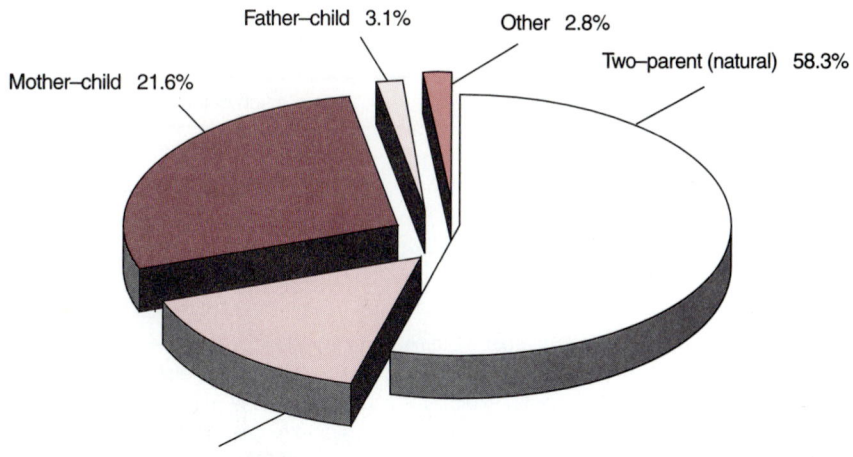

Father–child 3.1%   Other 2.8%

Mother–child 21.6%   Two–parent (natural) 58.3%

Two–parent (step) 14.2%

FIGURE 12.1

Living Arrangements of Children by Parents and Type of Family, 1990

Source: Family Research Council. (1992). *Free to be family: Helping mothers and fathers meet the needs of the next generation of American children.* Washington, DC: Author, based on data taken from U.S. Bureau of the Census, *Current Population Reports,* Series P-23, unpublished data. Reprinted with permission.

problems, everything from blatant discrimination to various social stigma (Edwards, 1995).

Understanding the factors that influence the development of persons with mental retardation requires that one understand the family environment, the dynamics of that environment, and the special needs of families of persons with mental retardation. Unlike other chapters in this book that focus on such matters as developmental periods, etiology, or legal issues, this chapter focuses on the family: the organization of families, the dynamics of family life, and the issues faced by families of persons with mental retardation. What follows is not a discussion of a storybook family, free from the stressors and problems of everyday living. Instead, the family is presented for what it is, a complex, dynamic, yet highly interdependent group of persons attempting to live, love, and work together.

ORGANIZATION OF THE FAMILY

Families may be organized along many different dimensions. This section offers a brief discussion of three such dimensions: family models, family development, and the family personality.

TABLE 12.1

Common Variations in Family Structure and Organization

Family type	Composition of family unit
Nuclear family	Husband, wife, children
Extended family	Nuclear family plus grandparents, uncles, aunts, and so on
Blended family	Husband, wife, plus children from previous marriage(s)
Common-law family	Man, woman, and possibly children living together as a family, although the former two have not gone through a formal legal marriage ceremony
Single-parent family	Household led by one parent (man or woman) possibly due to divorce, death, desertion, or never having married
Commune family	Men, women, and children living together, sharing rights and responsibilities, and collectively owning and/or using property, sometimes abandoning traditional monogamous marriages
Serial family	Man or woman has a succession of marriages, thus acquiring several spouses and different families over a lifetime, but one nuclear family at at time
Composite family	A form of polygamous marriage in which two or more nuclear families share a common husband (polygyny) or wife (polyandry), the former being more prevalent
Cohabitation	A more or less permanent relationship between two unmarried persons of the opposite sex who share a nonlegally binding living arrangement
Gay couples	Couples of the same gender who develop and maintain a homosexual relationship

Source: From *Family Therapy: An Overview*, 2nd Ed., p. 13, by I. Goldenberg and H. Goldenberg. Copyright © 1985 by Wadsworth, Inc. Reprinted with permission from Brooks/Cole Publishing Company, Pacific Grove, CA 93950.

FAMILY MODELS

The family represents the simplest yet oldest social unit of humankind. Whereas social scientists were once interested only in individuals, today they are interested in understanding people in general—large groups, small groups, and all groups in between. The family is one such example. Since the late 1960s, however, family psychology has been investigated with the same vigor as other, related subdisciplines of the behavioral sciences (Zigler, 1985). Consequently, and in light of the contributions of researchers from seemingly disparate disciplines, models have been developed that provide a framework for understanding the makeup of the family in much greater detail. The models that have been proposed borrow heavily from other disciplines and differ markedly from the ideal image of the American family of the 1950s. A brief discussion of three such models follows.

The family paradigms model of Reiss (1981) is based on a sociological framework focusing on the interactions of family members. This model classifies families into one of three different types based on their interpretation of and responses to events around them. Environmentally sensitive families comprise the first group and consist of persons who see their life events as both knowable and orderly; all family members are expected to contribute to the sharing of ideas and efforts of orderly family functioning. Interpersonally distant families consist primarily of detached family members, loners, and those for whom independence is critically important. Consequently, these family members put very little emphasis on interactions with others in the family. Consensus-sensitive families constitute the third group and are those families whose need for conformance and family order is so strong as to isolate them from the rest of society. Dissension is not tolerated, especially when it comes from outside the family, as family members quickly surrender their own ideas for what they believe to be the good of the family.

Beavers and Hampson (1993) offer an adaptability model that includes concepts typically used in the physical sciences. For example, families and family functioning may be placed on a grid in which one continuum ranges from severely dysfunctional to optimal, and the other continuum from centripetal to centrifugal (Figure 12.2). Those at the healthy end of the spectrum are more likely to be open, adaptable, and goal-oriented, while the severely dysfunctional families are most likely to be rigid, have poor communication patterns, use ineffective coping strategies, and be inappropriately content with their existing family structure. Beavers and Hampson's connection with the physical sciences comes in this major tenet, entropy, or the degree to which families tend toward disorder. **Centripetal forces** are those that draw a family together, while **centrifugal forces** are those that push a family apart. The ability to balance out the attractive (centripetal) and repelling (centrifugal) forces is a major determinant of healthy family functioning. As Figure 12.2 illustrates, the healthy family is one in which choices are respected and members are allowed to move, within limits, into and out of the family unit as life events dictate.

Biologically based models may take several different approaches. In the narrowest perspective, one may cite the continuation of the species as the sole reason for a family's existence. Within a broader perspective, people are considered to be biological systems that consist of and contribute to other, related biological systems. Those who take a still broader perspective may conceptualize families in terms of energy transformation and interactive elements, or they may define the family in terms of its evolutionary structure and view it as a specific subsystem moving toward equilibrium (balance) in light of internal and external forces. D. R. Miller and Sobelman (1985) contend that while some aspects of the family can indeed be reduced to chemical and biochemical components, a much broader definition is required to meet the needs of practicing professionals today.

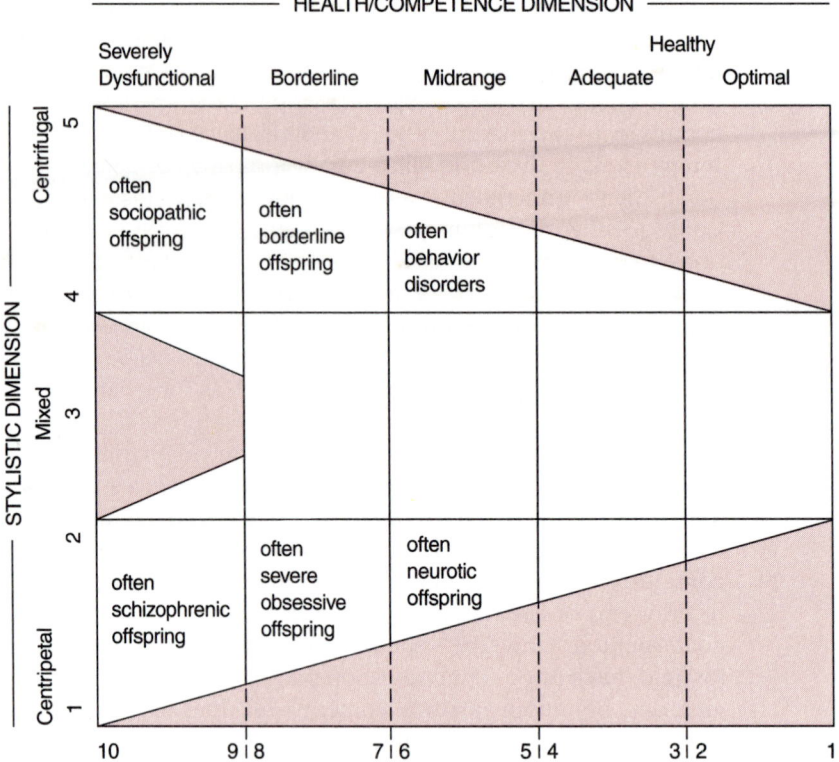

Health/Competence Dimensions

Severely Dysfunctional. Poor boundaries, confused communication, lack of shared attentional focus, stereotyped family process, despair, cynicism, [and/or] denial of ambivalence.

Borderline. Shifting from chaotic to tyrannical control efforts, boundaries fluctuate from poor to rigid, distancing depression, [and/or] outbursts of rage.

Midrange. Relatively clear communication, constant effort at control, "loving means controlling," distancing, anger, anxiety, or depression, [and/or] ambivalence handled by repression.

Adequate. Relatively clear boundaries, negotiating but with pain, ambivalence reluctantly recognized, some periods of warmth and sharing interspersed with control struggles.

Optimal. Capable negotiation, individual choice and ambivalence respected, warmth, intimacy, [and/or] humor.

FIGURE 12.2
Beavers and Hampson's Model of Family Functioning

Source: From "Measuring Family Competence" by W. R. Beavers and R. B. Hampson in *Normal Family Processes* (2nd ed., p. 78) edited by F. Walsh, 1993, New York: Guilford. Copyright 1993 by Guilford Press. Adapted by permission.

FAMILY DEVELOPMENT

Families are not referred to as "units" for lack of a better word. They are a collection of related, interdependent people with a shared sense of purpose, responsibility, and history. Their actions, behaviors, wishes, and intentions are often less a product of their own creation than of a desire to meet the needs of those around them. Their actions and interactions generally transcend any single member of the unit. For the individual family members to grow and develop, so must the family.

The notion that families develop along predictable lines is not a new one. In fact, some say that family psychology actually represents an elaboration of traditional developmental psychology; that is, the development of the individual. Duvall and Miller (1985) have divided the family life cycle into eight stages, beginning with married couples without children and ending with the retirement or death of both spouses. In between are the stages of families with infants, young children, adolescents, young adults, and middle adults (empty-nest years). Goldenberg and Goldenberg (1996) have identified a number of tasks families are expected to meet in their cycle of development. Separation from their families of origin, new behavioral patterns, acquisition of new friends, and the resolution of unmet needs at each of the respective stages are examples of stage-related tasks that must be addressed. For E. A. Carter and McGoldrick (1989), the family system is an intergenerational unit with three to four primary cohorts that move through life together: children, adults, and older adults. Much of Carter and McGoldrick's model is based on simple common sense, with the addition of the notion that the actions of people of each generation profoundly affect the other two generations, thereby creating and changing the actual course of development for each succeeding generation.

Just as most major theories of human development have failed to account adequately for nonnormative patterns of development for persons with disabilities, so too have most theories of family development. The literature is replete with studies addressing stressful life events, transition issues, and quality of life issues at various stages of normative patterns of family development; yet, the effect of persons with mental retardation on the family's growth and development is still far from certain. For example, whereas family care for a person with mental retardation terminated relatively early in life only a few decades ago, life expectancies are now commensurate with the population as a whole (Eyman & Borthwick-Duffy, 1994), making planning for the later years a necessity for many. This added concern may well add stress to families in ways unforeseen just a few years ago.

THE FAMILY PERSONALITY

As a family continues its journey through its life cycle, its members experience many alternating periods of stability, change, and readjustment. For most families, that means growth, or movement toward a more flexible, integrated, adaptable family unit. Not surprisingly, a family's pattern

Activities that are fun encourage bonding among family members.

of preferred responses to intra- and interfamilial events, hereafter referred to as its *personality*, is considered to be both a cause and a consequence of its development (Swenson, 1985). That is, families that are actively trying to develop are likely to find many of the rewards necessary for continued and adaptive family functioning; those that are not actively trying to develop are likely to be frustrated by their efforts to adjust to the stressors of life and to resort to familiar but less successful approaches to family functioning.

The ability to respond effectively to environmental challenges depends to a large extent on the integrity of a family's personality. A family's ability to organize itself, to solve problems, and to grow and change in light of challenges faced, positive as well as negative, all depend upon the family's level of health and well-being. At the heart of these tendencies are what many researchers refer to as *coping ability,* a family's collection of overt and covert strategies for responding to life's difficulties (Wills, Blechman, & McNamara, 1996).

Because most children enter a family through birth or adoption, and have little in the way of pre-established notions of family functioning, the parents generally set the tone for family functioning. As Hetherington and Blechman (1996) have suggested, there is no easy way of identifying which families are at greatest risk, how to reduce the risk of overwhelming stressors, or how to return to optimum levels of functioning once their development is hindered. What is considered healthy and adaptive in one environment may be considered dysfunctional and maladaptive in another. Adaptive behaviors are highly context-specific. For example, behaviors needed to survive in a war-torn country would be inappropriate in the American suburbs. Equally, an adolescent growing up in a serial family environment on "crack-street" in urban America may have few positive family role models from which to learn. When daily promises from unrelenting others include alluring alternatives to a particular lifestyle, children and youth can hardly be blamed for adopting the prevailing mores of a particular neighborhood, however negative. For persons with mental retardation, the analogies are equally justified.

FAMILY FUNCTIONING

Hearing for the first time that a child has a disability is upsetting for the entire family. Finding out that the disability is mental retardation is even more difficult. How a family actually responds to the subsequent challenges varies from family to family. Reaction to the news that a child has a disability, the long-term impact on family dynamics, and the presence of internal and external supports are three factors that are important to continued family development.

FAMILY REACTIONS

For many, the revelation that a child has a disability occurs later in childhood. Some parents respond to the news with a sense of relief that their concerns about the child were well founded, that the disability has a name, a predictable course of development, and the possibility of well-established treatments, but these parents are the exception. More typically, parents of children with mental retardation respond with shock, disbelief, or an overwhelming sense of loss (L. E. Powers, 1992). Foster and Berger (1985) have reported that the news is initially so devastating that it strikes at the heart of a family's value system, disrupting its equilibrium and causing the family unit to freeze in its developmental cycle. Batshaw, Perret, and Trachtenberg (1992) have outlined a number of steps that they believe fairly represent the stages families of children with mental retardation go through in their acceptance of the disability. A brief discussion of each of the five stages follows.

Denial

It is quite common for parents and family members to resist the notion that their loved one is different from others. Refusal to accept the new information may be particularly acute when it pertains to a child who looks normal, is somewhat shy or reserved in temperament, and is an only or eldest child. The greater the severity, the earlier the diagnosis, the more arduous the denial. Parents (or grandparents) who lack experience with children of similar age to their own child, especially those without a disability, may be particularly resistant to the information.

A Unique Parental Perspective

We who work with people who are retarded are always inspired by parents who do things that make their child a significant part of the family. It is typical for proud new parents to send out birth announcements of their new family member. Usually, these announcements are full of excitement and satisfaction. But how do you tell people that your newborn is retarded? Most of the time, this information is carefully disguised or withheld. To be sure, this is not an easy task, nor one that parents enjoy doing.

Sometimes interesting items come to our attention and we do not know from where they came or who gave them to us; the following material falls into this category. It is a real birth announcement, but its authors are unknown. It demonstrates one of the most positive parental attitudes we have seen. We have omitted the child's name, date, and time of birth because it is not necessary; the important message is contained in the parents' words. This child who is retarded is lucky to be introduced into family like this one.

We invite you to rejoice with us
at the birth of our daughter

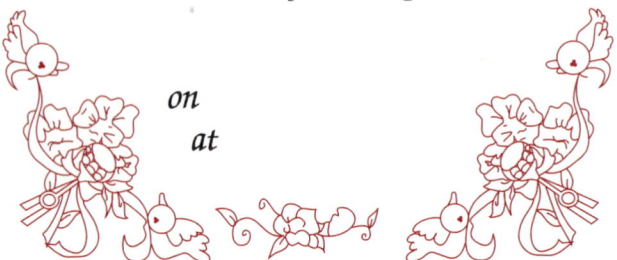

on

at

It is our belief as Latter-day Saints that we all lived a pre-earth life with our Heavenly Father. Certain valiant spirits were selected at that time for special missions during an earth life. One of these spirits has been chosen for our family. Our daughter is a child with Down Syndrome. We feel privileged to be entrusted with the care of this special child, who will return to her Heavenly Father at the end of her earth life and resume, for all eternity, her valiant status with her body and intellect completely restored.

Depression

Following an awareness that the threat of a disability is real and that the perceptions of qualified service providers (e.g., teachers, physicians, psychologists) have a basis in fact, family members often feel a weakening of their spirit, a sense of loss or even impending doom—and that the disability is greater than their resolve to overcome it. A general lack of interest in traditional social activities, routine health care, and normal daily activities are some of the many indicators of a brief depressive episode.

Anger and Guilt

The reader is referred to Rando's (1993) *Treatment of Complicated Mourning* text for a more complete discussion of the conditions and influences of loss, grief, and mourning.

Once the depression subsides and the family realizes that the disability is not likely to overwhelm them, their energy level starts to rise, and they begin to respond to the new and unfamiliar situation. Along with the increase in energy and unfamiliar feelings, however, comes a desire to fight back, to challenge the disability and challenge those they may consider to be responsible. Lack of knowledge about the disability and its causative factors often leads family members to strike out at unsuspecting others (e.g., self, friends, relatives, teachers, other professionals).

Bargaining

When parents realize that they, too, have a role to play in the course of the disability, they often set out in search of mitigating factors that will allow them to regain some control in their fight to overcome the disability. In an era of medical miracles, it is not uncommon for families to begin doctor-shopping, to search endlessly for someone or something that can diminish or even cure the child of the disability. Concessionary statements and proposals to health professionals, other relatives, and perhaps even to one's creator are not unusual avenues of recourse for families in this stage of resolution.

Acceptance

Accepting the reality of a situation that is unwanted and unpleasant remains an extremely difficult task. Once the family has accepted the permanence of the disability and found that its values and structures have remained relatively intact, they are free to continue their family functioning, growing and developing as a new family unit, living, loving, and learning to the fullest extent possible.

Although the stages presented here offer a useful schema for service providers who routinely work with families of persons with mental retardation, the stages are only a framework for better understanding the *process* of acceptance. Several caveats are in order. First, little empirical work has been done to verify the actual presence or invariant nature of these stages. Second, not all families proceed through the sequence at the same rate or with the same degree of success. Many never achieve full acceptance of the disability; many simply do not want to. Finally, the sense of loss experienced by the family is not for the child with the disability; rather, it is for the idealized "original" child, the one without the disability (L. E. Powers, 1992). Perhaps a comment by a mother of a child with Down syndrome offers a fitting perspective:

> The pain returns occasionally, but once most parents come to terms with their child's disability, they take the first step in the process of putting their lives back in their own control. Each time the pain brings on the familiar feelings of sadness, fear, and doubt, we as parents draw on our most potent reserves, the love we feel for our child. (Moeller, 1986, p. 151)

FAMILY DYNAMICS

Interpersonal relationships comprise the cornerstone of a family's existence. Inquiries into family relationships have generally taken one of two paths, caregiver–child attachments and child–other relationships. Both are embedded in larger social networks, and both have implications for persons with mental retardation. According to Collins and Gunnar (1990), secure attachments are the norm across cultures and subcultures. Yet, there are some cultures for which this is not the case. A number of interesting patterns in family dynamics have emerged in the literature pertaining to relationships involving children and families of children with mental retardation.

Many researchers have reported only the difficulties and extreme reactions of families of children with mental retardation. Foster and Berger (1985) have reported that these are often worst-case scenarios, and, even where demands are the greatest, many adults have modified their perspectives to "derive positive meaning from the experience of rearing a handicapped child" (p. 752). A commonly reported statistic among families of children with disabilities is the rate of marital breakups (e.g., M. H. Epstein, Cullinan, Quinn, & Cumblad, 1994; Hodapp & Krasner, 1995). However, there are also studies that contradict these findings (e.g., Dorner, 1975; McAndrew, 1976). Wikler (1981) found that when socioeconomic status was taken into account, divorce rates of parents of children with disabilities were no different from those of parents of children without disabilities. Not surprisingly, the major determinant of the psychological health and well-being of the child is the psychological health and well-being of the parents (Foster & Berger, 1985). The better the relationship between parents and the better integrated the family prior to the birth or adoption of a child with a disability, the better integrated the family afterward.

The relationship between a parent and child represents a special kind of relationship. Unlike work done in the 1960s in which the prevailing attitude about influence was primarily *of* the parents *on* the children, researchers now believe that there is a reciprocity of interactions between parents and their children (S. I. Powers, 1989). Within the literature on families there remains a tendency to focus on mother–child interactions in general and mother–child interactions for very young children specifically. One such example is a study conducted by Haldy and Hanzlik (1990) in which mothers of children with Down syndrome were found to feel as confident of their child-rearing abilities as mothers of children without Down syndrome, a feeling that decreased substantially as the child grew older. This focus is not without reason, given the differences in preferred methods of involvement between parents. There seems to be little difference in the frequency of interactions between mothers and fathers, individually, and their children; there is a difference in the *types* of activities demonstrated. Mothers demonstrate more positive interactions in caretaking roles, while fathers demonstrate more positive interactions in play-related roles (Collins & Gunnar, 1990). Furthering the themes of varied but predictable patterns of parent–child interaction were two studies that supported the notion that parents of children with disabilities experience more stress than parents of children without disabilities. No significant differences were found between both groups of parents in terms of levels of stress or coping ability (Beckman, 1991; Bolger, 1992).

The physical and emotional contact of siblings throughout life represents the most critical and enduring set of relationships life has to offer. Whereas child–parent and parent–child relationships routinely span 40 to 60 years, sibling relationships may last 60 to 80 years or more and may share a number of intimate, developmentally important tasks (Cicirelli, 1994; Powell & Gallagher, 1993). The challenges experienced by the brothers and sisters of persons with mental retardation are particularly complex. At a time when young siblings are still learning about themselves and others, it is difficult to know how to interact with others considered by society to be substantially different. Foster and Berger (1985) have reported three rather prominent themes that have emerged in studies of child–sibling interactions:

- *Shaken sense of identity*. This level of awareness often raises questions such as: Am I disabled as well? Perhaps I am normal now, but can I also become disabled later on? If the disability is hereditary, will my children be disabled? Why my brother or sister and not me?

- *Increased frustration*. Children who receive disproportionately less parental time and attention than a sibling with a disability often feel overlooked or taken for granted. Siblings without disabilities are often expected to assume responsibilities for tasks that their brother or sister cannot perform.

- *Adaptability and responsibility*. Children who are raised with a sibling with a disability often learn many of the benefits of shared responsibility. The very subtle pleasures and gratifications of helping others less capable as well as tendencies toward increased levels of maturation and compassion toward those who are different represent some of the many benefits of these relationships.

A comprehensive review of research by Powell and Gallagher (1993) suggests that the extant research of siblings with disabilities has resulted in fairly predictable conclusions. A major finding is that female siblings typically take on a greater share of the caretaking role, throughout life, than male siblings. Additionally, siblings without disabilities typically take on

A RITE OF PASSAGE

Following is a brief story about one family's attempt to provide their daughter, Lesley, with a reception that marked her entry into adulthood. This particular reception, considered by her parents and family to be an important developmental milestone, parallels that of many other young adults without mental retardation. More important, perhaps, is the realization that this reception occurred at a time when movement toward community involvement and full community inclusion was only just beginning. Irrespective of her disability and the social climate of the time, Lesley was entitled to all of the benefits and trimmings that most young women long for as they enter adulthood. For Lesley's family, the process of planning and preparing for this big occasion was as important as the event itself. Following are the words of Lesley and her mother as they reflect upon that big day nearly twenty years ago.

On Lesley's twenty-second birthday, we had a party for her at Eagle Creek State Park. The state park is not far from our home, is in the middle of a large nature preserve, and gives the appearance of being far from a large metropolitan area, which it is not. Though it was indeed a birthday party, it resembled a formal reception more than an actual birthday party. The reception was held on the grounds of the state park in a reception center, a large home formerly owned by the Eli Lilly foundation, the service arm of a large pharmaceutical company in Indianapolis and donated to Eagle Creek park for such activities.

Prior to her twenty-second birthday, we decided that every girl needed and deserved to have a formal reception of her own, one that required a lot of planning and preparation. As a part of our preparation, we were sure to include all of the formalities that seem so dear to a young woman's heart such as formal invitations, special napkins with her name and the date of the reception on them, and a beautiful, many layered cake. She needed to have the excitement of selecting the colors, planning the menu, planning the guest list, shopping for the cake, etc. It was to be a day for all to remember!

At the party itself we had a buffet, presents galore, and a guest book for people to sign as they entered the reception center. Similar to parties for other young adults without mental retardation, this guest list included immediate family members, friends,

Siblings of children with mental retardation typically demonstrate increased levels of leadership and care taking than siblings of children without mental retardation.

more leadership roles within the family than would otherwise be the case, a finding that generalizes to younger as well as older siblings. Finally, difficulties in overall levels of adjustment for siblings without a disability decreased as family size, socioeconomic status, and age differences in siblings increased. The negative aspects of growing up with a brother or sister with a disability should not be overlooked (e.g., anger, anxiety, sadness), but neither should the potential benefits. Children without disabilities who are the same sex and nearly the same age as the child with a disability stand to gain more from the relationship than others of opposite sex and a greater age difference, and both benefit more than children who do not have a sibling with a disability (J. Wilson, Blacher, & Baker, 1989).

and other relatives. Parents of friends were not invited unless Lesley or the invited guest dearly wanted them. The guest list numbered about forty people. Presents were listed according to guest so that "thank you" notes could be written. In one guest's words, "Lesley had a beautiful gown on, the food was great, and the band made for a nice, festive atmosphere." Lesley is forty-one now, and we have had several birthday parties for her since that summer afternoon in 1979. None, however, has matched the joy and splendor of her twenty-second birthday.

Lesley no longer works at a sheltered workshop. Instead she works around our home and at the Eagle Creek nature center on a regular basis. When not working, we enjoy walking and hiking along the trails of Eagle Creek as a family. She helps out around the home by taking care of her chores. Because we live on a small farm west of Indianapolis, we have many animals. Lesley takes care of her ducks, cats, dogs, goose, horse, and pony. Consequently, the dividing line between her chores at home and at work is often a fine one. Away from home, Lesley visits her sister Clare in Columbus, Ohio, at least once a year. They go shopping and do all of the things two sisters normally do. Her friend, Julie, also has her over to her house for overnight trips throughout the year. They do everything that friends do such as going out to eat, shopping, attending the State Fair, as well as many other activities.

Throughout Lesley's life, I have stressed the importance of her making her own decisions. I couldn't help but notice an almost universal failing with respect to this among the other mothers of Lesley's contemporaries. Whether it is raining or snowing, hot or cold, it is up to Lesley to dress appropriately, which she does very well. In addition, she takes full responsibility for her personal hygiene such as bathing, shampooing, brushing teeth, changing clothes, etc. I do the laundry and help her change the linens on her bed. In other words, we have continued to treat her just as we would any of our other adult children. This has not always been easy, however, as she certainly understands that there are many privileges that she will never attain—and it hurts her. Our means of responding to her, her needs, and her hurts, when they arise, is to simply talk about them and remember that no one has a perfect life and that we all have to be thankful for our blessings. We accept our disappointments and go on the best we can. Lesley has faith in God and in a life hereafter, which helps her immensely.

SUPPORT SERVICES

Families of persons with mental retardation face many demanding challenges. The challenges generally persist for the life of the person with mental retardation, affect virtually all life activity areas, and add a stressful dimension to life that most people would not, under other conditions, routinely accept. In short, families are committed to a lifestyle that is far different from that of most of their peers, thereby requiring a support system that is also far different from that of their peers. To do so means that they need **family support services,** services that will allow them to live as fully and as autonomously as possible in the community.

Parents' involvement in their children's
programs is welcome.

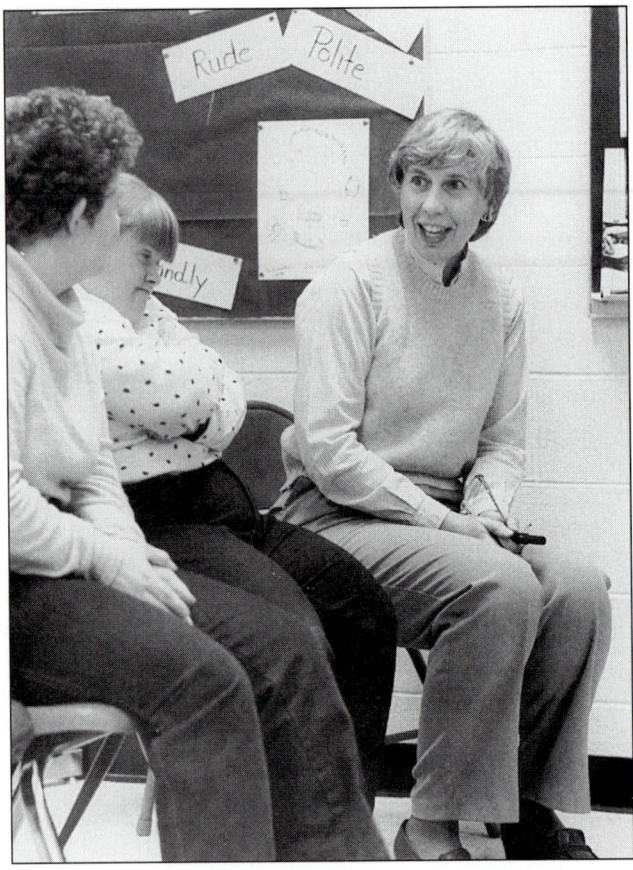

Prior to the 1980s, family support programs were largely child-based and were often housed in child-welfare agencies or organizations. The main purpose of these programs was to rescue children who had been hurt, abandoned, or neglected. Today, however, the purpose of most family support agencies is much broader in scope, is to minimize out-of-home placements, and offers to prevent problems through appropriate and timely intervention services (Cole, 1995).

Foremost among the list of natural supports needed by families is a social support system that allows the family to feel that they and their problems are valued by others (Flynt, Wood, & Scott, 1992). Acquaintances, friends, and significant others offer the family a multitude of options that are essential to offsetting the stressors that pervade their lives. Covert (1992) reports that, despite the need for social supports, many families experience a sense of isolation in their own communities; they lack an extended family with whom to share some of the burden and are often unable to rely on many of the personal connections that others without disabilities often take for granted.

Financial resources are also a major area of needed support. Despite the national trend toward deinstitutionalization and the fact that nearly 85 percent of all persons with disabilities live in their **natural homes** (homes with other family members) (Seltzer & Krauss, 1994), it seems ironic that only 1.5 percent of state dollars are earmarked for services to persons with developmental disabilities (Braddock, Hemp, Fujiura, Bachelder, & Mitchell, 1990). In addition, while state funding for family support services increased nearly 50 percent between 1988 and 1992, the number of families actually served during that same time period nearly doubled to reach an all-time high 105,500 families for the 37 states reporting such activity (Braddock, Hemp, Bachelder, & Fujiura, 1995). Given the difficulties Americans without disabilities are having with spiraling medical costs, it is not surprising that sizeable percentages (15 to 40 percent) of persons with severe disabilities report medical and equipment costs that are both excessive and burdensome (Covert, 1992). Expenditures such as a motorized wheelchair, a new van with modifications, or a computer to assist with communication can be more than an average family's budget may allow.

A third but certainly not final area of needed supports is in the area of coordinated services. The ability to coordinate efforts effectively cannot be underestimated. The presence of duplicate, redundant, or competing services can be just as frustrating as the general lack of necessary services. Consequently, the notion of *wraparound services* has evolved. The term **wraparound services** describes an organized, integrated approach to service delivery that allows for a specially designed treatment plan at a specific point in time. Similar to individualized education plans used in the schools, wraparound services result from a meeting or meetings held by a service coordinator (or case manager), treatment team, and the family. According to Karp (1996), such services allow the "service coordinators to wrap the services around children and their families rather than forcing children into existing service programs" (p. 299). Ironically, in a recent survey of desired community activities, all that families really wanted was "assistance and support that would help them function as much like other families as possible" (Covert, 1992, p. 147); in other words, they wanted the opportunity to be like every other family.

CONSULTATION WITH PROFESSIONALS

Years ago, families of children with mental retardation were encouraged to transfer the care of their child with mental retardation to the trained professionals of a state institution rather than care for them at home. Until recently, it has been argued that a professional bias against families exists and that few professionals consider family members to be anything more than the willing recipients of professional advice and services. Parents and other family members are accepting an increasing number of roles on behalf of their children with disabilities (e.g., teachers, political advocates, educational decision makers, and collaborators) (A. P. Turnbull & Turnbull, 1997). At a time when families of children without mental retardation appear to be abdicating the responsibilities of child rearing to organizations outside the home (e.g., boys/girls clubs, churches, schools), it seems ironic that families of children, adolescents, and adults with mental retardation are assuming a more prominent role in the service delivery process.

Understanding what families want in a helping relationship implies an understanding of what they do not want. They do not want to be told what is best for their child as much as they want options for care and action. Parents want to be seen as competent, capable, cooperative, and willing to pursue the right course of action once several paths have been identified. Parents want to be able to trust the professional relationship. Moeller (1986) has reported that the parents of people with disabilities are extremely vulnerable. Because of the extent to which they must rely on others for help, they often sense a loss of control in the care of their own child—and they are the ones who know the child best. Despite their need for "technical information, skills training, counseling, and support services" (Moeller, 1986, p. 155), the need for someone else to be knowledgeable as well as accepting of their child and to share the burdens as well as the joys is paramount. Consequently, many parents base their evaluation of a professional's services on the professional's emotional response to the family member, the disability, and the family's means of responding to the disability.

Since passage of the All Handicapped Children's Act of 1975 (the forerunner of the Individuals with Disabilities Education Act [IDEA]), services for children with special needs have become a well-accepted and highly utilized component of public education. More children and families of children with mental retardation are accessing services than ever before. Yet, Simpson (1990) has reported that even special educators are often uncomfortable attempting to meet the special needs of parents and family members, a finding underscored by McGrew, Gilman, and Johnson's (1989) findings in which 40 to 50 percent of the families in one school district indicated that specific priorities in their children's education were not being addressed by individualized educational plans. To help with this problem, and to give all involved a template for better understanding parent–professional relationships, Simpson (1990) has offered a model with five principal components (information exchange, partnership and advocacy training, home and community program implementation, counseling and consultation, and parent/family-coordinated service programs; Table 12.2). Within each component are a host of needs that may be addressed in many ways, each of which requires a broad-based, individualized program. Complementing the five components are five nonhierarchical levels of participation that allow for a range of options for family involvement.

B. L. Mallory (1986) has identified a number of assumptions that must be made in order for the parent–professional model to be a useful framework. The assumptions are as follows:

TABLE 12.2
A Model of Parent and Family Involvement

NEEDS				
Information exchange	Partnership and advocacy training	Home and community program implementation	Counseling and consultation	Parent/family-coordinated service programs
Diagnostic testing and evaluation feedback	Training on parent rights and responsibilities, especially under the Education For All Handicapped Children Act	Behavior management training	Support groups	Parent advocacy group
Initial informational exchanges		Home tutoring programs	Crisis intervention services	Parent advisory group
Initial and updated program descriptions	Training sessions on participating in IEP, progress report, and other conferences	Procedures for implementing specific education and training programs	Consultation for specific problems and issues	Parent and family classroom volunteers
Progress reports				Parent/family volunteer program
	Advocacy training and methods for identifying and using appropriate community and school resources		Conflict resolution	
LEVELS OF PARTICIPATION				
Recognition and Awareness	Ongoing Communication	Advocacy and Representation	Skill Development and Application	Partnership

Source: From *Conferencing Parents of Exceptional Children* (3rd ed., p. 32) by R. L. Simpson, 1996, Austin, TX: PRO-ED. Copyright 1996 by PRO-ED. Reprinted by permission.

Families of children with disabilities are more similar to other families than they are different. The disability is only one of many dimensions along which families may differ. Parents and service providers alike must operate from a non-pathological point of view when considering a family's needs. To define a family by the presence of a person with mental retardation does a grave injustice to the many other, more appropriate, defining characteristics of the family.

A longitudinal life-cycle perspective is necessary. It is not enough to consider the needs of the child, adolescent, or adult at any single point in time. Broader, long-term goals are necessary for the smooth transitioning of the person and family as they move through the life cycle.

Family members can provide valid and unique information not always available through other, formalized means. Families, better than any other single source, know the strengths and weaknesses of a person's repertoire of skills. Allowing parents and family members access to the assessment and decision-making process allows for shared responsibility, shared decision making, and a greater likelihood for success in more normative settings.

Interactions between families and community agencies are often difficult. Working within an educational system that has many decades of providing services to children with special needs is difficult enough; getting concurrence from agency personnel who have either no or limited experience with the same can be extremely difficult.

In many regions of the United States, appropriate and necessary services are already in place. Knowing that other, related services exist is only part of the mission of service agencies. Accessing the necessary services is often another hurdle that many families face. Getting agency personnel to emphasize service delivery and de-emphasize territorial limits will allow the true spirit of service delivery to emerge.

The mechanisms for designing and implementing social policies are often a barrier to service utilization. At the heart of this assumption is the need for preventative rather than remedial attention. Policies designed to respond only to the most acute needs of families of persons with disabilities unjustly penalize those with less obvious but, in the long run, equally important difficulties.

Families need the assistance of capable professionals. Professionals exist to help meet the needs of persons and families of persons with disabilities. Together, the two groups form an alliance that must be strong, resilient, and broadly based if the service delivery system is to work to the benefit of those for whom it is designed.

ISSUES IN FAMILY LIVING

Making life challenging for families of persons with mental retardation are a number of issues that families of persons without mental retardation respond to incidentally or without the same effort. This section focuses on such issues as home safety, religion, and planning for the later years.

Safety is an important issue for persons with mental retardation.

HOME SAFETY

Home safety has become an increasingly important issue for all families, particularly those of persons with mental retardation. Tymchuk, Hamada, Andron, and Anderson (1990) have stated that social service agencies and court personnel now consider that a person's ability to recognize, correct, and prevent dangerous situations from occurring in the home are major issues in custody/guardianship cases involving adults with mental retardation. Whether one lives in a foster home, group home, or natural family home, persons with and without mental retardation must always be cautious. Susceptibility to crime, accidents around the home, and an increased responsibility for oneself and others in times of emergencies are other examples of safety-related issues.

As the exodus from large public residential facilities continues, many will be leaving settings where twenty-four-hour supervision was provided and opportunities for accidents were minimized. Along with the many benefits of community living come many drawbacks. For persons with mental retardation, special care must be taken to reduce further the likelihood of accidents around the home. For example, what should a person do in case of a fire, ruptured plumbing, or a gas leak? How should a person respond

TABLE 12.3

Percent of Key Words on Product
Warning Labels at Each Reading Level

Source: From "An Analysis of the
Readability of Product Warning Labels:
Implications for Curriculum Development for
Persons with Moderate and Severe Mental
Retardation" by D. Fletcher and D. Abood,
1988, *Education and Training in Mental
Retardation, 23*(3), p. 226. Copyright 1988
by the Council for Exceptional Children.
Reprinted by permission.

Grade Level	Percent
1st	13
2nd	12
3rd	18
4th	12
5th	3
6th	24
7th	1
8th	4
9th	6
10th	2
*	5

*Not listed as core vocabulary at any grade
level (e.g., minimize, toxic, accumulate).

when an unexpected passerby knocks on the door and asks permission to
use the phone or when a member of the family suddenly becomes seriously
sick or injured? Access to hazardous household substances is another major
concern. Fletcher and Abood (1988) have reported that even among those
with mild mental retardation and a reading level of nearly fourth grade, 57
percent were unable to read important product warning labels because 42
percent of the words were at or above the sixth-grade level. Although words
such as "eyes," "milk," and "avoid" can be found on many warning labels,
so may such words as "inhale," "flammable," "discard," "inaccessible," and
"chlorine," words well beyond the reading ability of many persons with
mental retardation (Table 12.3).

RELIGION

Involvement in civic and religious activities is another area of interest for
many persons with mental retardation. While the Americans with Disabilities
Act of 1990 has mandated access to more facilities and programs than ever
before, the actual willingness of community leaders to embrace full community inclusion has been much slower to evolve. In contrast to the recent
emphasis on physical integration over the past few decades, spiritual integration has received only passing attention. This deficit exists despite a well-
accepted notion that parents frequently turn to religious organizations and
clergy for assistance in times of difficulty. According to Fewell (1986b), parents of persons with disabilities tend to look to religious leaders for support
in several key areas:

■ *Instrumental support.* Help with physical or financial supports of its members
   is a role that many religious communities willingly accept. Food, medical supplies, and money are often in short supply for the family of a person with a

severe disability. Many churches and synagogues have access to people and resources that can circumvent some of the delays typically encountered in obtaining community resources.

- *Emotional/social support*. The very strong bonds of support felt among families who have worshiped together for many years cannot be underestimated. Many clergy, elders, and long-standing church members enjoy the privilege of being considered more a family member than an outsider, yet with special skills and abilities useful in times of spiritual need.

- *Educational support*. Help in understanding how a disability occurs, how to care for a person with mental retardation, and even how to explain certain religious concepts to persons with disabilities are questions that often arise. Sunday school programs and social activities provide outlets and opportunities for normalization that are open to persons with and without disabilities and, at the same time, offer an important avenue for involvement in church life.

- *Structural support*. Accommodations to major life changes (e.g., birth, marriage, death) are another responsibility of church leaders. Many of the rituals and routines of religious activities offer church members a source of strength in difficult times. Gaining access to important religious roles and responsibilities is no more important for persons without mental retardation than it is for persons with mental retardation.

A publication sponsored by the National Organization on Disability entitled *That All May Worship: An Interfaith Welcome to People with Disabilities* (Thornburgh, 1992) is available to help church leaders with the process of spiritual integration.

If people with mental retardation are to be truly self-determined, that is, free to make their own decisions about important aspects of their lives, then spirituality offers an appropriate example. People with mental retardation are indeed active in their church communities, yet researchers have demonstrated that neither their care providers nor their clergy have well-developed strategies in place for helping foster growth and development in this all-too important area of everyday life (Riordan & Vasa, 1991; Weisner, Beizer, & Stolze, 1991).

Hoeksema (1995) has suggested that common sense can be a most helpful ally in helping others meet their religious needs without infringing on the wishes and preferences of others, particularly within large nonsectarian, public residential facilities. Simple strategies such as trying to see life from another's point of view, avoiding coercion of uninvolved others, honoring the past practices of persons living in the home, and assisting with self-advocacy and conflict resolution skills are all as useful in matters of religion as they are in other areas of daily living. If persons without mental retardation value and require spiritual support from church leaders, shouldn't persons with mental retardation be able to do to the same? The trend toward community adjustment in spiritual areas of daily living is only just beginning.

PLANNING FOR THE LATER YEARS

The graying of the American population referred to in Chapter 11 takes on a new appearance when one reduces the trend to a single family. Older adults with mental retardation represent a unique challenge for an increasing number of families today. Persons who were once strong, energetic, and responsible for family decisions frequently become less willing or less able to make the necessary decisions over time. When decisions of aging care-givers affect the life of an adult with mental retardation, another important transitional phase must be addressed—planning for the later years.

D. J. Anderson and Kloos (1992) have reported that older persons (over the age of sixty-five) with developmental disabilities represent the fastest growing group of people with disabilities (they represent approximately 12 percent of the total population of people over sixty-five). Because of im-provements in medicine, nutrition, education, and direct service delivery, persons with mental retardation, like those without mental retardation, are living longer than ever before. In most cases, that means living longer than their parents (Eyman & Borthwick-Duffy, 1994). Embedded in this new trend are new roles and expectations for virtually all family members, the parents, the siblings, and the adult offspring with mental retardation.

Parents of adult offspring are often faced with the difficult decision of determining when they can no longer care for their loved one. G. C. Smith, Majeski, and McClenny (1996) suggest that the difficulties of this perpetual state of parenthood are further exacerbated by such things as age-related decrements in the offsprings themselves, unavailability of resources for as-sisting with their care, and a chronic state of sorrow from the realization that the adult offspring had a less-than-typical life.

When parents are unable to care for the adult offspring, and out-of-family placements are not desired, the shift in residence is often to the home of a brother or sister. In a study of 140 adult siblings of adults who resided in the parental homes, Krauss, Seltzer, Gordon, and Friedman (1996) found that siblings maintained a connectedness with their brother or sister long after leav-ing home and that the siblings without mental retardation sustained "regular and personal contact, provided emotional support, and felt knowledgeable about the varied needs of their brother or sister with mental retardation" (p. 83). Approximately one third of the siblings surveyed intended to live with their sibling upon moving him or her out of the parental home.

For families who have not planned for the time when siblings or other family members must take over for the aging parents, the wait for services may be a long one. As recently as 1988, Seltzer found that 20 percent of the persons with mental retardation who were elderly were on a waiting list for services. Although only 5 percent of the people in Seltzer's sample required age-specific services (Seltzer, 1988), Englehardt, Brubaker, and Lutzer (1988) found that it was the caregivers' assessment of their ability to provide ser-vices that actually corresponded to the use of such support services. The fact that such a small percentage of people require age-related services is grati-fying but offset by the realization that family and residential stability are gen-erally tied to a family's and usually the parents' ability to cope—an ability that most often decreases with increasing age (Hogg & Moss, 1993). When the adult with mental retardation is living with a parent or sibling who is ag-ing, rather than in a public residential facility, vigilance in advocacy may be needed to balance the rigors of services and supports, inside and outside of

People with developmental disabilities over the age of sixty-five now represent the fastest growing group of people with disabilities in America.

The reader is referred to Chapter 1 for a personal perspective on preparation for the later years.

the home, and most certainly to see that the older adult's needs are met in a timely and respectful manner (Thorin, Yovanoff, & Irvin, 1996).

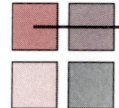

SUMMARY

ORGANIZATION OF THE FAMILY

- Whereas social scientists were once interested only in individuals, they are now concerned with understanding people in general, individually and collectively.
- The actions, behaviors, wishes, and intentions of family members are often less a product of the family itself than of a desire to meet the needs of those around them.
- A family's patterns of responses is considered to be both a cause and a consequence of its development.

FAMILY FUNCTIONING

- The news of a disability may be initially so devastating that it strikes at the heart of a family's value system.
- The major determinant of the psychological health and well-being of a child with mental retardation is the psychological health and well-being of the family.
- Foremost among the list of supports needed by families is a social support system that allows families to feel that they and their problems are valued by others.

CONSULTATION WITH PROFESSIONALS

- Families are assuming an increasingly greater role in the care and treatment of persons with mental retardation.
- Special educators are at times uncomfortable with meeting the broad-based needs of families of persons with severe disabilities.

ISSUES IN FAMILY LIVING

- Susceptibility to crime, accidents around the home, and an increased responsibility for oneself and others are many of the new concerns of persons with mental retardation as they move from an institution to a community-based home.
- Gaining access to important religious roles and responsibilities is as important for persons with mental retardation as it is for persons without mental retardation.
- Older adults with mental retardation represent the fastest growing age group of persons with mental retardation.

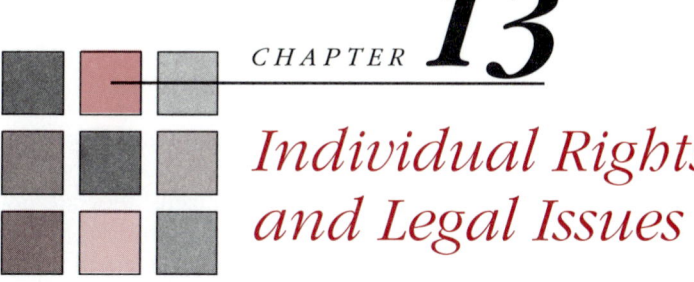

CHAPTER 13

Individual Rights and Legal Issues

After reading this chapter,
the student should be able to:

▪ Identify selected legal terminology.

▪ Understand fundamental concepts and legal bases for establishing the rights of persons who are mentally retarded.

▪ Discuss the legal history for establishing educational, institutional, and community rights.

▪ Recognize the issues related to withholding treatment and capital punishment.

Key Terms

consent agreement
educability
educational benefit
equal protection

habilitation
mitigating factor
procedural due
 process

quasi-suspect class
substantive due
 process

A review since the late 1960s indicates that advocates have made great gains for persons who are mentally retarded. These advocates, for the most part, have attempted to establish that certain rights pertain to all citizens; they are not privileges earned by a few. Much effort has been devoted to two fundamental activities: (a) establishing that persons with mental retardation are entitled to the same rights guaranteed all citizens, and (b) ensuring that those who are retarded have opportunities to exercise these rights.

The Arc of the United States regularly has played a critical role in securing the rights of persons with mental retardation.

THE CONTEXT FOR SECURING INDIVIDUAL RIGHTS

Wald (1976) has remarked that the rights to which all individuals, including those who are mentally retarded, are entitled are those that define a man or a woman as a human being. She suggested that these rights carry obligations for the individual as a member of society. For this reason, individuals who are mentally retarded must be accepted as contributing members of society if they are to secure the basic rights supposedly granted to all citizens.

To think that legal remedies alone will ensure the rights of those who are mentally retarded is simplistic. Society's acceptance of these people is influenced by a complex set of interactive factors. Townsend and Mattson (1981) have proposed a model that reflects the interrelationships of five major factors. Their model is presented in Figure 13.1. The factors that, according to them, crucially affect real change are:

1. Political coalitions (i.e., the evolution of various interest groups that advocate for resources to meet common goals)

2. Laws and judicial interpretations (i.e., the creation of rules that formalize and stabilize the agreements of diverse political coalitions)

3. Science and technology (i.e., the development of professional expertise to transform limited resources into effective practices that will meet the goals of various interest groups)

4. Personal satisfaction (i.e., the creation of working and living environments that allow individuals the opportunity to discover and pursue a variety of interests)

5. Public attitudes (i.e., the evolution of images, ideas, words, and behaviors that express the uniqueness and similarities of human interests) (p. 77)

FIGURE 13.1

A Multidisciplinary Concept of Rights

Source: Reprinted from *Analysis and Intervention in Developmental Disabilities, 1,* C. Townsend and R. Mattson, "The Interaction of Law and Special Education: Observing the Emperor's New Clothes," pp. 55–89, Copyright 1981, with kind permission from Pergamon Press Ltd, Headington Hill Hall, Oxford OX3 0BW, UK.

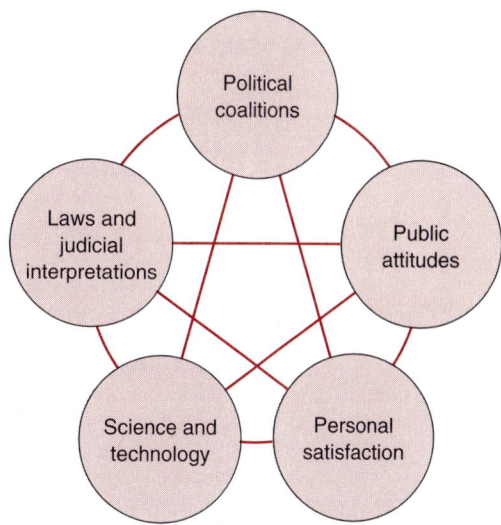

People with mental retardation have the same rights as other citizens.

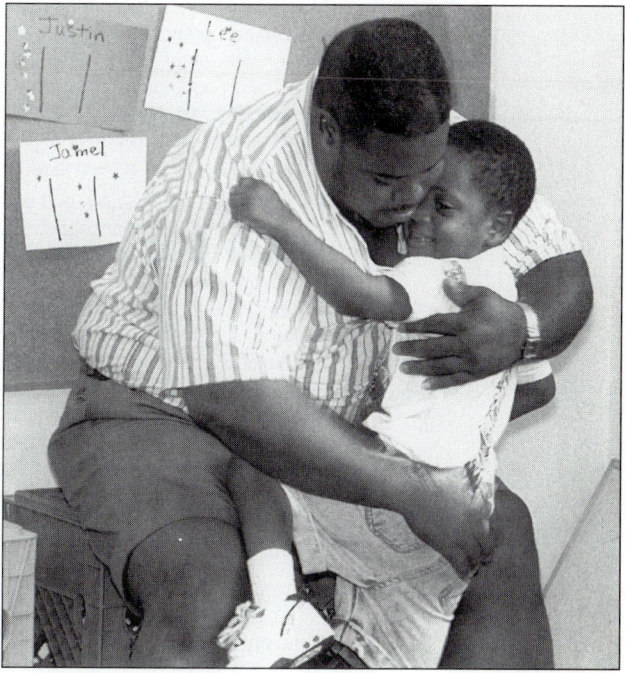

Turnbull (1993) noted that two compatible yet distinct ideologies that have emerged over time have resulted in important legal precedents and treatment outcomes. He suggested that the political ideology of egalitarianism and the human-service ideology of normalization (i.e., social role variation) have had a major impact on policy and law. Although focused on the right-to-education issue, he stated that these ideologies "supported each other,

TABLE 13.1

Selected Legal Terms

- *Cause of action.* The legal damage or injury on which a lawsuit is based. There must be a cause of action, or legal "wrong," for a court to consider a case; (in *Wyatt v. Stickney*, denial of treatment and maintenance of harmful conditions in institutions gave rise to causes of action for violation of constitutional rights).

- *Class action.* Most lawsuits are individual actions. A class action suit is brought by one or more named persons on their own behalf *and* on behalf of all persons in similar circumstances ("similarly situated"). A court's ruling in a class action suit applies to all members of the "class." For example, the court's ruling in the Willowbrook case applied to all 5,000 people who were residents of the Willowbrook State School when the suit was filed, not just the few in whose names the suit was filed.

- *Complaint.* A formal legal document submitted to a court by one or more persons (the plaintiffs), alleging that their rights have been violated. A complaint specifies one or more causes of action, names those who have allegedly violated the plaintiff's rights (the defendants), and demands that the defendants take certain corrective action (relief).

- *Consent agreement (consent judgment or consent decree).* A court-ratified and enforced agreement between the opposing parties in a suit, resolving the contested issues. Reached after the initiation of a lawsuit, a consent agreement, because it is ratified by a court, carries the same weight as any other court order. The Willowbrook case, *NY ARC v. Carey*, resulted in a consent agreement. For a plaintiff, a consent agreement minimizes the cost and time of continued litigation and avoids the risk of receiving an unfavorable ruling from the court.

- *Due process.* A right guaranteed under the 5th and the 14th Amendments to the U.S. Constitution. The concept of *substantive due process* refers to all citizens' fundamental rights to life, liberty, and property. For example, in *O'Connor v. Donaldson*, the Supreme Court ruled that the state of Florida had deprived Kenneth Donaldson of his rights under the 5th and 14th Amendments by involuntarily confining him in a custodial institution. *Procedural due process* refers to the fairness of procedures involved in any action that deprives people of their rights. Recent court rulings and legislation apply due process requirements to educational and treatment decisions. For instance, in *Mills v. Board of Education of the District of Columbia*, the court ruled that parents or guardians are entitled to due process regarding school classification and placement of their children. Courts have interpreted the right to due process to require at a minimum that a person receive *reasonable notice* and the opportunity for a *fair hearing* prior to being deprived of legal rights.

complemented each other, and drove the law and the right-to-education movement in the same direction" (p. 306). It is safe to say that these ideologies have extended beyond the area of education.

LEGAL BACKGROUND AND TERMINOLOGY

Proponents of any social change movement in today's world, such as the push for individual rights, need to become familiar with the language of law, because legal remedy is often one tool through which they can legitimize

TABLE 13.1

(continued)

- *Equal protection.* A right guaranteed by the 14th Amendment. This clause of the U.S. Constitution states that all citizens are entitled to equal protection under the law—that is, to be free from discrimination in the exercise of rights except where the state demonstrates a rational basis for compelling interest for apparently unequal treatment. In *Brown v. Board of Education of Topeka, Kansas*, the U.S. Supreme Court prohibited racial segregation in schools on the basis of the equal protection clause. The concept of equal protection has served as the foundation for landmark right-to-education and right-to-treatment suits on behalf of persons with disabilities.

- *Motion.* A request to the court in the context of a specific case to take some action relating to the case.

- *Ordinance.* A local law; that is, a city, town, or county law.

- *Petitioner.* The party appealing a court's decision to a higher court. Synonym for *appellant.* Also sometimes used to identify the plaintiff in certain courts or types of cases.

- *Plaintiff.* The party who brings a lawsuit alleging a violation of rights. The plaintiff is always named before the defendant in a case title; for example, Donaldson is the plaintiff in *Donaldson v. O'Connor.* Upon appeal, the order of names is reversed.

- *Precedent.* A prior court decision in a relevant case, cited in the interpretation of law or constitutional provision. A court may or may not accept a precedent as authoritative in interpreting the law in a specific case, depending on the factual similarities between the cases and the jurisdiction in which the precedent arose.

- *Relief.* The remedy to some legal wrong or violation of one's rights. Plaintiffs seek from the court certain types of relief against defendants, such as declaratory relief, injunctive relief, writs of *habeas corpus* (release), or money damages.

- *Remand.* An order by a higher court returning a case to a lower court for further action consistent with the higher court's decision.

- *Respondent.* The winning party at the trial level in a case that has been appealed. Synonym for *appellee.* Also used to mean the defendant in certain courts or cases.

Source: From *Understanding the Law: An Advocate's Guide to the Law and Developmental Disabilities* (pp. 3–11) by S. J. Taylor and D. Biklen, 1979, Syracuse, NY: Syracuse University and the Mental Health Law Project. Copyright 1979 by Syracuse University. Adapted by permission. The authors would like to thank Michael Lottman, Lee Carty, Harold Madorsky, and Lesley Lannan for their assistance in the preparation of this paper.

change. Advocates must understand the need for legal action, the significant legislation to date, the arguments upon which the court action is based, and the implications of judicial decisions and consent agreements. All these are addressed in this chapter.

One must also have some understanding of judicial language. Table 13.1 should assist the novice in legal terminology. It includes definitions of selected terms like "equal protection" and "due process" that are frequently used in judicial procedures and to which we refer throughout this chapter.

Stereotypes are all too often easy to make.

FUNDAMENTAL CONCEPTS

Throughout history, people with mental retardation have been misperceived in a number of ways, ranging from early thinking that they were demonically possessed to Justice Holmes's infamous perception of them as social parasites (*Buck v. Bell,* 1927). As noted in Chapter 2, the treatment accorded this group is very much a function of the sociopolitical influences of a given time. This treatment has included institutionalization for custodial and protective purposes, compulsory sterilization laws, exclusion from education and training, zoning ordinances that restrict the establishment of group homes, and withholding treatment from severely involved infants.

Prejudicial Attitudes

Misconceptions lead to faulty stereotyping and result in mistreatment.

The term *mental retardation* conjures up many misconceptions. Many of the general public associate this condition with sickness (Kurtz, 1977). All too often, individuals who are mentally retarded are perceived in negative ways and as a single homogeneous group. This happens, in part, because stereotypes are common and generalizations are easy to make. Such stereotypes and generalizations must be replaced by more accurate information and appropriate images.

Even professional thinking tends to accentuate the disabilities rather than the abilities of those who are retarded. Sociological perspectives are built on deviancy models (i.e., significant variance from the norm). Legal thinking has often used "differentness" as a basis for argument, particularly

FIGURE 13.2

A Model of Public Law

Source: From *Free Appropriate Public Education: The Law and Children with Disabilities* (4th ed., p. 4) by H. R. Turnbull, 1993, Denver, CO: Love Publishing Company. Copyright 1993 by Love Publishing Company. Adapted by permission.

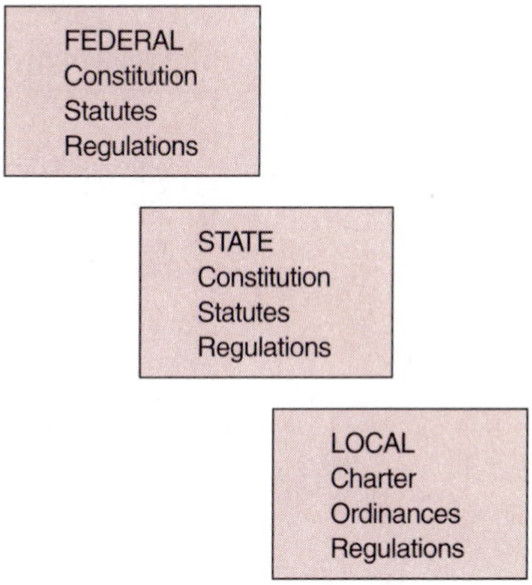

FEDERAL
Constitution
Statutes
Regulations

STATE
Constitution
Statutes
Regulations

LOCAL
Charter
Ordinances
Regulations

in equal protection claims. Attitudes and perspectives like these can easily lead to decisions and patterns of treatment that are antithetical to both egalitarianism and social role valorization. Attitudes and perspectives like these underscore the importance of public attitudes as important factors in the legal rights movement, as Townsend and Mattson (1981) have noted.

Best Interest versus Legal Right

From time to time, the principles of best interest and legal rights of an individual have come into conflict. When the state acts under the best interest principle, it does so in one of two ways. If the state acts in the best interest of the individual, it does so based on the theory of parens patriae (i.e., the state is the father of the country and of its citizens). If the state acts in the best interest of society, it does so based on the theory of police power (i.e., the power to impose restrictions on private rights that are related to the general welfare of the public). This legal principle can impose on the rights of an individual, as evidenced in many sterilization cases, in which the state interceded on behalf of the general welfare of the public. The principle of parens patriae may seem on face value to be harmless, but situations can arise in which its use negates the individual's right to due process under the law.

LEGAL BASES FOR ESTABLISHING RIGHTS

Different avenues are available for securing the rights of those who are mentally retarded. Turnbull (1993) presented a three-ladder model that shows parallel options at each level of legal authority (Figure 13.2). At each level, there is a fundamental governing document that is the most important source of law. Two major principles are noteworthy under this system of parallel governments: (a) federal, state, and local governments share responsibility and power, and (b) the federal Constitution and laws passed by Congress are the supreme law of the land.

TABLE 13.2

Constitutional Arguments Frequently Used in Litigation

Constitutional Argument	Constitutional Basis (Amendment)	Explanation	Example of Application
Equal protection	14th	No state shall deny to any person within its jurisdiction the equal protection of the laws	Right to education
Due process (substantive)	5th (federal) 14th (state)	Legislation must be reasonably related to the furtherance of a legitimate governmental objective	Right to appropriate classification Right to treatment
Due process (procedural)	5th (federal) 14th (state)	Guaranteed procedural fairness where the government would deprive one of property or liberty	Placement rights in the criminal justice system
Freedom from cruel and unusual punishment	8th	Protection from punishment that is found to be offensive to the ordinary person, that is unfair, or that is grossly excessive for the offense	Right to refuse treatment Right to treatment Rights in prison
Freedom from slavery and involuntary servitude	13th	No person shall be forced or coerced into working	Right to work (institutional)
Freedom of speech and the right to vote	1st	Free exercise of basic rights	Right to education

Federal Constitutional Arguments

The Fourteenth Amendment to the Constitution contains two frequently invoked clauses: the due process clause ("nor shall any State deprive any person of life, liberty, or property, without due process of law") and the equal protection clause ("nor deny to any person within its jurisdiction the equal protection of the laws"). Many of the rights secured and services established for those who are retarded have been achieved through litigation based on constitutional grounds, particularly on these two principles. Table 13.2 presents the constitutional arguments that have been used most frequently in cases involving persons who are mentally retarded. This table is only a brief guide to the constitutional basis for litigation; it is not a comprehensive list of all previous, present, or future bases for litigation.

Since the equal protection clause of the Fourteenth Amendment has been the backbone for many rights for persons, we will look at it more closely. There are three types of equal protection analyses (the application of equal protection to a specific claim): (a) rational basis analysis; (b) intermediate, or middle-tier, scrutiny standard; and (c) strict scrutiny analysis. Rothstein (1995) described these different levels of scrutiny as follows:

> If the individual affected by the practice is a member of a "suspect class" such as a racial minority, or if the right at issue is a "fundamental right" such as privacy, the practice will be strictly scrutinized (evaluated very carefully). Where the classification is not a specially protected class, or if the right is not an important one, the practice will usually be upheld if there is any rational basis for it. Individuals with disabilities have not been held to be members of a suspect class, but education has been recognized as deserving of "special constitutional treatment," and an intermediate test of heightened scrutiny has been applied. (p. 13)

When the courts apply the rational basis, or traditional, analysis, they use a two-pronged test. First, they ask whether the purposes for different treatment sought by the state are legitimate. Second, they investigate whether there exists a "rational" correspondence between the purposes of the state action and the classification.

The intermediate scrutiny standard is used when discriminatory practices are claimed against a group of people who share some of the characteristics of a "suspect class." A member of such a group is sometimes referred to as being a member of a **quasi-suspect class.** The United States Supreme Court decided in *Cleburne Living Center, Inc. v. City of Cleburne, Texas* (1984) not to grant suspect or quasi-suspect classification status to individuals who are mentally retarded. The Court stressed, however, that "irrational prejudice could not be the basis for unequal treatment" (Rothstein, 1995, p. 63).

The courts apply a strict scrutiny analysis where a practice affects a suspect classification or a fundamental interest. The state must demonstrate a compelling interest in order for the practice to be upheld.

Federal Statutes and Regulations

The Americans with Disabilities Act (ADA) of 1990 is arguably the most important piece of federal legislation ever enacted for persons with disabilities.

Another mechanism for securing the rights of citizens who are mentally retarded that has had and will continue to have significance is federal legislation and its accompanying regulations. As more federal legislation is enacted, reference to it will occur more frequently. This is particularly noteworthy in light of the Supreme Court's reluctance to apply either the intermediate or strict scrutiny standards—standards that make it easier to win equal protection claims (Bateman, 1986).

UNWELCOMED IMMIGRANTS

An article in *Sports Illustrated* ("From Russia with Love") featured a Soviet immigrant named Max Blank, a 6' 8½" tall high school basketball star; we were more interested in his younger brother. In describing the travels of the Blank family to the United States, *SI* reported:

> But the Blanks continued on to Italy; they spent eight months in the village of Ladispoli, west of Rome, waiting for a special waiver that would enable Max's younger brother, Yakov, a Down's syndrome child, to enter the U.S. A 1952 immigration statute prohibits the admission of aliens who are mentally retarded without such a waiver.

We located Section 212 of the Immigration and Naturalization Act entitled "General Classes of Aliens Ineligible to Receive Visas and Excluded from Admission." The first part of Section 212 is presented below.

General Classes of Aliens Ineligible to Receive Visas and Excluded from Admission

> Sec. 212 (a) Except as otherwise provided in this Act, the following classes of aliens shall be ineligible to receive visas and shall be excluded from admission into the United States:
>
> 1. Aliens who are feeble-minded;
> 2. Aliens who are insane;
> 3. Aliens who have had one or more attacks of insanity;
> 4. Aliens afflicted with psychopathic personality, epilepsy, or a mental defect;
> 5. Aliens who are narcotic drug addicts or chronic alcoholics;
> 6. Aliens who are afflicted with tuberculosis in any form, or with leprosy, or any dangerous contagious disease;
> 7. Aliens not comprehended within any of the foregoing classes who are certified by the examining surgeon as having a physical defect, disease, or disability, when determined by the consular or immigration officer to be of such a nature that it may affect the ability of the alien to earn a living unless the alien affirmatively establishes that he will not have to earn a living;
> 8. Aliens who are paupers, professional beggars, or vagrants;

The waiver about which the Blanks were waiting to hear is Form I-601, which is entitled "Application of Waiver of Grounds of Excludability." This form, along with a fee, is submitted to the office of Immigration and Naturalization Service when applying for permanent residency. Although there seem to be supportable arguments for excluding certain individuals from becoming citizens of this country, we will let you decide whether individuals with retardation should be one group of such individuals.

To date, the United States has enacted a number of major pieces of legislation in this area. A list and accompanying description of some of the more important laws are provided in Table 13.3. These legislative actions establish mandates and provide a legal basis for arguing against unfair treatment.

State Constitutions, Statutes, and Regulations

Since it is incumbent upon each state to provide education for its citizens by virtue of compulsory education laws, it would follow that this legislative mandate would be a strong basis for arguing that these same services be afforded

TABLE 13.3

Major Federal Legislation

Legislation	Year Enacted	Public Law No.	Features
Amendment to Vocational Rehabilitation Act	1973	93-112	* prohibited discrimination against persons with "handicaps" (Section 504 of the Act) * provided a functional definition of "handicap"— mental or physical impairments that limit one or more of a person's major life activities * included persons with conditions that would not be covered by later legislation (e.g., drug-alcohol addiction)
Education Amendments of the Elementary and Secondary Education Act 1965	1974	93-380	* provided increased funding to assist states in meeting the right-to-education requirements * required states to develop plans for implementing educational opportunities for all students with disabilities—this included procedural safeguards
Developmental Disabilities Assistance and Bill of Rights Act	1974	94-103	* broadened the term "developmental disabilities" * provided grants to states and university-affiliated programs
Education for All Handicapped Children Act [Individuals with Disabilities Education Act (IDEA)]	1975	94-142	* mandated a free, appropriate education for all students with "handicaps" in the least restrictive environment * provided for nondiscriminatory testing, individualized education programs, procedural safeguards, and parent participation * reauthorized most recently in 1997 as PL 105-17 * now named the Individuals with Disabilities Education Act (IDEA)
Handicapped Children's Protection Act	1986	99-372	* enacted in response to the Supreme Court's decision in *Smith v. Robinson* (1984) * allowed courts to award reasonable attorney's fees to parents if the parents complaint is successful
Americans with Disabilities Act	1990	101-336	* landmark civil rights legislation— designed to eliminate discrimination * provided civil rights protections to all persons with disabilities, including groups not previously addressed (e.g., HIV) * incorporated a functional definition similar to the Vocational Rehabilitation Act of 1973— limitations in one or more major life activities * stressed equal opportunity, independent living, and economic self-sufficiency. * addressed employment, public services (e.g., buildings, transportation), public accommodations (e.g., restaurants, museums), telecommunications

Some information used in this table taken from Drew, Logan, and Hardman (1992).

to students with disabilities. Although referring specifically to the right-to-education issue, Turnbull (1975) asserted the importance of state mandates in securing rights:

> The case law on the right to an education is not based solely upon federal and constitutional arguments. And not surprisingly, the federal equal-protection and due-process arguments are not as likely to be a secure ground for establishing the right to education as is the guarantee of education imposed on the state by its constitution or statutes. (p. 6)

Turnbull stated that nearly all states have constitutions containing provisions for educating their children, including those who are disabled, some of whom are mentally retarded.

Local Charters, Ordinances, and Regulations

These provisions also play an important role in determining the rights of individuals who are mentally retarded. City charters, for instance, typically specify the establishment of various boards (e.g., school boards) and commissions. Ordinances like those that control zoning can be critical in terms of securing housing opportunities for this population. Regulations developed and issued by people in positions of authority, that are based on policy decisions of various legislative bodies, also affect citizens who are retarded.

LEGAL PRECEDENTS FOR INDIVIDUAL RIGHTS

EDUCATIONAL RIGHTS

The importance of education is generally recognized and supported in our society. The Supreme Court, in the landmark *Brown v. Board of Education* (1954) decision, clearly commented on the value that education can have in one's life.

Today, education is perhaps the most important function of state and local governments. Both compulsory school attendance laws and great expenditures for education demonstrate our recognition of the importance of education to our democratic society. It is required in the performance of our most basic public responsibilities, even service in the armed forces. It is the very foundation of good citizenship. Today, it is a principal instrument in awakening children to cultural values, in preparing them for later professional training, and in helping them to adjust normally to their environment. It is doubtful that any child may reasonably be expected to succeed in life if denied the opportunity of an education. Such an opportunity, where the state has undertaken to provide it, is a right that must be made available to all on equal terms.

With the proliferation of legal cases, there has been a shift in focus from a systems-centered decision-making process to a more child-centered one.

Individual characteristics must be considered when educational decisions are made. Overriding concepts like appropriate education and least restrictive environment demand a child-centered perspective.

Right to Education

By many people, education is mistakenly considered a fundamental right that the authors of the Constitution clearly incorporated into this document. However, the Supreme Court, in *San Antonio Independent School District v. Rodriguez* (1973), stated that education is not a fundamental right guaranteed either explicitly or implicitly by the Constitution. Given this shocking statement, the *Rodriguez* decision has some encouraging implications for education. *Rodriguez* clearly addresses the importance of citizens' acquiring the basic skills required for exercising their First Amendment rights of free speech and involvement in the political mechanism of voting. Denial of educational services to any individual may impede the acquisition of these skills and may consequently be a denial of these constitutional rights. Although *Rodriguez* did not establish the right to education as fundamental, it did reaffirm the importance of education and implicitly denounced the denial of such services.

> The Constitution does not specifically address the issue of right to education.

Table 13.4 summarizes some of the early litigation affecting special education. As can be seen from Table 13.4, the arguments most frequently employed by plaintiffs in right-to-education cases include establishing the importance of education, using equal protection and due process claims, and addressing state and federal statutory provisions. For the most part, if education is provided to the public in general, these plaintiffs have argued, it should be available to all children, regardless of level of ability or type of impairment. Another critical factor established in the two major legal cases described next, *Pennsylvania Association for Retarded Children (PARC) v. Commonwealth of Pennsylvania* (1971) and *Mills v. Board of Education of the District of Columbia* (1972), is that all individuals who are mentally retarded can benefit from education or training. Without the prior establishment of this fact, opponents could have put up substantial opposition to providing educational services to many children and youth who were retarded and who had been excluded from schools. The issue of educability has been discussed professionally (Kauffman & Krouse, 1981; Noonan, Brown, Mulligan, & Rettig, 1982) and has been the focus of litigation (*Timothy W. v. Rochester School District*, 1988).

> The newer name of this organization is the Arc of Pennsylvania.

Keeping children who are mentally retarded out of school had been a long-standing practice, but in the early 1970s, legal challenges to exclusionary policies were successful. This litigation paved the way for later federal legislation that would significantly alter the availability of educational services to students who are disabled.

Early in January 1971, the Pennsylvania Association for Retarded Children and the parents of thirteen children who were mentally retarded filed a class action suit (*Pennsylvania Association for Retarded Children v. Commonwealth*

TABLE 13.4
Summary of Early Right-to-Education Litigation

Litigants	Year	Highest Level of Judicial Review	Issues	Implications of Litigations	Arguments Used
Brown v. Board of Education	1954	U.S. Supreme Court	Segregation of students by race Impact of racial segregation on the child's motivation to learn	Segregation by race unanimously declared unconstitutional Established importance of education for advancement Established policy in favor of equal educational opportunity Generalized the purposes of education, not its fundamentality	Equal protection
Pennsylvania Association for Retarded Children (PARC) v. Commonwealth of Pennsylvania	1972	U.S. District Court (PA)	Class action suit—challenging the exclusion of children with mental retardation from free public education Access to education for all citizens with mental retardation Particular learning needs of this population	Consent agreement of both parties Established a right to education for children with mental retardation Established that all children with mental retardation could gain from education and training Demanded appropriate education Demanded preschool services if normal children received such Provided tuition grant assistance Provided due process mechanisms Required the identification of children not already identified Provided for education in the least restrictive setting	Equal protection Due process State statutes
Mills v. Board of Education of District of Columbia	1972	U.S. District Court (DC)	Class action suit—exclusion of all exceptionalities Access to education Use of waiting lists	Extended the logic of *PARC* to all disability groups regardless of the degree of the impairment Gained procedural safeguards Required timetable of implementation Acknowledged alternatives placement	Equal protection Due process District of Columbia Code

TABLE 13.4
(continued)

Case	Year	Court	Issue	Outcome	Basis
San Antonio Independent School District v. Rodriguez	1973	U.S. Supreme Court	Claim that a discrimination exists due to being in a poorer school district Challenge to state-financing scheme Assertion that education is a fundamental right	Rejected wealth discrimination claim Left open the fundamentality of some identifiable quantum of education Reaffirmed the importance of education Indicated that denial of education could be used in terms of denial of freedom of speech and right to vote	Discrimination Equal protection
Lebanks v. Spears	1973	U.S. District Court	Challenged Louisiana's failure to provide education/training to a large number of children with mental retardation	Consent agreement Two features not found in *PARC* or *Mills* (1) Education—oriented toward making every child self-sufficient or employable (2) Educational services to adults who were not given services as children Acknowledged additional factors for evaluation in addition to intelligence	Equal protection
Maryland Association for Retarded Children v. Maryland	1974	Circuit Court of Baltimore County	Class action suit on behalf of children with mental retardation and those with physical handicaps being denied free public education	Began to address "appropriateness" issue Required the state to provide the necessary funding	State statutes
In the Interest of H.G., A Child	1974	Supreme Court of North Dakota	Equal educational opportunity	Involved the highest level of judicial review prior to PL 94-142 (1975)	State statutes Equal protection

of Pennsylvania) in federal court on behalf of all Pennsylvania residents who were mentally retarded between the ages of six and twenty-one who were excluded from receiving educational services. At issue was the prevailing policy that denied these school-age children access to public education. Expert testimony stressing the educational benefits (i.e., attainment of self-sufficiency for many, and some level of self-care for others) that all children with mental retardation could gain weighed heavily in this case.

Although settled by means of court-approved consent agreement in October, 1971, the PARC case had a profound impact on special education and children and youth with mental retardation. It established a precedent guaranteeing access to publicly supported education for all students who are mentally retarded. Through claims of violations of due process and equal protection rights, the plaintiffs were able to establish that certain Pennsylvania statutes were unconstitutional. Implications of this decision are listed in Table 13.4.

Not long after the consent agreement in PARC was reached, a civil suit (*Mills v. Board of Education of the District of Columbia,* 1972) was filed. In this case, the parents and guardians of seven children charged that the board of education was denying these children a publicly supported education. All the plaintiffs in this case qualified as disabled. In August 1972, Judge Waddy ruled in favor of the plaintiffs and in effect declared that a publicly supported education was the right of all children who were disabled, regardless of the type and severity of their condition. *Mills* actually extended many of the legal guarantees that the PARC case had achieved for children who were mentally retarded to children with other disabling conditions. The defendants claimed that funds were insufficient to provide education to all such students. Judge Waddy's reply reflected the attitude of many concerning the exclusionary practices so long in effect:

> The District of Columbia's interest in educating the excluded children clearly must outweigh its interest in preserving its financial resources. If sufficient funds are not available to finance all of the services and programs that are needed and desirable in the system, then the available funds must be expended equitably in such a manner that no child is entirely excluded from a publicly supported education consistent with his needs and ability to benefit therefrom. The inadequacies of the District of Columbia public school system, whether occasioned by insufficient funding or administrative inefficiency, certainly cannot be permitted to bear more heavily on the "exceptional" or handicapped child than on the normal child. (*Mills v. Board of Education,* 1972)

As noted in the preceding decision, limited financial resources are not sufficient reason to exclude students from receiving an appropriate education. But financial resources are limited, and even with PL 94-142 and its recent amendments in effect, financial issues will continue to demand attention.

After the PARC case and *Mills,* right-to-education suits were filed in many other states as well. Soon, all students who were mentally retarded were to gain the right to the free, appropriate public education that had previously been denied them, as many of the provisions formulated in the PARC consent agreement were later incorporated into the Education for All Handicapped Children Act, now known as the Individuals with Disabilities Education Act (IDEA).

The assumption of a right to education has not gone unchallenged. In 1988, a federal district court in New Hampshire decided in the case of *Timothy W. v. Rochester School District* that, if it seemed that a student could not benefit from special education, then the rights guaranteed under IDEA do not apply. This case involved a thirteen-year-old boy who was profoundly retarded and who had a host of other disabling conditions. He was described as operating at a most basic level and as not having made any progress over a long period of time. The court of appeals reversed the lower court's interpretation of IDEA to allow exclusion from public education in some cases, reaffirming the basic principles underlying the intent of IDEA. It is likely, particularly given harsh economic times, that the issue of educability and students' rights to an appropriate education may resurface.

Right to an Appropriate Evaluation and Classification

As noted earlier, the most frequent charges in litigation involving placement decisions have involved violations of equal protection and due process. MacMillan (1977) offers an explanation of the typical equal protection claim that can be raised in relation to special class placement for students who are mildly retarded: "The contention is made that a child placed in a special education class is denied equal educational opportunity because his options are reduced . . . and because the quality of the EMR [educable mentally retarded] program is poorer than that of the regular class" (p. 290).

As discussed in Chapter 3, many different terms, such as EMR, have been used and continue to be used to describe students with mild forms of mental retardation.

The due process arguments are based on the contention that the procedures (such as administration of certain tests) used to classify a child or to place a child in a special class may deny substantive due process. The denial of proper procedural safeguards before and after evaluation also violates the procedural due process clause of the Constitution. The thrust of the opposition to misclassification centers on the chronic effects of labeling a student. Many people vehemently object to the stigma associated with being placed in a class for students who are mentally retarded. Much of the criticism focuses on the segregation and isolation of special class placement.

The use of intelligence measures as the primary determinant for identification and placement decisions has long been under scrutiny. The problems associated with intelligence testing have come under fire in a number of legal suits. *Hobson v. Hansen* (1967), *Larry P. v. Riles* (1972), *Diana v. State Board of Education* (1970), and *PASE (Parents in Action on Special Education) v. Hannon* (1980) have specifically considered the use of intelligence tests for the purpose noted here.

In *Hobson v. Hansen* (1967), the practice of denying to poor school-age children educational services equal to those of the more affluent was determined to be unconstitutional. The court found that students were be-ing "tracked" into ability groups on the basis of instruments that seemed to be biased against African American students and those from lower socio-economic groups. Schools in the District of Columbia were no longer per-mitted to use IQ measures to place children in tracks, and a close review of classification practices was ordered. This case is important to those in-terested in mental retardation because it addressed the consequences of be-ing labeled mentally retarded.

In *Larry P. v. Riles* (1972), the Federal District Court for Northern California decided that standardized, invalidated IQ tests could not be used as the sole determinant in the identification and placement of African American students in segregated classes for students who were educably (i.e., mildly) mentally retarded. This decision was appealed, and in January of 1984, the Ninth Circuit Court of Appeals upheld by a two-to-one margin the lower court's opinion. Initially, intelligence tests could not be used to identify African American students as mentally retarded; in 1986 an ex-panded injunction was issued that banned the use of these instruments with African American students for any assessment purpose (Taylor, 1990). MacMillan and Balow (1991) noted that, as a repercussion of *Larry P.,* the three largest school districts in the state of California decided to ban the use of intelligence tests with all students, regardless of race, for special educa-tion purposes.

In 1988, however, a group of African American parents filed a complaint alleging that the 1986 order, which prevented their children from voluntar-ily taking IQ tests for purposes of placement in special education classes, vi-olated their due process and equal protection rights. The court found that the plaintiffs' due process rights had been violated and ordered that the 1986 modification be vacated (*Larry P. v. Riles,* 1992).

Turnbull (1993) makes two interesting observations about *Larry P.* First, he submits that this litigation was more a racial discrimination case than a special education case.

> Larry P. . . . was, as much as anything, a race discrimination case that put the court in the unenviable position of choosing among three possible explanations for the over-representation of minority children in special education (1) the tests and their invalidity, (2) the "gene pool" argument that minority children are in-herently less intelligent than nonminority children, and (3) the socioeconomic explanation of low performance on standardized tests. (p. 93)

The court chose to focus on the first explanation. Turnbull's second ob-servation is that neither court actually examined comprehensively whether these tests were racially biased. Nevertheless, the outcome of this decision was that schools were enjoined from placing African American students in classes for those who were educably mentally retarded primarily on the ba-sis of IQ scores.

Just as *Larry P.* specifically concerned the problems of African American children who were being misclassified, other cases brought in California have focused on the problems of other ethnic groups in placement decisions. In *Diana v. State Board of Education* (1970), the injured party, representing Spanish-speaking children, argued that many such students had been placed in classes for students who were mildly retarded on the basis of individual intelligence tests that were considered culturally biased. The children involved in this lawsuit spoke primarily Spanish but were given intelligence tests in English. Although *Diana* was settled out of court, it resulted in clear changes in the methods and procedures used for identifying and placing students in special classes.

It would be misleading to suggest that these were the only lawsuits involving appropriate classification and placement, or that all litigation has been decided in the same way. In a class action suit filed in an Illinois federal district court (*PASE [Parents in Action on Special Education] v. Hannon,* 1980), the use of intelligence tests to place minority students in special classes designed for children who were mentally retarded again came into question. This time, however, the court ruled differently, declaring the tests nondiscriminatory and this practice valid when additional measures are also employed. Unlike *Larry P.,* attorneys in this case closely examined specific intelligence tests for possible racial bias. So few items were found suspect that the court decided that these measures should be considered culturally neutral. The court went on to underscore the importance of clinical judgment in the interpretation of IQ results and the decision-making process.

The diametrically opposed findings in *PASE* and *Larry P.* have added more confusion to an already controversial area. The misuse of IQ measures continues to undergo professional scrutiny, as concern for misdiagnosis and misplacement remains a top priority in the referral and placement process. The effect of these decisions on practice has been mixed. Cordes (1984) remarks that some professionals believe there has been little change. Others (Polloway & Smith, 1983) contend that local education agencies have adopted a more conservative posture toward classifying minority students as mildly retarded. Certainly, assessment practices leading to eligibility decisions in such specific areas of the country as California have been dramatically affected as a result of litigation (MacMillan & Balow, 1991). But even in areas where a more conservative approach is evident (again, California), overrepresentation of minority students in classes for students who are mildly retarded continues (MacMillan, 1989). The problems are far from solved. As Taylor (1990) suggests, the issue of nondiscriminatory evaluation has not been put to rest.

W. B. v. Matula (1995) is another case relevant to the issue of identification and evaluation. A school district failed to identify and provide an appropriate education to a student. W. B., the parent of the student, sued, and the Third U.S. Circuit Court of Appeals held that the plaintiff was not precluded from seeking monetary damages. Some attorneys who specialize in the area

The inclusion of students with mental retardation was achieved on the basis of equal protection arguments.

of special education law believe that this is a major ruling for those seeking damages (Bleemer, 1995).

Right to an Appropriate Education

Once an appropriate education was mandated by the IDEA, it was inevitable that the term *appropriate education* would need to be defined. The issue is discussed routinely at Individualized Education Program (IEP) meetings, but it was never formally addressed until 1982. Then the U.S. Supreme Court ruled in the case *Board of Education of the Hendrick Hudson Central School District v. Rowley*—the first case argued on the basis of PL 94-142 to reach this highest level of judicial review.

Although the plaintiff named in this particular litigation, Amy Rowley, was a student with a hearing impairment, the case has significant implications for students who are mentally retarded. This is because the Court specified criteria for a "free appropriate public education" in the majority opinion written by Justice William Rehnquist:

> According to the definitions contained in the Act, a "free appropriate public education" consists of educational instruction specially designed to meet the unique needs of the handicapped child, supported by such services as are necessary to permit the child "to benefit" from the instruction. Almost as a checklist for adequacy under the Act, the definition also requires that such instruction

and services be provided at public expense and under public supervision, meet the State's educational standards, approximate the grade levels used in the State's regular education, and comport with the child's IEP. Thus, if personalized instruction is being provided with sufficient supportive services to permit the child to benefit from the instruction, and the other items on the definitional checklist are satisfied, the child is receiving a "free appropriate public education" as defined by the Act.

A number of important issues in interpreting the IDEA arose in this case, and they have had and will continue to have bearing on litigation. First, the Court discussed the importance of a "basic floor of opportunity" for students. The meaning of this concept is that all students should have reasonable opportunity for learning. The Court stressed that the Act intends students to obtain special instruction and related services that are individually developed to provide educational benefit to students with disabilities. Unfortunately, the term *educational benefit* suffers from the same ambiguity suffered by *appropriate education*.

The issue that has received the most attention involves the "level of education" to be provided to students. What type of services should be provided, and to what extent must they be offered? In *Rowley,* the U.S. Supreme Court reversed the Second Circuit Court of Appeals' ruling that Amy Rowley was entitled to an interpreter. The Court's interpretation of congressional intent in enacting PL 94-142 suggested that programs do not have to develop students to their maximum potential. The Court noted that language addressing this particular issue was "noticeably absent" in the federal statute.

The Rowley decision initially sent shock waves through the field of special education, as many thought that students with disabilities would suffer from school systems' taking narrow interpretations of this case. Special education professionals feared that schools would have too easy a time demonstrating that students were getting "educational benefit" in programs that were not providing needed supportive services (DuBow & Geer, 1984). Blatt's (1987) concern was that schools would (a) have more freedom to decide what is acceptable for students with special needs, (b) no longer be motivated to provide optimal programs, and (c) meet a "far lesser" standard. This scenario, fortunately, has not materialized.

The right to special services can also be argued on the basis of Section 504 of the Rehabilitation Act. Some students suspected of being mentally retarded may not qualify for services under the IDEA. Furthermore, some students have conditions that do not require special education, yet they may have a significant mental or physical impairment that requires certain services. The emerging issue with which schools must deal is whether students who are human immunodeficiency virus (HIV) positive are disabled. In the case of *Board of Education v. Arline* (1987), the Supreme Court ruled that a person with a contagious disease—in this case it was tuberculosis—is disabled under the intent of Section 504. Based on a 1987 amendment to the Rehabilitation Act and subsequent court decisions, Rothstein (1995) has concluded that acquired immune deficiency syndrome (AIDS) is a disability under Section 504 and the Americans with Disabilities Act, but not in all cases, under the IDEA.

Another case relevant to the issue of providing students with a free appropriate education is that of *Florence County School District Four v. Carter* (1993). In this case, Shannon Carter was a ninth grader who was classified as having a learning disability. Her parents were dissatisfied with her IEP, which stated that she would make four months grade equivalent gain during the academic year in reading and mathematics. The parents requested a hearing and the local educational officer and the state educational agency hearing officer concluded that the IEP was appropriate. Shannon's parents then unilaterally placed her in a private school that was not approved by the state. They also filed a lawsuit in federal court alleging that the IEP was inadequate. The federal court agreed that the IEP was inadequate and ordered tuition reimbursement. Both the Court of Appeals for the Fourth Circuit and the Supreme Court affirmed the decision of the lower court. The Court maintained that the private school had to be approved by the state only if the state, and not the parents, placed the student in the school.

Andry (1995) explained the decision of the courts by stating that as the unapproved private school provided an appropriate education, the courts wanted to emphasize "the importance of the education provided rather than the mere procedural aspect of whether or not a private school has gone through the state approval process" (p. 329). Both Andry (1995) and Opuda (1994) have cautioned that the Carter decision does not mean that parents who unilaterally place their children in unapproved private schools are guaranteed tuition reimbursement. Reimbursement is dependent on several conditions. The court must conclude both that the public school placement was inappropriate and that the private school provided a proper placement. Total reimbursement is possible only if the tuition of the private school is reasonable.

Right to an Appropriate Placement

Placing students who are mentally retarded in educational settings that are appropriate to their needs is becoming a major issue in the field. There is debate between those who want to maintain the guarantees of a continuum of service delivery options as specified in the IDEA and those who advocate full inclusion in general education settings as the only option. While this discussion will continue, some case law favoring integrated settings has been established. According to Turnbull (1993), an important case on which subsequent arguments have been based is *Daniel R. R. v. State Board of Education* (1989). A two-faceted test to determine whether a placement is appropriate and consistent with the concept of least restrictive environment (LRE) was developed by the Fifth Court of Appeals in this case. The *Daniel* test requires attention to the following components while considering other factors related to the student and school: Can a student be educated satisfactorily in the regular education classroom, with the use of supplementary aids and services? Has the school placed the student in the least restrictive setting to the maximum extent appropriate?

Several court cases also have given the concept of an appropriate education priority over inclusion ("The Courts' Impact on Special Education," 1996). In *Poolaw v. Bishop* (1995), the court decided that the LRE for a student who was deaf was a residential school. Issues related to appropriate placement will continue to be a source of litigation.

Right to Related Services

Under the IDEA, students are entitled to related services if needed, particularly if they allow a student to benefit from a free appropriate public education. It has not always been clear, however, whether certain services qualify as "related services," especially those that are more medically oriented and that many children with more severe forms of retardation need. This issue is important because purely medical services are not considered related services and therefore do not have to be provided as part of a student's individual program. This could exclude some students from receiving special education.

In *Irving Independent School District v. Tatro* (1984), the U.S. Supreme Court ruled that a student with spina bifida was entitled to clean intermittent catheterization services (i.e., a procedure that empties the bladder). The Court decided that this supportive service could be performed by a school nurse and technically did not qualify as an excludable medical service, thereby making it a related service. What is important in this case is that such services are viewed as creating an opportunity for learning that would otherwise be denied. In this case, the student would not be able to attend school without it. As in *Rowley,* the message here was that a student is entitled to supportive services to guarantee access to an appropriate, but not necessarily the best possible, education.

Other litigation has further delineated what is and what is not considered a related service under the IDEA. In *Department of Education v. Katherine Dorr* (1984), the Ninth Circuit Court of Appeals upheld a lower court ruling that tracheotomy cleaning and reinsertion—if the tube is dislodged—was a related service. Transportation to and from a placement that has been designated as appropriate for providing special services is considered a related service as found in two cases involving individuals who were mentally retarded: *Hurry v. Jones* (1984) and *Alamo Heights Independent School District v. State Board of Education* (1986).

The issue of whether psychotherapy is a related service has major implications for schools, because such a ruling might require expensive services (e.g., out-of-state residential placement) that public schools do not provide. Various litigation has produced differing outcomes. Several cases, including *T. G. v. Board of Education of Piscataway* (1983) and *Max M. v. Thompson* (1984), have contested this issue and found psychotherapy to be a related service. Other litigation, *McKenzie v. Jefferson* (1983), has found that the residential component of placement in a residential facility is medical, not educational, in nature and does not have to be paid for by a school district.

Turnbull (1993) remarked that certain factors tend to determine whether a service is related or medical. These include complexity, constancy, costs, and ultimate value of the service. A related factor is whether the required service is a traditional function of the school-based personnel or can be performed with minor modifications.

Right to Extended School Year

Another issue associated with the education of students with special needs is whether they and other students with disabilities are entitled under the IDEA to an extended school year (ESY) if it is deemed necessary to provide an appropriate education. As Sargent and Fiddler (1987) have summarized, a number of suits have focused on this topic, most of them filed in the early 1980s. While early cases took more interest in students with severe problems, others (e.g., *Georgia ARC v. McDaniel,* 1984) concerned students with milder disabilities.

The most celebrated case was *Armstrong v. Kline* (1979), originally filed in federal district court in Pennsylvania and later appealed to the Third Circuit Court of Appeals. The foremost issue in this litigation was that significant gaps (e.g., summer breaks) in the educational programs of certain students cause losses in skill development (regression) that require an unreasonable amount of time to make up (recoupment) and therefore entitle students to an extended school year. The decisions of both courts found the defendant's policy of limiting educational services to a maximum of 180 days inflexible, thus preventing students from receiving an appropriate education. Sargent and Fiddler (1987) note that the regression and recoupment question has remained the primary determinant in deciding which students qualify for ESY, even though research has yet to validate this concept. They also point out that courts have been concerned not only with that issue but with effects on an individual's self-sufficiency as well.

Right Not to Be Expelled

The Supreme Court ruled in *Honig v. Doe* (1988) that school districts cannot exclude students whose disruptive behaviors are at issue from appropriate programs until the matter is settled and proper due process procedures are exercised. An important aspect of this finding is that the disruptive behaviors in question must be related to the student's disability. As Turnbull (1993) noted, other interventions that do not result in a placement change are permissible. If a student with a disability, however, brings a gun to school, then that student can be placed in an alternative placement for a maximum of forty-five days (Underwood & Mead, 1995).

Another significant case is *J.B. v. Independent School District* (1995). A student committed an offense for which school administrators sought to expel him. The student had never been evaluated for special education ser-

The topic of change of placement is addressed in the 1997 reauthorization of IDEA.

vices. The parents requested an eligibility hearing and also requested that the "stay put provision" be used. Under this provision, a child's placement cannot be changed without parental permission or due process procedures. The court ruled that the parents could make the request. Expulsion proceedings were stopped, and under the "stay put" provision, the child remained in the general classroom ("The Courts Impact on Special Education," 1996).

INSTITUTIONAL RIGHTS

Institutions are addressed in the next chapter, but this section provides an introduction to the legal maneuverings that have become the backdrop for many changes in institutional settings. Much of this section is devoted to discussing a fundamental right that had been denied many of those confined to institutions for too long: the right to treatment.

The terms *treatment* and *habilitation* are often used interchangeably, although some professionals do make a distinction. Both imply the delivery of some type of service, and they have been at the center of much discussion concerning those living in large, segregated residential facilities. Baer (1981) interpreted the various courts' definitions of **habilitation** to mean "behavior change in the direction of those skills that cumulatively allow community living" (p. 91). Although this definition is very general, it does give a sense of purpose. Lakin and Bruininks (1985), analyzing the view of habilitation promoted in *Youngberg v. Romeo* (1982), remarked that the U.S. Supreme Court defines habilitation as something that ensures "safety and freedom from undue restraint." The usefulness of this perspective is questionable.

The treatment issue revolves around the notion that if individuals are placed, often involuntarily, in restrictive institutional settings, then constitutionally they are entitled to services. Many landmark cases have looked at this issue; a few are presented next. Most notable among them are *Wyatt v. Stickney* (1972), *New York Association for Retarded Children v. Rockefeller* (1973), *O'Connor v. Donaldson* (1974), *Halderman v. Pennhurst* (1977), and *Youngberg v. Romeo* (1982).

The legal impetus for reform was dramatized in the litigation of a landmark case, *Wyatt v. Stickney,* in 1972. This case had a direct impact on the adequacy of services in residential facilities for individuals who are mentally retarded. The plaintiffs in this class action suit built their case on the grounds that the residents of the Partlow State School (located in Tuscaloosa, Alabama) were being denied their right to treatment. While this was a class action suit, it was originally filed by the legal guardian of Ricky Wyatt against the Alabama Department of Mental Hygiene in 1970. Specifically, in *Wyatt,* Ricky Wyatt (named plaintiff) represented all residents in the state of Alabama who were involuntarily confined in the state's hospitals.

The decision of Judge Johnson of the District Court for the Middle District of Alabama, North Division, declared that the constitutional rights of those residents were being violated under the Fourteenth Amendment. The failure of this state to provide proper treatment in its residential facilities moved the court to draw up a precedent-setting twenty-two-page appendix that defined minimum treatment standards for the state school to adopt. The order and the decree of the Wyatt decision were comprehensive in their coverage of residents' right to treatment and habilitation, records and review, physical environment, medication, and admissions policies. Minimum treatment standards include the following:

1. Individuals who are borderline or mildly retarded shall not be placed in residential institutions.

2. Admission to a residential institution shall be granted following the determination that the client–environment match is the least restrictive habilitative setting.

3. Institutions must attempt to move residents in the following manner:
   a. To a less structured living environment
   b. From larger to smaller facilities
   c. From larger to smaller living units
   d. From group to individual residence
   e. From segregated to integrated community living
   f. From dependent to independent living

To summarize the importance of *Wyatt,* let us look at what it achieved. First, the case focused exclusively on individuals who were mentally retarded residing in institutions. Second, the court issued a set of minimum standards and monitoring procedures for residential facilities that would serve as a model to other states. Third, the case recognized the constitutional rights of these residents.

Of course, many judicial proceedings deal with essentially the same issues, and they sometimes reach diametrically opposed decisions. This was exactly the situation in the class action suit *Burnham v. Department of Public Health* (1972), in which a completely different decision from the Wyatt decision was reached. Judge Smith, presiding in the U.S. District Court for the Northern District of Georgia, recognized that individuals in mental institutions have a moral right to treatment. But he did not rule that there was a legal obligation for such treatment (Scheerenberger, 1976a). As a result, there was a legal discrepancy between *Wyatt* and *Burnham.* Resolution would come on appeal of *Wyatt* to the Fifth Circuit Court of Appeals (*Wyatt v. Aderholt,* 1974). The Court of Appeals essentially upheld the earlier decision of the Alabama federal court, re-emphasizing that residents have a constitutional right to treatment. Furthermore, this decision allowed the federal court to set standards and monitor their implementation.

In 1986, a consent agreement was approved in federal district court in Alabama, providing a settlement to this litigation, which had been initiated fourteen years earlier. Over the course of time, the original Wyatt case had been reopened periodically to review the status of the implementation of what the court had ordered in Judge Johnson's original decision (*Wyatt v. Hardin,* 1975; *Wyatt v. Ireland,* 1979). The latest action may be the end of this litigation, although the impact of the Wyatt case will remain. The 1986 agreement was conciliatory; both plaintiffs and defendants made compromises. But as Marchetti (1987) describes it, "It appeared that all parties to the litigation and the federal court were seeking a justifiable reason for returning the mental health system back to the state's 'control,' while protecting the rights of the class members" (p. 249). Marchetti provides an excellent chronology of the Wyatt litigation, a concise description of the consent decree, and an interesting discussion of the implications of this action.

Another case presented here because of the attention it received is *New York Association for Retarded Children v. Rockefeller* (1973). This case is commonly referred to as "the Willowbrook case," since the institution under scrutiny was the Willowbrook State School.

This case, like *Wyatt,* originated after complaints were voiced concerning reductions in staff. It focused on three major issues: overcrowding, understaffing, and the absence of community alternatives to institutionalization. Even though conditions did improve, the court's rulings were not as comprehensive and powerful as they had been in *Wyatt.* What may be most important about the Willowbrook case is the national attention it received. It made more people aware of the deplorable conditions and the lack of programming that existed in many such settings.

Another suit that had an impact on institutionalized people, decided by the Fifth Circuit Court of Appeals was *O'Connor v. Donaldson* (1974). Donaldson (the plaintiff) had been committed to an institution in 1957 by his father. It was determined that the defendants were aware at the time of Donaldson's placement that he was neither reckless nor dangerous to himself or others. Once he was institutionalized, Donaldson received neither adequate treatment nor therapy. The decision by the court awarded the plaintiff $38,000 in compensatory and punitive damages, which were to be paid personally by the defendants. In this particular case, the defendants were held personally liable. Subsequently, the case was sent to the court of appeals, where the original decision was upheld. *O'Connor v. Donaldson* is significant in that it established the illegality of involuntarily institutionalizing a person who is not dangerous and who is able to function without institutional care.

The first case concerning individuals who were retarded and residing in institutions to reach the U.S. Supreme Court was *Halderman v. Pennhurst* (1977). This case is fascinating because, in addition to the issues related to correcting unsatisfactory conditions at a large state-run facility (located in southeastern Pennsylvania), it ultimately sought to deinstitutionalize all residents, thereby closing down large, segregated facilities.

In the original action, begun in 1974, Terri Lee Halderman, a twenty-year-old resident of Pennhurst, filed suit on behalf of herself and all present and future residents of the facility, alleging that subhuman conditions and the lack of habilitative programming at Pennhurst violated their statutory and constitutional rights.

In the first phase of the nonjury trial, begun in 1977, the court spent thirty-two days hearing testimony to establish the truth of Halderman's allegations. By the end of this exposition, any illusions of Pennhurst State School and Hospital as a facility for the "care and training" of persons who were mentally retarded were erased. These excerpts from the opinion of presiding Judge Raymond Broderick suggest the quality of "care and training" afforded to residents there:

> Pennhurst is almost totally impersonal. Its residents have no privacy—they sleep in large, overcrowded wards, spend their waking hours together in large day rooms and eat in a large group setting. . . .
>
> All residents on Unit 7 go to bed between 8:00 and 8:30 P.M., are awakened and taken to the toilet at 12:00–12:30 A.M., and returned to sleep until 5:30 A.M. when they are awakened for the day, which begins with being toileted and then having to wait for a 7:00 A.M. breakfast.
>
> The physical environment at Pennhurst is hazardous to the residents, both physically and psychologically. There is often excrement and urine on ward floors, and the living areas do not meet minimal professional standards for cleanliness. Outbreaks of pinworms and infectious disease are common.
>
> Obnoxious odors and excessive noise permeate the atmosphere. Such conditions are not conducive to habilitation. Moreover, the noise level in the day rooms is often so high that many residents simply stop speaking.
>
> Residents' records commonly contain a notation that they would benefit from specific types of programming. However, such programming has, for the most part, been unavailable. The average resident receives only 1½ hours of programming per weekday and no programming on weekends. No one, except those in school, gets more than 3½ to 4 hours per day. If one factors out those programs which are not considered beneficial, the average drops to about 15 minutes per day.
>
> On the whole, the staff at Pennhurst appears to be dedicated and trying hard to cope with the inadequacies of the institution. Nearly every witness who testified concerning Pennhurst stated that it was grossly understaffed to adequately habilitate the residents.

The Broderick court held that confinement at Pennhurst clearly deprives residents of their right to nondiscriminatory habilitation, to minimally adequate care, to due process, equal protection, and freedom from harm, and to treatment by least restrictive means. Broderick ordered the eventual closing of Pennhurst and the establishment of suitable community settings to which residents could transfer. Moreover, he ordered that an individual program plan (IPP) be developed for each remaining resident and that monitoring procedures be established for the duration of the facility's operation.

Pennhurst officials and their various co-defendants appealed this decision in 1979 to the Third Circuit Court of Appeals. The appeals court affirmed the right of every individual who is retarded to receive habilitative care in the least restrictive setting possible as well as his or her private right of action to enforce this right. Although the appeals court did not mandate

Pennhurst's termination, it upheld thirty-eight of the forty-one paragraphs of Judge Broderick's order, along with his belief that persons with retardation would benefit most from community placement. The Third Circuit Court of Appeals based its judgment on statutory grounds—the 1974 Developmental Disabilities Assistance and Bill of Rights Act. The court stated that this legislation created substantive rights to habilitative services for individuals who were retarded.

In 1981, the U.S. Supreme Court reversed the appeals court decision. The high court recognized the inadequate conditions at Pennhurst but did not feel that the congressional intent of the Developmental Disabilities Act created rights and required adequate treatment. McCarthy (1983) summarized the Court's position: "The Supreme Court declared that the Act was not intended to create new substantive rights; it was designed to encourage, but not to mandate, better services for the developmentally disabled" (p. 519). McCarthy goes on to suggest that the Supreme Court position seems to be that it will strictly interpret funding legislation and will not demand that states provide services not explicitly stated in the laws.

In January 1984, out-of-court negotiations began between the parties involved in this case. By fall of that year, a settlement had been reached in which the state agreed to close Pennhurst, thus ending ten years of litigation. Although this famous case did not achieve all the outcomes desired by the plaintiffs, Pennhurst will remain a byword in the movement to close institutions.

In *Youngberg v. Romeo* (1982) the U.S. Supreme Court ruled that individuals who are severely retarded who were involuntarily confined to any state facility had a constitutional right to habilitative services to ensure their safety and freedom from undue restraint—a decidedly restrictive view of habilitation. The Court reasoned that this right is based on the substantive due process provisions of the Fourteenth Amendment. As H.R. Turnbull (1982) has indicated, the case affects professionals in significant ways. It spotlighted the roles of professionals and professional differences of opinion by acknowledging that there are various models of treatment and a lack of consensus about which is best. The Court also recognized that professionals in the field of mental retardation are in much better positions than judges or juries to make decisions about treatment. Lakin and Bruininks (1985) note that the Supreme Court seems to have established a more limited role for federal courts in decisions of this type.

COMMUNITY RIGHTS

Much of the litigation that was directed at securing reasonable treatment in institutional settings (e.g., *Wyatt*) also suggested that efforts be undertaken to establish living conditions in community settings for as many individuals as possible. In line with the goal of providing living conditions as close to normal as possible, advocates have championed the notion of community placement. The resultant community movement, as described in Chapter 11, has taken hold, and many more individuals who are mentally retarded are pursuing their lives in more inclusive ways (see the perspective on Charles Jackson in Chapter 1).

The right to live in community settings has not come without a struggle in many localities. This has been most obvious in community opposition to the establishment of group homes. R. R. Henderson and Vitello (1988) state that there are three kinds of barriers that can interfere with the community living movement: (a) local zoning ordinances, (b) state legislation that requires advance notification and in some cases permission from neighbors, and (c) restrictive covenants (e.g., people in a neighborhood are able to enforce a specific covenant to preserve the character of the neighborhood). Of the three situations, the first has received the most attention. It is discussed further next:

The case of *Cleburne Living Center, Inc. v. City of Cleburne, Texas* (1984) illustrates the problems that arise when a community opposes a group home. The principal obstacle in this case, as well as others like it, is the attempt to establish a group home in a "single-family residence" zone. In the past, group homes were commonly located in less desirable areas that were industrially or commercially zoned—areas for which permits were easier to obtain. In this case, the Cleburne Living Center, Inc., was notified that a special-use permit would have to be approved before it could establish a group home for adults who were mentally retarded. The city council denied this permit on the basis that such a "hospital for the feebleminded" violated a local zoning ordinance. A suit was filed in federal district court claiming that the constitutional rights of these adults were being violated. The federal court upheld the city's decision to deny the request. On appeal, the Fifth Circuit Court of Appeals reversed the district court's ruling, citing that the ordinance was unconstitutional. This case was eventually appealed to the U.S. Supreme Court, which also found the zoning ordinance to be a violation of the plaintiff's equal protection rights.

Adults with special needs living in community settings should be entitled to the same rights as other citizens. Gardner and Chapman (1985) have developed a list of rights that persons living in community-based residential programs should enjoy (presented in Table 13.5). This list is not exhaustive, but it does give a sense of the rights we take for granted that have not always been available to some citizens. To this list could be added other more controversial rights like the right to marry, the right to be parents, and the right to raise children. An overriding right for all is the right to associate with others.

LIFE-AND-DEATH ISSUES

Withholding Treatment

Within the last few years, much media attention has been given to the issue of withholding treatment from certain individuals with disabilities. Two celebrated cases have been *Guardianship of Philip B.* (1983) and *United States*

TABLE 13.5
Rights of Persons in Community-Based Residential Programs

Right to services in the least restrictive environment
Right to normalized living conditions
Right to dignity and respect
Right to freedom from discomfort and deprivation
Right to appropriate clinical, medical, and therapeutic services
Right to vote
Right to religious worship
Right to private communication
Right to free association
Right to physical exercise
Right to seasonal, clean, neat clothing
Right to manage personal funds
Right to bed, dresser, and storage area
Right to privacy
Right to access to public media
Right to adequate nutrition
Freedom from unnecessary medication and mechanical, chemical, or physical restraints
Freedom from involuntary servitude
Right to equal protection and due process

Source: From *Staff Development in Mental Retardation Services: A Practical Handbook* by J. F. Gardner and M. S. Chapman, 1985, Baltimore: Paul H. Brookes. Copyright 1985 by Paul H. Brookes. Reprinted by permission.

v. University Hospital, State of New York at Stony Brook (1984), better known as the Baby Jane Doe case. Both of these cases involve the major issues typically associated with all such cases: parental and family autonomy, appropriateness of governmental intervention, and the question of quality versus sanctity of life. What tends to be missing is concern for the best interest of the child.

The original Becker cases (*In re Phillip B.,* 1979) received much publicity. The earlier litigation was not successful in obtaining the corrective surgery Philip needed to prolong his life. Parental sovereignty won out over governmental interest in such matters. Later guardianship proceedings allowed Philip to have new, surrogate parents and to receive the corrective surgery that he needed. What is interesting in the Becker case is the legal means used to obtain the desired results: guardianship proceedings. Herr (1984) notes that "the jurisdiction of state courts to resolve Becker-type disputes does not depend on constitutional or section 504 violations . . . the remedy . . . was established under a traditional guardianship statute" (p. 38).

The other type of "withholding treatment" case is exemplified by the Baby Jane Doe case. In this type of case, unlike Becker, where the child is older and his abilities are known, the individual is a newborn and typically has severe and multiple disabilities. In this particular case, the hospital, with the parents' consent, chose not to perform certain surgical procedures to correct various physical problems. The government attempted to obtain the infant's medical records to determine whether the child's rights were being violated, taking the position that the treatment program selected (or the lack of one) might be in violation of Section 504. In this case, the federal district judge denied the government access to the child's medical records.

The Baby Jane Doe case and other situations like it have caused much professional reaction. Organizations such as the American Association on Mental Retardation, the ARC, and the Association for Persons with Severe Handicaps (TASH), have taken positions against withholding of treatment. TASH published a monograph on this topic entitled *Legal, Economic, Psychological, and Moral Considerations on the Practice of Withholding Medical Treatment from Infants with Congenital Defects* (1984).

Another effect of the Baby Jane Doe case is congressional action to include "Baby Doe" provisions in amendments to the Child Abuse Prevention and Treatment Act, originally enacted in 1974. The purpose of these provisions is to protect infants with disabilities. This legislation has been supported by a large number of professional organizations, with one notable exception—the American Medical Association. In this legislation, instances where treatment is withheld or withdrawn are referred to as medical neglect.

Capital Punishment

The other life-or-death issue involves the use of the death penalty with persons who are mentally retarded. Figures collected by the National Coalition to Abolish the Death Penalty and other sources indicate that, through mid-1997, over 400 persons have been executed in the United States since various states reinstated capital punishment in 1976. Approximately 2,500 persons live on death rows in the thirty-six states where the death penalty is applied (Perske, 1991). Persons known to be mentally retarded have been executed, and others are part of the group currently awaiting execution—estimates range from 12 to 20 percent. Perhaps the most celebrated case involving a person who was retarded who was sentenced to death involves Johnny Paul Penry. Penry was found guilty of murdering a twenty-two-year-old woman. During the sentencing phase, the judge in the case indicated to jurors that the death sentence could be invoked if a "yes" vote could be obtained on the following three questions (Perske, 1991):

- Did he deliberately commit the crime?
- Was the crime committed without provocation?
- Will he be dangerous in the future?

The jury took only forty-six minutes to answer "yes" to all three questions.

Perske (1991) chronicles that, not long before Penry was to be executed, the Supreme Court agreed to hear his case, *Penry v. Lynaugh* (1989), and focused on two important issues:

MRDD POSITION STATEMENT: CAPITAL PUNISHMENT AND INDIVIDUALS WITH MENTAL RETARDATION

It has been estimated that as many as one in eight persons on death row across the United States has mental retardation. Although a number of professional organizations have protested, most defendants with mental retardation are currently without meaningful protection from execution. In 1989, the Supreme Court in the *Penry* case ruled that the Constitution does not prohibit the execution of a person because of mental retardation even though that person does not meet the requirements of culpability. Without full comprehension of the law and its processes, there is a substantial chance that a person with mental retardation will be convicted and sentenced to death.

Deterrence and retribution have been advanced as two rationales for the death penalty. The *deterrence* theory of capital punishment holds that execution will not only prevent the punished from killing again but will also indirectly deter others. This is predicated on the assumption that the actor will weigh choices and possible consequences. In this re-

gard, the individual must be cognizant of the crimes for which the death penalty is imposed and believe execution is a probable consequence of conviction. For the individual with mental retardation, the goal of deterrence is problematic. The individual is unlikely to have premeditated his crime, may have acted on impulse and lacks the ability to think strategically while considering the future. If the fact that the commission of a certain act may forfeit life cannot be understood, the death penalty as a deterrent loses meaning.

Retribution also is problematic for the individual with mental retardation. Retribution requires that the punishment fit the crime and seeks to meet society's concern for vengeance and faith in the criminal justice system. By definition, the imposition of the death penalty should only be used to accomplish retribution when lesser punishment will not. Additionally, the criminal must be sufficiently culpable to warrant this most severe penalty. The mental and behavioral capacities of persons with mental retardation are

- Should jurors be advised to consider mental retardation as a mitigating factor when considering the death penalty?
- Is it cruel and unusual punishment to execute persons who are mentally retarded?

In five to four rulings on both issues, the Court agreed that mental retardation should be considered as a mitigating factor but did find that persons with mental retardation could be executed. Because the jurors in the Penry case had not considered mental retardation as a mitigating factor, the Court ordered that the case be retried. In this retrial, Penry was again found guilty of committing the crime. The jury, having been given the directive to consider mental retardation as a mitigating factor, found cause to sentence him to death once again.

Most major organizations dedicated to the interests of those who are mentally retarded unconditionally oppose the use of the death penalty with this group. The basic argument centers on the fact that, if one is mentally likely to preclude the level of culpability necessary to inflict the death penalty since they are challenged in their abilities to discriminate, communicate, control impulsivity, and recall. While these individuals may recognize an act as right or wrong, they often may not possess a full understanding of this concept and may not link prior action to later punishment. Many persons with mental retardation cannot comprehend such critical legal concepts as "right," "waiver," "elements of the offense charged," and Miranda warnings.

The Supreme Court has required for two decades that capital punishment be imposed only when it's served a valid deterrent or retributive purpose that a lesser sentence could not. Moreover, the Court has recognized that questions raised concerning the legitimate use of the death penalty in individual cases are essentially questions of personal responsibility, personal characteristics, and moral guilt. In the case of persons with mental retardation, the prudent course is to assume these individuals as a class cannot attain the level of culpability necessary to satisfy the deterrent and retributive goals of capital punishment.

The use of the death penalty for a person with mental retardation is improper and inhumane. Such action serves no legitimate societal interest. It can never satisfy society's demand that punishment must fit both the crime and the criminal's culpability. The individual and social harm of imposing the death penalty on a person who cannot satisfy a reasonable and societal standard of culpability is great.

Recognizing this fact, the Board of Directors of CEC-MR resolves that capital punishment of persons with mental retardation is cruel and inappropriate, is a tragic flaw in the legal system of the United States as it currently addresses the issues of justice for persons with mental retardation, and should not be imposed.

This statement was originally drafted by Dana Cooper, JD, and Kathleen Marshall, Ph.D. (University of South Carolina).

Source: From *MRDD Position Statement: Capital Punishment and Individuals with Mental Retardation* (Approved at the Board of Director's Meeting, October 3, 1992) by Division on Mental Retardation and Developmental Disabilities of the Council for Exceptional Children, 1992, Reston, VA: Council for Exceptional Children. Copyright 1992 by the Council for Exceptional Children. Reprinted by permission.

Given the recent waves of executions in those states where such punishment is allowed, great need exists to focus advocacy efforts on these important efforts.

retarded, then by definition one has limited intellectual and reasoning capacities. This not only affects the defendant's culpability with respect to a crime but also puts an individual who is retarded at great risk of being convicted and sentenced to death in our current criminal justice system. To illustrate professional thinking on this topic, a position statement of the Division on Mental Retardation of the Council for Exceptional Children opposing the use of the death penalty is presented in the accompanying box.

CONCLUSION: PERSISTING PROBLEMS

Much progress has been made in recent years with regard to guaranteeing the individual rights of persons who are mentally retarded, but the heyday of successful litigation may be over. It seems that courts have been stretched as far as they can go in certain areas (e.g., right to treatment) and that more conservative interpretations of the laws are being made. Blatt (1987) referred to some of the changes.

> More and more, the courts are (again) deciding on behalf of defendants rather than plaintiffs. More and more, the legislatures of our country are reluctant to either pass progressive legislation or to fully implement current legislation that would cost the taxpayers money—money which the legislators say the states do not have, and money which the taxpayers say they do not want to give for such purposes as providing the fullest educational opportunities for handicapped individuals. Here again, we have a situation for which nothing succeeds like failure and nothing fails like success. (p. 231)

A second concluding thought to consider relates to efforts to integrate persons who are mentally retarded into less restrictive settings; however, the substance of the message applies to much of what happens to those for whom we have concern and interest. H.R. Turnbull (1988) pointed out the difference between de jure and de facto integration:

> De jure integration occurs when the law overrides or allows for it by overriding various legal obstacles to it. This happens when group home legislation overrides local zoning, when *Pennhurst-Willowbrook* litigation compels the creation of community placements for people in institutions, when the Education of the Handicapped Act enforces a rebuttable presumption in favor of the "least restrictive" placement of disabled children in schools or when a Cleburne Court strikes down exclusionary zoning on Fourteenth Amendment grounds.
> De facto integration is a different matter. Its first stage consists of dissipated opposition to community placement and residences. But simple movement from a negative to a benign attitude does not assure integration. Its second stage consists of voluntary interaction of the nondisabled with people with retardation and their families. That voluntariness—the essence of noncompulsory giving and receiving—is still too elusive. But there is a reassuring element in all this. It is that negative conditions become muted and that benign conditions certainly are preferable to the disease of hostility and prejudice. Likewise, the benign sometimes is transformed to a positive, welcoming condition. (p. 59)

The challenge for all of us is to help create social conditions that are more positive, welcoming, and supportive to all.

FINAL THOUGHTS

Many of the issues in the field of special education and human services have been civil rights issues, and rights have been granted through processes other than education, psychology, or service delivery. We believe that anyone who studies mental retardation must, at some point, be able to articulate the individual rights guaranteed to all citizens who have this condition. Equally important is an understanding of the legal issues underlying these rights and the battles fought to secure them.

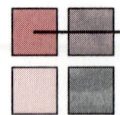

SUMMARY

CONTEXT FOR SECURING INDIVIDUAL RIGHTS

- Ideologies of egalitarianism and normalization have resulted in important precedents and treatment outcomes.
- Certain legal terms such as "equal protection" and "due process" must be understood.
- Persons with mental retardation historically have been vulnerable to purposely unequal treatment.
- There are instances when the best interests of an individual clash with one's legal rights.
- Mechanisms for securing rights are found at the federal, state, and local levels.

LEGAL PRECEDENTS FOR INDIVIDUAL RIGHTS

- Educational rights include the right to education, right to an appropriate evaluation and classification, right to an appropriate education, right to an appropriate placement, right to related services, right to an extended school year, and right not to be expelled.
- A noteworthy history of litigation exists that has tried to secure the right to treatment or habilitation for those confined to institutional settings.
- Two "life-and-death" issues affecting individuals with mental retardation are withholding treatment from newborns who are severely involved and the use of capital punishment.

CHAPTER 14

Institutional and Community Living

After reading this chapter,
the student should be able to:

- Discuss key factors associated with institutional living.
- Identify and describe many of the defining characteristics of the community living movement.
- Discuss many of the key issues that have influenced the direction of the deinstitutionalization movement today.

Key Terms

aversives
Cloak of Competence
community residential
  settings

deinstitutionalization
egalitarianism

public residential
  facilities (PRFs)
transition shock

Dramatic changes have occurred in the lives of adults with mental retardation since the 1960s. Yet, few have been as striking as the exodus of people from large public residential facilities to smaller community-based homes. Castellani (1987), referring to the broader classification of developmental disabilities, reported that: "There is simply no other area of human services in which fundamental changes in the context and structure of services, finance, clientele, and organization have been so dramatic and far-reaching in such a short period of time" (p. 149). For some, the transition has been a smooth one; for others, however, major challenges have accompanied even the most ordinary tasks. The purpose of this chapter is to introduce the reader to the influential factors associated with institutional and community living, especially those that are most relevant to the lives of persons with mental retardation.

INSTITUTIONAL LIVING

To most people, the word *institution* conjures up a multitude of unpleasant thoughts and images. Perhaps Burton Blatt (1987) said it best: "It is difficult to discuss institutions without engaging in controversy. After all, the Willowbrooks and Pennhursts of the world are famous for being infamous" (p. 159). Motion pictures such as *Awakenings* (Parkes, Lasker, & Marshall, 1991) and *One Flew over the Cuckoo's Nest* (Zaentz, Douglas, & Forman, 1975) have depicted many of the injustices often associated with institutional living. While there have been and will likely continue to be injustices that threaten the quality of life in such settings, it is not the placement in institutions alone that imperils a person's right to a happy, healthy, humane environment. Rather, it is the attitudes and practices of those who offer the care that define the quality of life people of all ability levels experience.

THE COMMITMENT PROCESS

Placement in an institution generally begins with a commitment. There are two formal procedures for admitting someone to an institutional setting, voluntary admission and involuntary commitment. Both forms of commitment require legal proceedings conducted according to the guidelines established in each locality. Nonetheless, one should have at least a cursory understanding of this process. Following is a brief description of how these two processes occur in the state of Mississippi.

In Mississippi, certification for voluntary admission to a regional treatment facility for persons with mental retardation begins when a person or the parent or legal guardian of a person with mental retardation files a written application with the director of a treatment facility. This application is accompanied by certificates from two physicians, or one physician and one psychologist, attesting to the person's need for treatment. Acceptance at the treatment facility depends on several factors, the two most important of which are the director's determination that the person will likely benefit from services available at the facility, and a preadmission evaluation. The preadmission evaluation includes an in-depth and individualized evaluation of the applicant's medical, psychological, nutritional, and social status. Persons seeking and receiving voluntary admission may elect to leave the regional treatment facility after a minimum of five days following written notification of intent to leave and barring no further formal appeals to the local chancery clerk for involuntary certification (Mississippi Code Ann., 1991). Voluntary admission is a relatively easy process, since all parties involved tend to agree upon the desired outcome.

It is important to realize that the procedures for admission and commitment described here represent only one system; notable differences are likely to be found in other locations throughout the country.

Involuntary commitment is also legal but is more problematic. The *Mississippi Code* (1991) provides an example representative of many jurisdictions. In the case of a parent- or guardian-initiated contact, the individual under consideration may not wish to be committed to an institution. A written affidavit for commitment is filed with the local chancery clerk complete with factual descriptions of relevant behaviors. Two physicians, or a physician and a psychologist, are requested to conduct a preliminary evaluation and determine if there is a need for institutionalization. Persons found in need of institutionalization as a result of the physical and psychological examination receive a formal hearing, under the direction of the court chancellor (judge), within ten days of certification. The director of an institution has both the right and the responsibility to apply to the court chancellor for a discontinuation of treatment for the person, to transfer the person to a less restrictive facility, or to return the person to the custody of the court if it is believed to be in the best interest of that person.

THE INSTITUTIONAL SETTING

Large public residential facilities are not unlike many other administratively complex organizations. **Public residential facilities (PRFs)** are state-supported facilities for persons with mental retardation and developmental disabilities designed to accommodate sixteen or more live-in residents at any one time. With quality of care a never-ending issue and many managed-care initiatives threatening even basic medical services, large PRFs are having to redefine their administrative and organizational structures accordingly. Inherent in such a structure is a system of services that is presumed to be

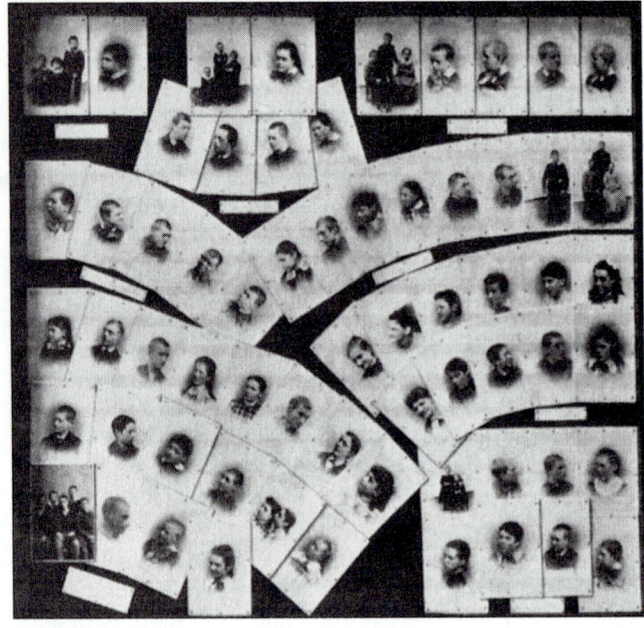

Institutions have changed in many ways since this bulletin board was assembled in the early 20th century. The small metal tags identified the eight groups of "pupils" from left to right, top to bottom, as "cretins, gelatinoids, hydrocephalic, isolated congenital cases, microcephalic, congenital (one of two or more cases occurring in a family), excitable, paralytic."

capable of meeting the needs of people of all life stages and across the broad range of disability levels. Figure 14.1 illustrates the *typical* structure of a large PRF offering services to persons with mental retardation.

As one can imagine, it takes a rather large number of people for a PRF to operate as intended. Most institutions require two very broad categories of people for effective operation: those who are admitted for services, generally referred to as the residents, and those who are hired to provide the necessary services, typically referred to as institutional staff. The operation of the institution occurs primarily on two levels, administrative and nonadministrative. People employed as administrators are responsible for management issues such as the budget, admissions, training, and coordination of services. Nonadministrative personnel are the staff members who implement the many treatment programs and services and provide the day-to-day tasks as outlined by administrative personnel.

Within the nonadministrative category are three classifications of institutional staff, all of which are essential to the smooth operation of a large PRF. First are the professional staff members licensed by the state to habilitate the resident toward adaptive functioning and an eventual return to the community. Examples of such staff members are nurses, physicians, psychologists, teachers, and therapists (e.g., occupational, speech, vocational). Second are the direct care staff members who often work in an educational, recreational, or health-care capacity and who are usually in direct and continuous contact with the residents. Examples of such service providers include cottage attendants, nursing assistants, and teaching assistants. The

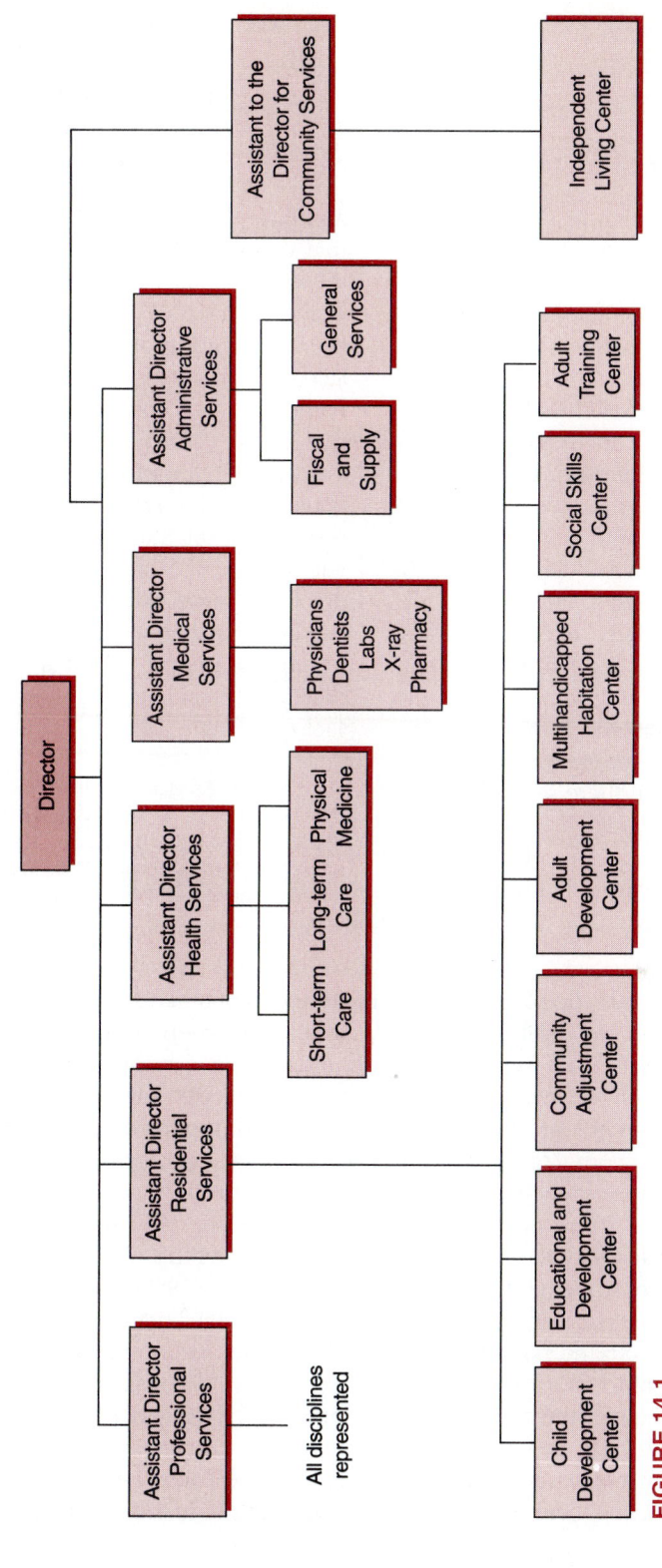

FIGURE 14.1
Schematic of a Large Public Residential Facility

THE IMPORTANCE OF DIRECT CARE PERSONNEL

Heidi is an older woman of German background who works in a unit of very low functioning residents. Every day she wakes up her assigned group, attends to their immediate needs, cleans their beds, bathes, dresses, and feeds them. While she is doing the tasks most of us would find less than enjoyable, she is talking to these uncommunicative and mostly unresponsive persons, as if they were her best friends or close relatives, about all sorts of topics. The fact that none of them ever contributes to the conversation does not seem to affect her at all.

After witnessing these events on more than one occasion, I asked her why she carried on the way she did with people who probably don't understand a word she was saying. She looked at me strangely and said, "Got to be a person in there somewhere."

I left that particular unit very humbled but with a renewed respect for those who mean so much to those we actually know so little

about. I was particularly struck by the idea that we don't know what is going on inside these individuals who perform so low on our existing measures of ability. Perhaps they hear and understand everything that is said to them but just can't communicate their feelings to us. (For a related example, read the book *Johnny Got His Gun,* by D. Trumbo [1959, Bantam Books]). On this particular day, I was also reminded of something that I tell students every time we visit such residential facilities: these individuals are much more like us than unlike us.

I also realized one other thing—to a small number of people, Heidi is more important than the President, the governor, Michael Jackson, Magic Johnson, or Roseanne Barr.

Source: From *Exceptional Children in Focus* (5th ed., pp. 71–72) by J. R. Patton, J. M. Kauffman, J. M. Blackbourn, and G. B. Brown, 1991, Upper Saddle River, NJ: Merrill/Prentice Hall. Copyright 1991 by Merrill/Prentice Hall. Reprinted by permission.

third type of staff members are the maintenance personnel, whose primary job responsibilities are to ensure the upkeep and operation of the physical plant itself (e.g., janitors, grounds keepers, repair personnel). Their contact with the residents is typically minimal. Not surprisingly, the attitudes and psychological well-being of these three groups of people are often far more powerful than the upper level policy decisions in determining whether those in their care will be abused, ignored, or genuinely served.

If services provided by institutions are reflective of the needs of the residents, then it can safely be said that the PRFs of today are markedly different from the PRFs of fifty years ago. In the 1950s, the average institution had in excess of 1,500 residents, with some facilities housing as many as several thousand people at any one time. The decline in daily residency since the mid-1960s has been both substantial and consistent (Figure 14.2). For example, the average daily population of residents in large PRFs was 65,078 in 1995, down from an all-time high of 228,500 in 1967. This 72 percent drop in residency is best quantified by the following population-based ratios. While there were 116 people (per 100,000 in the general population) in large

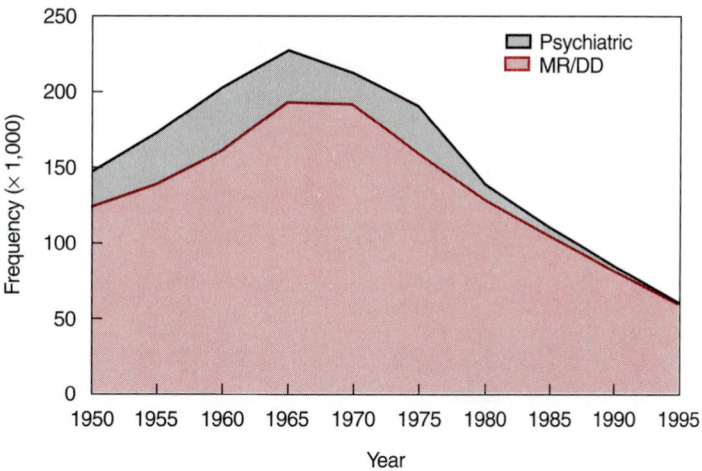

FIGURE 14.2

Average Daily Population of Persons with Mental Retardation and Related Conditions Living in Large Public Residential Facilities from 1950 through 1995

Source: Lakin, Prouty, and Bruininks (1996).

PRFs in 1967, there were only 25 people (per 100,000 in the general population) living in large PRFs in 1995. During 1995 alone, 5,333 persons with mental retardation and developmental disabilities were released from institutions, constituting 8.4 percent of the year's average daily population of residents (Lakin, Prouty, & Bruininks, 1996). By June 30, 1995, three states and the District of Columbia closed their last remaining facility (i.e., New Hampshire, Vermont, Rhode Island) (Stancliffe & Lakin, 1996). And, in the four-year period from 1992 through 1995, a total of 46 large public residential facilities closed, representing a closure rate of 11.5 facilities per year. As is the case with most descriptive statistics, however, there are great variations within and across public residential settings.

Not only have the facilities changed, but the characteristics of persons served in PRFs have changed as well. The nature of the disability is also much more complex than it was ten years ago; 57 percent of the residents had two or more diagnosed disabilities as opposed to 40 percent only five years earlier (Scheerenberger, 1992). The data presented in Table 14.1 give some indication of the characteristics of residents who typically inhabit institutions. For example, in a study of 288 large, state-operated facilities, C. C. White, Lakin, Bruininks, and Li (1991) reported that 42 percent had epilepsy, 21 percent had cerebral palsy, 6 percent were deaf, and 47 percent had behavioral disorders. This increasingly complex pattern of disabilities is further highlighted by the advancing age of the residential population, a population that is aging faster than even that of the U.S. population (Amado, Lakin, & Menke, 1990). Table 14.1 illustrates the inverse relationship between the number of residents

TABLE 14.1

Percentage of Residents of Large State-Operated Residential Facilities
According to Age, Level of Mental Retardation, and Functional Limitations

Resident Characteristics	Year			
	1977	1982	1987	1989
Age				
0 to 21 years	35.8	22.0	12.7	10.6
22 to 39 years	41.3	50.2	54.1	52.4
40 to 62 years	19.2	22.9	27.3	30.3
63 ≤ years	3.7	5.0	6.0	6.8
Level of Mental Retardation				
Borderline/Mild	10.4	7.1	7.2	6.7
Moderate	16.4	12.5	9.8	10.1
Severe	27.6	24.2	20.0	19.5
Profound	45.6	56.2	63.0	63.7
Functional Limitations				
Cannot walk	23.3	25.5	29.5	31.2
Cannot talk	43.5	49.1	54.8	55.3
Not toilet-trained	34.1	38.0	53.4	54.6
Cannot eat independently	21.4	35.0	37.8	38.2

Source: From *Persons with Mental Retardation and Related Conditions in State-Operated Residential Facilities: Year Ending June 30, 1989 with Longitudinal Trends from 1950 to 1989* (p. 28), by C. C. White, K. C. Lakin, R. H. Bruininks, and X. Li, 1991, Minneapolis, MN: University of Minnesota, Center for Residential and Community Services. Copyright 1991 by the University of Minnesota. Adapted by permission.

with borderline/mild mental retardation and those with profound mental retardation. In summary, residents today tend to be older, have greater levels of disability, and, as a result, have more extensive support needs.

FACTORS INFLUENCING INSTITUTIONALIZATION

Just as the characteristics and conditions of PRFs are markedly different from even a few decades ago, the factors influencing families toward placement of loved ones in institutions are also very different. The actual steps toward commitment comprise but one facet of the institutionalization process. Following is a brief description of other factors that might prompt the parents or guardians of a person with mental retardation to seek institutionalization.

Foremost among the factors leading to institutionalization are the characteristics of the individual. It is generally recognized that behavioral problems, and particularly those that interfere with social functioning, are the single greatest reason for placement in, or readmission to, a public residential facility. Campbell, Smith, and Wool (1982) found more maladaptive problems among those who were being considered for institutionalization than among those who were not being considered. Similarly, Bromley and Blacher (1992) found level of functioning and behavioral problems to be major determinants of placement for children with severe disabilities. With incidences of severe mental illness as high as 10 percent and minor mental illness as high as 60 percent among residents of large institutions (Parsons, May, & Menolascino, 1984), it stands to reason that the people most likely to be placed in institutions, and the people most likely to be retained in institutions in an era of deinstitutionalization, are those for whom behavioral and social functioning is most aberrant. The salient feature of these behavior problems is that they are of such severity that families are generally not able to handle the person at home.

Substantial and ongoing medical care represents a second factor that is very much related to the characteristics and conditions of the person (Spreat, Telles, Conroy, Feinstein, & Columbato, 1987). Different from persons without mental retardation and, to a large extent, different from persons with mental retardation living in community settings, persons living in PRFs tend to require an active and ongoing model of multidisciplinary medical care. That is, they do not simply require the support of a health-care professional intermittently, but, rather, they require the consistent, collaborative, and integrated input of several health-care professionals for simple daily living. With as many as 30 to 40 percent of people with mental retardation requiring supportive assistance from medical personnel other than physicians and dentists (e.g., physical therapists, speech/language therapists), demands for service are generally greatest among those with the more severe levels of disability, which, for now, means persons living in institutions.

Beyond the characteristics and needs of the individual are those of the family. There is no question that family characteristics and family life events influence the institutionalization process. For example, it is widely recognized that severe mental retardation does not favor any particular social class; yet, Eyman, Dingman, and Sabagh (1966) have found evidence to suggest that the decision to institutionalize may be very much related to one's level of socioeconomic status (SES), with earlier referrals coming from families from high SES backgrounds and proportionally more referrals coming from families of low SES backgrounds. Other factors such as number and type of daily stressors, number of parents in the home, complexity of a child's disability, level of parental education, and proximity to the out-of-home placement facility, are all associated with a family's degree of involvement in the placement process (Blacher & Baker, 1992; Bromley & Blacher, 1992).

See Chapter 12 for a more complete discussion of family considerations.

Family characteristics and degree of daily stressors notwithstanding, most parents choose institutionalization primarily out of concern for the child's welfare. This action results from concern about specific characteristics of their children in conjunction with the belief that the institutional setting is the best alternative possible—an orientation that is quickly changing. Some of the more common perceptions supporting this belief are listed below and derive from a number of sources: (a) the child's inability to develop independent living skills, (b) a notion that institutions are centers of special expertise and medical care, and (c) the view of institutional staff as loving, caring, and concerned persons (Larson & Lakin, 1991; Latib, Conroy, & Hess, 1984; Spreat et al., 1987). Family beliefs in favor of community residential placements are discussed later in the chapter. According to Spreat et al. (1987), 74 percent of the respondents in one study indicated that families were influenced to institutionalize their child by the advice of a physician, member of the clergy, or other professional. It may well be that there remains a serious and long-standing training problem among direct care physicians when it comes to mental retardation and disability-related issues (Guralnick, Heiser, Bennett, & Richardson, 1988).

COMMUNITY LIVING

Safford and Safford's (1996) text offers a nice, comprehensive review of the care and treatment of persons with disabilities throughout history.

Just as Hollywood has continued to sensationalize many of the injustices of institutional living, so, to, have they glamorized some of the potential benefits of integrated, community living. The motion picture *Forest Gump* (Finerman, Tisch, Starkey, & Zemekis, 1994) offers one example. Despite the recency of the community living movement, the notion that institutions are not appropriate for most persons with mental retardation is not a new one. Many of the programs in place today were first conceptualized as many as 200 years ago (Safford & Safford, 1996). If the overriding goal of the community living movement is to allow persons with mental retardation to live in settings that are as similar as possible to everyone else's, then they must be placed in residences that, as nearly as possible, mirror the contemporary American home. While many have been relocated to smaller, community-based placements, others still have not.

One trend that is illustrative of the vigor of the institutionalization movement from 1860 to 1980 is the rapid growth of PRFs during that period (Figure 14.3). More poignant perhaps is the finding that while the number of large public institutions has only recently begun to diminish, the drop in the number of persons living in large, state-operated institutions has continued unabated since the late 1960s.

ACCESS TO COMMUNITY SERVICES

Whereas access to an institution occurs primarily through a formal commitment process that is legally monitored, access to community residential services is much less rigid and is intended to be open to all. Following is a brief description of the process by which persons with mental retardation gain access to community residential settings, settings that more closely resemble natural family homes in traditional residential areas.

Most children with mental retardation today do not live in an institution; rather, they live at home with their natural families. Consequently, and as mentioned in Chapter 12, children with and without mental retardation currently reside in a wide range of family living options, some more beneficial

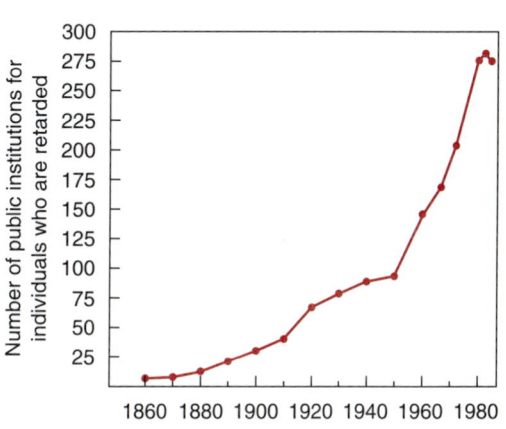

Historically, programming in institutions was minimal or nonexistant. (From Christmas in Purgatory: A Photographic Essay on Mental Retardation *(3rd ed.), Syracuse, NY. Permission granted by Human Policy Press.*

FIGURE 14.3
Number of Publicly Supported Institutions for Persons with Mental Retardation

Source: From "Community Placement and Adjustment of Deinstitutionalized Clients: Issues and Findings" by E. M. Craig and R. B. McCarver in *International Review of Research in Mental Retardation* (Vol. 12, p. 98) edited by N. R. Ellis and N. W. Bray, 1984, Orlando, FL: Academic Press. Copyright 1984 by Academic Press.

Children with mental retardation live in a wide range of family living options.

and supportive than others. Because children under the age of eighteen are not routinely expected to live on their own in our society, the notion of community settings applies mainly to adults living in the community. Exceptions to this are children with disabilities who are placed in family-type dwellings. Because these options represent a continuum of living options, the former would in all likelihood be a natural family home with the latter being a small community residential setting.

Placement in a community residential facility will most likely be pursued when the person reaches young adulthood and leaves school. Other young adults continue living with family members following the school years and may elect to pursue a community placement at a later date. In a small percentage of cases, that even means middle-adulthood when parents of an adult child with mental retardation can no longer take adequate care of the offspring at home. In any case, young, middle-age, and older adults should be allowed the opportunity to live in community residential settings when they so desire.

The most typical time—and some would say, the most appropriate time—for people with and without mental retardation to leave home and establish their own residence in the community is immediately after the school years. For the young adult with mental retardation exiting the public school system, recent legislation has mandated that a number of transition services be offered prior to leaving the public schools. Under the best possible circumstances, that means transition services that began when the student was in the ninth or tenth grade and culminate in a transition service delivery plan that includes, among other things, movement out of the natural family home and into a community residential facility. When that day comes, family and friends are recruited to help the young adult with the move. At this point, setting up a new home away from the family home is very much like that of any young adult moving away from home for the first time.

For young adults transitioning out of an institution, the procedures are a bit more formal. As one can imagine, much of the formality is traceable to the procedures for admission. Since it took certification by a judge and medical personnel to approve the admission, it often takes approval of judicial and medical personnel to grant the change of residential status. Generally, a request for transition is made to the person's case manager, and the service delivery team sets up an evaluation to formally process the request, similar in many ways to the multidisciplinary team evaluations conducted for the Individualized Education Program (IEP) at the elementary and secondary levels. A pretransition evaluation is conducted, and the person's likelihood for success is estimated for an alternative residential setting. The transition team then makes a recommendation to the director of the institution as to their decision and the reasons for that decision. If the evaluation is positive and the transition team is supportive of the move, a community support case manager is then involved and the transition scheduled. All of this assumes that there is room for the person in a community residential facility.

If the evaluation team determines that the person's likelihood for success in the new setting is not good, the request for transition may be denied. In such cases, parents or guardians can always appeal to the director of the institution for further consideration. The director has the option of either supporting the team's recommendation, overturning the team's recommendation, or suspending the decision until more data are gathered. When the director's evaluation follows the transition team's recommendation to maintain placement in the institution, family members or guardians then have the right to request that the person be withdrawn from the institution and reassigned to their care.

COMMUNITY SETTINGS

In Chapter 11 we presented information on congregate care facilities, large as well as small. There is a wide range of congregate care options in the community, most of which can be officially classified as community residential settings. **Community residential settings** are typically those with paid service providers and fifteen or fewer residents located in traditional residential neighborhoods. Many, though, are actual family homes and only resemble some of the smaller congregate care facilities on paper. Often, the distinctions are subtle and made based on the guidelines of the respective funding agencies. Just as no two public residential facilities are exactly alike, no two community residential settings are exactly alike, either.

The nation has indeed moved from an institution-based model of residential living to one that is primarily community-based. Whereas thirty years ago, 84 percent of people with mental retardation and developmental disabilities receiving residential services lived in large public residential facilities, today only about 32 percent do so. Further, over half (52 percent) of the 314,000 people receiving residential services in 1995 received them in community residential settings in which 6 or fewer people lived. More surprising perhaps is the realization that 24 percent (75,000) of those receiving services received them in a home with three or fewer people and that 13 percent of all persons receiving state-supported residential services received them in a home that they themselves owned or rented. The ratio of community residential settings to large PRF settings is also reflected in this trend. Of the 1,839 state-supported facilities serving people with mental retardation and developmental disabilities on June 30, 1995, only one in seven facilities was a large PRF (Prouty & Lakin, 1996).

At one end of the spectrum of community residential settings are intermediate care facilities for persons with mental retardation (ICF/MRs). These facilities serve as a residential hybrid between the large PRFs and the small family-type homes. While there are large ICF/MRs with room for sixteen or more persons at a given time (viz., PRFs), the ICF/MRs in this case meet the definition of community residential settings in that they are likely to have fifteen or fewer persons and, in most cases, reside in traditional residential neighborhoods. Further, they are generally staffed by a number of paid educational, medical, and social service personnel who also provide services similar to those offered in the larger institutional settings. For some persons with mental retardation leaving the institutional setting, an ICF/MR is a first stop along the community residential setting continuum.

At the other end of the community setting continuum are independent living settings and supervised apartments. In an increasing number of cases, these dwellings are owned or leased by the resident who lives in the dwelling; that is, they hold the mortgage or lease on the residence. Although a paid, professional staff member may have responsibility for some or all of the formal operations of the setting, the assistance (e.g., payment of rent, connection of utilities, contact with maintenance personnel) provided is one of support rather than overarching responsibility. The differences are certainly subtle, and, obviously, much depends upon the adjustment and adaptive capabilities of the persons in these settings.

Whereas a residential agency can hold the lease on a given setting and allow much freedom and responsibility on the part of the resident, in other settings, the resident holds the lease and yet has little in the way of formal responsibility. For this reason, Anderson, Polister, Prouty, and Lakin (1996) have defined two other classifications of community settings into which people are being placed with increasing frequency:

> *Foster family home.* A home owned or rented by an individual or family in which they live and provide care for one or more unrelated persons with mental retardation or developmental disabilities.

> *Own home.* A home owned or rented by one or more persons with mental retardation or developmental disabilities as the person(s)' own home in which personal assistance, instruction, supervision, and other support is provided as needed. (p. 54)

Not included in the aforementioned categories is the family home, a home that may or may not be owned or leased by a family member, but one in which the primary care for another is provided by a natural, biological, or adoptive relative. Irrespective of the range and pervasiveness of supports on-site, this is a home as opposed to a facility and is one that comes with all of the advantages and disadvantages of normal family living. These homes may or may not be licensed by the state for additional or reimbursable funds.

Nearly two-thirds of all persons receiving residential services in the United States do so in the home of a family member.

Approximately 22,000 people with mental retardation and developmental disabilities are spread across 13,000 foster family care settings in the United States, over half of which are concentrated in six states (i.e., Michigan, New Jersey, Pennsylvania, New York, Washington, Wisconsin). Further, four states accounted for 50 percent of the 33,000 residences in the United States with homes owned or leased by a recipient of residential services: California, Ohio, Wisconsin, and Florida. Finally, and not surprisingly, nearly two-thirds (216,000) of all persons receiving residential services in the United States reported receiving them in the home of a family member. Two states, California and New York, accounted for over half of all recipients, with 65,000 persons and 45,000 persons, respectively. A total of eight states, including the two just mentioned, reported that three of four (76 percent) recipients of residential services received them in a family member's home (i.e., Arizona, Connecticut, Florida, New Jersey, Ohio, Wisconsin) (Anderson et al., 1996).

The residential service system is indeed a fluid one. One might imagine from the above data that all movement for individuals as well as residential agencies, is one-directional—that is, that individuals with mental retardation and developmental disabilities are moving to smaller facilities at the same time that state and nonstate agencies are downsizing their entire residential service delivery system. While those trends are correct and supported by the data, there is also a great deal of movement that concerns service delivery personnel. For example, Bradley and Allard (1992) reported that of the 6,340 residential programs surveyed by the University of Minnesota's Center for Residential and Community Services in 1977, 38.4 percent "were no longer providing services to persons with developmental disabilities at the same address when the follow-up survey was conducted in 1982" (p. 285). Further, Conroy and Bradley (1985) found that 40 percent of the residences used for study in a 1980 to 1981 research project were not at the same address in the 1984 phase of the study. It is likely then, that some of the movement seen in community populations is not solely a function of enhanced service delivery, but, rather, due to the instability of the service delivery system itself. Change can indeed be good, particularly for people whose skills and abilities are such that new environments and locations can foster further growth and development. However, asking people to move and change for reasons that go beyond improved service delivery is an indictment of the system and a potential threat to the well-being of one of America's most vulnerable populations.

FACTORS INFLUENCING LIFE IN THE COMMUNITY

Because of the relatively recent nature of the deinstitutionalization movement, the concept of community adjustment is little more than a few decades old. More accurately, the concept is still evolving. Follow-up studies are typically conducted with one of two groups in mind: people who have recently left a special education program, who were discussed in Chapter 11, and persons who have recently been released from an institution. One of the earliest and most often cited studies on the community adjustment of adults with mental retardation is that of Edgerton (1967). A description of his project, now more than thirty years old, follows.

The study was designed to gain as much information as possible about the everyday lives of 53 men and women 20 to 75 years of age who were released from Pacific State Hospital in California between 1949 and 1958. In this study, Edgerton (1967) and his colleagues decided to focus on seven key areas of community adjustment: "where and how the ex-patients lived, making a living, relations with others in the community, sex, marriage, and children, 'spare time' activities, their perception and presentation of self, and their practical problems in maintaining themselves in the community" (pp. 16–17).

Interviews with the subjects and significant others (viz., employers, friends, relatives) were conducted, allowing Edgerton and his colleagues to gain much information about the subjects' lives in their respective communities. Approximately seventeen hours of investigation were devoted to each of the fifty-three people in the study. Edgerton found his subjects to be coping with life in the community relatively well, but with some difficulties. The authors point out that many of the subjects experienced complications dealing with stigma related to the label of mental retardation. He found these former residents to be clinging to a **Cloak of Competence;** that is, actively spending much time and energy denying their disability and attempting to present themselves as persons without mental retardation. Areas considered

Deinstitutionalization leads to normal living and activities for persons who are mentally retarded.

to be problematic by the subjects included making a living and managing sex, marriage, reproduction, and appropriate use of leisure time. To cope with these problems and to help pass as someone without mental retardation, many of the subjects developed relationships with people who could help them respond to problems of everyday living. Today, such a person is generally referred to as an advocate.

Twelve to fourteen years after the original study, Edgerton and Bercovici (1976) located and interviewed thirty of the original fifty-three subjects for further study. As in phase one (1960 and 1961), interviews and participant-observation methods were used to gather information about adjustment to the community. Unlike phase one, however, Edgerton and his colleagues videotaped the behaviors of subjects using a portable video camera. In addition to specific questions about current levels of adjustment, subjects were asked to compare their lives in 1972 and 1973 with their lives in 1960 and 1961. Ratings were assigned to the subject's responses by members of the investigative team and comparisons were made: eight subjects had improved, twelve had not changed, and ten appeared to have regressed. While the researchers noted that they were not able to predict very well from original data how a person would be doing at a later date, some general statements were warranted. As length of time in the community increased, subjects seemed to have fewer feelings of stigmatization, were less concerned with their mental retardation, and had less need for benefactors.

A number of points raised by the researchers are worth reiterating. First, adjustment is a complex and multiply determined concept. Second, as Edgerton and Bercovici (1976) pointed out, "social adjustment . . . may sometimes fluctuate markedly, not only from year to year, but from month to month or even from week to week" (p. 495). Third, what constitutes good social acceptance from the viewpoint of the person with mental retardation may differ substantially from acceptance criteria used by professionals. The following statement corroborates this:

> after many years of community living, persons once institutionalized as mentally retarded could . . . develop their own collective and individual views of what constitutes good social adjustment. If, as we suspect, our criteria of adjustment will continue to emphasize competence and independence while retarded persons themselves emphasize personal satisfaction, then our dilemma is even worse than we had all previously recognized. (Edgerton & Bercovici, 1976, p. 495)

In 1982, twenty years after the original study, Edgerton and his associates again located and interviewed as many of the subjects as possible from phases one and two of the study (Edgerton, Bollinger, & Herr, 1984). Of the original 53 subjects providing information in 1960 and 1961 (and 30 subjects in 1972 through 1975), only 15 people were available for participation in phase three of the study. This group was now much older and had an average age of fifty-six years. Using data-gathering techniques similar to those mentioned previously, researchers ranked the subjects according to the following areas of adjustment: life satisfaction, social competence, life stress, relative dependence on benefactors, quality of life, and degree of improvement in life circumstances over the last decade. Among those in the last category, three had improved, five were considered to be stable, and four were believed to be worse off than ten years previous. No agreement could be reached among the raters about the remaining three subjects, except that overall, the subjects conveyed an unshakable sense of optimism: "They believed that the future could be better and that their efforts could make a difference; they would pursue a better life by a variety of means" (Edgerton et al., 1984, p. 350).

Virtually thirty years after the first published study of persons exiting Pacific State Hospital, Edgerton (1993) reported that the general spirit of optimism previously demonstrated continued to grow unabated. That in growing older, the sixteen people (one more than in 1982) available for the study had, for the most part, grown wiser, stronger, and happier in their older adult years. As recently as 1992, the lives of those in the cohort had remained fairly stable. Although funding cutbacks decreased the frequency and duration of personal visits from the researchers, some members of the sample continued to be visited or called as often as every two weeks, others every four to six weeks. Though their lives were reportedly more stable, that does not mean that they were free of difficulty. Quite the opposite, the lives of adults in this thirty-year follow-up study appeared to be as encumbered with the difficulties of daily living as anyone else's in society.

Take the example of Richard, a sixty-five-year-old retired employee of a trucking company. Richard overcame the difficulties of transitioning from a state hospital into the community; yet not even limitations associated with illiteracy prevented him from claiming thirty-one years as a member of his local Teamsters Union. Unfortunately for Richard, the unshakable sense of optimism referred to earlier translated to an inability to recognize, or at least fully appreciate, the consequences of his actions. At nearly 300 pounds, requests by his doctors and others to improve his diet went ignored. Meals-on-wheels from the local hospital were taken to be supplements to his normal diet of burgers, fries, and sodas throughout the day. Yet, at sixty-eight years of age Richard died happy, fulfilled, and content with the direction his life had taken.

A second example is that of Hal and Midge, married to one another and both former residents of Pacific State Hospital. According to Edgerton (1993), Hal "speaks articulately and well, reads and writes, possesses extensive knowledge of the world, and gives no indication of being mentally retarded, no doubt because he was always incorrectly diagnosed (a post-release IQ test recorded 82)" (p. 213). Although estranged from Midge for a number of years, he continues to live and move throughout the community in such a way that few would ever suspect that he had at one time lived in Pacific State Hospital. At last contact, Midge lived with her brother and mother, helping to take care of both of them. Still technically married to Hal, there is no evidence of a continuing relationship; yet, she, too, was content, living in and moving about her own community in the way she felt most comfortable. Her own life difficulties notwithstanding, Midge, like so many others who also lived much of their earlier life in a state hospital, continued to demonstrate a courage, tenacity, and optimism that others without mental retardation would do well to emulate.

Longitudinal research on the community adjustment of adults leaving large PRFs since the 1960s now suggests that the majority of persons with mental retardation who are permitted to live in the community are reasonably successful and that their levels of success tend to stabilize over time (Edgerton, 1993). According to Heal, Sigelman, and Switzky (1978), three factors must be addressed when a person is preparing to leave an institution and enter community living: the characteristics of the person being released, the characteristics of the community environment into which the person is moving, and the interaction between the individual and the environment. Similar to findings reported in the postschool follow-up literature, adults with higher IQs tended to have an easier time adjusting than adults with lower IQs. A comparable pattern emerged for adaptive skills and social functioning, with occurrences of maladaptive (problem) behaviors the major determinant of either success or failure in the community. That is, the more extreme the maladaptive behaviors, the more likely a person was to fail at community living and be returned to an institution (Kearney & Smull, 1992; Scheerenberger, 1981).

ISSUES IN DEINSTITUTIONALIZATION

Securing the legal right-of-way for institutional reform is only the first of many steps in a long and sometimes arduous journey. The most crucial factor, public attitudes, cannot be changed overnight, and they cannot be changed by legislation alone. For the deinstitutionalization principle to be realized, in body and spirit, it must first be accepted as a legitimate and worthwhile social objective. The extent to which any particular social movement is supported at the individual and community levels varies from person to person and group to group. Successful institutional reform requires support in four different ways:

- Community and residential personnel must provide every opportunity for persons with mental retardation to be served in the least restrictive local setting possible.
- A person whose condition requires residential placement should be so placed no longer than is absolutely necessary.
- Persons living in institutions who can function in the community should be transferred to community-based settings as soon as possible.
- All phases of residential programming should emphasize independence and personal growth consonant with the deinstitutionalization principle.

Whereas the word **deinstitutionalization** once represented a simple reduction in admissions to large PRFs, it now represents a "general social commitment to increase access to real communities for persons with mental retardation" (Lakin, Bruininks, & Larson, 1992, pp. 198–199). Wolfensberger (1983) prefers the term *social role valorization* to deinstitutionalization and considers its goals to be twofold: (a) the reduction and prevention of stigma that devalue a person in the eyes of others and (b) changed perceptions on the part of society such that specific groups of people are no longer considered to be of lesser value than others.

Whether one wishes to use the term *deinstitutionalization, community adjustment,* or *social role valorization,* the principle remains the same, a continuum of opportunities *in the community* that more closely approximates the opportunities of persons without mental retardation. The notion of deinstitutionalization implies much more than life in a community residential setting but does assume that physical integration into a more normative living environment has already occurred. For until people actually live in more normative community settings, they are not yet free to participate in the full range of possibilities characteristically associated with community life. Three major developments have been primarily responsible for the community living movement:

FOSTER GRANDPARENT PROGRAM

If you have not visited a residential facility for individuals who are retarded recently, you may be surprised to see senior citizens on the grounds of the facility. These senior citizens are foster grandparents (FGPs).

The Foster Grandparent Program, a federally supported program that began in 1965, provides an opportunity for senior citizens who are sixty years or older and who have low income to serve individuals with special needs who are no older than twenty-one. The FGPs serve on a regular basis, usually four hours daily, five days a week, in such places as institutions, public schools, day care centers, and other nonprofit agencies. They bring their skills and experiences, as well as their kindness, patience, and understanding.

This program is beneficial to all parties involved. Institutions receive free assistance with their programs, and children benefit greatly from the additional attention. The foster grandparents receive the following benefits:

[N]ontaxable hourly stipend, which is not considered wages or compensation; transportation or transportation allowances; one meal per day; annual physical examinations; accident and liability insurance while on the job; uniforms (you will see them wearing smocks); vacation and sick leave; regular training; annual recognition.

In institutional settings, it is amazing to see persons with profound retardation who are unable to communicate in any traditional fashion respond positively to their FGP. Little language is used, because the physical proximity of the FGP is usually enough. FGPs are generally assigned two children each day and may provide companionship, attend to the personal needs of the individual (dressing, feeding, or toileting), and provide social contact. If you desire more information about this program, you can either contact the regional office of ACTION or call toll-free (800) 201-7106.

The first factor, exposure of abominable conditions in large PRFs, has already been presented and discussed. The second major development resides in the notion of **egalitarianism,** the belief that all people are created equal and that everyone is entitled to the same rights and privileges as others. The decades of the 1960s and 1970s were times of increased attention toward those who were at a social or cultural disadvantage. This particular time in our history was further characterized by a dedication to social reform and an enhanced commitment to equal opportunity for all (H. R. Turnbull, 1988). Looking back, this attitude has had a profound impact on the actions of many social service providers, especially those in the field of mental retardation.

The third principal factor relates to increased litigation and legislation for securing the rights of those who have been disenfranchised (see also Chapter 13). The first major court decision, *Wyatt v. Stickney* (1972), had a major impact on altering conditions in institutions and focused on a resident's right to treatment and habilitation. Another landmark case, and one that resulted in the closing of a large PRF, *Halderman v. Pennhurst State*

See Chapter 13 for a more complete discussion of the legal issues surrounding the care, treatment, and services provided to persons with mental retardation.

School and Hospital (1977), also had a significant effect on the rights of those living in institutions. Many arguments used to obtain services and privileges have been based on Section 1 of the 14th Amendment of the United States Constitution, which supports any attempts to establish or reaffirm rights for persons with mental retardation:

> All persons born or naturalized in the United States, and subject to the jurisdiction thereof, are citizens of the United States and of the State wherein they reside. No State shall make or enforce any law which shall abridge the privileges or immunities of citizens of the United States; *nor shall any State deprive any person of life, liberty, or property without due process of law;* nor deny to any person within its jurisdiction equal protection of the laws. [emphasis added]

ECONOMICS

People living in residential settings offering care to persons with mental retardation require access to quality medical care and equipment. Not surprisingly, the more people with disabilities in a given residence, the greater the potential costs for desperately needed goods and services. Proponents of the institutional model suggest that it is a practical and cost-effective way to offer the widest range of services to the greatest number of people. Consequently, the cost of care in all residential settings continues to rise, but none more quickly than those of large PRFs. Whereas the average annual rate of care in PRFs was about $750/person in 1950, the estimated average annual rate of care in 1996 will likely exceed $100,000 based on an anticipated rate of $278/day. Despite an increase in federal funding from $3.5 billion in 1977 to an estimated $23 billion in 1996, for the residential service system as a whole, the current approach to funding large institutions translates to proportionally more money for fewer people than ever before (e.g., $2.5 billion in 1977 to an estimated $5.5 billion in 1996) (R. Hemp, personal communication, January 30, 1997). An encouraging trend emerges when one considers that of the state, federal, and local funds allocated to residential services in 1992, approximately two thirds of the funds were allocated for community services with the remaining one third for services in large, residential facilities, the virtual opposite of 1977 (Figure 14.4).

Knobbe, Carey, Rhodes, and Horner (1995) conducted a comparative analysis of public program costs for community and institutional settings using 11 persons with severe mental retardation who had recently moved from large, public residential facilities into smaller, community-based settings in the state of Oregon. Although the community settings had modestly lower costs when compared with those of the institutions ($111,277 vs. $117,123), community settings "netted significant increases in variables such as resident's social networks, opportunities for integrated activities, and income" (p. 533). See Table 14.2 for a listing of the specified costs. Knobbe et al. attribute the lower costs of the community settings to two factors in particular, lower salaries and lower medical costs. However, not everything was less expensive in the community settings. Higher administrative costs due to larger management/resident ratios and higher daily liv-

FIGURE 14.4

Adjusted Spending Patterns for Congregate and Community Residential Services for Persons with Mental Retardation

Source: From The State of the States in Developmental Disabilities: An Overview (4th ed., p. 15) by D. Braddock, R. Hemp, L. Bachelder, and G. Fujiura, 1995, Washington, DC: American Association on Mental Retardation. Copyright 1995 by the American Association on Mental Retardation. Reprinted by permission.

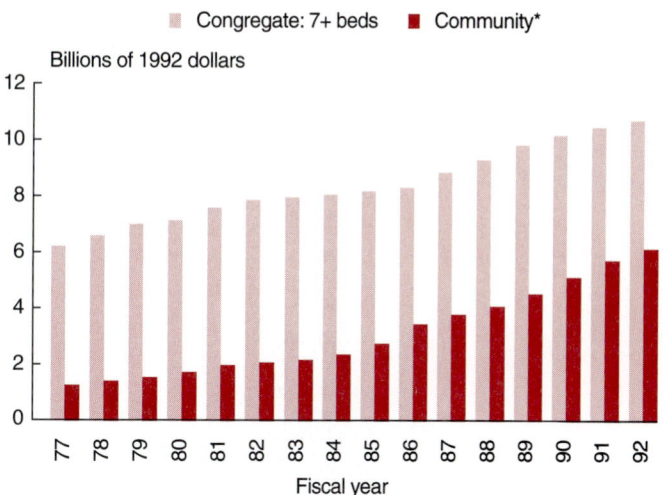

ing expenses for food, utilities, phone, maintenance, and room and board favored the large residential facilities. The difference in annual expenditures between ICF/MRs ($70,914) and home- and community-based services ($24,879), specifically, is even more pronounced (Prouty & Lakin, 1996). Several factors have contributed to the progressively escalating costs of PRFs (cf. Amado et al., 1990):

- Increased costs associated with building codes, payroll, personnel benefits, and technical equipment
- Increased need for medical and health-related specialists to accommodate an ever-increasing number of clients with more severe and more numerous disabilities
- Increased litigation and legislation mandating ever-improving facilities for client care

Existing large institutions cannot be depopulated until enough alternative sites have been constructed to accommodate the people being released into community settings. Furthermore, people cannot merely be released from institutions and sent home without adequate preparation and supports. Like all worthwhile endeavors, deinstitutionalization requires time, money, and effort on the part of all concerned. Whether or not a community has sufficient revenue to build new facilities for its citizens with mental retardation depends on a number of variables such as the local tax base, state and federal funding patterns, and priorities given to mental retardation/developmental disabilities services, and so on. Nonetheless, an understanding of economics provides only part of the picture necessary for understanding the broader issues of residential and community living.

TABLE 14.2

Public Program Costs for Institutional and Community-Based Residential Settings

	Average annual cost per person	
Costs	Institution[a]	CS[b]
Food	1,587	2,022
Medical	10,939	2,144
Utilities	1,569	1,429
Office	2,758	2,961
Cottage/house	1,983	1,995
Maintenance	402	2,080
Resident fees	(1,557)	(4,155)
Support staff		
Salaries	68,738	55,358
Benefits	27,633	13,391
Staff training	35	43
Administrative staff		
Salaries	1,351	17,452
Benefits	855	4,183
Job support	20	10,251
Agency transportation	99	587
Insurance[c]	789	789
Gas and vehicle maintenance	76	593
Total	117,277	111,123

[a]Adjusted to 1990 values using the Federal Reserve Index. [b]Community support. [c]The State of Oregon self-insures state-run programs. The value/cost of this insurance was calculated to be no different than community programs.

Source: From "Benefit–Cost Analysis of Community Residential versus Institutional Services for Adults with Severe Mental Retardation and Challenging Behaviors" by C. A. Knobbe, S. P. Carey, L. Rhodes, and R. Horner, 1995, *American Journal on Mental Retardation, 99*(5), p. 538. Copyright 1995 by the American Association on Mental Retardation. Reprinted by permission.

RELOCATION ISSUES

For the person pursuing deinstitutionalization, the road to full community inclusion is replete with obstacles. People uprooted from familiar settings and transplanted into new surroundings must often adapt very quickly. Yet, by definition, most if not all persons with mental retardation are assumed to have difficulty with adaptive functioning. Logically then, the rush to move a person from an institutional setting to a community residential setting may not mean a happier more fulfilling life initially and, instead, may even thwart the intended goals of the normalization process.

It is often difficult to discern which problems are the fault of the institution's transition team and which problems are the fault of the transition team in the receiving residence. Unfortunately, some problems are an inseparable part of the transition process and do not necessarily reflect lack of preparation or anticipation on the part of either team or the person who is changing residences. Oversights do occur and, when recognized, should be responded to as quickly as possible. Where the institution is to blame, difficulties can sometimes be averted or at least minimized with an extensive preparation program that involves contact with staff members from both the sending and receiving residences, visits to the new residence prior to the move, family participation in the adjustment process, and assignment of a personal advocate (chosen by the individual if possible) well before the move.

When problems arise that stem from the person's emotional response to change, patience and empathic counseling from staff members at both ends of the transition continuum are the most appropriate avenues of intervention. The person transitioning to the new setting should be reassured that feelings of anxiety and separation are normal and probably only temporary and that expectations of success (or failure) will heavily influence the new community member's ease of transition. The person who has been thoroughly prepared for the move will naturally have higher expectations for success than someone who is less well prepared.

Coffman and Harris (1980) have documented a set of symptoms that they call **transition shock,** a condition that is analogous to the adjustment problems of people who have recently gotten divorced, returned from war, been released from prison, or relocated to new countries. A number of common characteristics exist among these disenfranchised groups; for example:

- *Cue problems.* Responding inappropriately to cues that were relevant in the old environment but not in the new one (e.g., bells signaling mealtime in institutions), or failing to respond to cues peculiar to the new environment.

- *Value discrepancies.* Personal traits developed by rigid institutional routines (e.g., dependence, deference to others, and an inability to make decisions) that are not likely to be valued in the new community settings.

- *Emergence over time.* Problems associated with transition shock often do not occur immediately but rather incubate for a period of time (one to two weeks). Perhaps it is at this time that the special treatment afforded to newcomers gives way to routine.

Persons unfamiliar with developmental disabilities tend to forget that people with mental retardation experience the full range of human emotions. In addition, they fail to recognize that transition shock is an emotional reaction and that feelings of despondency, loneliness, anxiety, and hostility are no less proper for those with mental retardation than they are for persons without mental retardation. Heller (1984) reviewed the literature on relocation difficulties and noted the following general trends: no significant increase in mortality rates, some decreases in constructive behaviors, increases in physical/medical problems, and increases in social withdrawal. Heller pointed out that one's reactions will likely vary according to the characteristics of the person, degree of disruption, availability of support systems, and quality of the sending and receiving environments. Another critical factor in relocation research is the timing of the move. It seems that the impact of the move is most keenly felt during the first few weeks of the transition, thereby making it prudent to evaluate the person's adjustment initially and not simply deferring evaluation until later in the transition process.

When adjustment to the new setting does not go well, it often results in a return to the original setting. Opponents of community placement typically raise the issue of readmission to show that deinstitutionalization is not working. The data on readmissions are confusing and must be interpreted with caution. Between 1963 and 1974, the number of yearly releases from public institutions rose almost 150 percent. A more dramatic figure for the same period was the 500 percent increase in readmissions. For some (more than 40 percent in 1973), deinstitutionalization was largely a process of shuffling residents through a devastating experience in community living and then reeling them back into the institution (Scheerenberger, 1977). As indicated previously, the single greatest reason for the "revolving door" effect remains a general lack of support services to sustain the community placement.

The rate of readmissions seems to have decreased since the late 1970s. Whereas twenty years ago, the average readmission rate hovered around 20 percent (19 percent for E. M. Craig & McCarver, 1984; 18 percent for Scheerenberger, 1982), relevant figures had fallen to approximately 2 percent by the early 1990s (cf. Scheerenberger, 1992). The strength of Scheerenberger's (1992) most recent findings resides in the fact that the reported 1,172 readmissions represented 244 institutions nationwide with as many as 80,000 possible residents. Not so coincidentally, C. C. White et al. (1991) reported that half of all persons released from PRFs in 1989 went to group homes with fifteen or fewer people, 12 percent went to homes of parents or other relatives, and 18 percent went to other large residential facilities. The reasons more people are remaining in community settings very likely have to do with a deepening commitment to and general satisfaction with community-based settings. Table 14.3 illustrates the continued rate of decline of both admissions and readmissions between 1989 and 1991.

BEHAVIORAL CONTROL

Critics of institutions have long attested to the debilitating effects of congregate living on the social, emotional, and intellectual functioning of people. Yet, simple placement in a community residential facility is not enough to ensure an improved quality of life any more than simple physical integration alone ensures full community participation and adjustment. For that reason, some of the limitations so often associated with large PRFs can indeed surface in community residential settings. Presented here are many of the more noteworthy injustices typically associated with large residential facilities, injustices that should not occur in any type of facility, large or small.

Congregate living facilities are not in and of themselves debilitating, as many college residence halls, retirement communities, and professional

TABLE 14.3
New Admissions and Readmissions for Years 1988–1989 and 1990–1991

	New admissions		Readmissions	
Original setting	88–89	90–91	88–89	90–91
Less restrictive				
Parents or relatives	855	677	279	178
Foster/family care	161	117	131	108
Group homes (1 to 15 residents)	257	204	322	265
Boarding home	49	76	12	30
Semi-independent living	5	14	7	16
Independent living	30	24	11	13
Equally restrictive				
PRF (≤ 63 residents)	124	69	35	45
PRF (64 ≤ residents)	527	566	194	119
Private residential facility (64 ≤ residents)	98	75	41	68
Nursing home	80	75	43	20
Hospital/institution for mental illness	456	339	185	92
Correctional facility	94	94	13	22
Unknown	216	124	149	73
Total	2952	2454	1422	1049

Source: Adapted from *Public Residential Facilities for Persons with Mental Retardation* (Table 8, p. 7; Table 10, p. 8) by R. C. Scheerenberger, 1992, Madison, WI; National Association of Superintendents of Public Residential Facilities.

training facilities clearly demonstrate. Due to the large number of persons present and the funds that are generally available for program and service delivery, many congregate living facilities offer benefits that are otherwise unavailable in smaller, noncongregate settings. Instead, what people are objecting to are the callous and obdurate methods of behavioral control so often associated with unjust institutional living.

Unlike the congregate living facilities just mentioned where large group living is under the control of the person requesting the services, institutional living is most often provided at the request of others. In such cases, the congregate nature of care begins to encourage routinization and discourage opportunities for autonomy and self-determination—for the good of the group. Routinized feeding, toileting, dressing, and so on; mass movements at scheduled times; and the rationing of clothing and possessions are some such examples. However, when routine becomes overly rigid and the purpose turns from one of assistance to one of control, the service then becomes unjust and potentially abusive.

Strict adherence to routine is but one means of controlling behavior. Isolation, sometimes referred to as forced seclusion, is another type of behavioral control that is often justified as a deterrent to self-abuse. This typically involves removal of the offending resident to a solitary room or ward for a period of introspection and consideration about what went wrong. But

Adherence to routine is an effective means of controlling behavior.

isolation can be emotional as well as physical. For example, monitoring community trips, restricting outside travel, and rationing recreational and leisure time activities all constitute means by which individual isolation may occur. M. H. Lewis and Baumeister (1982) have made a clear case for the detrimental effects of isolation and restricted environmental opportunities on the health and well-being of the individual with mental retardation.

Mechanical restraints provide a third form of controlling behavior. Such devices as straitjackets (camisoles), restraining sheets on beds, and restraining chairs are sometimes used to calm recalcitrant residents or to inhibit self-destructive, aberrant behaviors. Biklen (1977) has documented countless incidents of overzealous restraining practices.

> We saw a teenage girl wearing a camisole being led into an isolation room where there was only a mat on the floor. The room was barren. One attendant spoke to another, "We took her over to the hospital this morning to give her an enema. We had to put the camisole on her in order to do it." The girl remained expressionless. I asked why she needed an enema. The attendant told me, "Well, she's on such heavy doses of tranquilizers, it's necessary." (p. 45)

Recent institutional reforms not withstanding, Biklen (1977) has concluded that the rigid, condemning living environment of most institutions for persons with mental retardation induces the very behavior it is designed to control. In the few facilities he examined with relaxed, accepting climates and no locked wards, Biklen found no evidence of acting-out behaviors that called for seclusion or physical restraints. But in the traditionally cold, regimented institutions where locked wards were part of the aversive treatment repertoire, he found that residents demonstrated maladaptive behavior for hours on end: upending furniture, banging heads, biting, kicking, and screaming—quite likely in response to their caged, isolated treatment. Though Biklen's observations were made in the mid-1970s, following his visits to six state schools and five hospitals, they nonetheless retain a sense of veracity and validity in that they are grounded in the reality of his observations and interpretations.

In contrast to the work of Biklen, where the institutional environment was considered to be the culprit, Bregman (1991) found evidence to suggest that psychological disturbances may actually be a major factor in institutional aberrant behavior. Across eight epidemiological studies, Bregman found a rate of psychopathology among persons with mental retardation ranging from 33 percent to 66 percent, several times higher than that of persons without mental retardation and consistent with the findings of B. K. Hill, Balow, and Bruininks (1985) relative to persons in need of psychotropic medications. Bregman further found that the psychiatric disturbances of persons with mild mental retardation mirrored those of persons without mental retardation. The pattern of disturbances for persons with moderate-to-severe mental retardation was noticeably different, with as many as one third of persons evidencing pervasive developmental disorders (characteristics of autism) along with the diagnosis of mental retardation. In a study involving more than 8,200 persons with mental retardation ranging from birth to ninety-eight years of age, McGrew, Ittenbach, Bruininks, and Hill (1991) found increasingly complex patterns of maladaptive behavior across the lifespan that were influenced substantially by both age and level of mental retardation. See Table 14.4 for a listing of examples of maladaptive behaviors exhibited according to facility type.

Aversive treatment techniques, usually referred to as **aversives,** represent yet another extreme form of behavior control. These techniques are designed to be uncomfortable, painful, and/or offensive in their efforts to eliminate problem behaviors. Over the years, aversives have taken may forms, ranging from simple verbal reprimands to electric shocks (Whitman, Hantula, & Spence, 1990). These techniques may evoke feelings of anger or even outrage on the part of others; however, in the context of extremely aggressive, disturbed, or life-threatening behaviors, they may take on a therapeutic orientation, one that is designed to help rather than hurt the client engaging in the extreme forms of maladaptive behavior.

For S. L. Harris and Handleman (1990), the issue of aversives is twofold: Does the aversive work better than other, nonaversive measures? and, if so, Are the benefits of the pain or discomfort ethically justifiable? At the heart of

TABLE 14.4

Percent of Residents Exhibiting Maladaptive Behavior As Reported by Direct Care Staff

Category of behavior	Private facility residents (N = 964)	State institution residents (N = 997)	State institution new admissions (N = 286)	State institution readmissions (N = 244)
Injures self	11.1%	21.7%	22.0%	21.3%
Injures other people	16.3%	30.3%	42.0%	38.5%
Damages property	11.1%	17.6%	19.2%	23.4%
Unusual or disruptive behavior	28.8%	34.3%	37.8%	41.0%
Breaks rules: won't follow routine	19.1%	18.8%	32.4%	33.2%
Refuses to go to day program	7.2%	11.7%	20.9%	25.8%
Has spent one of the last 30 days at home because of refusal to go	2.5%	5.7%	9.4%	13.8%
Has purposely run away	2.2%	3.6%	11.5%	13.5%
Has run away within the last six months	1.3%	2.5%	8.7%	8.2%
Has broken the law within the last year	1.5%	.5%	3.1%	7.4%
Court or law enforcement personnel involved	.7%	1%	1.4%	4.1%
Total with one or more types of behavior	47.3%	59.7%	68.5%	68.4%

Source: From *Residential Services for Adults with Developmental Disabilities* by R.H. Bruininks, B.K. Hill, K.C. Lakin, & C.C. White (1985), Logan: Utah State University, Developmental Center for Handicapped Persons. Reprinted by permission.

the controversy over aversive treatments is the argument that some behaviors may be better addressed through other, more appropriate means. For example, in a review of their earlier research, Reid, Parsons, and Schepis (1990) reported that approximately two thirds of the residents observed in twenty-two institutional settings were involved in nonproductive, off-task behaviors, a phenomenon that invites maladaptive behaviors. In such cases, appropriate supervision and empirically validated alternatives to aversives may offer a course of first resort. Although techniques such as these have been widely used as a means of controlling behaviors, W. I. Gardner and Cole (1990) contend that the use of aversive treatments such as those just described should be used only for the "duration of a current crisis" and only when other, more appropriate "treatment and management procedures have failed" (p. 237). In place of aversives, Gardner and Cole offer the options of ignoring behaviors, reinforcing functionally equivalent (or incompatible) behaviors, and more appropriate coping skills as possible preferable response options.

Many residents of institutions display maladaptive behaviors that can be most disruptive. Whether some of these behaviors are brought into these settings by the residents themselves or result from institutional placements is debatable. Logically, frustration and its manifestations that warrant restraints may be abated if residents are given meaningful ways to spend their time and are provided with an accepting, loving, and pleasant atmosphere in which to live. Otherwise, the natural, *normal* response may well be one of withdrawal, aggression, or even outright rebellion.

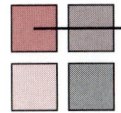

SUMMARY

INSTITUTIONAL LIVING

- Two formal procedures exist for admitting someone to an institutional setting, voluntary admission and involuntary commitment.

- Public residential facilities are large state-operated facilities that house sixteen or more residents at any one time.

- A number of factors influence the decision to institutionalize a person, including individual characteristics, family characteristics, and nonfamily factors.

COMMUNITY LIVING

- Most children with mental retardation live at home with their natural families.

- Community residential settings are those with fifteen or fewer residents located in traditional residential neighborhoods.

- Robert Edgerton's (1967) thirty-year follow-up study of persons exiting Pacific State Hospital from 1949 through 1958 remains the most well-known and highly cited study of deinstitutionalization to date.

ISSUES IN DEINSTITUTIONALIZATION

- Several factors are responsible for the success of the deinstitutionalization movement, including a reduction of the abominable living conditions of institutions, equal opportunities for all, and increased litigation on behalf of persons with mental retardation.

- Community-based settings cost less to operate than large PRFs.

- Persons with mental retardation experience a type of transition shock when moving out of institutions and into residential community settings.

- Isolation, mechanical restraints, and aversive techniques are some of the many means of behavioral control that have often been used to control aberrant behaviors.

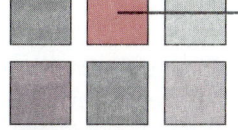

CHAPTER 15

Emerging and Future Issues

After reading this chapter,
the student should be able to:

- ▪ Identify key issues associated with public attitudes toward persons with mental retardation.

- ▪ Describe the critical issues associated with preparing persons with mental retardation for the demands of adulthood.

- ▪ Identify and describe many of the new and emerging issues in support services.

- ▪ Discuss major new advances in technology.

- ▪ Identify selected ways to prevent mental retardation.

- ▪ Identify and describe avenues of research for the coming decade.

Key Terms

absolute poverty	Human Genome	primary prevention
assistive technologies	Project	relative poverty
formal supports	informal supports	

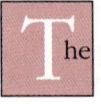he preceding chapters have identified many current issues affecting the field of mental retardation. New issues are emerging, and others are yet to develop. The intent of this chapter is to focus on those issues that will become major topics of interest. Describing the future includes both projecting present scenarios into the future and forecasting new situations.

PREDICTING THE FUTURE

The challenge of predicting the future is a monumental one. Basically, predictions are based on what we already know. Some error must always be acknowledged in any prediction, because we cannot foresee all the variables that will affect the future. A more appropriate name for this activity might be "probabilistic conjecture" (McHale, 1980). Despite the difficulties of prediction and the concomitant likelihood of error, we must persevere in our efforts and, at the very least, try to anticipate the future events.

The business of certain agencies, institutions, and professions is largely that of prediction. Insurance companies, for instance, rest their profit margins on their ability to predict the likelihood of certain events (life expectancies; auto accidents, injuries, and deaths; thefts and fires, etc.). Institutions of higher learning use certain variables such as high school grade-point average and SAT scores to predict success in college. The careers of meteorologists are made by good predictions and broken by poor ones, since they are constantly accountable to the public. Prediction is also used in medicine when prognoses are based on information about a patient. In all these examples, certain events are projected from existing knowledge.

Those of us interested in mental retardation are very much concerned about where we have been, where we are today, and where we will be in the future, but the best we can do without the gift of clairvoyance is to base our hunches on the trends and changes that the field is presently experiencing. Cain and Taber (1987) have identified three elements that define the relationship between the present and the future:

- **Continuity:** The future is always influenced by the past and the present.
- **Change:** The future is always influenced by unexpected events that break the continuity of history.

"What will my future be?"

> ■ Choice: The future is always influenced by the choices that people make when confronted with a new development.

These variables interact with one another and make it very difficult to predict the future with any certainty, particularly for situations involving complex human social systems.

Social forecaster John Naisbitt (1984) based his popular, insightful Megatrends on this premise: "The most reliable way to anticipate the future is by understanding the present" (p. xxiii). Unfortunately, the persistent element of the unknown lurks before us; therefore, to adopt a simplistic view of the future denies the possibility of unpredictable major turning points, or what Kuhn (1970) calls revolutionary change in scientific thinking. Naisbitt points out that, while certain broad tendencies can be noted (e.g., the shift from a national to a world economy), no one can predict what specific form our future society will take. Attempts to describe the future in detail, he feels, "are the stuff of science fiction and futuristic guessing games" (p. xxiii). A simplistic view of the future ignores the impact of sociopolitical factors that can significantly alter the course of events (e.g., the dissolution of the Soviet Union).

CHANGES IN SOCIETY

Before we can approach the topical issues, it is essential that we understand the changes and influences our society will probably experience. The social and economic structures of the Western world have progressed through three major stages (hunting and gathering, agricultural, and industrial) and are currently in a fourth stage (postindustrial).

Without question, the years ahead will be characterized by the themes of communication and information. To Naisbitt (1984), the "restructuring of America from an industrial to an information society will easily be as profound as the shift from an agricultural society to an industrial society" (p. 9). While the transition from agriculture to industry took about 100 years, the shift from industrial to an information-based society has taken only 20. Naisbitt believes the change has happened so quickly that many people are only just now realizing it.

Some of the changes that one can observe in the transition from an agricultural to an informational age are presented in Table 15.1. The table focuses on work-related issues, but it illustrates the magnitude of the other changes we have experienced and adumbrates those to come.

The pressures placed on an individual vary significantly with the demands of a given social system. The ability to succeed in school was not very important in the agricultural society of the early 18th century, when manual labor was esteemed. The industrial revolution introduced new demands

TABLE 15.1

Societal Changes through the Ages

	Agricultural Age	Industrial Age	Information Age
Defining technology	Craftsman	Clock	Instruction-based systems
Strategic resource	Raw materials: (seeds, water, soil)	Capital (money)	Ideas (minds)
Transforming resource	Natural energy (sun)	Processed energy (coal, electricity)	Synergy (minds working together)
Product	Food	Mass-produced items	Information
Organizing principle	Seasons	Product design	Inflow (information flow)
View of time	Cyclical	Steadily onward	Multiplexed
View of progress	Progress in history	Perfectibility of man and society	Merger of man and machine
Machine paradigm	Spindle	Heat engine	Organism (instruction-based machine)
Communication	Conversation (transfer ideas locally)	Face-to-face conference (transfer ideas by transporting people)	Teleconference (transfer ideas by transmitting images)

The transition from the Agricultural Age to the Industrial Age to the Information Age has changed the means, methods, and materials with which we work. This chart notes the changes that have taken place for a number of work-related items and activities.

Source: From "Rethinking How We Work: The Office of the Future" by S. E. Bleecker, 1987, *The Futurist, 21*(4) pp. 15–19. Copyright 1987 by World Future Society. Reprinted by permission.

Life continues to be more demanding and technologically challenging for individuals with mental retardation.

for semiskilled and skilled workers; ability and training for these jobs became mandatory for success in this era.

As we have advanced from an industrial to a postindustrial society, the types of skills necessary for success in social institutions, particularly in the workplace, have begun to change dramatically. The skills identified by employers as being important for employees in today's workplace include reading, writing, and computational skills; speaking and listening skills; learning-to-learn skills; problem-solving and creative thinking skills; personal management skills; teamwork skills; and leadership and organizational effectiveness skills (Carnevale, Gainer, & Meltzer, 1990).

FUTURE SCENARIOS

Trends

It seems evident that everyday life will continue to become more demanding and technologically sophisticated, and that these requirements will have a major effect on other areas as well. Some predictable changes in the near future follow:

■ The nature of work will be different. Many jobs will be more technically demanding, and many more jobs will be automated, thus reducing the number of positions in manufacturing and agriculture. Moreover, most of the available jobs will be in the service industry.

- Society will experience a significant aging effect. The number of older individuals will increase.

- Health care will become more sophisticated and more expensive. Questions as to how to ensure that all citizens have access to coverage remain, but changes are underway.

- Economic conditions in the United States (e.g., the federal budget deficit) will remain problematic, constraining spending in many areas, for example, services and health care (Amara, 1988).

- Educational systems will be different. It seems inevitable that schooling will become year-round, the school day will be longer, and technology will be used in innovative ways to deliver instruction and enhance learning (Halal & Liebowitz, 1996).

Some futurists describe 21st-century environments that may be quite different from what we are experiencing now. For instance, Dator (1988) and Macarov (1985) suggest that the future will be characterized as a "workless society" and suggest that efforts be directed at creating a society of full unemployment. This thinking is based on various notions: (a) technology will make a large workforce superfluous; (b) resources will be abundant; and (c) unemployment will always be with us. Macarov (1985) describes the situation in the following way:

> What is needed is a planned, conscious movement toward the highest technology possible, replacing human effort in every area for which changes in methods, machines, and material can be found. In short, the goal should be full unemployment. . . . This way, it will seem as a social good rather than a social ill. When only 10% of the population produces all the goods and services needed, the remaining "unemployed" 90% will look at unemployment in a much different light. (p. 22)

Whether or not this scenario will come to be is subordinate to the implications for teaching and service delivery inherent in the prediction. We should look beyond the present and even the near future to the distant future. If we are to prepare ourselves, our children, and their children for the future, we must start planning now. To do so, we must consider, as best we can, what the future might be like.

Implications for Individuals with Mental Retardation

Changes in the social, economic, and technological dimensions as well as in our lifestyles will have a profound impact on persons who are mentally retarded. In an informational society, it will be important to use developing technology to the advantage of those with retardation, on the one hand, and to prepare them to use various technologies, which will be very much part of everyday life, on the other. McHale (1980) suggests that some will be able to take advantage of future changes, and some will not, so that there will be

The importance of lifelong learning is becoming quite evident.

TABLE 15.2

Implications for the "Haves" and "Have Nots"

Information "Haves"	Information "Have Nots"
Become basis for elites in a restratified society	Training in applications of technology—how to use rather than why to use
More socially mobile, with diverse career paths and life-style opportunities	Will tend to be more locked in to particular jobs—less able to change occupations
Their acquisition of more and new knowledge becomes progressively easier	May tend to resign themselves to helplessness and alienation—will seek and use less and less information
Added capacity to create their own knowledge bases	Less able to cope with perplexing changes
More able to organize and associate at a distance through access to new techniques	Will become suspicious and hostile to the "knowledge people"
May possibly have more enlightened self-interest	Limited social mobility

Source: From "Mental Retardation and the Future: A Conceptual Approach" by J. McHale in *The Year 2000 and Mental Retardation* (pp. 19–70) edited by S. C. Plog and M. B. Santamour, 1980, New York: Plenum Press. Copyright 1980 by Plenum Press. Reprinted by permission.

"haves" and "have nots" in the informational society. The implications of this duality are presented in Table 15.2. Without assistance (i.e., planning and preparation), most persons with mental retardation will fall into the "have-not" category unless care is taken to consider requisite home, community, and workplace skills needed for success in tomorrow's environments. The paradox is that new developments, by and large, will be beneficial to this group (see the next section). But those with mental retardation are also at risk of being left behind as new types and levels of competence are created.

One of the outcomes of a technologically more advanced society is that certain demands of everyday life are made easier (by use of, e.g., pocket-size cellular telephones and new types of thermometers). But the limitation for many adults who are mentally retarded is that they do not know how to use these devices and—perhaps a more fundamental issue—they are unable to acquire them. This situation holds true for the ballooning use of computer technology as well.

The President's Committee on Mental Retardation (PCMR) brought together a group of futurists to consider the impact of change on those with retardation by the year 2000 (Plog, 1980). Selected questions this group raised and addressed (listed in Table 15.3) are noteworthy with regard to the next section of this chapter.

Mindful of these questions and of the necessity for caution about any prediction, let us examine some current scenarios and future directions. We must keep in mind that even the most extravagant predictions can be realized and that the pace at which the predicted becomes the reality is often faster than we might imagine.

A forthcoming publication, sponsored in part by the Arc U.S., and co-edited by Wehmeyer and Patton, focusing on mental retardation in the new millennium, is likely to update many of the topics addressed by the PCMR project.

TABLE 15.3
Questions to Consider about the Future and Mental Retardation

- To what degree will individuality be cherished and what will be the degree of tolerance toward deviation from normative patterns?
- To what extent will individual life be valued, particularly with reference to such practices as population control, abortion, and euthanasia?
- To what degree will procedures designed to shape an individual's own destiny be sanctioned, such as psychotechnology and genetic engineering?
- Can we expect an integrated and comprehensive effort by the biomedical and social sciences to reduce the incidence and severity of mental retardation?
- What will be the state of prenatal care, nutrition, intensive care for premature infants, genetic counseling, and family planning in the years to come?
- Is a centralized data system foreseeable for intervention purposes, and for tracking high-risk groups?

- Will the trend toward full citizenship rights for people with mental retardation continue?
- What will our judicial system be like 20 years from now?
- What is the employment outlook for people with mental retardation?
- What will be the governmental emphasis on human services?
- What will be the nature of governmental funding patterns?
- To what degree will education, including the impact of changing philosophy and technology, undergo significant changes?
- What will be the effects of the shrinking work week and increased leisure time?
- To what degree will the world of work and prevailing work-related ethics undergo changes?

Source: From *Strategies for Achieving Community Integration of Developmentally Disabled Citizens* (pp. 1–6) edited by S. C. Plog and M. B. Santamour, 1980, New York: Plenum Press. Copyright 1980 by Plenum Press. Adapted by permission.

CRITICAL AREAS OF CONCERN

Commensurate with the technological advances characteristic of a postindustrial society, changes will also emerge in social attitudes and perhaps in the concept of retardation itself. This section discusses ongoing activity and emerging trends in the areas of attitudes, preparation for adulthood, support systems, technology, and prevention of some forms of mental retardation.

Attitudes are eminently important because they are usually indicative of behavior. Harth (1977) has suggested that attitudes "represent a verbal statement about how one feels toward a particular construct" and that "people hold rather strong and divergent attitudes about mental retardation" (p. 4). In regard to persons with mental retardation, attitudes correlate strongly with (a) the availability of services and programs, (b) the amount of interaction between those with mental retardation and those without, and (c) the self-esteem of those who are mentally retarded (Guskin, 1977).

Historically, social attitudes toward deviant populations or individuals have placed the blame for the deviancy upon those who are different. Ryan's (1976) powerful book *Blaming the Victim* describes this phenomenon as it relates to placing the blame for poverty on the poor. As a result of this type of thinking, most intervention programs are designed to change

Chapter 2 highlights the impact of attitudes on the treatment of persons with mental retardation.

the individual, not the system. Rappaport (1977) proposes that what is required is a paradigm that involves a "person–environment fit," emphasizing the relationship between individuals and their social and physical environment. A perspective that includes this notion of person–environment fit would benefit persons who are mentally retarded by encouraging society to look more broadly at the full range of potentialities, needs, and problems of this group. What typically happens is that "we try to fit people into existing structures, rather than evaluate what is wrong with a social system that does not accept someone as she or he is" (Amado, 1988, p. 303). Society must move away from blaming the person to a more transactional model. There are signs that this is beginning to happen, as discussed later in the section on support systems.

The media can have a major impact on people's attitudes about those who are mentally retarded. Portrayals of persons with mental retardation in the media have changed for the better. In some cases, characters who are retarded are shown in positive and realistic ways (e.g., Corky, in "As Life Goes On."). Nevertheless, we must remain vigilant to misportrayals and stereotyping, and respond to such situations when they occur in order to prevent the dissemination of misinformation and the development of misperceptions.

PREPARATION FOR THE DEMANDS OF ADULTHOOD

A case has been made in Chapter 10 for adequately preparing individuals with mental retardation for the major demands of adulthood. These demands include employment/education; home and family; leisure pursuits; community involvement; physical/emotional health; and personal responsibility and relationships (Cronin & Patton, 1993). Ensuring that students acquire competence in dealing with adulthood will require innovative practices and will occur only if serious attention is directed to issues concerning curriculum, instructional technique, and transition planning.

Curricula must be based on what students will need in order to function in their likely subsequent environments. It must also be comprehensive in nature and must be (Polloway & Patton, 1997):

The topics of life skills and planning for adulthood are covered in depth in Chapter 10.

- Responsive to the needs of an individual student at the current time
- Reflective of the need to balance maximum integration with nondisabled peers against critical curricular needs
- Derived from a realistic appraisal of potential adult outcomes of individual students
- Sensitive to graduation goals and specific diploma track requirements (pp. 1–2)

To be responsive to the areas of adulthood identified here, curriculum development efforts must consider how best to prepare students for current and future workplace scenarios as well as for all the personal demands that

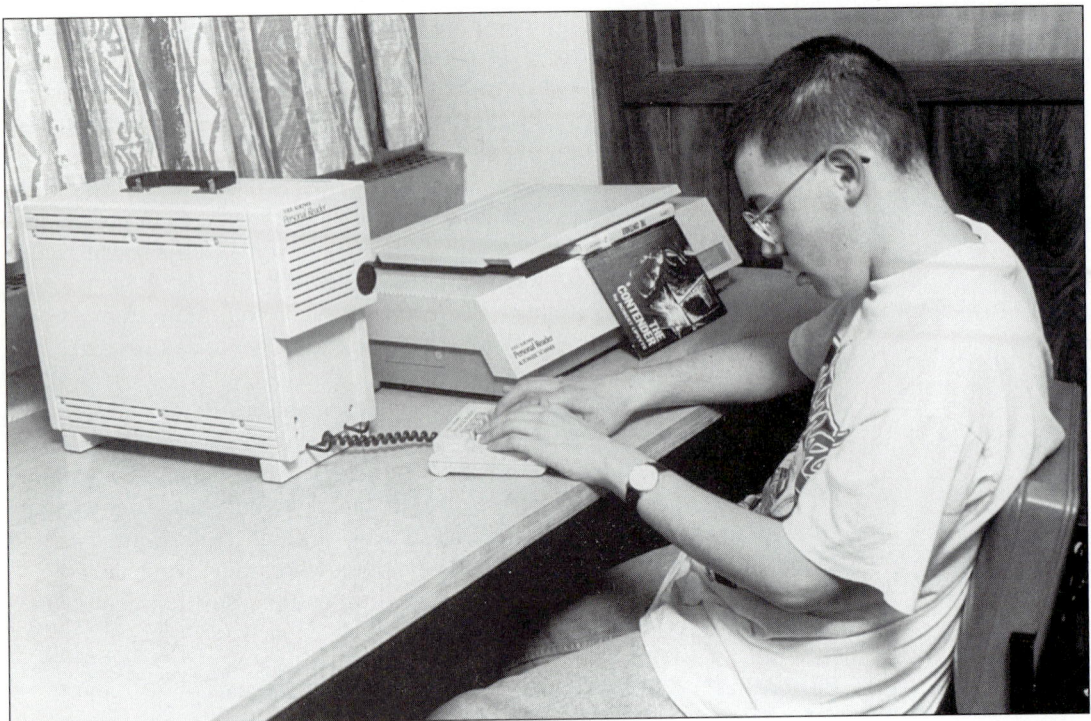

Curricula must be based on the needs of the students.

are part of adulthood. A more detailed sense of what must be taught is provided in Figure 15.1.

As discussed earlier in this chapter, employers themselves have identified important general job skills that are needed in today's and tomorrow's workplace. These include some skill areas that can be troublesome to students with mental retardation and, unfortunately, are not consistently part of their programs. If they are needed, then they will have to be taught, and resources are available for doing this (Wehman & Kregel, 1997).

Most students who are mentally retarded will need to be taught specific vocational skills prior to leaving formal schooling. It is critical that they be prepared vocationally to be part of an informational age workforce as opposed to preparing for a workforce that was needed in an industrial society. Apolloni and Feichtner (1991) note that the largest growth of jobs will be in the service industry. A listing of the occupations that are likely to grow the most in the near future can be found in Table 15.4.

To teach the skills needed for success in the workforce and in life, instruction should occur in community-based settings. Furthermore, it is suggested that instruction be performance based (Apolloni & Feichtner, 1991).

FIGURE 15.1

Areas of Required Competence

Source: Cronin and Patton (1993)

Employment/education
- General job skills
- General education/training considerations
- Employment setting
- Career refinement and re-evaluation

Home and family
- Home management
- Financial management
- Family life
- Child rearing

Leisure pursuits
- Indoor activities
- Outdoor activities
- Community/neighborhood activities
- Travel
- Entertainment

Community involvement
- Citizenship
- Community awareness
- Services/resources

Physical/emotional health
- Physical health
- Emotional health

Personal responsibility and relationships
- Personal confidence/understanding
- Goal setting
- Self-improvement
- Relationships
- Personal expression

These recommendations must be balanced against the need to have students in inclusive settings as much as possible. Establishing an equilibrium between these two requirements is possible but may require innovative options.

Transition planning for students who are mentally retarded must be based on a realistic evaluation of their needs, including all the major life domains (Clark & Patton, 1997). Transition plans should consider students' current and future environments as well as the nature of the support systems that students will have available to them when they leave school (this is discussed at length in the next section).

Pursuant to requirements mandated in the 1997 reauthorization of the Individuals with Disabilities Education Act (IDEA), statements of transition needs (by age fourteen) and transition services (by age sixteen) are required for all students who are disabled. As we know, legislating something does

TABLE 15.4
Service Industry Occupations

...cashiers; registered nurses, janitors and cleaners, including maids and household cleaners; truck drivers; waiters and waitresses; wholesale trade sales workers; nursing aides, orderlies, and attendants; sales workers, retail; accountants and auditors; teachers, kindergarten and elementary; secretaries; computer programmers; general office clerks; food preparation workers, excluding fast food; food preparation, fast food; computer system analysts, electronic data processing; electrical and electronic engineers; electrical and electronics technicians and technologists; guards; automotive and motorcycle mechanics; lawyers; cosmetologists and related workers; cooks, restaurant; maintenance repairers, general utility; bookkeeping, accounting, and auditing clerks; bartenders; computer operators, excluding peripheral equipment; physicians and surgeons; licensed practical nurses; carpenters; switchboard operators; food service and lodging managers; electricians; teacher aides and educational assistants; blue-collar worker supervisors; receptionists and information clerks; and mechanical engineers.

Source: Appolloni and Feichtner (1991)

not guarantee that it will be beneficial to those it is intended to help. Nevertheless, early transition planning is desirable, especially so, given that many students drop out of school. Equally important is the ensurance that the planning is comprehensive and relevant to students.

SUPPORT SYSTEMS

Within a rapidly changing service delivery system has come a heightened awareness of and need for stronger and better support systems for persons with mental retardation, with particular attention given to the development of natural support systems. While professionals and laypersons alike continue to disagree as to the best method of serving persons in community settings, few will argue that the face of residential services has changed markedly over the past several decades and will surely continue to do so for the foreseeable future (Lakin, Bruininks, & Larson, 1992). What has appeared to many to be a chaotic and unorganized system of service delivery may actually represent an evolution of opportunities, as persons with mental retardation move into new roles and new communities. As records of the Civil Rights era clearly document, members of dominant, established societies are often reluctant to share their resources and opportunities with smaller, less powerful segments of the population. Whether this issue involves persons of various religions, as was the case in the 1930s, persons of different races, as was the case in the 1960s, or persons of different ability levels, as is the case in the 1990s, the social realignment of opportunities and resources to new groups, however appropriate, does not generally come easily.

Some researchers, however, believe that the dilemmas faced by many service providers today result from a clash of perspectives pertaining to the issue of disabilities in general. Some see the problem as residing in the in-

The use of supports, both formal and informal, is a part of everyday life for all individuals.

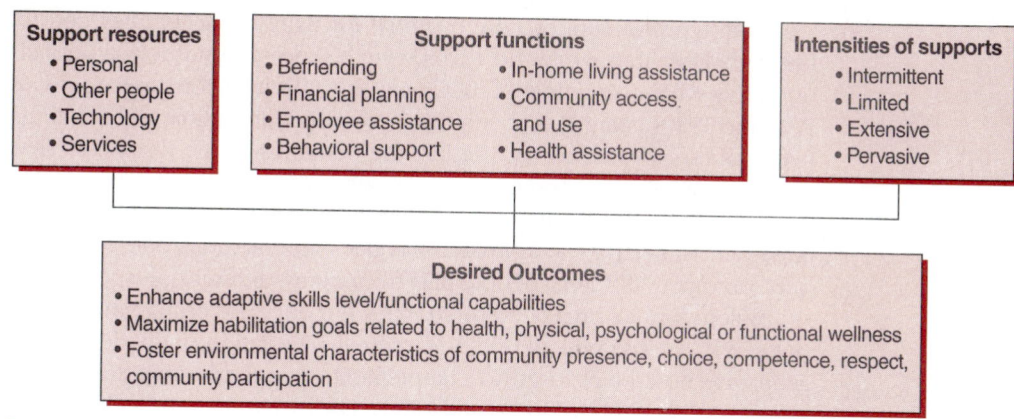

FIGURE 15.2
Supports-Outcome Model

Source: From *Mental Retardation: Definition Classification, and Systems of Support* (p. 102) by American Association on Mental Retardation, 1992, Washington, DC: American Association on Mental Retardation. Copyright 1992 by the American Association on Mental Retardation. Reprinted by permission.

dividual (rehabilitation paradigm), others in society (independent living paradigm), and still others in the process of service delivery itself (empowerment paradigm) (Racino, Taylor, Walker, & O'Connor, 1993).

While the issue of supports is certainly not a new one, the reframing of the American Association on Mental Retardation (AAMR) definition and classification system using supports as a major component in defining mental retardation certainly is. Some would even consider this change to be epochal. To show the interrelationships of such key factors as support resources, support functions, intensities of supports, and desired outcomes, the AAMR's (1992) schematic diagram of their supports-outcome model is provided in Figure 15.2.

Regardless of which paradigm one adopts, the realities of designing, providing, and accessing systems of support for persons with mental retardation remain both difficult and challenging. A subtle but necessary component of any paradigm is the issue of formal versus informal supports. Cooley (1989) distinguishes between formal and informal support services in this way: **Formal supports** are generally organized programs consisting of professionals trained to provide necessary and specific services for persons with disabilities (e.g., assistive technology, formal education, income assistance, medical services). **Informal supports,** on the other hand, are those services generally provided through intrapersonal or interpersonal means by either the person with the disability or the person's family, friends, or neighbors. While the skills of such persons may indeed be special (e.g., companionship, general problem solving, home modifications, transportation), they are generally not considered to be those of a trained professional.

Both types of supports are essential for daily living. Bradley and Knoll (1995) believe that while the 1970s were a time of rapid deinstitutionalization, they were also a time of increased specialization for service providers. With the 1980s came a new emphasis on individualization and meeting the needs of the whole person, not just the demands of the disability. That is, service providers no longer thought solely in terms of matching people to society but also of helping society meet the needs of people with mental retardation. This particular approach has been an ambitious one, requiring input from many different people and from many different perspectives.

Where formal, organized programs were once the primary means of social service delivery in the field of mental retardation, individualized programs are now being used to complement or replace altogether the more formal programs of the 1970s and 1980s. For many persons, including those whose support needs are extensive to pervasive, informal supports may provide the most basic and enduring supports of all (Figure 15.3).

Viewing a person with mental retardation as someone for whom skills and abilities are unique, just as their barriers and supports are unique, does much to free the person from the stigma of eternal clienthood (Bradley & Knoll, 1995). Beneath the new model of supports provided by AAMR is the assumption that skills and abilities change over time. So, too, should one's supports.

Inherent in this approach is the notion that evaluation of services is an ongoing activity for as long as services and supports are necessary. For the person relying upon a formal support system, strategies for change and planning for the future may take a path entirely different from that taken by a person whose support system consists primarily, or at least substantially, of informal and natural supports. The former will most certainly reflect the nuances of a system interested in efficiency, productivity, and the "common good," while the latter will be much more likely to emphasize the value systems of the person and family involved in the adjustment process.

The fact that some support systems rely more heavily on informal supports in no way detracts from the importance and integrity of the overall service delivery system. It does mean, however, that futures planning cannot

FIGURE 15.3

The Nature of Systems of Supports

Source: From *Mental Retardation: Definition Classification, and Systems of Support* (p. 144) by American Association on Mental Retardation, 1992, Washington, DC: American Association on Mental Retardation. Copyright 1992 by the American Association on Mental Retardation. Reprinted by permission.

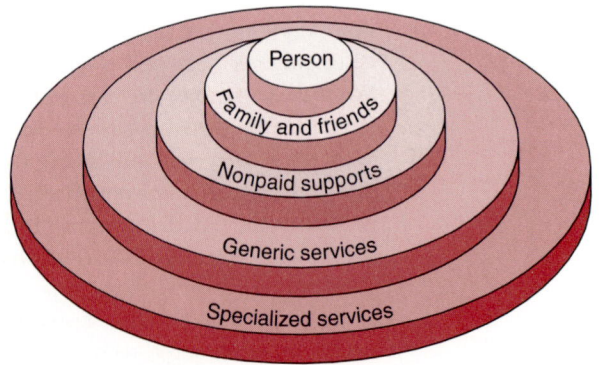

exist without definite and well-integrated resources (Taylor, Knoll, Lehr, & Walker, 1989). Where the privileges and opportunities of persons with mental retardation are concerned, the 21st century will very likely be no less individual-centered than were the 1980s; in fact, there is every reason to believe that it will be even more so.

The quest for a system of supports that enhances one's quality of life may be at first awkward and difficult, particularly if the person has been used to a support system consisting primarily of formal systems. While there is generally agreement that most families have the best interest of the person at heart, some families clearly do not. In the first case, families are generally in the best position to design a system of supports; in the second, a system consisting largely of formal supports is preferable.

Compounding the picture further is the notion on the part of many that service providers of large, highly routinized organizations consider family members more of a problem than a solution when difficulties are encountered. Whether or not either of these situations is true in any particular case, the result may be a carnival of services that frustrates all. In such a case, the need for some measure of quality assurance is paramount. Where there is no mechanism for quality assurance, the potential for error is great. Bradley (1988) has identified a sixfold purpose for an organized quality assurance program:

- Ensure that service providers have the capability to provide an acceptable level of service.
- Ensure that client services are consistent with accepted beliefs about what constitutes good practice.
- Ensure that a given commitment of resources produces a reasonable level of service.
- Ensure that services have the intended effects.
- Ensure that the limited supply of services is provided to the clients most in need.
- Ensure that the rights of persons with mental retardation are protected. (p. 279)

How these purposes are addressed will vary from person to person and from situation to situation. Bradley (1988) has further identified a number of techniques by which quality control measures can be included in the support system process, which has until recently focused primarily on the regulation of services. One such example is a private, outside evaluation team. Such a team has no official allegiances to either the person receiving services or the organizations providing them. Members of the team should be knowledgeable about service delivery to persons with mental retardation in general and about services in the given community specifically. A team such as this can generally offer a level of insight not usually obtainable through regular channels. Persons from a local college or university, mental health or mental retardation facility, or advocacy group may offer such services. Commitment to a quality support system is more than a commitment to a process; it is a commitment to persons and families of persons with mental retardation that everything is being done to ensure the highest possible quality of life.

ADVANCES IN TECHNOLOGY

Nowhere can there be more room for optimism than in the application of technology to the lives of persons with mental retardation. Many professional disciplines have joined together to influence seemingly divergent areas of service. This multidisciplinary flavor is embodied in a shared mission for many physical and social scientists, engineers, and health science personnel worldwide. One such example is in engineering, where researchers have contributed tremendously to the development of prosthetic limbs, orthotic devices, speech synthesizers, recording instruments, computerized wheelchairs, and a staggering array of computer-related services.

Medicine

Advances in biomedical technology are already revolutionizing services to persons with mental retardation. One very obvious example is the **Human Genome Project,** a concentrated, multinational effort to identify the location and function of all parts of the human genetic code. Because of this effort, scientists around the world are rapidly gaining ground on some of the most threatening diseases, disorders, and disabilities known to humankind. The importance of what is transpiring is reflected in Olesen's (1996) comments on genetic mapping:

> We're standing at the threshold of a golden age of biology. Over the next few decades, we'll begin to thoroughly understand biological processes and the causes of diseases. In fact, if you look back at where the computer industry was 10 or 15 years ago, that's where biological and genetic research is now. (p. 71)

Of the approximately 4,434 genetic disorders that affect people, mental retardation is believed to be a prominent feature in 448 (10 percent; Moser, 1992). The progress to date has been so rapid and successful that "it is likely that DNA markers for all the major genetic causes of mental retardation will be available by the year 2000, or not long thereafter" (Moser, 1992, p. 140).

While identification and mapping of known genes and biochemical pathways do not in themselves imply a cure, they do put scientists squarely on the path of forthcoming cures and treatments. Scientists from Japan's Institute for Future Technology recently released the results of a survey of 2,385 scientists worldwide representing sixteen different disciplines in which respondents were asked to identify the major scientific breakthroughs of the coming generation. Major breakthroughs and their estimated dates are as follows: cure for acquired immune deficiency syndrome (AIDS) (2003), nursing robots (2010), drugs to prevent cancer (2013), cure for Alzheimer's disease (2015) (Japanese Scientists, 1993). If mental retardation is believed to be a prominent feature in one of ten known genetic disorders, it stands to reason that breakthroughs in areas such as these will provide important advances in mental retardation as well.

Education and Rehabilitation

The use of technology with individuals with mental retardation is to be considered in employment, living, and community settings.

The effects of technology in general, and computer technology in particular, on key educational processes have been more subtle but equally essential. While the benefits of such technology are not limited to persons with mental retardation, the benefits to persons with mental retardation allow students, teachers, and parents access to information and processes in ways not possible even a few years ago.

In a review of research by Hannaford (1993), the same patterns of results observed in children without disabilities are observed in children with disabilities, relative to instructional technology. Following are a few of Hannaford's (1993, p. 12) key findings:

THE HIGHLY PROBABLE FUTURE

In 1994, the World Future Society published a list of 83 assumptions about the Year 2025. The following are some of the assumptions that, if they become reality, could have a dramatic impact on individuals with mental retardation.

- Everything will be smart—that is, responsive to its external or internal environment.
- All human diseases and disorders will have their linkages, if any, to the human genome identified.
- In several parts of the world, the understanding of human genetics will lead to explicit programs to enhance people's overall physical and mental abilities—not just prevent diseases.
- Robots and other automated machinery will be commonplace inside and outside the factory.
- Totally automated factories will be common but not universal.

- Virtual-reality technologies will be commonplace for training and recreation.
- Birth-control technologies will be universally accepted and widely employed.
- Identification cards will be universal. Smart cards will contain information such as nationality, medical history (perhaps even key data from one's genome), education, employment records, financial accounts, social security, credit status, and even religious and organizational affiliations.
- Genetic screening and counseling will be universally available and its use encouraged by many incentives and health choices.
- There will be more recreation and leisure time for the middle class in advanced nations.

Source: Coates, J. E. (1994). *The highly probable future: 83 assumptions about the year 2025.* Bethesda, MD: World Futures Society. Reprinted by permission.

- When computers are used, students tend to learn the material in less time.
- The use of computers seems to result in increased attention, motivation, and time on-task.
- Drill-and-practice is the most frequent type of program used. This type of program is most useful with lower-ability students but has been found to be effective overall.
- Use of computers leads to better social interaction when students work jointly than when they work in isolation or in traditional ways with traditional instruction.
- Teachers remain excited about the technology but do not spend much time actually using computers in the instructional process. Computers continue to be used in ways that are isolated from the instructional mainstream.

Light pens, touch screens, and verbal and audible interactive systems are some of the new developments undergoing evaluation (J. F. Gardner & Chapman, 1993). Intelligent tutoring systems are likely to be available in schools to assist teachers (Halal & Liebowitz, 1996). To help with the integration of computer technology into educational and rehabilitative programs, Jacobson (1989) has offered a number of ways in which computers may be useful to service personnel (Table 15.5).

Community Living

Whether the movement toward community living has accelerated the development of new assistive technologies or has merely occurred in concert with it, the benefits are the same. **Assistive technologies** are best described as "those technologies that an individual keeps and uses as a tool or an extension of their abilities" (Vanderheiden, 1992, p. 270). Communication devices, robotics, mobility aids, artificial intelligence problem-solving devices, and prostheses are some of the many technologies now available to persons with mental retardation living in community settings. Seven hundred entries were evaluated by judges at a recent Johns Hopkins University competition for technology benefiting persons with disabilities (Gardner & Chapman, 1993).

People who work with persons with mental retardation are well aware of the importance of transportation to independent living. For many, the importance translates to access to and experience with public transportation such as buses and subways. Vanderheiden (1992) envisions the day when a person will be able to go up to a bus stop, push a button, announce the destination, and, through visual or aural means, be told the time and number of the appropriate bus, if it is on time, where it currently is, and alternative bus routes or stops.

Devices using artificial intelligence are also receiving increased attention. Though these are not yet fully operational, Vanderheiden sees the day when persons with mental retardation will be able to use companion devices to help with everyday problem solving. Devices that track a person's progress, prompt for action with verbal cues, answer questions when posed,

TABLE 15.5

Microcomputer Applications for Program Management, Clinical Services, and Service Extension

Program management applications
Staff scheduling Documentation of participation in staff development activities Documentation of personnel evaluations Staff scheduling for workdays (attendance) Specialized and generic service resources directory Inventory Expenditures Satisfaction of key client documentation and records requirements Staff development instruction on an ad hoc, anecdotal schedule (programmed learning, interactive, and alternative format permitting training of staff whose schedules conflict with available group sessions).
Clinical service applications
Daily activity and training scheduling for staff and clients   Review of quarterly client progress (documentation of team process assessment results, automated client record updating periodically) Monitoring of assessment methodologies Scheduling of periodic or annual special assessments Documentation of incidents Documentation of medication use, frequency of seizures Assessment of intervention benefits together with indications of needs to alter intervention techniques or goals Service episodes for clinical services Consolidation of data from individual client records Monitoring resident progress (references to current goals; records of trials, prompt levels, and steps to criterion in task analyses and review of goal plan content specificity) Record of training instances Prompts to trainers by computer (computer-assisted training) Frequency, duration, and intensity records for focal behaviors, and records generation, and analysis Identification of environmental factors promoting maladaptive behavior, problem identification.
Service extension
Telecommunication capabilities for programmatic data between day and residential settings (networking) Extension of program activities from day program to natural family settings (modem or time sharing), and progress/program summaries for parent use, message-service capacities Documentation of program coordination and merging of material provided by community practitioners and other agencies in individual program file Preprogrammed instructional and guidance applications in everyday settings (reminder files, instructions, activities, schedules) using briefcase-size, or smaller, microcomputers as an aid to adaptation to independent living in the community.

Source: From "Microcomputer Applications in Public Residential Facilities" by J. W. Jacobson in *Transitions in Mental Retardation, Volume 4: Applications and Implications of Technology* (p. 130) edited by J. A. Mulick and R. F. Antonak, 1989, Norwood, NJ: Ablex. Copyright 1989 by Ablex. Reprinted by permission.

and instantly put the person in touch with others (e.g., family, friends, emergency personnel) are currently in development. The more sophisticated the community, the more sophisticated the assistive devices must be.

In a society that prides itself on technological breakthroughs such as cellular telephones, fax machines, programmable VCRs, and automobiles that can park themselves, seemingly easy tasks such as riding a bus, learning to read, or administering first aid to oneself or others often require much more sophisticated assistive technologies for success. For independence and successful daily living, the demands may be higher still. For persons with mental retardation, the potential benefits and rewards of new technological breakthroughs will certainly not be overlooked as the 21st century approaches.

PREVENTION

The PCMR published its report entitled Mental Retardation: Century of Decision (PCMR, 1976a). In this publication, the committee listed a number of goals, objectives, and recommendations to be achieved before the year 2000. Two of these goals are directly associated with prevention and discussed in the following sections:

- Goal: At least 50-percent reduction in the incidence of mental retardation from biomedical causes by the year 2000.
- Goal: Reduction of the incidence and prevalence of mental retardation associated with social disadvantages to the lowest level possible by the end of this century. (pp. 135, 137)

Prevention is a critical factor in controlling the incidence of mental retardation. Relatively few programs that are directed toward primary prevention currently exist, although "the greatest opportunities for prevention occur before conception and during pregnancy" (Grossman & Tarjan, 1987, p. 117)—that is, **primary prevention.** Unfortunately, most services provided are tertiary (see Chapter 5).

A relevant statistical feature common to both biomedical and psychosocial prevention is birthrate. This is a critical dimension in that it directly influences the incidence of mental retardation; as birthrate increases, so does the number of children who will likely be diagnosed as mentally retarded. Furthermore, as society becomes technologically more sophisticated, our ability to prevent some mental retardation by technical means is offset by our ability to keep alive infants who would not have survived in the past and who are at risk for having mental retardation. This raises critical ethical, moral, and legal questions.

Even though there is much to praise about recent technological advancements and their effects in preventing or minimizing mental retardation, we should be cautious about being too self-congratulatory. For instance, it is sadly ironic that even with our medical sophistication, the United States ranks high among industrialized nations in incidence of infant mortality.

Biomedical Issues

Biomedical intervention will undoubtedly have a great impact on the prevention of mental retardation in the future. Such intervention can be introduced at the preconceptive, prenatal (gestational), perinatal (birth), and postnatal stages of development.

Preconceptive prevention is a type of "quality control" (Fletcher, 1974). Smith and Smith (1978) stated that techniques safeguarding quality control and preventing mental retardation before conception include proper immunization against certain diseases, proper nutrition, diagnostic genetic intervention, and family planning. We can easily see that these strategies require some type of education or dissemination of information to prospective parents. Sometimes political savvy is needed. Since the purpose of these techniques is to minimize the incidence of mental retardation before conception (primary prevention), they rely heavily on early identification of high-risk situations and the delivery of appropriate education.

Genetic counseling can provide critical information for family planning after certain diagnostic tests have been conducted. Most genetic counseling centers provide fetal analysis and immediate postnatal testing in addition to screening prospective parents. Often, genetic analysis will identify carriers of defective genes whose future offspring have a chance of being affected. The ability to detect this situation early—before conception—can have a dramatic effect on prevention.

Another major concern during the preconceptive period is the health threat of various conditions like exposure to human immunodeficiency virus (HIV), which leads to AIDS, and of other communicable diseases (e.g., syphilis, herpes). These conditions can lead to mental retardation; for example, many children infected with HIV have central nervous system problems. That more infants who are being born have been affected by these diseases suggests that this area will command much attention in the future. The most effective intervention is education. Affected adults must be made aware of the consequences of these conditions on the children they bear.

Prenatal (gestational) prevention takes many forms. Adequate nutritional intake is a must for pregnant women if the birth of infants with physical and mental defects is to be avoided. Malnutrition can lead to premature births, low birth weight, and reduced mental functioning. This problem can be controlled. Through more efficient educational programs directed toward providing proper nutritional information and through technological advances like dietary supplements or nutritional meal systems delivered by mail (Beevy, 1978), the improper nutritional health of prospective mothers could be reduced drastically or (theoretically) eliminated completely.

Other preventive action is directed at eliminating or minimizing the effects of toxic substances and diseases that can damage the developing fetus. In addition to the risks of various teratogens (e.g., alcohol) covered in Chapter 5, other ingested substances may also have toxic implications. Prescribed medications can have serious teratogenic or cytotoxic (poisonous

See Table 5.4 for a listing of many different types of preventive options.

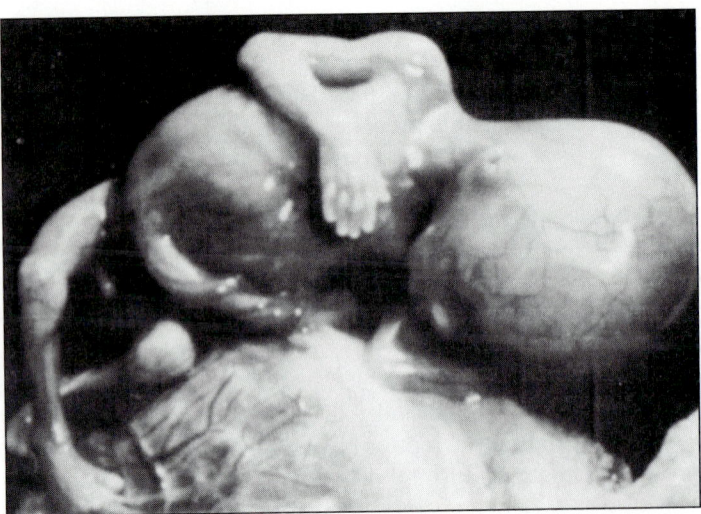

Not too long ago, photographs of a fetus were the stuff of science fiction. Surgery in utero to correct deformities is now a possibility.

to cells) effects on the unborn child as well. Pregnant women who require certain drugs for regulatory reasons (e.g., epilepsy) are faced with a difficult situation. They should not take medications, which they need, while pregnant and, if they must, they should keep them to a minimum during the first trimester. Furthermore, complications can arise from taking nonprescription drugs like aspirin, multivitamin preparations, or weight reduction agents.

Prenatal techniques such as sonography, ultrasound, amniocentesis, and chorionic villi sampling (CVS) can effectively diagnose defects in a developing fetus. These techniques are examples of innovations that are now available. It is possible to detect many (200 and 100, respectively) of the known genetic disorders through amniocentesis and CVS; however, this is far short of the 4,000+ known genetic disorders. In all likelihood, technological advances will increase the number of conditions that can be identified prenatally. These techniques or others like them will probably also allow us to detect problems earlier and with minimum risk to the mother and fetus. This ability, in combination with the techniques described next, will greatly contribute to the prevention of mental retardation or the alleviation of its effects.

Although the most highly developed of earthly creatures, *Homo sapiens* has the unenviable distinction of being the species with the longest period of vulnerability after birth. A neonate is quite helpless, and the probability of an infant's survival without assistance and protection is nil. As we know, various birth traumas (such as anoxia and breech birth) can account for a number of conditions associated with mental retardation. Although traumatic birth episodes will always be with us, the frequency of these unfortunate events will decrease as the field of obstetrics continues to develop innovative techniques.

With the continued sophistication of medical knowledge and service delivery, the science of screening newborns for metabolic deficiencies will continue to be perfected. Defects like phenylketonuria (PKU), hypoglycemia, galactosemia, and hypothyroidism, among others, can all be detected and treated early in an infant's life. What must be forestalled is the unacceptable paradox of researchers' developing the technology but not being able to apply it, for whatever (usually economic or political) reason.

Prevention of mental retardation in early childhood must emphasize the need to minimize environmental hazards, implement early stimulation projects, and reduce the incidence of accidents and child abuse. For instance, nursing infants can be at risk because breast milk can be contaminated by industrial chemicals (pesticides) that the mother has ingested through affected food (Elkington, 1985). The threat of lead poisoning has not gone away either, as children are still being exposed to high levels of this toxic substance. Unacceptable lead levels are being found in such places as water catchment systems and drinking fountains in various areas of the country.

If technology and, more important, its application to the problems associated with mental retardation continue to blossom, then there is a real chance that the incidence of mental retardation due to biomedical causes can be reduced 50 percent by the year 2000. But this goal cannot be achieved without public support and encouragement.

Psychosocial Issues

Predictions about causes related to psychological and social factors are more difficult to make because of their complexity. Socioeconomic status, poverty, race, environment, and culture have been related to retardation, but unfortunately, the questions they raise do not have simple answers. It would be marvelous to eliminate poverty and to attenuate the problems faced by people in lower socioeconomic classes, but we must be realistic. Even though the PCMR's goal of reducing the incidence and prevalence of mental retardation to the lowest level possible by the year 2000 is laudable, we face many entrenched institutional obstacles that make it unattainable.

First, regardless of our incontestable intention to eliminate poverty, this goal may be impossible. The perception of having eliminated poverty may indeed be achieved, but the reality of poverty will no doubt persist. In the 1976 Report to the President (PCMR, 1976a), the President's Committee cautioned that poverty should be viewed as a dual concept:

> The question of poverty is two-sided. **Absolute poverty** is officially measured in the United States as a fixed standard of real income based upon the prevailing cost of a minimum human diet. The percent of the population below this level has declined from 22.4 in 1959 to 11.9 in 1972. However, the proportionate distribution

of incomes in American society has changed very little in that time, with the lowest fifth of the population receiving a steady 4.5 to 5.5 percent of the aggregate income in each year in the United States from 1947 to 1972. This creates, the futurists suggest, a persistent condition of **relative poverty.** Projection of the continued decline of absolute poverty to near-zero could still leave the level of relative poverty unchanged. (pp. 42–43, emphasis added)

The correlates of poverty (e.g., malnutrition, inadequate medical care) have a direct impact on development.

Both dimensions of poverty pose continuing obstacles to the reduction of psychosocial causes of mental retardation in the future. Absolute poverty affects the ability of families to afford the necessities of life: housing, food, and adequate health care. Relative poverty (a person's economic and social standing) affects one's status, often leading to "a chronic state of failure, dependency, defeat, hopelessness, helplessness, cultural impoverishment, under- and unemployment, and broken families" (Nanus, 1980, p. 75). Both kinds of poverty will continue to stand in the way of reducing psychosocial causes of mental retardation.

Many more persons are finding it more difficult to make it in today's world. A group of "new poor" is developing that has been described as "a much less homogeneous group that includes structurally unemployed persons, young people whose upward mobility opportunities have been closed off, the mentally ill, and the 'voluntary poor' " (*The Futurist,* 1986, p. 44). This new group does not seem to use community resources (when available) to its advantage, either through lack of knowledge or unwillingness. For those who have children (and their numbers are increasing), the conditions in which they live do not contribute to quality child rearing. Whether some of these children are identified as mentally retarded at some time during their school careers is secondary to the fact that many of them will display learning-related problems with which school systems will have to deal initially and which society will have to address ultimately.

Our well-established notions and attitudes toward the concept of cultural deprivation may need to be rethought. Frequently, little acknowledgment is given to the strengths of children who arrive daily at school from what is called a "deprived" environment. Barring the financial distinction between middle and low socioeconomic status (SES), and the differences in educational opportunity that distinguish classes separated by income, there are few things intrinsically enriching about middle-class culture that would, by contrast, render lower class environments "deprived." A child's use of nonstandard English, for example, need not lead to the conclusion that the child's home life is substandard, because that language is a product of cultural factors not found in higher SES homes. The fact that most schools adhere to middle-class mores and standards ensures that problems will arise if we insist that the student from a non-middle-class background conform without question to this system. Ginsburg (1972) believes that children who are poor and who live in what we often refer to as "culturally deprived" environments actually have skills and strengths that are sufficient for adequate cognitive development, but that these skills and strengths are different from those of middle-class children. A heightened awareness of and sensitivity to diversity will continue to emerge as important considerations in delivering services to children from varying backgrounds.

None of what has been discussed here denies the importance of appropriate language development. The parental encouragement of language development and/or contact with well-designed early intervention programs that systematically develop language skills can help students do better in school. Preschool experiences seem to benefit all students. For this reason, many states are considering the implementation of publicly supported preschool classes for all students.

As the standard of living improves, as more programs directed toward upgrading impoverished areas increase, as more efforts to provide early intervention to children at risk for school failure are established, and as our conception of cultural deprivation matures, opportunities to prevent cases of mental retardation due to psychosocial causes will undoubtedly increase. Generalized amelioration will occur only if there are drastic changes in our social structure, and such changes are not likely. Finally, the goals proclaimed by the PCMR will need to be revisited, evaluated, and reformulated as we enter the next century.

AN AGENDA FOR FUTURE RESEARCH

Science, more often than not, deals with the unexpected, the unexplainable, and the unknown. Consequently, predictions of the future can often be as interesting as they are inaccurate. In an age when technological breakthroughs are apt to be as wonderful as they are astounding, it gives one reason to be optimistic. Yet, one must remain cautious, and predictions must be tempered with the realization that breakthroughs, however remarkable, may never come soon enough for those who may need them the most.

As long as there is mental retardation, there will continue to be a need for ongoing research about and for those with mental retardation. Such areas as etiology, development, education, and community living have potential significance. Beneath these areas of significance, however, lie equally important strata of developments waiting to be uncovered, theoretical and conceptual tenets that guide future investigations. Research, both basic and applied, should continue to be supported and encouraged by all members of the service delivery system. Persons and families of persons who rely on this research must demand the highest quality research possible. No longer should the decisions to proceed with major policy issues and practice strategies be made in the absence of sound and verifiable research. The costs to the persons with mental retardation, families of persons with mental retardation, and society are far too high.

While science and technology are designed to make great advances on a very wide front, when and where the new breakthroughs will actually come is, at this point, impossible to determine (Koshland, 1993). Rowitz (1992) has, however, identified 130 predictions of new developments in the field of mental retardation considered to be important as the 21st century approaches. The predictions are organized into four broad domains and are summarized next:

1. Conceptual Issues
   - Homogenizing of deviances into general classes (e.g., developmental disabilities)
   - Movement toward cognitive models and less reliance on psychomedical models
   - Quality of life as an international issue
2. Family Issues
   - Family organization, development, and functioning
   - Differential care arrangements of single parents
   - Sibling roles and development
3. Health Issues
   - Increased incidence and treatment of HIV infections
   - Implementation of actual coordinated service programs
   - Identification of marker genes for most/all genetic causes of mental retardation
4. Service and Policy Issues
   - Shortage of direct-service personnel at entry-level positions
   - Movement toward more and better integrated employment opportunities
   - Development of companion tools and reminder aids

FINAL THOUGHTS

We hope that the future will be characterized by improved conditions for those with special needs. There is good reason to believe that influences such as advocacy groups, interest groups, and most important, social attitudes, will continue to drive the quantity and quality of programs and services for those who are mentally retarded.

Blatt has given us much to think about in his many writings. In his last major publication, *The Conquest of Mental Retardation* (1987), he provided some thoughts that can help guide us as we prepare for the future.

> We will conquer mental retardation not only by better science, but by a better way of life. . . . Increasingly specialized knowledge about mental retardation will, in itself, do relatively little to ameliorate the problems faced by mentally retarded people. . . . In order to understand and respond to the voices of mentally retarded people, we must understand ourselves, our society, our institutions (in the broader sense), our values and our traditions. (p. 11)

We can influence the future in many ways by what we do or, at the very least, try to do today. We can no longer remain passive observers, but must become active participants in solutions to the problems and needs of persons who are mentally retarded. Our attention should focus not only on individuals with mental retardation but also on the public, because the key to the future rests there. Without positive public sentiment toward those who are mentally retarded, which must be nurtured by what happens today and reflected in financial support for our efforts, the outlook for this group is not favorable. Our highest priorities should be the inclusion of people who are mentally retarded in the worlds of all people, active participation on behalf of all advocates, and the continued search for new knowledge.

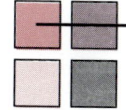

SUMMARY

PREDICTING THE FUTURE

- Much of what we can predict about the future is based on current developments in the field.

- The demands placed on persons with mental retardation have to be understood in terms of the emerging complexities of an information society.

- Everyday life is getting more complex as time progresses, and society is evolving into a scenario of "the haves"—those who have what it takes to adapt to future changes—and "the have nots"—those who do not have this ability.

CRITICAL AREAS OF CONCERN

- The public attitude toward those who are mentally retarded is changing due to increased media attention; however, many misconceptions and misperceptions remain.

- Many believe that the new definition and classification criteria of mental retardation represent a new beginning for the ways in which persons with mental retardation are viewed.

- Some futurists believe that most if not all of the major genetic causes of mental retardation will be known early in the 21st century.

- Many biomedical and psychosocial interventions, if invoked appropriately during various developmental periods, can prevent a significant number of persons from becoming mentally retarded.

AN AGENDA FOR THE FUTURE

- As long as there is mental retardation, there will continue to be a need for research about and for those with mental retardation.

- Persons, and families of persons, with mental retardation who rely on the research must demand the highest quality research possible.

Glossary

Absolute poverty The level below the federal government's officially measured fixed standard of necessary real income based upon prevailing cost of a minimum human diet.

Adaptive behavior "Degree and efficiency with which the individual meets the standards of personal independence and social responsibility expected of his age and cultural group" (Grossman, 1983, p. 1).

Advocacy The formal representation of one's interests in an effort to bring about changes in the broader social order.

American Association on Mental Retardation (AAMR) The nation's leading professional association of and for persons who are mentally retarded.

Amniocentesis Analysis of amniotic fluid during the second trimester of pregnancy to allow for biochemical analysis of fetal cells; can indicate presence of genetic and chromosomal disorders and indicate sex of fetus.

Annual goals Statements of what the student with disabilities can reasonably be expected to achieve in the course of one calendar year.

Anoxia Oxygen deprivation severe enough to cause permanent brain damage and retardation.

Aptitude test Standardized and norm-referenced assessment designed to measure an individual's potential ability to perform a specific task or the readiness to learn.

Assessment Collecting information through observation, testing, and task analysis to determine strengths and weaknesses for the purpose of making decisions.

Assistive technologies "Those technologies that an individual keeps and uses as a tool or extension of their abilities" (Vanderheiden, 1992, p. 270).

At risk A child who is in danger of substantial developmental delay because of medical, biological, or environmental factors if early intervention services are not provided.

Autosomes Twenty-two matched pairs of chromosomes (forty-four of normally present forty-six). *See* Sex chromosomes.

Aversives Treatment techniques considered to be an extreme form of behavior modification that is uncomfortable, painful, or otherwise offensive, and is generally used to eliminate maladaptive or problem behaviors.

Behavioral curricula   Theory of operant learning in which skills are taught according to the child's or infant's needs in the present or projected future environment. Skills are defined in behavioral terms with quantitatively stated criteria for performance.

Behavioral objectives   Statements that specify an observable behavior, the conditions under which it will occur, and the acceptable standard for accuracy against which to measure performance.

Career development   Curricula designed to give the individual a start in making a living.

Career education   Training that prepares individuals for all the roles to be assumed as adults, including the roles of worker, citizen, and family member.

Categorical program   Educational programs serving only students who are diagnosed with a specific disability and who are officially placed in a special education program.

Centrifugal forces   Experiences or interactions among family members that push them apart.

Centripetal forces   Experiences or interactions among family members that draw them together.

Cerebral palsy   Any neuromuscular disability resulting from damage to the brain at birth or during the first four years of life.

Chromosomes   Threadlike bodies containing genes (hereditary factors) occupying specific loci.

Cloak of competence   Refers to individuals who spend much time and energy denying their disability and attempting to present themselves as persons without mental retardation.

Cognitive-developmental theory   Proposed by Piaget; suggests that each individual progresses through stages of development where specific cognitive skills are acquired through interaction with and adaptation to the environment and perception of that environment. Includes four ordered stages of development.

Collaborative consultation   "An interactive process which enables people with diverse expertise to generate creative solutions to mutually defined problems" (Idol et al., 1986, p. 1).

Collaborative teaming   "An ongoing process whereby educators with different areas of expertise voluntarily work together to create solutions to problems that are impeding students' success, as well as to carefully monitor and refine these solutions" (Knackendofel et al., 1992, p. 1).

Community acceptance   The extent to which a person who is mentally retarded is accepted and supported in the community environment.

Community adjustment   An individual's ability to adjust to the multiple demands of life in the community.

Community-based instruction   Teaching a skill to a student in the actual environment as opposed to teaching the skill in a classroom with the expectation of transference, generalization, and application of knowledge when skill use is required.

Community-referenced instruction   Educational programs that are directly related to actual incidents that occur naturally in the environment.

Community-referenced instructional activities   Identifying skills that are necessary to function in public life.

Community residential settings   Typically, those with paid service providers and fifteen or fewer residents located in traditional residential neighborhoods.

Concrete operational stage   The period in Piaget's cognitive-developmental theory during which the child learns to classify and to solve concrete problems; lasts approximately from age seven to age eleven in children who are not mentally retarded.

Consent agreement   Legal agreement between opposing parties in a litigation that resolves the point of conflict and that is court sanctioned.

Consequences   Something produced by a cause or set of conditions. If made contingent, consequences can facilitate learning.

Criterion-referenced testing (CRT)   Measure of a child's skill in terms of a preestablished level of mastery in a given content area.

Cross-categorical program   A program reserved for students who are officially placed in a special education program but may serve students from more than one disability area. Students can be grouped according to their instructional needs rather than by disability.

Curriculum   A "master plan for selecting content and organizing learning experiences for the purpose of changing and developing learners' behavior and insights" (Armstrong, 1990, p. 4).

Curriculum-based assessment   A criterion-referenced type of test with test items drawn directly from the instructor's teaching materials, considered to be a highly effective measure of student performance.

Deinstitutionalization   Movement to decentralize large public institutions and move residents into smaller local centers and family settings, so as to provide the most natural and least restrictive environment in which persons who are disabled can live and maximize their potential.

Deletion   In genetics, a process where a portion of original genetic material is absent from a specific chromosomal pair.

Developmental curricula   Based largely on the work of Piaget; the teacher designs tasks related to children's normal developmental milestones, identifies deficits, and gears instruction to accelerating the rate of development of the child or infant who is disabled.

Developmental delay   A significant lag in one or more of the following areas of development: cognitive, speech/language, physical/motor, vision, hearing, psychosocial, and self-help skills when compared to age norms.

Developmental model   Suggests that cognitive development in individuals who are mentally retarded generally follows the same sequence as that of individuals who are not mentally retarded, but at a slower rate.

Developmental period   "Time between conception and the 18th birthday" in which a person grows mentally and physically (Grossman, 1983, p. 11).

Deviation IQ In contrast to ratio IQ, assumes IQ is normally distributed with 100 as average and a standard deviation that is the same for every age level.

Difference/deficit model Suggests that cognitive development in individuals who are mentally retarded is qualitatively different from that of individuals who are not mentally retarded and therefore requires different teaching strategies.

Disablism (Formerly handicapism.*)* "A set of assumptions and practices that promote differential and unequal treatment of people because of apparent or assumed physical, mental, or behavioral differences" (Bogdan & Biklen, 1977, p. 59).

Dominant inheritance Inheritance in which an individual gene has control or can mask the other gene in the pair.

Down syndrome A chromosomal anomaly that accounts for the largest percentage of cases of clinical moderate and severe retardation. Generally accompanied by such clinical manifestations as epicanthic folds, large tongue, broad flat bridge of nose, and poor muscle tone.

Dysfunctional families Those families that have failed at task resolution and, as a result, are arrested at earlier, less adaptive stages of development.

Early childhood special education A system of services for children from birth to five years of age who are disabled, developmentally delayed, or at risk of developmental delay, and their families.

Early intervention System of services that are usually provided free of charge for children who are disabled, developmentally delayed, or at risk of developmental delay, and their families.

Ecological inventory The process of setting educational goals for students who are mentally retarded based on the observation of performance by students who are not disabled in real-world settings.

Ecological model Instructional methodology designed to enhance the ability of persons with mental retardation to fully participate in the community. Includes the belief that people with disabilities have a right to participate in educational, economic, and social aspects of the community. Individualized programs of instruction are developed for each student, and skills are taught in the settings where they are to be used.

Economic integration The extent to which a person is able to obtain and disburse income as it relates to life in the community.

Educability The ability of an individual to learn from experience and to apply learning in various settings.

Educable mental retardation (EMR) Term used to refer to students whose abilities are adequate to become self-sufficient and learn academic skills through the upper elementary grades. The individual's score on an individual test of intelligence is approximately 55 to 70.

Educational benefit Learning that allows the highest degree of self-sufficiency possible.

Egalitarianism The belief that all people are created equal and that everyone is entitled to the same rights and privileges.

Ego-strength An intangible concept that refers to the organization and integrity of personality.

Employment integration An individual's adjustment to the routines, rhythms, and responsibilities of work.

Equal protection The principal of the 14th amendment, which allows the same rights and benefits to all citizens according to government practice unless there is a compelling reason to withhold these rights.

Etiology Cause, reason, or origin of a given condition.

Eugenics movement The science movement that manipulates breeding to improve the quality of the human race.

Expectancy Anticipation of the result of a task or situation based on previous experiences in similar situations.

Expectancy for failure Lower aspirations and goals intended to avoid additional failure; set by individuals who have accumulated failure experiences.

Expressivity Capacity of a gene to affect the phenotype of an organism.

Extensive supports Resources utilized by persons with disabilities to promote independence, productivity, and community integration. Extensive supports are provided regularly, in at least some environments, and on a long-term basis.

Family (1) A group of individuals consisting of immediate and distant relatives who are related through birth, adoption, or marriage. (2) A group of people who love and care for each other.

Family-directed assessment Assessment to study the resources, priorities, and concerns of the family and the identification of the supports and services necessary to enhance the family's capacity to meet the developmental needs of their infant or toddler with a disability.

Family support services "Services other than those basic residential and vocational/habilitative services that people with developmental disabilities require for normal community living" (Castellani et al., 1986, p. 71).

Feebleminded An obsolete British term for intelligence that coincides with the educational classification of educable mentally retarded or the American Association of Mental Retardation's classification of mild mental retardation.

Feedback Information given to the learner (or a system) following a specific response.

Formal operational stage The fourth stage in Piaget's cognitive-developmental theory, during which the child learns to think abstractly and reason by logic; begins around age eleven in children who are not mentally retarded.

Formal supports Generally, formally organized programs that consist of professionals trained to provide necessary and specific services for persons with disabilities (see Cooley, 1989).

Functional activities   Skills needed in the everyday home, community, vocational, and recreational environments.

Functional analysis   Examination of the content in which a behavior occurs and the function the behavior serves.

Functional curricula   A hybrid of the developmental and behavioral curricula that emphasizes teaching interrelated classes of behavior and generalization within task classes. It is developmental, yet behavioral in its emphasis on teaching skills that the infant or child needs now or will need later.

Gene   The basic biological unit within the chromosome influencing hereditary traits.

Gene therapy   A process of cloning a gene to perform the appropriate metabolic task (e.g., the conversion of phenylalanine to tyrosine in the case of phenylketonuria).

Genetics   The study of heredity and variation.

Grand mal seizure   The most severe type of epileptic seizure, in which the individual has violent convulsions, loses consciousness, and becomes rigid.

Grouping   Clustering material based on sameness prior to presentation.

Grouping of material   Clustering information prior to presentation to facilitate the learner's memory and recall.

Habilitation   The acquisition and use of skills to allow for successful functioning in independent living and employment.

Handicapism   See *Disabilism*.

Heritability   The proportion of total trait variance that is directly due to genetic, measurable factors.

Heterozygous   Having to do with pairs of genes carrying different traits.

Homme sauvage   Human savage.

Homozygous   Having to do with pairs of genes carrying the same trait.

Human Genome Project   A concerted, multinational effort to identify the location and function of all parts of the genetic code of humans.

Human rights committees (HRCs)   Began in the 1970s as a result of lawsuits and civil and human rights movements. HRCs are housed in an institution and are designed to protect the rights of persons living in institutional settings.

Hydrocephalus   A disorder resulting from blockage of cerebrospinal fluid in the cranial cavity that causes an enlarged head and undue pressure on the brain.

Incidence   The number of new cases of a condition identified within a population over a specific period of time.

Inclusion   Placing students who are disabled, regardless of the type or degree of disability, in general education classrooms in their home-school.

The general education teacher assumes primary responsibility for students who are included.

Inclusive environments   The placement of students with special learning needs in settings with peers who have no special learning needs.

Individual Family Service Plan (IFSP)   A document prepared as part of the voluntary component of PL 99-457, developed by a multidisciplinary team with the assistance of the child's parents or guardians, and detailing the year's plan for the child with disabilities aged birth to two and the child's family.

Individualized Education Program (IEP)   Individually written plan of yearly instruction by a committee required by the Individuals with Disabilities Education Act for every child or youth who is disabled.

Individuals with Disabilities Education Act (IDEA)   The 1990 amendment to PL 94-142, which modified PL 94-142 and changed the name of the law to reflect a sensitivity to preferred terminology.

Infant component   A voluntary component of PL 99-457, the Education of the Handicapped Amendments, that provides individual states with incentive grants to assist in the development of an interagency council whose purpose is to ensure planned, coordinated services for children with disabilities aged birth to two.

Informal supports   Those services generally provided through intra- or interpersonal means either by the person with the disability or by the person's family, friends, or neighbors (see Cooley, 1989).

Informed clinical opinion   An opinion formed by using at least 50 percent of a clinician's expertise in addition to the formal testing results to aid in determining eligibility for special education services.

Innate   Inherent; use of abnormal chromosome arrangements present from conception but most often not the product of hereditary exchange.

Input organization   Organization and storage of information so it can be recalled when needed.

Intelligence   Ability to adapt, achieve, solve problems, interpret incoming stimuli to modify behavior, accumulate knowledge, or respond to items on an intelligence test; cannot be measured directly.

Intelligence quotient (IQ)   A historically relevant term in which mental age is divided by chronological age and multiplied by 100; an index of intellectual performance relative to others in the same age group.

Interdisciplinary team   A group of individuals from varying professions responsible for developing comprehensive, appropriate educational programs for all students with disabilities.

Interpersonal relationships   An individual's ability to recognize and respond to the needs of others, and to interact appropriately with others.

Involuntary commitment   A legal procedure requiring a written affidavit, complete with descriptions of relevant behaviors, filed with the local chancery clerk. Two physicians or a physician and a psychologist must conduct a preliminary evaluation and determine if there is a need for institutionalization. Persons found eligible must receive a formal hearing with the court chancellor within ten days of certification.

Itinerant teacher A special educator who provides the general education teacher with consultation and some instructional services on a limited basis and gives support to the general education teacher, who has the major responsibility for the child's educational program.

Job coach A person who provides on-the-job training to individuals with disabilities.

Judgment-based assessment An appraisal according to a scale or checklist usually developed by a classroom teacher to measure abilities not typically identified by standardized instruments.

Karyotypes Graphic chromosomal pictures in descending order based on size.

Learned helplessness A pattern of submissiveness that develops in individuals when they believe that their actions are of no consequence and that outcomes are beyond their control.

Learning A process whereby practice or experience results in a change in behavior not due to maturation, growth, or aging; cannot be directly measured or observed.

Life skills Abilities necessary to function as an independent individual within the community.

Life skills curricula Instructional programs designed to teach individuals with disabilities those skills that will facilitate their inclusion as contributing members of their communities and their successful adjustment to adulthood.

Locus of control The hypothetical construct that people attempt to reach a goal within their own power (*internal locus of control*) or through events controlled by others (*external locus of control*).

Long-term memory The ability to retrieve information from storage after a few days or several years.

Mainstreaming The practice of placing students who are disabled in the general education classroom to the extent appropriate to their needs.

Maintenance The ability needed to retain skills or knowledge over time.

Mastery learning The teacher tests a concept, gives feedback, and then tests the concept again until the child has completely mastered the task.

Mediation (1) A memory strategy in which an individual connects a verbal label and information to be learned, (2) the process parents and school systems may use to agree upon identification, placement, and evaluation of a student with special needs.

Meiosis The division and pairing of gametes to form the genetic foundation for an embryo.

Memory The ability to retrieve stored information.

Mental age A measure of intellectual level (as performed on a mental measurement test) recorded independently of chronological age.

Mental retardation "Significantly subaverage general intellectual functioning resulting in or associated with concurrent impairments in adaptive behavior and manifested during the developmental period" (Grossman, 1983, p. 11).

Mental test An obsolete name for an intelligence test.

Metabolic disturbance See *Phenylketonuria*.

Mildly retarded A slight deviation below the normal range of intelligence and adaptive behavior. Individuals who are mildly retarded can usually benefit from academic instruction and are often referred to as educable mentally retarded.

Mitigating factor An element or agent of cause.

Modeling An approach to teaching where the teacher demonstrates part or all of the behavior to be learned, and the student repeats the action immediately.

Mosaicism (1) Uneven division of cells in mitosis, resulting in unequal or extra chromosomes, (2) a form of Down syndrome in which not all cells have unusual chromosome composition.

Myelomeningocele A condition characterized by a saclike mass on the spinal cord containing membrane tissue of the central nervous system and cerebrospinal fluid but no spinal nerves on the spinal cord.

Natural home A place of residence where one lives with biological or adoptive family members.

Natural supports The resources accessed by persons with disabilities that promote independence, productivity, and community integration. Natural supports are selected from resources preexisting in the person's environment and are provided without the aid of technology or services agencies.

Nature–nurture controversy The debate as to whether intelligence is either innate or acquired.

Noncategorical program An educational program designed to serve both students who are disabled and students who are not disabled but who need supplemental instruction.

Nondisjunction The failure of one pair of chromosomes to split correctly at meiosis resulting in a trisomy. Produces such conditions as Down syndrome (trisomy 21).

Normalization The process of providing for and, to the maximum extent possible, treating an individual with special needs in the mainstream of society as if the individual has no special needs.

Norm-referenced test A test that has been given to a large number of subjects and for which standard procedures for administration, scoring, and interpretation are published; standard procedures must be followed for results to be valid.

Observational learning Learning from watching demonstrations.

Ombudsman   One whose role is to protect the rights of individuals seeking services from government agencies.

Outerdirectedness   Looking to others for guidance or cues in developing appropriate responses in demanding situations.

Parity   Equal status of all members involved in the collaborative consultation process; no single individual is viewed as the expert, and all contributions are judged solely on their merit as a feasible solution to the problem.

Pedigree studies   Examination and research on a particular topic through generations.

Penetrance   The frequency of individuals within a particular population who manifest a hereditary condition caused by a dominant or double recessive gene. The failure to manifest the gene is a result of other genes and nongenetic factors.

Performance   Observable behavior; can be the basis for determining whether learning has occurred.

Personal satisfaction   The extent to which an individual's life has satisfaction and optimum quality.

Pervasive supports   Resources provided on a constant basis and across all environments to promote the independence, productivity, and community integration of persons with mental retardation. Pervasive supports are of a potentially life-sustaining nature.

Petit mal seizure   An epileptic seizure in which the individual loses consciousness, usually for less than half a minute; it may occur very frequently in some children.

Phenylketonuria (PKU)   An inherited metabolic disease resulting from the absence of an enzyme for digestion that causes a toxic buildup of substances in the blood and urine; if undiagnosed at birth, it causes mental retardation.

PL 94-142   The Education for All Handicapped Children Act of 1975 (now known as the Individuals with Disabilities Education Act, or IDEA). This law provides free appropriate public education in the least restrictive environment to all children and youth aged three to twenty-one who are disabled.

PL 99-457   A law extending the rights and privileges afforded to children who are disabled under PL 94-142 to children from birth to five years.

Polygenetic inheritance   Inheritance in which more than one gene pair affects the appearance of a particular trait.

Precision teaching   The teacher breaks a lesson into a hierarchy of skills.

Preoperational stage   The second stage in Piaget's cognitive-developmental theory, during which the child begins to use symbols and to imitate the actions of others; lasts from approximately age two to age seven in children without retardation.

Preschool component   A mandatory component of PL 99-457, the Education of the Handicapped Amendments, that requires states receiving funds under the law to provide a free appropriate preschool education with related services to all children with disabilities aged three to five.

Prevalence   The total number of cases of a disorder existing within a population at a particular place or at a particular time.

Primary prevention   Early prevention occurring prior to conception and during pregnancy as a critical factor in controlling the incidence of mental retardation.

Procedural due process   Guaranteed by the Fifth Amendment, the right to fairness in regard to property or liberty. In PL 94-142, it refers to the individual's right to a hearing, to be notified of a hearing, to be represented by counsel at a hearing, to be able to question and cross examine witnesses, and to present witnesses.

Profoundly retarded   People who are profoundly mentally retarded function at the lowest level of mental retardation and demonstrate retarded development in all areas, along with little communication or interaction with the environment. They are heavily dependent on others to meet their basic physical needs.

Psychotropic medications   Those medications for which the primary purpose is to control "mood, thought processes, or overt behavior" (Gadow & Poling, 1988, p. 40).

Public residential facility (PRF)   A public institutional setting designed to provide a residential treatment program for individuals who live there.

Quasi-suspect class   A group suspected of having a particular disorder.

Recessive inheritance   Inherited traits that do not express themselves when paired with dominant genes and are influential only when matched with another identical recessive gene.

Reciprocity   "Allowing all parties [involved in the collaborative consultation process] to have equal access to information and the opportunity to participate in problem identification, discussion, decision making and all final outcomes" (West et al., 1989, p. 1).

Recreational/leisure integration   The extent to which an individual harmonizes home and out-of-home free-time activities.

Regular class program   In special education, a system where the student is educated in the general education program but receives support through modification of general and special education materials.

Regular Education Initiative (REI)   A proposal advanced by the federal government that recommended fundamental changes in the ways in which students with mild learning-related disabilities are educated.

Related services   Supportive services (e.g., special transportation, speech or language therapy, occupational or physical therapy) needed to ensure that the special education program meets all of the student's educational needs.

Relative poverty A condition that affects an individual's status, often leading to "a chronic state of failure, dependency, defeat, hopelessness, helplessness, cultural impoverishment, under- and unemployment, and broken families" (Nanus, 1980, p. 75).

Residential facility Twenty-four-hour-a-day housing.

Residential integration Placing the residence of an individual with disabilities in a community.

Resource room A service delivery option in special education where students with special needs meet with a special education teacher apart from the general education classroom to receive extra help in the areas of greatest need.

Right to education Correct, free, and appropriate public school education for all children regardless of ability, age, race, religion, or gender.

Selective attention Focusing on particular dimensions of a learning task.

Self-contained special class A service delivery option in special education where similar students with special needs are placed with a special education teacher on a full-time basis.

Sensorimotor stage The first stage in Piaget's cognitive-developmental theory, during which the child makes purely physical responses to the environment; lasts from birth to approximately age two in children who are not mentally retarded.

Severe disabilities An educational term referring to the lowest level of intellectual functioning of an individual; also includes severe mental retardation, severely retarded, profoundly retarded, and severely disabled.

Severely retarded Individuals in this category function at a level between moderately and profoundly retarded. They show a high incidence of other disabilities, though they can generally communicate and can interact with the environment to some extent.

Sex chromosomes The pair of chromosomes that determines the gender of an individual. *See* Autosomes.

Short-term memory The ability to retrieve information from storage for a period between a few seconds and a few hours.

Short-term objectives Behaviorally stated objectives based on annual goals that provide a clear direction for instruction and ongoing evaluation of the progress of students with disabilities.

Six-hour retarded child A child who is considered mentally retarded at school but appears to function normally with family and peers outside of school.

Social integration An individual's general level of intra- and interpersonal functioning, particularly as it relates to persons who are mentally retarded.

Social role valorization Enhancement of the status of an individual's social role. This concept is the basis of deinstitutionalization: society's perceptions, rather than the individual with the disability, must change.

Sociopolitical forces Societal and civic strength.

Special day school An institution for students who are more severely disabled and who cannot function in the general school environment but who do not require residential care.

Special residential school Generally considered the most restrictive educational placement; usually considered only for students who are the most severely disabled and require twenty-four-hour care.

Standard deviation The unit used to measure the amount by which a particular score varies from the mean with respect to all the scores in a norm sample.

Stanford-Binet IV The *Stanford-Binet Intelligence Scale: Fourth Edition.* The most recent version of the original Binet-Simon Scale used in America after the turn of the century.

Sterilization The process of rendering an individual unable to produce offspring.

Subaverage general intellectual functions Refers to performance of at least one standard deviation below the mean on a standardized test of intelligence.

Subaverage intellectual functions "An IQ of 70 or below on standardized measures of intelligence. This upper limit is intended as a guideline; it could be extended through 75 or more, depending on the reliability of the test used" (Grossman, 1983, p. 11).

Substantive due process A right guaranteed in the Fifth Amendment whereby an individual is promised appropriate classification and treatment in legal pursuits.

Support services Assistive benefits essential to the education of a student with special needs as specified in the Individualized Education Program; also referred to as related services.

Supported employment The placement of individuals with special needs into competitive employment positions with a job coach who does on-the-job training and supervision to facilitate employment and enhance job retention.

Syndrome A group of characteristics that collectively indicate or designate a specific clinical disorder.

Teratogens Substances that can negatively affect prenatal development and result in a severely deformed fetus.

Trainable mental retardation (TMR) An educational term used for individuals functioning in the lower range of mental retardation who will not benefit from general education training but who require training in basic functional skills (e.g., self-help skills). Their score on an individual test of intelligence is usually 35 to 55.

Transition (1) A carefully planned educational process bridging the gap between school and employment and (2) the passage or change from one stage or level to the next (e.g., third to fourth grade, preoperational stage to concrete operations).

Transition education   The unifying vehicle for ensuring that an individual has a more than even chance to become a contributing member of society.

Transition programs   Programs designed to identify appropriate intervention and to provide training to facilitate the transition from level to level within school and from school to life after school.

Transition services   Those services, such as vocational rehabilitation or postsecondary vocational training, provided to individuals with disabilities and leading to employment.

Transition shock   A condition that is analogous to the adjustment problems of people who have recently gotten divorced, returned from war, been released from prison, or relocated to new countries.

Translocation   Exchange of a fragment of chromosomal material within the same chromosome or to another chromosome. Can result in Down syndrome.

Vocational education   A program aimed at preparing an individual for a specific occupation or upgrading of existing skills.

Voluntary admission   A legal procedure initiated when an individual or the parent or legal guardian of an individual who is mentally retarded files a written application with the director of a treatment facility accompanied by certificates from two physicians or one physician and one psychologist attesting to the individual's need for treatment.

Wechsler scales   The Wechsler Intelligence Scales used for identification and classification of countless preschool children, school-age children, adolescents, and adults for nearly half a century.

Wraparound services   A name given to an organized, integrated approach to service delivery that allows for a specially designed treatment plan at a specific point in time.

References

Abbeduto, L., & Nuccio, J.B. (1991). Relation between receptive language and cognitive maturity in persons with mental retardation. *American Journal on Mental Retardation, 96,* 143–149.

Abel, E.L., & Sokol, R.J. (1986). Fetal alcohol is now a leading cause of mental retardation. *Lancet, 2*(8517), 1222.

Abery, B.H. (1994). A conceptual framework for enhancing self-determination. In M.F. Hayden & B.H. Abery (Eds.), *Challenges for a service system in transition.* Baltimore: Brookes.

Abery, B.H., Thurlow, M.L., Bruininks, R.H., & Johnson, D.R. (1990). *The social support networks of transition age young adults with mental retardation.* Paper presented at the annual meeting of the American Association on Mental Retardation, Atlanta, GA.

Abery, B.H., Thurlow, M.L., Johnson, D.R. & Bruininks, R.H. (1989). *The social networks of young adults with developmental disabilities.* Paper presented at the annual meeting of the Association for Persons with Severe Handicaps, San Francisco.

Abroms, K.K., & Bennett, J.W. (1980). Current genetic and demographic findings in Down's Syndrome: How are they represented in college textbooks on exceptionality? *Mental Retardation, 18,* 101–107.

Achenbach, T.M. (1994). *Child Behavior Checklist.* Burlington: University of Vermont, Department of Psychiatry.

Adams, G.L. (1984). *Normative Adaptive Behavior Checklist.* San Antonio, TX: Psychological Corporation.

Alabiso, R. (1977). Inhibitory functions of attention in reducing hyperactive behavior. *American Journal of Mental Deficiency, 77,* 259–282.

Alamo Heights Independent School District v. State Board of Education, 790 F. 2d 1153 (1986).

Aldous, P. (1992). Twin studies go back to the womb. *Science, 257,* 165.

Algozzine, B., & Ysseldyke, J.E. (1981). Special education services for normal children: Better safe than sorry. *Exceptional Children, 48,* 238–243.

Allison, M. (1992). The effects of neurologic injury on the maturing brain. *Headlines, 3*(5), 2–10.

Amado, A.N. (1988). A perspective on the present and notes for new direction. In L.W. Heal, J.I. Haney, & A.N. Amado (Eds.), *Integration of developmentally disabled individuals into the community* (2nd ed., pp. 299–305). Baltimore: Brookes.

Amado, A.N. (1996). The role of agencies in supporting belonging. *Impact, 9*(4), 8.

Amado, A.N., Lakin, K.C., & Menke, J.M. (1990). *1990 Chartbook on services for people with developmental disabilities*. Minneapolis, MN: University of Minnesota, Center for Residential and Community Services.

Aman, M. (1986). *Aberrant Behavior Checklist*. East Aurora, NY: Slosson Educational Publications.

Amara, R. (1988). Health care tomorrow. *The Futurist, 22*(6), 16–20.

America 2000: An Education Strategy. (1991). Washington, DC: U.S. Government Printing Office.

American Association on Mental Deficiency. (1974). *AAMD Adaptive Behavior Scale—Revised*. Washington, DC: Author.

American Association on Mental Retardation. (1975). *Position papers of the AAMD*. Washington, DC: Author.

American Association on Mental Retardation. (1992). *Mental retardation: Definition, classification, and systems of supports* (9th ed.). Washington, DC: Author.

American Association on Mental Retardation. (1993). Self determination. In *Policy positions: On legislative and social issues* (pp. 8–10). Washington, DC: Author.

American Educational Research Association, American Psychological Association, & National Council on Measurement in Education. (1985). *Standards for educational and psychological testing*. Washington, DC: American Psychological Association.

American Psychiatric Association. (1980). *Diagnostic and statistical manual of mental disorders* (3rd ed.). Washington, DC: Author.

American Psychiatric Association. (1994). *Diagnostic and statistical manual of mental disorders* (4th ed.). Washington, DC: Author.

Americans with Disabilities Act, 42 U.S.C. 12101 (1990).

Anastasi, A. (1988). *Psychological testing* (6th ed.). New York: Macmillan.

Anderson, D.J., & Kloos, E.T. (1992). Health issues and placement decisions for older persons with disabilities. *Impact: Feature issue on family and empowerment, 5*(2), 17, 21.

Anderson, D.J., & Pollister, B. (in press). Psychotropic drug use among older persons with mental retardation. In E. Sutton, A. Factor, B. Hawkins, B. Heller, & G. Seltzer (Eds.), *Older adults with developmental disabilities: Optimizing choice and change*. Baltimore: Brookes.

Anderson, L., Dancis, J., & Alpert, M. (1978). Behavioral contingencies and self-mutilation in Lesch-Nyhan disease. *Journal of Consulting and Clinical Psychology, 46*, 529–536.

Anderson, L., Polister, B., Prouty, R.W., & Lakin, K.C. (1996). Number of residential settings and residents by type of living arrangement. In R.W. Prouty & K.C. Lakin (Eds.), *Residential services for persons with developmental disabilities: Status and trends through 1995* (pp. 54–59). Minneapolis: University of Minnesota, Institute on Community Integration.

Andry, H.H. (1995). Civil rights law—right to a free appropriate public education under the IDEA—reimbursement for private school tuition. *Tennessee Law Review, 62*, 313–330.

Apgar, V. (1953). A proposal for a new method of evaluation of the newborn infant. *Current Researches in Anesthesia and Analgesia, 32*, 260–264.

Apolloni, T., & Feichtner, S.H. (1991). Learners and workers in the year 2001. *The Journal for Vocational Special Needs Education, 14*(1), 5–10.

Armstrong, D.G. (1990). *Developing and documenting the curriculum*. Boston: Allyn & Bacon.

Armstrong v. Kline, 476 F, Supp. 583 (1979).

Arnold, M., & Serpas, D. (1992). Preparing teachers to address the needs of students with severe mental retardation. *Education, 113*(1), 80–84.

Association of Retarded Citizens of the United States. (1984). *How to provide for their future.* Arlington, TX: Author.

Aveno, A. (1987). A survey of leisure activities engaged in by adults who are severely retarded living in different residence and community types. *Education and Training in Mental Retardation, 22,* 121–127.

Aydlett, L.A. (1993). Assessing infant interaction skills in interaction-focused intervention. *Infants and Young Children, 5*(4), 1–7.

Baer, D. (1981). The nature of intervention research., In R. Schiefelbusch & D. Bricker (Eds.), *Early language: Acquisition and intervention* (pp. 559–573). Baltimore: University Park Press.

Bailey, D., & Wolery, M. (1984). *Teaching infants and preschoolers with handicaps.* Upper Saddle River, NJ: Merrill/Prentice Hall.

Baines, R.A. (1980). Unequal protection for the retarded? *Amicus, 4,* 128–132.

Baker, J.M., & Zigmond, N. (1995). The meaning and practice of inclusion for students with learning disabilities: Themes and implications from the five cases. *Journal of Special Education, 29*(2), 163–180.

Balkany, T.J., Downs, M.P., Jafek, B.W., & Krajicek, H.J. (1979). Hearing loss in Down's syndrome: A treatable handicap more common than generally recognized. *Clinical Pediatrics, 18,* 116–118.

Balla, D.A., & Zigler, E. (1979). Personality development in retarded persons. In N.R. Ellis (Ed.), *Handbook of mental deficiency: Psychological theory and research* (2nd ed., pp. 154–168). Hillsdale, NJ: Erlbaum.

Ballard, J., Ramirez, B., & Zantal-Weiner, K. (1987). *Public Law 94-142, Section 504, and Public Law 99-457: Understanding what they are and are not.* Reston, VA: Council for Exceptional Children.

Balthazar, E.E., & Stevens, H.A. (1975). *The emotionally disturbed, mentally retarded: A historical and contemporary perspective.* Upper Saddle River, NJ: Prentice Hall.

Bandura, A. (1969). *Principles of behavior modification.* New York: Holt, Rinehart, & Winston.

Barker, M. (1990, April). *Clinical overview of the Fragile X syndrome.* Paper presented at the 68th annual meeting of the Council for Exceptional Children, Toronto, Canada.

Barlow, C.F. (1978). *Mental retardation and related disorders.* Philadelphia, PA: Davis.

Barlow, D.H., & Durand, V.M. (1995). *Abnormal psychology: An integrated approach.* Pacific Grove, CA: Brooks/Cole.

Barnett, W.S. (1988). The economics of preschool special education under Public Law 99-457. *Topics in Early Childhood Special Education, 8,* 12–13.

Baroff, G.S. (1974). *Mental retardation: Nature, cause and management.* New York: Wiley.

Bateman, B. (1986). Equal protection for the handicapped. *Special Education Today,* p. 14.

Bates, W.J., Smeltzer, D.J., & Arnoczky, S.M. (1986). Appropriate and inappropriate use of psychotherapeutic medications for institutionalized mentally retarded persons. *American Journal of Mental Deficiency, 90*(4), 363–370.

Batshaw, M.L., Perret, Y., & Trachtenberg, S.W. (1992). Caring and coping: The family of a child with disabilities. In M.L. Batshaw, & Y. Perret, *Children with disabilities: A medical primer* (3rd ed., pp. 563–578). Baltimore: Brookes.

Baumeister, A.A., & Brooks, P.H. (1981). Cognitive deficits in mental retardation. In J.M. Kauffman & D.P. Hallahan (Eds.), *Handbook of special education* (pp. 87–107). Upper Saddle River, NJ: Prentice Hall.

Baumeister, A.A., & Hamlett, C.I. (1986). A national survey of state-sponsored programs to prevent fetal alcohol syndrome. *Mental Retardation, 24,* 169–173.

Beasley, C.R. (1982). Effects of a jogging program on cardiovascular fitness and work performance of mentally retarded adults. *American Journal of Mental Deficiency, 86,* 609–613.

Beavers, W.R. (1982). Healthy, midrange, and severely dysfunctional families. In F. Walsh (Ed.), *Normal family processes* (pp. 45–66). New York: Guilford.

Beavers, W.R., & Hampson, R.B. (1993). Measuring family competence. In F. Walsh (Ed.), *Normal family processes* (2nd ed., pp. 73–103). New York: Guilford.

Beck, J. (1972). Spina bifida and hydrocephalus. In V. Apgar & J. Beck (Eds.), *Is my baby alright? A guide to birth defects* (pp. 288–298, 400–414). New York: Simon & Schuster.

Beckman, P.J. (1991). Comparison of mothers' and fathers' perceptions of the effect of young children with and without disabilities. *American Journal on Mental Retardation, 95*(5), 585–595.

Bee, H.L. (1987). *The journey of adulthood.* New York: Macmillan.

Beevy, J. (1978, October). *Applications of biomedical and related technologies to instructional issues in the education of the severely and profoundly handicapped student.* Paper presented at the Annual Conference of the Severely/Profoundly Handicapped, Baltimore.

Begab, M.J. (1981). Issues in the prevention of psychosocial retardation. In M.J. Begab, H.C. Haywood, & H.L. Garber (Eds.), *Psychosocial influences in retarded performance: Issues and theories in development* (pp. 3–28). Baltimore, MD: University Park Press.

Beirne-Smith, M. (1991). Peer tutoring in arithmetic for children with learning disabilities. *Exceptional Children, 57,* 330–337.

Bellak, L., & Bellak, S.S. (1974). *Children's Apperception Test.* Larchmont, NY: C.P.S.

Bellamy, G.T. (1985). Severe disability in adulthood. *Newsletter of the Association for Persons with Severe Handicaps, 11,* 6.

Bellamy, G.T. (1990). Review of *Supported employment: Models, methods, and issues. Journal of the Association for Persons with Severe Handicaps, 15*(1), 261–265.

Bellamy, G.T., & Horner, R.H. (1987). Beyond high school: Residential and employment options after graduation. In M.E. Snell (Ed.), *Systematic instruction of persons with severe handicaps* (3rd ed., pp. 491–520). Upper Saddle River, NJ: Merrill/Prentice Hall.

Bellamy, G.T., Sowers, J., & Bourbeau, P.E. (1983). Work and work-related services: Postschool options. In M.E. Snell (Ed.), *Systematic instruction of the moderately and severely handicapped* (2nd ed., pp. 300–334). New York: Macmillan.

Bellinger, D.M., Rucker, H., & Polloway, E.A. (1997). Fragile X syndrome in males: Programmatic, behavioral and educational implications. *ERIC Document Reproduction Service* (information not available at time of publication).

Belmont, J.M. (1966). Long-term memory in mental retardation. *International Review of Research in Mental Retardation, 1,* 219–255.

Belmont, J.M. (1971). Medical-behavioral research in mental retardation. *International Review of Research in Mental Retardation, 5,* 1–81.

Belmont, J.M., & Butterfield, E.C. (1971). Learning strategies as determinants of memory deficiencies. *Cognitive Psychology, 2,* 411–420.

Belmont, J.M., & Butterfield, E.C. (1977). The instructional approach to developmental cognitive research. In R.V. Kail & J.W. Hagen (Eds.), *Perspectives on the development of memory and cognition* (pp. 437–481). Hillsdale, NJ: Erlbaum.

Bender, B., Fry, E., Pennington, B., Puck, M., Salonblatt, J., & Robinson, S. (1983). Speech and language development in 41 children with sex chromosomes anomalies. *Pediatrics, 71,* 262–266.

Bender, B.G., Puck, M.H., Salbenblatt, J.A., & Robinson, A. (1986). Cognitive development of children with sex chromosome abnormalities. In S.D. Smith (Ed.), *Genetics and learning disabilities* (pp. 175–201). San Diego: College-Hill Press.

Bennett, F.C. (1987). Infants at biological risk. In M.J. Guralnick & F.C. Gennett (Eds.), *Effectiveness of early intervention for at-risk and handicapped children* (pp. 79–112). New York: Academic Press.

Bennett, W.J. (1986). *What works: Research about teaching and learning.* Washington, DC: U.S. Government Printing Office.

Bercovici, S.M. (1983). *Barriers to normalization: The restrictive management of retarded persons.* Baltimore: University Park Press.

Berg, C., & Emanuel, I. (1987). Relationship of prenatal care to the prevention of mental retardation and other problems of pregnancy outcome. In *Developmental handicaps: Prevention and treatment* (pp. 45–70). (ERIC Document Reproduction Service No. 276 192)

Berg, W. (1992a, December). Factors to consider in developing a treatment plan. *Iowa News, 92*(9), 1–2. (Available from the Iowa Bureau of Special Education, Des Moines.)

Berg, W. (1992b, October). Conducting a functional analysis in the classroom. *Iowa News, 92*(7), 1–2. (Available from the Iowa Bureau of Special Education, Des Moines.)

Berger, M., & Foster, M. (1982). A family systems perspective on working with families of young handicapped children. *Journal of the Division for Early Childhood, 1*(1), 17–23.

Berkeley, T.R., & Ludlow, B.L. (1989). Toward a reconceptualization of the developmental model. *Topics in Early Childhood Special Education, 9*(3), 51–66.

Berkman, K.A., & Meyer, L.H. (1988). Alternative strategies and multiple outcomes in the remediation of severe self-injury: Going "all out" nonaversively. *Journal of the Association for Persons with Severe Handicaps, 13*(2), 76–86.

Bernabe, E.A., & Block, M.E. (1994). Modifying rules of a regular girls softball league to facilitate the inclusion of a child with severe disabilities. *Journal of the Association for Persons with Severe Handicaps 19*(1), 24–31.

Bernheim, K.F. (1989). Psychologists and families of the severely mentally ill: The role of family consultation. *American Psychologist, 44*(3), 561–564.

Bernstein, D.K., & Tiegerman, E. (1993). *Language and communication disorders in children.* Upper Saddle River, NJ: Prentice Hall.

Bijou, S.W. (1966). A functional analysis of retarded development. *International Review of Research in Mental Retardation, 1,* 1–19.

Biklen, D. (1977). The politics of institutions. In B. Blatt, D. Biklen, & R. Bogdan (Eds.), *An alternative textbook in special education* (pp. 29–84). Denver, CO: Love.

Biklen, D. (1990). Communication unbound: Autism and praxis. *Harvard Educational Review, 60,* 291–314.

Biklen, D., & Schubert, A. (1991). New words: The communication of students with autism. *Remedial and Special Education, 12*(6), 46–57.

Binet, A., & Simon, T. (1905). Methodes nouvelles pour le diagnostic du niveau intellectuel des anormaux. *Annee Psychologique, 11,* 191–244.

Blacher, J. (1984). Sequential stages of parental adjustment to the birth of a child with handicaps: Fact or artifact? *Mental Retardation, 22*(2), 55–68.

Blacher, J., & Baker, B.L. (1992). Toward meaningful family involvement in out-of-home placement settings. *Mental Retardation, 30,* 35–43.

Blackhurst, A.E., & Berdine, W.H. (1981). *An introduction to special education.* Boston: Little, Brown.

Blalock, G. (1988). Transitions across the lifespan. In B.L. Ludlow, A.P. Turnbull, & R. Luckasson (Eds.), *Transitions to adult life for people with mental retardation* (pp. 3–20). Baltimore: Brookes.

Blatt, B. (1987). *The conquest of mental retardation.* Austin, TX: Pro-Ed.

Bleck, E.E., & Nagel, D.A. (Eds.). (1975). *Physically handicapped children: A medical atlas for teachers.* Orlando, FL: Grune & Stratton.

Bleecker, S.E. (1987). Rethinking how we work: The office of the future. *The Futurist, 21*(4), 15–19.

Bleemer, R. (1995). Court allows special education damages trial. *New Jersey Law Journal, 142*(9), 6.

Bleyer, K. (1992). The Americans with Disabilities Act: Enforcement mechanisms. *Mental and Physical Disabilities Law Reporter, 16*(3), 347–350.

Block, M.E., & Rizzo, T.L. (1995). Attitudes and attributes of physical educators associated with teaching individuals with severe and profound disabilities. *Journal of the Association for Persons with Severe Handicaps, 20*(1) 80–87.

Bloom, B.S. (1964). *Stability and change in human characteristics.* New York: Wiley.

Board of Education v. Arline, 480 U.S. 273, 107 S. Cr. 1123, 94 L. Ed., 2d 307 (1987).

Board of Education of the Hendrick Hudson Central School District v. Rowley, 458 U.S. 176 (1982).

Board of Education v. Arline, 480 U.S. 273, 107 S. Ct. 1123, 94 L. Ed., 2d 307 (1987).

Bogdan, R. (1986). The sociology of special education. In R.J. Morris & B. Blatt (Eds.), *Special education: Research and trends* (pp. 344–359). New York: Pergamon.

Bogdan, R., & Biklen, D. (1977). Handicapism. *Social Policy, 7*(5), 59–63.

Bolger, M. (1992, May). *Stress, coping and psychological well-being in mothers and fathers of young children with a handicapping condition and typically developing children.* Paper presented at the annual meeting of the American Association on Mental Retardation, New Orleans.

Borkowski, J.G. (1985). Signs of intelligence: Strategy generation and metacognition. In S.R. Yssen (Ed.), *The growth of reflection in children* (pp. 105–144). Orlando, FL: Academic Press.

Borkowski, J.G., & Cavanaugh, J.C. (1979). Maintenance and generalization of skills and strategies by the retarded. In N.R. Ellis (Ed.), *Handbook of mental deficiency: Psychological theory and research* (2nd ed., pp. 569–617). Hillsdale, NJ: Erlbaum.

Borkowski, J.G., Peck, V.A., & Damberg, P.R. (1983). Attention, memory, and cognition. In J.L. Matson & J.A. Mulick (Eds.), *Handbook of mental retardation* (pp. 479–497). New York: Pergamon.

Borthwick-Duffy, S.A., & Eyman, R.K. (1990). Who are the dually diagnosed? *American Journal on Mental Retardation, 94,* 586–595.

Bouchard, T.J., Lykken, D.T., McGue, M., Segal, N.L., & Tellegen, A. (1990). Sources of human psychological differences: The Minnesota study of twins reared apart. *Science, 250,* 223–228.

Bowe, F. (1978). *Handicapping America: Barriers to disabled people.* New York: Harper & Row.

Bowe, F.G. (1993). Statistics, politics, and employment of people with disabilities. *Journal of Disability Policy Studies, 4*(2), 83–91.

Bower, A.C. (1978). Learning. In J.P. Das & D. Baine (Eds.), *Mental retardation for special educators* (pp. 48–81). Springfield, IL: Thomas.

Bowlby, J. (1960). Grief and mourning in infancy and early childhood. *Psychoanalytic Study of the Child, 15,* 1–9.

Bracken, B.A. (1987). Limitations of preschool instruments and standards for minimal levels of technical adequacy. *Journal of Psychoeducational Assessment, 4,* 313–326.

Braddock, D., Hemp, R., Bachelder, L., & Fujiura, G. (1995). *The state of the states in developmental disabilities: An overview* (4th ed.). Baltimore, MD: Brookes.

Braddock, D., Hemp, R., Fujiura, G., Bachelder, L., & Mitchell, D. (1990). *The state of the states in developmental disabilities.* Baltimore: Brookes.

Braden, J.P. (1992). The Differential Ability Scales and special education. *Journal of Psychoeducational Assessment, 10,* 92–98.

Braden, J.P. (1995). Review of the Wechsler Intelligence Scale for Children—Third edition. In J.C. Conoley & J.C. Impara (Eds.), *The twelfth mental measurements yearbook* (pp. 1098–1103). Lincoln, NE: University of Nebraska, Burus Institute.

Bradley, V.J. (1988). Ensuring the quality of services for persons with mental retardation. In B.L. Ludlow, A.P. Turnbull, & R. Luckasson (Eds.), Transitions to adult life for people with mental retardation—Principles and practices (pp. 275–292). Baltimore: Brookes.

Bradley, V.J., & Allard, M.A. (1992). The dynamics of change in residential services for people with developmental disabilities. In J.W. Jacobson, S.N. Burchard, & P.J. Carling (Eds.), *Community living for people with developmental and psychiatric disabilities* (pp. 284–302). Baltimore, MD: Johns Hopkins University Press.

Bradley V.J., & Knoll, J. (1995). Shifting paradigms in services to people with developmental disabilities. In O.C. Karan & S. Greenspan (Eds.), *The community revolution in rehabilitation services* (pp. 5–37). Boston: Butterworth-Heinemann.

Brady, P.M., Manni, J.L., & Winikur, D.W. (1983). Implications of ethnic disproportion in programs for the educable mentally retarded. *Journal of Special Education, 17,* 295–302.

Brandon, R.N. (1990). *Adaptation and environment.* Princeton, NJ: Princeton University Press.

Brantley, D. (1988). *Understanding mental retardation: A guide for social workers.* Springfield, IL: Thomas.

Bray, N.W. (1979). Strategy production in the retarded. In N.R. Ellis (Ed.), *Handbook of mental deficiency: Psychological theory and research* (2nd ed., pp. 699–737). Hillsdale, NJ: Erlbaum.

Bregman, J.D. (1991). Current developments in the understanding of mental retardation Part II: Psychopathology. *American Academy of Child and Adolescent Psychiatry, 30*(6), 861–872.

Bricker, D. (1986). An analysis of early intervention programs: Attendant issues and future directions. In R.J. Morris & B. Blatt (Eds.), *Special education: Research and trends* (pp. 28–65). Baltimore: University Park Press.

Bricker, D., & Cripe, J.J. (1992). *An activity-based approach to early intervention.* Baltimore: Brookes.

Bricker, D., & Veltman, M. (1990). Early intervention programs: Child-focused approaches. In S. Meisels & J. Shonkoff (Eds.), *Handbook of early childhood intervention* (pp. 373–399). New York: Cambridge University Press.

Bricker, W.A., & Dow, M.G. (1980). Early intervention with the young severely handicapped child. *The Journal of the Association for the Severely Handicapped, 5,* 130–142.

Brigance, A.H. (1982). *Brigance K and 1 Screen for Kindergarten and First Grade.* North Billerica, MA: Curriculum Associates.

Brigance, A.H. (1995). *Life Skills Inventory.* North Billerica, MA: Curriculum Associates.

Brinker, R.P. (1985). Interactions between severely mentally retarded students and other students in integrated and segregated public school settings. *Journal of Mental Deficiency, 89,* 587–594.

Brinker, R.P., & Thorpe, M.E. (1984). Integration of severely handicapped students and the proportion of IEP objectives achieved. *Exceptional Children, 51,* 168–175.

Brolin, D.E. (1978). *Life-centered career education: A competency-based approach.* Reston, VA: Council for Exceptional Children.

Brolin, D.E. (1982). *Vocational preparation of persons with handicaps* (2nd ed.). Upper Saddle River, NJ: Merrill/Prentice Hall.

Brolin, D.E. (1986). *Life-centered career education: A competency-based approach* (rev. ed.). Reston, VA: Council for Exceptional Children.

Brolin, D.E. (1989). *Life-centered career education: A competency based approach* (3rd ed.). Reston, VA: Council for Exceptional Children.

Brolin, D.E. (1992). *Life-Centered Career Education (LCCE) Knowledge and Performance Batteries.* Reston, VA: The Council for Exceptional Children.

Brolin, D.E. (1993). *Life centered career education: A competency-based approach* (4th ed.). Reston, VA: The Council for Exceptional Children.

Brolin, D.E., & D'Alonzo, B.J. (1979). Critical issues in career education for the handicapped student. *Exceptional Children, 45,* 246–253.

Brolin, D.E., & Kokaska, C.J. (1979). *Career education for handicapped children and youth.* Upper Saddle River, NJ: Merrill/Prentice Hall.

Brolin, J.C., & Brolin, D.E. (1979). Vocational education for special students. In D. Cullinan & M. Epstein (Eds.), *Special education for adolescents: Issues and perspectives.* Upper Saddle River, NJ: Merrill/Prentice Hall.

Bromley, B.E., & Blacher, J. (1992). Parental reasons for out-of-home placement of children with severe handicaps. *Mental Retardation, 29,* 275–280.

Bronicki, G.J., & Turnbull, A.P. (1987). Family professional interactions. In M.E. Snell (Ed.), *Systematic instruction of persons with severe handicaps* (3rd ed., pp. 9–35). Upper Saddle River, NJ: Merrill/Prentice Hall.

Brooks, D.N., Wooley, H., & Kanjilal, G.C. (1972). Hearing loss and middle ear disorders in patients with Down's syndrome. *Journal of Mental Deficiency Research, 16,* 21–29.

Brooks, P.H., & McCauley, C. (1984). Cognitive research in mental retardation. *American Journal of Mental Deficiency, 88,* 479–486.

Brooks-Gunn, J., & Luciano, L. (1985). Social competence in young handicapped children: A developmental perspective. In M. Sigman (Ed.), *Children with emo-*

tional disorders and developmental disabilities: Assessment and treatment (pp. 3–22). Orlando, FL: Grune & Stratton.

Brower, D.P., & Sullivan-Fleig, G. (1987). Involving parents in the educational process. In G.A. Robinson & E.A. Polloway (Eds.), *Best practices in mental disabilities* (Vol. 1, pp. 263–292). Des Moines: Iowa State Department of Education.

Brown, A.L. (1974). The role of strategic behavior in retardate memory. *International Review of Research in Mental Retardation, 7,* 55–111.

Brown, A.L., Campione, J.C., & Murphy, M.D. (1974). Keeping track of changing variables: Long-term retention of a trained rehearsal strategy by retarded adolescents. *American Journal of Mental Deficiency, 78,* 453–466.

Brown, L., Long, E., Udavari-Solner, A., Davis, L., Van Devon, P., Ahlgren, C., Johnson, F., Gruenewald, L., & Jorgensen, J. (1989). The home school: Why students with severe intellectual disabilities must attend the schools of their brothers, sisters, friends and neighbors. *The Journal for the Association of Persons with Severe Handicaps, 14*(1), 1–7.

Brown, L.F., Branston, M.B., Hamre-Nietupski, S.M., Johnson, F., Wilcox, B., & Gruenewald, L. (1979). A rationale for comprehensive, longitudinal interactions between severely handicapped students and nonhandicapped students and other citizens. *AAESPH Review, 4,* 3–14.

Brown, L.F., Branston, M.B., Hamre-Nietupski, S.M., Pumpian, I., Certo, N., & Gruenewald, L. (1979). A strategy for developing chronological-age-appropriate and functional curricular content for severely handicapped adolescents and young adults. *Journal of Special Education, 13,* 81–90.

Brown, L.F., Branston-McLean, M.B., Baumgart, D., Vincent, L., Falvey, M., & Schroeder, J. (1979). Using the characteristics of current and subsequent least restrictive environments in the development of curricular content for severely handicapped students. *The Journal of the Association for the Severely Handicapped, 4,* 407–424.

Brown, L.F., Nietupski, J., & Hamre-Nietupski, S. (1976). The criterion of ultimate functioning and public school services for severely handicapped students. In M.A. Thomas (Ed.), *Hey don't forget about me: Education's investment in the severely, profoundly, and multiply handicapped* (pp. 2–15). Reston, VA: Council for Exceptional Children.

Brown, L.F., Nisbet, J., Ford, A., Sweet, M., Shiraga, B., York, R., & Loomis, R. (1983). The critical need for nonschool instruction in educational programs for severely handicapped students. *The Journal of the Association for Persons with Severe Handicaps, 8,* 71–77.

Brown, L.F., Shiraga, B., York, J., Kessler, K., Strohm, B., Rogan, P., Sweet, M., Zanella, K., VanDeventer, P., & Loomis, R. (1984). Integrated work opportunities for adults with severe handicaps: The extended training option. *The Journal of the Association for Persons with Severe Handicaps, 9*(4), 262–269.

Brown v. Board of Education of Topeka, Kansas, 347 U.S. 483 (1954).

Bruininks, R.H. (1974). Physical and motor development of retarded persons. *International Review of Research in Mental Retardation, 7,* 209–261.

Bruininks, R.H. (1978). *Bruininks-Oseretsky Test of Motor Proficiency.* Circle Pines, MN: American Guidance Service.

Bruininks, R.H., Chen, T., Lakin, K., & McGrew, K.S. (1992). Components of personal competence and community integration for persons with mental retardation in small residential programs. *Research in Developmental Disabilities, 13,* 463–479.

Bruininks, R.H., Hill, B.K., Lakin, K.C., & White, C.C. (1985). *Residential services for adults with developmental disabilities.* Logan: Utah State University, Developmental Center for Handicapped Persons.

Bruininks, R.H., Morreau, L.E., Gilman, C.J., & Anderson, J.L. (1992). *Adaptive Living Skills Curriculum.* Chicago: Riverside.

Bruininks, R.H., Thurlow, M.L., & Gilman, C.J. (1987). Adaptive behavior and mental retardation. *The Journal of Special Education, 21*(1), 69–88.

Bruininks, R.H., Thurlow, M.L., Lewis, D.R., & Larson, N.W. (1988). Post-school outcomes for students in special education and other students one to eight years after high school. In R.H. Bruininks, D.R. Lewis, & M.L. Thurlow, (Eds.), *Assessing outcomes, costs and benefits of special education programs* (Report No. 88-1; pp. 9–111). Minneapolis: University of Minnesota, Institute on Community Integration.

Bruininks, R.H., Woodcock, R.W., Weatherman, R.F., & Hill, B.K. (1985a). *Development and standardization of the Scales of Independent Behavior.* Chicago: Riverside.

Bruininks, R.H., Woodcock, R.W., Weatherman, R.F., & Hill, B.K. (1985b). *Scales of Independent Behavior.* Chicago: Riverside.

Bruininks, R.H., Woodcock, R.W., Weatherman, R.F., & Hill, B.K. (1996a). *Scales of Independent Behavior—Revised (SIB-R).* Chicago: Riverside.

Bruininks, R.H., Woodcock, R.W., Weatherman, R.F., & Hill, B.K. (1996b). *Scales of Independent Behavior—Revised (SIB-R): Comprehensive manual.* Chicago: Riverside.

Buck v. Bell, 274 U.S. 200 (1927).

Bull, M., & LaVecchio, F. (1978). Behavior therapy for a child with Lesch-Nyhan syndrome. *Developmental Medicine & Child Neurology, 20,* 368–375.

Bunker, M.C., Lambdin, M.A., Lynch, H.T., Mickey, G.H., Roderick, T.H., Van Pelt, J.C., & Fosnot, H. (1972, April 30). *Parent Care.*

Burchard, S.N., & Thousand, J. (1988). Staff and manager competencies. In M.P. Janicki, M.W. Krauss, & M.M. Seltzer (Eds.), *Community residences for persons with developmental disabilities: Here to stay* (pp. 251–266). Baltimore: Brookes.

Bureau of the Census. (1991). *Statistical abstract of the United States: 1991* (111th ed.). Washington, DC: U.S. Department of Commerce, Economics and Statistics Administration.

Bureau of the Census. (1992). *Statistical abstract of the United States: 1992* (112th ed.). Washington, DC: U.S. Department of Commerce, Economics and Statistics Administration.

Bureau of the Census. (1995). *Statistical abstract of the United States: 1995* (115th ed.). Washington, DC: U.S. Department of Commerce, Economics and Statistics Administration.

Burke, P.J., McLaughlin, M.J., & Valdivieso, C.H. (1988). Preparing professionals to educate handicapped infants and young children: Some policy considerations. *Topics in Early Childhood Special Education, 8*(1), 73–80.

Burks, H.F. (1977). *Burks Behavioral Rating Scales: Preschool and Kindergarten Edition.* Los Angeles: Western Psychological Services.

Burnham v. Dept. of Public Health, 349 F. Supp. 1335 (N.D. Ga. 1972), Rev'd, 503 F. 2d 1319 (5th Cir. 1974).

Burt, C. (1966). The genetic determination of differences in intelligence. *British Journal of Psychology, 57,* 137–153.

Buyse, M.L. (1990). *Birth defects encyclopedia*. Dover, MA: Center for Birth Defects Information Services.

Bybee, J., & Zigler, E. (1992). Is outerdirectedness employed in a harmful or beneficial manner by students with and without mental retardation? *American Journal on Mental Retardation, 96,* 512–521.

Bzoch, K., & League, R. (1991). *Receptive–Expressive Emergent Language Test*. Austin, TX: Pro-Ed.

Cain, E.J., & Taber, F.M. (1987). *Educating disabled people for the 21st century*. Boston: College Hill.

Calvez, M. (1993). Social interactions in the neighborhood: A cultural approach to social integration of individuals with mental retardation. *Mental Retardation, 31*(6), 418–423.

Campbell, V., Smith, R., & Wool, R. (1982). Adaptive behavior scale differences in scores of mentally retarded individuals referred for institutionalization and those never referred. *American Journal of Mental Retardation, 86*(4), 425–428.

Campione, J.C., & Brown, A.L. (1978). Toward a theory of intelligence: Contributions from research with retarded children. *Intelligence, 2,* 279–304.

Campione, J.C., Brown, A.L., & Ferrara, R.A. (1982). Mental retardation and intelligence. In R.J. Sternberg (Ed.), *Handbook of human intelligence* (pp. 392–490). New York: Cambridge University Press.

Cancro, R. (Ed.). (1971). *Intelligence: Genetic and environmental influences*. Orlando, FL: Grune & Stratton.

Cantu, E.S., Stone, J.W., Wing, A.A., Langee, H.R., & Williams, C.A. (1990). Cytogenetic survey for autistic Fragile X carriers in a mental retardation center. *American Journal of Mental Retardation, 94,* 442–447.

Carlson, E. (1984). *Human genetics*. Lexington, MA: Heath.

Carnevale, A.P., Gainer, L.J., & Meltzer, A.S. (1990). *Workplace basics: The essential skills employers want*. San Francisco: Jossey-Bass.

Carney, I.H. (1987). Working with families. In F.P. Orelove & R. Sobsey (Eds.), *Multiple disabilities: A transdisciplinary approach* (pp. 315–338). Baltimore: Brookes.

Carroll, J.B. (1993). *Human cognitive abilities: A survey of factor analytic studies*. New York: Cambridge University Press.

Carta, J.J., Atwater, J.B., Schwartz, I.S., & McConnell, S.R. (1993). Developmentally appropriate practices and early childhood special education: A reaction to Johnson and McChesney-Johnson. *Topics in Early Childhood Special Education, 13,* 243–254.

Carter, C.H. (1975). *Handbook of mental retardation syndromes*. Springfield, IL: Charles C. Thomas.

Carter, E.A., & McGoldrick, M. (1989). Overview: The changing family life cycle: A framework for therapy. In E.A. Carter & M. McGoldrick (Eds.), *The changing family life cycle: A framework for therapy* (2nd ed., pp. 3–28). New York: Gardner.

Carter, J.L. (1975). Intelligence and reading achievement of EMR in three educational settings. *Mental Retardation, 13*(5), 26–27.

Cartwright, G.P., Cartwright, C.A., & Ward, M.E. (1989). *Educating special learners* (3rd ed.). Belmont, CA: Wadsworth.

Castellani, P.J. (1987). *The political economy of developmental disabilities*. Baltimore: Brookes.

Castellani, P.J., Downey, N.A., Tausig, M.B., & Bird, W.A. (1986). Availability and accessibility of family support services. *Mental Retardation, 24*(2), 71–79.

Cattell, J.M. (1963). Theory of crystallized intelligence: A critical experiment. *Journal of Educational Psychology, 54,* 1–22.

Cegelka, P.T. (1979). Career education. In D. Cullinan & M.H. Epstein (Eds.), *Special education for adolescents: Issues and perspectives* (pp. 155–184). Upper Saddle River, NJ: Merrill/Prentice Hall.

Cegelka, P.T., & Prehm, H.J. (1982). *Mental retardation: From categories to people.* Upper Saddle River, NJ: Merrill/Prentice Hall.

Census of Referred Suspected Mental Retardation. (1953). Reference not available.

Center for Demographic Policy. (1991). Drugs and babies: What lies ahead for the health, education, and legal systems? *CDP Newsletter, 2*(3), 1–4.

Centerpoint. (1996). *A Definition of Positive Supports, 1*(2). Orono, ME: Maine's Center for Interdisciplinary Education, Research, and Public Service in Developmental and Related Disabilities.

Certo, N., Haring, N.G., & York, R. (1984). *Public school integration of severely handicapped students.* Baltimore: Brookes.

Chalfant, J.C., & Pysh, M.V. (1989). Teacher assistance teams: Five descriptive studies of 96 teams. *Remedial and Special Education, 19*(6), 49–58.

Chamberlain, M.A. (1988). Employer's rankings of factors judged critical to job success for individuals with severe disabilities. *Career Development for Exceptional Individuals, 11*(2), 141–147.

Chan, K.S., & Rueda, R. (1979). Poverty and culture in education: Separate but equal. *Exceptional Children, 45,* 422–428.

Chaney, R.H., & Eyman, R.K. (1982). Etiology of mental retardation: Clinical vs. neuroanatomic diagnosis. *Mental Retardation, 20,* 123–132.

Chinn, P.C., Drew, C.J., & Logan, D.R. (1979). *Mental retardation: A life cycle approach* (2nd ed.). St. Louis: Mosby.

Christenson, S.L., Ysseldyke, J.E., & Thurlow, M.L. (1989). Critical instructional factors for students with mild handicaps: An integrative review. *Remedial and Special Education, 10*(5), 21–31.

Cicirelli, V.G. (1994). The longest bond: The sibling life cycle. In L. L'Abate (Ed.), *Handbook of developmental family psychology and psychopathology* (pp. 44–59). New York: Wiley.

Clark, G.M. (1996). Transition planning assessment for secondary-level students with learning disabilities. *Journal of Learning Disabilities, 29,* 79–92.

Clark, G.M. (1998). *Transition assessment.* Austin, TX: Pro-Ed.

Clark, G.M. (1979). *Career education for the handicapped child in the elementary classroom.* Denver: Love.

Clark, G.M., Carlson, B.C., Fisher, S., Cook, I.D., & D'Alonzo, B.J. (1991). Career development for students with disabilities in elementary schools: A position statement of the Division on Career Development. *Career Development for Exceptional Individuals, 14,* 109–120.

Clark, G.M., & Knowlton, H.E. (1987). From school to adult living: A forum on issues and trends. *Exceptional Children, 53,* 546–554.

Clark, G.M., & Kolstoe, O.P. (1990). *Career development and transition education for adolescents with disabilities.* Boston: Allyn & Bacon.

Clark, G.M., & Kolstoe, O.P. (1995). *Career development and transition education for adolescents with disabilities* (2nd ed.). Boston: Allyn & Bacon.

Clark, G.M., & Patton, J.R. (1997). *Transition Planning Inventory.* Austin, TX: Pro-Ed.

Clarke, J.T., Gates, R.D., Hogan, S.E., Barrett, M., & MacDonald, G.W. (1987). Neuropsychological studies on adolescents with phenylketonuria returned to phenylalanine-restricted diets. *American Journal of Mental Retardation, 92,* 255–262.

Clausen, J.A. (1967). Mental deficiency: Development of a concept. *American Journal of Mental Deficiency, 71,* 727–745.

Clausen, J.A. (1972a). Quo vadis, AAMD? *Journal of Special Education, 6,* 52–60.

Clausen, J.A. (1972b). The continuing problem of defining mental deficiency. *Journal of Special Education, 6,* 97–106.

Clayman, C.B. (Ed.). (1989). *The AMA encyclopedia of medicine.* New York: Random House.

Cleburne Living Center Inc. v. City of Cleburne, Texas, 735 F. 2d 832 (5th Cir. 1984).

Close, D.W., Sowers, J., Halpern, A.S., & Bourbeau, P.E. (1985). Programming for the transition to independent living for mildly retarded persons. In K.C. Lakin & R.H. Bruininks (Eds.), *Strategies for achieving community integration of developmentally disabled citizens* (pp. 161–176). Baltimore: Brookes.

Cnaan, R.A., Adler, I., & Ramot, A. (1986). Public reaction to establishment of community residential facilities for mentally retarded persons in Israel. *American Journal of Mental Deficiency, 90*(6), 677–685.

Coffman, T.L., & Harris, M.C. (1980). Transition shock and adjustments of mentally retarded persons. *Mental Retardation, 18*(3), 28–32.

Cohen, L. (1981). Ethical issues in withholding care from severely handicapped infants. *The Journal of the Association for the Severely Handicapped, 6*(3), 65–67.

Cohen, R.C. (1982). Individual differences in short-term memory. *International Review of Research in Mental Retardation, 11,* 43–77.

Cohn, M. (1992). Screening measures. In E.V. Nuttall, I. Romero, & J. Kalesnik (Eds.), *Assessing and screening preschoolers: Psychological and educational dimensions* (pp. 83–98). Boston: Allyn & Bacon.

Cole, E.S. (1995). Becoming family centered: Child welfare's challenge. *Families in Society: The Journal of Contemporary Services, 76*(3), 163–172.

Collins, W.A., & Gunnar, M.R. (1990). Social and personality development. *Annual Review of Psychology, 41,* 387–416.

Committee for Economic Development. (1991). *The unfinished agenda: A new vision for child development and education.* New York: Committee for Economic Development, Research and Policy Committee.

Conley, R.W. (1973). *The economics of mental retardation.* Baltimore: Johns Hopkins University Press.

Conley, R.W., Noble, J.J., & Elder, J.K. (1986). Problems with the service system. In W.E. Kiernan & J.A. Stark (Eds.), *Pathways to employment for adults with developmental disabilities* (pp. 67–84). Baltimore: Brookes.

Connis, R.T. (1979). The effects of sequential pictorial cues, self-recording, and praise on the job-task sequencing of retarded adults. *Journal of Applied Behavior Analysis, 12,* 355–361.

Conoley, J.C. (1990). Review of the K-ABC: Reflecting the unobservable. *Journal of Psychoeducational Assessment, 8,* 369–375.

Conoley, J.C., & Impara, J.C. (Eds.). (1985). *The twelfth mental measurements yearbook.* Lincoln: University of Nebraska, Buros Institute.

Conoley, J.C., & Kramer, J.J. (Eds.). (1989). *The tenth mental measurements yearbook.* Lincoln: University of Nebraska Lincoln, Buros Institute.

Conroy, J.W. (1996). The small ICF/MR program: Dimensions of quality and cost. *Mental Retardation, 34*(1), 13–26.

Conroy, J., & Bradley, V.J. (1985). *The Pennhurst Longitudinal Study: Combined report of five years of research and analysis.* Philadelphia: Temple University Developmental Disabilities Center.

Cooley, E. (1989). Community support. In G.H. Singer, & L.K. Irvin (Eds.), *Support for caregiving families: Enabling positive adaptation to disability* (pp. 143–157). Baltimore: Brookes.

Cordes, C. (1984). Will Larry P. face the supreme test? *Monitor, 15*(4), 1, 26–27.

Coulter, D.L. (1988a). Beyond Baby Doe: Does infant transplantation justify euthanasia? *The Journal of the Association for Persons with Severe Handicaps, 13,* 71–75.

Coulter, D.L. (1988b). The neurology of mental retardation. In F.J. Menolascino & J.A. Stark (Eds.), *Preventive and curative intervention in mental retardation* (pp. 113–152). Baltimore: Brookes.

Coulter, W.A., & Morrow, H.W. (Eds.). (1978). *Adaptive behavior: Concepts and measurements.* Orlando, FL: Grune & Stratton.

Council for Exceptional Children, Division on Mental Retardation and Developmental Disabilities. (1996). Position statement regarding assistive technology devices and services. *MRDD Express, 6*(3), 9.

Covert, S.B. (1992). Supporting families. In J. Nisbet (Ed.), *Natural supports in school, at work, and in the community for people with severe disabilities* (pp. 121–163). Baltimore: Brookes.

Craig, D.E., & Boyd, W.E. (1990). Characteristics of employers of handicapped individuals. *American Journal on Mental Retardation, 95*(1), 40–43.

Craig, E.M., & McCarver, R.G. (1984). Community placement and adjustment of de-institutionalized clients: Issues and findings. In N.R. Ellis & N.W. Bray (Eds.), *International review of research in mental retardation* (Vol. 12, pp. 95–122). Orlando, FL: Academic Press.

Cravioto, J., DeLicardie, E.R., & Birch, H.G. (1966). Nutrition, growth and neuro-integrative development: An experimental and ecological study. *Pediatrics, 38*(Suppl. 2), 319.

Crnic, L.S. (1984). Nutrition and mental development. *American Journal of Mental Deficiency, 88,* 526–533.

Crocker, A.C. (1992). Data collection for the evaluation of mental retardation prevention activities: The fateful forty-three. *Mental Retardation, 30,* 303–317.

Cromwell, R.L. (1963). A social learning approach to mental retardation. In N.R. Ellis (Ed.), *Handbook of mental deficiency: Psychological theory and research* (pp. 41–91). New York: McGraw-Hill.

Cronbach, L.J. (1969). Heredity, environment, and educational policy. *Harvard Educational Review, 39,* 338–347.

Cronin, M.E., & Patton, J.R. (1993). *Life skills instruction for all students with special needs: A practical guide for integrating real life content into the curriculum.* Austin, TX: Pro-Ed.

Crossley, R. (1988, October). *Unexpected communication attainments by persons diagnosed as autistic and intellectually impaired.* Paper presented at the annual meeting for the International Society for Augmentative and Alternative Communication, Los Angeles.

Crossley, R., & McDonald, A. (1980). *Annie's coming out.* New York: Penguin.

Cullari, S. (1984). Everybody is talking about the new institution. *Mental Retardation, 22,* 28–29.

Daker, M.G., Chidiac, P., Fear, C.N., & Berry, A.C. (1981, April). Fragile X in the normal male: A cautionary tale. *The Lancet, 1*(8223), 780.

Daniel, M. (1994). A review of the Differential Ability Scales. In R.J. Sternberg (Ed.), *Encyclopedia of human intelligence* (pp. 350–354). New York: Macmillan.

Daniel R.R. v. State Board of Education, 874 F. 2d 1036 (5th Cir. 1989).

Danielson, L.C., & Bellamy, G.T. (1989). State variation in placement of children with handicaps in segregated environments. *Exceptional Children, 55,* 448–455.

D'Arcy, E. (1968). Congenital defects: Mother's reactions to first information. *British Medical Journal, 3,* 796–798.

Das, J.P., Naglieri, J.A., & Kirby, J.R. (1994). *Assessment of cognitive processes: The PASS theory of intelligence.* Boston: Allyn & Bacon.

Dator, J. (1988). The futures of care and "normal" behavior: Implications for those who are mentally retarded. *Education and Training in Mental Retardation, 23,* 248–252.

Davis, M.R. (1981). *A discussion of phenylketonuria and a comparison of behavioral characteristics.* Unpublished manuscript, Lynchburg College, Lynchburg, VA.

de la Cruz, F. (1985). Fragile X syndrome. *American Journal of Mental Deficiency, 90,* 119–123.

Delaney, D., & Poling, A. (1990). Drug abuse among mentally retarded people: An overlooked problem? *Journal of Alcohol and Drug Education, 35,* 48–54.

Delaney, E.A., & Hopkins, T.F. (1987). *The examiner's handbook: An expanded guide for fourth edition users.* Chicago: Riverside.

Delaney, S., & Hayden, A. (1977). Fetal alcohol syndrome: A review. *AAESPH Review, 2,* 164–168.

Delpit, L.D. (1988). The silenced dialogue: Power and pedagogy in educating other people's children. *Harvard Educational Review, 58,* 280–298.

Deno, S.L., & Mirkin, P.K. (1980). Data based IEP development: An approach to substantive compliance. *Teaching Exceptional Children, 12,* 92–97.

Department of Education v. Katherine Dorr, 727 F. 2d 809 (1984).

DeStefano, L., & Wagner, M. (1990). *Outcome assessment in special education: Lessons learned.* Champaign, IL: University of Illinois, Transition Institute.

Dever, R.B. (1988). *Community living skills: A taxonomy.* Washington, DC: American Association on Mental Retardation.

Dewey, J. (1966). *Democracy and education.* New York: Macmillan.

Diana v. State Board of Education, C-70-37 R.F.P. (N.D. California, Jan. 7, 1970, and June 18, 1972).

Division for Early Childhood Task Force. (1993). *DEC recommended practices: Indicators of quality in programs for infants and young children with special needs and their families.* Pittsburgh, PA: Council for Exceptional Children, Division for Early Childhood.

Division on Mental Retardation and Developmental Disabilities of the Council for Exceptional Children. (1992). *MRDD position statement: Capital punishment and individuals with mental retardation.* Reston, VA: Author.

Dix, D. (1976). Memorial to the Legislature of Massachusetts, 1843. (Reprinted in M. Rosen, G.R. Clark, & M.S. Kivitz [Eds.], *The history of mental retardation: Collected papers* [Vol. 1, pp. 3–30]. Baltimore: University Park Press.) (Original work published 1843.)

Dmitriev, V., & Oelwein, P.L. (Eds.). (1990). *Advances in Down syndrome.* Austin, TX: Pro-Ed.

Dobzhansky, T. (1955). *Evolution, genetics, and man.* New York: Wiley.

Doll, E.A. (1935). A genetic scale of social maturity. *The American Journal of Orthopsychiatry, 5,* 180–188.

Doll, E.A. (1941). The essentials of an inclusive concept of mental deficiency. *American Journal of Mental Deficiency, 46,* 214–229.

Doll, E.A. (1947). *Social Maturity Scale.* Circle Pines, MN: American Guidance Service.

Doll, E.A. (1953). *Measurement of social competence: A manual for the Vineland Social Maturity Scale.* Circle Pines, MN: American Guidance Service.

Doll, E.A. (1962). Historical survey of research and management of mental retardation in the United States. In E.P. Trapp & P. Hinestein (Eds.), *Readings on the exceptional child* (pp. 21–68). New York: Appleton-Century-Crofts.

Doll, E. (1965). *Vineland Social Maturity Scale: Condensed manual of directions* (1965 ed.). Circle Pines, MN: American Guidance Service.

Donaldson, M.D.C., Chu, C.E., Cooke, A., Wilson, A., Greene, S.A., & Stephenson, J.B.P. (1994). The Prader-Willi syndrome. *Archives of Disease in Childhood, 70,* 58–63.

Dorland's Medical Dictionary (23rd ed.). (1957). Philadelphia: Saunders.

Dorner, S. (1975). The relationship of physical handicap to stress in families with an adolescent with spina bifida. *Developmental Medicine and Child Neurology, 17,* 765–776.

Downey, J., Elkin, E.J., Ehrhardt, A.A., Meyer-Bahlburg, H.F., Bell, J.J., & Morishima, A. (1991). Cognitive ability and everyday functioning in women with Turner syndrome. *Journal of Learning Disabilities, 24,* 32–39.

Drew, C.J., Hardman, M.L., & Hart, A.W. (1996). *Designing and conducting research in education and social science.* Needham Heights, MA: Allyn & Bacon.

Drew, C.J., Hardman, M.L., & Logan, D.R. (1996). *Mental retardation: A life cycle approach* (6th ed.). Upper Saddle River, NJ: Merrill/Prentice Hall.

Drew, C.J., Logan, D.R., & Hardman, M.L. (1992). *Mental retardation: A life cycle approach* (5th ed.). Upper Saddle River, NJ: Merrill/Prentice Hall.

Drinkwater, S., & Demchak, M. (1995). The Preschool Checklist: Integration of children with severe disabilities. *Teaching Exceptional Children, 28*(1), 4–8.

Dubow, S., & Geer, S. (1984). Special education law since Rowley. *Clearinghouse Review, 17,* 1001–1007.

Dugdale, R.L. (1877). *The Jukes, a study in crime, pauperism, disease and heredity.* New York: Putnam.

Duker, P. (1975). Behavior control of self-biting in a Lesch-Nyhan patient. *Journal of Mental Deficiency Research, 19,* 11–19.

Dunn, L.M. (Ed.). (1963). *Exceptional children in the schools.* New York: Holt, Rinehart, & Winston.

Dunn, L.M. (1968). Special education for the mildly retarded—Is much of it justifiable? *Exceptional Children, 35,* 5–22.

Dunn, L.M. (1973a). Children with mild general learning disabilities. In L.M. Dunn (Ed.), *Exceptional children in the schools: Special education in transition* (2nd ed., pp. 126–133). New York: Holt, Rinehart, & Winston.

Dunn, L.M. (Ed.). (1973b). *Exceptional children in the schools: Special education in transition* (2nd ed.). New York: Holt, Rinehart, & Winston.

Dunn, L.M., & Dunn, L.M. (1981). *Peabody Picture Vocabulary Test—Revised.* Circle Pines, MN: American Guidance Service.

Dunst, C.J., Trivette, C.M., & Thompson, R. (1990). Supporting and strengthening family functioning: Toward a congruence between principles and practice. *Prevention in Human Services, 9*(1), 19–43.

Durand, V.M., & Carr, E. (1985). Self-injurious behavior: Motivating conditions and guidelines for treatment. *School Psychology Review, 14*(2), 171–176.

Duvall, E.M. (1977). *Marriage and family development* (5th ed.). Philadelphia: Lippincott.

Duvall, E.M., & Miller, B.C. (1985). *Marriage and family development* (6th ed.). New York: Harper & Row.

Edgar, E. (1987). Secondary programs in special education: Are many of them justifiable? *Exceptional Children, 53,* 555–561.

Edgerton, R.B. (1967). *The cloak of competence: Stigma in the lives of the mentally retarded.* Berkeley: University of California Press.

Edgerton, R.B. (1984). Anthropology and mental retardation: Research approaches and opportunities. *Culture, Medicine, & Psychiatry, 8,* 25–48.

Edgerton, R.B. (1990). Quality of life from a longitudinal research perspective. In R.L. Schalock (Ed.), *Quality of life: Perspectives and issues* (pp. 149–160). Washington, DC: American Association on Mental Retardation.

Edgerton, R.B. (1993). *The cloak of competence* (revised and updated). Berkeley: University of California Press.

Edgerton, R.B., & Bercovici, S.M. (1976). The cloak of competence: Years later. *American Journal of Mental Deficiency, 80,* 485–497.

Edgerton, R.B., Bollinger, M., & Herr, B. (1984). The cloak of competence: After two decades. *American Journal of Mental Deficiency, 88,* 345–351.

Edmister, P., & Ekstrand, R.E. (1987). Preschool programming: Legal and educational issues. *Exceptional Children, 54,* 130–136.

Education Commission of the States. (1988). *Drawing in the family: Family involvement in the schools* (P188-2). Denver, CO: ECS Distribution Center.

Education for All Handicapped Children Act of 1975, P.L. 94-142, §326.4, 34 U.S.C. (1992).

Edwards, R. (1995, September). Psychologists foster the new definition of family. *APA Monitor,* p. 38.

Egan, G. (1994). *The skilled helper: A problem-management approach to helping* (5th ed.). Pacific Grove, CA: Brooks/Cole.

Elkington, J. (1985). *The poisoned womb.* New York: Viking Penguin.

Elliott, C.D. (1990). *Differential Ability Scales.* San Antonio, TX: Psychological Corporation.

Elliott, C.D., Murray, D.J., & Pearson, L.S. (1979). *British Ability Scales.* Windsor, England: National Foundation for Educational Research.

Ellis, N.R. (1963). The stimulus trace and behavioral inadequacy. In N.R. Ellis (Ed.), *Handbook of mental deficiency* (pp. 134–158). New York: McGraw-Hill.

Ellis, N.R. (1969). A behavioral research strategy in mental retardation: Defense and critique. *American Journal of Mental Deficiency, 73,* 557–566.

Ellis, N.R. (1970). Memory processes in retardates and normals. *International Review of Research in Mental Retardation, 4,* 1–32.

Enderle, J., & Severson, S. (1991). *Enderle-Severson Transition Rating Scale.* Moorehead, MN: Practical Press.

Engel, E. (1977). One hundred years of cytogenetic studies in health and disease. *American Journal of Mental Deficiency, 82,* 109–117.

Englehardt, J.L., Brubaker, T.H., & Lutzer, V.D. (1988). Older caregivers of adults with mental retardation: Service utilization. *Mental Retardation, 26*(4), 191–195.

Epstein, C.J. (1988). New approaches to the study of Down syndrome. In F.J. Menolascino & J.A. Stark (Eds.), *Preventive and curative intervention in mental retardation* (pp. 35–60). Baltimore: Brookes.

Epstein, M.H., Cullinan, D., & Polloway, E.A. (1986). Patterns of maladjustment among mentally retarded children and youth. *American Journal of Mental Deficiency, 91,* 127–134.

Epstein, M.H., Cullinan, D., Quinn, K.P., & Cumblad, C. (1994). Characteristics of children with emotional and behavioral disorders in community-based programs designed to prevent placement in residential facilities. *Journal of Emotional and Behavioral Disorders, 2*(1), 51–17.

Epstein, M.H., Polloway, E.A., Patton, J.R., & Foley, R. (1989). Mild retardation: Student characteristics and services. *Education and Training of the Mentally Retarded, 24,* 7–16.

Erikson, E.H. (1950). *Identity and the life cycle.* New York: International Universities Press.

Erikson, E.H. (1968). *Identity: Youth and crisis.* New York: Norton.

Estes, W.K. (1970). *Learning theory and mental development.* New York: Academic Press.

Eyman, R.F., Call, T.E., & White, J.F. (1991). Life expectancy of persons with Down syndrome. *American Journal of Mental Retardation, 95,* 603–612.

Eyman, R.K., & Borthwick-Duffy, S.A. (1994). Trends in mortality rates and predictors of mortality. In M.M. Seltzer, M.W. Krauss, & M.P. Janicki (Eds.), *Life course perspectives on adulthood and old age* (pp. 93–105). Washington, DC: American Association on Mental Retardation.

Eyman, R.K., Dingman, H., & Sabagh, G. (1966). Association of characteristics of retarded patients and their families with speed of institutionalization. *American Journal of Mental Deficiency, 71,* 93–99.

Fallen, N.H., & Umansky, W. (1985). *Young children with special needs* (2nd ed.). Upper Saddle River, NJ: Merrill/Prentice Hall.

Falvey, M.A. (1986). *Community-based curriculum: Instructional strategies for students with severe handicaps.* Baltimore: Brookes.

Family Research Council. (1992). *Free to be family: Helping mothers and fathers meet the needs of the next generation of American children.* Washington, DC: Author.

Farber, B. (1968). *Mental retardation: Its social context and social consequences.* Boston: Houghton Mifflin.

Fernald, D.C. (1976). The Lesch-Nyhan syndrome, cerebral palsy, mental retardation and self-mutilation. *Journal of Pediatric Psychology, 1*(3), 51–55.

Ferrara, M.L. (1992). *Substance abuse treatment program for persons with mental retardation.* Austin, TX: Texas Commission on Alcohol and Drug Abuse.

Feuerstein, R., Miller, R., Hoffman, M.B., Rank, Y., Mintzker, Y., & Jensen, M.R. (1981). Cognitive modifiability in adolescence: Cognitive structure and the effects of intervention. *Journal of Special Education, 15,* 269–287.

Fewell, R.R. (1986a). A handicapped child in the family. In R.R. Fewell & P.F. Vadasy (Eds.), *Families of handicapped children: Needs and supports across the lifespan* (pp. 3–34). Austin, TX: Pro-Ed.

Fewell, R.R. (1986b). Supports from religious organizations and personal beliefs. In R.R. Fewell & P.F. Vadasy (Eds.), *Families of handicapped children: Needs and supports across the life span* (pp. 297–316). Austin, TX: Pro-Ed.

Fewell, R.R., & Kelly, J.F. (1983). Curriculum for young handicapped children. In S.G. Garwood (Ed.), *Educating handicapped children* (pp. 407–433). Rockville, MD: Aspen.

Fewell, R.R., & Vadasy, P.F. (1986). *Families of handicapped children: Needs and supports across the life span*. Austin, TX: Pro-Ed.

Field, S., & Hoffman, A. (1996). *Steps to self-determination*. Austin, TX: Pro-Ed.

Finerman, W., Tisch, S., Starkey, S. (Producers), & Zemekis, R. (Director). (1994). *Forest Gump* [Film]. New York: Paramount.

Fishler, K., Azen, C.G., Henderson, R., Friedman, E.G., & Koch, R. (1987). Psychoeducational findings among children treated for phenylketonuria. *American Journal of Mental Retardation, 92,* 65–73.

Flanagan, D.P., Genschaft, J.L., & Harrison, P.L. (Eds.). (1997). *Contemporary intellectual assessment: Theories, tests, and issues*. New York: Guilford.

Fletcher, D., & Abood, D. (1988). An analysis of the readability of product warning labels: Implications for curriculum development for persons with moderate and severe mental retardation. *Education and Training in Mental Retardation, 23*(3), 224–227.

Fletcher, J. (1974). *The ethics of genetic control: Ending reproductive roulette*. Garden City, NY: Anchor.

Fletcher, J. (1975). The "right" to live and the "right" to die. In M. Kohl (Ed.), *Beneficent euthanasia* (pp. 44–53). Buffalo, NY: Prometheus.

Florence County School District Four v. Carter, 114 S.Ct. 361 (1993).

Flynn, L.L., & McCollum, J. (1989). Support systems: Strategies and implications for hospitalized newborns and families. *Journal of Early Intervention, 13,* 173–182.

Flynt, S.W., Wood, T.A., & Scott, R.L. (1992). Social support of mothers of children with mental retardation. *Mental Retardation, 30*(4), 233–236.

Foley, K. (1988). School/community based programs for students with moderate to profound mental retardation. *Pointer, 32*(2), 22–26.

Folio, M.R., & Fewell, R.R. (1983). *Peabody Developmental Motor Scales and Activity Cards*. Chicago: Riverside.

Folling, A. (1934). Uber Ausscheidung von Phenylbrenztraubensaure in den Harn als Stoffwechselanomalie in Verbindung mit Imbezilitat. *Zeitschrift fur Physiologisch Chemie, 227,* 169–176.

Ford, A., & Miranda, P. (1984). Community instruction: A natural cues and corrections decision model. *The Journal of the Association for Persons with Severe Handicaps, 9,* 79–88.

Forness, S.R., & Polloway, E.A. (1987). Physical and psychiatric diagnosis of pupils with mild mental retardation currently being referred for related services. *Education and Training of the Mentally Retarded, 22,* 221–228.

Forrest, M. (Ed.). (1987). More integration/education. Downsville, Ontario: Roeher Institute.

Foster, M., & Berger, M. (1985). Research with families with handicapped children: A multilevel systemic perspective. In L. L'Abate (Ed.), *The handbook of family psychology and therapy* (Vol. 2, pp. 741–780). Pacific Grove, CA: Brooks/Cole.

Foster-Johnson, L., & Dunlap, G. (1993). Using functional assessment to develop effective individualized interventions for challenging behaviors. *Teaching Exceptional Children, 25*(3), 44–50.

Foxx, R.M., Faw, G.D., Taylor, S.D., Davis, P.K., & Fulia, R. (1993). "Would I be able to . . . "? Teaching clients to assess the availability of their living style preferences. *American Journal of Mental Retardation, 98*(2), 235–248.

Frankenburg, W.K. (1984). A survey of state guidelines for identification of mental retardation. *Mental Retardation, 22*(1), 17–20.

Frankenburg, W.K., Dodds, J., Archer, P., Bresnick, B., Maschka, P., Edelman, N., & Shapiro, H. (1989). *Denver II*. Denver, CO: Denver Developmental Materials.

Fredricks, B. (1987, June). Back to the future: Integration revisited. *The Association for Persons with Severe Handicaps Newsletter*, p. 1.

Friend, J., & McNutt, G. (1984). Resource room programs: Where are we now? *Exceptional Children, 51,* 150–155.

Fuchs, D., & Fuchs, L.S., (1991). Framing the REI debate: Abolitionists versus conservationists. In J.W. Lloyd, N.N. Singh, & A.C. Repp (Eds.), *The regular education initiative: Alternative perspectives on concepts, issues, and models* (pp. 241–255). Sycamore, IL: Sycamore Publishing.

Fuchs, D., Fuchs, L.S., & Bahr, M.W. (1990). Mainstream assistance teams: A scientific basis for the art of consultation. *Exceptional Children, 57,* 128–139.

Fuchs, D., Fuchs, L., Benowitz, S., & Barringer, K. (1987). Norm-referenced tests: Are they valid for use with handicapped students? *Exceptional Children, 54,* 263–272.

Fuchs, L.S., & Fuchs, D. (1990). Curriculum-based assessment. In C.R. Reynolds & R.W. Kamphaus (Eds.), *Handbook of psychological and educational assessment of children: Intelligence and achievement* (pp. 435–455). New York: Guilford.

Furlong, M.J., & LeDrew, L. (1985). IQ = 68 = mildly retarded? Factors influencing multidisciplinary team recommendations on children with FS IQs between 63 and 75. *Psychology in the Schools, 22,* 5–9.

Gadow, K.D. & Poling, A.D. (1988). *Pharmacotherapy and mental retardation*. Boston: College-Hill.

Gage, N.L. (1972). IQ heritability, race differences, and educational research. *Phi Delta Kappan, 53,* 308–312.

Gallagher, J.J., Beckman, P.J., & Cross, A.H. (1983). Families of handicapped children: Sources of stress and its amelioration. *Exceptional Children, 50,* 10–19.

Gallahue, D.L. (1989). *Understanding motor development: Infants, children, adolescents* (2nd ed.). Indianapolis, IN: Benchmark.

Galton, F. (1869). *Hereditary genius*. London: Macmillan.

Garber, H.L. (1988). *The Milwaukee project: Preventing mental retardation in children at risk*. Washington, DC: American Association on Mental Retardation.

Garber, H.L., & Heber, R.F. (1973). *The Milwaukee project: Early intervention as a technique to prevent mental retardation*. Storrs: University of Connecticut.

Garber, H.L., & Heber, R.F. (1981). The efficacy of early intervention with family rehabilitation. In M.J. Begab, H.C. Haywood, & H.L. Garber (Eds.), *Psychosocial influences in retarded performance: Strategies for improving competence* (Vol. 2, pp. 71–87). Baltimore: University Park Press.

Garber, H.L., & McInerney, M. (1982). Sociobehavioral factors in mental retardation. In P.T. Cegelka & H.J. Prehm (Eds.), *Mental retardation: From Categories to people*. Upper Saddle River, NJ: Merrill/Prentice Hall.

Gardner, H. (1983). *Frames of mind: The theory of multiple intelligences*. New York: Basic Books.

Gardner, H. (1993). *Frames of mind: The theory of multiple intelligences* (2nd ed.). New York: Basic Books.

Gardner, J.F., & Chapman, M.S. (1985). *Staff development in mental retardation services: A practical handbook*. Baltimore: Brookes.

Gardner, J.F., & Chapman, M.S. (1993). *Developing staff competencies for supporting people with developmental disabilities: An orientation handbook* (2nd ed.). Baltimore: Brookes.

Gardner, W.I., & Cole, C.L. (1990). Aggression and related conduct difficulties. In J.L. Matson (Ed.), *Handbook of behavior modification with the mentally retarded* (2nd ed., pp. 225–251). New York: Plenum.

Gaylord-Ross, R., & Chadsey-Rusch, J. (1991). Measurement of work-related outcomes for students with severe disabilities. *Journal of Special Education, 25*(3), 291–304.

Geiger, W., Brownsmith, K., & Forgnone, C. (1978). Differential importance of skills for TMR students perceived by teachers. *Education and Training of the Mentally Retarded, 13,* 259–264.

Geik, I., Gilkerson, L., & Sponseller, D.B. (1982). An early intervention training model. *Journal of the Division for Early Childhood, 5,* 42–52.

Georgia Association for Retarded Citizens v. McDaniel, 704F. 2d 902 (11th Cir. 1984).

Gertsen, R., Crowell, F., & Bellamy, T. (1986). Spillover effects: Impact of vocational training on the lives of severely retarded clients. *American Journal of Mental Deficiency, 19,* 501–506.

Gifford, J.L., Rusch, F.R., Martin, J.E., & White, D.M. (1984). Autonomy and adaptability: A proposed technology for maintaining work behavior. *International Review of Research in Mental Retardation, 12,* 285–318.

Gilhool, T.K. (1976). The right to community services. In M. Kindred, J. Cohen, D. Penrod, & T. Shaffer (Eds.), *The mentally retarded citizen and the law* (pp. 172–213). New York: Free Press.

Ginsburg, H. (1972). *The myth of the deprived child: Poor children's intellect and education*. Upper Saddle River, NJ: Prentice Hall.

Ginzberg, E., & Bray, D.W. (1953). *The uneducated*. New York: Columbia University Press.

Glass, G.V. (1983). Effectiveness of special education. *Policy Studies Review, 2*(Special No. 1), 65–78.

Glidden, L.M., & Zetlin, A.G. (1992). Adolescence and community adjustment. In L. Rowitz (Ed.), *Mental retardation in the year 2000* (pp. 101–114). New York: Springer-Verlag.

Gnezda, M.T., & Smith, S.L. (1989). *A child care and early childhood education policy: A legislator's guide*. Denver, CO: National Conference of State Legislators.

Goddard, H.H. (1907). Psychological work among the feeble-minded. *Journal of Psycho-Asthenics, 12*(1–4), 22.

Goddard, H.H. (1911). A revision of the Binet scale. *Training School, 8,* 56–62.

Goddard, H.H. (1912). *The Kallikak family*. New York: Macmillan.

Goddard, H.H. (1917). Mental tests and the immigrant. *Journal of Delinquency, 2,* 243–277.

Goddard, H.H. (1920). *Feeble-mindedness: Its causes and consequences*. New York: Macmillan.

Gold, M.W. (1976). Task analysis of a complex assembly task by the retarded blind. *Exceptional Children, 43,* 78–84.

Gold, M.W. (1980). An alternative definition of mental retardation. In M.W. Gold (Ed.), *"Did I say that?" Articles and commentary on the Try Another Way System* (pp. 145–150). Champaign, IL: Research Press.

Goldberg, R.T., McLean, M.M., LaVigne, R., Fratolillo, J., & Sullivan, F.T. (1990). Transition of persons with developmental disability from extended sheltered employment to competitive employment. *Mental Retardation, 28,* 299–304.

Goldenberg, I., & Goldenberg, H. (1985). *Family therapy: An overview* (2nd ed.). Pacific Grove, CA: Brooks/Cole.

Goldenberg, I., & Goldenberg, H. (1996). *Family therapy: An overview* (4th ed.). Pacific Grove, CA: Brooks/Cole.

Goldman, J.J. (1988). Prader-Willi syndrome in two institutionalized older adults. *Mental Retardation, 26,* 97–102.

Gollay, E., Freedman, R., Wyngaarden, M., & Kurtz, N.R. (1978). *Coming back: The community experiences of deinstitutionalized mentally retarded people.* Cambridge, MA: Abt.

Gollin, E.S. (1985). Ontogeny, phylogeny, and causality. In E.S. Gollin (Ed.), *The comparative development of adaptive skills: Evolutionary implications* (pp. 1–18). Hillsdale, NJ: Erlbaum.

Googins, B. (1989). Support in integrated work settings: The role played by industry through employee assistance programs. In W.E. Kiernan & R.L. Schalock (Eds.), *Curriculum considerations in inclusive classrooms* (pp. 85–100). Baltimore: Brookes.

Gordon, E. (1990a). *Family support services and residential options for the mentally retarded in the U.S.: New service paradigms and models.* Pittsburgh, PA: Health and Welfare Planning Association. (ERIC Document Reproduction Service No. ED 334 749)

Gordon, E. (1990b). *Four years of follow-up of mentally retarded school completers.* Pittsburgh, PA: Health and Welfare Planning Association. (ERIC Document Reproduction Service No. ED 344 748)

Gordon, J.R. (1991). *A diagnostic approach to organizational behavior* (3rd ed.). Boston: Allyn & Bacon.

Gottesman, I.I. (1963). Genetic aspects of intelligent behavior. In N.R. Ellis (Ed.), *Handbook of mental deficiency: Psychological theory and research* (pp. 253–296). New York: McGraw-Hill.

Gottlieb, J. (1975). Public, peer, and professional attitudes toward mentally retarded persons. In M.J. Begab & S.A. Richardson (Eds.), *The mentally retarded in society: A social science perspective* (pp. 99–125). Baltimore: University Park Press.

Gottlieb, J., & Budoff, M. (1973). Social acceptability of retarded children in nongraded schools differing in architecture. *American Journal of Mental Deficiency, 78,* 15–19.

Gould, R. (1978). *Transformations: Growth and change in adult life.* New York: Simon & Schuster.

Gould, S.J. (1981). *The mismeasure of man.* New York: Norton.

Graham, F.K., Ernhart, C.B., Thurston, D., & Craft, M. (1962). Development three years after perinatal anoxia and other potentially damaging experiences. *Psychological Monographs, 76* (Whole No. 522).

Graham, M., & Scott, K.G. (1988). The impact of definitions of higher risks on services to infants and toddlers. *Topics in Early Childhood Special Education, 8,* 23–28.

Gray, G. (1975). Educational service delivery. In W.J. Cegelka (Chair), *Educating the 24-hour retarded child.* Symposium conducted at the National Training Meeting on Education of the Severely and Profoundly Retarded. Arlington, TX: National Association for Retarded Citizens.

Great Lakes Area Regional Resource Center. (1986). *"Medically fragile" handicapped children: A policy research paper*. Columbus: Ohio State University.

Greenspan, S. (1979). Social intelligence in the retarded. In N.R. Ellis (Ed.), *Handbook of mental deficiency: Psychological theory and research* (2nd ed., pp. 483–531). Hillsdale, NJ: Erlbaum.

Greenspan, S. (1981a). Defining childhood social competence: A proposed working model. In B.K. Keough (Ed.), *Advances in special education* (Vol. 3, pp. 1–39). Greenwich, CT: JAI Press.

Greenspan, S. (1981b). Social competence and handicapped individuals: Practical implications of a proposed model. In B.K. Keough (Ed.), *Advances in special education* (Vol. 3, pp. 41–82). Greenwich, CT: JAI Press.

Greenspan, S. (1994). Review of the 1992 AAMR manual. *American Journal of Mental Retardation, 98,* 544–549.

Greenspan, S. (1997). The role of intelligence in a broad model of personal competence. In D.P. Flanagan, J.O. Genshaft, & P.L. Harrison (Eds.), *Contemporary intellectual assessment: Theories, tests, and issues* (pp. 131–150). New York: Guilford.

Greenspan, S. (in press). Dead manual walking?: Why the 1992 AAMR definition needs redoing. *Education and Training in Mental Retardation and Developmental Disabilities.*

Greenspan, S., & Driscoll, J. (1997). The role of intelligence in a broad model of personal competence. In D.P. Flanagan, J.O. Genshaft, & P.L. Harrison (Eds.), *Contemporary intellectual assessment: Theories, tests, and issues* (p. 133). New York: Guilford.

Greenspan, S., & Granfield, J.M. (1992). Reconsidering the construct of mental retardation: Implications of a model of social competence. *American Journal on Mental Retardation, 96,* 442–453.

Gresham, F.M. (1982). Misguided mainstreaming: The case for social skills training with handicapped children. *Exceptional Children, 48,* 422–433.

Gresham, F.M., MacMillan, D.L., & Siperstein, G.N. (1995). Critical analysis of the 1992 AAMR definition: Implications for school psychology. *School Psychology Quarterly, 10,* 1–19.

Griesbach, L.S., & Polloway, E.A. (1991). *Fetal alcohol syndrome*. (ERIC Document Reproduction Service No. 326 035)

Grossman, H.J. (Ed.). (1973). *Manual on terminology and classification in mental retardation*. Washington, DC: American Association on Mental Retardation.

Grossman, H.J. (Ed.). (1977). *Manual on terminology and classification in mental retardation*. Washington, DC: American Association on Mental Retardation.

Grossman, H.J. (Ed.). (1983). *Classification in mental retardation*. Washington, DC: American Association on Mental Retardation.

Grossman, H.J., & Tarjan, G. (1987). *AMA handbook on mental retardation*. Chicago: American Medical Association, Division of Clinical Science.

Gruenewald, L., Schroeder, J., & Yoder, D. (1982). Considerations for curriculum development and implementation. In B. Campbell & V. Baldwin (Eds.), *Severely handicapped/hearing impaired students* (pp. 163–180). Baltimore: Brookes.

Guardianship of Phillip B., 139 Cal. App. 3d 407, 188 Cal. Rptr. 781 (app. 1983).

Guilford, J.P. (1967). *The nature of human intelligence*. New York: McGraw-Hill.

Guilford, J.P. (1985). The structure-of-intellect model. In B.B. Wolman (Ed.), *Handbook of intelligence: Theories, measurements, and applications* (pp. 225–266). New York: Wiley.

Guralnick, M.J. (1991). The next decade of research on the effectiveness of early intervention. *Exceptional Children, 58,* 174–183.

Guralnick, M.J., Heiser, K.E., Bennett, F.C., & Richardson, H.B. (1988). A systems approach to training pediatricians in the field of developmental disabilities. In M.D. Powers (Ed.), *Expanding systems of service delivery for person with developmental disabilities* (pp. 233–253). Baltimore, MD: Brookes.

Guralnick, M.J., & Weinhouse, E. (1984). Peer-related social interactions of developmentally delayed young children: Their development and characteristics. *Developmental Psychology, 20,* 815–827.

Guskin, S.L. (1977). Paradigms for research on attitudes toward the mentally retarded. In P. Mittler (Ed.), *Research to practice in mental retardation* (Vol. 1, pp. 23–33). Baltimore: University Park Press.

Guterman, B.R. (1995). The validity of categorical learning disabilities services: The consumer's view. *Exceptional Children, 62,* 112–124.

Guttmacher, M., & Weihofen, H. (1952). *Psychiatry and the law.* New York: Norton.

Haggard, H.W., & Jellinek, E.M. (1942). *Alcohol explained.* Garden City, NY: Doubleday.

Hagner, D., & Salomone, P.R. (1989). Issues in career decision making for workers with developmental disabilities. *Career Development Quarterly, 38,* 148–158.

Halal, W.E., & Liebowitz, J. (1996). Telelearning: The multimedia revolution in education. In E. Cornish (Ed.), *Exploring your future: Living, learning, and working in the information age* (pp. 95–100). Bethesda, MD: World Future Society.

Halderman v. Pennhurst State School and Hospital, 446 F. Supp. 1295 (E.D. Pa. 1977), aff'd in part, remanded in part. Nos. 84-1490, 78-1564, 78-1602 (3rd Cir. Dec. 13, 1979).

Haldy, M.B., & Hanzlik, J.R. (1990). A comparison of perceived competence in child-rearing between mothers of children with Down syndrome and mothers of children without delays. *Education and Training in Mental Retardation, 25*(2), 132–141.

Hallahan, D.P., Keller, C.E., McKinney, J.D., Lloyd, J.W., & Bryan, T. (1988). Examining the research base of the regular education initiative: Efficacy studies and the adaptive learning environment model. *Journal of Learning Disabilities, 21,* 29–35.

Hallahan, D.P., & Reeve, R.E. (1980). Selective attention and distractibility. In B. Keogh (Ed.), *Advances in special education. Vol. 1: Basic constructs and theoretical orientations.* Greenwich, CO: JAI Press.

Halle, J.W., Silverman, N.A., & Regan, L. (1983). The effects of a data-based exercise program on physical fitness of retarded children. *Education and Training of the Mentally Retarded, 18*(3), 221–225.

Halpern, A.S. (1985). Transition: A look at the foundations. *Exceptional Children, 51,* 479–486.

Halpern, A.S. (1992). Transition: Old wine in new bottles. *Exceptional Children, 58,* 202–212.

Halpern, A.S. (1993). Quality of life as a conceptual framework for evaluating transition outcomes. *Exceptional Children, 59,* 486–498.

Halpern, A.S. (1994). The transition of youth with disabilities to adult life: A position statement of the Division on Career Development and Transition, The Council for Exceptional Children. *Career Development for Exceptional Individuals, 17,* 115–124.

Halpern, A.S., Herr, C.M., Wolf, N.K., Doren, B., Johnson, M.D., & Lawson, J.D. (1997). *Next step: Student transition and evaluation planning.* Austin, TX: Pro-Ed.

Halpern, A.S., Nave, G., Close, D.W., & Nelson, D. (1986). An empirical analysis of the dimensions of community adjustment for adults with mental retardation in semi-independent living programs. *Australia and New Zealand Journal of Developmental Disabilities, 12*(3), 147–157.

Hamilton, D.I., & Bishop, G.D. (1976). Attitudinal and behavioral effects of initial integration of white suburban neighborhoods. *Journal of Social Issues, 32,* 47–67.

Hannaford, A.E. (1993). Computers and exceptional individuals. In J.D. Lindsey (Ed.), *Computers and exceptional individuals* (2nd ed., pp. 3–26). Austin, TX: Pro-Ed.

Hanson, M.J. (1984). *Atypical infant development.* Austin, TX: Pro-Ed.

Hanson, M.J., & Schwarz, R.H. (1978). Results of a longitudinal intervention program for Down's syndrome infants and their families. *Education and Training of the Mentally Retarded, 13,* 403–407.

Harbin, G.L. (1988). Implementation of P.L. 99-457: State technical assistance needs. *Topics in Early Childhood Special Education, 8*(1), 24–36.

Hardman, M.L., Drew, C.J., Egan, M.W., & Wolf, B. (1993). *Human exceptionality: Society, school, and family* (4th ed.). Boston: Allyn & Bacon.

Hardman, M.L., Drew, C.J., & Egan, M.W. (1996). *Human exceptionality: Society, school, and family* (5th ed.). Boston: Allyn & Bacon.

Haring, N.G., McCormick, L., & Haring, T.G. (1994). *Exceptional children and youth* (6th ed.). Upper Saddle River, NJ: Merrill/Prentice Hall.

Harrington, T.F., & O'Shea, A.J. (1992). *The Harrington-O'Shea Career Decision-Making System.* Circle Pines, MN: American Guidance Service.

Harris, L., & Associates, Inc. (1986). *International Center for the Disabled survey of disabled Americans: Bring disabled Americans into the mainstream.* New York: Author.

Harris, S.L., & Handleman, J.S. (1990). Using aversive procedures: An overview of the issues. In S.L. Harris & J.S. Handleman (Eds.), *Aversive and nonaversive interventions: Controlling life-threatening behavior by the developmentally disabled* (pp. 1–10). New York: Springer-Verlag.

Harrison, P.L. (1987). Research with adaptive behavior scales. *The Journal of Special Education, 21*(1), 37–68.

Harrison, P.L., Kaufman, A.S., Kaufman, N.L., Bruininks, R.H., Rynders, J., Ilmer, S., Sparrow, S.S., & Cicchetti, D. (1990). *AGS Early Screening Profiles.* Circle Pines, MN: American Guidance Service.

Harrison, P.L., & Robinson, B. (1995). Best practices in the assessment of adaptive behavior. In A. Thomas & J. Grimes (Eds.), *Best practices in school psychology— III* (pp. 753–762). Washington, DC: National Association of School Psychologists.

Harth, R. (1977). Attitudes and mental retardation: Review of the literature. In C.J. Drew, M.L. Hardman, & H.P. Bluhm (Eds.), *Mental retardation: Social and educational perspectives* (pp. 4–14). St. Louis, MO: Mosby.

Hasazi, S.B., Gordon, L.R., & Roe, C.A. (1985). Factors associated with employment status of handicapped youth exiting high school from 1979 to 1983. *Exceptional Children, 51,* 455–469.

Haskins, R. (1989). Beyond metaphor: The efficacy of early childhood education. *American Psychologist, 44,* 274–282.

Havinghurst, R.J. (1953). *Human development and education.* New York: Longmans, Green.

Hawkes, N. (1979). Tracing Burt's descent into scientific fraud. *Science, 205,* 673–675.

Hawaii Transition Project. (1987). Transition Resources. Honolulu: University of Hawaii, Department of Special Education.

Hayden, A.H., & Pious, C.G. (1979). The case for early intervention. In R. York & E. Edgar (Eds.), *Teaching the severely handicapped* (Vol. 4). Seattle, WA: American Association for the Education of the Severely/Profoundly Handicapped.

Hayden, M.F., & Abery, B.H. (Eds.). (1994). *Challenges for a service system in transition: Ensuring quality community experiences for persons with developmental disabilities.* Baltimore, MD: Brookes.

Hayden, M.F., & DePaepe, P. (1994). Waiting for community services: The impact on persons with mental retardation and other developmental disabilities. In M.F. Hayden & B.H. Abery (Eds.), *Challenges for a service system in transition* (pp. 000–000). Baltimore: Brookes.

Haywood, H.C. (1979). What happened to mild and moderate mental retardation? *American Journal of Mental Deficiency, 83,* 429–439.

Haywood, H.C., & Paour, J. (1992). Alfred Binet (1857–1922): Multifaceted Pioneer. *Psychology in Mental Retardation and Developmental Disabilities, 18,* 1–4.

Heal, L.W., Borthwick-Duffy, S.A., & Saunders, R.R. (1996). In J.W. Jacobson & J.A. Mulick (Eds.), *Manual of diagnosis and professional practice in mental retardation* (pp. 199–209). Washington, DC: American Psychological Association.

Heal, L.W., Copher, J.I., DeStefano, L., & Rusch, F.R. (1988, May). *A comparison of successful and unsuccessful placements of secondary students with mental handicaps into competitive employment.* Paper presented at the annual meeting of the American Association on Mental Retardation, Washington, DC. (ERIC Document Reproduction No. ED 305 811)

Heal, L.W., & Rusch, F.R. (1994). Prediction of residential independence of special education high school students. *Research in Developmental Disabilities, 15*(3), 223–243.

Heal, L.W., Sigelman, C.K., & Switzky, H.N. (1978). Research on community residential alternatives for the mentally retarded. *International Review of Research in Mental Retardation, 9,* 209–249.

Healey, K.N., & Masterpasqua, F. (1992). Interpersonal cognitive problem-solving among children with mild mental retardation. *American Journal on Mental Retardation, 96,* 367–372.

Healy, A., Keesee, P.D., & Smith, B.S. (1985). *Early services for children with special needs: Transition actions for family support.* Iowa City: University of Iowa, Division of Developmental Disabilities.

Hearnshaw, L.S. (1979). *Cyril Burt, psychologist.* Ithaca, NY: Cornell University.

Heber, R.F. (1959). A manual on terminology and classification in mental retardation. *Monograph Supplement to the American Journal of Mental Deficiency, 62.*

Heber, R.F. (1961). A manual on terminology and classification in mental retardation (rev. ed.). *Monograph Supplement to the American Journal of Mental Deficiency, 64.*

Heber, R.F. (1964). Personality. In H.A. Stevens & R.F. Heber (Eds.), *Mental retardation: A review of research* (pp. 143–174). Chicago: University of Chicago Press.

Heber, R.F., & Garber, H. (1967). The Milwaukee project: A study of the use of family intervention to prevent cultural-familial mental retardation. In B.Z. Friendlender (Ed.), *The exceptional infant: Assessment and intervention.* New York: Appleton-Century-Crofts.

Heber, R.F., & Garber, H. (1971). An experiment in prevention of cultural-familial mental retardation. In D.A. Primrose (Ed.), *Proceedings of the Second Congress of the International Association for the Scientific Study of Mental Deficiency.* Warsaw: Polish Medical Publishers.

Heller, T. (1984). Issues in adjustment of mentally retarded individuals to residential relocation. In N.R. Ellis & N.W. Bray (Eds.), *International review of research in mental retardation* (Vol. 12, pp. 123–147). Orlando, FL: Academic Press.

Henderson, N.D. (1982). Human behavior genetics. *Annual Review of Psychology, 33,* 403–440.

Henderson, R.A., & Vitello, S.J. (1988). Litigation related to community integration. In L.W. Heal, J.I. Haney, & A.R. Novak Amado (Eds.), *Integration of developmentally disabled individuals into the community* (2nd ed., pp. 272–282). Baltimore: Brookes.

Herr, E.L. (1977). *The emerging history of career education: A summary view.* Washington, DC: National Advisory Council on Career Education.

Herr, S.S. (1984). The Phillip Becker case resolved: A chance for habilitation. *Mental Retardation, 22*(1), 35–39.

Herrnstein, R. (1971, September). I.Q. *The Atlantic Monthly, 228,* 43–65.

Herrnstein, R. (1982, August). IQ testing and the media. *The Atlantic Monthly, 250,* 68–74.

Herrnstein, R., & Murray, C. (1994). *The bell curve: Intelligence and class structure in American life.* New York: The Free Press.

Hetherington, E.M., & Blechman, E.A. (Eds.). (1996). *Stress, coping, and resiliency in children and families.* Mahwah, NJ: Erlbaum.

Hetherington, E.M., & Martin, B. (1986). Family factors and psychopathology in children. In H.C. Quay & J.S. Werry (Eds.), *Psychopathological disorders of childhood* (3rd ed., pp. 332–390). New York: Wiley.

Heward, W.L. (1996). *Exceptional children: An introduction to special education* (5th ed.). Upper Saddle River, NJ: Merrill/Prentice Hall.

Hewett, F.M., & Forness, S. (1977). *Education of exceptional learners* (2nd ed.). Boston: Allyn & Bacon.

Heyne, L., Storley, C., Rone, C., Levine, B., & Denelle, D. (1996). Elders and preschoolers supporting each other: The JCC Intergenerational Program. *Impact, 9*(4), 10–11.

Hill, B.K., Balow, B.A., & Bruininks, R.H. (1985). A national study of prescribed drugs in institutions and community residential facilities for mentally retarded people. *Psychopharmacology Bulletin, 21,* 279–284.

Hill, B.K., Lakin, K.C., Bruininks, R.H., Amado, A.N., Anderson, D.J., & Copher, J.I. (1989). *Living in the community: A comparative study of foster homes and small group homes for people with mental retardation* (Report No. 28). Minneapolis: University of Minnesota, Center for Residential and Community Integration.

Hill, B.K., Lakin, K.C., Sigford, B.B., Hauber, F.A., & Bruininks, R.H. (1982). *Programs and services for mentally retarded people in residential facilities* (Report No. 16). Minneapolis: University of Minnesota, Institute on Community Integration.

Hill, M., Hill, J.W., Wehman, P., & Banks, D. (1985). An analysis of monetary and nonmonetary outcomes associated with competitive employment of mentally retarded persons. In P. Wehman & J.W. Hill (Eds.), *Competitive employment for persons with mental retardation* (pp. 110–133). Richmond, VA: Virginia Commonwealth University, Rehabilitation, Research, and Training Center.

Hill, M.L., Wehman, P.H., Kregel, J., Banks, P.D., & Metzler, H.M. (1987). Employment outcomes for people with moderate and severe disabilities: An eight-year longitudinal analysis of supported competitive employment. *Journal of the Association of Severe Disabilities, 12*(3), 182–189.

Hilliard, L.T., & Kirman, B.H. (1965). *Mental deficiency* (2nd ed.). London: Churchill.

Hobson v. Hansen, 269 F. Supp. 401 (D.D.C. 1967, aff'd sub norm).

Hodapp, R.M., & Krasner, D.V. (1995). Families of children with disabilities: Findings from a national sample of eighth-grade students. *Exceptionality, 5*(2), 71–81.

Hodgkinson, H.L. (1985). *All one system: Demographics of education, kindergarten through graduate school.* Washington, DC: Institute for Educational Leadership.

Hodgkinson, H.L. (1989). *The same client: The demographics of education and service delivery systems.* Washington, DC: Institute for Educational Leadership, Center for Demographic Leadership.

Hoefnagel, D., Andrew, E.D., Mireault, N.G., & Berndt, W.O. (1965). Hereditary choreoathetosis, self-mutilation, and hyperuricemia in young males. *New England Journal of Medicine, 273,* 130–135.

Hoeksema, T.B. (1995). Supporting the free exercise of religion in the group home context. *Mental Retardation, 33*(5), 289–294.

Hogg, J., & Moss, S. (1993). Characteristics of older people with intellectual disabilities in England. *International Review of Research in Mental Retardation, 19,* 71–96.

Hollinger, C., & Jones, R. (1970). Community attitudes toward slow learners and mental retardates: What's in a name? *Mental Retardation, 8*(1), 1–23.

Holm, V.A., Cassidy, S.B., Butler, M.G., Hanchett, J.M., Greenswag, L.R., Whitman, B.Y., & Greenberg, F. (1993). Prader-Willi syndrome: Consensus diagnostic criteria. *Pediatrics, 182,* 398–402.

Holm, V.A., Sulzbacher, S.J., & Pipes, P.L. (Eds.). (1981). *Prader-Willi syndrome.* Baltimore, MD: University Park Press.

Holman, J., & Bruininks, R.H. (1985). Assessing and training adaptive behaviors. In K.C. Lakin & R.H. Bruininks (Eds.), *Strategies for achieving community integration of developmentally disabled citizens* (pp. 73–104). Baltimore: Brookes.

Honig v. Doe, 108 S. Ct. 592, 98 L. ED. 2d 686 (1988).

Hoover, J.J. (1988). *Curriculum adaptation for students with learning and behavior problems: Principles and practices.* Lindale, TX: Hamilton.

Hopkins, G.A. (1982). A comparison of cytogenetic groups of children with Down's syndrome on verbal and nonverbal measures. *Exceptional People Quarterly, 1,* 329–342.

Hopkins, T.F. (1988). The fourth edition of the Stanford-Binet: Alfred Binet would be proud . . . *Measurement and Evaluation in Counseling and Development, 21,* 40–42.

Horn, E., & Fuchs, D. (1987). Using adaptive behavior in assessment and intervention: An overview. *The Journal of Special Education, 21*(1), 11–26.

Horn, J.L. (1985). Remodeling old models of intelligence. In B.B. Wolman (Ed.), *Handbook of intelligence: Theories, measurements, and applications* (pp. 267–300). New York: Wiley.

Horn, J.L., & Cattell, R.B. (1966). Refinement of the theory of fluid and crystallized general intelligence. *Journal of Educational Psychology, 57,* 253–270.

Horne, R.L. (1991). *The education of children and youth with special needs: What do the laws say?* Washington, DC: National Information Center for Children and Youth with Disabilities. (ERIC Document Reproduction Service No. ED 333 640).

Horner, R.H., Dunlap, G., Koelgel, R.L., Carr, E.G., Sailor, W., Anderson, J., Albin, R.W., & O'Neill, R.E. (1990). Toward a technology of "nonaversive" behavioral support. *Journal of the Association for Persons with Severe Handicaps, 15,* 60–69.

Houston, J. (1987, April). Panel initiates planning. *A vision for the future.* Montgomery: Alabama State Department of Education.

Howell, K.W., Rueda, R., & Rutherford, R.B. (1983). A procedure for teaching self-recording to moderately retarded students. *Psychology in the Schools, 20,* 202–209.

Hoyt, K.B. (1982). Career education—Beginning of the end? Or a new beginning? *Career Development for Exceptional Individuals, 5,* 3–13.

Hresko, W.P., & Brown, L. (1984). *Test of Early Socioemotional Development.* Austin, TX: Pro-Ed.

Hresko, W.P., Reid, D.K., & Hammill, D.D. (1991). *Test of Early Language Development.* Austin, TX: Pro-Ed.

Huberty, T.J., Koller, J.R., & Ten Brink, T.D. (1980). Adaptive behavior in the definition of mental retardation. *Exceptional Children, 46,* 256–261.

Hughes, C., Rusch, F.R., & Curl, R.M. (1990). Extending individual competence, development of natural support, and promoting social acceptance. In F.R. Rusch (Ed.), *Supported employment: Models, methods, and issues* (pp. 181–197). Sycamore, IL: Sycamore.

Humphrey, G., & Humphrey, M. (Eds. & Trans.). (1962). *Wild boy of Aveyron.* New York: Appleton-Century-Crofts.

Hungerford, R.H., DeProspo, C.J., & Rosenweig, I.E. (1948). The non-academic pupil. *Philosophy of occupational education.* New York: Association of New York City Teachers of Special Education.

Hunt, J.M. (1961). *Intelligence and experience.* New York: Ronald Press.

Hunt, J.M. (1969). *The challenge of incompetence and poverty: Papers on the role of early education.* Urbana: University of Illinois Press.

Hunt, N. (1967). *Nigel Hunt: The diary of a mongoloid youth.* New York: Garrett.

Hurry v. Jones, 734 F. 2d 829 (1st Cir. 1984).

Hurwitz, N. (1975). Communications networks and the urban poor. *Equal Opportunity Review,* pp. 1–5. (ERIC Document Reproduction Service No. 109 292)

Ianacone, R.N., & Leconte, P.J. (1986). Curriculum-based vocational assessment: A viable response to a school-based service delivery issue. *Career Development for Exceptional Individuals, 9,* 113–120.

Idol, L., Paolucci-Whitcomb, P., & Nevin, A. (1986). *Collaborative consultation.* Austin, TX: Pro-Ed.

Idol, L., & West, J.F. (1993). *Effective instruction of difficult to teach students.* Austin, TX: Pro-Ed.

In re Phillip B., 92 Cal. App. 3rd 796 (1979).

Individuals with Disabilities Education Act, 42 U.S.C. 99457 (1990).

Ingalls, R.P. (1978). *Mental retardation: The changing outlook.* New York: Wiley.

Inhelder, B. (1968). *The diagnosis of reasoning in the mentally retarded.* New York: Day.

Intagliata, J., & Rinck, C. (1985). Psychoactive drug use in public and community residential facilities for mentally retarded persons. *Psychopharmacology Bulletin, 21*(2), 268–278.

Interdisciplinary Working Party on Issues in Severe Communication Impairment. (1988). *D.E.A.L. Communication Center operation. A statement of concern.* Melbourne, Australia: Author.

Irving Independent School District v. Tatro, 104 S. Ct. 3371 (1984).

Itard, J.M. (1962). *Wild boy of Aveyron*. New York: Appleton-Century-Crofts. (G. Humphrey, & M. Humphrey Eds. and Trans.) (Original work published 1801)

Ittenbach, R.F. (1989). *Race, gender, and maternal education differences on three measures of the Early Screening Profiles* (Doctoral dissertation, University of Alabama, 1989). *Dissertation Abstracts International, 51/03*A.

Ittenbach, R.F., Abery, B.H., Larson, S.A., Spiegel, A.N., & Prouty, R.W. (1994). Community adjustment of young adults with mental retardation: Overcoming barriers to inclusion. *Palaestra, 10*(2), 32–42.

Ittenbach, R.F., Bruininks, R.H., Thurlow, M.L., & McGrew, K.S. (1993). Community adjustment of young adults with mental retardation: A multivariate analysis of adjustment. *Research in Developmental Disabilities, 14,* 275–290.

Ittenbach, R.F., Esters, I.G., & Wainer, H. (1997). The history of test development. In D.P. Flanagan, J.L. Genschaft, & P.L. Harrison (Eds.), *Contemporary intellectual assessment: Theories, tests, and issues* (pp. 17–31). New York: Guilford.

Ittenbach, R.F., Harrison, P.L., & Deck, M.D. (1989). Issues in preschool screening. *Alabama ACD Journal, 15*(2), 37–44.

Ittenbach, R.F., Larson, S.A., Spiegel, A.N., Abery, B.H., & Prouty, R.W. (1993). Community adjustment of young adults with mental retardation: A developmental perspective. *Palaestra, 9*(4), 19–24.

Ittenbach, R.F., & Lawhead, W.F. (1997). Historical and philosophical foundations of single-case research. In R.D. Franklin, D.B. Allison, & B.S. Gorman (Eds.), *Design and analysis of single-case research*. Hillsdale, NJ: Erlbaum.

Ittenbach, R.F., Spiegel, A.N., McGrew, K.S., & Bruininks, R.H. (1992). Confirmatory factor analysis of early childhood ability measures within a model of personal competence. *Journal of School Psychology, 30,* 307–323.

Jacobson, J.W. (1989). Microcomputer applications in public residential facilities. In J.A. Mulick & R.F. Antonak (Eds.), *Transitions in mental retardation, Volume 4: Applications and implications of technology* (pp. 128–154). Norwood, NJ: Ablex.

Jacobson, J.W., & Mulick, J.A. (1996). *Manual on diagnosis and professional practice in mental retardation*. Washington, DC: American Psychological Association.

Japanese scientists predict the future. (1993). *Science, 259,* 461.

Jaquish, C., & Stella, M.A. (1986). Helping special needs students move from elementary to secondary school. *Counterpoint, 7*(1), 1.

Jastak, J., MacPhee, H., & Whiteman, M. (1963). *Mental retardation: Its nature and incidence*. Newark: University of Delaware Press.

J.B. v. Indep. Sch. Dist., 21 IDELR 1157 (D. Minn. 1995).

Jenkins, J.R., Speltz, M.L., & Odom, S.L. (1985). Integrating normal and handicapped preschoolers: Effects on child development and social interaction. *Exceptional Children, 52,* 7–18.

Jenkins, M.W. (1987). Effect of a computerized individual education program (IEP) writer on time savings and quality. *Journal of Special Education, 8*(3), 55–66.

Jensen, A.R. (1969). How much can we boost IQ and scholastic achievement? *Harvard Educational Review, 39,* 1–123.

Jensen, A.R. (1973). *Educability and group differences*. New York: Harper & Row.

Jensen, A.R. (1981). *Straight talk about mental tests*. New York: Free Press.

Johnson, C.F., Koch, R., Peterson, R.M., & Friedman, E.G. (1978). Congenital and neurological abnormalities in infants with phenylketonuria. *American Journal of Mental Deficiency, 82,* 375–379.

Johnson, D.R., Bruininks, R.H., & Thurlow, M.L. (1987). Meeting the challenge of transition service planning through improved interagency cooperation. *Exceptional Children, 53,* 522–530.

Johnson, D.R., & Lewis, D.R. (1994). Supported employment: Program models, strategies, and evaluation perspectives. In M.F. Hayden & B.H. Abery (Eds.), *Challenges for a service system in transition* (pp. 449–482). Baltimore: Brookes.

Johnson, G.O. (1959). Here and there the Onondaga census—Fact or artifact. *Exceptional Children, 25,* 226–231.

Johnson, L.J., & Beauchamp, K.D. (1987). Preschool assessment measures: What are the teachers using? *Journal of the Division for Early Childhood, 12,* 70–76.

Johnson, T.E., Chandler, L.L., Kerns, G.M., & Fowler, S.A. (1986). What are parents saying about school transitions? *Journal of the Division for Early Childhood, 11,* 10–17.

Jones, K.L., Smith, D.W., Ulleland, C.N., & Streissguth, A.P. (1973). Patterns of malformation in offspring of chronic alcoholic mothers. *The Lancet, 1*(1267), 1271.

Jordan, T.E. (1976). *The mentally retarded* (4th ed.). Upper Saddle River, NJ: Merrill/Prentice Hall.

Juel-Nielsen, N. (1965). Individual and environment: A psychiatric-psychological investigation of monozygotic twins reared apart. *Acta Psychiatra et Neurologica Scandinaviae* (Monograph Suppl. No. 183).

Kagan, J. (1970). On class differences and early development. In V. Denenberg (Ed.), *Education of the infant and young child.* New York: Academic Press.

Kail, R.V., & Cavanaugh, J.C. (1996). *Human development.* Pacific Grove, CA: Brooks/Cole.

Kamin, L.J. (1974). *The science and politics of IQ.* Hillsdale, NJ: Erlbaum.

Kamphaus, R.W. (1987). Conceptual and psychometric issues in the assessment of adaptive behavior. *The Journal of Special Education, 21*(1), 27–36.

Kanner, L.A. (1964). *A history of the care and study of the mentally retarded.* Springfield, IL: Thomas.

Kaplan, O.L. (1943). Mental decline in older morons. *American Journal on Mental Deficiency, 47*(3), 277–285.

Karnes, M.B. (1986). Future directions in early childhood education for exceptional children. In J.J. Gallagher & B.B. Weiner (Eds.), *Alternative futures in special education* (pp. 42–64). Reston, VA: Council for Exceptional Children.

Karp, N. (1996). Individualized wrap-around services for children with emotional, behavior, and mental disorders. In E.H. Singer, L.E. Powers, & A.L. Olson (Eds.), *Redefining family support: Innovations in public–private partnerships* (pp. 291–310). Baltimore, MD: Brookes.

Karpinski, R. (1993). Bellcore prototypes hint at multimedia future. *Telephony, 225,* 17.

Kastner, L.S., Reppucci, N.D., & Pezzoli, J.J. (1979). Assessing community attitudes toward mentally retarded persons. *American Journal of Mental Deficiency, 84,* 137–144.

Kastner, T. (1988). AIDS and mental retardation. *AAMR News & Notes, 1*(4), 2, 4.

Kauffman, J.M. (1987). Research in special education: A commentary. *Remedial and Special Education, 85*(6), 57–62.

Kauffman, J.M., & Krouse, J. (1981). The cult of educability: Searching for the substance of things hoped for, the evidence of things not seen. *Analysis & Intervention in Developmental Disabilities, 1,* 53–60.

Kauffman, J.M., & Payne, J.S. (1975). *Mental retardation: Introduction and personal perspectives.* Upper Saddle River, NJ: Merrill/Prentice Hall.

Kaufman, A.S. (1979). *Intelligent testing with the WISC-R*. New York: Wiley.

Kaufman, A.S. (1989). *Has anybody ever really measured adult intelligence?* Paper presented at the annual meeting of the American Psychological Association, Atlanta, GA.

Kaufman, A.S. (1990). *Assessing adolescent and adult intelligence*. Boston: Allyn & Bacon.

Kaufman, A.S. (1994). *Intelligent testing with the WISC-III*. New York: Wiley.

Kaufman, A.S., Harrison, P.L., & Ittenbach, R.F. (1990). Intelligence testing in the schools. In T.B. Gutkin & C.R. Reynolds (Eds.), *The handbook of school psychology* (2nd ed., pp. 289–327). New York: Wiley.

Kaufman, A.S., & Kaufman, N.L. (1983a). *Kaufman Assessment Battery for Children* (K-ABC). Circle Pines, MN: American Guidance Service.

Kaufman, A.S., & Kaufman, N.L. (1983b). *Kaufman Assessment Battery for Children: Interpretive manual*. Circle Pines, MN: American Guidance Service.

Kaye, K. (1985). Toward a developmental psychology of the family. In L. L'Abate (Ed.), *The handbook of family psychology and therapy* (Vol. 1, pp. 38–72). Pacific Grove, CA: Brooks/Cole.

Kearney, F.J., & Smull, M.W. (1992). People with mental retardation leaving mental health institutions: Evaluating outcomes after five years. In J.W. Jacobson, S.N. Burchard, & P.J. Carling (Eds.), *Community living for people with developmental and psychiatric disabilities* (pp. 183–196). Baltimore, MD: Johns Hopkins University Press.

Keith, T.Z., Fehrman, P.G., Harrison, P.L., & Pottebaum, S.M. (1987). The relation between adaptive behavior and intelligence: Testing alternative explanations. *Journal of School Psychology, 24,* 31–43.

Kemp, D.R. (1983). Assessing human rights committees: A mechanism for protecting the rights of institutionalized mentally retarded persons. *Mental Retardation, 21,* 13–16.

Kennedy, C.H., Horner, R.H., & Newton, J.S. (1989). Social contacts of adults with severe disabilities living in the community: A descriptive analysis of relationship patterns. *The Journal of the Association for Persons with Severe Handicaps, 14,* 190–196.

Kennedy, C.H., & Itkonen, T. (1994). Some effects of regular class participation on the social contacts and social networks of high school students with severe disabilities. *Journal of the Association for Persons with Severe Handicaps, 19*(1), 1–10.

Kennedy, D.W., Austin, D.R., & Smith, R.W. (1989). *Special recreation: Opportunities for persons with disabilities*. Philadelphia: Sanders.

Kenowitz, L., Zweibel, S., & Edgar, E. (1978). Determining the least restrictive educational opportunity for the severely and profoundly handicapped. In N.G. Haring & D.D. Bricker (Eds.), *Teaching the severely handicapped* (Vol. 3, pp. 48–73). Seattle, WA: American Association for the Education of the Severely/Profoundly Handicapped.

Keogh, B.K. (1988). Improving services for problem learners. Rethinking and restructuring. *Journal of Learning Disabilities, 21,* 19–22.

Keogh, B.K. (1990). Narrowing the gap between policy and practice. *Exceptional Children, 57,* 186–190.

Keogh, B.K., & Daley, S.E. (1983). Early identification: One component of comprehensive services for at-risk children. *Topics in Early Childhood Special Education, 3*(3), 7–16.

Kidd, J.W. (1977). Comments from the executive director: The definitional dilemma. *Education and Training of the Mentally Retarded, 12,* 303–304.

Kidd, J.W. (1979). An open letter to the Committee on Terminology and Classification of AAMD from the Committee on Definition and Terminology of CEC-MR. *Education and Training of the Mentally Retarded, 14,* 74–76.

Kiernan, W.E., & McGaughey, M. (1991). *Employee assistance programs: A support mechanism for the worker with a disability.* Boston: Children's Hospital, Training and Research Institute for People with Disabilities.

King, B.H., DeAntonio, C., McCracken, J.T., & Forness, S.R. (1994). Psychiatric consultation in severe and profound mental retardation. *American Journal of Psychiatry, 151*(12), 1802–1808.

Kirk, S.A. (1964). Research in education. In H.A. Stevens & R.F. Heber (Eds.), *Mental retardation: A review of research* (pp. 57–99). Chicago: University of Chicago Press.

Klein, N.K., & Campbell, P. (1990). Preparing personnel to serve at-risk and disabled infants, toddlers, and preschoolers. In S.J. Meisels & J.P. Shonkoff (Eds.), *Handbook of early childhood intervention* (pp. 679–699). New York: Cambridge University Press.

Klein, N.K., & Sheehan, J. (1987). Staff development: A key issue in meeting the needs of young handicapped children in day care settings. *Topics in Early Childhood Special Education, 7*(1), 13–27.

Kleinberg, J., & Galligan, B. (1983). Effects of deinstitutionalization on adaptive behavior of mentally retarded adults. *American Journal of Mental Deficiency, 88*(1), 21–27.

Knackendofel, E.A., Robinson, S.M., Deshler, D.D., & Schumaker, J.B. (1992). *Collaborative problem solving.* Lawrence, KS: Edge Enterprises.

Kneedler, R.D., & Hallahan, D.P. (1981). Self-monitoring of on-task behavior with learning disabled children: Current studies and directions. *Education Quarterly, 2*(3), 73–82.

Knobbe, C.A., Carey, S.P., Rhodes, L., & Horner, R.H. (1995). Benefit–cost analysis of community residential versus institutional services for adults with severe mental retardation and challenging behaviors. *American Journal on Mental Retardation, 99*(5), 533–541.

Knowles, M. (1990). *The adult learner: The neglected species.* Houston, TX: Gulf.

Koch, R., Friedman, E.C., Azen, C., Wenz, E., Parton, P., Ledue, X., & Fishler, K. (1988). Inborn errors of metabolism and the prevention of mental retardation. In F.J. Menolascino & J.A. Stark (Eds.), *Preventive and curative intervention in mental retardation* (pp. 61–90). Baltimore: Brookes.

Koehler, R.S., Schalock, R.L., & Ballard, B.L. (1989). *Personal growth habilitation manual.* Hastings: Mid-Nebraska Mental Retardation Services.

Kokaska, C.J. (1968). The occupational status of the educable mentally retarded: A review of the follow-up studies. *Journal of Special Education, 2,* 369–377.

Kolstoe, O.P. (1972). *Mental retardation: An educational viewpoint.* New York: Holt, Rinehart, & Winston.

Kolstoe, O.P. (1975). Secondary programs. In J.M. Kauffman & J.S. Payne (Eds.), *Mental retardation: Introduction and personal perspectives* (pp. 312–334). Upper Saddle River, NJ: Merrill/Prentice Hall.

Kolstoe, O.P. (1981). Career education for the handicapped: Opportunities for the '80s. *Career Development for Exceptional Individuals, 4,* 3–13.

Kopp, C.B., Baker, B.L., & Brown, K.W. (1992). Social skills and their correlates: Preschoolers with developmental disabilities. *American Journal on Mental Retardation, 96,* 357–366.

Koshland, D.E. (1993). Science and society. *Science, 260,* 143.

Kotlowitz, A. (1991). *There are no children here: The story of two boys growing up in the other America.* New York: Anchor Books.

Kozol, J. (1988). *Rachel and her children: Homeless families in America.* New York: Crown.

Kozol, J. (1991). *Savage inequalities: Children in America's schools.* New York: Crown.

Krajicek, M., & M. Thompkins, R. (1993). *The medically fragile infant.* Austin, TX: Pro-Ed.

Krauss, M., Seltzer, M.M., Gordon, R., & Friedman, D.H. (1996). Binding ties: The roles of adult siblings of persons with mental retardation. *Mental Retardation, 34*(2), 83–93.

Kregel, J., Wehman, P., Seyfarth, J., & Marshall, K. (1986). Community integration of young adults with mental retardation: Transition from school to adulthood. *Education and Training of the Mentally Retarded, 21*(1), 35–42.

Krieg, F.J., Brown, P., & Ballard, J. (1995). *Transition: School to work.* Bethesda, MD: National Association of School Psychologists.

Kubler-Ross, E. (1969). *On death and dying.* New York: Macmillan.

Kugel, R.B. (1967). Familial mental retardation: Fact or fancy? In J. Hellmuth (Ed.), *The disadvantaged child* (Vol. 1, pp. 43–63). New York: Bruner/Mazel.

Kugel, R.B., & Parsons, M.H. (1967). *Children of deprivation: Changing the course of familial retardation.* Washington, DC: Children's Bureau.

Kuhn, T.S. (1970). *The structure of scientific revolutions* (2nd ed.). Chicago: University of Chicago Press.

Kurtz, R.A. (1977). *Social aspects of mental retardation.* Lexington, MA: Lexington Books.

Lachar, D. (1990). *Personality Inventory for Children.* Los Angeles: Western Psychological Services.

Lachiewicz, A., Harrison, C., Spiridigliozzi, G.A., Callanan, N.P., & Livermore, J. (1988). What is the Fragile X syndrome? *North Carolina Medical Journal, 49,* 203–208.

Lagomarcino, T.R., & Rusch, F.R. (1990). *An analysis of the reasons for job separations in relation to disability, placement, job type, and length of employment.* (ERIC Document Reproduction Service No. ED 331 235)

Lakin, K.C. (1983). Research-based knowledge and professional practices in special education for emotionally disturbed persons. *Behavioral Disorders, 8,* 128–137.

Lakin, K.C. (1988). Strategies for promoting the stability of direct care staff. In M.P. Janicki, M.W. Krauss, & M.M. Seltzer (Eds.), *Community residences for persons with developmental disabilities: Here to stay* (pp. 231–238). Baltimore: Brookes.

Lakin, K.C., & Bruininks, R.H. (1985). Challenges to advocates of social integration of developmentally disabled persons. In K.C. Lakin & R.H. Bruininks (Eds.), *Strategies for achieving community integration of developmentally disabled citizens* (pp. 313–330). Baltimore: Brookes.

Lakin, K.C., Bruininks, R.H., Hill, B.K., & Hauber, F.A. (1982). Turnover of direct-care staff in a national sample of residential facilities for mentally retarded persons. *American Journal of Mental Deficiency, 87,* 64–72.

Lakin, K.C., Bruininks, R.H., & Larson, S.A. (1992). The changing face of residential services. In L. Rowitz (Ed.), *Mental retardation in the year 2000* (pp. 197–250). New York: Springer-Verlag.

Lakin, K.C., Hill, B.K., & Bruininks, R.H. (1988). Trends and issues in the growth of community residential services. In M.P. Janicki, M.W. Krauss, & M.M. Seltzer

(Eds.), *Community residences for persons with developmental disabilities: Here to stay* (pp. 25–43). Baltimore: Brookes.

Lakin, K.C., Hill, B.S., Chen, T., & Stephens, S.A. (1989). *Persons with mental retardation and related conditions in mental retardation: Selected findings from the 1987 National Medical Expenditure Survey.* Minneapolis: University of Minnesota, Center for Residential and Community Services.

Lakin, K.C., Prouty, R.W., & Bruininks, R.H. (1996). Longitudinal trends in large state-operated residential facilities, 1950–1995. In R. Prouty & K.C. Lakin (Eds.), *Residential services for persons with developmental disabilities: Status and trends through 1995* (Report No. 43, pp. 23–29). Minneapolis: University of Minnesota, Institute on Community Integration.

Lambert, N., Nihira, K., & Leland, H. (1993a). *AAMR Adaptive Behavior Scale—School* (2nd ed.). Austin, TX: Pro-Ed.

Lambert, N., Nihira, K., & Leland, H. (1993b). *AAMR Adaptive Behavior Scale—School (2nd ed.): Technical manual.* Austin, TX: Pro-Ed.

Landesman, S. (1986). Quality of life and personal life satisfaction: Definition and measurement issues. *Mental Retardation, 24,* 141–143.

Langness, L.L., & Levine, H.G. (Eds.). (1986). *Culture and retardation: Life histories of mildly mentally retarded persons in American society.* Boston: Reidel.

Larry P. v. Riles, C-71-2270 (RFP, District Court for Northern California 1972).

Larry P. v. Riles, 495 F.Supp. 926 (N.D. Cal. 1979) *aff'd,* 793 F.2d 969 (9th Cir. 1984).

Larry P. v. Riles, No. C-71-2270 RFP, 1992 Lexis 13677 (N.D. Cal. 1992).

Larson, S.A., & Lakin, K.C. (1989). Deinstitutionalization of persons with mental retardation: Behavioral outcomes. *The Journal of the Association for Persons with Severe Handicaps, 14,* 324–332.

Larson, S.A., & Lakin, K.C. (1991). Parent attitudes about residential placement before and after deinstitutionalization: A research synthesis. *The Journal of the Association for Persons with Severe Handicaps, 16,* 25–38.

Laski, F.J. (1991). Achieving integration during the second revolution. In L.H. Meyer, C.A. Peck, & L. Brown (Eds.), *Critical issues in the lives of people with severe disabilities* (p. 409). Baltimore: Brookes.

Latib, A., Conroy, J., & Hess, C.M. (1984). Family attitudes toward deinstitutionalization. In N.R. Ellis & N.W. Bray (Eds.), *International review of research in mental retardation* (Vol. 12; pp. 67–93). Orlando, FL: Academic Press.

LaVor, M.L. (1977). Federal legislation for exceptional children: Implications and a view of the field. In R.D. Kneedler & S.G. Tarver (Eds.), *Changing perspectives in special education.* Upper Saddle River, NJ: Merrill/Macmillan.

Laurent, J., Swerdlik, M., & Ryburn, M. (1992). Review of validity research on the Stanford-Binet Intelligence Scale: Fourth Edition. *Psychological Assessment, 4*(1), 102–112.

Lawrence, E.A., & Winschel, J.F. (1975). Locus of control: Implications for special education. *Exceptional Children, 41,* 483–490.

Lehr, D.M., & Brown, F. (1984). Perspectives on the severely handicapped. In E.L. Meyen (Ed.), *Mental retardation: Topics of today and issues of tomorrow* (pp. 41–65). Reston, VA: Council on Exceptional Children.

Lejeune, J., Gautier, M., & Turpin, R. (1959). Etudes des chromosomes somatiques de neuf enfants mongoliers. *Academie de Science, 248,* 1721–1722.

Leland, H.W. (1978). Theoretical considerations of adaptive behavior. In W.A. Coulter & H.W. Morrow (Eds.), *Adaptive behavior: Concepts and measurements* (pp. 21–44). Orlando, FL: Grune & Stratton.

Leland, H.W. (1983). Assessment of adaptive behavior. In K.D. Paget & B.A. Bracken (Eds.), *The psychoeducational assessment of preschool children* (pp. 191–206). Orlando, FL: Grune & Stratton.

Lemperle, G. (1985). Plastic surgery. In D. Lane & B. Stratford (Eds.), *Current approaches to Down's syndrome* (pp. 131–145). New York: Holt, Rinehart, & Winston.

Lemperle, G., & Rada, D. (1980). Facial plastic surgery in children with Down's syndrome. *Plastic & Reconstructive Surgery, 66,* 337–342.

Lesch, M., & Nyhan, W.L. (1964). A familial disorder of uric acid metabolism and central nervous system function. *American Journal of Medicine, 36,* 561–570.

Levinson, D.J. (1978). *The seasons of a man's life.* New York: Knopf.

Levitan, S.A., & Taggart, R. (1977). *Jobs for the disabled.* Baltimore: Johns Hopkins University Press.

Levy, P.H., Levy, J.M., Freeman, S., Feiman, J., & Samowitz, P. (1988). Training and managing community residence staff. In M.P. Janicki, M.W. Krauss, & M.M. Seltzer (Eds.), *Community residences for persons with developmental disabilities: Here to stay* (pp. 239–250). Baltimore: Brookes.

Lewis, E.O. (1929). *Report of the mental deficiency committee* (Part 4). London: H.M. Stationery.

Lewis, M.H., & Baumeister, A.A. (1982). Stereotyped mannerisms in mentally retarded persons: Animal models and theoretical analyses. In N.R. Ellis & N.W. Bray (Eds.), *International review of research in mental retardation* (Vol. 11; pp. 123–161). Orlando, FL: Academic Press.

Lewontin, R., Rose, S., & Kamin, C. (1984). *Not in our genes.* New York: Pantheon Books.

Libby, J.D., Polloway, E.A., & Smith, J.D. (1983). Lesch-Nyhan syndrome: A review. *Education and Training of the Mentally Retarded, 18,* 226–231.

Lichtenstein, R., & Ireton, J. (1984). *Preschool screening: Identifying young children with developmental and educational problems.* Orlando, FL: Grune & Stratton.

Lieberman, L.M. (1992). Preserving special education . . . for those who need it. In W. Stainback & S. Stainback (Eds.), *Controversial issues confronting special education: Divergent perspectives* (pp. 13–25). Boston: Allyn & Bacon.

Lilly, S.M. (1986). The relationship between general and special education: A new face on an old issue. *Counterpoint, 10,* 1.

Lindley, L. (1990). Defining TASH: A mission statement. *TASH Newsletter, 16*(8), 1.

Linstone, H.A. (1977). *The postindustrial society and mental retardation.* Paper presented to the President's Committee on Mental Retardation, Washington, DC.

Linstone, H.A. (1980). The postindustrial society and mental retardation. In S.C. Plog & M.B. Santamour (Eds.), *Strategies for achieving community integration of developmentally disabled citizens* (pp. 123–154). New York: Plenum.

Loeb, P.A. (1996). *Independent Living Scales.* San Antonio, TX: Psychological Corporation.

Loevinger, J. (1976). *Ego development.* San Francisco: Jossey-Bass.

Loevinger, J. (1987). *Paradigms of personality.* New York: Freeman.

Lovett, D.L., & Harris, M.B. (1987). Important skills for adults with mental retardation: The client's point of view. *Mental Retardation, 25,* 351–356.

Lubin, R.A., Schwartz, A.A., Zigmond, W.B., & Janicki, M.P. (1982). Community acceptance of residential programs for developmentally disabled persons. *Applied Research in Mental Retardation, 3,* 191–200.

Luckasson, R., Coulter, D.L., Polloway, E.A., Reiss, S., Schalock, R.L., Snell, M.E., Spitalnik, D.M., & Stark, J.A. (1992). *Mental retardation: Definition, classification, and systems of support* (9th ed.). Washington, DC: American Association on Mental Retardation.

Luckasson, R., Coulter, D., Polloway, E.A., Reiss, S., Schalock, R., Snell, M., Spitalnik, D., & Stark, J. (1992). *Mental retardation: Definition, diagnosis and systems of support.* Washington, DC: American Association on Mental Retardation.

Lumsden, C.J., & Wilson, E.O. (1985). The relation between biological and cultural evolution. *Journal of Social Biology Structures, 8,* 343–359.

Lund, K.A., & Bos, C.S. (1981). Orchestrating the preschool classroom: The early schedule. *Teaching Exceptional Children, 14,* 121–125.

Luria, A.R. (1966). *Higher cortical functions in man.* New York: Basic Books.

MacAndrew, C., & Edgerton, R. (1964). The everyday life of institutionalized "idiots." *Human Organization, 23,* 312–313.

Macarov, D. (1985). Overcoming unemployment: Some radical proposals. *The Futurist, 19*(2), 19–24.

MacMillan, D.L. (1977). *Mental retardation in school and society.* Boston: Little, Brown.

MacMillan, D.L. (1982). *Mental retardation in school and society.* (2nd ed.). Boston: Little, Brown.

MacMillan, D.L. (1989). "New" EMRs. In G.A. Robinson, J.R. Patton, E.A. Polloway, & L.R. Sargent (Eds.), *Best practices in mental retardation* (pp. 1–20). Reston, VA: Council for Exceptional Children, Division on Mental Retardation and Developmental Disabilities.

MacMillan, D.L., & Balow, I.H. (1991). Impact of Larry P. on education programs and assessment practices in California. *Diagnostique, 17,* 57–69.

MacMillan, D.L., & Borthwick, S. (1980). The new educable mentally retarded population: Can they be mainstreamed? *Mental Retardation, 18,* 155–158.

MacMillan, D.L., Gresham, F.M., & Siperstein, G.N. (1993). Conceptual and psychometric concerns over the 1992 AAMR definition of mental retardation. *American Journal of Mental Retardation, 98,* 325–335.

MacMillan, D.L., Gresham, F.M., & Siperstein, G.N. (1996). A challenge to the viability of mild mental retardation as a diagnostic category. *Exceptional Children, 62,* 356–371.

Mallory, B.L. (1986). Interactions between community agencies and families over the life cycle. In R.R. Fewell & P.F. Vadasy (Eds.), *Families of handicapped children: Needs and supports across the life span* (pp. 317–356). Austin, TX: Pro-Ed.

Mallory, B.M. (1977). The ombudsman in a residential institution: A description of the role and suggested training areas. *Mental Retardation, 15*(5), 14–17.

Maloney, M.P., & Ward, M.P. (1978). *Mental retardation and modern society.* New York: Oxford University Press.

Manni, J.L., Winikur, D.W., & Keller, M. (1980). *The status of minority group representation in special education programs in the state of New Jersey.* Trenton: New Jersey State Department of Education. (ERIC Document Reproduction Service No. ED 203 575)

March of Dimes. (n.d.). *Public health education information sheet: Neurofibromatosis.* White Plains, NY: Author.

Marchetti, A.G. (1987). Wyatt v. Stickney: A consent decree. *Research in Developmental Disabilities, 8,* 249–259.

Mardell-Czudnowski, C.D., & Goldenberg, D.S. (1990). *Developmental Indicators for the Assessment of Learning—Revised.* Circle Pines, MN: American Guidance Service.

Marder, C., & D'Amico, R. (1992). *How well are youth with disabilities really doing? A comparison of youth with disabilities and youth in general.* Menlo Park, CA: SRI International.

Marino, P.E., Landrigan, P.J., Graef, J., Nussbaum, A., Bayan, G., Boch, K., & Boch, S. (1990). A case report of lead poisoning during renovation of a Victorian farmhouse. *American Journal of Public Health, 80,* 1183.

Marland, S.P. (1971). Career education now. *The Education Digest, 36,* 9–11.

Marland, S.P. (1972). Career education: Every student headed for a goal. *American Vocational Journal, 47*(3), 34–36.

Marlowe, M., Errera, J., & Jacobs, J. (1983). Increased lead and cadmium disorders among mentally retarded children and children with borderline intelligence. *American Journal of Mental Deficiency, 87,* 477–483.

Marshall County transition school prepares students for employment. (1992, May). *Alabama Education,* p. 6.

Martin, E.W. (1972). Individualism and behaviorism as future trends in educating handicapped children. *Exceptional Children, 38,* 517–525.

Martin, J.E., & Huber Marshall, L.H. (1996). *Choicemaker self-determination transition assessment.* Longmont, CO: Sopris West.

Martin, R.P. (1991). Assessment of social and emotional behavior. In B.A. Bracken (Ed.), *The Psychoeducational assessment of preschool children* (2nd ed., pp. 450–464). Boston: Allyn & Bacon.

Masland, R., Sarason, S., & Gladwin, T. (1958). *Mental subnormality.* New York: Basic Books.

Matson, J.L. (1988). *The Psychopathology Inventory for Mentally Retarded Adults.* Orland Park, IL: International Diagnostic Systems.

Matthews, W.S., Barabas, G., Cusack, E., & Ferrari, M. (1986). Social quotients of children with phenylketonuria before and after discontinuation of dietary therapy. *American Journal of Mental Deficiency, 91,* 92–94.

Maurer, S., Teas, S., & Bates, P. (1980). *Project A.M.E.S.* Des Moines: Iowa Department of Public Instruction.

Max M. v. Thompson, 566 F. Supp. 1330, 592 F. Supp. 1437, 592 F. Supp. 1450 (N.D. IL. 1984).

May, D.C. (1988). Plastic surgery for children with Down syndrome: Normalization or extremism? *Mental Retardation, 26,* 17–19.

May, D.C., & Morazas, D.S. (1994). Are elderly people with mental retardation being included in community senior citizen centers? *Education and Training in Mental Retardation and Developmental Disorders, 29*(3), 229–235.

May, D.C., & Turnbull, N. (1992). Plastic surgeons' opinions of facial surgery for individuals with Down syndrome. *Mental Retardation, 30,* 29–33.

Mayo, L.W. (1962). *A proposed program for national action to combat mental retardation.* Report to the President's Committee on Mental Retardation. Washington, DC: U.S. Government Printing Office.

McAfee, J.K., & Sheller, M.C. (1987). Accommodation of adults who are mentally retarded in community colleges: A national study. *Education and Training in Mental Retardation, 22,* 262–267.

McAndrew, I. (1976). Children with a handicap and their families. *Child: Care, Health, and Development, 2,* 213–237.

McBride, J.W., & Forgnone, C. (1985). Emphasis of instruction provided LD, EH, and EMR students in categorized and cross-categorical programming. *Journal of Research & Development in Education, 18*(4), 50–54.

McCarney, S.B. (1995). *Adaptive Behavior Evaluation Scale: Revised.* Columbia, MO: Hawthorne Educational Services.

McCarney, S.B., & Leigh, J. (1990). *Behavioral Evaluation Scale—II* (BES—II). Columbia, MO: Hawthorne Educational Services.

McCarthy, M.M. (1983). The Pennhurst and Rowley decisions: Issues and implications. *Exceptional Children, 49,* 517–522.

McCarver, R.B., & Craig, E.M. (1974). Placement of the retarded in the community: Prognosis and outcome. *International Review of Research in Mental Retardation, 7,* 145–207.

McCubbin, H.I., Joy, C.B., Cauble, A.E., Comeay, J.K., Patterson, J.M., & Needle, R.H. (1980). Family stress and coping: A decade of review. *Journal of Marriage and the Family, 42*(4), 125–141.

McDaniel, G. (1977). Successful programs for young handicapped children. *Educational Horizons, 56*(1), 26–27, 30–33.

McDonnell, A., McDonnell, J., Hardman, M., & McCune, G. (1991). Educating students with severe disabilities in their neighborhood school: The Utah elementary integration model. *Remedial and Special Education, 12*(6), 34–45.

McDonnell, J., & Hardman, M. (1995). Planning the transition of severely handicapped youth from school to adult services: A framework for high school programs. *Education and Training of the Mentally Retarded, 20*(4), 275–286.

McGrew, K.S., & Bruininks, R.H. (1989). The factor structure of adaptive behavior. *School Psychology Review, 18,* 64–81.

McGrew, K.S., & Bruininks, R.H. (1990). Defining adaptive and maladaptive behavior within a model of personal competence. *School Psychology Review, 19*(1), 53–73.

McGrew, K.S., & Bruininks, R.H. (1991, March). *Dimensions of personal competence and adjustment in the community.* Paper presented at the International Conference on Mental Retardation, Hong Kong.

McGrew, K.S., Bruininks, R.H., & Johnson, D.R. (1996). Confirmatory factor analytic investigation of Greenspan's model of personal competence. *American Journal on Mental Retardation, 100*(5), 533–545.

McGrew, K.S., Bruininks, R.H., Thurlow, M., & Lewis, D. (1992). An empirical analysis of multidimensional measures of community adjustment for young adults with mental retardation. *American Journal of Mental Retardation, 96,* 475–487.

McGrew, K.S., Gilman, C.J., & Johnson, S.D. (1989). *Family needs survey results: Responses from parents of young children with disabilities.* Minneapolis: University of Minnesota, Institute on Community Integration.

McGrew, K.S., Ittenbach, R.F., Bruininks, R.H., & Hill, B.S. (1991). Factor structure of maladaptive behavior across the lifespan of persons with mental retardation. *Research in Developmental Disabilities, 12,* 181–199.

McGrew, K.S., Johnson, D.R., & Bruininks, R.H. (1994). Factor analysis of community adjustment outcome measures for young adults with mild to severe disabilities. *Psychoeducational Assessment, 12*(1), 55–66.

McHale, J. (1980). Mental retardation and the future: A conceptual approach. In S.C. Plog & M.B. Santamour (Eds.), *The year 2000 and mental retardation* (pp. 19–70). New York: Plenum.

McKenzie v. Jefferson, 566 F. Supp 43 (D.D.C. 1983).

McKinney, J.D., & Hocutt, A.M. (1988). Policy issues in the evaluation of the Regular Education Initiative. *Learning Disabilities Focus, 4*(1), 15–23.

McKusick, V.A. (1983). *Mendelian inheritance in man: Catalogs of autosomal dominant, autosomal recessive, and X-linked phenotypes.* (6th ed.) Baltimore: Johns Hopkins University Press.

McLaren, J., & Bryson, S.E. (1987). Review of recent epidemiological studies of mental retardation: Prevalence, associated disorders and etiology. *American Journal of Mental Retardation, 92,* 243–254.

McLaughlin, M.J., Smith-Davis, J., & Burke, P.J. (1986). *Personnel to educate the handicapped in America: A status report.* College Park: University of Maryland, Institute for the Study of Exceptional Children and Youth.

McLaughlin, P.J., & Wehman, P. (1992). *Developmental disabilities.* Boston: Andover Medical.

McLaughlin, P.J., & Wehman, P. (1996). *Mental retardation and developmental disabilities* (2nd ed.). Austin, TX: Pro-Ed.

McLoughlin, J.A., & Lewis, R. (1990). *Assessing special students* (3rd ed.). Upper Saddle River, NJ: Merrill/Prentice Hall.

McNeil, M.C., Polloway, E.A., & Smith, J.D. (1984). Feral and isolated children: Historical review and analysis. *Education and Training of the Mentally Retarded, 19,* 70–79.

Meador, D.M., Osborn, R.G., Owens, M.H., Smith, E.C., & Taylor, T.L. (1991). Evaluation of environmental support in group homes for persons with mental retardation. *Mental Retardation, 29,* 159–164.

Mecham, M.J. (1989). *Utah Test of Language Development—3.* Salt Lake City, UT: Communication Research Associates.

Mehlinger, H. (1988). Technology and teaching. In D.E. Orlosky (Ed.), *Society, schools, and teacher preparation: A report of the Commission on the Future Education of Teachers* (pp. 38–47). Washington, DC: American Association of College for Teacher Education.

Meins, W. (1995). Symptoms of major depression in mentally retarded adults. *Journal of Intellectual Disability Research, 39*(1), 41–45.

Meisels, S.J., & Wiske, M.S. (1988). *Early Screening Inventory* (2nd ed.). New York: Columbia University, Teacher's College Press.

Menolascino, F.J., & Egger, M.L. (1978). *Medical dimensions of mental retardation.* Lincoln: University of Nebraska Press.

Mercer, C.D. (1991). *Students with learning disabilities* (4th ed.). Upper Saddle River, NJ: Merrill/Prentice Hall.

Mercer, C.D., & Mercer, A.R. (1993). *Teaching students with learning problems* (4th ed.). Upper Saddle River, NJ: Merrill/Prentice Hall.

Mercer, C.D., & Snell, M.E. (1977). *Learning theory research in mental retardation: Implications for teaching.* Upper Saddle River, NJ: Merrill/Prentice Hall.

Mercer, J.R. (1973a). Labeling the mentally retarded. Berkeley: University of California Press.

Mercer, J.R. (1973b). The myth of 3% prevalence. In G. Tarjan, R.K. Eyman, & C.E. Meyers (Eds.), *Sociobehavioral studies in mental retardation: Monographs of the*

American Association on Mental Deficiency, 1, 1–8. Washington, DC: American Association on Mental Deficiency.

Mercer, J.R. (1978a). *System of Multicultural Pluralistic Assessment: Parent interview manual.* San Antonio, TX: Psychological Corporation.

Mercer, J.R. (1978b). Theoretical constructs of adaptive behavior: Movement from a medical to a social-ecological perspective. In W.A. Coulter & H.W. Morrow (Eds.), *Adaptive behavior* (pp. 59–82). Orlando, FL: Grune & Stratton.

Mercer, J.R., & Lewis, J.F. (1978). *System of Multicultural Pluralistic Assessment* (SOMPA). San Antonio, TX: Psychological Corporation.

Mercer, J.R., & Lewis, J.F. (1982). *Adaptive Behavior Inventory for Children.* San Antonio, TX: Psychological Corporation.

Meryash, D.L. (1992). Characteristics of Fragile X relatives with different attitudes towards terminating an affected pregnancy. *American Journal of Mental Retardation, 96,* 528–535.

Mesibov, G.B. (1976). Mentally retarded people: 200 years in America. *Journal of Clinical Child Psychology, 5*(3), 25–29.

Messick, S. (1988). The once and future issues of validity: Assessing the meaning and consequences of measurement. In H. Wainer & H.I. Braun (Eds.), *Test validity* (pp. 33–45). Hillsdale, NJ: Erlbaum.

Meyer, L.H., Eichinger, J., & Park-Lee, S. (1987). A validation of program quality indicators in educational services for students with severe disabilities. *Journal of the Association for Persons with Severe Handicaps, 12*(4), 251–263.

Meyer, L.H., & Putnam, J. (1988). Social integration. In V. Van Hasselt, P. Strain, & M. Hersen (Eds.), *Handbook of developmental and physical disabilities* (pp. 107–133). New York: Pergamon.

Meyers, C.E., & MacMillan, D.L. (1976). Utilization of learning principles in retardation. In R. Koch & J. Dobson (Eds.), *The mentally retarded child and his family: A multidisciplinary handbook* (2nd ed., pp. 323–348). New York: Bruner/Mazel.

Meyers, C.E., Nihira, K., & Zetlin, A. (1979). The measurement of adaptive behavior. In N.R. Ellis (Ed.), *Handbook of mental deficiency: Psychological theory and research* (2nd ed., pp. 431–481). Hillsdale, NJ: Erlbaum.

Meyers, R. (1980). *Like normal people.* New York: McGraw-Hill.

Miller, D.R., & Sobelman, G. (1985). Models of the family: A critical review of alternatives. In L. L'Abate (Ed.), *The handbook of family psychology and therapy* (Vol. 1, pp. 3–37). Pacific Grove, CA: Brooks/Cole.

Miller, L.J. (1988). *Miller Assessment for Preschoolers.* San Antonio, TX: Psychological Corporation.

Miller, R. (1996). *The developmentally appropriate inclusive classroom in early education.* Albany, NY: Delmar.

Miller, T.L., & Reynolds, C.R. (Eds.). (1984). Special issue: Kaufman Assessment Battery for Children. *The Journal of Special Education, 18* (Whole No. 3).

Mills v. Board of Education of District of Columbia, 348 F. Supp. 866 (D.D.C. 1972).

Millsaps, P.A., Thackrey, M., & Cook, B.J. (1987). Dimensional structure of the Adaptive Behavior Inventory for Children (ABIC): Analyses and implications. *Journal of Psychoeducational Assessment, 5,* 61–66.

Mississippi Code Ann. § 41-21-43 through § 41-21-103 (Supp. 1991).

Mithaug, D.E., Horiuchi, C.N., & Fanning, P.N. (1985). A report on the Colorado statewide follow-up survey of special education students. *Exceptional Children, 51,* 397–404.

Mithaug, D.E., Martin, J.E., & Agran, M. (1987). Adaptability instruction: The goal of transitional programming. *Exceptional Children, 53,* 500–505.

Moeller, C.T. (1986). The effect of professionals on the family of a handicapped child. In R.R. Fewell & P.F. Vadasy (Eds.), *Families of handicapped children: Needs and supports across the life span* (pp. 149–166). Austin, TX: Pro-Ed.

Monat-Hallar, R.K. (1992). *Understanding & expressing sexuality: Responsible choices for individuals with developmental disabilities.* Baltimore: Brookes.

Morgan, D. (1981). *A primer on individualized education programs for exceptional children.* Reston, VA: Foundation for Exceptional Children.

Morgan, D.P., & Rhode, G. (1983). Teachers' attitudes toward IEPs: A two-year follow-up. *Exceptional Children, 50,* 64–67.

Morreau, E., & Bruininks, R.H. (1992). *Checklist of Adaptive Living Skills.* Chicago: Riverside.

Morris, R. (1983). *Evolution and human nature.* New York: Seaview/Putnam.

Morsink, C.V., & Lenk, L.L. (1992). The delivery of special education programs and services. *Remedial and Special Education, 13,* 33–43.

Moser, H.W. (1992). Prevention of mental retardation. In L. Rowitz (Ed.), *Mental retardation in the year 2000* (pp. 140–148). New York: Springer-Verlag.

Mosier, H.D., Grossman, H.J., & Dingman, H.F. (1965). Physical growth in mental defectives. *Pediatrics, 36,* 465–519.

Mueller, D.J., Chase, C.I., & Walden, J.D. (1988). Effects of reduced class size in primary classes. *Educational Leadership, 45*(5), 48–50.

Naglieri, J.A. (1985). *Matrix Analogies Test—Expanded Form.* San Antonio, TX: Psychological Corporation.

Naglieri, J.A., & Das, J.P. (1990). Planning, attention, simultaneous, and successive (PASS) cognitive processes as a model for intelligence. *Journal of Psychoeducational Assessment, 8,* 303–337.

Naisbitt, J. (1984). *Megatrends: Ten new directions transforming our lives.* New York: Warner.

Nanus, B. (1980). Living and working in the year 2000: Some implications for mental retardation policy. In S.C. Plog & M.B. Santamour (Eds.), *Strategies for achieving community integration of developmentally disabled citizens* (pp. 71–96). New York: Plenum.

National Institute on Disability and Rehabilitation Research. (1994). *Chartbook: Summary of data on children and youth with disabilities in the United States.* Washington, DC: U.S. Department of Education.

Nativio, D.G., & Belz, C. (1990). Childhood neurofibromatosis. *Pediatric Nursing, 16,* 575–580.

Neely, C.W. (1991). Family bonds: A mother's story about Fragile X syndrome. *LDA/Newsbriefs, 24*(4), 3, 6, 8.

Neisworth, J.T., & Bagnato, S.J. (1988). Developmental retardation. In V.B. Van Hasselt & M. Hersen (Eds.), *Psychological evaluation of the developmentally and physically disabled* (pp. 179–212). New York: Plenum.

Neisworth, J.T., & Smith, R.M. (1978). *Retardation: Issues, assessment and intervention.* New York: McGraw-Hill.

New York Association for Retarded Children v. Rockefeller, 357 F. Supp. 752 (E.D. N.Y. 1973). Final consent judgment entered, Civil Nos. 72C 356, 72C 357 (E.D. N.Y. entered May 5, 1975).

Newman, H.H., Freeman, F.N., & Holzinger, K.J. (1937). *Twins: A study of heredity and environment.* Chicago: University of Chicago Press.

Nietupski, J.A., & Hamre-Nietupski, S.M. (1979). Teaching auxiliary communication skills to severely handicapped students. *AAESPH Review, 4*(2), 107–123.

Nietupski, J.A., & Hamre-Nietupski, S.M. (1987). An ecological approach to curriculum development. In L. Goetz, D. Guess, & K. Stremel Campbell (Eds.), *Innovative program design for individuals with dual sensory impairments* (pp. 225–253). Baltimore: Brookes.

Nietupski, J.A., Hamre-Nietupski, S.M., Schuetz, G., & Ockwood, L. (1980). The delivery of communication therapy services to severely handicapped students: A plan for change. *The Journal of the Association for the Severely Handicapped, 6*(1), 13–23.

Nihira, K. (1969). Factorial dimensions of adaptive behavior in adult retardates. *American Journal of Mental Deficiency, 73,* 868–878.

Nihira, K., Leland, H., & Lambert, N. (1993a). *AAMR Adaptive Behavior Scale—Residential and Community* (2nd ed.). Austin, TX: Pro-Ed.

Nihira, K., Leland, H., & Lambert, N. (1993b). *AAMR Adaptive Behavior Scale—Residential and Community (2nd ed.): Technical manual.* Austin, TX: Pro-Ed.

Nirje, B. (1969). The normalization principle and its human management implications. In R.B. Kugel & W. Wolfensberger (Eds.), *Changing patterns in residential services for the mentally retarded* (pp. 179–195). Washington, DC: U.S. Government Printing Office.

Nisbet, J., & Hagner, D. (1988). Natural supports in the workplace: A reexamination of supported employment. *Journal of the Association for Persons with Severe Handicaps, 13,* 260–267.

Nolley, D., & Nolley, B. (1984). Microcomputer data analysis at a clinical mental retardation site. *Mental Retardation, 22,* 85–89.

Noonan, M.J., Brown, F., Mulligan, M., & Rettig, M.A. (1982). Educability of severely handicapped persons: Both sides of the issue. *The Journal of the Association for Persons with Severe Handicaps, 7,* 3–12.

Nyhan, W.L. (1976). Behavior in the Lesch-Nyhan syndrome. *Journal of Autism & Childhood Schizophrenia, 6,* 235–252.

Nyhan, W.L., Johnson, H.G., Kaufman, I.A., & Jones, K. (1980). Serotonergic approaches to the modification of behavior in the Lesch-Nyhan syndrome. *Applied Behavior in Mental Retardation, 1,* 25–40.

O'Connell, J.C. (1986). Managing small group instruction in an integrated preschool setting. *Teaching Exceptional Children, 18,* 166–171.

O'Connor, N. (1966). The prevalence of mental defect. In A.A. Clarke & A.D. Clarke (Eds.), *Mental deficiency: The changing outlook* (rev. ed., pp. 23–43). New York: Free Press.

O'Connor, N. (1975). Imbecility and color blindness. *American Journal of Mental Deficiency, 62,* 83–87.

O'Connor v. Donaldson, 493 F. 2nd 507 (5th Cir. 1974), vacated and remanded on the issue of immunity, 95 S. Ct. 258b (1975).

Olbrisch, R.R. (1982). Plastic surgical management of children with Down's syndrome: Indications and results. *British Journal of Plastic Surgery, 35,* 195–200.

Olesen, D.E. (1996). The top ten technologies for the next ten years. In E. Cornish (Ed.), *Exploring your future: Living, learning, and working in the information age* (pp. 67–71). Bethesda, MD: World Future Society.

Olswang, L.B., & Bain, B.A. (1988). Assessment of language in developmentally disabled infants and preschoolers. In T.D. Wachs & R. Sheehan (Eds.), *Assessment of young developmentally disabled children* (pp. 285–320). New York: Plenum.

Opuda, M.J. (1994, April). *Home school, private schools, parochial schools—What are a public school's special education obligations?* Paper presented at the annual international convention of the Council for Exceptional Children. Denver CO. (ERIC Document Reproduction Service No. ED 384 174)

Orelove, F.P., & Sobsey, R. (1984). *Educating individuals with multiple disabilities.* Baltimore: Brookes.

Orelove, F.P., & Sobsey, R. (1987). *Multiple disabilities: A transdisciplinary approach.* Baltimore: Brookes.

Ormerod, J.J., & Huebner, E.S. (1988). Crisis intervention: Facilitating parental acceptance of a child's handicap. *Psychology in the Schools, 25,* 422–428.

Osgood, C., Gorsuch, L., & McGrew, B. (1966). *Survey of mental retardation services in the Kansas City metropolitan area.* Kansas City, MO: Institute for Community Studies.

Otto, P.L., Sulzbacher, S.I., & Worthington-Roberts, B.S. (1982). Sucrose-induced behavior changes of persons with Prader Willi syndrome. *American Journal of Mental Deficiency, 86,* 335–341.

Ouellete, E.M. (1984). *Developmental handicaps: Prevention and treatment, II. A cooperative project between University affiliated facilities and state MCH/CC programs.* Rockville, MD: Office for Maternal and Child Health Services. (ERIC Document Reproduction Service No. ED 276 193)

Page, E.G. (1972). Miracle in Milwaukee: Raising the I.Q. *Educational Researcher, 15,* 8–16.

Page, E.G., & Grandon, G.M. (1981). Massive intervention and child intelligence: The Milwaukee Project in critical perspective. *Journal of Special Education, 15,* 239–256.

Paige, D.M. (1975). Nutritional deficiency and school performance. In R.A. Haslam & P.J. Valletutti (Eds.), *Medical problems in the classroom* (pp. 253–279). Baltimore: University Park Press.

Parker, R. (1991a). *OASIS-2 Aptitude Survey.* Austin, TX: Pro-Ed.

Parker, R. (1991b). *OASIS-2 Interest Schedule.* Austin, TX: Pro-Ed.

Parkes, W.F., Lasker, L. (Producers), & Marshall, P. (Director). (1991). *Awakenings* [Film]. Burbank, CA: Columbia Pictures.

Parsons, C.L., Iacone, T.A., & Rozner, L. (1987). Effect of tongue reduction on articulation in children with Down's syndrome. *American Journal of Mental Deficiency, 91,* 328–332.

Parsons, J.A., May, J.G., & Menolascino, F.J. (1984). The nature and incidence of mental illness in mentally retarded individuals. In F.J. Menolascino & J.A. Stark (Eds.), *Handbook of mental illness in the mentally retarded* (pp. 3–43). New York: Plenum.

Pasamanick, B. (1959). Influence of sociocultural variables upon organic factors in mental retardation. *American Journal of Mental Deficiency, 64,* 316–320.

PASE (Parents in Action on Special Education) v. Hannon, U.S. District Court, N.D. Ill., No. 74 (3586) (July 1980).

Patrick, J.L., & Reschly, D.L. (1982). Relationship of state educational criteria and demographic variables to school-system prevalence of mental retardation. *American Journal of Mental Deficiency, 86,* 351–360.

Patterson, D. (1987). The causes of Down syndrome. *Scientific American, 52,* 112–118.

Patton, J.R., Blackbourn, J.M., & Fad, K.S. (1996). *Exceptional individuals in focus* (6th ed.). Upper Saddle River, NJ: Merrill/Prentice Hall.

Patton, J.R., Cronin, M.E., & Jairrels, V. (1997). Curricular implications of transition: Life skills instruction as an integral part of transition education. *Remedial and Special Education, 18,* 294–306.

Patton, J.R., Cronin, M.E., & Wood, S. (1998). *Techniques for integrating life skills topics into existing content areas.* Unpublished manuscript.

Patton, J.R., & Dunn, C. (1998). *Transition from school to young adulthood for students with special needs: Basic concepts and recommended practices.* Austin, TX: Pro-Ed.

Patton, J.R., Kauffman, J.M., Blackbourn, J.M., & Brown, J.B. (1991). *Exceptional children in focus* (5th ed.). Upper Saddle River, NJ: Merrill/Prentice Hall.

Patton, J.R., & Polloway, E.A. (in press). Mild mental retardation. In N. Haring, L. McCormick, & T.G. Haring (Eds.), *Exceptional children and youth* (6th ed.). Upper Saddle River, NJ: Merrill/Prentice Hall.

Payne, J.S., Polloway, E.A., Smith, J.E., & Payne, R.A. (1981). *Strategies for teaching the mentally retarded* (2nd ed.). Upper Saddle River, NJ: Merrill/Prentice Hall.

Peck, C.A., Donaldson, J., & Pezzoli, M. (1990). Some benefits nonhandicapped adolescents perceive for themselves from their social relationships with peers who have severe handicaps. *The Journal of the Association for Persons with Severe Handicaps, 15*(4), 241–249.

Pennhurst State School v. Halderman, 451 U.S. 1, 101 S. Ct. 1531, 67, L. Ed. 2nd 694 (1981).

Pennsylvania Association for Retarded Children (PARC) v. Commonwealth of Pennsylvania, Civil Action No. 71-42, 3-Judge Court (E.D. Pa., 1971).

Pennsylvania Association for Retarded Children (PARC) v. Commonwealth of Pennsylvania, 334 F.Supp. 1257 (E.D. Pa. 1971), 343 F.Supp. 279 (E.D. Pa. 1972).

Penrose, L.S. (1966). *The biology of mental defect* (rev. ed.). Orlando, FL: Grune & Stratton.

Penry v. Lynaugh, 109 S.C. 2934 (1989).

Perske, R. (1991). *Unequal justice? What can happen when persons with retardation or other developmental disabilities encounter the criminal justice system.* Nashville, TN: Abingdon Press.

Peters, J.M., Templeman, T.P., & Brostrom, G. (1987). The school and community partnership: Planning transition for students with severe handicaps. *Exceptional Children, 53,* 531–536.

Peterson, N.L. (1986). *Early intervention for handicapped and at-risk children.* Denver: Love Publishing.

Peterson, N.L. (1987). *Early intervention for handicapped and at-risk children: An introduction to early childhood special education.* Denver, CO: Love.

Piaget, J. (1952). *The origins of intelligence in children.* New York: International Universities Press.

Piaget, J. (1969). *The theory of stages in cognitive development.* New York: McGraw-Hill.

Piaget, J., & Inhelder, B. (1969). *The psychology of the child.* New York: Basic Books.

Piper, W. (1976). *The little engine that could.* New York: Platt & Munk/Grosset & Dunlap. (Original work published 1930)

Pipitone, P. (1992). Acquired pediatric brain damage: Diverse causes. *Headlines, 3*(5), 5.

Plog, S.C. (1980). The year 2000 and mental retardation: An interpretation and critique. In S.C. Plog & M.B. Santamour (Eds.), *Strategies for achieving community integration of developmentally disabled citizens* (pp. 201–226). New York: Plenum.

Plog, S.C., & Santamour, M.B. (Eds.). (1980). *Strategies for achieving community integration of developmentally disabled citizens.* New York: Plenum Press.

Plomin, R. (1994). *Genetics and experience: The interplay between nature and nurture.* Thousand Oaks, CA: Sage.

Polloway, E.A., Epstein, M.H., & Cullinan, D. (1985). Prevalence of behavior problems among educable mentally retarded students. *Education and Training of the Mentally Retarded, 20,* 3–13.

Polloway, E.A., Epstein, M.H., Patton, J.R., Cullinan, D., & Luebke, J. (1986). Demographic, social and behavioral characteristics of students with educable mental retardation. *Education and Training of the Mentally Retarded, 21,* 27–34.

Polloway, E.A., & Patton, J.R. (1993). *Strategies for teaching learners with special needs* (5th ed.). Upper Saddle River, NJ: Prentice Hall.

Polloway, E.A., & Patton, J.R. (1997). *Strategies for teaching learners with special needs* (6th ed.). Upper Saddle River, NJ: Merrill/Prentice Hall.

Polloway, E.A., Patton, J.R., Epstein, M.H., & Smith, T.E. (1989). Comprehensive curriculum for students with mild handicaps. *Focus on Exceptional Children, 21*(8), 1–12.

Polloway, E.A., & Rucker, H. (1997). Etiology: Biological and environmental considerations. In T.E.C. Smith, C.A. Dowdy, E.A. Polloway, & G.E. Blalock (Eds.), *Children and adults with learning disabilities* (pp. 160–187). Boston: Allyn & Bacon.

Polloway, E.A., & Smith, J.D. (1983). Changes in mild mental retardation: Population, programs, and perspectives. *Exceptional Children, 50,* 149–159.

Polloway, E.A., & Smith, J.D. (1984). The right to life: A survey of attitudes among the staff of a residential facility for mentally retarded persons. In J.D. Smith & E.A. Polloway (Eds.), *Special education in transition* (pp. 83–88). Lynchburg, VA: Vahnity Press.

Polloway, E.A., & Smith, J.D. (1987). Current status of the mild mental retardation construct: Identification, placement, and programs. In M.C. Wang, M.C. Reynolds, & H.J. Wahlberg (Eds.), *The handbook of special education: Research and practice* (pp. 1–22). New York: Pergamon.

Polloway, E.A., Smith, J.D., Patton, J.R., & Smith, T.E.C. (1996). Historical changes in mental retardation and developmental disabilities. *Education and Training in Mental Retardation and Developmental Disabilities, 31,* 3–12.

Poolaw v. Bishop, 67 F.3rd 830 (9th Cir. 1995).

Porter, M.E., & Stodden, R.A. (1986). A curriculum-based vocational assessment procedure: Addressing the school-to-work transition needs of secondary schools. *Career Development for Exceptional Individuals, 9,* 121–128.

Porteus, S.D. (1965). *Porteus Mazes.* San Antonio, TX: Psychological Corporation.

Powell, T.H., Aiken, J.M., & Smylie, M.A. (1982). Treatment of involuntary euthanasia for severely handicapped newborns: Issues of philosophy and public policy. *Journal of the Association for the Severely Handicapped, 7*(4), 3–10.

Powell, T.H., & Gallagher, P.A. (1993). *Brothers and sisters—A special part of exceptional families* (2nd ed.). Baltimore, MD: Brookes.

Powell, T.H., Panscofar, E.L., Streers, D.E., Butterworth, J., Itzkowitz, J.S., & Rainforth, B. (1991). *Supported employment: Providing integrated employment opportunities for persons with disabilities.* New York: Longman.

Powers, L.E. (1992). Disability and grief: From tragedy to challenge. In G.H. Singer & L.E. Powers (Eds.), *Families, disability, and empowerment: Active coping skills and strategies for family interventions* (pp. 119–149). Baltimore, MD: Brookes.

Powers, S.I. (1989). Family systems throughout the lifespan: Interactive consultations of development, meaning, and behavior. In K. Kreppner & R.M. Lerner (Eds.), *Family systems and lifespan development* (pp. 271–287). Mahwah, NJ: Erlbaum.

President's Committee on Mental Retardation (PCMR). (1970). *The six-hour retarded child.* Washington, DC: U.S. Government Printing Office.

President's Committee on Mental Retardation (PCMR). (1976a). *Mental retardation: Century of decision*. Washington, DC: U.S. Government Printing Office.

President's Committee on Mental Retardation (PCMR). (1976b). *Mental retardation: The known and the unknown*. Washington, DC: U.S. Government Printing Office.

President's Committee on Mental Retardation (PCMR). (1978, March). *Untitled*. Washington, DC: PCMR Newsclipping Service.

Prosser, C.L. (1986). *Adaptational biology: Molecules to organisms*. New York: Wiley.

Prout, H.T., & Sheldon, K.L. (1984). Classifying mental retardation in vocational rehabilitation: A study of diagnostic practices and their adherence to accepted guidelines. *Rehabilitation Counseling Bulletin, 28*, 125–131.

Prouty, R., & Lakin, K.C. (Ed.). (1996). *Residential services for persons with developmental disabilities: Status and trends through 1995*. Minneapolis: University of Minnesota, Institute on Community Integration.

Pueschel, S.M. (1991). Ethical considerations relating to prenatal diagnosis of fetuses with Down syndrome. *Mental Retardation, 29*, 185–190.

Pueschel, S.M., Hays, R.M., & Mendoza, T. (1983). Familial X-linked mental retardation syndrome associated with minor congenital anomalies. *American Journal of Mental Deficiency, 87*, 372–376.

Pugach, M.C., & Johnson, L.J. (1989). Prereferral interventions: Progress, problems, and challenges. *Exceptional Children, 56*, 217–226.

Quinn, J.M., Sherman, J.A., Sheldon, J.B., Quinn, L.M., & Harchik, A.E. (1992). Social validation of component behaviors of following instructions, accepting criticism, and negotiating. *Journal of Applied Behavior Analysis, 25*(2), 401–413.

Racino, J.A., Taylor, S.J., Walker, P., & O'Connor, S. (1993). Introduction. In J. Racino, P. Walker, S. O'Connor, & S. Taylor (Eds.), *Housing, support, and community: Choice and strategies for adults with disabilities* (pp. 1–30). Baltimore: Brookes.

Rainforth, B., & York, J. (1991). Handling and positioning. In F. Orelove & D. Sobsey (Eds.), *Educating children with multiple disabilities: A transdisciplinary approach* (pp. 79–118). Baltimore: Brookes.

Ramey, C.T., & Ramey, S.L. (1992). Effective early intervention. *Mental Retardation, 30*, 337–345.

Ramey, C.T., et al. (1985). Project CARE: A comparison of two early intervention strategies to prevent retarded development. *Topics in Early Childhood Special Education, 5*(2), pp. 15–16.

Rando, T.A. (1993). *Treatment of complicated mourning*. Champaign, IL: Research Press.

Rappaport, J. (1977). *Community psychology: Values, research, and action*. New York: Holt, Rinehart, & Winston.

Raven, J.C. (1938). *Standard Progressive Matrices*. London: Lewis.

Raynes, N.V., Bumstead, D.C., & Pratt, M.W. (1974). Unitization: Its effect on residential care practices. *Mental Retardation, 12*(4), 120–124.

Reber, M. (1992). Dual diagnosis: Psychiatric disorders and mental retardation. In M. Batshaw & Y.M. Perret (Eds.), *Children with disabilities: A medical primer* (3rd ed., pp. 421–440). Baltimore: Brookes.

Reed, E.W., & Reed, S.C. (1965). *Mental retardation: A family study*. Philadelphia: Saunders.

Rehabilitation Research and Training Center. (1988). What the research shows: New horizons for supported employment. *RRTC, 4*(2). (ERIC Document Reproduction Service No. 298 749)

Reid, D.H., Parsons, M.B., & Schepis, M.M. (1990). Management practices that affect the relative utility of aversive and nonaversive procedures. In S.L. Harris, & J.S.

Handleman (Eds.), *Aversive and nonaversive interventions: Controlling life-threatening behavior by the developmentally disabled* (pp. 144–162). New York: Springer-Verlag.

Reiss, D. (1981). *The family's construction of reality.* Cambridge, MA: Harvard University Press.

Reiss, S.P. (1987). *Reiss Screen for Maladaptive Behavior.* Worthington, OH: International Diagnostic Systems.

Repp, A.C. (1983). Teaching the mentally retarded. Upper Saddle River, NJ: Prentice Hall.

Reschly, D. (1981). Evaluation of the effects of SOMPA measures on classification of students as mildly mentally retarded. *American Journal of Mental Deficiency, 86,* 16–20.

Reschly, D. (1982). Assessing mild mental retardation: The influence of adaptive behavior, sociocultural status, and prospects for nonbiased assessment. In C.R. Reynolds & T.B. Gutkin (Eds.), *The handbook of school psychology* (pp. 209–242). New York: Wiley.

Reschly, D. (1985). Best practices: Adaptive behavior. In A. Thomas & J. Grimes (Eds.), *Best practices in school psychology* (pp. 353–368). Kent, OH: National Association of School Psychologists.

Reschly, D. (1988). Incorporating adaptive behavior deficits into instructional programs. In G.A. Robinson, J.R. Patton, E.A. Polloway, & L.R. Sargent (Eds.), *Best practices in mental disabilities* (Vol. 2, pp. 53–80). Des Moines: Iowa State Department of Education.

Reschly, D., Robinson, G., Volmer, L., & Wilson, L. (1988). *Iowa mental disabilities research report: Final report and executive summary.* Des Moines: Iowa State Department of Education.

Resnick, O. (1988). Nutrition, neurotransmitter regulation and developmental pharmacology. In F.J. Menolascino & J.A. Stark (Eds.), *Preventive and curative intervention in mental retardation* (pp. 161–176). Baltimore: Brookes.

Resource Center on Substance Abuse and Prevention and Disabilities. (1992). *Mental retardation: A look at alcohol and other drug abuse prevention.* Washington, DC: U.S. Department of Health and Human Services, Office for Substance Abuse Prevention.

Restak, R. (1975, September). Genetic counseling for defective parents: The danger of knowing too much. *Psychology Today,* pp. 21–23, 92–93.

Reynolds, C.R. (1984a). The K-ABC [Special issue]. *The Journal of Special Education, 18*(3).

Reynolds, C.R. (1984b). A review of the Kaufman Assessment Battery for Children (K-ABC). In R.J. Sternberg (Ed.), *Encyclopedia of human intelligence* (pp. 633–638). New York: Macmillan.

Reynolds, C.R. (1988). Sympathy not sense: The appeal of the Stanford-Binet fourth edition. *Measurement & Evaluation in Counseling and Development, 21,* 45.

Reynolds, C.R., & Clark, J.H. (1983). Assessment of cognitive abilities. In K.D. Paget & B.A. Bracken (Eds.), *The psychoeducational assessment of preschool children* (pp. 163–189). Orlando, FL: Grune & Stratton.

Reynolds, M.C. (1989). A historical perspective: The delivery of special education to mildly disabled and at-risk students. *Remedial and Special Education, 10*(6), 7–11.

Reynolds, M.C., Wang, M.C., & Walberg, H.J. (1987). The necessary restructuring of special and regular education. *Exceptional Children, 20*(5), 1–8.

Rice, F.P. (1986). *Adult development and aging.* Boston: Allyn & Bacon.

Rich, D. (1985). *The forgotten factor in school success: The family.* Washington, DC: Home and School Institute.

Richards, B.W., Sylvester, R.E., & Brooker, C. (1981). Fragile X-linked mental retardation: The Martin-Bell syndrome. *Journal of Mental Deficiency Research, 25,* 253–258.

Rimland, B. (1992). Facilitated communication: Now the bad news. *Autism Research Review International, 6*(1), 3.

Riordan, J., & Vasa, S.F. (1991). Accommodations for and participation of persons with disabilities in religious practice. *Education and Training in Mental Retardation, 26*(2), 151–155.

Roberts, R.N., Wasik, B.H., Casto, G., & Ramey, C.T. (1991). Family support in the home: Programs, policy and social change. *American Psychologist, 46,* 131–137.

Robinault, I.P., & Denhoff, E. (1973). The multiple dysfunctions called cerebral palsy. In A.B. Cobb (Ed.), *Medical and psychological aspects of disability.* Springfield, IL: Thomas.

Robinson, N.K., & Robinson, H.B. (1976). *The mentally retarded child* (2nd ed.). New York: McGraw-Hill.

Rogers, R.C., & Simensen, R.J. (1987). Fragile X syndrome: A common etiology of mental retardation. *American Journal of Mental Deficiency, 91,* 445–449.

Roistacher, R.C., Holstrom, E.I., Cantril, A.H., & Chase, J.T. (1982). *Toward a comprehensive data system on the demographic and epidemiological characteristics of the handicapped population: Final report.* Washington, DC: National Institute of Handicapped Research. (ERIC Document Reproduction Service No. ED 182 465)

Rosen, J.W., & Burchard, S.N. (1990). Community activities and social support networks: A social comparison of adults with and adults without mental retardation. *Education and Training in Mental Retardation, 25,* 193–203.

Rosen, M., Clark, G., & Kivitz, M.S. (1977). *Habilitation of the handicapped: New dimensions in programs for the developmentally disabled.* Baltimore: MD: Brookes.

Rothstein, L.F. (1995). *Special education law.* New York: Longman.

Rotter, J.B. (1954). *Social learning and clinical psychology.* Englewood Cliffs, NJ: Prentice Hall.

Rovet, J. (1993). The psychoeducational characteristics of children with Turner syndrome and adolescents with insulin-dependent diabetes mellitus. *Journal of Learning Disabilities, 26,* 333–341.

Rowitz, L. (1992). Predictions for the 1990s and beyond. In L. Rowitz (Ed.), *Mental retardation in the year 2000* (pp. 353–366). New York: Springer-Verlag.

Rusch, F.R. (1983). Competitive vocational training. In M.E. Snell (Ed.), *Systematic instruction of the moderately and severely handicapped* (2nd ed., pp. 503–525). Upper Saddle River, NJ: Merrill/Prentice Hall.

Rusch, F.R., Chadsey-Rusch, J., & Johnson, J.R. (1991). Supported employment: emerging opportunities for employment integration. In L.H. Meyer, C.A. Peck, & L. Brown (Eds.), *Critical issues in the lives of people with severe disabilities* (pp. 145–170). Baltimore: Brookes.

Rusch, F.R., Enchelmaier, J.F., & Kohler, P.D. (1994). Employment outcomes and activities for youths in transition. *Career Development for Exceptional Individuals, 17*(1), 1–15.

Rusch, F.R., & Phelps, L.A. (1987). Secondary special education and transition from school to work: A national priority. *Exceptional Children, 53,* 487–492.

Rushton, J.P. (1995). *Race, evolution, and behavior: A life history perspective*. New Brunswick, NJ: Transaction.

Russel, A.T., & Forness, S.R. (1985). Behavioral disturbance in mentally retarded children in TMR and EMR classrooms. *American Journal of Mental Deficiency, 89,* 338–344.

Ryan, C.S., & Coyne, A. (1985). Effects of group homes on neighborhood property values. *Mental Retardation, 23,* 241–245.

Ryan, W. (1976). *Blaming the victim* (rev. ed.). New York: Vintage.

Rynders, J.E., & Horrobin, J.M. (1990). Always trainable? Never educable? Updating educational expectations concerning children with Down syndrome. *American Journal of Mental Retardation, 95,* 77–83.

Rynders, J.E., & Schleien, S.J. (1991). *Together successfully: Creating recreational and educational programs that integrate people with and without disabilities.* Arlington, TX: ARC.

Rynders, J.E., Spiker, D., & Horrobin, J.M. (1978). Underestimating the educability of Down's syndrome children: Examination of methodological problems in recent literature. *American Journal of Mental Deficiency, 82,* 440–448.

Safford, P.L., & Safford, E.J. (1996). *A history of childhood and disability*. New York: Teachers College Press.

Sailor, W., & Guess, D. (1983). *Severely handicapped students: An instructional design.* Boston: Houghton Mifflin.

Sailor, W., Halvorsen, A., Anderson, J., Goetz, O.L., Gee, K., Doering, K., & Hunt, P. (1986). Community intensive instruction. In R. Horner, L. Meyer, & H.D. Fredericks (Eds.), *Education of learners with severe handicaps: Exemplary service strategies* (pp. 251–288). Baltimore: Brookes.

Salvia, J., & Ysseldyke, J.E. (1991). *Assessment* (5th ed.). Boston: Houghton Mifflin.

Salvia, J., & Ysseldyke, J.E. (1995). *Assessment* (6th ed.). Boston: Houghton Mifflin.

San Antonio Independent School District v. Rodriguez, 411 U.S. (1973).

Sandoval, J. (1992). Using the DAS with multi-cultural populations: Issues of test bias. *Journal of Psychoeducational Assessment, 10,* 88–91.

Sarason, S.B. (1985). *Psychology and mental retardation: Perspectives in change.* Austin, TX: Pro-Ed.

Sargent, L.R., & Fiddler, D.A. (1987). Extended school year programs: In support of the concept. *Education and Training of the Mentally Retarded, 22,* 3–11.

Sayegh, Y., & Dennis, W. (1965). The effect of supplementary experiences upon the behavioral development of infants in institutions. *Child Development, 36*(1), 81–90.

Scarr, S., & Carter-Saltzman, L. (1982). Genetics and intelligence. In R.J. Sternberg (Ed.), *Handbook of human intelligence* (pp. 798–896). Cambridge, UK: Cambridge University Press.

Scarr-Salapatek, S. (1971a). Race, social class and IQ. *Science, 174,* 1285–1295.

Scarr-Salapatek, S. (1971b). Unknowns in the IQ equation. *Science, 174,* 1223–1228.

Schakel, J.A. (1987, June). Preschool practices, problems, & issues: A summary of the results of the Preschool Interest Group Questionnaire. *Preschool Interests,* p. 3.

Schalock, R.L. (1986). *Transition from school to work*. Washington, DC: National Association of Rehabilitation Facilities.

Schalock, R.L., & Kiernan, W.E. (1990). *Habilitation planning for adults with developmental disabilities*. New York: Springer-Verlag.

Schalock, R.L., & Koehler, R.S. (1988). *Individual assessment/planning for home and community living skills*. Hastings: Mid-Nebraska Mental Retardation Services.

Schalock, R.L., & Lilley, M.A. (1986). Placement from community based mental retardation programs: How well do clients do after 8–10 years? *American Journal of Mental Deficiency, 90,* 669–676.

Schalock, R.L., McGaughey, M.J., & Kiernan, W.E. (1989). Placement into nonsheltered employment: Findings from national employment surveys. *American Journal on Mental Retardation, 94,* 80–87.

Scheerenberger, R.S. (1976a). *Current trends and status of public residential facilities for the mentally retarded, 1974.* Madison, WI: National Association of Superintendents of Public Residential Facilities for the Mentally Retarded.

Scheerenberger, R.S. (1976b). *Deinstitutionalization and institutional reform.* Springfield, IL: Thomas.

Scheerenberger, R.S. (1977). A study of public residential facilities, 1976. *Mental Retardation, 15*(5), 5.

Scheerenberger, R.S. (1981). Deinstitutionalization: Trends and difficulties. In R.H. Bruininks, C.E. Meyers, B.B. Sigford, & K.C. Lakin (Eds.), *Deinstitutionalization and community adjustment of mentally retarded people* (pp. 3–13). Washington, DC: American Association on Mental Retardation.

Scheerenberger, R.S. (1982). Public residential services, 1981: Status and trends. *Mental Retardation, 20,* 210–215.

Scheerenberger, R.S. (1992). *Public residential facilities for persons with mental retardation: FY 1990–91.* Madison, WI: National Association of Superintendents of Public Residential Facilities for the Mentally Retarded.

Scheerenberger, R.S., & Felsenthal, D. (1977). Community settings for mentally retarded persons: Satisfaction and activities. *Mental Retardation, 15*(4), 3–7.

Scheiderman, G., Lowden, J.A., & Rae-Grant, Q. (1978). Tay-Sachs and related storage diseases: Family planning. *Mental Retardation, 16,* 13–15.

Schleien, S.J., Certo, N.J., & Muccino, A. (1984). Acquisition of leisure skills by a severely handicapped adolescent: A data based instructional program. *Education and Training of the Mentally Retarded, 19*(4), 297–305.

Schleien, S.J., Meyer, L.H., Heyne, L.A., & Brandt, B.B. (1995). *Lifelong leisure skills and lifestyles for persons with developmental disabilities.* Baltimore: Brookes.

Schleien, S.J., & Ray, M.T. (1988). *Community recreation and persons with disabilities:* Strategies for integration. Baltimore: Brookes.

Schleien, S.J., Ray, M.T., & Green, F.P. (1996). *Community recreation and people with disabilities: Strategies for inclusion* (2nd ed.). Baltimore: Brookes.

Schultz, D.P., & Schultz, S.E. (1987). *A history of modern psychology* (4th ed.). San Diego: Harcourt Brace Jovanovich.

Schultz, D.P., & Schultz, S.E. (1996). *A history of modern psychology* (6th ed.). San Diego: Harcourt Brace Jovanovich.

Schultz, F.R. (1983). Phenylketonuria and other metabolic diseases. In J.A. Blackman (Ed.), *Medical aspects of developmental disabilities in children birth to three* (pp. 197–201). Iowa City: University of Iowa Press.

Schumaker, J.B., & Deshler, D.D. (1988). Implementing the regular education initiative in secondary schools: A different ball game. *Journal of Learning Disabilities, 21,* 36–42.

Schuster, J.W. (1990). Sheltered workshops: Financial and philosophical liabilities. *Mental Retardation, 28,* 233–239.

Schutz, R.P. (1988). New directions and strategies in habilitation services: Toward meaningful employment outcomes. In L.W. Heal, J.I. Haney, & A.R. Novak Amads

(Eds.), *Integration of developmentally disabled individuals into the community* (2nd ed.). Baltimore: Brookes.

Scott, G.M., Smith, T.E.C., Hendricks, M.D., & Polloway, E.A. (1997). *Prader-Willi syndrome: A review and implications for educational interventions*. Manuscript submitted for publication.

Scudder, R.R., & Tremain, D.H. (1992). Repair behaviors of children with and without mental retardation. *Mental Retardation, 30,* 277–282.

Seguin, E.O. (1846). *Traitement moral, hygiene et education des idiots et des autres enfants arrieres*. Paris: Baillier.

Seligman, M.E. (1975). *Helplessness: On depression, development, and death*. San Francisco: Freeman.

Sells, C.J., & Paeth, S. (1987). Health and safety in day-care. *Topics in Early Childhood Special Education, 7*(1), 61–72.

Seltzer, M.M. (1984). Correlates of community opposition to community residences for mentally retarded persons. *American Journal of Mental Deficiency, 89*(1), 1–8.

Seltzer, M.M. (1988). Structure and patterns of service utilization by elderly persons with mental retardation. *Mental Retardation, 26*(4), 181–185.

Seltzer, M.M. (1992). Family caregiving across the full lifespan. In L. Rowitz (Ed.), *Mental retardation in the year 2000* (pp. 85–100). New York: Springer-Verlag.

Seltzer, M.M., & Krauss, M.W. (1994). Aging parents with resident adult children: The impact of life-long care giving. In M.M. Seltzer, M.W. Krauss, & M.P. Janicki (Eds.), *Life course perspectives on adulthood and old age* (pp. 3–18). Washington, DC: American Association on Mental Retardation.

Semmel, M.I., Abernathy, T.V., Butera, G., & Lesat, S. (1991). Teacher perceptions of the regular education initiative. *Exceptional Children, 58,* 9–24.

Seymour, H.N., & Wyatt, T. (1992). Speech and language assessment of preschool children. In E.V. Nuttall, I. Romero, & J. Kalesnik (Eds.), *Assessing and screening preschoolers: Psychological and educational dimensions* (pp. 193–212). Boston: Allyn & Bacon.

Sherman, J.A., Sheldon, J.B., Harchik, A.E., Edwards, K., & Quinn, J.M. (1992). Social evaluations of behaviors comprising three social skills and a comparison of the performance of people with and without mental retardation. *American Journal on Mental Retardation, 96,* 419–431.

Shields, J. (1962). *Monozygotic twins*. New York: Oxford University Press.

Shipe, D., Neisman, L.E., Chung, C.Y., Darnell, A., & Kelley, S. (1968). The relationship between cytogenetic constitution, physical stigmata, and intelligence in Down's syndrome. *American Journal of Mental Deficiency, 72,* 789–797.

Showers, B. (1985). Teachers coaching teachers. *Educational Leadership, 42*(7), 43–48.

Simpson, R.L., (1990). *Conferencing parents of exceptional children* (2nd ed.). Austin, TX: Pro-Ed.

Singer, G.H., & Irvin, L.K. (Eds.). (1989). *Support for caregiving families: Enabling positive adaptation to disability*. Baltimore: Brookes.

Sitlington, P.L. (1996). Transition to living: The neglected components of transition programming for individuals with learning disabilities. *Journal of Learning Disabilities, 29,* 31–39, 52.

Sitlington, P.L., Neubert, D.A., Begun, W., Lombard, R.C., & Leconte, P.J. (1996). *Assess for success: Handbook on transition assessment*. Reston, VA: Division on Career Development and Transition, Council for Exceptional Children.

Skeels, H.M. (1942). A study of the effects of differential stimulation on mentally retarded children: A follow-up report. *American Journal of Mental Deficiency, 46,* 340–350.

Skeels, H.M. (1966). Adult status of children with contrasting early life experiences. *Monographs of the Society for Research in Child Development, 31.*

Skeels, H.M., & Dye, H.B. (1939). A study of the effects of differential stimulation on mentally retarded children. *Convention Proceedings of the American Association on Mental Deficiency, 44,* 114–136.

Skinner, B.F. (1953). *Science and human behavior.* New York: Macmillan.

Skrtic, T.M. (1991). The special education paradox: Equity as a way to excellence. *Harvard Educational Review, 61*(2), 148–206.

Sloan, S.Z., & L'Abate, L. (1985). Intimacy. In L. L'Abate (Ed.), *The handbook of family psychology and therapy* (Vol. 1, pp. 405–427). Pacific Grove, CA: Brooks/Cole.

Sloan, W., & Harmon, H.H. (1947). Constancy of IQ in mental defectives. *Pedagogical Seminary and Journal of Genetic Psychology, 71*(2), 177–185.

Sloan, W., & Stevens, H.A. (1976). *A century of concern: A history of the American Association on Mental Deficiency 1876–1976.* Washington, DC: American Association on Mental Retardation.

Smith, B.J., & Strain, P.S. (1984). The argument for early intervention (Fact sheet). *ERIC Digest.* Reston, VA: Council for Exceptional Children.

Smith, B.J., & Strain, P.S. (1988). Early childhood special education in the next decade: Implementing and expanding P.L. 99-457. *Topics in Early Childhood Special Education, 8*(1), 34–47.

Smith, B.J., Vincent, L., Toole, A., Garland, C., Dunst, C., McCarten, K., Williamson, G., Jesien, G., McLean, M., Seitlin, S., Karnes, M.B., McCollum, J., Monahan, R., & Odom, S. (1987, March). *Position statements and recommendations relating to PL 99-457 and other federal and state early childhood policies.* Reston, VA: Council for Exceptional Children.

Smith, D.D., & Smith, J.O. (1978). Trends. In M.E. Snell (Ed.), *Systematic instruction of the moderately and severely handicapped* (pp. 478–493). Upper Saddle River, NJ: Merrill/Prentice Hall.

Smith, D.W., & Wells, M.W. (1983). Use of a microcomputer to assist staff in documenting resident progress. *Mental Retardation, 21,* 111–115.

Smith, D.W., & Wilson, A.A. (1973). *The child with Down's syndrome (mongolism).* Philadelphia: Saunders.

Smith, G.C., Majeski, R.A., & McClenny, B. (1996). Psychoeducational support groups for aging parents: Development and preliminary outcomes. *Mental Retardation, 34*(3), 172–181.

Smith, J.D. (1981). Down's syndrome, amniocentesis and abortion: Prevention or elimination? *Mental Retardation, 19,* 8–11.

Smith, J.D. (1984). Pediatric euthanasia, handicapped infants, and special education: A challenge to our advocacy. *Exceptional Children, 51,* 335–337.

Smith, J.D. (1985). *Minds made feeble: The myth and legacy of the Kallikaks.* Rockville, MD: Aspen Systems.

Smith, J.D. (1987). *The other voices: Profiles of women in the history of special education.* Seattle, WA: Special Child.

Smith, J.D. (1988a). *Psychological profiles of conjoined twins: Heredity, environment and identity.* New York: Praeger.

Smith, J.D. (1988b, September). CEC-MR position statement on the right of children with mental retardation to life sustaining medical care and treatment. *CEC-Report,* p. 2.

Smith, J.D. (1989a). On the right of children with mental retardation to life sustaining medical care and treatment: A position statement. *Education and Training in Mental Retardation, 24,* 3–6.

Smith, J.D. (1994). Reflections on mental retardation and eugenics, old and new: Mensa and the human genome project. *Mental Retardation, 32,* 234–238.

Smith, J.D. (1995). *Pieces of purgatory: Mental retardation in and out of institutions.* Pacific Grove, CA: Brooks-Cole.

Smith, J.D. (in press). Mental retardation as an educational construct: Time for a new shared view? *Education and Training in Mental Retardation and Developmental Disabilities.*

Smith, J.D., & Nelson, K.R. (1989). *The sterilization of Carrie Buck: Was she feeble-minded or society's pawn?* Far Hills, NJ: New Horizon Press.

Smith, J.D., & Polloway, E.D. (1993). Institutionalization, involuntary sterilization, and mental retardation: Profiles from the history of the practice. *Mental Retardation, 31,* 208–214.

Smith, J.E., & Payne, J.S. (1980). *Teaching exceptional adolescents.* Columbus, OH: Merrill.

Smith, M.A., & Schloss, P.J. (1988). Teaching to transition. In P.J. Schloss, C.A. Hughes, & M.A. Smith (Eds.), *Community integration for persons with mental retardation* (pp. 1–16). Austin, TX: Pro-Ed.

Smith, S.W. (1990). Individualized Education Programs (IEPs) in special education—From intent to acquiescence. *Exceptional Children, 57,* 6–14.

Snell, M.E. (Ed.). (1987). *Systematic instruction of persons with severe handicaps* (3rd ed.). Upper Saddle River, NJ: Merrill/Prentice Hall.

Snell, M.E. (1993). *Instruction of students with severe disabilities* (4th ed.). New York: Macmillan.

Snell, M.E., & Renzaglia, A.M. (1986). Moderate, severe, and profound handicaps. In N.G. Haring & L. McCormick (Eds.), *Exceptional children and youth* (4th ed., pp. 271–310). Upper Saddle River, NJ: Merrill/Prentice Hall.

Snyderman, M., & Rothman, S. (1987). Survey of expert opinion on intelligence and aptitude testing. *American Psychologist, 42,* 137–144.

Soeffing, M. (1975). Abused children are exceptional children. *Exceptional Children, 42,* 126–133.

Sonnier, C. (1991). *Implementing early intervention services for infants and toddlers with disabilities* (P.L. 101-476, Part H). Denver, CO: National Conference of State Legislatures.

Sontag, E. (1989, October). *Keynote address.* Second international conference of CEC-MR, Davenport, IA.

Sontag, E., Burke, P., & York, R. (1973). Considerations for serving the severely handicapped in the public schools. *Education and Training of the Mentally Retarded, 8*(2), 20–26.

Sparrow, S.S., Balla D.A., & Cicchetti, D.V. (1984a). *Vineland Adaptive Behavior Scales: Interview Edition, Expanded Form.* Circle Pines, MN: American Guidance Service.

Sparrow, S.S., Balla D.A., & Cicchetti, D.V. (1984b). *Vineland Adaptive Behavior Scales: Interview Edition, Survey Form.* Circle Pines, MN: American Guidance Service.

Sparrow, S.S., Balla D.A., & Cicchetti, D.V. (1985). *Vineland Adaptive Behavior Scales: Classroom Edition Form*. Circle Pines, MN: American Guidance Service.

Spearman, C.E. (1927). *The abilities of man*. New York: Macmillan.

Spitz, H.H. (1966). The role of input organization in the learning and memory of mental retardates. *International Review of Research in Mental Retardation, 2,* 29–56.

Spitz, H.H. (1973). Consolidating facts into the schematized learning and memory of mental retardates. *International Review of Research in Mental Retardation, 6,* 149–168.

Spitz, H.H. (1979). Beyond field theory in the study of mental deficiency. In N.R. Ellis (Ed.), *Handbook of mental deficiency: Psychological theory and research* (2nd ed., pp. 121–141). Hillsdale, NJ: Erlbaum.

Spooner, F., & Spooner, D. (1984). A review of chaining techniques: Implications for future research and practice. *Education and Training of the Mentally Retarded, 20,* 114–124.

Spradlin, J.E. (1968). Environmental factors and the language development of retarded children. In S. Rosenberg & J.H. Koplin (Eds.), *Developments in applied psycholinguistic research* (pp. 261–290). New York: Macmillan.

Spreat, S., Telles, J.L., Conroy, J.W., Feinstein, C., & Colombatto, J.J. (1987). Attitudes toward deinstitutionalization: National survey of families of institutionalized persons with mental retardation. *Mental Retardation, 25,* 267–274.

Spring, J.H. (1986). *The American school 1642–1985*. New York: Longman.

Springer, N.S., & Fricke, N.L. (1975). Nutrition and drug therapy for persons with developmental disabilities. *American Journal of Mental Deficiency, 80,* 317–322.

Spruill, J. (1988). Review of the *Stanford-Binet Intelligence Scale: Fourth Edition. Test Critiques, 6,* 114–127.

Staddon, J.E. (1983). *Adaptive behavior and learning*. New York: Cambridge University Press.

Staff. (1991). Facilitated communication reports generate heated controversy. *Autism Research Review International, 5*(1), 1, 6.

Staff. (1992). A facilitated communication "horror story." *Autism Research Review International, 6*(1), 1, 3.

Stainback, S., & Stainback, W. (1992). Schools as inclusive communities. In W. Stainback & S. Stainback, (Eds.), *Controversial issues facing special education: Divergent perspectives* (pp. 29–43). Boston: Allyn & Bacon.

Stancliffe, R., & Lakin, K.C. (1996). *Cost-effectiveness of different models of community support for persons with developmental disabilities leaving Minnesota's regional treatment centers*. Minneapolis: University of Minnesota, Institute on Community Integration.

Stark, J.A., & Goldsbury, T. (1988). Analysis of labor and economics: Needs for the next decade. *Mental Retardation, 26,* 363–368.

Stark, J.A., & Goldsbury, T. (1990). Quality of life from childhood to adulthood. In R.L. Schalock (Ed.), *Quality of life: Perspectives and issues* (pp. 71–83). Washington, DC: American Association on Mental Retardation.

Stark, J.A., Menolascino, F.J., & Goldsbury, T.L. (1988). An updated search for the prevention of mental retardation. In F.J. Menolascino & J.A. Stark (Eds.), *Preventive and curative intervention in mental retardation* (pp. 3–25). Baltimore: Brookes.

Stein, Z., & Susser, M. (1975). Public health and mental retardation: New power and new problems. In M. Begab & S.A. Richardson (Eds.), *The mentally retarded and society: A social science perspective* (pp. 53–73). Baltimore: University Park Press.

Stephens, W.E. (1966). Category usage of normal and subnormal children on three types of categories. *American Journal of Mental Deficiency, 71,* 266–273.

Stephens, W.E. (1972). Equivalence formation by retarded and nonretarded children at different mental ages. *American Journal of Mental Deficiency, 77,* 311–313.

Sternberg, R.J. (1985). *Beyond IQ: A triarchic theory of intelligence.* New York: Cambridge University Press.

Sternberg, R.J. (1988). *The triarchic mind: A new theory of human intelligence.* New York: Viking.

Sternberg, R.J. (1997). The triarchic theory of intelligence. In D.P. Flanagan, J. Genshaft, & P.L. Harrison (Eds.), *Contemporary intellectual assessment: Theories, tests and issues* (pp. 92–104). New York: Guilford.

Sternberg, R.J., & Spear, L.C. (1985). A triarchic theory of mental retardation. *International Review of Research in Mental Retardation, 13,* 301–326.

Stevens, H.A. (1964). Overview of mental retardation. In H.A. Stevens & R. Heber, (Eds.), *Mental retardation* (pp. 3–15). Chicago: University of Chicago Press.

Stevenson, H.W. (1972). *Children's learning.* Upper Saddle River, NJ: Prentice Hall.

Stewart, A.J., Sokol, M., Healy, J.M., Chester, N.L., & Weinstock-Savoy, D. (1982). Adaptation to life changes in children and adults: Cross-sectional studies. *Journal of Personality and Social Psychology, 43,* 1270–1281.

Stoddard, K. (1992). The changing role of teachers: Refocus on the family. *LD Forum, 17*(1), 15–17.

Stodden, R.A., & Boone, R. (1987). Assessing transition services for handicapped youth: A cooperative interagency approach. *Exceptional Children, 53,* 537–545.

Stokes, T.F., & Baer, D.M. (1977). An implicit technology of generalization. *Journal of Applied Behavior Analysis, 10,* 349–367.

Strain, P.S., & Cardisco, L.K. (1983). Child characteristics and outcomes related to mainstreaming. In J. Anderson & T. Black (Eds.), *Issues in preschool mainstreaming* (pp. 46–47). Chapel Hill, NC: TADS.

Streissguth, A.P., & LaDue, R.A. (1987). Fetal alcohol: Teratogenic causes of developmental disabilities. In S.R. Schroeder (Ed.), *Toxic substances and mental retardation: Neurobehavioral toxicology and teratology* (pp. 1–32). Washington, DC: American Association on Mental Deficiency.

Strichart, S.S., & Gottlieb, J. (1983). Characteristics of mild mental retardation. In T.L. Miller & E.E. Davis (Eds.), *The mildly handicapped student* (pp. 37–65). Orlando, FL: Grune & Stratton.

Stricklan, S.P. (1971). Can slum children learn? *American Education, 7*(6), 3–7.

Stroud, M., & Sutton, E. (1988). *Expanding options for older adults with developmental disabilities: A practical guide to achieving community access.* Baltimore: Brookes.

Strully, J. (1986, November). *Our children and the regular education classroom: Why settle for anything less than the best?* Paper presented at the annual meeting of The Association for Persons with Severe Handicaps, San Francisco.

Strully, J. (1987, October). *All children can learn together: No more segregation of any kind.* Paper presented at the annual meeting of the Iowa Chapter of the Association for Persons with Severe Handicaps.

Strully, J.L., & Strully, C.F. (1989). Friendships as an educational goal. In S. Stainback, W. Stainback, & M. Forest (Eds.), *Educating all students in the mainstream of regular education* (pp. 59–68). Baltimore: Brookes.

Stuart v. Nappi, 443 F. Supp. 1235 (D. Conn 1978).

Sugai, G. (1985). Case study: Designing instruction from IEPs. *Teaching Exceptional Children, 17,* 239.

Sundram, C.J., & Stavis, P.F. (1994). Sexuality and mental retardation: Unmet challenges. *Mental Retardation, 32*(4), 255–264.

Swenson, C.H. (1985). Personality development in the family. In L. L'Abate (Ed.), *The handbook of family psychology and therapy* (Vol. 1, pp. 73–101). Pacific Grove, CA: Brooks/Cole.

T.G. v. Board of Education of Piscataway, 576 F. Supp. 420 (D.N.J. 1983).

Tarjan, G., Wright, S.W., Eyman, R.K., & Keeran, D.V. (1973). Natural history of mental retardation: Some aspects of epidemiology. *American Journal of Mental Deficiency, 77,* 369–379.

TASH. (The Association for Persons with Severe Handicaps). (1984). *Legal, economic, psychological, and moral considerations on the practice of withholding medical treatment from infants with congenital defects.* Seattle, WA: Author.

Taylor, A.R., Asher, S.R., & Williams, G.A. (1987). The social adaptation of mainstreamed mildly retarded children. *Child Development, 58,* 1321–1334.

Taylor, R.L. (1990). The Larry P. decision a decade later: Problems and future directions. *Mental Retardation,* iii–v.

Taylor, S.J. (1988). Caught in the continuum: A critical analysis of the principles of the least restrictive environment. *Journal of the Association for Persons with Severe Handicaps, 13*(1), 41–53.

Taylor, S.J., & Biklen, D. (1979). *Understanding the law: An advocate's guide to the law and developmental disabilities.* Syracuse, NY: Syracuse University and the Mental Health Law Project.

Taylor, S.J., & Bogdan, R. (1990). Quality of life and the individual's perspective. In R.L. Schalock (Ed.), *Quality of life: Perspectives and issues* (pp. 27–40). Washington, DC: American Association on Mental Retardation.

Taylor, S.J., Knoll, J.A., Lehr, S., & Walker, P.M. (1989). Families for all children: Value-based services for children with disabilities and their families. In G.H. Singer & L.K. Irvin (Eds.), *Support for caregiving families: Enabling positive adaptation to disability* (pp. 41–53). Baltimore: Brookes.

Temple University Developmental Disabilities Center. (1990). *The final report on the 1990 National Consumer Survey of people with developmental disabilities and their families.* Philadelphia: Author.

Terman, L.M. (1916). *The measurement of intelligence.* Boston: Houghton Mifflin.

Terman, L.M., & Merrill, M.A. (1937). *Measuring intelligence.* Boston: Houghton Mifflin.

Terman, L.M., & Merrill, M.A. (1960). *Stanford-Binet Intelligence Scale.* Boston: Houghton Mifflin.

The Association for Persons with Severe Handicaps (TASH). (1990). *Definition of severe disabilities.* Washington, DC: Author.

The courts' impact on special education. (1996, June). *CEC Today, 2,* 1, 13, 15.

The Futurist. (1986). The new poor: Jobless and homeless in the United States. *20*(2), 44.

Thompson, P.R. (1974). Keynote address. In J. Moore & V. Engleman (Eds.), *The severely, multiply handicapped: What are the issues? Proceedings from the Regional, Topical Conference* (pp. 70–76). Salt Lake City: University of Utah.

Thorin, E., Yovanoff, P., & Irvin, L. (1996). Dilemmas faced by families during their young adults' transitions to adulthood: A brief report. *Mental Retardation, 34*(2), 117–120.

Thornburgh, G. (1992). *That all may worship: An interfaith welcome to people with disabilities.* Washington, DC: National Organization on Disability.

Thorndike, E.L. (1927). *The measurement of intelligence.* New York: Columbia University, Teacher's College Press.

Thorndike, R.L., Hagen, E.P., & Sattler, J.M. (1986a). *Stanford-Binet Intelligence Scale: Fourth Edition.* Chicago: Riverside.

Thorndike, R.L., Hagen, E.P., & Sattler, J.M. (1986b). *The Stanford-Binet Intelligence Scale: Fourth Edition: Guide for administering and scoring.* Chicago: Riverside.

Thurlow, M.L. (1992). Issues in the screening of preschool children. In E. Nuttall, I. Romero, & J. Kalesnik (Eds.), *Assessing and screening preschoolers: Psychological and educational dimensions* (pp. 67–82). Boston: Allyn & Bacon.

Thurlow, M.L., Bruininks, R.H., & Lange, C.M. (1989). *Assessing post-school outcomes for students with moderate to severe mental retardation* (Report No. 89-1). Minneapolis: University of Minnesota, Institute on Community Integration.

Thurlow, M.L., Bruininks, R.H., Wolman, C., & Steffens, K. (1989). *Post-school occupational and social status of persons with moderate, severe, and profound mental retardation* (Report No. 89-3). Minneapolis: University of Minnesota, Institute on Community Integration.

Thurstone, L.L. (1938). Primary mental abilities. *Psychometric Monographs,* No. 1.

Tilson, G.P., Luecking, R.G., & Donovan, M.R. (1994). Involving employers in transition: The Bridges Model. *Career Development for Exceptional Individuals, 17*(1), 77–89.

Timothy W. v. Rochester School District, EHLR 559:480 (D.N.H. 1988).

Todis, B., & Walker, H.M. (1993). User perspectives on assistive technologies in educational settings. *Focus on Exceptional Children, 26*(3), 1–2.

Townsend, C., & Mattson, R. (1981). The interaction of law and special education: Observing the emperor's new clothes. *Analysis & Intervention in Developmental Disabilities, 1,* 75–89.

Tredgold, A.F. (1937). *A textbook of mental deficiency.* Baltimore: Wood.

Treffert, D.A. (1989). *Extraordinary people: Understanding "idiot savant."* New York: Harper & Row.

Trumbow, D. (1959). *Johnny get your gun.* New York: Bantam.

Tucker, S.M. (1978). *Fetal monitoring and fetal assessment in high-risk pregnancy.* St. Louis: C.V. Mosby.

Turkington, C. (1987). Special talents. *Psychology Today, 20,* 42–46.

Turnbull, A.P. (1982). Preschool mainstreaming: A policy and implementation analysis. *Education Evaluation and Policy Analysis, 4*(3), 281–291.

Turnbull, A.P. (1988). The challenge of providing comprehensive support to families. *Education and Training in Mental Retardation, 23,* 261–272.

Turnbull, A.P., Brotherson, M.J., Bronicki, G.J., Benson, H.A., Houghton, J., Roeder-Gordon, C., & Summers, J.A. (1985). *How to plan for my child's adult future: A three-part process to future planning.* Lawrence, KS: University Affiliated Facility, Bureau of Child Research, Future Planning Project.

Turnbull, A.P., Summers, J.A., & Brotherson, M.J. (1984). *Working with families with disabled members: A family systems approach*. Lawrence: University of Kansas, Kansas University Affiliated Facility.

Turnbull, A.P., Summers, J.A., & Brotherson, M.J. (1986). Family life cycle: Theoretical and empirical implications and future directions for families with mentally retarded members. In J.J. Gallagher & P.M. Vietze (Eds.), *Families of handicapped persons* (pp. 45–65). Baltimore: Brookes.

Turnbull, A.P., & Turnbull, H.R. (1985). *Parents speak out: Then & now* (2nd ed.). Upper Saddle River, NJ: Merrill/Prentice Hall.

Turnbull, A.P., & Turnbull, H.R. (1997). *Families, professionals, and exceptionality: A special partnership* (3rd ed.). Upper Saddle River, NJ: Prentice Hall.

Turnbull, A.P., Turnbull, H.R., III, Shank, M., & Leal, D. (1995). *Exceptional lives: Special education in today's schools*. Upper Saddle River, NJ: Merrill/Prentice Hall.

Turnbull, H.R. (1975). *Legal aspects of the developmentally disabled*. Topeka, KS: National Organization on Legal Problems of Education.

Turnbull, H.R. (1980, April 18). *Legal issues and challenges in special education*. Paper presented at the University of Virginia's Spring Special Education Forum, Charlottesville.

Turnbull, H.R. (1983). *Free appropriate public education: The law and children with disabilities* (2nd ed.). Denver, CO: Love.

Turnbull, H.R. (1986). *Free appropriate public education: The law and children with disabilities* (3rd ed.). Denver, CO: Love.

Turnbull, H.R. (1988). Ideological, political, and legal practices in the community-living movement. In M.P. Janicki, M.W. Krauss, & M.M. Seltzer (Eds.), *Community residences for persons with developmental disabilities: Here to stay* (pp. 15–24). Baltimore: Brookes.

Turnbull, H.R. (1993). *Free appropriate public education: The law and children with disabilities* (4th ed.). Denver, CO: Love.

Turnure, J., & Zigler, E. (1964). Outer-directedness in the problem solving of normal and retarded children. *Journal of Abnormal and Social Psychology, 69*, 427–436.

Tymchuk, A.J., Hamada, D., Andron, L., & Anderson, S. (1990). Home safety training with mothers who are mentally retarded. *Education and Training in Mental Retardation, 25*(3), 142–149.

Ullman, L.P., & Krasner, L. (1969). *A psychological approach to abnormal behavior*. Upper Saddle River, NJ: Prentice Hall.

Ulrich, D.A. (1985). *Test of Gross Motor Development*. Austin, TX: PRO-ED.

Underwood, J.K., & Mead, J.F. (1995). *Legal aspects of special education and pupil services*. Boston: Allyn & Bacon.

United States v. University Hospital, State University of New York at Stonybrook, 729 F. 2d 144 (2d Cir. 1984).

Urbach, P. (1974). Progress and degeneration in the "IQ debate." *British Journal of Philosophy of Science, 25*, 99–135.

U.S. Congress, House of Representatives. (1991). *House report 102-198*. Individuals with Disabilities Education amendments of 1991, Committee on Education and Labor. Washington, DC: U.S. Government Printing Office.

U.S. *Constitution,* Amend. XIV, Sec. 1.

U.S. Department of Commerce. (1996). *Current population reports: Population projections of the United States by age, sex, race, and Hispanic origin: 1995 to 2050* (pp. 25–1130). Washington, DC: Bureau of the Census, Economics and Statistics Administration.

U.S. Department of Education. (1983). *To assure the free appropriate public education of all handicapped children: Fifth annual report to Congress on the implementation of The All Handicapped Children Act of P.L. 94-142*. Washington, DC: Office of Special Education and Rehabilitative Services.

U.S. Department of Education. (1988). To assure the free appropriate public education of all handicapped children: Tenth annual report to Congress on the implementation of the All Handicapped Children's Act of P.L. 94-142. *Federal Register*. Washington, DC: Author.

U.S. Department of Education. (1990). *To assure the free appropriate public education of all handicapped children: Twelfth annual report to Congress on the implementation of the Education of the Handicapped Act*. Washington, DC: U.S. Department of Education, Office of Special Education and Rehabilitative Services.

U.S. Department of Education. (1991). *To assure the free appropriate public education of all handicapped children: Thirteenth annual report to Congress on the implementation of the Education of the Handicapped Act*. Washington, DC: U.S. Department of Education, Office of Special Education and Rehabilitative Services.

U.S. Department of Education. (1992). *To assure the free appropriate public education of all handicapped children: Fourteenth annual report to Congress on the implementation of the Education of the Handicapped Act*. Washington, DC: U.S. Department of Education, Office of Special Education and Rehabilitative Services.

U.S. Department of Education. (1994). *Sixteenth annual report to Congress on the implementation of the Individuals with Disabilities Education Act*. Washington, DC: Office of Special Education Programs, U.S. Department of Education.

U.S. Department of Education. (1995). *To assure the free appropriate public education of all handicapped children: Seventeenth annual report to Congress on the implementation of the Individuals with Disabilities Education Act*. Washington, DC: Office of Special Education and Rehabilitative Services.

U.S. Department of Education. (1996). *Eighteenth annual report to congress on the implementation of the Individuals with Disabilities Education Act*. Washington, DC: Office of Special Education Programs, U.S. Department of Education.

U.S. Department of Health and Human Services. (1990). *Task II: Federal programs for persons with disabilities*. Washington, DC: U.S. Government Printing Office.

Utley, C.A., Lowitzer, A.C., & Baumeister, A.A. (1987). A comparison of the AAMD's definition, eligibility criteria, and classification schemes with state departments of education guidelines. *Education and Training in Mental Retardation, 22*, 35–43.

Vanderheiden, G.C. (1992). A brief look at technology and mental retardation in the 21st century. In L. Rowitz (Ed.), *Mental retardation in the year 2000* (pp. 268–278). New York: Springer-Verlag.

Vernon, P.E. (1950). *The structure of human abilities*. New York: Wiley.

Vernon-Levett, P. (1991). Head injuries in children. *Pediatric Trauma, 3*, 411–421.

Viadero, D. (1991). Law to aid handicapped infants faces critical test. *Education Week, 10*(27), 27–29.

Vincent, L.J. (1986). Testimony before the Subcommittee on Select Education, July 29. *House report 99-120*. Washington, DC: U.S. Government Printing Office.

Vincent, L., Davis, J., Brown, P., Broome, K., Miller, J., & Gruenewald, L. (1983). *Parent inventory of child development in nonschool environments*. Madison, WI:

Madison Metropolitan School District Early Childhood Program, Active Decision Making by Parents Grant.

Vincent, L.J., Poulsen, M.K., Cole, C.K., Woodruff, G., & Griffith, D.R. (1991). *Born substance abused, educationally vulnerable.* Reston, VA: Council for Exceptional Children.

Vogelsberg, R.T. (1986). Vermont's employment training programs. In F.R. Rusch (Ed.), *Competitive employment: Service delivery models, methods, and issues* (pp. 35–50). Baltimore: Brookes.

Vogelsberg, R.T., & Schutz, R.P. (1988). Establishing community employment programs for persons with severe disabilities: Systems designs and resolutions. In M.D. Powers (Ed.), *Expanding Systems of Service Delivery for Persons with Developmental Disabilities.* Baltimore: Brookes.

Voorhees, P.J. (1996). Travel training for person's with cognitive or physical disabilities: An overview. *NICHCY Transition Summary, 9,* 7–9.

Wacker, D. (1992a, September). Functional analysis of severe problem behaviors. *Iowa News, 92*(6), 1–2. (Available from the Iowa Bureau of Special Education, Des Moines).

Wacker, D. (1992b, November). Matching treatment to the function of problematic behavior. *Iowa News, 92*(8), 1–2. (Available from the Iowa Bureau of Special Education, Des Moines).

Wagner, M., Newman, L., & Shaver, D. (1989). *The National Longitudinal Transition Study of Special Education Students: Report on procedures for the first wave of data collection* (1987). Menlo Park, CA: SRI International.

Wald, P.M. (1976). Personal and civil rights of mentally retarded citizens. In M. Kindred, J. Cohen, D. Penrod, & T. Shaffer (Eds.), *The mentally retarded citizen and the law* (pp. 2–30). New York: Free Press.

Walker, N.W. (1987). The Stanford-Binet, 4th edition: Haste does seem to make waste. *Measurement & Evaluation in Counseling and Development, 20,* 135–138.

Wallace, G., Larsen, S.C., & Elksin, L.K. (1992). *Educational assessment of learning problems: Testing for teaching* (2nd ed.). Boston: Allyn & Bacon.

Wallin, J.W. (1955). *Education of mentally handicapped children.* New York: Harper & Row.

Walters, J., & Walters, L.H. (1980). Parent-child relationships: A review, 1970–1979. *Journal of Marriage and Family Therapy, 42*(4), 80–95.

Wannarachue, N., Ruvalcaba, R., & Kelley, V.C. (1975). Hypogonadism in Prader-Willi syndrome. *American Journal of Mental Deficiency, 79,* 592–603.

Warren, K.R., & Bast, R.J. (1988). Alcohol-related birth defects: An update. *Public Health Reports, 103,* 638–642.

Warren, S.F., & Abbeduto, L. (1992). The relation of communication and language development to mental retardation. *American Journal on Mental Retardation, 97,* 125–130.

Watson, J.B. (1930). *Behaviorism* (rev. ed.). Chicago: University of Chicago Press.

W.B. v. Matula, 67 F.3rd 484 (3rd. Cir. 1995).

Webb, S., Hochberg, M.S., & Sher, M.R. (1988). Fetal alcohol syndrome: Report of a case. *Journal of American Dental Association, 116,* 196–198.

Wechsler, D. (1939). *The measurement of adult intelligence.* Baltimore: Williams & Wilkins.

Wechsler, D. (1949). *Wechsler Intelligence Scale for Children.* San Antonio, TX: Psychological Corporation.

Wechsler, D. (1955). *Wechsler Adult Intelligence Scale*. San Antonio, TX: Psychological Corporation.

Wechsler, D. (1958). *The measurement and appraisal of adult intelligence* (4th ed.). Baltimore: Williams & Wilkins.

Wechsler, D. (1967). *Wechsler Preschool and Primary Scale of Intelligence*. San Antonio, TX: Psychological Corporation.

Wechsler, D. (1974). *Wechsler Intelligence Scale for Children—Revised*. San Antonio, TX: Psychological Corporation.

Wechsler, D. (1981a). *Wechsler Adult Intelligence Scale—Revised*. San Antonio, TX: Psychological Corporation.

Wechsler, D. (1981b). *Wechsler Adult Intelligence Scale—Revised: Manual*. San Antonio, TX: Psychological Corporation.

Wechsler, D. (1989a). *Wechsler Preschool and Primary Scale of Intelligence—Revised*. San Antonio, TX: Psychological Corporation.

Wechsler, D. (1989b). *Wechsler Preschool and Primary Scale of Intelligence—Revised: Manual*. San Antonio, TX: Psychological Corporation.

Wechsler, D. (1991a). *Wechsler Intelligence Scale for Children—Third Edition*. San Antonio, TX: Psychological Corporation.

Wechsler, D. (1991b). *Wechsler Intelligence Scale for Children—Third Edition: Manual*. San Antonio, TX: Psychological Corporation.

Wehman, P. (1990). School-to-work: Elements of successful programs. *Teaching Exceptional Children, 23*(1), 40–43.

Wehman, P. (1995). *Individual transition plans: The teacher's curriculum guide for helping youth with special needs*. Austin, TX: Pro-Ed.

Wehman, P., Hill, J.W., & Koehler, F. (1979). Helping severely handicapped persons enter competitive employment. *AAESPH Review, 4,* 274–290.

Wehman, P., & Kregel, J. (1985). A supported work approach to competitive employment of individuals with moderate and severe handicaps. *The Journal of the Association for Persons with Severe Handicaps, 10*(1), 3–11.

Wehman, P., & Kregel, J. (1997). *Functional curriculum for elementary, middle, and secondary age students with special needs*. Austin:, TX: Pro-Ed.

Wehman, P., Kregel, J., & Barcus, J.M. (1985). From school to work: A vocational transition model for handicapped students. *Exceptional Children, 52,* 25–37.

Wehman, P., Kregel, J., & Seyfarth, J. (1985). Transition from school to work for individuals with severe handicaps: A follow-up study. *The Journal of the Association for Persons with Severe Handicaps, 10,* 132–136.

Wehman, P., Parent, W., Wood, W., Talbert, C.M., Jasper, C., Miller, S., Marchant, J., & Walker, R. (1989). From school to competitive employment for young adults with mental retardation: Transition in practice. *Career Development for Exceptional Individuals, 12,* 97–105.

Wehman, P., Wood, W., Everson, J.M., Goodwyn, R., & Conley, S. (1988). *Vocational education for multihandicapped youth with cerebral palsy*. Baltimore: Brookes.

Wehmeyer, M. (1993). Self-determination as an educational outcome. *Impact, 6*(4), 16–17, 26.

Weisner, T.S., Beizer, L., & Stolze, L. (1991). Religion and families of children with developmental delays. *American Journal on Mental Retardation, 95*(6), 647–662.

Weissman, R.A., & Littman, D.C. (1996). Early intervention. In P.J. McLaughlin & P. Wehman (Eds.), *Mental retardation and developmental disabilities* (pp. 29–48). Austin, TX: Pro-Ed.

West, J.F., Idol, L., & Cannon, G. (1989). *Collaboration in the schools*. Austin, TX: Pro-Ed.

Westling, D.L. (1986). *Introduction to mental retardation*. Upper Saddle River, NJ: Prentice Hall.

White, B.L. (1975). *The first three years*. Upper Saddle River, NJ: Prentice Hall.

White, C.C., Lakin, K.C., Bruininks, R.H., & Li, X. (1991). *Persons with mental retardation and related conditions in state-operated residential facilities: Year ending June 30, 1989 with longitudinal trends from 1950 to 1989*. Minneapolis: University of Minnesota, Institute on Community Integration.

White, C.C., Prouty, R.W., Lakin, K.C., & Blake, E.M. (1992). *Persons with mental retardation and related conditions in state-operated residential facilities: Year ending June 30, 1990 with longitudinal trends from 1950 to 1990*. Minneapolis: University of Minnesota, Institute on Community Integration.

White, K.R., & Casto, G. (1989). What is known about early intervention. In G. Tingey (Ed.), *Implementing early intervention* (pp. 3–20). Baltimore: Brookes.

White House. (1991, February). *The national education goals: A second report to the nation's governors*. Washington, DC: Author.

Whitman, T.L. (1990). Self-regulation and mental retardation. *American Journal on Mental Retardation, 94,* 347–362.

Whitman, T.L., Borkowski, J.G., Schellenbach, C.J., & Nath, P.S. (1987). Predicting and understanding developmental delay of adolescent mothers: A multidimensional approach. *American Journal of Mental Deficiency, 92,* 40–56.

Whitman, T.L., Hantula, D.A., & Spence, B.H. (1990). Current issues in behavior modification with mentally retarded persons. In J.L. Matson (Ed.), *Handbook of behavior modification with the mentally retarded* (2nd ed., pp. 9–50). New York: Plenum.

Widaman, K.F., & McGrew, K.S. (1996). The structure of adaptive behavior. In J.W. Jacobson & J.A. Mulick (Eds.), *Manual of diagnosis and professional practice in mental retardation* (pp. 97–110). Washington, DC: American Psychological Association.

Widaman, K.F., Reise, S.P., & Clatfelter, D.L. (1994, March). *Assessing the measurement structure of adaptive behavior: Factor analytic versus item response theory approaches*. Paper presented at the Gatlinburg Conference on Research and Theory in Mental Retardation and Developmental Disabilities, Gatlinburg, TN.

Widaman, K.F., Stacy, A.W., & Borthwick-Duffy, S.A. (1993). Construct validity of dimensions of adaptive behavior: A multitrait–multimethod evaluation. *American Journal on Mental Retardation, 98,* 219–234.

Widerstrom, A.H., Mowder, B.A., & Sandall, S.R. (1991). *At-risk and handicapped newborns and infants*. Upper Saddle River, NJ: Prentice Hall.

Wiederholt, J.L., & Chamberlain, S.P. (1989). A critical analysis of resource programs. *Remedial and Special Education, 10*(6), 15–27.

Wikler, L. (1981). Chronic stresses of families of mentally retarded children. *Family Relations, 30,* 281–288.

Wilbur, H. (1976). *Eulogy to Edouard Sequin. Remarks made at Seguin's funeral, Clamecy, France, 1880*. (Reprinted in M. Rosen, G.R. Clark, & M.S. Kivitz [Eds.], *The history of mental retardation: Collected papers* [Vol. 1, pp. 181–187]. Baltimore: University Park Press.)

Wilcox, B., & Bellamy, G.T. (1982). *Design of high school programs for severely handicapped students*. Baltimore: Brookes.

Will, M.C. (1984). *OSERS programming for the transition of youth with disabilities: Bridges from school to working life*. Washington, DC: U.S. Department of Education, Office of Special Education and Rehabilitative Services.

Williams, H.G. (1991). Assessment of gross motor functioning. In B.A. Bracken (Ed.), *The Psychoeducational assessment of preschool children* (2nd ed., pp. 284–316). Boston: Allyn and Bacon.

Williams, H.M. (1963). *Education of the severely retarded child*. Washington, DC: U.S. Government Printing Office.

Williams, W., Brown, L., & Certo, N. (1975). Basic components of instructional programs. *Theory Into Practice, 14,* 123–136.

Wills, T.A., Blechman, E.A., & McNamara, G. (1996). Family support, coping and competence. In E.M. Hetherington & E.A. Blechman (Eds.), *Stress, coping, and resiliency in children and families* (pp. 107–134). Mahwah, NJ: Erlbaum.

Wilson, E.O. (1975). *Sociobiology: The new synthesis*. Cambridge, MA: Belknap Press.

Wilson, J., Blacher, J., & Baker, B.L. (1989). Siblings of children with severe handicaps. *American Journal on Mental Retardation, 27,* 167–173.

Winick, M. (1969). Malnutrition and brain development. *Journal of Pediatrics, 74,* 667.

Winking, D.L., DeStefano, L., & Rusch, F.R. (1988). *Supported employment in Illinois: Job coach issues*. Champaign, IL: University of Illinois, Secondary Transition Intervention Effectiveness Institute. (ERIC Document Reproduction Service No. 295 407)

Wolery, M. (1991). Instruction in early childhood special education:. "Seeing through a glass darkly . . . knowing in part." *Exceptional Children, 58,* 127–134.

Wolery, M., Baily, D., & Sugai, G. (1988). *Effective teaching: Principles and procedures of applied behavior analysis with exceptional students*. Boston: Allyn & Bacon.

Wolf, M.M. (1978). Social validity: The case for subjective measurement or how applied behavior analysis is finding its heart. *Journal of Applied Behavior Analysis, 11*(2), 203–214.

Wolfensberger, W. (1972). *The principle of normalization in human services*. Toronto: National Institute on Mental Retardation.

Wolfensberger, W. (1975). *The origin and nature of our institutional models*. Syracuse, NY: Center on Human Policy.

Wolfensberger, W. (1983). Social role valorization: A proposed new term for the principle of normalization. *Mental Retardation, 21,* 234–239.

Wolfensberger, W. (1985). An overview of social role valorization and some reflections on elderly mentally retarded persons. In M.P. Janicki & H.M. Wisniewski (Eds.), *Expanding systems of service delivery for persons with developmental disabilities* (pp. 127–148). Baltimore: Brookes.

Wolman, B.B. (Ed.). (1985). *Handbook of intelligence: Theories, measurements, and applications*. New York: Wiley.

Wolraich, M.L. (1983). Hydrocephalus. In J.A. Blackman (Ed.), *Medical aspects of developmental disabilities in children birth to three* (pp. 137–141). Iowa City: University of Iowa Press.

Woodcock, R.W., & Johnson, M.B. (1977). *Woodcock-Johnson Psychoeducational Battery*. Chicago: Riverside.

Woodcock, R.W., & Johnson, M.B. (1989). *Woodcock-Johnson Psychoeducational Battery—Revised*. Chicago: Riverside.

Woodward, W.M. (1963). The application of Piaget's theory to research in mental deficiency. In N.R. Ellis (Ed.), *Handbook of mental deficiency* (pp. 297–324). New York: McGraw-Hill.

Woodward, W.M. (1979). Piaget's theory and the study of mental retardation. In N.R. Ellis (Ed.), *Handbook of mental deficiency: Psychological theory and research* (2nd ed., pp. 169–195). Hillsdale, NJ: Erlbaum.

World Health Organization (WHO). (1978). *International classification of diseases (9th rev.)*. Washington, DC: Author.

Wright, B., King, M.P., & National Conference of State Legislatures Task Force on Developmental Disabilities. (1991). *Americans with developmental disabilities.* Washington, DC: Author.

Wuerch, B.B., & Voeltz, L.M. (1981). *Ho'onanea program: A leisure curriculum component for severely handicapped children and youth.* Baltimore: Brookes.

Wyatt v. Aderholt, 368 F. Supp. 1382, 1383 (M.D. Ala. 1974).

Wyatt v. Hardin, Civil Action No. 3195-N (M.D. Ala. 1975).

Wyatt v. Ireland, Civil Action No. 3195-N (M.D. Ala. 1979).

Wyatt v. Stickney, 344 F. Supp. 387, 344 F. Supp. 373 (M.D. Ala. 1972), 334 F. Supp. 1341, 325 F. Supp. 781 (M.D. Ala. 1971), 772 aff'd sub nom. *Wyatt v. Aderholt,* 503 F.2d 1305 (5th Cir. 1974).

Yerkes, R.M. (1921). Reference not available.

Youngberg v. Romeo, 102 S. Ct. 2452 (1982).

Ysseldyke, J.E., Algozzine, B., & Thurlow, M.L. (1992). *Critical issues in special education.* Boston: Houghton Mifflin.

Zaentz, S., Douglas, M. (Producers), & Forman, M. (Director). (1975). *One flew over the cuckoo's nest* [Film]. New York: Thorn EMI.

Zantal-Weiner, K. (1987). *Child abuse and handicapped children.* Reston, VA: ERIC Clearinghouse on Handicapped and Gifted Children.

Zarfas, D.E., & Wolf, L.C. (1979). Maternal age patterns and the incidence of Down's syndrome. *American Journal of Mental Deficiency, 83,* 353–359.

Zeaman, D., & House, B.J. (1963). The role of attention in retardate discrimination learning. In N.R. Ellis (Ed.), *Handbook of mental deficiency: Psychological theory and research* (pp. 159–223). Hillsdale, NJ: Erlbaum.

Zeaman, D., & House, B.J. (1979). A review of attention theory. In N.R. Ellis (Ed.), *Handbook of mental deficiency: Psychological theory and research* (2nd ed., pp. 63–120). Hillsdale, NJ: Erlbaum.

Zetlin, A.G., & Murtaugh, M. (1988). Friendship patterns of mildly learning handicapped and nonhandicapped high school students. *American Journal on Mental Retardation, 92*(5), 447–454.

Zetlin, A.G., & Turner, J.L. (1985). Transition from adolescence to adulthood: Perspectives of mentally retarded individuals and their families. *American Journal of Mental Deficiency, 89*(6), 570–579.

Zigler, E. (1966). Research on personality structure in the retardate. *International Review of Research in Mental Retardation, 1,* 77–108.

Zigler, E. (1969). Development versus difference theories of mental retardation and problems of motivation. *American Journal of Mental Deficiency, 73,* 536–556.

Zigler, E. (1973). The retarded child as a whole person. In D.K. Routh (Ed.), *The experimental psychology of mental retardation* (pp. 231–322). Chicago: Aldine.

Zigler, E. (1985). Foreword. In L. L'Abate (Ed.), *The handbook of family psychology and therapy* (Vol. 1, p. v). Pacific Grove, CA: Brooks/Cole.

Zigler, E., & Balla, D.A. (1981). Issues in personality and motivation in mentally retarded persons. In M.J. Begab, H.C. Haywood, & H.L. Garber (Eds.), *Psychosocial influences in retarded performance: Issues and theories of development* (Vol. 1, pp. 197–218). Baltimore, MD: University Park Press.

Zigler, E., Balla, D.A., & Hodapp, R. (1984). On the definition and classification of mental retardation. *American Journal of Mental Deficiency, 89,* 215–230.

Zigler, E., & Black, K.B. (1989). America's family support movements: Strengths and limitations. *American Journal of Orthopsychiatry, 59,* 6–19.

Zigler, E., & Seitz, V. (1982). Social policy and intelligence. In R.J. Sternberg (Ed.), *Handbook of human intelligence* (pp. 586–641). Cambridge: Cambridge University Press.

Zigman, W.S., Schupf, N., Lubin, R.A., & Silverman, W.P. (1987). Premature regression of adults with Down syndrome. *American Journal of Mental Retardation, 92,* 161–168.

Zimmerman, I.L., Steiner, B.G., & Pond, R.E. (1992). *Preschool Language Scales—3.* San Antonio, TX: Psychological Corporation.

Zingg, R.M. (Ed.). (1966). *Feral man and cases of extreme isolation of individuals.* New York: Archon Books. (Original work published 1942)

Zingg, R.M. (1940). Feral man and extreme cases of isolation. *American Journal of Psychology, 53,* 487–517.

Zirpoli, T. (1986). Child abuse and children with handicaps. *Remedial and Special Education, 7*(2), 39–48.

Zucker, S.H., & Polloway, E.A. (1987). Issues in identification and assessment in mental retardation. *Education and Training in Mental Retardation, 22,* 69–76.

About the Authors

Mary Beirne-Smith

Mary Beirne-Smith is Associate Professor and Chair of the Programs in Special Education at The University of Alabama. Her previous experience includes general and special education classroom teaching and public school administration. Her research interests center around academic interventions for students with mild learning disorders. She is currently involved in implementing a collaborative consultation project with several local education agencies. She is also researching motivation and goal setting for students with mild disabilities. Mary received her M.Ed. and Ed.D. from the University of Virginia.

Richard F. Ittenbach

Richard F. Ittenbach is an Associate Professor in the Educational Psychology program at the University of Mississippi where he teaches classes in principles of psychometrics, statistics, and research design. He received his B.S. degree in secondary science education from Butler University, his M.Ed. in counseling from Auburn University, and his Ed.S. and Ph.D. in educational research and educational/school psychology, respectively, from The University of Alabama. He has written numerous articles on the adjustment of persons with mental retardation, young adult development, and issues related to the measurement of mental and special abilities. His articles have appeared in such journals as the *American Journal on Mental Retardation, Educational and Psychological Measurement, Journal of Counseling Psychology, Journal of School Psychology, Measurement and Evaluation in Counseling and Development,* and *Research in Developmental Disabilities.*

James R. Patton

James R. Patton is the Executive Editor at Pro-ed and Adjunct Associate Professor at the University of Texas at Austin. He has experience teaching students with special needs at the elementary, secondary, and post-secondary levels. His research interests include curriculum development, life-long learning, instructional methodology, and teaching science. Currently he is developing integrated curricula and life skills programs. Jim earned his B.S. from the University of Notre Dame and his M.Ed. and Ed.D. from the University of Virginia.

Cynthia W. Jackson

Cynthia W. Jackson is a doctoral student at The University of Alabama in mild learning behavior disorders. Her experience includes psychometrics and the teaching of students with special needs at the preschool, elementary, secondary, and post-secondary levels. Cynthia's research interests include the development of attitudes in children and teachers toward individuals with special needs, practices necessary to ensure the successful integration of students with special needs into the general education classroom, and transition services. She received a B.S. in elementary education with endorsements in English and social studies at the secondary level from John Brown University and an M.S. in learning disabilities with an endorsement in mental retardation from the University of Central Arkansas.

Veda Jairrels

Veda Jairrels is an Associate Professor of Exceptional Student Education at Clark Atlanta University in Atlanta, Georgia. She was a special education teacher in New York City Public Schools for several years where she taught students with learning disabilities and behavioral disorders. Veda is interested in the issue of cultural diversity and how it affects the teacher preparation process and curriculum. She received her A.B. and law degrees from Indiana University and her M.A. and Ph.D. degrees from Columbia University and The University of Alabama, respectively. She is a member of the Pennsylvania Bar.

Edward A. Polloway

Edward A. Polloway is Dean of the School of Education and Human Development at Lynchburg College, Virginia. His previous experience includes teaching elementary and special education public school classes. He has published numerous books, chapters, and journal articles and is two-time president of MR/DD. He received his B.A. from Dickinson College and his M.Ed. and Ed.D. from the University of Virginia.

J. David Smith

J. David Smith is Professor of Educational Psychology at the University of South Carolina. He is also Coordinator of Programs in Special Education at USC. His career has included work as a special education teacher, counselor, and Peace Corps Volunteer. He has written numerous books and articles. He received his B.S. and M.S. from Virginia Commonwealth University, and his M.Ed. and Ed.D. from Columbia University.

Shannon H. Kim

Shannon H. Kim is a doctoral student in educational psychology at the University of Mississippi. She has provided psychological services to persons with Prader Willi Syndrome as an employee of the Mississippi Department of Mental Health. Additional experiences include working with persons who have mild, moderate, severe, and profound levels of mental retardation in residential and vocational settings. Shannon's research interests include issues of transition, services to individuals with dual diagnoses, and the study of genetic syndromes. She received her M.Ed. in 1994 from the University of Mississippi.

Mitylene Arnold

Mit Arnold, Ed.D., is Associate Professor of Special Education at the University of Mississippi. She holds a B.A. from Baylor University, and has been a classroom teacher in Austin, Texas, and Madison, Georgia. She completed the Master's and Doctoral degrees at the University of Georgia, where she served as Project Director at the University Affiliated Program for Developmental Disabilities.

Name Index

Kaufman, J. S., 455
Kaufman, N. L., 113, 282
Kearney, F. J., 498
Keith, T. Z., 120
Keller, C. E., 325
Keller, M., 204, 205
Kelly, J. F., 295, 296
Kennedy, C. H., 244, 395, 396
Keogh, B. K., 272, 315, 325
Kessler, K., 400
Kiernan, W. E., 394, 411
King, B. H., 240
King, M. P., 381
Kirby, J. R., 102, 103, 115
Kirman, B. H., 62
Kloos, E. T., 440
Knackendofel, E. A., 325, 326
Knobbe, C. A., 500, 502
Knoll, J., 524, 525
Koch, R., 143, 145, 146
Kohler, P. D., 251
Koller, J. R., 86
Kolstoe, O. P., 63, 137, 357–359, 379, 383, 384
Kopp, C. B., 210
Koshland, D. E., 536
Kotlowitz, A., 168
Kozol, J., 169, 170
Krajicek, H. J., 224
Krasner, D. V., 428
Krasner, L., 85
Krauss, M., 433, 440
Kregel, J., 247, 251, 402, 520
Krieg, F. J., 389, 390
Krouse, J., 455
Kugel, R. B., 170
Kuhn, T. S., 513
Kurtz, R. A., 448

Lachar, D., 282
Lachiewicz, A., 152
Lagomarcino, T. R., 362
Lakin, K. C., 120, 324, 394, 404, 467, 471, 485, 486, 488, 492, 493, 498, 501, 522
Lamabdin, M. A., 89
Lambert, N., 125, 126, 285
Landrigan, P. J., 163
Lange, C. M., 388, 391

Langee, H. R., 153
Langness, L. L., 200
Lannan, L., 447
Larson, S. A., 120, 388, 393, 396, 403, 408, 488, 498, 522
Lasker, L., 480
Laski, F. J., 324
Latib, A., 488
Laurent, J., 109
LaVecchio, F., 146
LaVigne, R., 362
LaVor, M. L., 51
Lawhead, W. F., 106
Lawrence, E. A., 206
Lawson, J. D., 377
League, R., 285
Leal, D., 304
Leconte, P. J., 369, 384
LeDrew, L., 86
Ledue, X., 143, 145, 146
Lehr, D. M., 190, 191
Lehr, S., 525
Leigh, J., 282
Leland, H., 125, 126, 285
Lemperle, G., 224
Lenk, L. L., 299
Lesat, S., 325
Lesch, M., 146
Levine, B., 257
Levine, H. G., 200
Levinson, D. J., 391, 393
Lewis, D., 259, 394
Lewis, J. F., 130
Lewis, M. H., 506
Lewis, R., 277
Lewontin, R., 181–183
Li, X., 485, 486
Libby, J. D., 146
Liebowitz, J., 516, 528
Lindley, L., 239
Littman, D. C., 266
Livermore, J., 152
Lloyd, J. W., 325
Loeb, P. A., 130
Logan, D. R., 229, 290
Lombard, R. C., 369
Loomis, R., 400
Lottman, M., 447
Lubin, R. A., 150, 407

Luciano, L., 282
Luckasson, R., 54, 72, 73, 82
Ludlow, B. L., 296
Luebke, J., 203, 204, 210, 212, 229, 230
Luecking, R. G., 399
Lumsden, C. J., 117
Lund, K. A., 298
Luria, A. R., 103
Lutzer, V. D., 440
Lykken, D. T., 104
Lynch, H. T., 89

Macarov, D., 516
MacDonald, G. W., 145
MacMillan, D. L., 80, 91, 93, 200, 218, 221, 229, 231, 314, 459–461
Madorsky, H., 447
Majeski, R. A., 258, 440
Mallory, B. L., 434
Maloney, M. P., 30, 41
Manni, J. L., 86, 204, 205
Marchant, J., 382
Marchetti, A. G., 469
Marino, P. E., 163
Marland, S. P., 355
Marlowe, M., 163
Marshall, K., 402
Marshall, L. H., 377
Marshall, P., 480
Martin, J. E., 377
Martin, R. P., 282
Masland, R., 43
Masterpasqua, F., 210
Matthews, W. S., 145
Mattson, R., 444, 449
May, D. C., 151, 254
May, J. G., 240, 487
Mayo, L. W., 45, 46
McAndrew, I., 428
McBride, J. W., 230
McCarney, S. B., 130, 282
McCarthy, M. M., 471
McCarver, R. B., 489, 504
McCauley, C., 215, 218
McClenny, B., 258, 440
McCollum, J., 293
McConnell, S. R., 292
McCracken, J. T., 240

McCune, G., 245
McDaniel, G., 266
McDonnell, A., 245
McDonnell, J., 245, 246
McGoldrick, M., 423
McGrew, K. S., 117, 118, 120, 394, 434, 507
McGue, N. L., 104
McHale, J., 512, 516, 517
McInerney, M., 271
McKinney, J. D., 325
McLaren, J., 136, 162
McLaughlin, P. J., 381, 382, 385
McLean, M. M., 362
McLoughlin, J. A., 277
McNamara, G., 424
McNeil, M. C., 32
Mead, J. F., 466
Mecham, M. J., 285
Mehlinger, H., 298
Meins, W., 241
Meltzer, A. S., 515
Menke, J. M., 404, 485, 501
Menolascino, F. J., 138, 143, 144, 150, 158, 160, 240, 487
Mercer, A. R., 318
Mercer, C. D., 207, 209, 219, 318, 321
Mercer, J. R., 83–85, 90, 117, 130, 131
Messick, S., 106
Metzler, H. M., 251
Meyer, L. H., 255, 402
Meyer-Bahlburg, H. F., 155
Meyers, C. E., 124, 218
Mickey, G. H., 89
Miller, B. C., 423
Miller, D. R., 421
Miller, S., 382
Millsap, P. A., 117
Mireault, N. G., 146
Mirkin, P. K., 332
Mitchell, D., 433
Moeller, C. T., 434
Monat-Hallar, R. K., 410
Morazas, D. S., 254
Morgan, D. P., 332
Morishima, A., 155
Morreau, E., 130

Morrow, H. W., 131
Morsink, C. V., 299
Mosier, H. D., 224
Moss, S., 440
Mowder, B. A., 143, 160, 161
Mueller, D. J., 317
Mulick, J. A., 80–82, 529
Mulligan, M., 455
Murphy, M. D., 219
Murray, C., 177
Murray, D. J., 113
Murtaugh, M., 396

Naglieri, J. A., 102, 103, 113, 115
Naisbitt, J., 513, 514
Nanus, B., 534
Nativio, D. G., 142
Nave, G., 394
Neely, C. W., 152
Neisworth, J. T., 227, 277, 281
Nelson, D., 394
Nelson, K. R., 39
Neubert, D. A., 369
Nevin, A., 325
Newman, H. H., 179
Newman, L., 204
Newton, J. S., 395
Nietupski, J., 231
Nihira, K., 117, 118, 125, 126, 285
Nirje, B., 47, 246
Noble, J. J., 401
Nolley, B., 332
Nolley, D., 332
Noonan, M. J., 455
Nuccio, J. B., 221
Nussbaum, A., 163
Nyhan, W. L., 146

O'Connor, N., 225
O'Connor, S., 523
Olbrisch, R. R., 224
Olesen, D. E., 526
Olswang, L. B., 285
Opuda, M. J., 464
Orelove, F. P., 192
O'Shea, A. J., 383
Ouellette, E. M., 159

Page, E. G., 175
Paige, D. M., 227
Paolucci-Whitcomb, P., 325
Paour, J., 107
Parent, W., 382
Parker, R., 383
Parkes, W. F., 480
Parsons, C. L., 224
Parsons, J. A., 240, 487
Parsons, M. B., 508
Parsons, M. H., 170
Parton, P., 143, 145, 146
Pasamanick, B., 164
Patrick, J. L., 86
Patton, J. R., 28, 44, 53, 54, 203–204, 210–212, 218, 221, 227, 229–231, 297, 302, 338, 342, 344, 352, 357, 365–367, 369, 378, 484, 519, 521
Payne, J. S., 209, 218, 384
Payne, R. A., 218
Pearson, L. S., 113
Peck, C. A., 396
Peck, V. A., 219
Pennington, B., 154, 155
Penrose, L. S., 62, 63
Perret, Y., 425
Perske, R., 474
Peterson, N. L., 172
Peterson, R. M., 145
Pezzoli, M., 396
Phelps, L. A., 364
Piaget, J., 117, 213, 295
Pious, C. G., 266
Piper, W., 23
Pipitone, P., 162
Plog, S. C., 517, 518
Plomin, R., 103
Polister, B., 493
Polloway, E. A., 32, 44, 53–54, 72, 73, 82, 86, 88, 92, 142, 146, 152, 153, 155, 156, 159, 160, 177, 203–204, 206, 210, 212, 218, 221, 227, 229–231, 297, 302, 338, 342, 344, 378, 461, 519
Pond, R. E., 285
Porteus, S. D., 114
Pottebaum, S. M., 120
Poulsen, M. K., 159, 160

Powell, T. H., 429
Powers, L. E., 425, 428
Powers, M. D., 400
Powers, S. I., 428
Prosser, C. L., 116
Prouty, R. W., 388, 393, 396, 403, 404, 408, 485, 492, 493, 501
Puck, M., 154, 155
Pueschel, S. M., 187
Pugach, M. C., 325
Pumpian, I., 231

Quinn, J. M., 210, 407
Quinn, K. P., 428
Quinn, L. M., 407

Racion, J. A., 523
Rada, D., 224
Rainforth, B., 226
Ramey, C. T., 267
Ramey, S. L., 267
Ramot, A., 407
Rando, T. A., 427
Rappaport, J., 519
Raven, J. C., 114
Ray, M. T., 253, 403
Reber, M., 201, 211
Reeve, R. E., 218
Regan, R., 229
Reid, D. H., 508
Reid, D. K., 285
Reise, S. P., 117
Reiss, D., 420
Reiss, S., 54, 72, 73, 82
Renzaglia, A. M., 231
Repp, A. C., 85
Reschly, D., 61, 86, 88, 131, 224
Resnick, O., 163
Rettig, M. A., 455
Reynolds, C. R., 113, 290
Reynolds, M. C., 313, 314, 324
Rhode, G., 332
Rhodes, L., 500, 502
Rice, F. P., 393
Richardson, H. B., 488
Riordan, J., 254, 439
Rizzo, T. L., 244
Robinault, I. P., 226
Robinson, B., 122

Robinson, G., 224
Robinson, H. B., 91, 204, 210
Robinson, N. K., 91, 204, 210
Robinson, S., 155
Robinson, S. M., 325, 326
Roderick, T. H., 89
Rogan, P., 400
Rogers, R. C., 152
Roistacher, R. C., 94, 95
Rone, C., 257
Rose, S., 181–183
Rosen, J. W., 396
Rosenzweig, I. E., 355
Rothstein, L. F., 451, 463
Rovet, J., 155
Rowitz, L., 536
Rozner, L., 224
Rucker, H., 142, 152, 153, 155, 160
Rueda, R., 165, 167
Rusch, F. R., 248, 251, 362–364, 390
Rushton, J. P., 104
Russell, A. T., 210
Ryan, C. S., 407
Ryan, W., 518
Ryburn, M., 109
Rynders, J. E., 151

Sabagh, G., 487
Safford, E. J., 245, 488
Safford, P. L., 245, 488
Salonblatt, J., 154, 155
Salvia, J., 100, 280
Sandall, S. R., 143, 160, 161
Sandoval, J., 113
Santamour, M. B., 517, 518
Sarason, S. B., 28, 43, 62
Sargent, L. R., 466
Sattler, J., 107, 108, 282
Saunders, R. R., 406
Scarr, S., 147, 180
Scarr-Salapatek, S., 178
Schakel, J. A., 290
Schalock, R. L., 54, 72, 73, 82, 248, 394, 411
Scheerenberger, R. S., 247, 468, 485, 498, 504
Schepis, M. M., 508
Schleien, S. J., 253, 402, 403

Schultz, D. P., 107
Schultz, F. R., 145
Schultz, S. E., 107
Schumaker, J. B., 325, 326
Schupf, N., 150
Schutz, R. P., 400
Schwartz, A. A., 407
Schwartz, I. S., 292
Scot, R. L., 432
Scott, G. M., 155, 156
Scott, K. G., 184
Scudder, R. R., 221
Seguin, E. O., 6, 33, 245
Seitz, V., 182
Seligman, M. E., 206
Seltzer, M. M., 407, 433, 440
Semmel, M. I., 325
Serpas, D., 251
Severson, S., 369
Seyfarth, J., 247, 402
Seymour, H. N., 285
Shank, M., 304
Shaver, D., 204
Sheldon, J. B., 210, 407
Sher, M. R., 158
Sherman, J. A., 210, 407
Shields, J., 180
Shiraga, B., 400
Showers, B., 325
Sigelman, C. K., 497
Silverman, N. A., 229
Silverman, W. P., 150
Simensen, R. J., 152
Simpson, R. L., 434
Siperstein, G. N., 80, 93
Sitlington, P. L., 369
Skeels, H. M., 171, 172
Skinner, B. F., 296
Skrtic, T. M., 324
Smith, B. J., 266
Smith, D. W., 226, 332
Smith, G. C., 258, 440
Smith, J. D., 32, 37–39, 42, 44, 53, 54, 80, 86, 92, 146, 176–178, 180, 181, 190, 192, 461
Smith, J. E., 218, 384
Smith, R., 486
Smith, R. M., 227
Smith, R. W., 396

Smith, S. W., 332
Smith, T. E., 342
Smith, T. E. C., 44, 53, 54, 155, 156
Smull, M. W., 498
Snell, M. E., 54, 72, 73, 82, 207, 209, 219, 231, 244, 248
Sobelman, G., 421
Sobsey, R., 192
Sokol, M., 117
Sokol, R. J., 158
Sontag, E., 159
Sparrow, S. S., 127, 285
Spear, L. C., 219
Spearman, C. E., 102
Spence, B. H., 507
Spiegel, A. N., 120, 388, 393, 396, 403, 408
Spiker, D., 151
Spiridigliozzi, G. A., 152
Spitalnik, D. M., 54, 72, 73, 82
Spitz, H. H., 217
Spradlin, J. E., 221
Spreat, S., 240, 487, 488
Spruill, J., 109
Stacy, A. W., 117
Staddon, J. E., 116
Stainback, S., 324
Stainback, W., 324
Stancliffe, R., 485
Stark, J. A., 54, 72, 73, 82, 150, 158, 163, 362, 406
Starkey, S., 488
Stavis, P. F., 410
Steffens, K., 388, 391
Steiner, B. G., 285
Stella, M. A., 230
Stephens, W. E., 218
Stephenson, J. B. P., 155
Sternberg, R. J., 102, 219
Stevens, H. A., 210, 218, 237
Stewart, A. J., 117
Stilington, P. L., 361
Stoddard, K., 159
Stolze, L., 439
Stone, J. W., 153
Storley, C., 257
Strain, P. S., 266
Strohm, B., 400

Strully, C. F., 244
Strully, J. L., 244
Sugai, G., 296, 332
Sullivan, F. T., 362
Summers, J. A., 305
Sundram, C. J., 410
Sweet, M., 400
Swenson, C. H., 424
Swerdlik, M., 109
Switzky, H. N., 497

Tager, F. M., 512
Talbert, C. M., 382
Tarjan, G., 60, 530
Taylor, A. R., 396
Taylor, R. L., 460, 461
Taylor, S. D., 388
Taylor, S. J., 246, 447, 523, 525
Tellegen, A., 104
Telles, J. L., 240, 487, 488
Ten Brink, T. D., 86
Thackrey, M., 117
Thorin, E., 441
Thornburg, G., 439
Thorndike, E. L., 102
Thorndike, R., 107, 108, 282
Thurlow, M. L., 121, 291, 347, 352, 388, 391, 394, 396
Thurston, D., 162
Thurstone, L. L., 102
Tiegerman, E., 221
Tilson, G. P., 399
Tisch, S., 488
Todis, B., 299
Townsend, C., 444, 449
Trachtenberg, S. W., 425
Tredgold, A. F., 66, 69, 82
Tremain, D. H., 221
Trumbo, D., 484
Turkington, C., 151
Turnbull, A. P., 304, 305, 433, 471, 477
Turnbull, H. R., 304, 433, 445, 449, 454, 460, 464
Turnbull, N., 151
Turner, J. L., 254
Turnure, J., 220

Turpin, R., 149
Tymchuk, A. J., 437

Ulman, L. P., 85
Ulrich, D. A., 289
Underwood, J. K., 466

Vanderheiden, G. C., 528
VanDeventer, P., 400
Van Pelt, J. C., 89
Vasa, S. F., 254, 439
Veltman, M., 266
Vernon, P. E., 102
Vernon-Levett, P., 162
Vincent, L. J., 159, 160, 267
Vogelsberg, R. T., 400
Volmer, L., 224

Wagner, M., 204, 389
Wainer, H., 106
Walberg, H. J., 324
Wald, P. M., 444
Walden, J. D., 317
Walker, H. M., 299
Walker, P., 523, 525
Walker, R., 382
Walsh, F., 422
Wang, M. C., 324
Ward, M. P., 30, 41
Warren, K. R., 158
Warren, S. F., 221
Watson, J. B., 164
Weatherman, R. F., 128, 285
Webb, S., 158
Wechsler, D., 101, 109–111, 114, 520
Wehman, P., 247, 381–382, 384, 385, 402
Wehman, P. H., 251
Wehmeyer, M., 55
Weihofen, H., 63
Weinhouse, E., 210
Weinstock-Savoy, D., 117
Weisner, T. S., 439
Weissman, R. A., 266
Wells, M. W., 332
Wenz, E., 143, 145, 146
West, J. F., 326

Westling, D. L., 205, 232
White, B. I., 266
White, C. C., 485, 486, 504
White, J. F., 150
Whitman, B. Y., 155
Whitman, T. L., 209, 507
Widerstrom, A. H., 143, 160, 161
Widman, K. F., 117, 118
Wiederholt, J. L., 318, 319
Wikler, L., 428
Wilbur, H., 33
Wilcox, B., 244
Will, M. C., 353, 364
Williams, C. A., 153
Williams, G. A., 396
Williams, H. G., 289
Wills, T. A., 424
Wilson, A., 155, 226
Wilson, E. O., 117
Wilson, J., 430
Wilson, L., 224

Wing, A. A., 153
Winikur, D. W., 86, 204, 205
Winschel, J. F., 206
Wolery, M., 266, 296
Wolf, B., 51
Wolf, M. M., 281
Wolf, N. K., 377
Wolfensberger, W., 64, 245, 246, 399
Wolman, C., 388, 391
Wolraich, M. L., 157
Wood, S., 366
Wood, T. A., 432
Wood, W., 382
Woodcock, R. W., 128, 285
Woodruff, G., 159, 160
Woodward, W. M., 214
Wool, R., 486
Wooley, H., 224
Wright, B., 381
Wyatt, T., 285

Yerkes, R. M., 40
York, J., 226, 400
Yovanoff, P., 441
Ysseldyke, J. E., 100, 280, 324, 347, 352

Zaentz, S., 480
Zanella, K., 400
Zantal-Weiner, K., 162
Zeaman, D., 215
Zemekis, R., 488
Zetlin, A. G., 117, 254, 393, 396
Zigler, E., 86, 88, 116, 181, 182, 207, 213, 220, 420
Zigman, W. S., 150
Zigmond, N., 325
Zigmond, W. G., 407
Zimmerman, I. L., 285
Zingg, R. M., 32
Zirpoli, T., 162, 228
Zucker, S. H., 86, 88

Subject Index

American Medical Association, 474

American Psychiatric Association, 68, 75, 237

American Psychological Association, 80–81, 100

American Society of Plastic and Reconstructive Surgeons, 222

America 2000 strategy, 53–54

Amniocentesis, 186–187

Anencephaly, 192

Anger and family interactions, 427

Annual goals, 331

Apgar test of vital signs, 188

Appropriate education, 347, 462–464

Appropriate outcomes, 250–254

Architectural supports, 259–260

Artificial intelligence, 528

Assessment, 44. *See also* Intelligence testing
  adaptive behavior, 115–131
  curriculum-based, 280–281, 327–328, 384
  early childhood intervention programs, 276–291
  educational programming, 326–337
  key terms, 99
  severe mental retardation, 243
  summary, 132–133
  theories of intelligence, 100–106
  transitional planning process, 367, 369
  vocational preparation, 383–384

Assistive technologies, 528

Association for Persons with Severe Handicaps (TASH), 239, 412, 474

Association for Retarded Citizens (ARC), 412, 413

At risk children, 53, 94, 270–272

Attention variables, 215–217

Attitudes toward deviant populations, social, 518–519

Authentic contexts, teaching tasks in, 20, 48, 249–250

Authoritarianism, 167

Autism, 153

Autosomes, 140

Aversive treatment techniques, 507–508

Awakenings (film), 480

Bank-Mikkelsen, N. E., 47

Behavioral analysis perspective, 84–85

Behavior management
  assessment, behavioral criterion-referenced, 328
  curriculum, 296
  Ezell, Dan, 20
  goals, 333
  institutional living, 486–487, 504–509
  new behaviors over time, maintaining, 341
  Nunnally, Jerry, 23, 25

Best interest *vs.* legal right, 449

Binet, Alfred, 39, 107–109

Bioethical issues, 55

Biologically based family models, 421

Biomedical technology, 140, 526–527, 531–533

Blaming the Victim (Ryan), 518

Blood-group incompatibility, 157–158

Blood tests, 186

Board of Directors of the Division on Mental Retardation and Developmental Disabilities (CEC-MRDD), 301, 476

Brain injury in young children, 162

Broad-based model of assessment and intervention, 122–123

Brody, Garry S., 222

Bruininks-Oseretsky Test of Motor Proficiency, 289

Bureau of Education for the Handicapped (BEH), 46

Burt, Sir Cyril, 176

Camera, electronic panning, 299, 300–302

Capital punishment, 474–476

Career development. *See also* Employment; Vocational preparation

defining, 357
  issues in, 363–364
  Marland, Sidney P., 355–356
  models of, 357–360
  research, 361–363
  vocational development and, 377–378

Case management program, 10

Categorical programs, 318–320

Cattell, James M., 106

Causes of mental retardation. *See* Etiology

Center-based services, 294–295

Centrifugal/centripetal forces and family functioning, 421

Cerebral palsy, 226

Changing Patterns in Residential Services for the Mentally Retarded (Nirje), 47

Checklist of Adaptive Living Skills, 130

Children. *See also* Early childhood intervention programs; Education; Family, the; Pregnancy
  feral, 31–33
  right to life after birth of, 191, 193
  sibling interactions, 429–430
  transplanting organs from infants, 192
  withholding treatment, 472–474

Chorionic villi sampling (CVS), 186, 532

Chromosomes
  autosomes, 140
  Down syndrome, 149–151
  fragile X syndrome, 152–153
  karyotyping, 147
  Klinefelter's syndrome, 153–155
  meiosis, 147–149
  Prader-Willi syndrome, 155–156
  sex, 140–141, 146
  Turner's syndrome, 155

Civil rights, 47

Clark, Gary, 4–9

Classification, 66–68, 76, 95